Chemotherapy of Infection

William B. Pratt, M.D.
Associate Professor of Pharmacology
University of Michigan

New York
Oxford University Press
1977

I would like to thank the authors, journals, and publishers for their permission to
reprint the following figures and tables in this text:

Fig. 1-2: J. W. Costerton *et al.*, *Bacteriol. Revs.* 38:87 (1974). American Society for
Microbiology
Figs. 2-4, 2-6, 2-7: J. L. Strominger *et al.*, *Fed. Proc.* 26:9 (1967). Federation of American
Societies for Experimental Biology
Fig. 2-5: M. Matsuhashi *et al.*, *J. Biol. Chem.* 242:3191 (1967). American Society of Biological
Chemists
Fig. 2-8: D. J. Tipper and J. L. Strominger, *Proc. Natl. Acad. Sci.* 54:1133 (1965). National
Academy of Sciences
Fig. 2-11: B. B. Levine, *J. Exptl. Med.* 112:1131 (1960). The Rockefeller University Press
Fig. 2-12: B. B. Levine and Z. Ovary, *J. Exptl. Med.* 114:875 (1961). The Rockefeller University
Press
Fig. 2-13: B. C. Brown *et al.*, *J. Am. Med. Assoc.* 189:599 (1964). The American Medical
Association
Fig. 3-5: E. Jawetz, *Ann. Rev. Pharmacol.* 8:151 (1968). Reproduced with permission from
Annual Review of Pharmacology. Vol. 8. Copyright © 1968 by Annual Reviews, Inc. All
rights reserved
Fig. 3-6: R. C. Moellering and A. N. Weinberg, *J. Clin. Invest.* 50:2580 (1971). The American
Society for Clinical Investigation, Inc.
Fig. 3-7: R. A. Chan *et al.*, *Ann. Int. Med.* 76:773 (1972). American College of Physicians
Fig. 3-8: J. Schacht, *J. Acoust. Soc. Am.* 59:940 (1976). American Institute of Physics
Fig. 4-1: C. L. Wisseman *et al.*, *J. Bacteriol.* 67:662 (1954). American Society for Microbiology
Fig. 4-2: S. Peskta, *Proc. Natl. Acad. Sci.* 64:709 (1969). National Academy of Sciences
Fig. 4-3: C. F. Weiss *et al.*, *New Eng. J. Med.* 262:787 (1960). The Massachusetts Medical
Society
Fig. 4-4: W. R. Best, *J. Am. Med. Assoc.* 201:99 (1967). The American Medical Association
Figs. 5-1, 5-2: D. D. Woods, "The biochemical mode of action of the sulfonamides," *J. Gen.
Microbiol.* 29:687 (1962). Cambridge University Press
Fig. 6-2: Reprinted with permission from W. R. Veatch *et al.*, *Biochemistry* 13:5249 (1974).
American Chemical Society. Copyright by the American Chemical Society
Fig. 8-1: H. Tiitinen, *Scand. J. Resp. Dis.* 50:110 (1969). Munksgaard International Publishers
Ltd.
Fig. 8-2: J. R. Mitchell *et al.*, *Ann. Int. Med.* 84:181 (1976). American College of Physicians
Fig. 9-1: S. C. Kinsky *et al.*, *Biochim. Biophys. Acta* 152:174 (1968). Elsevier Publishing Co.
Fig. 9-2: T. E. Andreoli, *Ann. N.Y. Acad. Sci.* 235:448 (1974). New York Academy of Science
Fig. 10-1: L. T. Coggeshall, in *Textbook of Medicine*, ed. by P. B. Beeson and W. McDermott.
W. B. Saunders Co., 1963
Fig. 10-3: H. Polet and C. F. Barr, *Am. J. Trop. Med. Hyg.* 17:672 (1968). American Society of
Tropical Medicine and Hygiene
Fig. 10-4: S. N. Cohen and K. L. Yielding, *J. Biol. Chem.* 240:3123 (1965). American Society of
Biological Chemists
Fig. 10-7: E. Beutler, *J. Lab. Clin. Med.* 49:84 (1957). D. V. Mosby Co.
Fig. 10-11: I. M. Rollo, *Brit. J. Pharmacol.* 10:208 (1955). The Macmillan Co.
Fig. 11-2: A. P. Grollman, *J. Biol. Chem.* 243:4089 (1968). American Society of Biological
Chemists

Preface

The field of chemotherapy has several different sources of information—the clinical sciences, pharmacology, biochemistry, molecular biology, and microbiology (including virology, bacteriology, mycology, parasitology, and immunology). It is the goal of this book to integrate information from all of these areas in describing the drugs used to treat infectious diseases. My aim has been to make the book both comprehensive and concise.

This textbook provides the details of the action, pharmacology, and adverse effects of the antibacterial, antifungal, antiparasitic, and antiviral drugs. The emphasis is on the understanding of mechanisms—both the mechanisms by which the drugs affect the organisms and the biochemical and pathophysiological basis for toxicities, side effects, and hypersensitivity reactions. Whenever the effects of a group of drugs on a biochemical process are presented, a summary of the appropriate biochemistry (including diagrams of the relevant biochemical pathways) is included in the discussion. Although this book presents detailed information on the various drugs in current clinical use, it is not intended to be a therapeutic guide. In some specific cases dosage recommendations are included, but this has been done only when I have felt that fundamental pharmacological concepts would be reinforced by showing how they are translated into a therapeutic regimen.

This book has evolved from my shorter text, *Fundamentals of Chemotherapy*, which was published by Oxford in 1973, although it differs from the earlier text in many ways. One-fifth of that book was devoted to a discussion of anticancer drugs. Because some of the concepts involved in the treatment of cancer are quite different from those involved in the treatment of infection, I have now chosen to make treatment of infection the subject of a separate effort.

Chemotherapy of Infection is divided into four parts according to type of organism. The first part consists of eight chapters dealing with the drugs used to treat infection due to bacteria. Chapter 1 is entirely new, and it covers those properties of the bacterium or of the patient that determine whether the response to antimicrobial therapy will be successful. There are some concepts, such as selective toxicity, superinfection, drug resistance, and resistance transfer, that must be learned before chemotherapy can be really understood. These concepts are presented in Chapter 1; discussions throughout the text provide specific examples. The following two chapters cover the major groups of bactericidal antibiotics: Chapter 2, the penicillins, cephalosporins, and other inhibitors of cell wall synthesis; Chapter 3, the aminoglycosides, which act by inhibiting bacterial protein synthesis. In organizing the presentation of the other antibacterial drugs, I have continued the method of grouping them, as far as possible, by their biochemical mechanism of action. Thus, Chapter 4 covers the common bacteriostatic inhibitors, of protein synthesis (e.g., chloramphenicol, the lincomycins, erythromycin, the tetracyclines); Chapter 5, the antimetabolites (e.g., the sulfonamines, trimethoprim); Chapter 6, some less commonly used antibiotics that act on the permeability of the cell membrane (e.g., the polymxins). This organization has not been followed in the last two chapters of Part I; these new chapters deal with drugs used to treat urinary tract infections and tuberculosis.

Parts II, III, and IV of the text covers the drugs used to treat fungal, parasitic, and viral diseases. Chapter 9, antifungal drugs, has been greatly expanded to include a detailed discussion of such newer drugs as flucytosine, miconazole, and clotrimazole. And Part III, antiparasitic drugs, has been expanded from two to three chapters. Throughout the text, I discuss some key experiments, both basic and clinical, to give readers a background for understanding how some major information has been obtained. I have also used many figures and tables to present and consolidate information.

Students who read this book should find ample opportunity to utilize their knowledge of the basic medical sciences while they arrive at an understanding of the many drugs employed to treat infectious disease. Clinicians, or teachers, who wish a concise description of the mechanisms of the drug effects should also find it a useful text. With this in mind, I have provided extensive references to other texts, reviews, and research papers. The broad input of information into the field of chemotherapy can be appreciated from the fact that, in addition to general sources, references to articles in over 160 biomedical journals, representing a wide range of subdisciplines, have been included. In the process of gleaning information from these diverse subdisciplines, some

oversimplification may have occurred. Thus, I welcome comments from the readers.

The University of Michigan   W. B. P.
Ann Arbor
April 1977

Acknowledgments

I would like to thank the many people who have made this effort possible. Keen students are an important stimulus to textbook writing and in this respect I am grateful for the interest and enthusiasm of the medical and graduate students at Stanford and the University of Michigan. I am deeply indebted to the entire faculty of the Department of Pediatrics at Yale Medical School, for providing me with an intensive and excellent educational experience that was most important to stimulating my efforts on this book. In addition to my colleagues at Stanford, who were acknowledged in the preface to the earlier text, I would like to thank several of my current colleagues on the faculty at the University of Michigan who were kind enough to provide suggestions for this book or review parts of the manuscript. They include Drs. Frederick Neidhardt, Raymond Ruddon, Jochen Schacht, Wendell Weber, and Harvey Whitfield. I am indebted to a graduate student, Ms. Julianne Sando, who read and provided valuable editorial comment on the entire manuscript. I also thank my wife, Dr. Diana Pratt, for making time in her busy schedule to read proof. Finally, I owe a great deal to both Diana and Sean for being my family and for tolerating me during this effort.

Contents

Part I
Drugs Employed in the Treatment of Bacterial Infection

Chapter 1
Determinants of Bacterial Response
to Antimicrobial Agents

Introduction

The formal definition of an antibiotic restricts the use of the term to chemicals that are produced by microorganisms and that have the capacity to inhibit the growth of, or to kill, bacteria and other microorganisms. This definition distinguishes between chemicals produced by microorganisms and antimicrobial compounds synthesized by chemists (e.g., sulfonamides, trimethoprim, isoniazid). The distinction is rather academic, and one finds that the word antibiotic is now often used to include both these groups of antimicrobial agents.

The central concept of antibiotic action is that of "selective toxicity"—that is, the growth of the infecting organism is selectively inhibited, or the organism is killed, without damage to the cells of the host. The ideal antibiotic would have no deleterious effect on the patient but would be lethal to the organism. There is no ideal antibiotic. Perhaps penicillin G in the nonallergic patient comes as close to this goal as any antimicrobial drug.

To obtain selectivity of action the antibiotics exploit differences between the biochemistry of the infecting agent and that of the host. With the penicillins, for example, the basis for the selective effect is quite clear; they inhibit cell wall synthesis, a process that does not take place in mammalian cells, which lack a cell wall. This explains the selective action of the penicillins but not their relative lack of toxicity. Other inhibitors of cell wall synthesis, which include bacitracin, cycloserine, and vancomycin, also inhibit biochemical processes unique to bacterial cells, but when given systemically, such antibiotics act on the cells of the host in other ways, and this makes them quite toxic.

It is important that those who are beginning their study of antimicrobial agents do not confuse the concept of selective toxicity with that of therapeutic index, also called therapeutic ratio, which is the ratio of the toxic dose to the effective dose of a drug. In some cases, the selective toxicity will parallel the therapeutic index, as for the penicillins (see above). The polyene antibiotics (e.g., amphotericin B) have both a low degree of selective toxicity and a low therapeutic index. That is, they show little selectivity of action against fungi versus mammalian cells, and they are also quite toxic. With other antibiotics, there is little relationship between selective cellular toxicity and therapeutic index. Let us take the aminoglycosides as an example. These antibiotics are very selective with respect to killing bacterial versus host cells, but for some members of this class, unrelated effects on the patient's nervous system, kidneys, or inner ear (hearing, balance) result in a lower margin for therapeutic error than would be predicted on the basis of their selective action on cell viability. Major sections of this book will be devoted to explanations of the mechanisms of the selective action of antibiotics on microorganisms. Equally important sections will be devoted to explanations of the mechanisms by which these drugs cause the undesirable effects that contribute to the therapeutic index and thus impose limitations on their clinical use.

Antibiotic Effect—"Cidal" versus "Static"

In the chemotherapy of infectious disease, the goal is to assist the body in ridding itself of the infecting organism. In general, the human body is extraordinarily well equipped to fight bacterial invasion. The skin is very efficient at preventing entry of organisms, by virtue of both its physical properties and its ability to produce unsaturated fatty acids, which have antibacterial action. The mucous membranes and their secretions also efficiently prevent entry of microorganisms. And once invasion has taken place, the bacterium is confronted with a well-orchestrated set of responses, including antibody production, the complement system, inflammatory responses, cellular migration and phagocytosis, and intracellular killing mechanisms.[1] The overall effect of the host defense is bacterial death, and the system is very effective. Most infections do not require therapy; they are taken care of by the body's defense mechanisms, and the individual may never be aware of them. For some infections, however, treatment with antibiotics may be required.

Antibiotics exert an effect in the patient that is either bactericidal or bacteriostatic. Those antibiotics that are bacteriostatic (e.g., chloramphenicol, erythromycin, tetracyclines) inhibit bacterial cell replication but do not kill the organism. Other antibiotics (e.g., penicillins, cephalosporins, aminoglycosides) are bactericidal; they cause microbial cell death and lysis. A few compounds (e.g., sulfonamides) are either cidal or static according to the composition of the environment (blood, pus, urine, etc.) in which the infecting organisms are growing. These two effects can be demonstrated *in vitro* and are illustrated schematically in Figure 1-1.

Treatment with a bacteriostatic drug stops bacterial growth, thereby allowing the host defenses to catch up in their battle. Treatment with a bactericidal agent superimposes the killing effect of the drug on the effect of the host defense. This is clearly somewhat oversimplied, since bactericidal drugs at low concentrations sometimes have a bacteriostatic effect, and bacteriostasis, if continued long enough, will be accompanied by a decrease in bacterial viability.

The distinction between the two types of antibiotics, cidal and static, is important in choosing a drug for therapy. In a patient

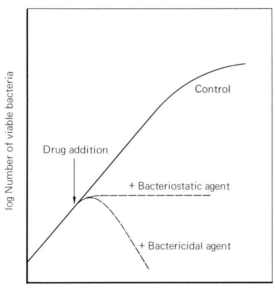

Time

Figure 1-1 Bacteriostatic and bactericidal effects of antibiotics. A suspension of bacteria in the log phase of growth is divided into three parts. A bacteriostatic drug, such as chloramphenicol, is added to one culture and a bactericidal agent, such as penicillin, to another; the third is a control. At various times, samples are taken from each culture, diluted, and plated on agar with new growth medium. The number of colonies obtained is a measure of the number of viable cells per culture.

with a severe infection, it is usually better (assuming that other considerations, such as organism sensitivity and the distribution properties and the clinically undesirable effects of the drugs do not dictate otherwise) to choose a bactericidal, rather than a bacteriostatic, antibiotic. In some cases, the patient's natural ability to fight an infection may be lowered. This occurs, for example, in patients with disorders of the immune system, in patients with lymphoreticular diseases or diabetes mellitus, and in severely debilitated patients. Also, a growing number of patients are under treatment with drugs having immunosuppressive effects, and they often have virtually no ability to fight infection. In these cases, almost total reliance must be placed on a chemotherapeutic effect that is unaided by host defense mechanisms, and bactericidal antibiotics must be employed.

DETERMINANTS OF BACTERIAL RESPONSE TO THERAPY

There are numerous reasons why a patient may not respond to therapy with antibiotics. One of the major factors is that the wrong antibiotic may have been prescribed, since these drugs are extensively misused by physicians.[2] The majority of cases of antibiotic misuse are probably due to inappropriate choices based on considerations that do not fall within the purview of this book. These would include the administration of antibiotics for treating infections (e.g., viral conditions) against which they are inactive, the use of antibiotics in conditions of noninfectious etiology because of misdiagnosis, and inappropriate prophylactic antibiotic therapy. Antibiotics are commonly administered to hospitalized patients who show no evidence of infection; in fact, in some hospitals much of the antibiotic use may fall into this category.[3] It is also clear that there is considerable misuse of antibiotics by the patients themselves. Many outpatients fail to initiate or more often, fail to properly complete their proscribed course of therapy.

Host Determinants

Some of the factors a physician must consider when treating an infection with an antimicrobial drug include: the sensitivity of the organism to the drug; the appropriate dosage, route of administration, and duration of therapy; and the special features of the patient that may alter the way a drug is handled by the body.

These features, the host determinants, may result in an inadequate concentration of the active drug at the site of infection or they may render the patient more likely to suffer adverse drug effects.[4] The host determinants of particular importance in determining undesirable toxic and side effects will be discussed in detail with each drug as it is presented in subsequent chapters. In this introduction, it is appropriate to mention a few host determinants that affect the response of the bacterium to the drug. Some examples have been given above. These include poor phagocytic activity, immunosuppression, serious disease of noninfectious etiology (diabetes mellitus, neoplasms), and physical debilitation, all of which compromise the ability of the patient to call on or utilize his full complement of host defenses.

If a sufficient concentration of antibiotic is not achieved at the site of infection, therapy will obviously fail. Thus, it is necessary to consider the distribution properties of the drug in choosing the antibiotic and its route of administration. For example, if a patient has a meningitis that requires the use of an aminoglycoside, the drug will have to be administered intrathecally, since these drugs do not pass through either normal or inflamed meninges in sufficient quantity to achieve reliable therapeutic levels in the cerebrospinal fluid. Although the polymyxins are extensively bound in some tissues, they are not of value in the treatment of most tissue infections because the concentration of free drug available to act on bacteria is too low. These are examples of distribution patterns not altered by the host.

Normally, very low levels of penicillins are achieved in the cerebrospinal fluid. But when the meninges are inflamed, much higher cerebrospinal fluid levels are attained, and thus these drugs are very useful in treating meningitis. This alteration in the permeability barrier is therapeutically advantageous. In other cases, the host determinant may be altered in a manner that is disadvantageous to therapy. For example, nitrofurantoin, a drug used to treat urinary tract infections, achieves high levels in the urine when renal function is normal. If a patient has impaired renal function, however, the level of drug in the urine is insufficient for an appropriate antibacterial effect. In another example, some patients who have a genetically determined rapid rate of metabolic inactivation of the antituberculous drug isoniazid respond poorly when the drug is given at weekly intervals. In daily therapy the therapeutic effect is no different from that of patients with slower inactivation rates. But when the dosage interval is extended to once a week, the rapid metabolizers inactivate the drug so fast that drug levels are low enough to compromise the bacterial response.

If a patient continues to demonstrate symptoms of infection despite appropriate antibiotic therapy, several host determinants must be considered. Is there an occult abscess responsible for the continuing problem? If such a focus of infection is located, it requires surgical drainage. Is there an obstruction (e.g., in the lungs or in the biliary or urinary tracts) creating conditions of stasis under which bacteria can multiply in poorly perfused pockets of infection? If so, surgical intervention may be necessary. Are there mechanical factors involved, such as a foreign body, or retained suture material that requires removal? Are continuous portals of bacterial entry being maintained unnecessarily or inappropriately (e.g., intravenous catheters left in for long periods of time, an unnecessary use of or inappropriate maintenance of a urinary catheter)? These are examples of host determinants that are subject to analysis and correction, but are often ignored by physicians who favor adding, or changing to, another antibiotic.

Some aspects of the host defense mechanisms are compromised when tissue necrosis and localized abscesses exist. For example, phagocytes function very poorly in such suppurative regions, and the local bactericidal response is diminished. The conditions of acidity, low oxygen tension, and lack of nutrients that impair phagocytic function in such areas can also affect bacterial growth. Since organisms that are not dividing are not killed by certain bactericidal drugs (e.g., penicillins, aminoglycosides), the bacterial response to the antibiotic may also be compromised. Abscess walls may be poorly vascularized; consequently, delivery of drug to the infection site is poor, and the local concentration of antibiotic may be inadequate. Thus, in an abscess, both the host's response to the organism and the organism's response to the antibiotic may be compromised. Such closed infections require surgical drainage; reliance on chemotherapy alone is usually useless.

Superinfection

Another factor entering into the therapeutic response is difficult to classify as either a host or a bacterial determinant. While a patient is being treated with an antibiotic, he can become superinfected with organisms other than those causing the original infection. This problem is more common when antibiotics having a broad spectrum of action or antibiotic combinations are employed. The organisms responsible for producing this secondary infection are usually normal residents of the host. The human body harbors a variety of microflora existing in ecologically balanced communities. The bowel is the largest and most obvious example of such a community. Other important areas normally colonized with bacteria include the oropharynx, skin, vagina, the genital and perineal areas, the external ear canals, and the conjunctivae. Usually resident bacteria in these areas are harmless and some even perform important functions for the host, such as the synthesis of vitamin K by coliform organisms. The harmless resident bacteria also serve to control the growth of potentially pathogenic organisms.

The ecological balance of the microbial colonies is maintained by a variety of mechanisms referred to collectively as microbial antagonism. Two principal mechanisms of antagonism are competition for nutrients and the production of compounds that inhibit the growth of other organisms. Some enteric bacilli, for example, produce colicins, proteins that kill sensitive bacteria in very specific ways. These colicins often act at the bacterial membrane to elicit such responses as inhibition of macromolecular synthesis, degradation of DNA, or inhibition of oxidative phosphorylation. The nature of the cell response depends on the colicin involved. Resident bacteria can also alter the chemical environment so that it is unfavorable for the growth of less desirable organisms. For example, lactobacilli in the adult vagina help maintain an acidic pH (4.0 to 4.5), which is probably not optimal for the growth of a number of potential pathogens.

If the ecological balance of these microbial communities is disturbed as it is when an antibiotic acts upon important resident bacteria, other microbes normally kept in check in the ecosystem can multiply and possibly cause complications. This phenomenon has been called superinfection. The superinfecting organism may be a bacterium or a fungus and is either initially resistant to the antibiotic or has become resistant during therapy. The degree of discomfort and patient risk that can attend the complication of superinfection ranges from superficial irritation or mild diarrhea to severe pneumonia or acute enteritis. The risk of creating conditions that would lead to flora overgrowth and superinfection must be considered by the physician in the rational administration of antibiotics. It is important that the physician be aware of the general spectrum of action of an antibiotic, that he be attuned to the signs and symptoms signaling the presence of superinfection, and that he carefully consider the necessity for continuing the antibiotic treatment if superinfection ensues. The concept of superinfection has only been introduced here; it will be discussed in more detail in Chapter 4 and throughout the text.

Bacterial Determinants

Intrinsic Resistance

The most obvious determinant of bacterial response to an antibiotic is the presence or absence of the target for the drug action. If an organism lacks the receptor for the drug, it will not respond and is therefore inherently insensitive to the antibiotic action. The polyenes (e.g., amphotericin B, nystatin) are antibiotics that kill fungi by altering the permeability of the cell membrane. These drugs bind tightly to sterols in the fungal cell membrane, and the presence of sterol is required for drug action. Since bacterial membranes do not contain sterols, they are insensitive to the antibiotic. Most bacteria do not respond to isoniazid, a drug used to treat tuberculosis. Isoniazid is effective against the mycobacteria because it inhibits the synthesis of mycolic acids, which are unique components of mycobacterial cell walls. Since other bacteria do not have the biochemical pathway containing the target for the drug action, they are inherently insensitive.

Bacteria often contain the drug receptor but they do not respond because the concentration of antibiotic at the target site is inadequate. Although the organism is not insensitive, for all practical purposes it behaves as if it were with respect to the chemotherapeutic goal. The failure of fungi to respond to rifampin is an example of this type of intrinsic resistance. The site of action of rifampin is in the cell interior where inhibition of DNA-dependent RNA polymerase occurs. Although fungal polymerases are inhibited by the antibiotic, rifampin is not particularly effective against fungi because it does not readily pass through the fungal cell envelope to its site of action. This intrinsic resistance of the fungus can be altered by simultaneous exposure to a polyene antibiotic. In the presence of a low concentration of amphotericin B, the permeability of the cell membrane is altered and the barrier to rifampin entry lowered. Rifampin now enters the organism, sufficient concentrations of drug are achieved at the site of action, and the synthesis of fungal RNA is inhibited.

Another example of intrinsic resistance on the part of an organism that contains appropriate drug targets is provided by the gram-negative bacilli. The difference in the permeability barrier provided by the cell envelopes of gram-negative and gram-positive organisms is important in determining sensitivity patterns to the penicillins. Gram-positive bacteria are encased in a cell membrane surrounded by a peptidoglycan wall. In these organisms, the penicillins have very easy access to their target site, the transpeptidase enzyme, which is attached to the external surface of the cytoplasmic membrane. The gram-negative envelope is more complex, and in general, it is less permeable to the antibiotic. As shown in Figure 1-2, the gram-negative cell envelope has a second membrane external to the peptidoglycan wall. A penicillin therefore must pass through a charged area at the surface of the outer membrane, traverse the hydrophobic membrane interior, and diffuse through the periplasmic space before reaching its site of action. Some penicillins (penicillin G and the other narrow-spectrum compounds) that are effective against gram-positive bacteria do not readily pass through the cell envelope of most gram-negative bacilli. The chemical modifications that yielded the broad-spectrum penicillins (e.g., ampicillin, carbenicillin) apparently make it possible for these drugs to pass more easily through the external layers of the envelope and thus be effective against many gram-negative infections.

Escape from the Antibiotic Effect

Sometimes bacteria are sensitive to an antibiotic and sufficient concentrations are achieved at the site of action, but the organism is able to escape the consequences of the drug effect. Sulfonamides prevent the normal production of purines, thymidine, methionine, and serine by blocking the synthesis of the folate cofactor. But if these compounds are present in the environment, the bacterium may be able to utilize them as precursors for further biochemical synthesis and escape the consequences of the drug blockade.

Another example of escape is that of the failure of penicillin therapy in some cases of pyelonephritis caused by penicillin-

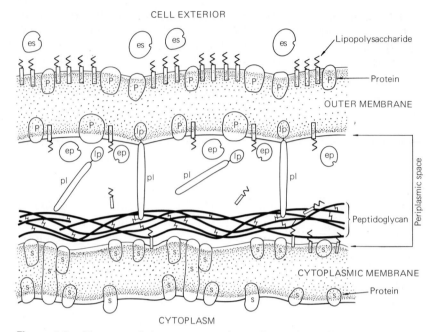

Figure 1-2. Diagram of the gram-negative cell envelope. The three-layered gram-negative envelope consists of two membranes separated by a periplasmic space containing the cross-linked peptidoglycan. Hydrophobic regions are here stippled. Each membrane has protein as well as phospholipid and lipopolysaccharide components: s and p designate the protein components of these membranes. There are also extramembrane proteins. Some of these enzymes are at the cell surface (es) and others are localized in the periplasmic zone (ep). The outer membrane is attached to the peptidoglycan wall by lipoprotein bridges; pl and lp refer to the protein and lipid portions of these bridging units. (Adapted from Costerton *et al.*[5])

sensitive organisms.[6] The penicillins act by inhibiting cell wall synthesis. If bacteria are growing in an appropriately high osmotic environment, they can escape the consequences of the antibiotic effect by converting to the L-form, a state in which the organism does not have a cell wall. These wall-free bacteria have been recovered from penicillin-treated cases of pyelonephritis by culture in special hypertonic medium. When penicillin therapy is stopped, these L-forms may be able to revert to eubacteria and the infection may continue.

Acquired Drug Resistance

A population of organisms can lose its sensitivity to an antibiotic while the patient is under treatment. In some cases, the loss of sensitivity may be slight, but often, organisms become resistant to any clinically achievable concentration of drug. The relative abundance of resistant organisms in a microbial population increases as continuing antibiotic therapy preferentially eliminates drug-sensitive cells. This process of enrichment is called selection, and the continuing presence of the antibiotic is said to exert a selective pressure in favor of the resistant organisms.

Microorganisms become less sensitive to antibiotics through a variety of biochemical mechanisms. The major mechanisms of resistance determined for clinical microbial isolates will be discussed as each drug is presented in subsequent chapters. In addition to the clinically important mechanisms, some unique modes of resistance studied only in laboratory strains will be discussed. These examples will be presented either because the resistance mechanism has played an important role in defining the biochemical mechanism of the drug action or to point out some of the ingenious ways in which microorganisms can change in order to live in the presence of antibiotics.

Most antibiotic resistance in microorganisms fits one of several general mechanisms, which may be classified as follows:[7]

1. Decreased Drug Uptake—The principal mechanism of tetracycline resistance in bacteria
2. Increased Destruction of Drug—The principal mechanism of resistance to the penicillins, aminoglycosides, and chloramphenicol
3. Decreased Conversion of a Drug to the Active Growth Inhibitory Compound—The antifungal drug flucytosine must be converted in the organism to fluorouracil, which is further metabolized to the active form of the drug. Fungi become resistant to flucytosine by losing the activity of enzymes along the activation pathway
4. Increased Concentration of a Metabolite Antagonizing the Drug Action—This has been shown to occur rarely in bacteria resistant to sulfonamides and in fungi resistant to flucytosine
5. Altered Amount of Drug Receptor—Some organisms become resistant to trimethoprim by synthesizing large amounts of dihydrofolate reductase, the target of the drug

action. The alteration may be in the direction of less receptor as well. In the rare instances in which fungi have become resistant to polyenes, the resistant organisms were found to synthesize decreased amounts of the membrane sterols to which these antibiotics must bind in order to produce the drug effect

6. Decreased Affinity of Receptor for the Drug—This mechanism has been defined in bacteria resistant to sulfonamides, trimethoprim, streptomycin, erythromycin, rifampin, and several other antibiotics

Microbial populations, particularly large inocula, often contain a few resistant organisms before the initiation of therapy. In some cases, the initial population is comprised solely of drug-sensitive cells, but one or a few organisms subsequently become resistant and are selected out during therapy. Drug resistance is acquired in two ways: it may arise *de novo* by mutation or it may be transferred to the infecting organism from other bacteria in the form of extrachromosomal pieces of DNA that contain the information for the resistance mechanism. This transfer of resistance will be discussed in the next section of the chapter.

The chromosomal type of resistance that arises because of mutation may change antibiotic sensitivity greatly or moderately, depending upon the location, type, and biological consequence of the mutation. For example, a single point mutation in the part of a gene coding for the receptor site of a drug may have one of several effects. The receptor protein may be altered so that it will no longer be able to bind the drug, although it still can carry out its biological function (assuming that the protein is an enzyme) sufficiently well to permit survival of the microorganism. This would constitute an example of a large-step mutation to drug insensitivity and it is not common. Or the receptor protein may be altered so that it has less affinity for the drug. In this case, the antibiotic is still effective, but higher concentrations are required. Additional mutational events, each conferring a small degree of resistance by one of the general mechanisms outlined above, will lead eventually to the production of organisms that are resistant to the concentrations of antibiotic achievable in therapy. This is called the multiple-step pattern of resistance as opposed to the facultative large-step pattern. It has been well documented that the mutations that lead to resistance occur as random events in the bacterial population.[7] Thus, they occur whether or not the antibiotic is present and the drug only exerts a selection pressure.

R-Factors and the Problem of Infectious, Multiple Drug Resistance

Occasionally, one bacterial strain confers resistant properties on a previously drug-sensitive strain by transferring to it an extrachromosomal piece of DNA called an R-factor. If, for example, the R-factor contains the gene for penicillinase, the bacterium will then be able to synthesize its own penicillin inactivating enzyme. Most clinical isolates of antibiotic-resistant gram-negative bacteria harbor R-factors, and this mode of antibiotic resistance constitutes a major problem in the field of chemotherapy of infection.

The First Observations

At the end of World War II, the sulfonamides were introduced into Japan for the treatment of bacillary dysentery. As a result, the incidence of the disease decreased by about 80 per cent within 2 years.[8] After 1949, however, the incidence of dysentery rose above the level observed at the end of the war. This higher incidence was seen despite the extensive use of sulfonamides; most of the Shigella strains isolated from cases at that time were found to be resistant to the drug. After 1952, newer antibiotics, such as streptomycin, chloramphenicol, and the tetracyclines, were used to treat the sulfonamide-resistant shigellae. With the advent of these newer drugs, the number of dysentery patients fell somewhat, but within only 4 years it became clear that their therapeutic usefulness was also diminishing rapidly. After 1952, Japanese workers isolated one strain of Shigella from each dysentery epidemic and tested it for resistance to streptomycin, chloramphenicol, and the tetracyclines (see Table 1-1). By 1958, a number of the strains being recovered were simultaneously resistant to two or three of these antibiotics. Many of the strains listed in the table were resistant to sulfonamides as well.

In epidemiological studies, Shigella strains isolated from some patients were completely sensitive, whereas serologically identical strains isolated from other patients in the same epidemic were resistant to a number of drugs. Stool cultures from a single patient were sometimes found to contain both sensitive and multiple drug-resistant strains of the same serological type. Finally, it was observed that the administration of chloramphenicol alone to patients infected with sensitive Shigella could result in the appearance of organisms that were resistant to many drugs. These findings were tied together when one of the Japanese investigators

Table 1-1 **Antibiotic resistance in shigellae isolated from epidemics of bacillary dysentery in Japan**

One strain of *Shigella* was isolated from each epidemic of bacillary dysentery occurring in Japan from 1953 to 1969 and tested for resistance to streptomycin (Sm), tetracycline (Tc), and chloramphenicol (Cm). (Data from Watanabe.[28])

					Number of strains resistant to:			
Year	Number of strains tested	Sm	Tc	Cm	Sm, Cm	Sm, Tc	Cm, Tc	Sm, Cm, Tc
1953	4900	5	2	0	0	0	0	0
1956	4399	8	4	0	0	0	1	0
1958	6563	18	20	0	7	2	0	193
1960	3396	29	36	0	61	9	7	308

postulated that multiple drug resistance might be transferred from multiple drug-resistant *E. coli* to shigellae in the patient's intestinal tract. It was demonstrated that multiple drug-resistant *E. coli* could be cultured *in vitro* with sensitive *Shigella* and that the multiple resistance could then be transferred to the shigellae without the simultaneous transfer of a number of genetic markers that are a part of the genome of *E. coli*.[9]

The Mechanism

Since the original observations of drug resistance transfer, we know a great deal more about the mechanisms by which drug resistance determinants are maintained and transmitted from cell to cell.[10] The genes coding for drug resistance are located in circular pieces of extrachromosomal DNA called R-determinants. In *Enterobacteriaceae*, R-determinants can be transferred to other bacteria after they become linked to another extrachromosomal piece of DNA called a resistance transfer factor or RTF. The complete unit is called an R-factor (Figure 1-3). The RTF contains the information required for bacterial conjugation, permitting the transmission of drug resistance genes to the appropriate recipient bacteria. Both R-determinants and RTF can exist as separate closed circles of DNA or combined as a complete R-factor.[11] Each unit (R-determinant, RTF, or the combination of the two) is called a plasmid; it contains its own genes for replication and it replicates autonomously, that is, its replication is not linked to that of the chromosomal DNA. Plasmids usually determine resistance to more than one antibiotic and are classified according to incompatibility groups. Plasmids of the same incompatibility group are

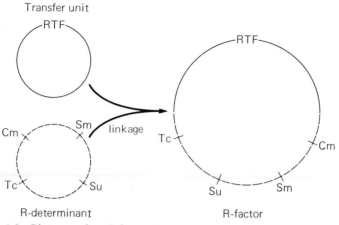

Figure 1-3 Diagram of an R-factor that contains information for determining resistance to tetracycline (Tc), sulfonamide (Su), streptomycin (Sm), and chloramphenicol (Cm). Genetic determinants for antibiotic resistance (R-determinants) can exist independently of the transfer factor or in combination with it.[12] The transfer unit contains the genetic information that directs the transfer of the whole plasmid during bacterial conjugation.

similar (they possess considerable DNA homology), but they cannot stably coexist with each other. They can, however, cohabitate with each member of any other incompatibility set, and a bacterial cell may contain multiple plasmids as long as they belong to different incompatibility groups.

R-factors are responsible for most of the drug resistance observed clinically among the Enterobacteriaceae and they cause the rapid spread of drug resistance through a microbial population, even among different strains. *Staphylococcus aureus*, a gram-positive organism, also contains plasmid elements analogous to R-factors. These plasmids do not have RTF (the transfer factor) and therefore are not transmitted by conjugation as in the gram-negative bacteria. Transmission occurs at a lower frequency by transduction with bacteriophage. The plasmids of S. *aureus* also determine multiple drug resistance. Most of the penicillin resistance encountered in this organism clinically is due to penicillinase produced from plasmids, not from chromosomal genes.

The Clinical and Epidemiological Problem

Few physicians outside the specialty of infectious disease realize the extent to which R-factors are responsible for the antibiotic resistance they encounter clinically. The physician must be aware of some of the properties of R-factors in order to understand the real and the possible clinical significance of this form of resistance transmission. Nonpathogenic coliform organisms can serve as a reservoir of resistance that can be transmitted to pathogens. In some cases, this may pose a serious therapeutic dilemma. For example, multiple drug resistance (including resistance to the drug of choice) has been found in isolates from cases of such severe diseases as cholera and typhoid fever. The presence of carbenicillin resistance in *Pseudomonas* infecting patients in a burn unit has been shown to be due to R-factor transmitted determinants derived from other bacteria resident in the alimentary tract.[13] Treatment of a patient with an antibiotic to which R-factor—mediated resistance determinants exist is followed by rapid conversion of the gut flora to the appropriate resistance pattern (sometimes as many as 90 per cent of all strains isolated are resistant within a few days).[13] Since the resistance determinants are usually multiple, one can enrich for coliform resistance to penicillins or kanamycin, for example, while treating a patient with a tetracycline. When antibiotic treatment is ended, the percentage of resistant flora usually declines. This implies that R-factors confer some growth disadvantage on the host bacteria.

The way antibiotic use can affect the resistance pattern of coliform bacteria can be appreciated from the data of Table 1-2.[14] In this study, researchers sampled the effluent of sewers draining hospitals and adjacent residential areas. Coliform bacteria were cultured and antibiotic sensitivity was determined on each strain. From the data, it is clear that there was a high incidence of resistance in coliform organisms cultured from the sewers of general hospitals as compared to sewage draining from residential areas or a mental hospital. It was confirmed in the study that a much wider variety of antibiotics and many more courses of treatment were prescribed in the general hospitals than in the large mental hospital.

In the above study, the coliform bacilli in the sewage from general hospitals had a much higher proportion of antibiotic resistance, more R-factors, and a greater proportion of R-factors carrying multiple resistance than sewage organisms from residential and other sources. Despite this enrichment in the effluent from general hospitals, it was calculated that 95 per cent of the R-factors in the total sewage output of this English city did not originate in hospitals. Thus, since the normal population appears

Table 1-2 **Antibiotic resistance of coliform bacilli from sewers serving isolated premises**

Coliform organisms were cultured from effluent of sewers serving restricted premises, such as hospitals or adjacent residential areas. The coliform bacilli were then tested for antibiotic sensitivity by the disk method. (Excerpted from Linton et al.[14])

Area	Premises	Number of samples	Percentage of coliform bacilli resistant to:		
			Streptomycin	Chloramphenicol	Tetracycline
A	General hospital	3	48.8	0.4	24.3
	Residential area	3	0.6	0.007	0.1
B	General hospital	3	34.7	0.7	32.0
BC	Residential area	3	6.5	0.02	1.3
C	Mental hospital	2	9.5	0.03	0.4

to be the greatest source of R-factors, one must ask what contributes to this drug resistance reservoir. The answer to the question is probably quite complex and it is certainly not yet defined.

One factor that may contribute to the maintenance of the pool of transmissible drug resistance plasmids is the selective pressure created by the widespread use of antibiotics in animal feeds. The economic advantage of this practice has been clearly demonstrated. Antibiotics kill intestinal microorganisms that commonly infect livestock living under crowded conditions and cause diarrhea and a decreased growth rate.[15] The prolonged use of antibiotics in animal feed results in the presence of R-factors in a high percentage of the coliform organisms.[16]

Drug resistance can be transferred from animal flora to the resident flora of man. This has been shown, for example, in an outbreak of tetracycline-resistant salmonellosis that was traced back to calves that had been treated with the antibiotic. Some data also suggest that the multiple drug resistance of *E. coli* in the gut of humans who work with livestock may result from the transfer of resistance from animal strains.[17] On the basis of prudent judgment a few antibiotics that are critical to the treatment of human disease are now excluded from use in animal feeds.

Many people feel that the drug resistance occurring in the animal population could reduce the effectiveness of drug therapy in man. Although there is, as yet, no proof that the use of antibiot-

ics in animal feeds is a major factor responsible for the maintenance of R-factors in human coliform organisms, it is possible. Much more information must be generated on the natural history of R-factors in our environment before we will be able to entertain the possibility of reducing this form of drug resistance by the use of a rational scientific approach.

REFERENCES

1. B. D. Davis, R. Dulbecco, H. N. Eisen, H. S. Ginsberg, and W. B. Wood: *Microbiology* (second edition), New York: Harper & Row, 1973, pp. 627–665.

2. C. M. Kunin, T. Tupasi, and W. A. Craig: Use of antibiotics: A brief exposition of the problem and some tentative solutions. *Ann. Int. Med.* 79:555 (1973).

3. W. E. Scheckler and J. V. Bennett: Antibiotic usage in seven community hospitals. *J. Am. Med. Assoc.* 213:264 (1970).

4. L. Weinstein and A. C. Dalton: Host determinants of response to antimicrobial agents. *New Eng. J. Med.* 279:467–473; 524–531; 580–588 (1968).

5. J. W. Costerton, J. M. Ingram, and K. J. Cheng: Structure and function of the cell envelope of gram-negative bacteria. *Bact. Rev.* 38:87 (1974).

6. L. B. Guze and G. M. Kalmanson: Persistence of bacteria in "protoplast" form after apparent cure of pyelonephritis in rats. *Science* 143:1340 (1964).

7. A. Goldstein, L. Aronow, and S. M. Kalman: *Principles of Drug Action*, New York: John Wiley & Sons, 1974, pp. 517–567.

8. T. Watanabe: Infective heredity of multiple drug resistance in bacteria. *Bacteriol. Rev.* 27:87 (1963).

9. T. Akiba, K. Koyama, Y. Ishiki, S. Kimura, and J. Fukushima: On the mechanism of the development of multiple-drug-resistant clones of *Shigella. Japan, J. Microb.* 4:219 (1960).

10. D. R. Helinski: Plasmid determined resistance to antibiotics: Molecular properties of R factors. *Ann. Rev. Microbiol.* 27:437 (1973).

11. S. N. Cohen and C. A. Miller: Non-chromosomal antibiotic resistance in bacteria; molecular nature of R-factors isolated from *Proteus mirabilis* and *Escherichia coli. J. Mol. Biol.* 50:671 (1970).

12. T. Watanabe and T. Fukasawa: Episome-mediated transfer of drug resistance in Enterobacteriaceae, transfer of resistance factors by conjugation. *J. Bacteriol.* 81:669 (1961).

13. M. H. Richmond: "R Factors in Man and His Environment" in *Microbiology—1974* ed. by D. Schlessinger. Washington: American Society of Microbiology, 1975, pp. 27–35.

14. K. B. Linton, M. H. Richmond, R. Bevan and W. A. Gillespie: Antibiotic resistance and R factors in coliform bacilli isolated from hospital and domestic sewage. *J. Med. Microbiol.* 7:91 (1974).

15. T. H. Jukes: Antibiotics in meat production. *J. Am. Med. Assoc.* 232:292 (1975).

16. E. S. Anderson: The ecology of transferable drug resistance in the enterobacteria. *Ann. Rev. Microbiol.* 22:131 (1968).

17. F. J. Marsik, J. T. Parisi and J. C. Blenden: Transmissible drug resistance of *Escherichia coli* and *Salmonella* from humans, animals, and their rural environments. *J. Infect. Dis.* 132:296 (1975).

Chapter 2
The Inhibitors
of Cell Wall Synthesis
The Penicillins
The Cephalosporins
Vancomycin
Bacitracin
Cycloserine

Discovery of the Penicillins

The discovery of penicillin is a now classic story of serendipity in scientific investigation. In 1928, Fleming noted that bacteria growing in culture in the vicinity of a contaminating mold were lysed.[1] He followed up this observation by culturing the mold in broth and demonstrating that filtrates of the broth were bactericidal in vitro. Almost a decade later, a group at Oxford led by H. W. Florey isolated a crude preparation of the bactericidal agent from cultures of Penicillium notatum. These investigators subsequently demonstrated the usefulness of this antibiotic in the treatment of bacterial infections in man. Although the basic unit of the penicillins has been synthesized, penicillin is produced commercially by isolation from cultures of mold that have been genetically altered to produce a very high yield.

In many cases, a detailed knowledge of the structure of an antibiotic is not particularly critical for developing an understanding of the current state of knowledge regarding its mechanism of action. For the penicillin group, however, a knowledge of the basic structure of the molecule is critical for understanding, at the molecular level, the basis of the mechanism of action, the development of bacterial cell resistance, and the mechanisms underlying the allergic response. The molecule penicillin G is composed of a thiazolidine ring attached to a four-membered (β-lactam) ring and a side chain attached in peptide linkage to the β-lactam ring. The four-membered ring is somewhat strained, and a number of important ring-opening reactions take place here. The cephalosporins, another group of compounds isolated from fungi, have the same mechanism of action as the penicillins and a similar structure with the characteristic β-lactam ring.

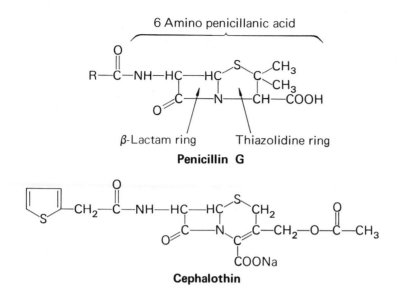

6 Amino penicillanic acid

Penicillin G

Cephalothin

MECHANISM OF ACTION

Site of Action

The cell wall of a bacterium forms a rather rigid skeleton on the outer surface of the cell membrane. The bacterial cell membrane, in essence, encases a volume hypertonic to the environment of the organism. Although the cell membrane is critical to the maintenance of the osmotic gradient between the organism and its environment, it is not strong enough in itself to keep the hypertonic sac from rupturing by osmotic shock. Thus, the cell wall, which encases the cell membrane as a continuous, highly cross-linked molecule, prevents the cell membrane from rupturing. The penicillins inhibit the formation of cross-links between the units of the cell wall. As a result a strong cell wall network is not made. Continued activity of a group of bacterial surface enzymes, called autolysins, leads to cleavage of previously synthesized cell wall, creating weak points through which the cell membrane extrudes and where membrane rupture eventually occurs. The ruptured cell is, of course, no longer viable. Thus, the penicillins are bactericidal agents. The critical role of the autolysins in bringing about cell death after exposure to the penicillins and other drugs that inhibit cell wall synthesis will be expanded upon later.

When the bacterium is growing in a medium isotonic to the cytoplasm, exposure to penicillin, rather than rupturing the bacterium, can lead to the production of organisms that have no cell wall.[2] Such bacteria, encased solely in their cell membranes, are called protoplasts or spheroplasts. The principal site of synthesis of the cell wall of many bacteria lies in a narrow growth zone that extends in a girdle around the organism. If *Escherichia coli*, for

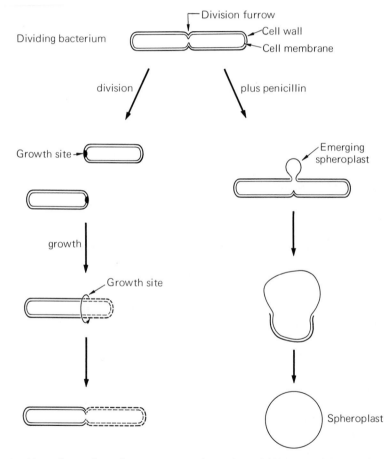

Figure 2-1 Normal cell growth and division compared to the formation of penicillin spheroplasts. Normal cell wall synthesis often takes place at a growth site that encircles the cell. In the presence of penicillin, cross-linking of the cell wall units is inhibited, and the cell membrane then protrudes out of the structurally defective cell wall.

Table 2-1 **Incorporation of isotopes into cell wall, cell protein, and nucleic acid in *Staphylococcus aureus***

Penicillin was introduced into cultures of *S. aureus,* and the cultures were incubated for 20 minutes with radioactive leucine or phosphate. Incorporation as counts per minute per milligram protein. (From Nathenson and Strominger,[4] Table 1.)

Culture	Incorporation of [14C]lysine into:		Incorporation of 32P inorganic phosphate into:	
	Cell wall	Cell protein and nucleic acid	Cell wall	Cell protein and nucleic acid
Control	34,800	5,100	155,000	11,600
Penicillin (100 μg/ml)	3,290	4,960	48,900	11,600

example, are exposed to penicillin, small protrusions of the cell membrane emerge at this division furrow.[3] One model of the sequence of events in bacterial cell growth and in the production of penicillin spheroplasts is presented schematically in Figure 2-1.

Early experiments demonstrated that exposure of *Staphylococcus aureus* to penicillin resulted in a marked inhibition of radioactive precursor (leucine or phosphate) incorporation into the cell wall but not into bacterial protein or nucleic acid[4] (Table 2-1). It was clear that the process of cell wall biosynthesis would have to be explained in order to understand its inhibition by antibiotics.

Inhibition of Cell Wall Synthesis

Synthesis of a bacterial cell wall can be divided into three stages according to where in the cell the reactions are taking place (Figure 2-2). The first series of reactions, resulting in the production of the basic cell wall building block (the UDP-acetylmuramyl-pentapeptide), takes place inside the cell. Cycloserine, a very toxic antibiotic that is employed rarely in the treatment of tuberculosis, inhibits one of the terminal reactions in this sequence. In the second stage of cell wall synthesis, the precursor unit is carried from inside the cell membrane outside. During this process, a number of modifications occur in the chemical structure of the basic repeating unit of the cell wall, and the units are linked covalently to the preexisting cell wall. The antibiotics vancomycin and bacitracin act during this second stage. The third stage of the process is a single reaction that takes place outside the cell

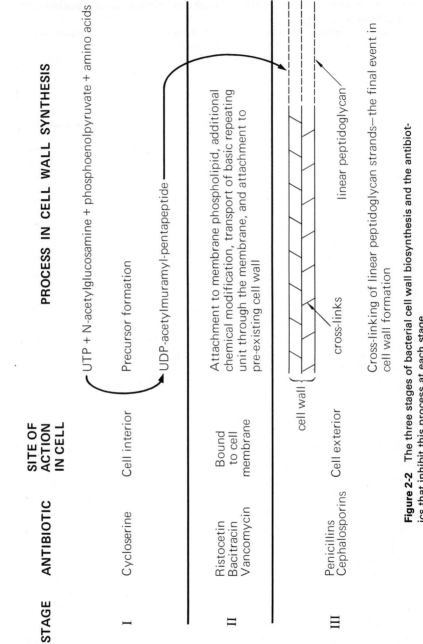

Figure 2-2 The three stages of bacterial cell wall biosynthesis and the antibiotics that inhibit this process at each stage.

membrane and results in the cross-linking of linear molecules to form the highly cross-linked, tough outer envelope of the cell. This cross-linking reaction is inhibited by the penicillins and cephalosporins.

Stage I—Precursor Formation

The sequence of reactions comprising the first stage of cell wall synthesis in *S. aureus* is presented in Figure 2-3. In the first reaction, UTP is bound covalently to N-acetylglucosamine-1-P to form UDP-N-acetylglucosamine. Subsequent reactions add a three-carbon unit from phosphoenolpyruvate and three amino acids to form a UDP-acetylmuramyltripeptide. In the final reaction of this stage, a D-alanyl-D-alanine dipeptide is joined to the UDP-acetylmuramyltripeptide to produce the UDP-acetylmuramyl-pentapeptide, which is then available to participate in the second stage of cell wall synthesis. Exposure of bacteria to the

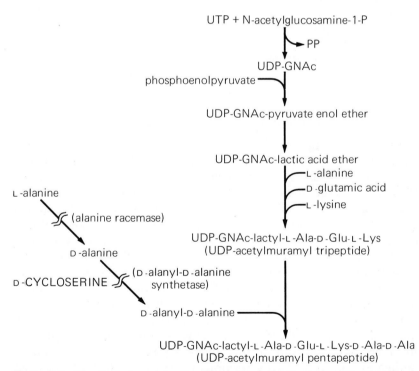

Figure 2-3 The first stage of cell wall synthesis in *S. aureus*. The reactions inhibited by D-cycloserine are indicated by the break marks.

antibiotics that inhibit stages II and III of cell wall synthesis will result in an accumulation of the pentapeptide in the cell.

Exposure of organisms to cyloserine prevents the formation of the pentapeptide. D-Cycloserine is a structural analog of D-alanine. The antibiotic is a competitive inhibitor of both alanine racemase and D-alanyl-D-alanine synthetase. Both enzymes bind the antibiotic 100 times as strongly ($K_i = 5 \times 10^{-5}$ M) as they bind the normal substrate ($K_m = 5 \times 10^3$ M).[5] It is postulated that the drug has a higher affinity for the enzymes because it has a more rigid ring structure that maintains it in the appropriate conformation for occupying the substrate sites. The natural alanine substrate is more flexible and would assume the appropriate conformation only rarely.[6]

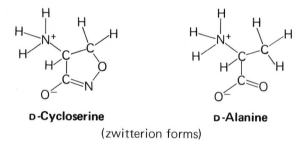

D-Cycloserine   D-Alanine

(zwitterion forms)

Stage II—Formation of a Linear Peptidoglycan

In the second stage of cell wall synthesis, the two uridine nucleotides UDP-acetylmuramyl pentapeptide and UDP-N-acetylglucosamine are linked together to form a linear polymer (Figure 2-4). During this stage, the cell wall precursor units are attached to the cell membrane. In the first reaction, the sugar pentapeptide becomes attached by a pyrophosphate bridge to a phospholipid bound to the cell membrane. Then a second sugar derived from UDP-N-acetylglucosamine is added to form a disaccharide (-pentapeptide)-P-P-phospholipid. In S. aureus, this molecule is further modified by a series of reactions resulting in the addition of five glycines to the ε-amino group of lysine. In this unusual reaction sequence glycyl-tRNA serves as the amino acid donor molecule.[7] The modified disaccharide is subsequently separated from the phospholipid and is covalently bonded to an acceptor molecule (i.e., preexisting portions of cell wall) to form a linear peptidoglycan polymer. In the terminal reaction of stage II, the

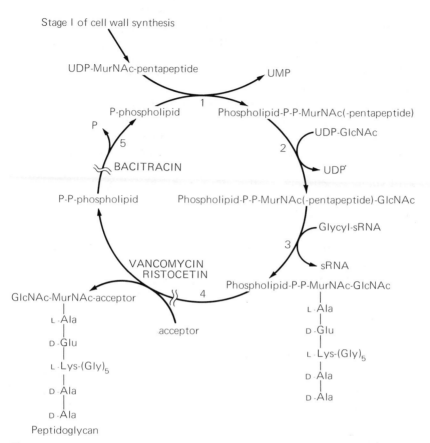

Stage I of cell wall synthesis

UDP-MurNAc-pentapeptide → UMP

P-phospholipid

Phospholipid-P-P-MurNAc(-pentapeptide)

UDP-GlcNAc

UDP'

BACITRACIN

P-P-phospholipid

Phospholipid-P-P-MurNAc(-pentapeptide)-GlcNAc

Glycyl-sRNA

sRNA

Phospholipid-P-P-MurNAc-GlcNAc
|
L-Ala
|
D-Glu
|
L-Lys-(Gly)_5
|
D-Ala
|
D-Ala

VANCOMYCIN
RISTOCETIN

GlcNAc-MurNAc-acceptor
|
L-Ala
|
D-Glu
|
L-Lys-(Gly)_5
|
D-Ala
|
D-Ala

acceptor

Peptidoglycan

Figure 2-4 The second stage of cell wall synthesis in *S. aureus*. An ATP-requiring amidation of glutamic acid that occurs between reaction 2 and reaction 3 has been omitted. The sites of inhibition by bacitracin, vancomycin, and ristocetin are indicated by the break marks. (Modified from Strominger *et al.* [6])

phospholipid carrier molecule with two phosphate groups attached is dephosphorylated with the release of inorganic phosphate. The resulting phospholipid can again bind the end product of stage I synthesis, the UDP-N-acetylmuramyl pentapeptide, and continue on another cycle of the membrane-bound reactions.

During the course of the stage II reactions, the basic repeating units of the cell wall are put together to form a long polymer. All the events up to this point occur either inside the cell or at the cell membrane. It is postulated that the lipid intermediates formed probably represent a mechanism for transporting the prefabricated units of the cell wall through the cell membrane to the exterior site where they are utilized for cell wall synthesis.[5] Two antibiotics that are employed clinically, vancomycin and bacitracin, inhibit the utilization of the lipid intermediates for the synthesis of the peptidoglycan.

Vancomycin and ristocetin (ristocetin is too toxic to be used clinically) inhibit the reaction in which the finished unit is separated from the membrane-bound phospholipid and attached to the acceptor molecule (Reaction 4, Figure 2-4). Both these antibiotics inhibit the formation of peptidoglycan from the appropriate second-stage precursors at the same concentration at which they inhibit cell growth.[8] As seen in Table 2-2, exposure to penicillin will only inhibit the second-stage process at a concentration of antibiotic more than 6000 times that required to inhibit growth. In the presence of vancomycin or ristocetin, there is a normal synthesis of lipid intermediates, but they cannot be utilized for synthesis of the peptidoglycan (Figure 2-5).

Release of the wall precursor unit from the phospholipid that attaches it to the cell membrane and its subsequent attachment to the growing cell wall (Reaction 4, Figure 2-4) are directed by an enzyme called peptidoglycan synthetase. The mechanism by which vancomycin inhibits the synthetase reaction is now being defined in some detail. It was observed that vancomycin-treated bacteria retained the drug tightly bound to cell wall precursor units.[10] It was then demonstrated that vancomycin binds very

Table 2-2 **Antibiotic sensitivity of cell growth and of peptidoglycan synthetase in Staphylococcus aureus**
Antibiotics were introduced into cultures of growing cells, and cell growth and peptidoglycan synthetase activity were measured. The enzyme activity was assayed by incubating a particulate enzyme preparation from drug-treated cells with radioactive-labeled UDP-N-acetylmuramyl-pentapeptide and the appropriate substrates and then determining the amount of radioactivity incorporated into peptidoglycan. (From Anderson et al.[8])

| | Antibiotic concentration (μg/ml) required for 50 per cent inhibition of: | |
Antibiotic	Growth	Peptidoglycan synthesis by particulate enzyme
Ristocetin	12	12
Vancomycin	6	6
Bacitracin	35	35
Penicillin	0.04	>250

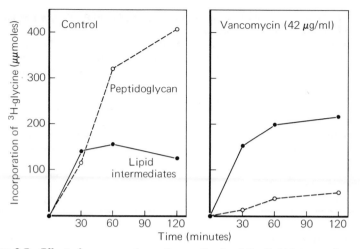

Figure 2-5 Effect of vancomycin on the synthesis of the lipid intermediates and peptidoglycan. A particulate enzyme preparation from *S. aureus* was incubated with [³H]glycine, tRNA, amino acid activating enzymes, and the appropriate substrates for stage II synthesis. The amount of glycine incorporated into peptidoglycan and lipid intermediates was determined at various times in the presence and absence of vancomycin. (From Matsuhashi *et al.*[9])

tightly to peptides that contain D-alanyl-D-alanine at the free carboxyl end.[11] The mechanism of action of vancomycin, as it is understood at this time, is as follows: The drug receptor is the membrane-bound cell wall precursor unit. Vancomycin binds with high affinity to the acyl-D-alanyl-D-alanine portion of this molecule. There is a rather strict requirement for the presence of two alanines in the D configuration for tight binding of the drug to occur.[12] It is postulated that the presence of the rather large vancomycin molecule tightly bound to the peptide side chain of the precursor unit provides enough stearic hinderance to prevent it from occupying the substrate site on the synthetase enzyme. Thus, step 4 in Figure 2-4 is blocked, and the membrane-bound intermediates formed in steps 1, 2, and 3 will accumulate in the presence of the drug. The physical nature of the drug-receptor complex is now being studied by utilizing such powerful techniques as nuclear magnetic resonance spectroscopy to determine the type of intermolecular interactions involved in the binding of vancomycin to acyl-D-alanyl-D-alanine units in solution.[13,14] The vancomycin story provides an elegant example of the development of knowledge regarding the mechanism of a drug action

Table 2-3 **Effect of antibiotics on the hydrolysis of lipid-P-^{32}P by a particulate enzyme from *Micrococcus lysodeikticus***

Particulate enzyme from *M. lysodeikticus* was incubated with lipid-P-^{32}P labeled only in the terminal phosphate. After incubation with and without an antibiotic, lipid phosphate and inorganic phosphate were separated and assayed for radioactivity. Results as counts per minute of inorganic phosphate released from lipid-P-[32]P. (From Siewert and Strominger.[15])

Antibiotic	Inorganic phosphate recovered (cpm)
None	1040
Bacitracin (153 μg/ml)	361
Vancomycin (40 μg/ml)	1001
Ristocetin (40 μg/ml)	1075

from the level of gross observation of the cell killing effect down to some understanding of the atomic perturbations that accompany the interaction of the drug with its receptor.

Bacitracin inhibits peptidoglycan synthesis by inhibiting the dephosphorylation of lipid pyrophosphate to lipid phosphate (Reaction 5, Figure 2-4), a step essential to the regeneration of the lipid carrier.[15] This is demonstrated by the experiment that provided the data for Table 2-3. Bacitracin inhibited the liberation of inorganic phosphate from lipid pyrophosphate, whereas vancomycin and ristocetin had no effect on this process.

In S. aureus, the lipid that attaches the precursor units to the cell membrane during the second stage of cell wall synthesis is a 55-carbon isoprenyl phosphate.[16] The dephosphorylation of the lipid pyrophosphate is carried out by a membrane-associated phosphatase.[17] Bacitracin forms a very tight complex with magnesium ion and the C_{55}-isoprenyl pyrophosphate,[18] and the formation of this complex is responsible for the inhibition of cell wall synthesis by the drug.[19] The precise details of how the association of the drug with the substrate blocks the dephosphorylation mechanism are not yet clear. Since the C_{55}-isoprenyl pyrophosphate must be dephosphorylated before it can act as an acceptor for another pentapeptide precursor unit, bacitracin effectively blocks further cell wall synthesis.

Stage III—Cross-Linking of the Peptidoglycan

This terminal event in cell wall synthesis takes place outside the cell membrane. There is no ATP available at the extracellular site to act as a source of energy for the reaction, which is a transpeptidation. The energy for the reaction is derived from the peptide bond linking the two terminal D-alanine residues of each polypeptide side chain. As seen in Figure 2-6, the transpeptidase enzyme directs the splitting of the terminal D-alanyl-D-alanine linkage and forms a peptide bond between the terminal glycine of the pentaglycine side chain and the penultimate D-alanine of an adjacent peptidoglycan strand. Thus, each polypeptide side chain of each repeating unit becomes covalently linked to the side chains in two neighboring peptidoglycan strands.

The penicillins and the cephalosporins are inhibitors of this transpeptidation.[20] In the presence of penicillin, fibrous material, which can be seen by electron microscopy, accumulates at the growing point of the bacterium.[21] These fibers presumably represent the accumulating peptidoglycan strands, which cannot cross-link. In certain organisms, exposure to penicillin under

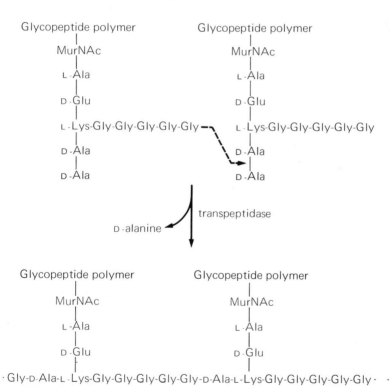

Figure 2-6 The third stage of cell wall synthesis in *S. aureus:* cross-linking of peptidoglycan polymers by the joining of the peptide side chains with the elimination of D-alanine. (Modified from Strominger *et al.*[6])

experimental conditions can be shown to effect secretion of linear uncross-linked peptidoglycan into the growth medium.[22] The inhibition of transpeptidases by both penicillins and cephalosporins has been demonstrated in cell-free enzyme preparations that catalyze the cross-linking reaction.[23,24] In vitro inhibition occurs at the same drug concentrations that are effective in killing the organisms. This is consistent with the conclusion that inhibition of transpeptidase activity is the important event that accounts for the penicillin effect.

The mechanism of the inhibition of transpeptidase by penicillin has not been directly demonstrated, but there is substantial evidence in support of the following model. The structure of the penicillins is similar to that of the D-alanyl-D-alanine terminus of the polypeptide side chain of peptidoglycan.[25] Figure 2-7 shows this similarity in drawings of stereo models of the antibiotic and the dipeptide. The arrows point to the CO-N bond in the β-lactam ring of penicillin and the analogous peptide bond in D-alanyl-D-alanine. It is postulated that the penicillins and cephalosporins

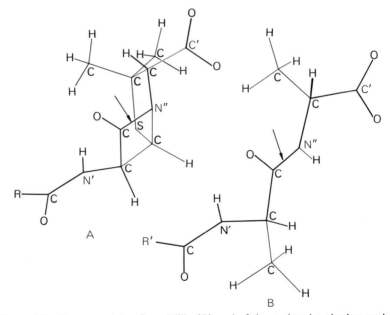

Figure 2-7 Stereomodels of penicillin (A) and of the D-alanyl-D-alanine end of the peptidoglycan strand (B). The arrows indicate the CO-N bond in the β-lactam ring of penicillin and the CO-N bond in the D-alanyl-D-alanine at the end of the peptidoglycan strand. (From Strominger *et al.*[6])

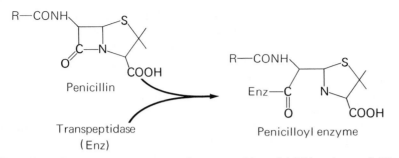

Figure 2-8 Proposed mechanism of transpeptidase inhibition by penicillin. Penicillin occupies the D-alanyl-D-alanine substrate site of transpeptidase, the reactive four-membered (β-lactam) ring is broken by cleavage at the CO-N bond, and the antibiotic becomes linked to the enzyme by a covalent bond. (From Tipper and Strominger.[25])

occupy the D-alanyl-D-alanine substrate site of the transpeptidase enzyme. In addition, the available evidence suggests that the antibiotic becomes covalently bound to the enzyme. This is supported by the observation that penicillin inhibition of transpeptidase is not reversed by washing the particulate enzyme preparation or by digestion with penicillinase.[23] According to this model, a penicillin would occupy the substrate site of transpeptidase, with the C-N bond of the β-lactam ring in the same orientation as the C-N peptide bond between the two D-alanines. This is the peptide bond that is cleaved as part of the normal action of the enzyme. The highly reactive C-N bond of the β-lactam ring of the antibiotic opens in a similar manner, but a covalent bond with the transpeptidase is formed, and the enzyme is irreversibly inactivated (Figure 2-8). This model is intellectually very attractive, and it is consistent with most experimental observations. It is not absolutely necessary that the drug bind covalently to the enzyme in order to be active. In some organisms, the β-lactam antibiotics occupy the substrate site of transpeptidase without the subsequent formation of a covalent bond.[26] In this case, enzyme inhibition is readily reversible.

The Attempt to Isolate the Penicillin-Receptor Complex

To better understand the nature of the drug-receptor interaction, much research effort has focused on isolating and characterizing penicillin-protein complexes from bacterial cells. The status of this work has been reviewed by Blumberg and Strominger.[27] It would at first seem to be a simple matter to expose bacterial cells or particulate enzyme preparations to radioactive penicillin and then examine the type of binding complexes that form. There are several major problems, however. In some bacteria, enzymes other than transpeptidases are inhibited by the β-lactam antibiotics. The D-alanine carboxypeptidases[28] (enzymes that hydrolyze the peptide bond between terminal D-alanine residues of cell wall units) and some endopeptidases[29] (enzymes that have an autolytic function, cleaving the cross-linkages of cell walls) are inhibited by the penicillins. The occurrence of tight penicillin binding does not necessarily represent penicillin-bound transpeptidase. *Bacillus subtilis* membranes, for example, have been shown to contain five penicillin-binding components, and the major component is a D-alanine carboxypeptidase, not transpeptidase.[30] This drug-protein complex does not represent the important interaction with respect to cell killing because inactivation of carboxypeptidase by penicillins and cephalosporins is clearly not lethal in *B. subtilis*.[31] But the carboxypeptidase has been solubilized and purified with retention of enzymatic activity,[32] permitting the study of the penicillin-enzyme interaction in some detail. Definitive studies of penicillin-transpeptidase binding have not been carried out because transpeptidases have not been separated from bacterial membranes with retention of cross-linking activity.

Despite these limitations, the study of bacterial penicillin-binding components has yielded valuable information. The *B. subtilis* carboxypeptidase is irreversibly inactivated by the penicillins,[33] and the bound drug is not released from the enzyme by a variety of procedures that denature the protein.[34] Some data suggest that the penicillin may be linked to the enzyme via a sulfur bridge.[35,36] This might indicate that the antibiotic forms a covalent bond with a sulfhydryl group in the substrate site of the carboxypeptidase. Since the antibiotic does seem to bind covalently to carboxypeptidase, this interaction may serve as a model system similar to the binding of the β-lactam antibiotics to transpeptidases. One interesting possibility is that the D-alanine carboxypeptidases constitute a different physical state of the transpeptidases, which are capable only of hydrolyzing the peptide bond between the two terminal D-alanine residues and thus cannot direct cross-link formation. It also seems clear that one organism may contain several transpeptidases, making it more difficult to define the lethal drug-receptor interaction.[37] For example, there is evidence that *S. aureus*, the organism we have used to describe the three stages of cell wall synthesis, contains two transpeptidases and two penicillin-binding components.[24,30]

Why Bacteria are Killed by Antibiotics that Inhibit Cell Wall Synthesis

The antibiotics that inhibit cell wall synthesis are all bactericidal upon addition to growing cultures of sensitive cells. Although we have described how these drugs inhibit various steps in the process of cell wall biosynthesis, such a description does not completely explain how they cause cell lysis and death. Cell lysis in many (and perhaps all) penicillin-sensitive organisms requires the continuous action of cell wall autolytic enzymes. The natural biological role for the autolysins is subject to speculation. They may be required to make nicks in the cell wall that serve as points of attachment for new peptidoglycan units[38] or they may be necessary to separate two daughter cells from one another during division.[39] The growth of the cell wall may require both autolytic and synthetic activity. Inhibition of biosynthesis in the presence of continued cell wall autolysis would produce weak points through which the cell membrane could extrude and eventually rupture would occur. This attractive hypothesis could be tested if one were able to examine the response to these antibiotics in bacteria that have very little autolytic activity.

The hypothesis has been tested in two ways. First, in mutants of Bacillus subtilis and Bacillus licheniformis with greatly reduced autolytic activity, very high concentrations of vancomycin or cycloserine are required to produce even a slow lysis of the organism.[40] The second approach has exploited the observation that the autolytic activity of Pneumococcus is suppressed when cells are grown in the presence of ethanolamine rather than choline.[41] This is due to the inability of the autolytic enzymes of this organism to hydrolyze ethanolamine-containing cell walls. It was then shown that cycloserine and penicillin did not lyse the ethanolamine-containing cells. When the cells were allowed to reincorporate choline into the cell wall, the normal lytic response to the antibiotics reappeared.[42]

In the case of both the autolysin-deficient mutants and the ethanolamine-containing Pneumococcus, low concentrations of antibiotic stopped cell growth, but the bacteria remained fully viable. Thus, the antibiotic effect had been converted from a bactericidal to a bacteriostatic one. These experiments also demonstrate a unique mechanism of production of multiple antibiotic resistance by the modification of an enzymatic process that is unaffected by the drug but necessary for expression of the drug effect (e.g., lysis).

Broad-Spectrum Penicillins versus Narrow-Spectrum Penicillins

Although most of the penicillins are relatively ineffective in inhibiting the growth of gram-negative organisms, a few (e.g., ampicillin and carbenicillin) are quite effective in treating infections due to certain gram-negative bacteria. These are the broad-spectrum penicillins. In this context "broad spectrum" is not equivalent to the term as it is applied to such truly broad-spectrum antibiotics as chloramphenicol or the tetracyclines. It merely refers to a broader spectrum of action than that of penicillin G and the penicillinase-resistant penicillins. In this restricted sense, the cephalosporins are also broad spectrum. Although the concept of broad versus narrow spectrum of action of the penicillins is of immense clinical importance, very little is known about why the broad-spectrum penicillins are effective against gram-negative organisms. As can be seen in Figure 2-9, there is very little difference in structure between penicillin G and the broad-spectrum agents. Currently, it is assumed that these minor structural differences permit the broad-spectrum penicillins to pass through the restrictive lipopolysaccharide-containing outer membrane of the gram-negative organism (see Chapter 1, Figure 1-2) to the transpeptidase enzyme that is bound to the cytoplasmic membrane. This is inferred from the observation that a particulate transpeptidase-containing preparation from a gram-negative organism like *E. coli* is as sensitive to inhibition by penicillin G as by the broad-spectrum drug, ampicillin.[28] Ampicillin kills the cells at the same concentration at which it inhibits the enzyme *in vitro*. But penicillin G kills the bacterium only at concentrations which are much higher than those required to inhibit the particulate enzyme. Thus, it appears that the broad-spectrum drug readily penetrates to the site of action, whereas narrow-spectrum agents like penicillin G do not.

PHARMACOLOGY OF PENICILLIN G AND ITS FORMULATIONS

Penicillin G is the prototype compound in the penicillin series, and it is appropriate to begin a review of the penicillins with a summary of the pharmacology of this drug and its formulations.

Penicillin G is benzylpenicillin (see Figure 2-9 for structure). It has a narrow spectrum of action and is sensitive to inactivation by penicillinase. It is still the drug of choice for the treatment of non-penicillinase-producing strains of most cocci, gram-positive bacilli, and spirochetes (Table 2-4). The two major limitations to the use of penicillin G in the treatment of the common infections cited in Table 2-4 are the production of penicillinase by the infecting organism and the presence of penicillin allergy. Both problems will be discussed later in this chapter.

Absorption

Approximately one-third of an oral dose of penicillin G is absorbed from the gastrointestinal tract, primarily from the duodenum.[44] Maximum blood levels are reached in about 45 minutes. Penicillin G is unstable in acid,[45] and though one would assume from this that maximum absorption of penicillin G would be achieved if the drug were ingested when the gastric pH is highest, this is not the case. For maximum absorption, penicillin G should be taken either 1 hour before or 2 to 3 hours after a meal, as it has been clearly shown that the absorption is highest when the stomach is empty.[46] This, however, is the time when the pH is the lowest. Apparently the longer retention time of the drug in the food-containing stomach results in more extensive inactivation despite the higher pH. There is a great deal of variability in the amount of penicillin G that is absorbed with each oral administration in the same patient. This variability is probably due to different degrees of acid inactivation.

When penicillin G is administered intramuscularly, maximum blood levels are achieved in 15 minutes. In more severe infections, the antibiotic is administered parenterally at first, and oral penicillin is then utilized as the patient's condition permits. A schematic drawing of the relative blood levels and durations of action of penicillin G administered in various forms is presented in Figure 2-10. There are two parenteral preparations of penicillin G that are very slowly absorbed from the site of intramuscular injection—procaine penicillin G and benzathine penicillin G. Procaine penicillin G yields peak blood levels in 2 to 4 hours, and the blood concentration declines to negligible levels by about 24 hours. Benzathine penicillin G is dissolved much more slowly, and very low serum levels of the antibiotic are detectable for 3 to 4 weeks after administration. Since these two forms of the antibiotic result in low blood levels, they must be employed only in the treatment of organisms that are very sensitive to penicillin G. An

Name	Side chain	Stability in acid	Spectrum of action	Sensitivity to penicillinase	Advantage
Penicillin G		Poor	Narrow	Sensitive	Cheapest
Phenoxymethyl penicillin (Pen V)		Good	Narrow	Sensitive	Better oral absorption than penicillin G
Methicillin		Poor (not given orally)	Narrow	Resistant	For parenteral treatment of infections due to penicillinase-producing organisms
Oxacillin		Good	Narrow	Resistant	For oral and parenteral treatment of infections due to penicillinase-producing organisms
Dicloxacillin		Good	Narrow	Resistant	For oral treatment of infections due to penicillinase-producing organisms
Cloxacillin		Good	Narrow	Resistant	

Name					Resistant	
Nafcillin	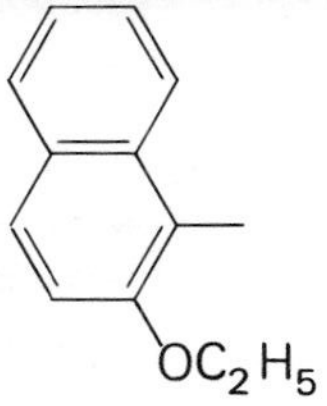	Poor		Narrow	Resistant	No important advantage over oxacillin or cloxacillins (on a weight basis, this the most potent of the penicillinase-resistant penicillins against staphylococci)
Ampicillin	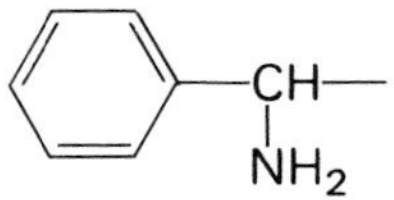	Fair		Broad	Sensitive	
Amoxicillin		Good		Broad	Sensitive	For treatment of infections due to gram-negative, non-resistant organisms
Carbenicillin		(not given orally)		Broad	Sensitive	
Carbenicillin indanyl sodium		Good		Broad	Sensitive	

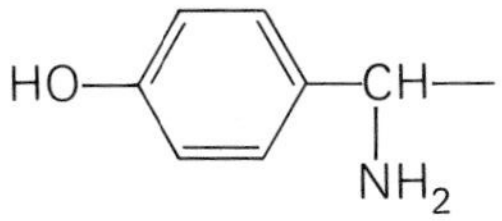

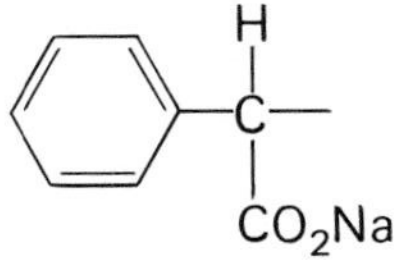

Nafcillin — OC₂H₅

Ampicillin — CH—NH₂

Amoxicillin — HO— CH—NH₂

Carbenicillin — H—C—CO₂Na

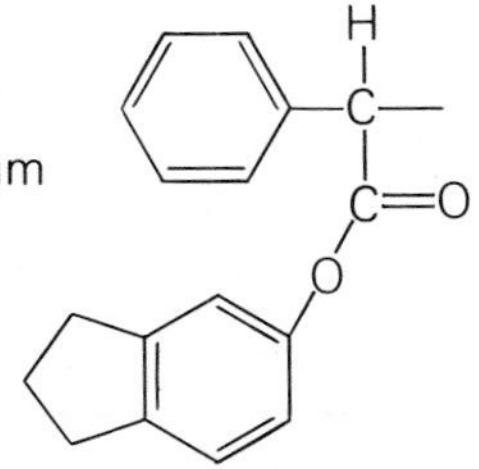

Carbenicillin indanyl sodium

Figure 2-9 Properties and advantages of a selected list of common penicillins.

Table 2-4 Pathogenic bacteria and appropriate drugs to consider for therapy
(From *The Medical Letter*.[43])

Infecting organism	Drug of first choice	Alternative drugs
GRAM-POSITIVE COCCI		
Staphylococcus aureus		
non-penicillinase-producing	Penicillin G or V	A cephalosporin; clindamycin; vancomycin
penicillinase-producing	A penicillinase-resistant penicillin	Same alternative drugs as for non-penicillinase-producing strains
Streptococcus pyogenes (Group A) and Groups B, C, and G	Penicillin G or V	An erythromycin
Streptococcus, viridans group	Penicillin G with or without streptomycin	A cephalosporin; vancomycin; an erythromycin with streptomycin
Streptococcus, Enterococcus group endocarditis or other severe infection	Ampicillin or penicillin G with streptomycin, kanamycin, or gentamicin	Vancomycin
uncomplicated urinary tract infection	Ampicillin or penicillin G	A tetracycline; trimethoprim-sulfamethoxazole
Streptococcus, anaerobic	Penicillin G	Clindamycin; a tetracycline; an erythromycin
Streptococcus (Diplococcus) pneumoniae	Penicillin G or V	An erythromycin; a cephalosporin; chloramphenicol
GRAM-NEGATIVE COCCI		
Neisseria gonorrhoeae	Penicillin G	Ampicillin; spectinomycin; a tetracycline
Neisseria meningitidis	Penicillin G	Chloramphenicol; a sulfonamide
GRAM-POSITIVE BACILLI		
Bacillus anthracis (anthrax)	Penicillin G	An erythromycin; a tetracycline
Clostridium perfringens (welchii)	Penicillin G	An erythromycin; a tetracycline
Clostridium tetani	Penicillin G	A tetracycline
Corynebacterium diphtheriae	An erythromycin	Penicillin G
Listeria monocytogenes	Ampicillin with or without	A tetracycline; an erythromycin

ENTERIC GRAM-NEGATIVE BACILLI

Bacteroides

oropharyngeal strains — Penicillin G — Clindamycin; chloramphenicol; ampicillin; a tetracycline

gastrointestinal strains — Clindamycin — Chloramphenicol; ampicillin; a tetracycline

Enterobacter — Gentamicin — Tobramycin; kanamycin; chloramphenicol; a tetracycline; carbenicillin

Escherichia coli

community-acquired — Ampicillin — Gentamicin; a tetracycline; a cephalosporin; kanamycin; chloramphenicol

hospital acquired — Gentamicin — Ampicillin; carbenicillin; a cephalosporin; tobramycin; kanamycin; a tetracycline; chloramphenicol

Klebsiella pneumoniae — Gentamicin with or without a cephalosporin — Tobramycin; kanamycin; a tetracycline; a cephalosporin; chloramphenicol

Proteus mirabilis — Ampicillin — Amoxicillin; kanamycin; a cephalosporin; gentamicin; tobramycin; chloramphenicol

other *Proteus* — Gentamicin — Tobramycin; kanamycin; carbenicillin; a tetracycline; chloramphenicol

Providencia (Proteus inconstans) — Gentamicin — Tobramycin; kanamycin; carbenicillin; trimethoprim-sulfamethoxazole; chloramphenicol

Table 2-4 Pathogenic bacteria and appropriate drugs to consider for therapy
(From *The Medical Letter*.[43])

Infecting organism	Drug of first choice	Alternative drugs
ENTERIC GRAM-NEGATIVE BACILLI		
Salmonella typhi	Chloramphenicol	Ampicillin; amoxicillin; trimethoprim-sulfamethoxazole
other *Salmonella*	Ampicillin	Amoxicillin; chloramphenicol; trimethoprim-sulfamethoxazole
Serratia	Gentamicin	Kanamycin; trimethoprim-sulfamethoxazole; chloramphenicol; carbenicillin
Shigella	Ampicillin	Trimethoprim-sulfamethoxazole; chloramphenicol
OTHER GRAM-NEGATIVE BACILLI		
Acinetobacter (Mima, Herellea)	Gentamicin	Tobramycin; kanamycin; chloramphenicol
Bordetella pertussis (whooping cough)	An erythromycin	Ampicillin
Brucella (brucellosis)	A tetracycline with or without streptomycin	Chloramphenicol with or without streptomycin; trimethoprim-sulfamethoxazole
Calymmatobacterium granulomatis (granuloma inguinale)	A tetracycline	Streptomycin
Francisella tularensis (tularemia)	Streptomycin	A tetracycline; chloramphenicol
Haemophilus ducreyi (chancroid)	A sulfonamide	A tetracycline; streptomycin
Haemophilus influenzae meningitis or epiglottitis	Chloramphenicol	Ampicillin
other infections	Ampicillin or amoxicillin	A tetracycline; trimethoprim-sulfamethoxazole; a sulfonamide
Leptotrichia buccalis (Vincent's infection)	Penicillin G	A tetracycline; an erythromycin
Pasteurella multocida	Penicillin G	A tetracycline

Pseudomonas aeruginosa urinary tract infection	Carbenicillin	Gentamicin; tobramycin; a polymyxin
other infections	Gentamicin or tobramycin with carbenicillin	Streptomycin with chloramphenicol
Pseudomonas (Actinobacillus) mallei (glanders)	Streptomycin with a tetracycline	A sulfonamide
Pseudomonas pseudomallei (melioidosis)	A tetracycline with or without chloramphenicol	
Spirillum minor (rat bite fever)	Penicillin G	A tetracycline; streptomycin
Streptobacillus moniliformis (rat bite fever, Haverhill fever)	Penicillin G	A tetracycline; streptomycin
Vibrio cholerae (cholera)	A tetracycline	Trimethoprim-sulfamethoxazole
Yersinia pestis (bubonic plague)	Streptomycin	A tetracycline; chloramphenicol
ACTINOMYCETES		
Actinomyces israelii (actinomycosis)	Penicillin G	A tetracycline
Nocardia	A sulfonamide	Trimethoprim-sulfamethoxazole; a sulfonamide with minocycline or ampicillin or erythromycin; cycloserine
SPIROCHETES		
Borrelia recurrentis (relapsing fever)	A tetracycline	Penicillin G
Leptospira	Penicillin G	A tetracycline
Treponema pallidum (syphilis)	Penicillin G	A tetracycline; an erythromycin

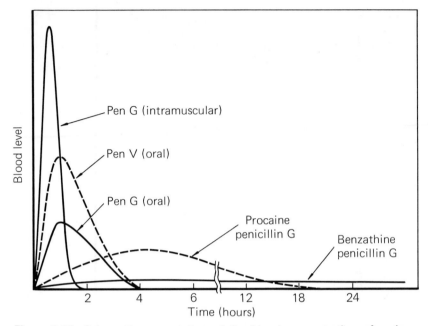

Figure 2-10 Schematic presentation of the blood concentration of various forms of penicillin G plotted as a function of time after oral or intramuscular administration.

example of the appropriate use of procaine penicillin G is the treatment of uncomplicated gonococcal infection. The non-penicillinase-producing forms of this organism are sensitive to the antibiotic at low concentration, and the administration of 4.8 million units of procaine penicillin G on a single office visit is adequate for eradication of the organism in a high percentage of cases. Obviously, benzathine penicillin G can be employed only with organisms that are exquisitely sensitive to the antibiotic, such as group A beta-hemolytic streptococci. Some physicians, in lieu of daily oral therapy, will treat selected patients with a single injection of benzathine penicillin G at monthly intervals as prophylaxis against rheumatic heart disease.

Distribution and Excretion
Penicillin G is distributed widely throughout the body spaces. Passage into joint, ocular, and cerebrospinal fluids is poor in the absence of inflammation, however. In the patient with inflamed

meninges, the drug will enter the cerebrospinal fluid. This is fortunate, since the increased permeability that occurs with inflammation permits entry of enough penicillin to make these drugs useful in the treatment of meningitis caused by sensitive organisms.

Penicillin is rapidly excreted by the kidney. Most of an intramuscular dose of penicillin G (80 to 90 per cent) is excreted by the kidney within an hour and a half. This rapid clearance is accomplished by tubular secretion (about 80 per cent) and by glomerular filtration (about 20 per cent). The tubular secretion mechanism is shared with a wide variety of organic acids. Since the penicillins are not inactivated by metabolism to any significant extent, it is the active form of the antibiotic that is cleared by the tubular transport mechanism. Thus, the levels of the antibiotic attained in the urine are many times greater than in the blood. The very high urine level achieved with both the penicillins and the cephalosporins is an obvious advantage in the treatment of urinary tract infections.

The fact that other organic acids (e.g., probenecid) are transported by the same renal tubular system has been exploited therapeutically. When penicillin was both scarce and expensive, probenecid was often given with the penicillin. Probenecid competes for the tubular transport of penicillin and longer lasting, higher levels of the drug result. Although this is not routinely done now, there are still many occasions when it is useful. For example, it has been demonstrated that the percentage of complete cures obtained in uncomplicated gonococcal infection treated with a single administration of benzathine penicillin G is increased when 1 g of probenecid is administered by mouth just before the injection.[47] A similar active transport system for organic acids exists in the choroid plexus. In this case, organic acids like Diodrast, PSP, and the penicillins are transported from the cerebrospinal fluid to the blood.[48,49] This transport system may account in part for the low levels of penicillin seen in the cerebrospinal fluid after systemic administration. It has been shown in animals that the administration of probenecid decreases the rate of efflux of penicillin from the cerebrospinal fluid to the blood. In animals given penicillin intravenously, pretreatment with probenecid increases the concentration of penicillin in the cerebrospinal fluid as a result of the combined blockade of the active transport systems for penicillin in both the choroid plexus and the kidney.[50] This effect could be used in the development of an important therapeutic regimen in the treatment of meningitis, particularly during the recovery stage as the functional barrier to penicillin entry returns.

Toxicity

The penicillins have the lowest toxicity of any of the antibiotics and, in fact, are among the least toxic of all drugs. The oral penicillin preparations can cause diarrhea, a problem that is greater in infants and young children than in adults. Often the physician can switch to a parenteral route of administration for a couple of days and then resume oral therapy without a return of the diarrhea. Both potassium and sodium salts of penicillin G are marketed, and with the administration of large amounts of the antibiotic the physician must be aware that he is giving the patient large quantities of salt as well. This is, of course, particularly important in patients with compromised cardiac and renal function. With the use of very high doses (on the order of 50 million units) of penicillin, it has become apparent that neurotoxicity can develop.[51] The symptoms include hyperreflexia and seizures. Since penicillin is excreted almost entirely by the kidney, it must be remembered that in patients with severe renal insufficiency very high levels of penicillin can build up with continuous administration of large amounts of the drug (>10 million units per day). Thus, the patient may develop neurotoxicity if the dosage is not modified.[52] In the case of patients with renal insufficiency who are receiving daily amounts of penicillin in the usual range, it is not necessary to lower the drug dose. Rarely, when large doses of penicillin are given for a prolonged period (typically, at least 10 million units daily for a week or more), hemolysis can take place. This, however, represents a hypersensitivity, not a toxicity. Penicillin becomes bound to red cell membranes and antibodies then react with this complex.[53] Penicillin is one of the most common causes of drug-induced hemolysis. Cessation of therapy is followed by complete recovery.

THE SPECIALIZED PENICILLINS

Numerous penicillins have been developed with such therapeutically desirable features as increased stability to acid, less binding to serum protein, resistance to digestion by penicillinases, and a broad spectrum of antibacterial action.

Phenoxymethyl Penicillin (Penicillin V)

Penicillin V has the same spectrum of antibacterial action as penicillin G and is readily digested by penicillinases. Penicillin V is more stable in acid than penicillin G, and thus, higher and more consistent blood levels are achieved with this form of the antibiotic. Penicillin V is available by generic prescription and costs, on the average, a little bit more than penicillin G. In treating appropriately sensitive infections, the more reliable absorption and higher blood levels achieved with penicillin V often make this the preferred form for oral administration.

The Penicillinase-Resistant Penicillins

Structural modifications in the side chain of these penicillins (Figure 2-9) provide enough steric hinderance to keep them from being utilized as good substrates by the penicillinase enzymes. Methicillin is the compound that has been in clinical use the longest and the one with which physicians have had the greatest experience. It is rapidly inactivated by acid and thus is given only parenterally. Oxacillin is another preparation that is widely used parenterally. It binds to serum protein somewhat more than methicillin but is less often associated with the production of interstitial nephritis (described below under hypersensitivity reactions). The two penicillinase-resistant penicillins with the best oral absorption are dicloxacillin and cloxacillin. Of the two, more complete absorption and higher blood levels are obtained with dicloxacillin.

The penicillinase-resistant penicillins have a narrow spectrum of action, similar to that of penicillin G, and their primary use is in the treatment of infection due to penicillinase-producing staphylococci. Because numerous penicillinase-producing pathogens have emerged in recent years, there has been an increasing tendency to treat common infections usually sensitive to penicillin G with one of the penicillinase-resistant penicillins. One example of this practice is the unnecessary use of expensive penicillinase-resistant penicillins in the treatment of beta-hemolytic streptococcal pharyngitis. There is a very low incidence of penicillinase production by the organisms, and the drug of choice is penicillin G or V.

Broad-Spectrum Penicillins

The broad-spectrum penicillins, in addition to their effectiveness against the range of bacteria normally sensitive to penicillin

G, are active against some gram-negative rods as well. The increased spectrum of action of this group can be appreciated from a perusal of the section of Table 2-4 presenting antibiotics recommended for treatment of infections due to various gram-negative bacilli. As can be seen from the structures of ampicillin and carbenicillin (Figure 2-9), the increased spectrum of action is achieved by the addition of an amino or a carboxyl group to the side chain of penicillin G. All the broad-spectrum penicillins are sensitive to digestion by penicillinases. Therefore, they have no role in the treatment of infections due to penicillinase-producing organisms.

There are very specific indications for the use of broad-spectrum penicillins. These drugs, however, are frequently employed inappropriately. The use of ampicillin or amoxicillin to obtain a broader spectrum of antibacterial action than is required should be discouraged. This is especially true in the treatment of a mild infection that is probably of gram-positive etiology. In such a case, one often hears physicians say that they wish to have "a little broader coverage," and for this purpose they choose to initiate therapy with a broad-spectrum penicillin or a cephalosporin. There is no sound basis for this practice, and it can be harmful. No antibiotic should be employed in a catch-all manner. In the treatment of mild and moderate infection, it is a good general rule to start therapy with the narrowest spectrum antibiotic that is effective against the organism. This reduces the chance of superinfection, and it decreases the selection pressure for the development of resistant organisms (see Chapter 1). One should not assume that superinfection is a problem that is peculiar to the use of the very broad-spectrum antibiotics like the tetracyclines and chloroamphenicol. It is a problem with almost any antibiotic, and the chances of encountering superinfection increase as the spectrum of drug action becomes greater. The broad-spectrum penicillins, like the cephalosporins, are widely overused.

Ampicillin and amoxicillin are amino-substituted, broad-spectrum penicillins. Ampicillin was introduced many years ago and clinicians have had more experience with this drug than with the other broad-spectrum penicillins. Ampicillin is active against several common gram-negative bacilli, including most strains of *Escherichia coli, Haemophilus influenzae, Shigella,* and *Proteus mirabilis.* Amoxicillin is a newer form of ampicillin that is more readily absorbed from the gastrointestinal tract, and it produces serum levels two and a half times higher than those achieved with the same dose of ampicillin.[54] In contrast to ampicillin, the absorption of amoxicillin is not decreased by food. The urine levels achieved with amoxicillin are approximately twice those obtained with ampicillin.[54,55]

Tests in vitro demonstrate that amoxicillin has a spectrum of action similar to ampicillin.[56] There is an interesting exception to the observation that the two antibiotics are nearly equivalent at the same free drug concentration. This exception is found in the treatment of bacillary dysentery (shigellosis). It has been demonstrated that the serum concentration of antibiotic, not the intraluminal intestinal concentration, is the critical determinant of effectiveness against this infection.[57] Even though higher and more reliable blood levels of amoxicillin are achieved, oral ampicillin is more effective in the treatment of Shigella infection.[58] The reason for the greater effectiveness of ampicillin is not well understood. In the absence of human serum, the two antibiotics have an equivalent effect in vitro against Shigella. The difference in clinical efficacy seems to be determined by the presence of serum, although the two drugs bind to serum protein to about the same degree.[59] This difference in the clinical effectiveness of these two similar drugs would not be predicted from known pharmacological or microbiological principles. It is an example that is presented here to emphasize the fact that host factors can modify drug response so that rational prediction does not always match the clinical result.

Hetacillin is an ampicillin derivative that is rapidly and completely hydrolyzed in the body to ampicillin. Ampicillin is therefore the active form of this drug. Conversion to ampicillin is complete so it is given in the same dosage as ampicillin itself.

Carbenicillin is a carboxyl-substituted, broad-spectrum penicillin. This compound is given only parenterally. Indanyl carbenicillin is a more acid stable form that is well absorbed from the gastrointestinal tract. It is hydrolyzed in the body to produce carbenicillin, the active form of the drug, and metabolic products derived from indanol. Carbenicillin is effective against Pseudomonas and indole-positive Proteus strains, whereas other penicillins are not. Unfortunately, when carbenicillin is used alone in the treatment of deep Pseudomonas infection, resistance emerges rapidly.[60] Thus, although mild infections with this organism are often treated with carbenicillin alone, serious infections should be treated with a combination of carbenicillin and gentamicin or tobramycin. The use of these drug combinations for the treatment of *Pseudomonas* has been shown to have a synergistic effect both *in vitro* and clinically,[61,62] and it should slow the emergence of antibiotic resistence. The proposed mechanism of this synergism will be discussed in the next chapter.

It is interesting to note that the rate at which resistance to carbenicillin develops when it is employed in the single drug therapy of urinary tract infections is extremely low. This is probably because the urine concentrations achieved as a result of the tubular secretion mechanism are so high that any penicillinase-producing organisms present are killed instead of being selected. Large doses of carbenicillin are often required for treatment of *Pseudomonas* infection. The normal serum half-life of 1.0 hour increases to about 16 hours in severe uremia, and a reduction of the dosage and lengthening of the dosage interval then become necessary.[63]

The use of carbenicillin should remain restricted to organisms like *Pseudomonas*, indole-positive *Proteus*, *Enterobacter*, *Serratia*, and some sensitive strains of anaerobic bacteria. The widespread use of this antibiotic against organisms that can be readily treated with another penicillin should be discouraged for two reasons. First, carbenicillin is expensive. Second, widespread use will increase the incidence of carbenicillin-resistant *Pseudomonas*. Since carbenicillin is the least toxic of the three types of drugs that are effective in the treatment of *Pseudomonas aeruginosa*, great care should be taken not to compromise its usefulness. It should be added here that most strains of *Klebsiella* respond poorly to carbenicillin,[56] and superinfection with this organism is an important problem in the type of patient who requires carbenicillin therapy.

THE CEPHALOSPORINS

As we have just seen, no penicillins with a broad spectrum of action are penicillinase resistant. The cephalosporins have a relatively broad spectrum of action and are resistant to most penicillinases. They are active against most common pathogenic gram-positive cocci (enterococci being a major exception) as well as a variety of gram-negative organisms (e.g., *E. coli*, *P. mirabilis*, *Klebsiella*—see Table 2-4). *Pseudomonas* strains are not sensitive to the cephalosporins,[64] and superinfection with this organism can be a problem in patients treated with these antibiotics. For all practical purposes, the antimicrobial spectrum of action of the various cephalosporins discussed in this section is the same, and their differences are largely pharmacological.[65] New cephalosporins are being licensed at a rapid rate and no attempt will be made here to cover all of them. The student who is beginning his study of the antibiotics may be overwhelmed if he sets them all to memory. In practice it may help to pick one parenteral and one oral preparation and learn how to use each one well.

The fact that the cephalosporins are broad spectrum (in the restricted sense of that term as it was applied to the penicillins) and penicillinase resistant has both positive and negative aspects. It is often very useful to have these two properties combined in a therapeutic situation. However, some physicians tend to use the cephalosporins in situations in which the narrower spectrum penicillins are more appropriate. This has the obvious drawback of increasing the chances of superinfection and of selecting for resistant organisms that may become a worse problem than the initial infection. These drugs are generally overused.

Pharmacology

The body handles the cephalosporins and the penicillins in a similar manner. Some of the cephalosporins are metabolized to a greater extent than the penicillins. For example, about 30 per cent of a dose of cephalothin appears in the urine as the deacetyl compound.[66] The cephalosporins are secreted by the same renal tubular transport system as the penicillins, but in general, their serum half-lives are longer (e.g., 2 hours for cephazolin versus less than 30 minutes for most penicillins). The distribution of the cephalosporins is also similar to that of the penicillins. Passage of these drugs into the cerebrospinal fluid increases with meningeal inflammation,[67] but the drug levels attained are unpredictable. In general, the response of meningitis (even meningitis caused by organisms proven to be sensitive) to the cephalosporins is unreliable.[68] There are several recorded cases of patients with bacteremia who developed meningitis due to cephalothin-sensitive organisms while they were receiving the drug.[69] Given their poor penetration across the blood-brain barrier and the variable clinical results, the cephalosporins should not be used to treat severe infections of the central nervous system.

Toxicity

The principal toxicity associated with the cephalosporins is a nephrotoxicity. This is unrelated to the interstitial nephritis of allergic etiology that is occasionally observed with the penicillins. The cephalosporins cause a proximal tubular necrosis,[70] and the results of animal studies have demonstrated that this has a clear dose dependency.[71] Nephrotoxicity has rarely been associated with cephalothin therapy,[72] but the presence of impaired renal function or concurrent treatment with nephrotoxic drugs (e.g., aminoglycosides, see Chapter 3) may increase the risk. Cephaloridine, in contrast, has been implicated in a substantial number of cases of acute renal failure. The biochemical mechanism responsible for the nephrotoxic effect is unknown. It is interesting that the administration of probenecid prevents the development of nephrotoxicity in some model animal systems.[73] All the cephalosporins produce phlebitis upon intravenous administration. Hypersensitivity to the cephalosporins and bacterial resistance will be discussed later in this chapter.

The Cephalosporin Preparations

Several cephalosporins are available for parenteral administration. Cephalothin has received the most extensive clinical use. Cefazolin has been introduced more recently, and it seems likely that it will replace cephalothin as the principal preparation for intramuscular use. Although the protein binding of cefazolin is somewhat higher than that of cephalothin (84 versus 65 per cent), the serum concentration of free antibiotic achieved with cefazolin is about three times that obtained with an equivalent dose of cephalothin.[74] The serum half-life of cefazolin is four times as long as that of cephalothin (1.8 hours versus 30 minutes).[75] The level of drug obtained in joint fluid is nearly the same as that in serum. Although cefazolin has a slower rate of renal clearance than cephalothin, high urine concentrations are nevertheless achieved.[74] Cephazolin is well tolerated[76] and less painful than cephalothin when given by intramuscular injection.[77] Other parenteral cephalosporin preparations include cephaloridine, cephapirin, and cephradine. This latter compound can also be given orally. The reader is referred to the literature for a review of the pharmacology of these preparations as well as others that have not been released for clinical use in the United States.[77]

There are several acid-stable cephalosporins that can be administered orally. Cephalexin and cephradine are both absorbed well. Cephaloglycin, however, is poorly absorbed, and there does not seem to be any reason for using it. High urine concentrations are achieved with cephalexin. When a cephalosporin is being used to treat a severe infection, therapy is generally started with intravenous cephalothin or cefazolin. As the patient's condition improves, parenteral administration may be stopped and therapy continued with oral cephalexin.

HYPERSENSITIVITY REACTIONS

Estimates of the incidence of allergic reaction to the penicillins range from 1 to 5 per cent of patient courses of treatment.[78] The reactions encompass virtually every sort of allergic manifestation. Their onset may be immediate, accelerated (occurring 1 to 72 hours after administration), or delayed for several days or even weeks (Table 2-5). Allergic responses to any of the penicillins can occur, and reactions are less frequent in children than in adults. Manifestations of allergy may be seen after any route of drug administration, but anaphylaxis (and perhaps other types of

Table 2-5 Allergic reactions to penicillins
(Modified from Levine et al.,[78] Table 1.)

IMMEDIATE ALLERGIC REACTIONS
  (occur 2 to 30 minutes after penicillin)
  Urticaria
  Flushing
  Diffuse pruritis
  Hypotension or shock
  Laryngeal edema
  Wheezing
ACCELERATED URTICARIAL REACTIONS
  (1 to 72 hours)
  Urticaria or pruritis
  Wheezing or laryngeal edema
  Local inflammatory reactions
LATE ALLERGIC REACTIONS
  (more than 72 hours)
  Morbilliform eruptions (occasionally occur as early as 18 hours after intiation of
    penicillin)
  Urticarial eruptions
  Erythematous eruptions
  Recurrent urticaria and arthralgia
  Local inflammatory reactions
SOME RELATIVELY UNUSUAL LATE REACTIONS
  Immunohemolytic anemia
  Drug fever
  Acute renal insufficiency
  Thrombocytopenia

allergic reaction) is less common with the oral than with the parenteral route.[79] The incidence of anaphylactic reaction appears to be higher in people with a history of atopy (e.g., asthma, hay fever, and other allergic diseases).[80]

Over the past several years, the study of drug allergy has become a clearly defined field of inquiry that incorporates the techniques of both immunology and pharmacology. The reader is referred to two of the many general reviews in this area.[81,82] Because of the high incidence of allergy to the penicillins and the large patient population exposed to these antibiotics (penicillin is apparently the major cause of anaphylaxis in man[83]), much of the research has been directed to defining the mechanisms underlying penicillin allergy. Most of our current understanding of allergic responses to drugs in general has evolved from the study of penicillin hypersensitivity.

Immunochemistry

Before small molecules (such as most drugs) can elicit an immune response, they must become associated in an irreversible manner with large molecules in the host tissues. Antibodies to the complete antigen, the hapten-protein conjugate, then form. The hapten may be the unaltered drug, a metabolite, or a chemical degradation product. In the case of the penicillins, it is clear that penicillin itself is not the major form of the molecule that functions as a hapten. Rather, penicillin G can undergo a ring cleavage in solution to form small amounts of several degradation products.[84] One of the products resulting from the nonenzymatic cleavage of the thiazolidine ring is D-benzylpenicillenic acid. This is a very reactive isomer of penicillin, which can react irreversibly with sulfhydryl groups or amino residues in tissue proteins to form hapten-protein conjugates. The proposed mechanism is presented in Figure 2-11. Of primary importance is the reaction of D-benzylpenicillenic acid with the ε-amino group of lysine residues on proteins to form D-benzylpenicilloyl derivatives of tissue proteins, which then function as complete penicillin antigens.

The results of one experiment supporting the proposal that the D-benzylpenicilloyl-ε-aminolysyl units are the primary antigenic determinants are presented in Figure 2-12. Serum from rabbits, which were exposed to penicillin G, contained an anti-penicillin antibody that precipitated when the serum was incubated with

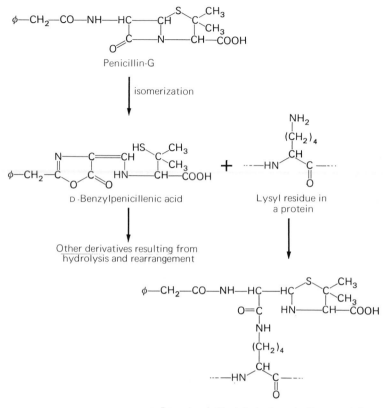

Figure 2-11 Proposed chemical pathway for the formation of the penicillin antigen. A very small percentage of penicillin G is isomerized at physiological pH to D-benzylpenicillenic acid, which then reacts with the ε-amino group of lysyl residues in proteins to form the complete penicillin antigen. (From Levine.[84])

antigen—human gamma globulin containing a number of D-benzylpenicilloyl groups. These antigen-antibody precipitation reactions were carried out in the presence of increasing amounts of penicillin or penicilloylamide compounds to determine what concentration of penicillin G or penicillin derivative effectively competed for the antigen sites on the rabbit anti-penicillin serum antibodies. The more effective a compound was in associating with the antibody (thus preventing precipitation by the gamma globulin antigen) the more closely it would resemble the complete penicillin antigen that elicited antibody production. As seen

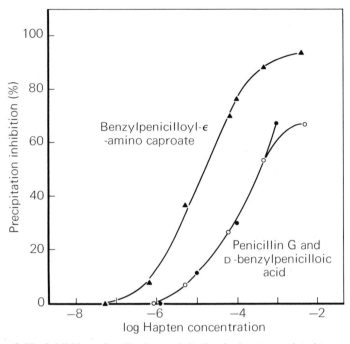

Figure 2-12 Inhibition of antibody precipitation by haptens related to penicillin. Rabbit anti-penicillin G serum was incubated with D-benzylpenicilloyl human gamma globulin in the presence of various concentrations of D-benzylpenicilloyl-ε-aminocaproate (▲ ---- ▲). D-benzylpenicilloic acid (●———●), or penicillin G (○———○). The amount of precipitate in each incubation was then assayed. (Data from Levine and Ovary.[85])

in Figure 2-12, D-benzylpenicilloyl-ε-amino caproate, an analog of the ε-aminolysyl derivative, was effective in blocking the precipitation at one-hundredth the concentration at which penicillin G or D-benzylpenicilloic acid were effective. Similar experiments using serum from patients with penicillin allergy have shown that the majority of the antibodies formed are specific for the penicilloyl-lysyl group.[85] There is now some evidence suggesting that penicillin itself can react with amino groups on proteins and form complete antigens without having to first proceed through the penicillenic acid intermediate.[86]

Penicillenic acid is not the only degradation product of penicillin that is capable of eliciting an antibody response. Others induce the production of antibodies that are different from the penicilloyl type—they are called minor determinants. Both the major and minor determinants elicit antibodies of several immunoglobulin classes. But at the risk of oversimplifying, it can be said that IgG is more often specific for the penicilloyl group and IgE reacts with a wider range of penicillin determinants, both major and minor. The IgE antibodies are responsible for the production of the wheal and flare reactions observed in skin testing and for such important immediate reactions as anaphylaxis.[87] In contrast, the serum sickness syndrome is an example of an allergic reaction mediated by antibodies of the IgG class (and possibly also by IgM).

Apparently allergic responses to commercial penicillin preparations are not always due to complete antigen formed between penicillin derivatives and tissue protein. Some preparations of penicillin have been found to contain a high-molecular-weight material responsible for producing allergic reactions.[88,89] In some cases, these high-molecular-weight antigens have penicilloyl specificity. They are probably penicilloyl-protein conjugates that are formed during the biosynthetic process used in production. There is also evidence indicating that if allergic patients are given skin tests using fresh preparations of penicillin from which the high-molecular-weight contaminant has been removed, the incidence of reaction decreases.[90,91]

Skin Testing for Hypersensitivity

A classic method of testing for drug allergy is to inject a small amount of the drug intradermally; if erythema develops, the patient is sensitive. This method of testing with penicillin is unsatisfactory for two reasons: (1) Intradermal injection of penicillin can precipitate a full-blown anaphylactic response in the patient; (2) the results are unreliable. One factor that apparently contributes to the rather high incidence of false negatives is the phenomenon described by the curves in Figure 2-12. A small amount of the penicillin in the test injection is altered and forms the hapten-protein conjugate, but this complete antigen is prevented from reacting with the small amount of antibody in the area of injection because of competition for antibody sites by the relatively large amount of unaltered penicillin. A more reliable test substance than penicillin itself has been developed from the antigenic determinant we have just discussed; it is a penicilloyl derivative of lysine. Penicilloyl-polylysine is a multivalent antigen of approximately 20 lysine residues and 12 to 15 penicilloyl groups per unit. It is not immunogenic, its diffusion from the site of injection is slow because of its molecular size, and systemic response is rare. A small amount of the clear penicilloyl-polylysine solution is administered intradermally, and after 20 minutes the injected area is examined for evidence of a wheal and erythema response. The reaction is graded negative, 2+, or 4+ depending on the magnitude of the response.

The results of this test are more reliable, and the test is certainly much less dangerous than one using only the drug itself as the test substance. A positive test reaction, however, is by no means an absolute indication that the patient will have an allergic reaction if he is subsequently treated with penicillin. The data from one survey of the predictive value of penicilloyl-polylysine testing are presented in Figure 2-13. In this survey approximately 0.5 per cent of people who had no reaction on skin testing developed an allergic reaction after therapy with penicillin.[92] Of 206 severely ill patients who had a 4+ response to penicilloyl-polylysine and were treated with penicillin, 21 developed an allergic response. Of the people who had both a positive skin test and a previous history of penicillin sensitivity, 27 per cent who were subsequently treated exhibited allergic symptoms. Also in the same study, 50 per cent of the people who had a positive history of

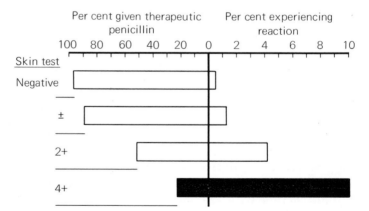

Figure 2-13 Relationship between the results of skin tests with penicilloyl-polylysine and subsequent reaction to penicillin. Skin tests with penicilloyl-polylysine were evaluated by the size of the wheal and by erythema: −, no response; ±, ambiguous response, wheal larger than initial bleb but less than 12 mm in diameter; 2+, positive, wheal 12 to 20 mm in average diameter; and 4+, strongly positive, wheal more than 20 mm in diameter. The positive-responding patients were treated with penicillin only when it was felt that the need outweighed the risk. (From Brown *et al.*[92])

penicillin sensitivity had a negative skin test. This could be explained by the following: (1) the patient may have given an inaccurate history; (2) antibody levels may have declined; (3) the antigenic determinants may have been different.

Testing with benzylpenicilloyl-polylysine (PPL) is helpful, but the physician cannot rely on this test alone for predicting a patient's reaction to subsequent penicillin therapy. Patients who have a negative skin test with PPL may have developed an allergic response to minor determinants that do not react to the penicilloyl group. The use of the word "minor" to describe these determinants is unfortunate, since the clinical consequences of treating these patients with a penicillin can be major. People who are sensitive to minor determinants are more likely to experience an immediate anaphylactic reaction upon therapeutic administration of the drug. Thus, it is critical to identify the patient's response to testing with the minor determinants as well as to PPL. There is no preparation of minor determinants available commercially, but pharmacies in the larger hospitals can prepare an appropriate test mixture. The minor determinant mixture (MDM) usually contains crystalline benzylpenicillin, 20 mM; sodium benzylpenicilloate, 10 mM; and sodium-α-benzylpenicilloyl-amine, 10 mM.

The predictive value of skin testing with both PPL and MDM is indicated by the data in Table 2-6. Skin tests with PPL, MDM, and a diluent control were performed on 217 patients with a history of penicillin hypersensitivity.[93] Of the 185 patients in whom both skin tests were negative, only one accelerated reaction occurred when penicillin was given therapeutically. There were no immediate reactions. Thirty-two patients (15 per cent) had positive skin tests with PPL, MDM, or both. This is considerably higher than the 3 per cent rate of positive response that is obtained upon skin testing ward patients chosen at random.[94] Seven patients who were negative to PPL, and who might have been considered at low risk if judged on the results of that test alone, were positive to MDM. These data indicate that negative immediate skin tests to PPL and MDM virtually exclude the possibility that the patient will experience an immediate (possibly life-threatening) allergic reaction to penicillin. A negative response also markedly reduces the probability of an accelerated reaction.

The use of the two test procedures can be of great help to the physician. It has been shown that the procedure can be applied by house officers in a ward setting in a useful and safe manner.[95,96] When MDM is not available, aqueous penicillin G can be used as a

Table 2-6 **Relation of immediate skin tests with PPL and MDM to the occurrence of immediate and accelerated allergic reactions to penicillin**
In skin test-positive patients, penicillin therapy was started by gradual administration. In skin test-negative patients, penicillin therapy was initiated without an attempt at desensitization. (From Levine *et al.*[93])

Patients with history of penicillin allergy	Skin tests: PPL	MDM	Immediate or accelerated reaction to penicillin therapy
185	−	−	One had a mild accelerated urticarial reaction
9	+	−	Not treated with penicillins
4	−	+	Not treated with penicillins
8	+	+	Not treated with penicillins
8	+	−	Five of eight had accelerated urticarial reactions
3	−	+	Two had accelerated reactions (urticarial or diffuse flush); one had an immediate urticarial reaction

substitute.[81] PPL testing can be initiated with an intradermal injection. If this is negative, one may proceed to MDM (or penicillin G) scratch testing and then intradermal injection. No one should be tested for a drug sensitivity without trained personnel, syringes, epinepherine, and appropriate airway support immediately available.

It would be advantageous to have a method of testing for drug allergies that did not expose patients to the risk of injecting the antigen. Such methods have been developed, but they are not yet rapid and definitive enough to be of clinical use. Hemagglutination techniques can be used to detect penicilloyl-specific IgG and IgM; the antibodies, however, are nearly ubiquitous. In one study, for example, anti-penicillin antibodies were detected in virtually all patients examined, even those who denied ever having had penicillin therapy.[94] The presence of some classes of IgG antibodies may actually mitigate against the production of allergic reactions. Sometimes benzylpenicilloyl-specific IgG antibodies act as "blocking antibodies" in competition with penicilloyl-specific IgE units.[94] Radioimmunological assay techniques (RAST) have been employed to detect penicilloyl-specific IgE antibodies, and there appears to be a good correlation between the RAST test results and those obtained by skin testing with penicillin.[97] This type of approach holds some promise of developing into a rapid, practical method of testing samples of serum for the presence of multiple antibodies to both major and minor determinants.

Treatment of the Patient with Penicillin Hypersensitivity

When a patient with a history of penicillin allergy presents with an infection for which penicillin therapy is indicated, the physician may choose to treat with another antibiotic or he may test for penicillin hypersensitivity and proceed according to those results. In the case of mild or moderate infections, one most often chooses another antibiotic. Table 2-4 presents several alternatives to the drug of first choice for infections of different etiologies. The infecting organism should, of course, be cultured and its drug sensitivity determined, but therapy is usually initiated before the results of sensitivity tests are known. In choosing an alternative to penicillin, there are several facts one should keep in mind.

Patients who are allergic to one penicillin must be assumed to be allergic to all penicillins. There are cases in which patients have been shown to be allergic to one penicillin and not to others, but they are only of academic interest.[98] Clinically, a physician should never assume that he can substitute one penicillin for another in the treatment of the allergic patient. It is safest, in these cases, to choose an antibiotic that is not a member of the β-lactam group. The cephalosporins are allergenic, and there is some cross-reaction between the penicillins and cephalosporins. The major determinant of cephalosporin allergy is a cephaloyl hapten analogous to the penicilloyl structure.[100] Cross-reactivity has been demonstrated both by serum tests[101,102] and by skin testing.[103] It is not possible to give an exact figure for the number of penicillin hypersensitive people who are also allergic to the cephalosporins—estimates vary from 5 to 30 per cent. In one study, nine of 22 patients proven to be allergic to penicillin developed eosinophilia when they were treated with cephalothin.[104] Probably a reasonable estimate is that about 5 to 10 per cent of patients with penicillin hypersensitivity will have some allergic reaction if they are given a cephalosporin. Several papers have reported cases of anaphylaxis following administration of a cephalosporin to patients who were allergic to the penicillins.[105] Thus, in patients with a history of an immediate reaction to the penicillins, cephalosporin antibiotics should not be used. Some physicians use these drugs to treat infections in patients with a history of mild penicillin allergy. But it is clear that there is a risk of cross-reaction (although the risk is certainly lower than if a penicillin were used), and the cephalosporin should only be given when appropriate precautions for treating an immediate reaction have been taken.

In the case of serious infection (e.g., a septicemia, meningitis, or endocarditis) for which a penicillin is clearly the drug of choice, then one should skin test with both PPL and MDM. If the skin testing is negative, therapy with a penicillin may be initiated. If one or both of the skin tests are positive, treatment with another carefully chosen, potent antimicrobial is probably warranted.[106] In certain cases, in which the benefit of penicillin therapy outweighs the risk of immediate allergic reaction (for example, with an enterococcal endocarditis), treatment with a penicillin is begun with graduated doses of antibiotic according to a prudent desensitization schedule.[81,107] This is a dangerous procedure that should be carried out only in a hospital with maximum support and trained personnel available. Desensitization should be attempted only in life-threatening situations in which there is no equally effective alternative antibiotic. Desensitization may permit therapy with the penicillins to proceed, but often it simply does not work. If desensitization is successful, the response of the patient to skin testing may change from positive to negative during therapy.[107,108] This may be due to depletion of the skin-sensitive IgE by the antigen and to the blocking action of increased IgG.

One possible method for controlling the allergic response may be to utilize stable univalent haptens to block the association of the multivalent antigens with the antibody. For example, in vitro studies like the one presented in Figure 2-12 have shown that a stable, synthetic penicilloyl hapten (benzylpenicilloylformyllysine) is very efficient at blocking anti-penicilloyl antibodies.[109] This observation has been extended by administering the synthetic penicilloyl hapten to several patients who had allergic reactions and who required further penicillin therapy.[110] Most of the patients were able to continue or resume penicillin treatment without allergic symptoms under cover of the hapten. There is probably only a very small subgroup of the population in which this specific competing monovalent hapten would be effective, and the potential for the use of the technique is very limited. But it is a magnificent demonstration of the translation of basic molecular principles into therapy.

Several precautions can minimize the complications of penicillin allergy: (1) Always ask the patient about previous allergic reactions. (2) If the patient is given penicillin by injection, he should remain in the clinic or office 30 minutes after receiving the drug. (3) If the patient is to be given procaine or benzathine penicillin, some physicians prefer to give a small amount of penicillin G first and then inject the long-lasting preparation 30 minutes later. This is prudent, since it decreases the chance of having to treat a patient for a reaction when a lot of antigen is already in the body in a slow-release form. (4) Always have a syringe containing epinepherine (1:1000) on hand. (5) When using an alternative antibiotic, never substitute another penicillin. (6) Remember that the cephalosporins are not always safe alternatives and that the patient is usually best treated with a non-β-lactam antibiotic. (7) Skin testing with PPL and MDM (or penicillin G) can be very helpful, particularly in identifying those patients who have a high risk of developing an immediate reaction.

Interstitial Nephritis

Numerous specific reactions to the penicillins have been studied in detail, and the reader is referred to the review by Parker for an entré into the literature.[81] One rare complication of penicillin use that is particularly important to keep in mind if a patient's renal function begins to decline during therapy is interstitial nephritis. The clinical picture of the syndrome is characterized by fever, rash, and eosinophilia, with hematuria and proteinuria. When penicillin therapy is stopped, there is usually recovery. The syndrome is more common with methicillin, but it can also be seen with penicillin G and ampicillin.[111,112] Both tubular damage and an interstitial accumulation of mononuclear cells and eosinophils are seen in specimens obtained by renal biopsy.[113] There are no glomerular abnormalities nor is there evidence of arteritis. The nephritis usually develops after high doses of methicillin or penicillin G, but this is clearly an allergic condition, not a toxicity. Methicillin haptenic groups have been demonstrated at the tubular basement membrane, and one patient was shown to have antitubular basement membrane antibodies.[114] This finding suggests that penicillin may bind to the tubular basement membrane to form an antigen that can elicit the production of antitubular basement membrane antibodies. These antibodies are thought to be capable of reacting with the normal tubular basement membrane to produce the pathological changes of interstitial nephritis.

Ampicillin Rashes

The incidence of skin rashes is about twice as high with ampicillin as with the other penicillins. In one study of 422 patients treated with ampicillin, for example, rashes occurred in 9.5 per cent.[115] Most rashes associated with ampicillin are pruritic, maculopapular eruptions; a few are urticarial.[116] Although the variation is great, the time of onset of the maculopapular rashes associated with ampicillin is later (median 7 days) than penicillin rashes in general. The incidence of ampicillin rashes seems to be higher in children than in adults. Since ampicillin is given to a tremendous number of people each year, it would be especially disturbing if rashes appearing at such a high frequency represented allergic sensitization. The maculopapular rash does not, however, seem to have an allergic basis. The results of both skin testing and in vitro studies indicate that the rash is not mediated by IgE, and readministration of ampicillin to patients who have had the maculopapular type of rash produced no reaction.[116,117] The urticarial rashes seen with ampicillin probably have an allergic basis, but the mechanism of the more common maculopapular rash is unknown.

The incidence of rashes in patients with infectious mononucleosis who are also treated with ampicillin is extremely high (about 90 per cent).[118,119] Again, the ampicillin rash is a pruritic, maculopapular eruption having a later onset and perhaps a somewhat different distribution than the similar rash that normally appears in 10 to 15 per cent of patients with mononucleosis.[120] There is also a marked increase in the frequency of rashes in patients who are taking allopurinol. In one large study, the incidence of rashes was 7.5 per cent in patients treated with ampicillin but 22 per cent in patients receiving both allopurinol and ampicillin.[121] It is not clear yet whether the incidence of ampicillin rash is increased with hyperuricemia or whether a drug interaction with allopurinol is involved.

RESISTANCE TO THE PENICILLINS

Mechanisms of Resistance

When the penicillins first came into wide use in the 1940s, relatively few infections due to penicillin-resistant gram-positive organisms were encountered. For example, no resistant strains were found in a study of 29 clinical isolates of S. aureus obtained in 1942.[122] During the late 1940s and the 1950s, however, an increasing proportion of S. aureus strains isolated from patients were found to be resistant to the penicillins. The growing incidence of resistance in S. aureus was accompanied by more frequent problems with penicillin resistance in other organisms as well.

Bacteria can become resistant to the action of penicillins in several ways. In the upper urinary tract, organisms can become refractory to the action of penicillins because L-forms (bacteria without cell walls) are created, and they can survive if the tonicity of the environment is high enough to prevent cell rupture. This is an example of escape from the therapeutic effect of the drug but not true resistance. Earlier in this chapter we reviewed a mechanism by which an alteration in a cell wall lytic enzyme resulted in resistance.[40] It would seem that the gram-negative bacilli have what might be described as a natural resistance to the narrow-spectrum penicillins in the form of a cell envelope that impedes entry of the drug. A potential mechanism of resistance that involves alterations of this envelope is suggested by the observation that the chemical composition of the outer-membrane lipopolysaccharide of an E. coli strain resistant to the broad-spectrum compound ampicillin is altered.[123] But the principal mechanism by which bacteria become resistant to the penicillins and cephalosporins is by producing enzymes that inactivate the drugs.

Resistance to the penicillins results from the production of one of two enzymes by the bacterium (Figure 2-14). By far the most common mechanism is the production of penicillinase. This enzyme, a β-lactamase, cleaves the four-membered, β-lactam ring of the penicillin. As described earlier in the chapter, an intact β-lactam ring is an absolute requirement for the inhibition of the transpeptidase, and cleavage of the ring destroys antibacterial activity.

Transfer of Penicillin Resistance

Penicillinases clearly existed before the introduction of penicillin into therapy, but few strains of bacteria produced them. With the selection pressure caused by widespread antibiotic use, penicillinase-producing strains became more prevalent. It is interesting to speculate about what caused the β-lactamases to evolve in the first place. One set of candidates for the progenitors of the β-lactamases are the transpeptidases. One can speculate that muta-

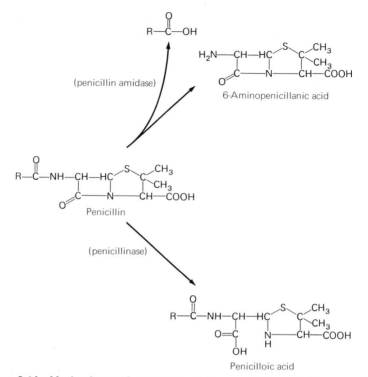

Figure 2-14 Mechanisms of resistance to the penicillins. Resistance to the penicillins usually arises from bacterial production of one of two enzymes—penicillin amidase or penicillinase. Penicillinase production is by far the more common form of resistance.

tions may have permitted a transition from the membrane-bound transpeptidase to a membrane-bound carboxypeptidase. The carboxypeptidases cleave the peptide linkage between D-alanyl-D-alanine units, but they cannot form a peptide bond like the transpeptidases. As we have seen, the catalytic sites of the carboxypeptidases are occupied by the penicillins, and the β-lactam ring of the antibiotic is opened. Further mutation resulting in release of the carboxypeptidase from its membrane-bound location and additional modification of the catalytic site might produce a soluble enzyme that efficiently hydrolyzes the β-lactam ring of penicillin—a penicillinase.[124] Those few strains of bacteria that acquired the ability to produce β-lactamases may have had some selective advantage if the enzymes acted as detoxifiers of penicillins and cephalosporins present in their natural environment.[125] This route of evolution is, of course, hypothetical, and alternative theories propose that the penicillinases evolved as peptidases that are required in the process of sporulation.[126] The former hypothesis, however, is intriguing, since it provides a perspective for thinking about the potential interrelationship between the enzymes that act in a specific manner on the β-lactam structure, both as drug receptors and as instruments of bacterial resistance.

The increase in S. aureus penicillin resistance that occurred as the clinical use of penicillin increased was not due just to selection of a few strains of mutant organisms that were capable of producing penicillinase before the introduction of the drug. The genetic information determining the production of resistance to the penicillins is carried in most cases in DNA that is located extrachromasomally in plasmids. Both the genes determining penicillinase structure and the genes controlling its production can be carried in a single plasmid, and this information can be transferred from one organism to another by transduction in vivo.[127,128] Analysis of staphylococci isolated from hospital patients confirms the important role of plasmids in determining penicillinase production in the clinical environment.[129,130] In the enterobacteria the genes determining penicillinase are also frequently located in plasmids. In this case the plasmids often contain determinants for resistance to other antibiotics and they can be transferred from one bacterium to another by conjugation (see discussion of multiple drug resistance in Chapter 1). The problem of penicillin resistance in S. aureus has been reviewed from an epidemiological standpoint by Rolinson,[131] and a detailed review of the role of plasmids in antibiotic resistance in this organism has been published recently by Lacey.[132] It is not possible to extend this discussion here except to note that, because of extrachromosomal resistance transfer and the selective pressure of widespread antibiotic use, by 1960 many hospitals were reporting 60 to 80 per cent of their S. aureus isolates resistant to penicillin. It was fortunate that methicillin, the first of the penicillinase-resistant penicillins, was introduced at about that time.

Penicillinase Production

There are many different β-lactamases, and they can be distinguished from each other by differences in pH optima, immunological differences, etc.[133] Several penicillinases have been purified to homogeneity and the amino acid sequence of some of them has been determined. The β-lactamases vary considerably with respect to substrate specificity. Strictly interpreted, "penicillinase" refers only to enzymes that hydrolyze penicillins, whereas β-lactamases that cleave cephalosporins are called cephalosporinases. But more and more enzymes that act on a spectrum of substrates in both antibiotic groups are being identified,[134] and the term penicillinase is often used for β-lactamases in general. The production of penicillinase can often be increased by exposing the bacterium to a penicillin. All of the penicillins, including the penicillinase-resistant penicillins, and the cephalosporins can act as inducers of the enzyme.[135]

Penicillinases are synthesized inside the cell and then transferred through the membrane to the external surface. In general, gram-positive bacteria produce large amounts of β-lactamase, and much of it is released into the surrounding growth medium. This is called exopenicillinase. In contrast, gram-negative organisms usually produce penicillinase in smaller amounts, and it remains largely in association with the surface structures external to the plasma membrane.[136]

The immediate fate of newly synthesized penicillinase varies somewhat from one type of organism to another. One model system that has been studied in some detail is the gram-positive organism B. licheniformis. This bacterium has a single structural gene for penicillinase,[137] but the enzyme can clearly exist in hydrophilic or hydrophobic forms. The enzyme secreted into the medium is hydrophilic. The majority of the exopenicillinase is directly secreted into the medium, but it may also be derived from cell-bound forms of the enzyme.[138] Although some of the cell-bound enzyme is in direct association with the plasma membrane (we shall refer to this hydrophobic form as membrane penicillinase), the majority is contained in vesicles located in the periplasmic space or in superficial mesosome-like structures.[139] The vesicles apparently function as a specialized apparatus for penicillinase packaging and perhaps excretion. When the bacterium is exposed to inducers (e.g., a penicillin), there is a rapid increase in penicillinase production accompanied by the formation of numerous vesicles with a high enzyme activity.[139] The hydrophobic membrane penicillinase is a phospholipoprotein with a molecular weight of 33,000 in contrast to 29,000 for the exoenzyme.[140] Cleavage of the membrane penicillinase with trypsin yields a phospholipopeptide and a hydrophilic penicillinase differing from the exopenicillinase only by the absence of the amino-terminal lysine residue.[141] Thus, the catalytic portion of the membrane associated enzyme is covalently linked via a peptide bridge to a phospholipid, which is responsible for its hydrophobic character and presumably anchors the enzyme to the membrane.

The vesicle and membrane forms of penicillinase should not be considered merely as precursors of the free exoenzyme. Indeed, they play a very important role in protecting the cell from the action of penicillins. Penicillinase synthesizing gram-negative bacteria can attain a high level of penicillin resistance with the production of a relatively small amount of enzyme. As mentioned before, the gram-negative bacteria have a certain intrinsic resistance due to the barrier function of the outer membrane.[142] The cell-bound penicillinases of these organisms can apparently provide an effective level of activity in the periplasmic space. Thus, any antibiotic that penetrates the surface layers is destroyed on its way to the target, the transpeptidase enzyme attached to the cytoplasmic membrane (see Figure 1-2).

Gram-positive organisms can secrete large amounts of penicillinase into the surrounding medium. For example, when fully induced, clinical isolates of S. aureus can synthesize up to 0.1 per cent of their dry weight as penicillinase.[136] The β-lactamases of gram-positive organisms frequently have a very high affinity for their substrates and an impressive drug destroying activity may be achieved in the local environment. Occasionally, infections have been noted to be clinically resistant to penicillin therapy even though the pathogen cultured from the infection site remained sensitive to antibiotic testing in vitro. Such apparent clinical resistance happens rarely with streptococcal infections in the respiratory tract.[143] The major pathogen is protected from the drug because the exopenicillinase produced by other organisms (e.g., staphylococci) inactivates the antibiotic.

The Penicillinase-resistant Penicillins

As one might expect, the effectiveness of a penicillin against penicillinase-producing organisms is an inverse function of its affinity for the penicillinase enzyme. The affinity constants of three penicillins for staphylococcal penicillinase are presented in Table 2-7. It is evident that methicillin, which is used to treat penicillin-resistant infections, has an affinity for the substrate site of penicillinase some four orders of magnitude less than penicillin G, which is readily hydrolyzed. Thus, methicillin is not inacti-

Table 2-7 **Affinity of penicillins for** *Staphylococcus aureus* **penicillinase**
The K_m was determined for each compound with free penicillinase in the broth from a culture of *S. aureus.* (From Novick[144])

Antibiotic	Effectiveness in treatment of penicillinase-producing organisms	K_m (μM)
Penicillin G	Ineffective	2.5
Phenoxymethyl penicillin	Ineffective	3.8
Methicillin	Effective	28,000

vated to any significant extent by staphylococcal penicillinase. Some other penicillinases, like that of *Bacillus cereus*, for example, will hydrolyze methicillin very slowly.[145]

It is entirely possible that minor mutations occurring at the gene locus governing the structure of the substrate site could result in the production of altered penicillinases with the ability to readily hydrolyze the penicillinase-resistant penicillins. These penicillins, however, have been used widely since the early 1960s, and super-penicillinases capable of attacking the methicillin-oxacillin group have not become a problem.[146] Methicillin resistance that is not due to hydrolysis by penicillinase does occur.

Resistance to the Penicillinase-resistant Penicillins

There are now numerous reports of methicillin-resistant staphylocci causing hospital infections. The methicillin-resistant strains are resistant to many antibiotics.[147,148] Table 2-8 presents some data from a study of several cases of methicillin-resistant staphylococcal infections at the Boston City Hospital. In the strains tested there was resistance not only to the penicillinase-resistant penicillins but also to the other β-lactam antibiotics and to a number of antibiotics of widely differing structures and mechanisms of action. The methicillin-resistant infections that have been reported in the literature, like those in this Boston study, have remained sensitive to vancomycin.[149]

Methicillin resistance is clearly not due to a penicillinase.[146] Although almost all the methicillin-resistant strains of staphylococci produce penicillinase, it has been shown that segregants that have lost the ability to produce penicillinase retain methicillin resistance.[150] Cells that are methicillin resistant often differ from sensitive staphylococci in their morphology and their capacity to produce certain enzymes and pigments.[132] Most methicillin-resistant strains are also resistant to streptomycin, tetracyclines, and some metal ions.[151] The degree of methicillin resistance varies considerably within single strains according to such environmental conditions as temperature and pH.[152] But the biochemical mechanism of methicillin resistance is not known.

The inheritance pattern for methicillin resistance is unusual. Apparently the determinants for the resistance occur in plasmids.[153] Methicillin resistance can be transduced, but the ability of staphylococci to act as recipients for this transduction is highly specific.[154] This is fortunate. If transfer of this type of resistance did occur readily, very difficult therapeutic problems could evolve.

It is difficult to predict how much of a problem resistance to the penicillinase-resistant penicillins will become. The incidence so far has been spotty. Although it has not been common in the United States, some hospitals in Europe have had a high incidence of methicillin resistance in seriously ill patients. In one Danish hospital, for example, the incidence of methicillin-resistant strains grown from blood cultures of patients with staphylococcal bacteremia was reported to be 45 per cent.[155] Most of the methicillin-resistant infections probably represent nosocomial

Table 2-8 Relative sensitivity of methicillin-sensitive and methicillin-resistant strains of *Staphylococcus aureus* to various antibiotics
The minimum concentration of antibiotic required to prevent visible growth in cultures of *S. aureus* isolated from patients at the Boston City Hospital was determined. Results as concentration of drug at which growth was totally inhibited in 50 per cent of the strains tested. (Table constructed from data of Barrett *et al.*[148])

Antibiotic	Antibiotic concentration required for growth inhibition (μg/ml): Methicillin-sensitive (291 strains)	Methicillin-resistant (22 strains)	Approximate-fold resistance
Methicillin	1.3	40	34
Cloxacillin	0.24	18	75
Cephalothin	0.24	20	83
Erythromycin	0.24	>100	>400
Tetracycline	1.6	70	44
Chloramphenicol	5	60	12
Vancomycin	2	1.4	0
Bacitracin	20	15	0

problems.[149] In other words, these organisms probably reside in the hospital environment and are rarely, if ever, involved in similar infections contracted in the community.[150] The incidence of methicillin resistance overall seems to be rising, but the rate of increase is slow.[156]

It is easy to see what a difficult therapeutic problem these resistant organisms present. Since these strains are resistant to other drugs that are useful against staphylococci, the therapeutic choice becomes very limited. Vancomycin is the drug of choice for treatment.

VANCOMYCIN AND BACITRACIN

Vancomycin

This is the most potent antibiotic against staphylococci. Vancomycin is used to treat severe staphylococcal infections, particularly in penicillin-hypersensitive patients, and staphylococcal infections caused by strains resistant to the penicillinase-resistant penicillins. It is an alternative to penicillins in the treatment of endocarditis caused by *Enterococcus* or *Streptococcus viridans*. The drug is very toxic and difficult to administer.

For systemic use, vancomycin must be given intravenously, and it readily causes thrombophlebitis. Severe drug fever is very common and occasionally patients will experience an acute hypotensive reaction. In some cases, the addition of a small amount of hydrocortisone to the infusion may make fever and thrombophlebitis less of a problem. Patients routinely complain of bothersome circumoral paresthesias. Vancomycin is severely ototoxic and nephrotoxic. It is cleared almost entirely by the kidney, and in the presence of renal insufficiency the dosage must be carefully adjusted.[157]

Since vancomycin is both poorly absorbed from the gastrointestinal tract and very effective against staphylococci, it is especially useful in the treatment of staphylococcal enterocolitis. The drug is administered orally in this life-threatening condition. Patients tend to vomit the drug back up, but vomiting can be controlled by administering the antibiotic through a nasogastric tube that has been passed beyond the pylorus.

Bacitracin

The use of bacitracin is restricted to the topical treatment of superficial infections. An injectable form is available, but there is no clinical indication for its use. When given systemically, the drug is very nephrotoxic. The spectrum of antibacterial action includes the gram-positive organisms. It is particularly effective against such common skin pathogens as staphylococci and streptococci.

The topical preparations often contain other antimicrobials like neomycin and polymyxin. Some preparations also contain corticosteroids. The rationale behind the inclusion of a corticosteroid with the antibiotics is subject to some dispute. The shotgun use of both the steroid and the antibiotics permits treatment of dermatitis of both infectious and noninfectious etiology without having to make a definitive diagnosis. When one must deal with large numbers of patients this is convenient. Those who use the combined preparations draw support from the argument that the steroid reduces local discomfort and itching, thus decreasing irritation of the involved area by scratching. One can also argue, however, that the inclusion of the corticosteroid would seem to be frankly counterproductive in the case of superficial infection, since it suppresses both the local reaction and the healing process. When the dermatitis is not due to infection, antibiotics are clearly being used when they are not needed and the patient is exposed to the risk of developing hypersensitivity to one of the antibiotic components. There is good reason to question the role of these antibiotic-corticosteroid combinations in therapy. They are certainly overused and their efficacy against mild superficial infections is not well documented.

REFERENCES

1. H. W. Florey: *Antibiotics,* Vol. I (ed. H. W. Florey *et al.* New York:) Oxford University Press, 1949.

2. J. Lederberg: Bacterial protoplasts induced by penicillin. *Proc. Natl. Acad. Sci. U.S.* 42:574 (1956).

3. W. D. Donachie and K. J. Begg: Growth of the bacterial cell. *Nature* 227:1220 (1970).

4. S. G. Nathenson and J. L. Strominger: Effects of penicillin on the biosynthesis of the cell walls of *Escherichia coli* and *Staphylococcus aureus. J. Pharmacol. Exp. Therap.* 131:1 (1961).

5. U. Roze and J. L. Strominger: Alanine racemase from *Staphylococcus aureus:* Conformation of its substrates and its inhibitor, D-cycloserine. *Mol. Pharmacol.* 2:92 (1964).

6. J. L. Strominger, K. Izaki, M. Matsuhashi, and D. L. Tipper: Peptidoglycan transpeptidase and D-alanine carboxypeptidase: Penicillin-sensitive enzymatic reactions. *Fed. Proc.* 26:9 (1967).

7. M. Matsuhashi, C. P. Dietrich, and J. L. Strominger: Incorporation of

glycine into the cell wall glycopeptide in *Staphylococcus aureus:* Role of sRNA and lipid intermediates. *Proc. Natl. Acad. Sci. U.S.* 54:587 (1965).

8. J. S. Anderson, M. Mitsuhashi, M. A. Haskin, and J. L. Strominger: Lipid-phosphoacetylmuramyl-pentapeptide and lipid-phospho-disaccharide-pentapeptide: Presumed membrane transport intermediates in cell wall synthesis. *Proc. Natl. Acad. Sci. U.S.* 53:881 (1965).

9. M. Matsuhashi, C. P. Dietrich, and J. L. Strominger: Biosynthesis of the peptidoglycan of bacterial cell walls: The role of soluble ribonucleic acid and of lipid intermediates in glycine incorporation in *Staphylococcus aureus, J. Biol. Chem.* 242:3191 (1967).

10. A. N. Chatterjee and H. R. Perkins: Compounds formed between nucleotides related to the biosynthesis of bacterial cell wall and vancomycin. *Biochem. Biophys. Res. Commun.* 24:489 (1966).

11. H. R. Perkins: Specificity of combination between mucopeptide precursors and vancomycin or ristocetin. *Biochem. J.* 111:195 (1969).

12. M. Nieto and H. R. Perkins: Modification of the acyl-D-alanyl-D-alanine terminus affecting complex formation with vancomycin. *Biochem. J.* 123:789 (1971).

13. J. P. Brown, J. Feeney, and A. S. V. Burgen: A nuclear magnetic resonance study of the interaction between vancomycin and acetyl-D-alanyl-D-alanine in aqueous solution. *Mol. Pharmacol.* 11:119 (1975).

14. J. P. Brown, L. Terenius, J. Feeney, and A. S. V. Burgen: A structure-activity study by nuclear magnetic resonance of peptide interactions with vancomycin. *Mol. Pharmacol.* 11:126 (1975).

15. G. Siewert and J. L. Strominger: Bacitracin: an inhibitor of the dephosphorylation of lipid pyrophosphate, an intermediate in biosynthesis of the peptidoglycan of bacterial cell walls. *Proc. Natl. Acad. Sci. U.S.* 57:767 (1967).

16. Y. Higashi, J. L. Strominger, and C. C. Sweeley: Biosynthesis of the peptidoglycan of bacterial cell walls: XXI. Isolation of free C_{55}-isoprenoid alcohol and of lipid intermediates in peptidoglycan synthesis from *Staphylococcus aureus. J. Biol. Chem.* 245:3697 (1970).

17. K. J. Stone and J. L. Strominger: Mechanism of action of bacitracin: Complexation with metal ion and C_{55}-isoprenyl pyrophosphate. *Proc. Natl. Acad. Sci. U.S.* 68:3223 (1971).

18. D. R. Storm and J. L. Strominger: Complex formation between bacitracin peptides and isoprenyl pyrophosphates: The specificity of lipid-peptide interactions. *J. Biol. Chem.* 248:3940 (1973).

19. D. R. Storm and J. L. Strominger: Binding of bacitracin to cells and protoplasts of *Micrococcus lysodeikticus. J. Biol. Chem.* 249:1823 (1974).

20. D. J. Tipper and J. L. Strominger: Biosynthesis of the peptidoglycan of bacterial cell walls: Inhibition of cross-linking by penicillins and cephalosporins. *J. Biol. Chem.* 243:3169 (1968).

21. P. Fitz-James and R. Hancock: The initial structural lesion of penicillin action in *Bacillus megaterium. J. Cell Biol.* 26:657 (1965).

22. D. Mirelman, R. Bracha, and N. Sharon: Penicillin-induced secretion of a soluble, uncross-linked peptidoglycan by *Micrococcus luteus* cells. *Biochemistry* 13:5045 (1974).

23. K. Izaki, M. Matsuhashi, and J. L. Strominger: Biosynthesis of the peptidoglycan of bacterial cell walls: Peptidoglycan transpeptidase and

D-alanine carboxypeptidase; penicillin-sensitive enzymatic reaction in strains of Escherichia coli. J. Biol. Chem. 243:3180 (1968).

24. D. Mirelman and N. Sharon: Biosynthesis of peptidoglycan by a cell wall preparation of Staphylococcus aureus and its inhibition by penicillin. Biochem. Biophys. Res. Commun. 46:1909 (1972).

25. D. J. Tipper and J. L. Strominger: Mechanism of action of penicillins: A proposal based on their structural similarity to acyl-D-alanyl-D-alanine. Proc. Natl. Acad. Sci. U.S. 54:1133 (1965).

26. G. G. Wickus and J. Strominger: Penicillin-sensitive transpeptidation during peptidoglycan biosynthesis in cell-free preparations from Bacillus megaterium. J. Biol. Chem. 247:5307 (1972).

27. P. M. Blumberg and J. L. Strominger: Interaction of penicillin with the bacterial cell: Penicillin-binding proteins and penicillin-sensitive enzymes. Bact. Rev. 38:291 (1974).

28. K. Izaki, M. Matsuhashi, and J. L. Strominger: Glycopeptide transpeptidase and D-alanine carboxypeptidase; penicillin-sensitive enzymatic reactions. Proc. Natl. Acad. Sci. U.S. 55:656 (1966).

29. D. Bogdanovsky, E. Bricas, and P. Dezélée: Sur L'identité de la mucopeptidase et de la carboxypeptidase I d'Escherichia coli, enzymes hydrolysant des liaisons de configuration D-D et inhibée par la penicilline. C. R. Acad. Sci., Paris, Ser. D. 269:390 (1969).

30. P. M. Blumberg and J. L. Strominger: Five penicillin-binding components occur in Bacillus subtilis membranes. J. Biol. Chem. 247:8107 (1972).

31. P. M. Blumberg and J. L. Strominger: Inactivation of D-alanine carboxypeptidase by penicillins and cephalosporins is not lethal in Bacillus subtilis. Proc. Natl. Acad. Sci. U.S. 68:2814 (1971).

32. P. M. Blumberg and J. L. Strominger: Isolation by affinity chromatography of the penicillin-binding components from membranes of Bacillus subtilis. Proc. Natl. Acad. Sci. U.S. 69:3751 (1972).

33. J. N. Umbreit and J. L. Strominger: D-alanine carboxypeptidase from Bacillus subtilis membranes: II. Interaction with penicillins and cephalosporins. J. Biol. Chem. 248:6767 (1973).

34. P. M. Blumberg, R. Yocum, E. Willoughby, and J. L. Strominger: Binding of [^{14}C]penicillin G to the membrane-bound and the purified D-alanine carboxypeptidases from Bacillus stearothermophilus and Bacillus subtilis and its release. J. Biol. Chem. 249:6828 (1974).

35. P. J. Lawrence and J. L. Strominger: Biosynthesis of the peptidoglycan of bacterial cell walls: XV. The binding of radioactive penicillin to the particulate enzyme preparation of Bacillus subtilis and its reversal with hydroxylamine or thiols. J. Biol. Chem. 245:3653 (1970).

36. P. J. Lawrence and J. L. Strominger: Biosynthesis of the peptidoglycan of bacterial cell walls: XVI. The reversible fixation of radioactive penicillin G to the D-alanine carboxypeptidase of Bacillus subtilis. J. Biol. Chem. 245:3660 (1970).

37. J. L. Strominger, P. M. Blumberg, H. Suginaka, J. Umbreit, and G. G. Wickus: How penicillin kills bacteria: Progress and problems. Proc. R. Soc. Lond. B 179:369 (1971).

38. G. D. Shockman: Symposium on the fine structure and replication of bacteria and their parts. IV. Unbalanced cell-wall synthesis: Autolysis and cell-wall thickening. Bacteriol. Rev. 29:345 (1965).

39. C. Forsberg and H. J. Rogers: Autolytic enzymes in growth of bacteria. *Nature* 229:272 (1971).

40. H. J. Rogers and C. W. Forsberg: Role of autolysins in the killing of bacteria by some bactericidal antibiotics. *J. Bacteriol.* 108:1235 (1971).

41. A. Tomasz: Biological consequences of the replacement of choline by ethanolamine in the cell wall of *Pneumococcus*: Chain formation, loss of transformability, and loss of autolysis. *Proc. Natl. Acad. Sci. U.S.* 59:86 (1968).

42. A Tomasz, A. Albino, and E. Zanati: Multiple antibiotic resistance in a bacterium with suppressed autolytic system. *Nature* 227:138 (1970).

43. The choice of antimicrobial drugs. *Med. Letter* 18:9 (1976).

44. C. H. Rammelkamp and C. S. Keefer: The absorption, excretion, and distribution of penicillin. *J. Clin. Invest.* 22:425 (1943).

45. C. H. Rammelkamp and J. D. Helm: Studies on the absorption of penicillin from the stomach. *Proc. Soc. Expt. Biol. Med.* 54:324 (1943).

46. W. McDermott, P. A. Bunn, M. Benoit, R. DuBois, and M. E. Reynolds: The absorption, excretion and destruction of orally administered penicillin. *J. Clin. Invest.* 25:190 (1946).

47. R. H. Meade: Gonorrhea: The minimum effective dose. *New Eng. J. Med.* 283:42 (1970).

48. J. R. Pappenheimer, S. R. Heisey, and F. F. Jordan: Active transport of Diodrast and phenolsulfonphthalein from cerebrospinal fluid to blood. *Am. J. Physiol.* 200:1 (1961).

49. R. L. Dixon, E. S. Owens, and D. P. Rall: Evidence of active transport of benzyl-^{14}C-penicillin from the cerebrospinal fluid to blood. *J. Pharm. Sci.* 58:1106 (1969).

50. R. Spector and A. V. Lorenzo: The effects of salicylate and probenecid on the cerebrospinal fluid transport of penicillin, aminosalicylic acid and iodide. *J. Pharm. Expt. Ther.* 188:55 (1974).

51. H. Smith. P. I. Lerner, and L. Weinstein: Neurotoxicity and massive intravenous therapy with penicillin. *Arch. Int. Med.* 120:47 (1967).

52. C. S. Bryan and W. J. Stone: "Comparably massive" penicillin G therapy in renal failure. *Ann. Int. Med.* 82:189 (1975).

53. G. Garraty and L. D. Petz: Drug-induced immune hemolytic anemia. *Am. J. Med.* 58:398 (1975).

54. H. C. Neu: Antimicrobial activity and human pharmacology of amoxicillin. *J. Infect. Dis.* 129 Suppl.:S123 (1974).

55. W. M. Kirby, R. C. Gordon, and C. Regamey: The pharmacology of orally administered amoxicillin and ampicillin. *J. Infect. Dis.* 129 Suppl.:S154 (1974).

56. M. Finland, J. E. McGowan, C. Garner, and C. Wilcox: Amoxicillin: *In vitro* susceptibility of "Blood Culture Strains" of gram-negative bacilli and comparisons with penicillin G, ampicillin, and carbenicillin. *J. Infect. Dis.* 129 Suppl.:S132 (1974).

57. K. C. Haltalin, J. D. Nelson, L. V. Hinton, H. T. Kusmiesz, and M. Sladoje: Comparison of orally absorbable and nonabsorbable antibiotics in shigellosis. *J. Pediat.* 72:708 (1968).

58. J. D. Nelson and K. C. Haltalin: Amoxacillin less effective than ampicillin against *Shigella in vitro* and *in vivo*: Relationship of efficacy to activity in serum. *J. Infect. Dis.* 129 Suppl.:S222 (1974).

59. H. C. Neu and E. B. Winshell: *In vitro* antimicrobial activity of 6-[D(−)-α-amino-β-hydroxyphenyl-acetamide]-penicillanic acid, a new semisynthetic penicillin. *Antimicrob. Agents Chemother.* 11:407 (1971).

60. W. L. Hewitt and R. E. Winters: The current status of parenteral carbenicillin. *J. Infect. Dis.* 127 Suppl.:S120 (1973).

61. M. Sonne and E. Jawetz: Combined action of carbenicillin and gentamicin on *Pseudomonas aeruginosa in vitro*. *Appl. Microbiol.* 17:893 (1969).

62. C. B. Smith, J. N. Wilfert, P. E. Dans, T. A. Kurrus, and M. Finland: *In vitro* activity of carbenicillin and results of treatment of infections due to *Pseudomonas* with carbenicillin singly and in combination with gentamicin. *J. Infect. Dis.* 122 Suppl.:S14 (1970).

63. C. M. Kunin: Antibiotic usage in patients with renal impairment. *Hospital Practice* 7:141 (1972).

64. L. D. Sabath, C. Wilcox, C. Garner, and M. Finland: *In vitro* activity of cephazolin against recent clinical bacterial isolates. *J. Infect. Dis.* 128 Suppl.:S320 (1973).

65. W. L. Hewitt: The cephalosporins-1973. *J. Infect. Dis.* 128 Suppl.:S312 (1973).

66. C. H. O'Callaghan and P. W. Muggleton: The formation of metabolites from cephalosporin compounds. *Biochem. J.* 89:304 (1963).

67. N. J. Vianna and D. Kaye: Penetration of cephalothin into the spinal fluid. *Am. J. Med. Sci.* 254:216 (1967).

68. D. J. Brown, A. W. Mathies, D. Ivler, W. S. Warren, and J. M. Leedom: Variable results of cephalothin therapy for meningococcal meningitis. *Antimicrob. Agents Chemother.* 10:432 (1970).

69. R. J. Mangi, R. S. Kundargi, R. Quintiliani, and V. Andreole: Development of meningitis during cephalothin therapy. *Ann. Int. Med.* 78:347 (1973).

70. F. Silverblatt, M. Turck, and R. Bulger: Nephrotoxicity due to cephaloridine: A light- and electron-microscopic study in rabbits. *J. Infect. Dis.* 122:33 (1970).

71. F. Silverblatt, W. O. Harrison, and M. Turck: Nephrotoxicity of cephalosporin antibiotics in experimental animals. *J. Infect. Dis.* 128 Suppl.:S367 (1973).

72. D. P. Pasternak and B. G. Stephens: Reversible nephrotoxicity associated with cephalothin therapy. *Arch. Int. Med.* 135:599 (1975).

73. B. M. Tune: Relationship between the transport and toxicity of cephalosporins in the kidney. *J. Infect. Dis.* 132:189 (1975).

74. W. A. Craig, P. G. Welling, J. C. Jackson, and C. M. Kunin: Pharmacology of cefazolin and other cephalosporins in patients with renal insufficiency. *J. Infect. Dis.* 128 Suppl.:S347 (1973).

75. W. M. M. Kirby and C. Regamey: Pharmacokinetics of cefazolin compared with four other cephalosporins. *J. Infect. Dis.* 128 Suppl.:S341 (1973).

76. J. A. Gold, J. J. McKee, and D. S. Ziv: Experience with cefazolin: An overall summary of pharmacologic and clinical trials in man. *J. Infect. Dis.* 128 Suppl.:S415 (1973).

77. R. C. Moellering and M. N. Schwartz: The newer cephalosporins. *New Engl. J. Med.* 294:24 (1976).

78. B. B. Levine, A. P. Redmond, H. E. Voss, and D. M. Zolov: Prediction of penicillin allergy by immunological tests. *Ann. N.Y. Acad. Sci.* 145:298 (1967).

79. R. P. Spark: Fatal anaphylaxis due to oral penicillin. *Clin. Pathol.* 56:407 (1971).

80. K. F. Austen: Systemic anaphylaxis in the human being. *New Eng. J. Med.* 291:661 (1974).

81. C. W. Parker: Drug allergy. *New Eng. J. Med.* 292:511,732, and 957 (1975).

82. A. Goldstein, L. Aronow, and S. M. Kalman: Drug allergy in *Principles of Drug Action,* New York: John Wiley and Sons, 1974, pp. 489–515.

83. H. Welch, C. N. Lewis, H. I. Weinstein, and B. B. Boeckman: Severe reactions to antibiotics. A nationwide survey. *Antibot. Med.* 4:800 (1957).

84. B. B. Levine: Studies on the mechanism of the formation of the penicillin antigen; Delayed allergic cross-reactions among penicillin G and its degradation products. *J. Exptl. Med.* 112:1131 (1960).

85. B. B. Levine and Z. Ovary: Studies on the mechanism of the formation of the penicillin antigen. *J. Exptl. Med.* 114:875 (1961).

86. C. W. Parker: Mechanisms of penicillin allergy. *Pathobiol. Ann.* 2:405 (1972).

87. K. Ishizaka and T. Ishizaka: Human reaginic antibodies and immunoglobulin E. *J. Allergy* 42:330 (1968).

88. F. R. Batchelor, J. M. Dewdney, J. G. Feinberg, and R. D. Weston: A penicilloylated protein impurity as a source of allergy to benzylpenicillin and 6-aminopenicillanic acid. *Lancet* 1:1175 (1967).

89. G. T. Stewart: Allergenic residues in penicillins. *Lancet* 1:1177 (1967).

90. E. T. Knudsen, O. P. W. Robinson, E. A. P. Croydon, and E. C. Tees: Cutaneous sensitivity to purified benzylpenicillin. *Lancet* 1:1184 (1967).

91. G. T. Stewart: Allergy to penicillin and related antibiotics: Antigenic and immunochemical mechanism. *Ann. Rev. Pharmacol.* 13:309 (1973).

92. B. C. Brown, E. V. Price, and M. B. Moore: Penicilloyl-polylysine as an intradermal test of penicillin sensitivity. *J.A.M.A.* 189:599 (1964).

93. B. B. Levine and D. Zolov: Prediction of penicillin allergy by immunological tests. *J. Allergy* 43:231 (1969).

94. B. B. Levine, A. P. Redmond, M. J. Fellner, H. E. Voss, and V. Levytska: Penicillin allergy and the immune response of man to penicillin. *J. Clin. Invest.* 45:1895 (1966).

95. N. F. Adkinson, W. L. Thomson, W. C. Maddrey, and L. M. Lichtenstein: Routine use of penicillin skin testing on an inpatient service. *New Eng. J. Med.* 285:22 (1971).

96. M. J. Fellner, A. I. Weidman, M. V. Klaus, and R. L. Baer: The usefulness of immediate skin tests to haptens derived from penicillin. *Arch. Derm.* 103:371 (1971).

97. L. Wide and L. Juhlin: Detection of penicillin allergy of the immediate type by radioimmunoassay of reagins (IgE) to penicilloyl conjugates. *Clinical Allergy* 1:171 (1971).

98. R. G. VanDellen, W. E. Walsh, G. A. Peters, and G. J. Gleich:

Differing patterns of wheal and flare skin reactivity in patients allergic to the penicillins. *J. Allergy* 47:230 (1971).

99. B. B. Levine: Antigenicity and cross-reactivity of penicillins and cephalosporins. *J. Infect. Dis.* 128 Suppl.:S364 (1973).

100. F. R. Batchelor, J. M. Dewdney, and D. Gazzard: Penicillin allergy: The formation of the penicillin determinant. *Nature* 206:362 (1965).

101. P. Spath, G. Garratty, and L. Petz: Studies on the immune response to penicillin and cephalothin in humans: II. Immunohematologic reactions to cephalothin administration. *J. Immunol.* 107:860 (1971).

102. J. M. T. Hamilton-Miller and E. P. Abraham: Specificities of haemagglutinating antibodies evoked by members of the cephalosporin C family and benzylpenicillin. *Biochem. J.* 123:183 (1971).

103. R. L. Perkins and S. Saslaw: Experiences with cephalothin. *Ann. Int. Med.* 64:13 (1966).

104. S. L. Merrill, A. Davis, B. Smolens, and S. M. Finegold: Cephalothin in serious bacterial infection. *Ann. Int. Med.* 64:1 (1966).

105. J. F. Scholand, J. I. Tennenbaum, and G. J. Cerilli: Anaphylaxis to cephalothin in a patient allergic to penicillin. *J. Am. Med. Assoc.* 206:130 (1968).

106. G. O. Westenfelder and P. Y. Paterson: Life-threatening infection: Choice of alternate drugs when penicillin cannot be given. *J. Am. Med. Assoc.* 210:845 (1969).

107. M. J. Fellner, E. Van Hecke, M. Rozan, and R. L. Baer: Mechanisms of clinical desensitization in urticarial hypersensitivity to penicillin. *J. Allergy* 45:55 (1970).

108. S. A. Gillman, J. L. Korotzer, and Z. H. Haddad: Penicillin desensitization: *Clinical Allergy* 2:63 (1972).

109. A. L. deWeck and C. H. Schneider: Specific inhibition of allergic reactions to penicillin in man by a monovalent hapten. I Experimental immunological and toxicologic studies. *Int. Arch. Allergy* 42:782 (1972).

110. A. L. deWeck and J. P. Girard: Specific inhibition of allergic reactions to penicillin in man by a monovalent hapten. II Clinical studies. *Int. Arch. Allergy* 42:798 (1972).

111. G. E. Brauninger and J. S. Remington: Nephropathy associated with methicillin therapy. *J. Am. Med. Assoc.* 203:103 (1968).

112. D. N. Gilbert, R. Gourly, A. d'Agostino, S. H. Goodnight, and H. Worthen: Interstitial nephritis due to methicillin, penicillin and ampicillin. *Ann. Allergy* 28:378 (1970).

113. D. S. Baldwin, B. B. Levine, R. T. McCluskey, and G. R. Gallo: Renal failure and interstitial nephritis due to penicillin and methicillin. *New Eng. J. Med.* 279:1245 (1968).

114. W. A. Border, D. H. Lehman, J. D. Egan, H. J. Sass, J. E. Glode, and C. B. Wilson: Antitubular basement-membrane antibodies in methicillin-associated interstitial nephritis. *New Eng. J. Med.* 291:381 (1974).

115. S. Shapiro, D. Slone, and V. Siskind: Drug rash with ampicillin and other penicillins. *Lancet* 2:969 (1969).

116. C. W. Bierman, W. E. Pierson, S. J. Zeitz, L. S. Hoffman, and P. P. VanArsdel: Reactions associated with ampicillin therapy. *J. Am. Med. Assoc.* 220:1098 (1972).

117. Z. H. Haddad and J. L. Korotzer: *In vitro* studies on the mechanism of penicillin and ampicillin drug reactions. *Int. Arch. Allergy* 41:72 (1971).

118. B. M. Patel: Skin rash with infectious mononucleosis and ampicillin. *Pediatrics* 40:910 (1967).

119. H. Pullen, N. Wright, and J. M. Murdoch: Hypersensitivity reactions to antibacterial drugs in infectious mononucleosis. *Lancet* 2:1176 (1967).

120. P. E. Weary, J. W. Cole, and L. H. Hickam: Eruptions from ampicillin in patients with infectious mononucleosis. *Arch. Derm.* 101:86 (1970).

121. Boston Collaborative Drug Surveillance Program: Excess of ampicillin rashes associated with allopurinol or hyperuricemia. *New Eng. J. Med.* 286:505 (1972).

122. C. H. Rammelkamp and T. Moxon: Resistance of *Staphylococcus aureus* to the action of penicillin. *Proc. Soc. Expt. Biol. Med.* 51:386 (1942).

123. D. A. Monner, S. Jonsson, and H. G. Boman: Ampicillin-resistant mutants of *Escherichia coli* K-12 with lipopolysaccharide alterations affecting mating ability and succeptibility to sex-specific bacteriophages. *J. Bacteriol.* 107:420 (1971).

124. E. F. Gale, E. Cundliffe, P. E. Reynolds, M. H. Richmond, and M. J. Waring: Inhibitors of bacterial cell wall synthesis in *The Molecular Basis of Antibiotic Action*, London: John Wiley and Sons, 1972, pp. 49–120.

125. M. R. Pollock: The function and evolution of penicillinase. *Proc. R. Soc. Lond. B* 179:385 (1971).

126. J. H. Ozer and A. K. Saz: Possible involvements of β-lactamase in sporulation in *Bacillus cereus*. *J. Bacteriol.* 102:65 (1970).

127. R. P. Novick: Analysis by transduction of mutants affecting penicillinase formation in *Staphylococcus aureus*. *J. Gen. Microbiol.* 33:121 (1963).

128. R. P. Novick and S. I. Morse: *In vivo* transmission of drug resistance factors between strains of *Staphylococcus aureus*. *J. Expt. Med.* 125:45 (1967).

129. K. G. H. Dyke, M. T. Parker, and M. H. Richmond: Penicillinase production and metal-ion resistance in *Staphylococcus aureus* isolated from hospital patients. *J. Med. Microbiol.* 3:125 (1970).

130. R. W. Lacey and M. H. Richmond: The genetic basis of antibiotic resistance in *S. aureus*: The importance of gene transfer in the evolution of this organism in the hospital environment. *Ann. N.Y. Acad. Sci.* 236:395 (1974).

131. G. N. Rolinson: Bacterial resistance to penicillins and cephalosporins. *Proc. R. Soc. Lond. B* 179:403 (1971).

132. R. W. Lacey: Antibiotic resistance plasmids of *Staphylococcus aureus* and their clinical importance. *Bacteriol. Rev.* 39:1 (1975).

133. N. Citri: Penicillinase and other β-lactamases in *The Enzymes* Vol. IV (ed. P. D. Boyer) New York, Academic Press, 1971, pp. 23–46.

134. G. G. Jackson, V. T. Lolans, and B. G. Gallegos: Comparative activity of bacterial β-lactamases on penicillins and cephalosporins. *J. Infect. Dis.* 128 Suppl.:S327 (1973).

135. D. L. Swallow and P. H. A. Sneath: Studies on staphylococcal penicillinase. *J. Gen. Microbiol.* 28:461 (1962).

136. M. H. Richmond and N. A. C. Curtis: The interplay of β-lactamases and intrinsic factors in the resistance of gram-negative bacteria to penicillins and cephalosporins. *Ann. N.Y. Acad. Sci.* 235:553 (1974).

137. D. J. Sherratt and J. F. Collins: Analysis by transformation of the penicillinase system in *Bacillus licheniformis*. *J. Gen. Microbiol.* 76:217 (1973).

138. M. G. Sargent and J. O. Lampen: A mechanism for penicillinase secretion in *Bacillus licheniformis*. *Proc. Natl. Acad. Sci. U.S.* 65:962 (1970).

139. B. K. Ghosh, J. O. Lampen, and C. C. Remsen: Periplasmic structure of frozen-etched and negatively stained cells of *Bacillus licheniformis* as correlated with penicillinase formation. *J. Bacteriol.* 100:1002 (1969).

140. S. Yamamoto and J. O. Lampen: Purification of plasma membrane penicillinase from *Bacillus licheniformis* 749/C and comparison with exoenzyme. *J. Biol. Chem.* 251:4095 (1976).

141. S. Yamamoto and J. O. Lampen: The hydrophobic membrane penicillinase of *Bacillus licheniformis* 749/C: Characterization of the hydrophilic enzyme and phospholipopeptide produced by trypsin cleavage. *J. Biol. Chem.* 251:4102 (1976).

142. H. G. Boman, K. Nordstrom, and S. Normark: Penicillin resistance in *Escherichia coli* K12: Synergism between penicillinases and a barrier in the outer part of the envelope. *Ann. N.Y. Acad. Sci.* 235:569 (1974).

143. L. Weinstein and A. C. Dalton: Host determinants of response to antimicrobial agents. *New Engl. J. Med.* 279:580 (1968).

144. R. P. Novick: Staphylococcal penicillinase and the new penicillins. *Biochem. J.* 83:229 (1962).

145. G. N. Rolinson, S. Stevens, F. R. Batchelor, J. C. Wood, and E. B. Chain: Bacteriological studies on a new penicillin-BRL.1241. *Lancet* 2:564 (1960).

146. K. G. H. Dyke: Penicillinase production and intrinsic resistance to penicillins in methicillin-resistant cultures of *Staphylococcus aureus*. *J. Med. Microbiol.* 2:261 (1969).

147. R. J. Bulger: A methicillin-resistant strain of *Staphylococcus aureus*. *Ann. Int. Med.* 67:81 (1967).

148. F. F. Barrett, R. F. McGehee, and M. Finland: Methicillin-resistant *Staphylococcus aureus* at Boston City Hospital. *New Eng. J. Med.* 279:441 (1968).

149. E. J. Benner and F. H. Kayser: Growing clinical significance of methicillin-resistant *Staphylococcus aureus*. *Lancet* 2:741 (1968).

150. S. Seligman: Penicillinase-negative variants of methicillin-resistant *Staphylococcus aureus*. *Nature* 209:994 (1966).

151. S. J. Seligman: Magnesium-ion susceptibility of methicillin-resistant *Staphylococcus aureus*. *J. Med. Microbiol.* 7:403 (1974).

152. L. D. Sabath and S. J. Wallace: Factors influencing methicillin resistance in staphylococci. *Ann. N.Y. Acad. Sci.* 182:258 (1971).

153. R. W. Lacey: Genetic control in methicillin-resistant strains of *Staphylococcus aureus*. *J. Med. Microbiol.* 5:497 (1972).

154. S. Cohen and H. M. Sweeney: Transduction of methicillin-resistance in *Staphylococcus aureus* dependent on an unusual specificity of the recipient strain. *J. Bacteriol.* 104:1158 (1970).

155. P. Bülow: Staphylococci in Danish hospitals during the last decade: Factors influencing some properties of predominant epidemic strains. *Ann. N.Y. Acad. Sci.* 182:21 (1971).

156. M. T. Parker and J. H. Hewitt: Methicillin resistance in *Staphylococcus aureus*. *Lancet* 1:800 (1970).

157. *The Medical Letter Handbook of Antimicrobial Therapy* (1976).

Chapter 3

Bactericidal Inhibitors of Protein Synthesis (The Aminoglycosides)
Gentamicin
Streptomycin
Neomycin
Kanamycin
Paromomycin
Tobramycin
Amikacin

Introduction

The aminoglycoside group of antibiotics includes a large number of structurally related polycationic compounds composed of amino sugars connected by glycosidic linkages. They are all derived from different species of *Streptomyces*. Gentamicin, streptomycin, neomycin, kanamycin, and tobramycin are employed clinically in the treatment of bacterial infections. Another aminoglycoside, paromomycin, is used to treat cestodiasis (tapeworm infection, see Chapter 12). The aminoglycosides all inhibit protein synthesis and they are all bactericidal. They affect protein synthesis in the bacterial cell similarly, but there are probably slight differences in their mechanisms of action at the level of the drug interaction with the ribosomal receptor site.

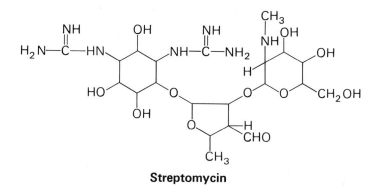

Streptomycin

Protein Synthesis in Bacteria

It is appropriate to review our current understanding of protein synthesis[1-3] before discussing inhibition of the process by drugs. The synthesis of proteins, which, for the purpose of this discussion, equals the process of messenger RNA (mRNA) translation, can be conveniently divided into three stages—initiation, elongation, and termination.

The first stage in protein synthesis is the formation of an initiation complex (Figure 3-1). In bacteria the first or N-terminal amino acid for all proteins is formylmethionine. Formylmethionine and its appropriate transfer RNA (tRNA) are first united under the direction of an aminoacyl-tRNA-synthetase to form aminoacyl-tRNA. The mRNA becomes attached to the 30S subunit, a process that requires the participation of a soluble protein called an initiation factor (F_3). The formylmethionine-charged tRNA then combines with the mRNA-30S-ribosomal complex. The anticodon triplet portion of the tRNA is juxtaposed to the start signal (AUG initiation codon) on the mRNA. This requires the participation of

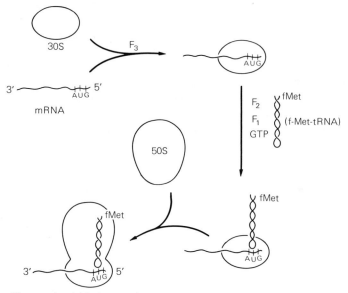

The complete initiation complex

Figure 3-1 Steps in the formation of the 70S initiation complex in bacteria. F_1, F_2, and F_3 represent the initiation factors. The process of initiation is described in detail in the text.

two additional initiation factors (F_1 and F_2) and GTP. In the next step, the 50S ribosomal subunit becomes bound to the mRNA-30S-tRNA-amino acid complex in a reaction also requiring GTP. The initiation factors and the guanosine nucleotide, which are required for the correct association of all of the components, are released during the last two stages of assembly. The initiation complex is now complete.

Chain elongation (Figure 3-2) commences with the insertion of a second aminoacyl-tRNA in the ribosomal acceptor (A) site, a process that requires the participation of GTP and two elongation factors (EF-Tu and EF-Ts). The first two tRNA's are now oriented appropriately with their anticodon ends opposite their respective code triplets on the mRNA and their attached amino acids adjacent to each other on the surface of the 50S portion of the ribosome. The two amino acids then become linked by a peptide bond under the direction of a peptidyl transferase enzyme. The peptidyl transferase system is composed of one, or several, of the more than 30 protein components of the 50S ribosomal subunit. The carboxyl group of formylmethionine is linked to the amino group of the second amino acid, and the dipeptide is now attached to the second tRNA, which is occupying the A site. After the formation of the peptide bond, a complicated translocation takes place. The tRNA for formylmethionine is released from the P site, the tRNA with the attached dipeptide moves from the A to the P site, and the 30S subunit moves one codon along the mRNA. Elongation factor G (EF-G) and GTP hydrolysis are required for this three part process to occur. The A site is now unoccupied and ready to receive the next aminoacyl-tRNA directed by the next code triplet on the mRNA. The process of elongation continues with the addition of single amino acid units until a termination sequence containing code triplets UAA, UGA, or UAG in the mRNA signals that the protein chain is complete.

When one of these nonsense (terminator) codons appears in the A site, no aminoacyl-tRNA is bound. Instead, the ribosome binds a protein, called a termination release factor, which recognizes the terminator codon. This release factor activates peptidyl transferase, which hydrolyzes the bond joining the now fully synthesized protein to the tRNA occupying the P site. After release of the protein, the deacylated tRNA is released from the P site, and mRNA is detached from the ribosome. The mechanisms of these two events are not well understood, although it appears that EF-G, GTP, and an additional factor may be required. The ribosomes are

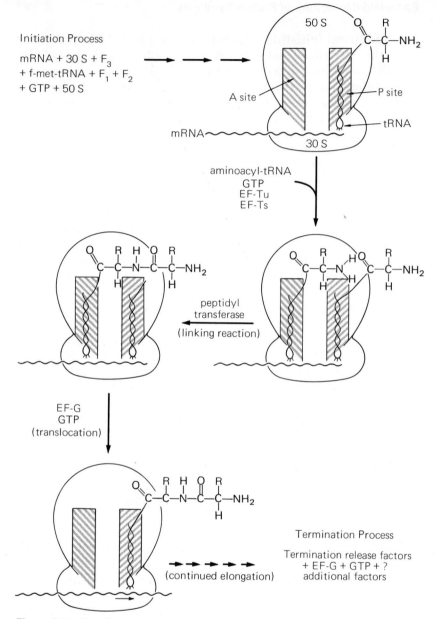

Figure 3-2 Protein synthesis in bacteria. This schematic presentation of this process is described in detail in the text. The shapes representing the tRNA and the ribosome are, of course, highly schematic and are not intended to represent their actual form. F_1, F_2, and F_3 refer to the three initiation factors and EF-Tu, EF-Ts, and EF-G represent the three elongation factors. As described in the text, these factors and the termination release factors are soluble proteins required for the processes of protein synthesis.

apparently released as 70S units, which then become dissociated into 30S and 50S subunits in a process that requires the participation of a ribosome dissociation factor.[4] This factor is apparently the same as initiation factor 3. The 30S and 50S subunits then return to the cycle of events at initiation.

MECHANISM OF ACTION

Inhibition of Protein Synthesis

Most of the work on the mechanism of action of the aminoglycoside antibiotics has been carried out with streptomycin; it has been reviewed by Pestka[5] and by Weisblum and Davies.[6] When growing bacteria are exposed to streptomycin, there is a rapid inhibition of protein synthesis.[7] It is now well established that the site of streptomycin action is the 30S ribosomal subunit. There are multiple effects as a result of this interaction, but it is clear that inhibition of protein synthesis is responsible for the bactericidal effect of the drug. The theories regarding the mechanism of inhibition of protein synthesis by streptomycin have evolved along two somewhat different paths. According to one interpretation (Luzzatto et al.[8]), streptomycin irreversibly blocks protein synthesis at the stage of initiation.

In one experiment that lends support to this conclusion, streptomycin was added to a culture of growing E. coli in which stable RNA had been labeled with radioactive uracil, the cells were lysed at various times after the streptomycin was added, and the lysate was centrifuged on a sucrose gradient.[8] Over a period of several minutes the ^{14}C activity disappeared from the polysome region and appeared in the 70S region of the sucrose gradient. The largest polysomes were the first to disappear, followed by the smaller units until most of the radioactivity in the portion of the gradient occupied by the polyribosomes had been shifted to 70S material. The disappearance of polysomes is interpreted to mean that protein synthesis in progress when the streptomycin was added continues, but that new protein synthesis does not start, presumably due to an inability of the initiation complex to function. If the rate of chain elongation were reduced by streptomycin without a change in the rate of initiation, one would expect polysomes to accumulate.

The 70S units that accumulate are called "streptomycin monosomes," and they are incapable of protein synthesis. The accumulation of the 70S monosomes takes place at the expense of 50S and

30S ribosomes as well as polyribosomes. These streptomycin monosomes consist of a complex of 30S and 50S ribosomal particles, mRNA, and streptomycin. The streptomycin is bound very tightly, and the 70S units accumulate irreversibly in the cell. This accumulation of 70S monosomes at the expense of both large and small ribosomal units is what one would expect if the effect of streptomycin were to "freeze" protein synthesis at the initiation complex stage. Thus the drug allows the initiation complex to form, but this streptomycin-bound complex is inactive. There is a good correlation between the accumulation of 70S monosomes and the loss of cell viability after exposure to streptomycin. This model of the effect of streptomycin on bacterial protein synthesis is schematically presented in Figure 3-3.

The model of Luzzatto et al. emphasizes only the effect of streptomycin on initiation. Davis and his co-workers,[9] however, have demonstrated an inhibitory effect of streptomycin on protein synthesis directed by purified polysomes under conditions in which initiation does not take place.[10] Thus, streptomycin can interact with both free 30S subunits and ribosomes that are attached to mRNA in the polysome structure. The interaction with a ribosome in the polysome structure incompletely blocks protein synthesis, whereas the interaction before initiation completely blocks it. Luzzatto et al.[8] propose that the streptomycin-containing 70S units are abnormal initiation complexes that accumulate irreversibly in the cell, sequestering the mRNA in this form. Modolell and Davis[11] argue that streptomycin permits normal initiation, but that chain extension is blocked and there is a slow breakdown of the 70S initiation complex, with the accompanying release of fMet-tRNA. Thus, the two models differ with regard to the stability of the streptomycin-bound initiation complex, but they agree with regard to the observation that the initiation complex cannot function at all in protein synthesis.

In E. coli K12, Wallace and Davis have shown that some polysomes can be recovered from streptomycin-treated cells even when inhibition of protein synthesis is virtually complete.[12] They demonstrated that polysomes are not formed if either new mRNA synthesis or normal initiation is inhibited. Thus, they suggest that the polysomes observed in this bacterium result from the reattachment of streptomycin-bound ribosomes to initiation sites on newly synthesized mRNA by means of the normal initiation process. The polysomes are inactive, that is, they do not incorporate radioactive amino acid into polypeptide. One might expect that streptomycin-bound ribosomes that reinitiate on mRNA would

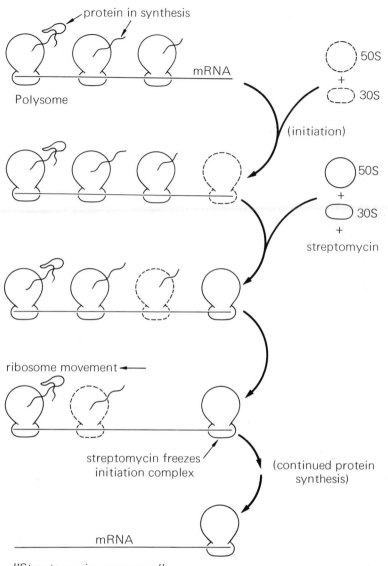

protein in synthesis

mRNA

Polysome

50S
+
30S

(initiation)

50S
+
30S
+
streptomycin

ribosome movement ←

streptomycin freezes
initiation complex

(continued protein
synthesis)

mRNA

"Streptomycin monosome"

Figure 3-3 Schematic presentation of the mechanism of action of streptomycin proposed by Luzzatto *et al.*[8] Streptomycin blocks bacterial protein synthesis at initiation. After intact bacteria are exposed to streptomycin, polysomes become rapidly depleted, and 70S particles, the "streptomycin monosomes," build up. Although the formation of the initiation complex is not affected, the complex formed in the presence of streptomycin cannot synthesize protein and remains fixed in position. It is proposed that ribosomes beyond the initiation stage are able to continue their movement and detachment so that a 70S complex of mRNA and 50S and 30S units with bound streptomycin results. In effect, the initiation complex is "frozen."

form 70S monosomes, since the drug-containing initiation complex cannot move along the mRNA, and thus leave the N-terminal initiator codon open to be occupied by subsequent initiation units. The fact that polysomes are formed implies that either intragenic AUG (initiation) codons in the mRNA are accessible or that streptomycin causes a misreading so that other codons are read as if they were AUG, and the initiation process is permitted. The polysomes in the streptomycin-treated cells turn over rapidly and are maintained in the presence of continued RNA production by a cyclic process of ribosome release and abortive reinitiation.

Let us now review again the two interpretations of streptomycin blockade of protein synthesis. According to the model of Luzzatto et al.,[8] streptomycin binds to the 30S ribosomal subunit, which can then enter into an initiation complex. But these are aberrant initiation complexes that cannot synthesize protein and remain "frozen" with their attached mRNA. In the model of Davis and his co-workers, the drug-bound subunit can form an initiation complex in the normal manner, but due to a distortion in the A site, it cannot efficiently bind aminoacyl-tRNA,[13] and there is no chain elongation. The streptomycin-bound ribosomes are not permanently frozen in this model, but slowly dissociate from the mRNA as 70S ribosomes. This is a critical point in the difference between the two proposals. The experiments of Davis et al. indicate that the 70S streptomycin-bound material, which accrues in the cell, is composed of both ribosomes that have dissociated from the mRNA and monosomes, that is, initiation complexes with their attached mRNA. Wallace and Davis[14] have also obtained data supporting the concept that streptomycin-bound 70S ribosomes have an impaired ability to respond to the factor that promotes their dissociation into the respective 30S and 50S subunits. They have demonstrated that the drug-bound 30S particles that are recycled to the free state are not inert but are capable of reattaching to initiation regions of any available mRNA. Thus, they propose that the binding of streptomycin to the ribosomal subunit results in a cycle of initiation, blockade of chain extension, gradual release of ribosomes, and reinitiation.

Any explanation of streptomycin action must take into account the dominance of sensitivity over resistance in heterozygotes.[15] The heterozygote contains both streptomycin-sensitive and streptomycin-resistant ribosomal subunits. Wallace and Davis[12] propose that this can be accounted for in their model of the action of streptomycin (see Figure 3-4). In the heterozygote, as in bacteria

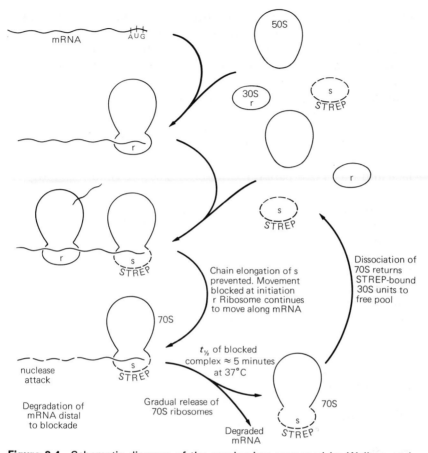

Figure 3-4 Schematic diagram of the mechanism proposed by Wallace and Davis[12] to explain how heterozygotes are killed by streptomycin (STREP). The heterozygote contains both STREP-sensitive (s) and STREP-resistant (r) 30S subunits. There is a roughly equivalent chance of initiation occurring with either one. As with the model of Luzzatto et al. (Figure 3-3), the initiation complex formed with a STREP-bound 30S subunit cannot synthesize polypeptide and move along the mRNA. The half-life of the complex is long (about 5 minutes at 37°C), and apparently extensive degradation of the mRNA distal to the block takes place. The STREP-bound 70S ribosome is gradually released from the degrading mRNA. Streptomycin binding also results in slower dissociation of the 70S ribosome into 50S and 30S subunits.[14] Nevertheless, the STREP-bound 30S units are returned to the free pool where they can compete with resistant units for attachment to newly synthesized mRNA and block protein synthesis. The sensitive ribosomes can thus prevent the resistant ribosomes from supporting virtually any protein synthesis.

that contain only sensitive 30S units, the mRNA that enters into an initiation complex with a drug-bound ribosome is blocked for a long time. The half-life of the streptomycin-containing complex in the cell at 37°C is 5 minutes. This can be compared to the normal initiation rate of 15 to 20 ribosomes per second. During this time, degradation of mRNA distal to the blocked initiation site occurs. The eventual release of the streptomycin-bound ribosome from the remaining mRNA permits reentry of sensitive 30S subunits into the free subunit pool where they can again compete with resistant ribosomes for attachment to new messenger. Wallace and Davis compare the drug-bound sensitive unit's ability to interfere with the function of the resistant particle to an antimetabolite that blocks the utilization of the normal metabolite. As the sensitive ribosomes cycle through the system they are never completely bound up to mRNA as in the model of Luzzatto et al.,[8] and they are continually available to prevent the resistant ribosomes from supporting any protein synthesis.

A critical question that remains unanswered is why total blockade of protein synthesis by streptomycin kills cells, whereas total blockade by some other antibiotics (chloramphenicol, tetracyclines, etc.) is bacteriostatic. The answer is perhaps related to the possibility that streptomycin binds so tightly that it remains associated with the 30S unit for a long time after the free drug concentration declines, whereas the bacteriostatic agents, which are weakly bound and more rapidly dissociated, permit renewed cell growth.

The Receptor

The aminoglycoside antibiotics have a selective toxicity because they bind only to bacterial ribosomes. They differ from chloramphenicol and erythromycin in that they interact with the 30S subunit of the ribosome. This site of interaction was first indicated by experiments that utilized ribosomes from streptomycin-sensitive and streptomycin-resistant cells to support poly U-directed protein synthesis.[16] The 70S ribosome can be dissociated into its 50S and 30S subunits by lowering the Mg^{++} concentration; raising the Mg^{++} concentration permits reassociation. Accordingly, cell extracts of E. coli were made in buffer of low Mg^{++} concentration and centrifuged on a sucrose gradient to separate the heavier 50S subunits from the 30S particles. Cross-over experiments were then carried out by raising the concentration to produce hybrid

70S ribosomes with one subunit from sensitive cells and one from resistant cells. These reassociated ribosomes were then incubated with poly U and streptomycin in an appropriate system for protein synthesis. The results of the experiment, summarized in Table 3-1, demonstrate that substantial inhibition of protein synthesis is achieved only when the 30S subunit is derived from sensitive cells.

This type of experiment has been carried further by Nomura and his co-workers; they separated purified 30S ribosomes into 16S RNA and more than 20 different proteins, which could be fractionated by phosphocellulose column chromatography.[17] These proteins and the 16S RNA were then reassociated into 30S ribosomal subunits that support protein synthesis. Protein-synthesizing experiments utilizing such reconstituted ribosomes prepared with 30S ribosomal protein purified from streptomycin-sensitive and streptomycin-resistant cells demonstrate that a single protein (designated P_{10} in accordance with its migration on polyacrylamide gel electrophoresis) determines the streptomycin sensitivity of the reconstituted particles (Table 3-2).[18]

Clearly the P_{10} protein is necessary not only for streptomycin sensitivity but also for streptomycin binding. This has been demonstrated by incubating reconstituted 30S particles with radioactive dihydrostreptomycin and then separating the bound 30S-streptomycin complex from the free drug by filtration.[18] The

Table 3-1 The effect of streptomycin on the incorporation of phenylalanine in a system utilizing hybrid ribosomes from sensitive and resistant cells

Ribosomes reconstituted from 30S and 50S subunits purified from streptomycin-sensitive and streptomycin-resistant *E. coli* were added to a phenylalanine incorporation system directed by poly U. Incubations were carried out with or without streptomycin ($5 \times 10^{-5}M$), and the amount of radioactivity incorporated into the acid-insoluble form was assayed. The results are presented as the average per cent inhibition of incorporation by streptomycin for four experiments. (Data from Davies.[16])

Constitution of hybrid ribosomes:		Inhibition of phenylalanine incorporation by streptomycin (%)
30S	50S	
Sensitive	Sensitive	62
Sensitive	Resistant	60
Resistant	Resistant	6
Resistant	Sensitive	15

Table 3-2 Poly U-directed phenylalanine incorporation activity of reconstituted 30S ribosomal particles and their sensitivity to streptomycin

RNA prepared from 30S ribosomes and 30S ribosomal protein purified by phosphocellulose chromatography from streptomycin-sensitive and streptomycin-resistant E. coli were reconstituted into 30S subunits. Two protein fractions were prepared: the protein P_{10}, which was essentially pure, and the protein mixture containing all the other 30S subunit proteins except P_{10}. Particles were reconstituted in the combinations indicated and assayed for their activity in poly U-directed phenylalanine incorporation with or without streptomycin ($5 \times 10^{-5}M$). Values in counts per minute of phenylalanine incorporated per incubation: S, sensitive; r, resistant; Sm, streptomycin. (Data from Ozaki et al.[18])

Origin of proteins used for reconstituted 30S subunits: All proteins but P_{10}	P_{10}	Incorporation activity (cpm): −Sm	+Sm	Inhibition by streptomycin (%)
S	S	6354	4153	35
S	r	6209	5755	7
S	—	2926	3116	0
r	r	4214	4031	4
r	S	4236	2771	35

Table 3-3 Binding of dihydrostreptomycin to reconstituted 30S ribosomal particles

30S particles reconstituted from 16S RNA and purified 30S subunit protein from streptomycin-sensitive or streptomycin-resistant E. coli were incubated at 30 °C with radioactive dihydrostreptomycin (3.4 μg/ml). After 20 minutes, the bound drug-30S complex was separated from the free drug by filtration on cellulose acetate. The radioactive drug remaining on the filter was assayed in a scintillation counter; values in counts per minute of dihydrostreptomycin bound per 1.5 OD_{260} units of 30S particles: S, sensitive; r, resistant. (From Ozaki et al.[18])

Origin of proteins used for reconstituted 30S subunits: All proteins but P_{10}	P_{10}	Dihydrostreptomycin bound (cpm)
S	S	1198
S	r	65
S	—	83
r	r	31
r	S	691
Control 30S (S)		943
Control 30S (r)		35

results presented in Table 3-3 show that there is significant binding of dihydrostreptomycin to ribosomes only when the P_{10} in the reconstituted ribosome is derived from sensitive cells. In dialysis experiments, P_{10} alone (that is, not in combination with RNA as a reconstituted 30S particle) does not bind the drug, whereas complete 30S particles under the same conditions bind well. Therefore some structure involving both P_{10} and other components of the 30S subunit of the ribosome is essential to the formation of the complete functioning receptor site for the drug.

Distortion of the Fidelity of Translation

One result of the interaction of streptomycin (or other aminoglycoside antibiotics) with the ribosome is a higher frequency of incorrect codon-anticodon interaction. This effect on the fidelity of messenger translation can be seen in vitro as an increased incorporation of the "wrong" amino acid in protein synthesis directed by synthetic mRNA.[19] The effect can be also seen in vivo as "phenotypic suppression": that is, the drug masks the phenotypic expression of certain mutations.

An example of the misreading seen with streptomycin is presented in Table 3-4. Under routine assay conditions, poly U directs the incorporation of phenylalanine (codes UUU and UUC) much more readily than leucine, isoleucine, or serine, all of which have codons that differ from a phenylalanine codon by only one base. In the presence of streptomycin, neomycin, or

Table 3-4 **Amino acid incorporation with poly U in the presence of aminoglycoside antibiotics**
A subcellular protein-synthesizing system prepared from *E. coli* was incubated with poly U and a mixture of 20 amino acids; one amino acid was ^{14}C-labeled. Incubation was with or without aminoglycoside (4 μg/ml). Values represent the incorporation of the amino acid as per cent poly U-directed incorporation of phenylalanine in the absence of drug: Sm, streptomycin; Nm, neomycin; Gm, gentamicin. (Data from Davies *et al.*[19])

| Amino acid incorporated | No drug | Relative incorporation: | | |
		+Sm	+Nm	+Gm
Phenylalanine	100	60	40	55
Leucine	5	10	6	15
Isoleucine	8	30	37	55
Serine	4	20	48	100

gentamicin, however, the incorporation of isoleucine relative to phenylalanine increases several-fold.[19] This misreading effect of streptomycin has also been examined in a poly-U-directed protein-synthesizing system utilizing ribosomes with reconstituted 30S particles, and the presence of protein P_{10} from sensitive cells was found to be a prerequisite for extensive streptomycin-induced incorporation of "wrong" amino acids (isoleucine, serine, and tyrosine).[18]

The distortion of codon recognition in intact, growing bacteria should result in the frequent insertion of "wrong" amino acids and a consequent alteration in (or loss of) activity of proteins. If distortion led to false UGA, UAA, or UAG (termination codons) recognition, then premature chain termination would result. Formerly, it was thought that the bactericidal effect of streptomycin was due to the production of faulty protein in the bacterium exposed to the drug. Altered protein is certainly produced in the bacterium, but extensive misreading can be demonstrated in some mutant bacteria without the occurrence of cell death.[20] This and other evidence reviewed by Pestka[5] demonstrate that miscoding and cell killing are independent phenomena resulting from the same drug receptor interaction.

Phenotypic Suppression and Streptomycin Dependence

That streptomycin induces misreading of the genetic code can be demonstrated in the intact bacterium by the ability of the drug to reverse the effect of certain mutations. For example, an E. coli mutant was isolated that required an arginine-containing medium for growth. In the presence of sublethal concentrations of streptomycin, however, growth could proceed in the absence of arginine.[21] Thus, the drug was able to suppress the phenotypic expression of the mutation. It was found that when the mutant bacterium was grown without streptomycin, ornithine transcarbamylase activity was absent. This enzyme converts ornithine to citrulline, a reaction necessary for the synthesis of arginine by the bacterium. The mutant was shown to possess a defective structual gene that led to the production of an inactive enzyme, and thus no arginine could be produced. Exposure to streptomycin apparently introduced enough ambiguity into the reading process so that an amino acid acceptable for enzyme activity was occasionally inserted during translation. In this way, the mutation became phenotypically corrected by streptomycin at the level of translation. Enough active enzyme molecules were then produced so that cells in the presence of streptomycin grew in an arginine-free medium. These mutants are called "conditionally streptomycin dependent," which means that another compound, such as an amino acid, can be substituted for streptomycin to support growth. As one would predict, the aminoglycosides can phenotypically suppress mutations of the nonsense (termination) or missense (wrong amino acid) type, but they do not suppress the expression of frame shift mutations.[22]

There is another form of streptomycin dependence in which streptomycin is needed for growth, and only this drug, or perhaps one of the other aminoglycosides, can support growth. Genetic analysis in E. coli has demonstrated that sensitivity to streptomycin, single-step resistance to high concentrations of the drug, and streptomycin dependence are determined by multiple alleles at a single genetic locus, the Sm locus.[23] The Sm locus seems to be the locus for the P_{10} protein. These streptomycin-dependent mutants contain altered ribosomes that are too restricted to be functional in the absence of drug. When streptomycin is present, it binds to the altered 30S subunit, presumably restoring it to a more normal configuration.[24] These drug-bound ribosomes function well enough to permit sufficient protein synthesis for cell growth.[25] When the drug is removed, the rate of protein synthesis declines.[26]

The phenomenon of mutation to antibiotic dependence is of bacteriological and genetic interest, but it is not of importance in the clinical treatment of infection. Bacterial drug dependence has been found for chloramphenicol and other antibiotics as well, but the case of streptomycin is the most fully understood.

Differences between the Mechanisms of Action of Streptomycin and the Other Aminoglycosides

Like streptomycin, the other aminoglycosides also bind to the 30S subunit, inhibit protein synthesis, and cause misreading of the genetic code. The various drugs show differences in the pattern of misreading. This can be seen by comparing the relative incorporation of phenylalanine and serine in Table 3-4, for example. As the concentration of neomycin, kanamycin, or gentamicin is raised from 10^{-6} to $10^{-4}M$, there is a several-fold increase in the amount of misreading.[27] In contrast, misreading by streptomycin remains constant over the concentration range. This is consistent with the interpretation that neomycin, kanamycin, and gentamicin may interact with additional, weaker binding sites on the 30S ribosomal subunit.

One clear demonstration that there is a difference between the interaction of streptomycin with the 30S subunit and that of the other clinically useful aminoglycosides is derived from ribosomal mutants. Some single-step mutants to high level streptomycin resistance have an altered P_{10} protein but are not resistant to neomycin, kanamycin, paromomycin, or gentamicin.[28] It may very well be that in the complex configuration of the 30S subunit all the aminoglycosides occupy a primary binding site of which one component is the P_{10} protein. The other aminoglycosides may interact strongly with other portions of the complete binding site, permitting them to effectively distort the structure of the 30S subunit even in the presence of an altered P_{10} protein. Streptomycin may lack these additional strong interactions, and the alteration in the P_{10} protein thus obliterates streptomycin binding.

There are clear differences in the clinical spectra of action of the aminoglycosides. These differences may be determined in part by disparities in the ability of the ribosomes to bind the drug and by different degrees of distortion of the ribosome structure. The primary determinants of the sensitivity patterns, however, are probably differences in drug penetration into bacteria and differences in the capacities of bacteria to chemically alter the drugs.

COMBINED THERAPY WITH AMINOGLYCOSIDES AND OTHER ANTIBIOTICS

When an organism is exposed simultaneously to two antibiotics to which it is sensitive, the response to the combination will fall into one of three patterns—indifference, antagonism, or synergism.[29]

(1) The indifferent (or additive) response is diagrammed in Figure 3-5 (left). The response to the drug combination is more effective than the response to either antibiotic alone and represents, roughly, a summation of the two drug effects. This is probably the most frequent outcome when two drugs are combined in therapy. Often the added benefit of the second drug is not clinically significant. (2) The combination may produce less of a response than one of the drugs alone. This is drug antagonism. Such antagonism may, for example, occur when streptomycin and chloramphenicol are combined.[30] Treatment with a bactericidal

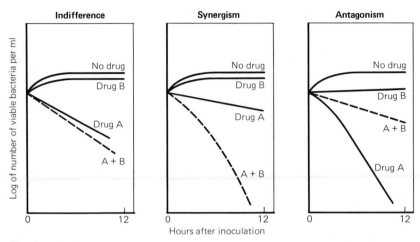

Figure 3-5 Patterns of response to therapy with two antibiotics. The response of bacteria suspended in growth medium to exposure to drug A or B alone is represented by the solid lines. The dashed lines represent the responses to simultaneous administration of the two drugs. (From Jawetz.[29])

drug (streptomycin) in combination with a bacteriostatic drug (chloramphenicol) sometimes leads to a response that is less than that of the bactericidal drug alone.[29] A common explanation of this observation is that many bactericidal agents will have a killing effect only on cells that are growing and actively synthesizing protein and that bacteriostatic drugs prevent such growth and thereby counter the effect of a bactericidal drug. This explanation is simplistic. It fits certain situations perhaps, but it does not fit others. In the above example, it may be that chloramphenicol, by retarding the breakdown of polysomes,[31] tends to slow the entry of 30S subunits into the free pool where they can be occupied by streptomycin and produce a complete blockade of protein synthesis.

Antagonism is obviously not a clinically desirable response, but it does occur. The following is a clinical example of drug antagonism. The mortality of patients with acute bacterial meningitis (due to *Haemophilus influenzae, Diplococcus pneumoniae,* or *Neisseria meningitidis*) treated with ampicillin alone was compared to the mortality of a comparable group on a regimen of ampicillin and chloramphenicol (supplemented with 2 days of streptomycin therapy).[32] The mortality with the single drug was

3.9 per cent; the mortality with the combined antibiotic treatment was 11.7 per cent. There is no easy way to determine whether a particular antibiotic combination will result in therapeutic antagonism. From a theoretical point of view, it is reasonable to avoid combinations of bactericidal and bacteriostatic agents when one is seeking additional antibacterial action by adding a second antibiotic to the therapeutic regimen. (3) A combination of antibiotics may have greater effect than the sum of the two individual drug effects. This is called a synergistic response, and it is seen in specific cases with mixtures of two bactericidal drugs. The combination of gentamicin and carbenicillin is synergistic *in vitro* for some strains of *Pseudomonas*.[33] Such a synergistic response is also seen in the clinical treatment of severe *Pseudomonas* infection.[34] The combination of a penicillin and an aminoglycoside is synergistic in many strains of enterococci[35] and in *Strep. viridans.*[29]

It has been shown that all the antibiotics that inhibit bacterial cell wall synthesis (cycloserine, bacitracin, vancomycin, and the β-lactam antibiotics) are synergistic with streptomycin against sensitive strains of enterococci in culture.[36] A mechanism for the synergism is suggested by the experiment presented in Figure 3-6.[37] When suspensions of enterococci are incubated with radioactive streptomycin, very little antibiotic becomes associated with the bacteria. But when the growing bacteria are exposed to penicillin as well as to radioactive streptomycin, increasing amounts of radioactivity are recovered with the organism. This suggests that the bacterial cell wall may function as a barrier to the entry of the aminoglycoside. In the presence of the penicillin, this barrier is disrupted and higher intracellular levels of the aminoglycoside are attained. Thus, the role of the penicillin in the synergistic pair is to permit the streptomycin to have a greater effect. This would seem to be a rational explanation for the synergism between penicillins and aminoglycosides observed in other organisms as well (e.g., carbenicillin and gentamicin against *Pseudomonas*). One would predict from this mechanism that, if an organism is highly resistant to gentamicin alone, there would be no synergy when it was treated with a combination of a penicillin and an aminoglycoside. This is the case. It has been shown with the combination of penicillin and streptomycin in enterococci[36] with high-level streptomycin resistance and with the combination of carbenicillin and gentamicin in highly gentamicin-resistant *P. aeruginosa.*[38]

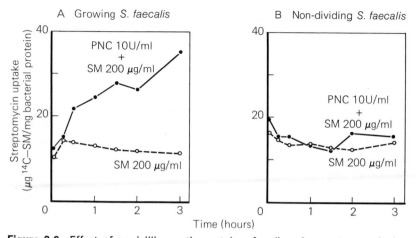

Figure 3-6 Effect of penicillin on the uptake of radioactive streptomycin by *Streptococcus faecalis*—a possible mechanism for synergism. Carbon fourteen-labeled streptomycin ([^{14}C]-SM) was added to suspensions of *S. faecalis* in the presence or absence of 10 units/ml of penicillin (PNC). At various times, aliquots of the bacterial suspensions were filtered and the amount of radioactivity remaining on the filter with the bacteria was assayed. Graph A shows the effect of penicillin on streptomycin uptake in growing cultures and Graph B the effect in suspensions of nondividing bacteria. One explanation of the data is that penicillin, in inhibiting cell wall synthesis in the growing bacterium, lowers the permeability barrier to streptomycin entry. Since higher intracellular streptomycin levels are obtained in the presence of penicillin, the combination of the two drugs is synergistic. (From Moellering and Weinberg.[37])

PHARMACOLOGY OF THE AMINOGLYCOSIDE ANTIBIOTICS

Since gentamicin is currently the most important of the aminoglycosides with respect to the treatment of the more common gram-negative infections, we will focus on that drug in this discussion. The reader is referred to the first and second international symposia on gentamicin for an extensive presentation of the subject.[39,40]

Absorption
All of the aminoglycosides are very poorly absorbed from the gastrointestinal tract, so they are routinely administered parenterally. They are absorbed well from intramuscular injection sites, and peak blood levels are achieved in about 1 hour. The fact that aminoglycosides are not absorbed from the gut is exploited when neomycin or kanamycin is given orally to kill the bowel

flora before intestinal surgery. Although kanamycin has a marked effect on the gastrointestinal flora after oral administration, there is little effect after parenteral administration. The aminoglycosides in general are excreted primarily in their unchanged form by the kidney, and very little of the parenterally administered drug reaches the intestine. After systemic administration, somewhat more gentamicin than kanamycin may be excreted into the bile. Nevertheless, if the cystic duct is not obstructed, the bile concentration will be less than half that of the serum.[41] When the bile gentamicin is diluted by the intestinal contents, the concentration of drug is apparently inadequate to seriously depress the bowel flora. Neomycin and gentamicin are sometimes applied topically, and absorption through the intact skin is minimal. Gentamicin, however, is applied topically to patients with extensive burn injury, and enough absorption can take place through large areas of burn-damaged skin to produce systemic toxicity.

There is a special precaution that should be taken with regard to the stability of gentamicin. If gentamicin is mixed in the same intravenous solution with carbenicillin, the gentamicin will slowly lose its antibacterial activity.[42] When gentamicin is being given intravenously, it should be infused over a period of 1 to 2 hours to prevent the possibility of neuromuscular blockade.

Distribution

Although the passage of aminoglycosides into several body fluid spaces is restricted, high enough concentrations are achieved in some fluids in the presence of adequate serum levels to permit therapy. The concentration of gentamicin in pleural and pericardial fluid, for example, ranges from one-fourth to one-half the serum concentration.[43] Gentamicin does pass across the placenta, and the concentration of gentamicin in human fetal serum has been found to range from 20 to 40 per cent of the maternal serum concentration.[44] This is important, since gentamicin is used to treat gram-negative infections during gestation, and hearing loss (an important aminoglycoside toxicity) has been reported in children born of mothers treated with other aminoglycosides (e.g., streptomycin) during pregnancy.[45]

The passage of aminoglycosides into the cerebrospinal fluid is negligible in the absence of meningeal inflammation.[46] Even in the presence of meningitis the levels of drug attained in the cerebrospinal fluid are low and erratic.[47] This is important in choosing an appropriate antibiotic and its method of administration for the treatment of gram-negative bacillary meningitis. The relative abilities of several antibiotics useful in the treatment of gram-negative infections to diffuse from the blood into the spinal fluid is presented in Table 3-5. When an aminoglycoside is used in the treatment of meningitis, it must be given intrathecally to consistently achieve therapeutic spinal fluid concentrations. The half-life of gentamicin in the cerebrospinal fluid is about 5.5 hours when the drug is administered intrathecally with concomitant intramuscular therapy.[48] To maintain therapeutic concentrations of the drug in the cerebrospinal fluid, 4-mg injections are given intrathecally every 18 hours along with appropriate intramuscular administration for maintenance of adequate serum levels (3 to 5 mg/kg daily when renal function is normal).

There is a great deal of individual variability in the serum concentrations achieved with a given gentamicin dosage, even in patients with normal renal function.[43] Several factors may contribute to this variability. Gentamicin apparently distributes into a volume approximating the extracellular fluid space. The percentage of body weight represented by the extracellular fluid space varies considerably with age and body habitus. Thus, since dosage is calculated according to body weight, considerable variation could result on this basis. Another interesting variable that can affect the peak serum concentration is the presence or absence of

Table 3-5 **Relative diffusion of gram-negative antimicrobial agents from blood into cerebrospinal fluid**
Because high-level resistance of gram-negative bacilli to sulfonamides and tetracyclines is common, these drugs are not used in the initial treatment of meningitis, before the sensitivity of the infecting organism has been determined. In general, the cephalosporins (Cephalothin; Cephaloridine) penetrate into the cerebrospinal fluid with meningeal inflammation better than the aminoglycosides but not as well as the penicillins. Results in treating meningitis with the cephalosporins have been poor (see Chapter 2); they should not be used in treating infection of the central nervous system. (From Rahal.[47])

Excellent with or without inflammation	Good only with inflammation	Minimal or not good with inflammation	No passage with inflammation
Sulfonamides Chloramphenicol	Ampicillin Carbenicillin Cephalothin Cephaloridine	Tetracycline Streptomycin Kanamycin Gentamicin Tobramycin	Polymyxin B Colistin

fever. Experiments with volunteers subjected to drug-induced (etiocholanolone) fever suggest that the average serum concentration of gentamicin may be reduced by as much as 40 per cent compared with control individuals who were injected with the pyrogen but did not develop fever.[49] Measurements of the serum half-life and determination of the renal clearance of the antibiotic suggest that these parameters were not affected by the presence of fever, and the mechanism of the effect remains unknown. It is not yet possible to fully evaluate the clinical significance of the temperature effect, but it constitutes an interesting example of the subtle ways in which host factors can affect the serum concentration of an antibiotic.

Excretion

The aminoglycosides are not metabolized to any significant extent and are excreted in their active forms almost entirely by glomerular filtration. If renal function is impaired, the blood levels of these drugs, which are all toxic to eighth nerve function, will rise rapidly with a consequent increased risk of toxic effects. In order to prevent a toxic reaction, it is important to adjust the dose of these drugs when renal function declines.

Aminoglycoside concentrations that are much higher than peak blood levels can occur in the urine. Urinary tract infections are treated with a lower maintenance dose (1.5 mg/kg/daily in the patient with normal renal function) than are infections elsewhere in the body.[43] Since these drugs have a greater antibacterial effect in an alkaline environment, bicarbonate should be given when aminoglycosides are used to treat urinary tract infections. The effectiveness of gentamicin against S. *aureus*, for example, is 17 times greater *in vitro* at pH 8 than at pH 6.[50]

Modification of Gentamicin Dosage with Renal Failure

Impaired renal function affects the serum levels of several antibiotics, including the aminoglycosides, the polymyxins, vancomycin, the penicillins, the cephalosporins, and the tetracyclines.[51] Gentamicin will be used as an example of how the dosage of an antibiotic may be modified in the presence of reduced renal function. To determine the effective dosage, the physician must appropriately assess the extent to which the patient's ability to excrete the drug is compromised. Since gentamicin and creatinine are both excreted predominantly by glomerular filtration (without tubular resorption), the creatinine clearance rate will give an approximation of the gentamicin clearance rate. Of course, this would not be true if significant amounts of gentamicin were inactivated metabolically or excreted by organs other than the kidney.

The dosage of gentamicin required to maintain an effective antibacterial serum level depends upon the rate of drug excretion. This relationship is presented in Figure 3-7. To construct this nomogram, the rate of gentamicin excretion and the creatinine clearance were determined in several patients with various degrees of depressed renal function.[52] From the nomogram one can determine the maintenance dose of gentamicin required to obtain a safe antibacterial serum concentration of drug. Above a creatinine clearance of 70 ml/minute, the rate of gentamicin excretion is reasonably constant.[52] To use the nomogram, a loading

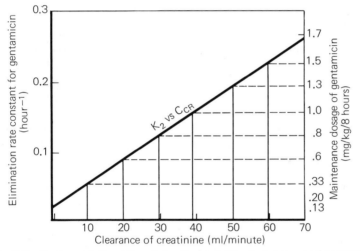

Figure 3-7 Nomogram for determining the maintenance dosage of gentamicin to be given to patients with various degrees of renal failure. The elimination rate constant (K_2) for gentamicin was calculated from the values for the plasma half-life of the drug in 20 patients with differing degrees of renal failure. The elimination rate constant (left ordinate) when plotted against the creatinine clearance (C_{CR}) values determined in the same patients yields a straight line up to a creatinine clearance of 70 ml/minute. On the right ordinate is plotted the maintenance dosage of gentamicin (in milligrams per kilogram) that must be administered every 8 hours to sustain a safe antibacterial serum concentration between 3 and 8 µg/ml. The solid and dashed lines in the grid provide easier reading of the maintenance dosage at each ten units of creatinine clearance. (From Chan *et al.*[52])

dose of 1.7 mg/kg body weight is administered initially. Even if the patient has severely compromised renal function and requires a very low maintenance dose of antibiotic, a loading dose must be administered in order to achieve adequate initial serum levels after the drug has equilibrated in the body to its distribution volume (roughly 24 per cent of the body weight for gentamicin[53]). By drawing a line from the patient's creatinine clearance value to the sloping line, one can read off the dose of gentamicin that must be administered every 8 hours to maintain the serum concentration in an appropriate range for therapy.

Another approach to therapy is to alter the dosage interval rather than the amount of drug administered. There is a simple (although very rough) relationship between the serum creatinine concentration and the gentamicin half-life. It has been shown that, for clinical purposes, the serum half-life of gentamicin can be estimated by multiplying the value of the serum creatinine (mg/100 ml) by four and substituting hours as the unit of measure.[54] For example, a patient with a serum creatinine of 3 has an approximate gentamicin half-life of 12 hours. In one method of calculating the dosage for a patient with compromised renal function, a 2 mg/kg dose of gentamicin is given initially, followed by the same dose every third half-life (in this example, every 36 hours).[53] A similar method of determining kanamycin dosage from serum creatinine levels has also been worked out from experimental data.[55] Another way of rapidly estimating a maintenance regimen for gentamicin is to give 1.1 mg/kg at a dosage interval of eight times the serum creatinine (in hours). Thus, a patient with a serum creatinine of 3 would receive 1.1 mg/kg every 24 hours.

Although these methods are useful for calculating a drug dosage and dosage interval based on some assessment of the degree of renal dysfunction, estimates of the rate of gentamicin excretion based on serum creatinine values are nevertheless very imprecise, and the most accurate guide to therapy is to routinely assay serum gentamicin levels and adjust the dosage accordingly.[56] Enzymatic[57] or bacteriological[58] assays are regularly available in many hospitals. A radioimmunoassay will soon become commercially available. The enzymatic assay, based on the transfer of [^{14}C]adenylate to gentamicin is more accurate and rapid than the bacteriological assays.[59,60] The bacteriological assays are agar-diffusion methods based on comparing zones of bacterial growth inhibition, in the presence of the patient's serum, to the effect of graded concentrations of gentamicin.

Patients who are undergoing intermittent hemodialysis must have their antibiotic doses adjusted according to the rate at which the drug is dialyzed. For this purpose it is necessary to know the serum half-life of the drug during the dialysis. The half-life of gentamicin during hemodialysis is about 6 hours.[61] Creatinine is cleared more rapidly by the artificial kidney, so measurements of creatinine dialysance do not provide an appropriate guideline for therapy.

The reader is referred to the literature for precise recommendations on modifying the dosage of the other antibiotics that are markedly affected by compromised renal function.[51,62,63]

THERAPEUTIC APPLICATIONS

Gentamicin

Gentamicin has a broad antibacterial spectrum against gram-negative bacteria. It is very effective against *Escherichia coli, Proteus mirabilis,* indole-positive *Proteus, Klebsiella, Enterobacter, Serratia,* and *Pseudomonas aeruginosa* (cf. Table 2-4). *Salmonella* and *Shigella* are often gentamicin-sensitive. Because gentamicin is effective against a broad range of gram-negative bacteria, it is employed in most antibiotic regimens for treating undefined sepsis. Gentamicin is active against most strains of *S. aureus.* It is generally more potent than kanamycin and it is less ototoxic.

Table 3-6 presents a list of some common gram-negative bacilli and antibiotics that are useful in treating mild or severe infections with these organisms. In all cases of gram-negative infection, the antibiotic sensitivity of the organism must be determined. This table is only a guide for initial drug administration— it does not replace careful culturing and sensitivity testing. It must also be remembered that the antibiotic sensitivity of an organism may vary considerably from place to place, and this, as well as the anatomical location and severity of the infection, will affect the choice of antibiotic.

As mentioned in Chapter 2, mild infections due to *P. aeruginosa* can often be treated with carbenicillin alone. In deep-seated and severe infections, however, both carbenicillin and gentamicin

Table 3-6 **Examples of appropriate antibiotics for the treatment of infections due to some common gram-negative bacilli**

Infecting organism	Mild infection	Severe infection
Haemophilus influenzae	Ampicillin	Ampicillin* (plus chloramphenicol initially)
Escherichia coli	Ampicillin	Ampicillin†
Klebsiella	Cephalexin	Gentamicin
Enterobacter	Gentamicin	Gentamicin
Proteus mirabilis	Ampicillin	Ampicillin
Indole-positive *Proteus*	Gentamicin	Gentamicin
Pseudomonas aeruginosa	Carbenicillin	Carbenicillin (plus gentamicin)

*An increasing number of ampicillin-resistant *H. influenzae* strains are being isolated from cases of meningitis.[64] In children over two months old, treatment of *Haemophilus* meningitis or epiglottitis should include chloramphenicol until the organism's sensitivity is known.[65]

†*Escherichia coli* strains in the hospital environment are often resistant to ampicillin, and gentamicin is often employed to treat severe infections acquired in hospital.

should be used. This combination is employed for two reasons: (1) The combination is synergistic in many strains of *Pseudomonas*.[34,66] (2) When carbenicillin is used alone, resistant organisms can emerge rapidly.[67] The use of the two drugs decreases the probability of resistance emerging during therapy. Gentamicin has been employed topically in the treatment of patients with burns. In addition to the risk of toxicity due to absorption from the denuded skin of the burn area, such treatment selects for gentamicin-resistant gram-negative pathogens such as *Pseudomonas*. This may compromise the effectiveness of the drug in treating infections acquired by other patients in the hospital environment.

Tobramycin

This is a new aminoglycoside with a spectrum of action similar to that of gentamicin.[68,69] It is significantly more active *in vitro* against *Pseudomonas* than is gentamicin.[68,70] Some strains of *P. aeruginosa* that are resistant to gentamicin retain sensitivity to tobramycin.[71] The pharmacology of tobramycin is similar to that of gentamicin.[72] Studies in animals suggest that tobramycin may be slightly less ototoxic than gentamicin, but there is, as yet, no reason to suspect that this is true for humans.[73] The role of tobramycin in therapy is now being defined. It is particularly useful in the treatment of infections due to *P. aeruginosa*.

Kanamycin

Kanamycin has a broad antibacterial activity among the gram-negative bacilli. It is not effective against *Pseudomonas*. Kanamycin is less active on a molar basis than either gentamicin or tobramycin,[69] and it is more toxic. Gentamicin is now utilized in many cases for which kanamycin was formerly the drug of choice.

Amikacin

Amikacin is a new semisynthetic derivative of kanamycin. It is effective against many gram-negative strains that have become resistant to other aminoglycosides. The pharmacology of amikacin is the same as that of kanamycin. In order to preserve the effectiveness of amikacin, it is appropriate to restrict its usage to the treatment of serious infections caused by susceptible gram-negative strains that are resistant to kanamycin, gentamicin, and tobramycin.

Neomycin

This drug is not administered parenterally. Like kanamycin, it is sometimes given orally to reduce the intestinal flora. The primary use of this antibiotic is topical. Neomycin is available in topical preparations both alone and in combination with such antibiotics as polymyxin B and bacitracin. Some preparations also contain a glucocorticoid. The corticosteroid-antibiotic combinations are discussed in the section on bacitracin in Chapter 2.

The topical neomycin-containing preparations (of which there are at least 100 different forms) are overused, and their efficacy in most cases is doubtful.[74] Ototoxicity can occur by absorption of neomycin from wounds that are being irrigated with the antibiotic.[75] Although the more common use of the antibiotic in local application to superficial skin infections is not associated with toxicity, sensitization to neomycin frequently occurs.[76] Especially after long-term therapy, neomycin can produce contact dermatitis, which is, in many cases, clinically similar to the condition being treated.[77] When there is such a conversion from a complex of signs and symptoms of infectious origin to an allergic contact dermatitis, the patient benefits from withdrawal of therapy rather than continuation. It stands to reason that systemic administra-

tion of the other aminoglycoside antibiotics in the person who has
been so sensitized may result in a hypersensitivity reaction.

Streptomycin

The role of streptomycin in therapy has declined considerably
since the advent of the newer aminoglycosides, the broad-spectrum penicillins and the cephalosporins. It is still employed in
combination with a penicillin to treat bacterial endocarditis due
to S. viridans and enterococcus. Many physicians now employ
gentamicin and ampicillin or penicillin G for this latter indication
however. Streptomycin is still used in the treatment of tuberculosis (see discussion of tuberculosis therapy in Chapter 8). Streptomycin, either alone or in combination with another antibiotic, is
still useful in the treatment of several rather uncommon infections
including plague (Yersinia pestis), tularemia (Francisella tular-
ensis), glanders (Actinobacillus mallei), and severe cases of bru-
cellosis (Brucella abortus) (see Table 2-4).

Treatment of Sepsis of Unknown Etiology

There is a special case in which the use of an antibiotic for a
"shotgun" effect is required. When a patient presents with a
septicemia of unknown etiology, treatment must begin immediately after the cultures are obtained, and the antibiotics used must
have a broad enough spectrum to cover the potential pathogens. A
combination of antibiotics is used to ensure an adequate antibacterial spectrum of activity until the results of culturing and sensitivity testing are known. Gram-negative bacilli have been
accounting for an increasing proportion of bacteremias and of
deaths from these infections.[78] Because of its broad antibacterial
action against the gram-negative bacilli and its efficacy against
such gram-positive organisms as S. aureus, gentamicin is usually
employed as one member of a drug pair in the treatment of
undiagnosed bacteremia. The other is often cephalothin.

Other combinations may be appropriate in specific clinical
situations. If Pseudomonas is suspected, as in a patient with a
well-characterized wound infection with P. aeruginosa who
becomes septic, the combination of carbenicillin and gentamicin
(or tobramycin) is appropriate. In the patient who becomes septic
after abortion or gastrointestinal surgery or in the patient with
abdominal or pelvic abscess, there is good reason to administer

clindamycin or chloramphenicol in addition to gentamicin. This is done because clindamycin and chloramphenicol are effective against anaerobes, in particular *Bacteroides fragilis*, which can enter the bloodstream from these sources. If the patient has had genitourinary instrumentation, there may be an increased probability of enterococcus, and a combination of ampicillin and gentamicin might be employed.

Patients who are neutropenic are unable to respond to infections effectively. In such patients, infections can spread rapidly, and they must be treated promptly. The classical clinical signs of infection may be reduced due to the absence of vigorous inflammatory response. Thus, in patients with leukemia, or with other neoplasms and neutropenia, antimicrobial therapy may have to be initiated when the patient becomes febrile and before the results of culturing are known. Gram-negative organisms are a major cause of morbidity in this group, and the combination of carbenicillin and cephalothin can be used (on the basis of empirical success) to initiate therapy.[79,80] This combination is easier to employ in the patient with renal failure as well. The margin of allowable error is greater and the calculation of a safe dosage is easier than with combinations containing gentamicin.

Antibiotic Preparation of the Bowel for Colonic Surgery

There is a special case of the prophylactic use of antibiotics in bowel surgery. Before elective colon surgery, many surgeons give oral antibiotics to "sterilize the bowel" with the intention of reducing the risk of postoperative complication due to infection with gram-negative enteric organisms. The goal of this bowel preparation is to eliminate bacteria from the intestine without achieving high blood levels of antibiotic or irritating the bowel mucosa. The antibiotic regimen is combined with a low residue diet and cleansing enemas for 2 to 3 days before surgery.

One of the potential dangers of this treatment is that it can disturb the balance of the normal bacterial flora, resulting in an overgrowth of pathogenic organisms. Because an increased incidence of postoperative diarrhea and staphylococcal and yeast infection has been reported, there is some controversy over the value of preoperative antibiotic preparation of the bowel. Some surgeons feel that there may be less wound complication and diarrhea in patients who do not receive antibiotics before open colon resection.[81] Thieme and Fink[82] studied the use of neomycin or a poorly absorbed sulfa, or a combination of the two, for bowel preparation before colonic surgery. They found that the change in flora did not result in staphylococcal overgrowth leading to staphylococcal enterocolitis or staphylococcal wound infection. There is at present no clear resolution to the controversy. Since the colon is the largest reservoir of bacteria in the body, and the risk of infection after elective operations on the colon can be high, it seems clear that bowel antisepsis will continue to be a widely used procedure for some time. There is a group of surgeons, however, who place their reliance on careful surgical technique and thorough mechanical cleansing of the bowel.

Many drug combinations have been used for preoperative bowel preparation. These have included a non-absorbable sulfa, neomycin, or kanamycin. Now a single aminoglycoside is generally used; kanamycin may be preferable to neomycin. It should be cautioned that resistance to kanamycin is increasing in bowel flora. If a patient who has received kanamycin preoperatively does develop an infection as a result of spillage of the bowel contents, the infection is likely to be more difficult to treat than if he had not received antibiotics. Because selection of multiple drug resistance determinants can occur there is not only an increased chance that the organism will be resistant to some or all of the aminoglycosides but to other classes of antibiotics as well. Preoperative treatment with both kanamycin and metronidazole (an antibiotic that is effective against anaerobic organisms—see Chapter 11) has been reported to significantly suppress both aerobic and anaerobic bacteria.[83] In a study involving 50 patients undergoing elective colonic surgery, 11 out of 25 control patients had postoperative wound infections but only two of 25 in the antibiotic pretreatment group developed infections. The results of this study are encouraging, but the size of the patient population is limited and the advantages of preoperative antibiotics have not yet been proven. A discussion of the possible advantages and complications of intestinal antisepsis has been presented by Cohn.[84]

TOXICITY OF THE AMINOGLYCOSIDES

The aminoglycosides have a toxic action on the kidney and the inner ear and they can produce a neuromuscular blockade. It is possible that all these toxicities may be the result of the same general biochemical effect.

Neurotoxicity

At very high concentrations, the aminoglycosides can produce a non-depolarizing type of neuromuscular blockade. This was first observed when neomycin was found to produce respiratory arrest after intraperitoneal administration. Neuromuscular blockade can occur after intravenous or intramuscular administration of aminoglycosides in patients who are receiving ether anesthesia or a neuromuscular blocking agent during anesthesia.[85] Patients with myasthenia gravis are predisposed to neuromuscular blockade and constitute a high risk group.[86]

The aminoglycosides dramatically reduce the amount of acetylcholine released from motor nerve terminals.[87] There is also a weak antagonism to the stimulating action of acetylcholine on striated muscle, but the effect on transmitter release seems to be the major cause of neuromuscular blockade. The effect is therefore predominantly prejunctional and not postjunctional, like that of curare. The paralysis produced by aminoglycosides is completely reversed by calcium.[86] Since calcium is required for the release of acetylcholine from the prejunctional membrane, it is postulated that the aminoglycosides (which are polycations) bind to the required calcium-binding sites on the presynaptic membrane to produce paralysis. Consistent with this hypothesis, neomycin has been shown to prevent the reuptake of calcium or its rebinding to superficial sites on the cell membrane in vascular smooth muscle preparations.[88] The neuromuscular reaction is potentially fatal, since respiratory paralysis may occur. The condition is treated by administering calcium gluconate and an anticholinesterase drug like neostigmine.

Ototoxicity

The aminoglycosides are ototoxic. Both the hearing and balance functions of the inner ear can be affected. Some of the aminoglycosides (e.g., streptomycin and gentamicin) mainly affect vestibular function, whereas others (e.g., kanamycin) mainly affect hearing. At a high enough concentration, both balance and hearing will be affected by all these antibiotics. If loss of hearing or balance is not extensive, termination of the drug therapy will usually result in complete return to normal function. After extensive damage, however, a permanent decrease in hearing acuity or even complete deafness can occur.

Patients being treated with aminoglycosides must have their vestibular and auditory function tested frequently. It is not enough to casually test for loss of hearing acuity by observing if the patient responds to questions asked in a low tone of voice. The first hearing loss that takes place is in the high-tone range, and there can be considerable loss of function before there is any noticeable change in the range of normal conversational speech. A patient thus can suffer significant loss of ability to appreciate music, for example, if the drug is stopped only when the hearing decrement is readily apparent by voice testing. For this reason, patients receiving aminoglycosides should have their hearing acuity tested frequently by audiometry. One can use quantitative caloric stimulation to monitor for labyrinthine toxicity in the bedridden patient. If a patient is too young to understand or is unable to respond appropriately, audiometry cannot be employed, and one must rely on cruder testing methods.

Ototoxicity is the most frequent toxic effect that limits therapy with the aminoglycosides. Great caution must thus be taken to ensure appropriate reduction of the drug dosage in patients with compromised renal function. If possible, the aminoglycosides should not be used with other drugs that are ototoxic. Ethacrynic acid, a diuretic, is ototoxic. Severe, permanent hearing loss following intravenous ethacrynic acid administration has been reported in patients receiving aminoglycosides.[89] The effect is rapid and the mechanism of the interaction is unknown.[90]

The aminoglycosides are concentrated many-fold in the inner ear fluids,[91] and it seems clear that their primary effect is on the peripheral sensory portions of the inner ear, not on the eighth nerve itself.[92,93] The biochemistry of this aminoglycoside toxicity is now being studied in the minute tissues of the inner ear. When the guinea pig cochlea is perfused with artificial perilymph containing a high concentration of neomycin, there is a rapid reduction in its ability to generate an acoustic current (ac) potential in response to a sound stimulus.[94] The generation of the ac potential is used to measure the physiological state of the cochlea, which acts to transduce sound waves transmitted in the perilymph into electrical events that are relayed to the acoustical center in the brain. If radioactive phosphate is added to an artificial perilymph perfusing the cochlea, it becomes incorporated into membrane phospholipids. It has been shown that neomycin decreases incorporation of the phosphate into phosphatidylinositol diphosphate, one of the phospholipid components of the membranes.[94,95] If

guinea pigs are subcutaneously injected with large doses of neomycin for 3 weeks, and the cochlea are then perfused for a short
time with radioactive phosphate, the effect of the systemically
administered drug can be studied in detail. The cochlea can be
rapidly fixed to prevent biochemical degradation, and the individual components of the cochlea removed by microdissection. It
has thus been shown that neomycin decreases incorporation of
phosphate into phosphatidylinositol diphosphate but not into
other phospholipids in both the organ of Corti and the stria
vascularis.[95] This location of the drug effect on phosphotidylino-
sitol metabolism agrees with the localization of early changes
viewed by histological means.[93] Neomycin and the other aminoglycosides have also been shown to competitively inhibit the
binding of radioactive calcium ion to homogenates of these tissues[95] and to phosphoinositides in artificial membranes.[96]

These data and additional observations concerning the effects
of neomycin on phospholipid metabolism can be integrated into a
model of aminoglycoside toxicity (see Figure 3-8).[97] In order to
understand the model it is important to realize that relationships
between calcium binding and polyphosphoinositide metabolism
have been established in other cell membrane systems.[98] It has

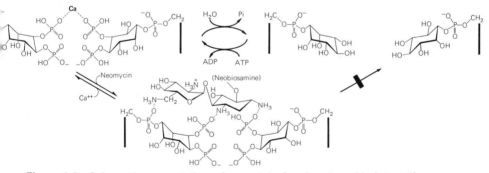

Figure 3-8 Schematic presentation of a model of aminoglycoside interaction
with membrane phosphoinositide metabolism. The glycerol backbone and fatty
acid side chains of the phospholipid are indicated by the heavy bars. In the
model, the phosphate groups on the inositol part of the phospholipid bind
calcium and the hydrolysis of monoester phosphate groups liberates calcium
and alters membrane permeability (upper right).[99] Rephosphorylation by ATP
returns the phosphatidylinositol to its calcium binding form. The aminoglycoside (neomycin) occupies the calcium binding site, altering the membrane
permeability and preventing the phosphorylation-dephosphorylation cycle. See
the text for details. (From Schacht.[97])

been postulated that, when the polyphosphoinositides are acted upon by a phosphomonoesterase, their phosphate groups are cleaved, liberating calcium and changing membrane permeability to cations. Subsequent phosphorylation of the same groups may restore the membrane to its original state.[99] In the model, the aminoglycosides, which are strongly cationic molecules and do not readily pass through membranes (for example, they are not absorbed from the gastrointestinal tract and do not pass into the cerebrospinal fluid), occupy calcium binding sites provided by negatively charged phosphate groups of the polyphosphoinositides in the membrane. A possible binding arrangement for neomycin is presented in Figure 3-8. The neomycin-bound phosphoinositide is a poor substrate for the dephosphorylating enzyme, and its role in the membrane physiology is consequently impaired. For the incorporation of radioactive phosphate into phosphoinositol diphosphate to be inhibited by neomycin, the phosphomonoesterase must be the rate limiting step in the cycle of phosphorylation-dephosphorylation events. This aspect of the model is also consistent with the available biochemical evidence.[95]

This model cannot be used to explain the irreversible damage that can result from aminoglycoside toxicity. Of course, one can propose that multiple sites of drug binding might impose conformational changes on the membrane and disrupt both its structure and function. Physical studies of neomycin effects on synaptosome (nerve ending) membranes and synthetic lipid monolayers have shown that inhibition of calcium binding and membrane conformational changes are reversibile at low drug concentrations, but at higher concentrations, a second type of interaction becomes evident.[96] Unlike the low dose effects, these changes with high doses are noncompetitive and not readily reversible. It is tempting to speculate that the effects of this interaction at high drug concentration precipitate the gross membrane changes observed with the scanning electron microscope.[92] For the model to be useful, the biochemical observations upon which it is based must pertain only to ototoxic antibiotics. This is the case with respect to the antibiotics that have been studied so far.[97] There are several reasons for presenting the model here despite its early stage of development. It provides a testable framework within which to examine the ototoxicity of these drugs, and it may provide a rationale for considering the three major toxicities of the aminoglycosides as different expressions of the same membrane event in the ear, in the kidney, and at the neuromuscular junction.

That the data supporting this model have been obtained from biochemical studies of the changes produced by drugs in minute regions of the cochlea is very impressive. The experiments themselves represent an extraordinary technical accomplishment. Further studies of the effects of aminoglycosides on synthetic phosphoinositide-containing membranes are now under way. These studies may permit the definition of the structural requirements for the toxic effect and open the way to the design of aminoglycoside compounds with even less toxicity.

Nephrotoxicity

The aminoglycosides can produce a nephrotoxicity that is usually reversible upon cessation of therapy. Kanamycin and neomycin are more nephrotoxic than streptomycin and, although gentamicin is one of the least nephrotoxic of the group, renal insufficiency can occur with it as well and patients should have routine BUN and serum creatinine assays performed during therapy.[100] The physician must always think of potential additive toxicities when prescribing combination therapy. As mentioned earlier in this chapter, the combination of gentamicin and a cephalosporin is useful under certain clinical conditions. The cephalosporins are also nephrotoxic and there have been a few reports of acute tubular necrosis occurring during therapy with gentamicin and cephalothin.[101] Another example of a drug interaction at this level concerns the use of methoxyflurane, an anesthetic that can potentiate the nephrotoxicity of the aminoglycosides.[102]

The mechanism of aminoglycoside nephrotoxicity is not known in detail. These antibiotics accumulate in the renal parenchyma,[103] and neomycin has been shown to alter phosphoinositide metabolism in the kidney in much the same way as it does in the cochlea.[95] The pathological changes produced in animal models primarily involve the renal tubules.[104]

RESISTANCE TO THE AMINOGLYCOSIDES

It was demonstrated some time ago that resistance to an antibiotic could develop either gradually in small steps or that resistance to a high level of the same drug could develop suddenly.[105] The former process is called a multi-step resistance pattern, and it results from the selection of several mutations, often in a number of different genes. Each mutation confers a small amount of resistance, and a cumulative effect builds up in the bacterial culture. The second type of resistance development, called the large-step pattern, is the type of mutation that was discussed earlier in the chapter: a mutation at the Sm locus which resulted in an alteration of the 30S ribosomal subunit protein, P_{10}, making the mutant cells insensitive to streptomycin. In the large-step type of resistance, a mutation in a single gene leads to a very high degree of resistance or to drug insensitivity. This type of high-level ribosomal resistance to the aminoglycosides occurs in very few clinical isolates.

The most important type of aminoglycoside resistance under clinical conditions is due to drug inactivating enzymes.[106] In contrast to the ribosomal type of resistance, the inactivating enzymes are determined by extrachromosomal genes (plasmids) that can be transmitted by conjugation. The aminoglycosides are inactivated by acetylation of amino groups or phosphorylation or adenylation of hydroxyl groups. The aminoglycoside inactivating enzymes are not inducible. This contrasts with penicillinases, produced by R-factors, which are generally inducible (Chapter 2). There are various patterns of aminoglycoside resistance. Some of the inactivating enzymes can modify a few of the aminoglycosides but not others, and an enzyme may be able to chemically modify several aminoglycosides but not markedly affect their antibacterial activity. For example, acetylation of kanamycin A inactivates the drug, but a similarly modified gentamicin (N-acetylgentamicin C) retains substantial antibiotic activity.[107] This reinforces a clinical point. If an infection becomes resistant to therapy with one aminoglycoside, the physician may still be able to employ another. To determine whether this is possible, the antibiotic sensitivity of the microorganism must be monitored at appropriate intervals. These R-factor-mediated resistances spread readily and the overuse of antibiotics promotes that spread. For example, antibiotic resistance in *Pseudomonas* is promoted by large scale topical application of gentamicin in some burn units.[108]

REFERENCES

' 1. J. Lucas-Lenard and F. Lipmann: Protein biosynthesis. *Ann. Rev. Biochem.* 40:409 (1971).

2. R. Haselkorn and L. B. Rothman-Denes: Protein synthesis. *Ann. Rev. Biochem.* 42:397 (1973).

3. H. Weissbach and N. Brot: The role of protein factors in the biosynthesis of proteins. *Cell* 2:137 (1974).

4. B. D. Davis: Role of subunits in the ribosome cycle. *Nature* 231:153 (1971).

5. S. Pestka: Inhibitors of ribosome functions. *Ann. Rev. Microbiol.* 25:487 (1971).

6. B. Weisblum and J. Davies: Antibiotic inhibitors of the bacterial ribosome. *Bact. Rev.* 32:493 (1968).

7. D. T. Dubin, R. Hancock, and B. D. Davis: The sequence of some effects of streptomycin in *Escherichia coli*. *Biochim. Biophys. Acta* 74:476 (1963).

8. L. Luzzatto, D. Apirion, and D. Schlessinger: Polyribosome depletion and blockage of the ribosome cycle by streptomycin in *Escherichia coli*. *J. Mol. Biol.* 42:315 (1969).

9. B. J. Wallace, P. -C. Tai, E. L. Herzog, and B. D. Davis: Partial inhibition of polysomal ribosomes of *Escherichia coli* by streptomycin. *Proc. Natl. Acad. Sci. U.S.* 70:1234 (1973).

10. P. -C. Tai, B. J. Wallace, E. L. Herzog, and B. D. Davis: Properties of initiation-free polysomes of *Escherichia coli*. *Biochemistry* 12:609 (1973).

11. J. Modolell and B. D. Davis: Breakdown by streptomycin of initiation complexes formed on ribosomes of *Escherichia coli*. *Proc. Natl. Acad. Sci. U.S.* 67:1148 (1970).

12. B. J. Wallace and B. D. Davis: Cyclic blockade of initiation sites by streptomycin-damaged ribosomes in *Escherichia coli*: An explanation for dominance of sensitivity. *J. Mol. Biol.* 75:377 (1973).

13. J. Modolell and B. D. Davis: Mechanism of inhibition of ribosomes by streptomycin. *Nature* 224:345 (1969).

14. B. J. Wallace, P. -C. Tai, and B. D. Davis: Effect of streptomycin on the response of *Escherichia coli* ribosomes to the dissociation factor. *J. Mol. Biol.* 75:391 (1973).

15. J. Lederberg: Streptomycin resistance: A genetically recessive mutation. *J. Bacteriol.* 61:549 (1951).

16. J. E. Davies: Studies on the ribosomes of streptomycin-sensitive and resistant strains of *Escherichia coli*. *Proc. Natl. Acad. Sci. U.S.* 51:659 (1964).

17. P. Traub and M. Nomura: Structure and function of *Escherichia coli* ribosomes; VI. Mechanism of assembly of 30S ribosomes studied *in vitro*. *J. Mol. Biol.* 40:391 (1969).

18. M. Ozaki, S. Mizuchima, and M. Nomura: Identification and functional characterization of the protein controlled by the streptomycin-resistant locus in *E. coli*. *Nature* 222:333 (1969).

19. J. Davies, L. Gorini, and B. D. Davis: Misreading of RNA codewords induced by aminoglycoside antibiotics. *Mol. Pharmacol.* 1:93 (1965).

20. L. Gorini and E. Kataja: Streptomycin-induced oversuppression in *E. coli*. *Proc. Natl. Acad. Sci. U.S.* 51:995 (1964).

21. L. Gorini and E. Kataja: Phenotypic repair by streptomycin of defective genotypes in *E. coli*. *Proc. Natl. Acad. Sci. U.S.* 51:487 (1964).

22. H. J. Whitfield, R. G. Martin, and B. N. Ames: Classification of aminotransferase (C Gene) mutants in the histidine operon. *J. Mol. Biol.* 21:335 (1966).

23. K. Hashimoto: Streptomycin resistance in *Escherichia coli* analyzed by transduction. *Genetics* 45:49 (1960).

24. L. Gorini, R. Rosset, and R. A. Zimmermann: Phenotypic masking and streptomycin dependence. *Science* 157:1314 (1967).

25. C. R. Spotts and R. Y. Stanier: Mechanism of streptomycin action on bacteria; a unitary hypothesis. *Nature* 192:633 (1961).

26. C. R. Spotts: Physiological and biochemical studies on streptomycin dependence in *Escherichia coli*. *J. Gen. Microbiol.* 28:347 (1962).

27. J. Davies and B. D. Davis: Misreading of ribonucleic acid code words induced by aminoglycoside antibiotics: The effect of drug concentration. *J. Biol. Chem.* 243:3312 (1968).

28. J. Davies: Bacterial resistance to aminoglycoside antibiotics. *J. Infec. Dis.* 124 Suppl.:S7 (1971).

29. E. Jawetz: The use of combinations of antimicrobial drugs. *Ann. Rev. Pharmacol.* 8:151 (1968).

30. P. Plotz and B. D. Davis: Absence of a chloramphenicol-insensitive phase of streptomycin action. *J. Bacteriol.* 83:802 (1962).

31. M. H. Dresden and M. B. Hoagland: Polyribosomes of *Escherichia coli*: Breakdown during glucose starvation. *J. Biol. Chem.* 242:1065 (1967).

32. P. F. Wehrle, A. W. Mathies, J. M. Leedom, and D. Ivler: Bacterial meningitis. *Ann. N.Y. Acad. Sci.* 145:488 (1967).

33. M. Sonne and E. Jawetz: Combined action of carbenicillin and gentamicin on *Pseudomonas aeruginosa* in vitro. *Appl. Microbiol.* 17:893 (1969).

34. C. B. Smith, J. N. Wilfert, P. E. Dans, T. A. Kurrus, and M. Finland: In vitro activity of carbenicillin and results of treatment of infections due to *Pseudomonas* with carbenicillin singly and in combination with gentamicin. *J. Infec. Dis.* 122:S14 (1970).

35. E. Jawetz and M. Sonne: Penicillin-streptomycin treatment of enterococcal endocarditis: A re-evaluation. *New. Eng. J. Med.* 274:710 (1966).

36. R. C. Moellering, C. Wennersten, and A. N. Weinberg: Studies on antibiotic synergism against enterococci. I. Bacteriologic studies. *J. Lab. Clin. Med.* 77:821 (1971).

37. R. C. Moellering and A. N. Weinberg: Studies on antibiotic synergism against enterococci. II. Effect of various antibiotics on the uptake of ^{14}C-labeled streptomycin by enterococci. *J. Clin. Invest.* 50:2580 (1971).

38. R. M. Kluge, H. C. Standiford, B. Tatem, V. M. Young, S. C. Schimpff, W. H. Greene, F. M. Calia, and R. B. Hornick: The carbenicillin-gentamicin combination against *Pseudomonas aeruginosa*: Correlation of effect with gentamicin sensitivity. *Ann. Int. Med.* 81:584 (1974).

39. *International Symposium on Gentamicin: A New Aminoglycoside Antibiotic. J. Infect. Dis.* vol. 119, pp. 341–540 (1969).

40. *Second International Symposium on Gentamicin: An Aminoglycoside Antibiotic. J. Infect. Dis.* 124 Suppl.:S1–S300 (1971).

41. H. A. Pitt, R. A. Roberts, and W. D. Johnson: Gentamicin levels in the human biliary tract. *J. Infect. Dis.* 127:299 (1973).

42. P. Noone and J. R. Pattison: Therapeutic implications of interaction of gentamicin and penicillins. *Lancet* 2:575 (1971).

43. L. J. Riff and G. G. Jackson: Pharmacology of gentamicin in man. *J. Infect. Dis.* 124 Suppl.:S98 (1971).

44. R. E. Kauffman, J. A. Morris, and D. L. Azarnoff, Placental transfer and fetal urinary excretion of gentamicin during constant rate maternal infusion. *Pediat. Res.* 9:104 (1975).

45. N. Conway and B. D. Birt: Streptomycin in pregnancy: Effect on the foetal ear. *Brit. Med. J.* 2:260 (1965).

46. V. Rodriguez, D. Stewart, and G. P. Bodey: Gentamicin sulfate distribution in body fluids. *Clin. Pharm. Ther.* 11:275 (1970).

47. J. J. Rahal: Treatment of gram-negative bacillary meningitis in adults. *Ann. Int. Med.* 77:295 (1972).

48. J. J. Rahal, P. H. Hyams, M. S. Simberkoff, and E. Rubinstein: Combined intrathecal and intramuscular gentamicin for gram-negative meningitis: Pharmacologic study of 21 patients. *New Eng. J. Med.* 290:1394 (1974).

49. J. E. Pennington, D. C. Dale, H. Y. Reynolds, and J. D. MacLowry: Gentamicin sulfate pharmacokinetics: Lower levels of gentamicin in blood during fever. *J. Infect. Dis.* 132:270 (1975).

50. M. Barber and P. M. Waterworth: Activity of gentamicin against pseudomonas and hospital staphylococci. *Brit. Med. J.* 1:203 (1966).

51. C. M. Kunin: Antibiotic usage in patients with renal impairment. *Hospital Practice* 7:141 (1972).

52. R. A. Chan, E. J. Benner, and P. D. Hoeprich: Gentamicin therapy in renal failure: A nomogram for dosage. *Ann. Int. Med.* 76:773 (1972).

53. R. E. Cutler, A. -M. Gyselynck, P. Fleet, and A. W. Forrey: Correlation of serum creatinine concentration and gentamicin half-life *J. Am. Med. Assoc.* 219:1037 (1972).

54. M. C. McHenry, T. L. Gavan, R. W. Gifford, N. A. Geurkink, R. A. van Ommen, M. A. Town, and J. G. Wagner: Gentamicin dosages for renal insufficiency: Adjustments based on endogenous creatinine concentration. *Ann. Int. Med.* 74:192 (1971).

55. R. E. Cutler and B. M. Orme: Correlation of serum creatinine concentrations and kanamycin half-life. Therapeutic implications. *J. Am. Med. Assoc.* 209:539 (1969).

56. M. Barza, R. B. Brown, D. Shen, M. Gibaldi, and L. Weinstein: Predictability of blood levels of gentamicin in man. *J. Infect. Dis.* 132:165 (1975).

57. D. H. Smith, B. van Otto, and A. L. Smith: A rapid chemical assay for gentamicin. *New. Eng. J. Med.* 286:583 (1972).

58. R. E. Winters, K. D. Litwack, and W. L. Hewitt: Relation between dose and levels of gentamicin in blood. *J. Infect. Dis.* 124 Suppl.:S90 (1971).

59. I. Phillips, C. Warren, and S. E. Smith: Serum gentamicin assay: A comparison and assessment of different methods. *J. Clin. Pathol.* 27:447 (1974).

60. R. Daigneault, M. Gagné, and M. Brazeau: A comparison of two methods of gentamicin assay: An enzymatic procedure and an agar diffusion technique. *J. Infect. Dis.* 130:642 (1974).

61. M. Danish, R. Schultz, and W. J. Jusko: Pharmacokinetics of gentamicin and kanamycin during hemodialysis. *Antimicrob. Agents Chemother.* 6:841 (1974).

62. W. M. Bennett, I. Singer, and C. H. Coggins: Guide to drug usage in

adult patients with impaired renal function: A supplement. *J. Am. Med. Assoc.* 223:991 (1973).

63. *The Medical Letter Handbook of Antimicrobial Therapy.* (1976).

64. Center for Disease Control: Morbidity and Mortality Weekly Report. 24:205 (1975).

65. Committee on Infectious Diseases: Ampicillin-resistant strains of *Haemophilus influenzae* type B. *Pediatrics* 55:145 (1975).

66. V. T. Andreole: Synergy of carbenicillin and gentamicin in experimental infection with *Pseudomonas. J. Infect. Dis.* 124 Suppl.:S46 (1971).

67. T. A. Hoffman and W. E. Bullock: Carbenicillin therapy of *Pseudomonas* and other gram-negative bacillary infections. *Ann. Int. Med.* 73:165 (1970).

68. M. E. Levison, R. Knight, and D. Kaye: *In vitro* evaluation of tobramycin, a new aminoglycoside antibiotic. *Antimicrob. Agents Chemother.* 1:381 (1972).

69. A. V. Reynolds, J. M. T. Hamilton-Miller, and W. Brumfitt: Newer aminoglycosides—amikacin and tobramycin: An *in-vitro* comparison with kanamycin and gentamicin. *Brit. Med. J.* 3:778 (1974).

70. R. M. Laxer, E. Mackay, and M. I. Marks: Antimicrobial activity of tobramycin against gram-negative bacteria and the combination of ampicillin/tobramycin against *E. coli. Chemotherapy* 21:90 (1975).

71. R. K. Holmes, B. H. Minishew, and J. P. Sanford: Resistance of *Pseudomonas aeruginosa* to aminoglycoside antibiotics. *J. Infect. Dis.* 130 Suppl.:S163 (1974).

72. B. R. Meyers and S. Z. Hirschman: Pharmacologic studies on tobramycin and comparison with gentamicin. *J. Clin. Pharmacol.* 12:321 (1972).

73. R. E. Brummett, D. Himes, B. Saine, and J. Vernon: A comparative study of the ototoxicity of tobramycin and gentamicin. *Arch. Otolaryngol.* 96:505 (1972).

74. Topical neomycin: *Med. Letter* 15:101 (1973).

75. J. E. Davia, A. W. Siemsen, and R. W. Anderson: Uremia, deafness, and paralysis due to irrigating antibiotic solutions. *Arch. Int. Med.* 125:135 (1970).

76. North American Contact Dermatitis Group: Epidemiology of contact dermatitis in North America: 1972. *Arch. Dermatol.* 108:537 (1973).

77. E. Epstein: Allergy to dermatologic agents. *J. Am. Med. Assoc.* 198:103 (1966).

78. J. E. McGowan, B. W. Barnes, and M. Finland: Bacteremia at Boston City Hospital: Occurrence and mortality during 12 selected years (1935–1972), with special reference to hospital-acquired cases. *J. Infect. Dis.* 132:316 (1975).

79. J. Klastersky, A. Henri, C. Hensgens, and D. Daneau: Gram-negative infections in cancer: Study of empiric therapy comparing carbenicillin-cephalothin with and without gentamicin. *J. Am. Med. Assoc.* 227:45 (1974).

80. V. Rodriguez, M. Burgess, and G. P. Bodey: Management of fever of unknown origin in patients with neoplasms and neutropenia. *Cancer* 32:1007 (1973).

81. M. A. Polacek and P. Sanfelippo: Oral antibiotic bowel preparation and complications in colon surgery. *Arch. Surg.* 97:412 (1968).

82. E. T. Thieme and G. Fink: A study of the danger of antibiotic preparation of the bowel for surgery. *Surgery* 67:403 (1970).

83. J. Goldring, A. Scott, W. McNaught, and G. Gillespie: Prophylactic oral antimicrobial agents in elective colonic surgery. *Lancet* 2:997 (1975).

84. I. Cohn: Intestinal antisepsis. *Surg. Gynec. Obstet.* 130:1006 (1970).

85. C. B. Pittinger, Y. Eryasa, and R. Adamson: Antibiotic-induced paralysis. *Anesth. Analg.* 49:487 (1970).

86. C. Pittinger and R. Adamson: Antibiotic blockade of neuromuscular function. *Ann. Rev. Pharmacol.* 12:169 (1972).

87. O. Vital Brazil and J. Prado-Franceschi: The nature of neuromuscular block produced by neomycin and gentamicin. *Arch. Int. Pharmacodyn.* 179:78 (1969).

88. F. R. Goodman, G. B. Weiss, and H. R. Adams: Alterations by neomycin of ^{45}Ca movements and contractile responses in vascular smooth muscle. *J. Pharm. Expt. Ther.* 188:472 (1974).

89. W. D. Meriwether, R. J. Mangi, and A. S. Serpick: Deafness following standard intravenous dose of ethacrynic acid. *J. Am. Med. Assoc.* 216:795 (1971).

90. B. A. West, R. E. Brummett, and D. L. Himes: Interaction of kanamycin and ethacrynic acid. *Arch. Otolaryngol.* 98:32 (1973).

91. H. F. Stupp: Untersuchung der antibiotikaspiegel in den innenohrflüssigkeiten und ihre bedeutung für die spezifische ototoxizität der aminoglykosidantibiotika. *Acta Oto-Laryng.* Suppl.262:1–85 (1970).

92. J. Wersäll, B. Bjorkroth, A. Flock, and P. -G. Lundquist: Experiments on ototoxic effects of antibiotics. *Adv. Oto.* 20:14 (1973).

93 J. E. Hawkins: "Biochemical aspects of ototoxicity" in *Biochemical Mechanisms in Hearing and Deafness*, ed. by M. M. Paparella. Springfield: Charles C. Thomas, 1970. pp. 323–339.

94. A. L. Nuttall, D. M. Marques, E. Stockhorst, and J. Schacht: Neomycin effects on cochlea microphonics and phospholipid metabolism. *J. Acoust. Soc. Am.* 57:S60 (1975).

95. A. Orsulakova, E. Stockhorst, and J. Schacht: Effect of neomycin on phosphoinositide labeling and calcium binding in guinea pig inner ear tissues in vivo and in vitro. *J. Neurochem.* 26:285 (1976).

96. S. Lodhi, N. D. Weiner, and J. Schacht: Interactions of neomycin and calcium in synaptosomal membranes and polyphosphoinositide monolayers. *Biochim. Biophys. Acta* 426:781 (1976).

97. J. Schacht: Biochemistry of neomycin ototoxicity. *J. Acoust. Soc. Am.* 59:940 (1976).

98. J. T. Buckley and J. H. Hawthorne: Erythrocyte membrane polyphosphoinositide metabolism and the regulation of calcium binding. *J. Biol. Chem.* 247:7218 (1972).

99. M. Kai and J. N. Hawthorne: Physiological significance of polyphosphoinositides in brain. *Ann. N.Y. Acad. Sci.* 165:761 (1969).

100. J. N. Wilfert, J. P. Burke, H. A. Bloomer, and C. B. Smith: Renal insufficiency associated with gentamicin therapy. *J. Infect. Dis.* 124 Suppl.:S148 (1971).

101. F. Cabanillas, R. C. Burgos, R. C. Rodriguez, and C. Baldizon: Nephrotoxicity of combined cephalothin-gentamicin regimen. *Arch. Int. Med.* 135:850 (1975).

102. R. I. Mazze and M. J. Cousins: Combined nephrotoxicity of gentamicin and methoxyflurane anesthesia in man. *Br. J. Anesth.* 45:394 (1973).

103. F. C. Luft and S. A. Kleit: Renal parenchymal accumulation of aminoglycoside antibiotics in rats. *J. Infect. Dis.* 130:656 (1974).

104. J. C. Kosek, R. I. Mazze and M. J. Cousins: Nephrotoxicity of gentamicin. *Lab. Invest.* 30:48 (1974).

105. M. Demerec: Origin of bacterial resistance to antibiotics. *J. Bacteriol.* 56:63 (1948).

106. R. Benveniste and J. Davies: Mechanisms of antibiotic resistance in bacteria. *Ann. Rev. Biochem.* 42:471 (1973).

107. R. Benveniste and J. Davies: Enzymatic acetylation of aminoglycoside antibiotics by *Escherichia coli* carrying an R factor. *Biochemistry* 10:1787 (1971).

108. J. A. Shulman, P. M. Terry, and C. E. Hough: Colonization with gentamicin-resistant *Pseudomonas aeruginosa*, pyocine type 5, in a burn unit. *J. Infect. Dis.* 124 Suppl.:S18 (1971).

Chapter 4

Bacteriostatic Inhibitors of Protein Synthesis
Chloramphenicol
Erythromycin
Lincomycin
Clindamycin
Spectinomycin
The Tetracyclines

Introduction

Chemotherapeutic drugs have been discovered in a number of ways. Only rarely has their discovery been the result of the logical design of a compound that was intended to interfere with a particular biochemical reaction in a predictable way. Upon occasion, drugs have been discovered by following up a chance observation in the laboratory. More often, drugs used in the treatment of infectious disease have been discovered in search programs that screen chemicals and extracts of plants and fungi for antibacterial properties. These procedures, which are exceedingly repetitive have yielded the bulk of the useful antibiotics. Chloramphenicol, erythromycin, the aminoglycosides, and the tetracyclines were all isolated from soil actinomycetes discovered in large screening programs. Literally thousands of antibacterial compounds have been found in such screening programs, but the majority are not marketed either because they are too toxic to the patient or offer no advantages over antibiotics already in use.

ANTIBIOTICS THAT ACT ON THE 50S RIBOSOMAL SUBUNIT

There is no inherently logical order in which to present the bacteriostatic antibiotics that act by inhibiting protein synthesis. They will be presented in this chapter according to their locus of action on the bacterial ribosome. The antibiotics chloramphenicol, erythromycin, lincomycin, and clindamycin all inhibit bacterial protein synthesis, and they all bind to the 50S subunit of the bacterial ribosome. These drugs are not all structural analogs of each other, and a knowledge of their structure does not afford any particular insight into their mechanism of action at our current level of understanding. The extensive literature dealing with the mechanism of action of the antibiotics presented in this chapter has been reviewed in detail by Pestka.[1]

CHLORAMPHENICOL

Chloramphenicol was originally isolated from a soil actinomycete, *Streptomyces venezuelae*. It has the simple structure shown below and is now produced by chemical synthesis rather than by fermentation.

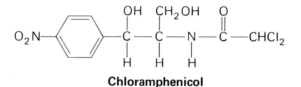

Chloramphenicol

Mechanism of Action

The Receptor

It was demonstrated very early that exposure of bacteria to chloramphenicol stopped protein synthesis immediately with no immediate effect on the synthesis of nucleic acids (Figure 4-1).[2] The ability of an organism's ribosomes to bind chloramphenicol is related to it's sensitivity to growth inhibition by the drug.[3] Table 4-1 shows that only 70S ribosomes have the ability to bind the drug. The binding is readily reversible, and if a chloramphenicol-treated culture is diluted with new growth medium, the culture will begin growing again.

It is clear that interaction of chloramphenicol with the ribosome is responsible for the inhibition of protein synthesis by the drug. This inhibition of protein synthesis is maximal when one molecule of chloramphenicol is bound per ribosome.[4] The results presented in Table 4-2 show that chloramphenicol inhibits protein synthesis in a cell-free system only when 70S ribosomes are present.[5] There is very little inhibition when protein synthesis is directed by a soluble fraction from *E. coli* and 80S ribosomes prepared from yeast. This is the basis for the selective toxicity of chlorampheni-

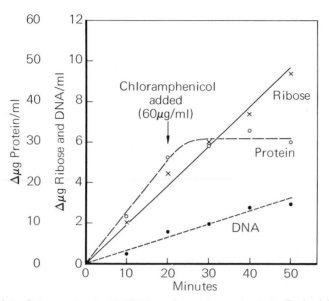

Figure 4-1 Chloramphenicol inhibition of protein synthesis in *Escherichia coli*. Chloramphenicol was added to *E. coli* in the logarithmic phase of growth, and portions of the culture were sampled at various time intervals and assayed for total cell protein and nucleic acid. The values represent the average of triplicate analyses expressed as increments in micrograms per milliliter over the initial concentration. (Reprinted from Wisseman *et al.*[2])

col. This selectivity is not complete, however. Although most protein synthesis in mammalian cells takes place on 80S ribosomes, the small amount of protein synthesis that takes place in mitochondria is inhibited by chloramphenicol.[6] It is hypothesized that mitochondria may have arisen from primitive infecting organisms that gradually became obligatory endosymbionts.[7] The mitochondria direct the synthesis of their own ribosomes, which behave in many ways like their bacterial 70S counterparts. As will be described later in this chapter, it is suspected that one of the major toxic effects of chloramphenicol may be explained on the basis of its inhibition of mitochondrial protein synthesis.

Chloramphenicol binds only to the 50S subunit of the bacterial ribosome.[8] The 50S subunit can be separated into its protein and RNA components and then reconstituted. The reconstituted unit will bind chloramphenicol,[9] and some preliminary data suggest that one ribosomal protein in particular is required for the formation of a competent drug receptor site.[10,11] The binding of chlor-

Table 4-1 **Relationship between sensitivity to growth inhibition by chloramphenicol and the ability of isolated ribosomes to bind the radioactive-labeled drug**
Here ^{14}C-labeled chloramphenicol was added to ribosome suspensions prepared from various sources, and the amount of drug bound was assayed by centrifuging the samples and determining the radioactivity in the ribosomal pellet. The results are expressed as picograms of chloramphenicol bound per milligram of ribosomes. (Data compiled from Vazquez.[3])

Type of organism	Source of ribosomes	Response to chloram-phenicol	Type of ribosome	*In vitro* binding to ribosomes
Bacterial	*Staphylococcus aureus*	Sensitive	70S	18
	Bacillus megaterium	Sensitive	70S	30
	Escherichia coli B	Sensitive	70S	29
Yeast	*Saccharomyces fragilis*	Resistant	80S	Less than 1
Protozoan	*Strigomonas*	Resistant	80S	Less than 1
Mammal	Rat liver	—	80S	Less than 1

amphenicol to ribosomes is inhibited by lincomycin and such macrolide antibiotics as erythromycin, carbomycin, and oleandomycin.[12] But since the binding of erythromycin is not inhibited by chloramphenicol, it is clear that the binding sites are not identical.[13] Thus, it is likely that the receptor sites of erythromycin and chloramphenicol overlap or interact in some way. The lincomycins also have their receptor sites in close proximity to, or shared with, the others.

Table 4-2 **Effect of chloramphenicol on [^{14}C]lysine incorporation with yeast and *Escherichia coli* supernatant and ribosomes**
Ribosomal and soluble (105,000 × g supernatant) fractions were prepared from *E. coli* and the yeast *S. fragilis.* The ribosomes and supernatant were incubated with [^{14}C]lysine and nonradioactive amino acids with or without chloramphenicol (2 μmoles/ml), and the amount of radioactivity incorporated into trichloroacetic acid-insoluble material was assayed. The results are expressed as counts per minute incorporated per incubation. (From So and Davie.[5])

Supernatant	Ribosomes	Chloram-phenicol	Amino acid incorporation: Experi-ment 1	Experi-ment 2	Average inhibition (%)
Escherichia coli	*Escherichia coli*	−	5,625	3,905	95
		+	196	239	
Escherichia coli	*Saccharomyces fragilis*	−	4,804	10,369	14
		+	4,460	8,236	

Inhibition of Protein Synthesis

In reviewing what we know of the mechanism of chloramphenicol action, it is useful to refer to the sequence of events in protein synthesis presented in Figure 3-2. It is clear that chloramphenicol does not preferentially inhibit the initiation of new protein chains or chain termination and detachment from ribosomes.[4] The binding of aminoacyl-tRNA[14] and the binding of mRNA[4] to the 30S ribosome subunit is not affected by the drug.

In the presence of chloramphenicol, newly formed, pulse-labeled mRNA enters poly-ribosomes of all sizes without concomitant synthesis of protein.[15] It would then seem that in the presence of chloramphenicol, ribosomes attach to and move along mRNA (a process that requires translocation) without producing peptide bonds. The conclusion that chloramphenicol inhibits peptide bond formation was also reached by the use of several different experimental approaches.[1,16] The uncoupling of translocation and peptide bond formation is difficult to understand. It is postulated that chloramphenicol binding by the ribosome distorts ribosomal components and thus relaxes the requirement for the coupling of peptide bond formation and ribosome movement. In this case, translocation would continue in an ordered manner by virtue of the correct orientation of the tRNA molecules in the acceptor and donor sites on the ribosome.

If we visualize the orientation of the amino acid-charged tRNA on the ribosome, the tRNA is attached to the 30S portion in that region of the molecule containing the anticoden triplet. The region of the tRNA containing the attached amino acid must be correctly oriented on the surface of the 50S portion of the ribosome for peptide bond formation to take place. This can be inferred from the fact that the enzyme directing the synthesis of the peptide bond (peptidyl transferase) is a structurally integral part of the 50S ribosome subunit. If the binding of tRNA at the codon recognition site is undisturbed, then translocation might very well proceed in the presence of chloramphenicol. One would predict that a disturbance in the binding of the amino acid-containing end of the tRNA to the 50S subunit would interfere with peptide bond formation.

This prediction has been tested directly: tRNA charged with tritium-labeled phenylalanine was digested with T_1 ribonuclease. After this limited digestion, a [^{3}H]phenylalanine-pentanucleotide was isolated. It was presumed that this radioactive amino acid-oligonucleotide represented the aminoacyl portion of an amino

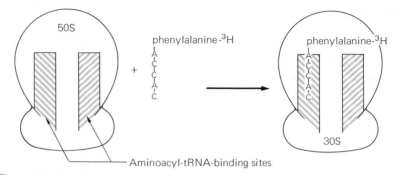

Figure 4-2   A schematic illustration of the binding of phenylalanyl-oligonucleotide to ribosomes. The binding of phenylalanyl-oligonucleotide to the ribosome
is used here as a model of the specific binding of the amino acid-containing end
of a complete aminoacyl-tRNA. The binding that does occur between the phenylalanyl-tRNA and the ribosome is inhibited by chloramphenicol but not by
erythromycin. (Adapted from Pestka.[17])

acid-charged tRNA. Several antibiotics were then tested for their
effect on the ability of ribosomes to bind the radioactive phenylal-
anine-oligonucleotide (Figure 4-2).[17] Chloramphenicol markedly
inhibited the binding at concentrations that inhibited protein
synthesis in in vivo systems. Subsequently, several other amino
acid-oligonucleotides have been synthesized, and chloramphenicol inhibits the binding of all of them to bacterial ribosomes.
Isomers of chloramphenicol that do not prevent bacterial growth
do not prevent the binding of the amino acid-oligonucleotides.[18]
There is evidence that this system mimics the association between
the amino-acyl-terminal of the tRNA and the 50S ribosomal subunit.[19,20] These experiments, and others not discussed here, support the conclusion that chloramphenicol inhibits protein synthesis by binding in a reversible manner to the 50S ribosome subunit
and by preventing the attachment of the amino acid-containing
end of the aminoacyl-tRNA to its binding region in the A site.
This apparently prevents the appropriate association of peptidyl
transferase with its amino acid substrate, and the peptide bond
cannot be formed.

Pharmacology and Toxicity of Chloramphenicol

Chloramphenicol is well absorbed from the gastrointestinal tract,
with peak serum levels attained in approximately 2 hours. The
drug readily passes into body fluid spaces, including the cerebro-

spinal fluid.[21] The concentration of chloramphenicol in the cerebrospinal fluid is about one-half that in plasma. Under conditions of normal hepatic function, chloramphenicol is almost totally metabolized in the liver by conjugation to the glucuronide. Studies in rats demonstrate that administration of phenobarbital markedly increases the rate of metabolism, leading to a significant reduction in the serum level of the active drug.[22]

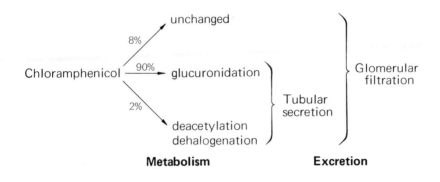

Metabolism   **Excretion**

The glucuronide is neither toxic nor active against bacteria. It is excreted by the kidney, but the dosage of chloramphenicol does not have to be modified in the patient with compromised renal function.[23] Even though higher levels of the drug build up in the patient who excretes it in reduced amounts, they are not of great consequence because it is the nontoxic glucuronide form that is present. If a patient has combined hepatic and renal failure, it would seem reasonable to lower the dosage. In situations in which there is extensive parenchymal damage in the liver, the capacity to conjugate substances with glucuronic acid is reduced (as evidenced by increases in the serum level of unconjugated bilirubin). The incidence of bone-marrow toxicity due to chloramphenicol is higher in patients with hepatic insufficiency, and the physician should be particularly observant with this group.[24] There are no good guidelines for dosage reduction in the presence of compromised hepatic function.

Chloramphenicol is a broad-spectrum antibiotic, and bacterial and fungal superinfections can occur during therapy. Hypersensitivity reactions are not common, however. The most important undesirable effects of chloramphenicol are on the hematopoietic system and these are considered in the next section. There is a potentially fatal toxic reaction to chloramphenicol that occurs in newborn infants. The complex of symptoms is called the "gray syndrome," and it is characterized by abdominal distention, vomiting, progressive pallid cyanosis, irregular respiration, hypothermia, and finally vasomotor collapse.[25] It develops because the liver of a newborn infant is unable to conjugate chloramphenicol to the glucuronide. In addition to an inability to metabolize the drug, infants have depressed rates of glomerular filtration and tubular secretion. As a result, high levels of the unaltered drug build up in the newborn (Figure 4-3), even though the dose of the drug, after adjustment for body weight and surface area, would be appropriate for an older baby. Termination of therapy upon early development of symptoms often reverses the process. The biochemical mechanism of this toxicity is not known. The syndrome has also been reported in older children (e.g., 25 months) who have high serum chloramphenicol levels.[26] These patients may conceivably have had a defect in glucuronidation although there was no gross evidence of this. Because of gray syndrome toxicity lower dosages (based on body weight) and special caution are employed with infants less than 1 month old.

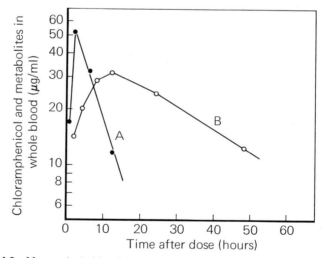

Figure 4-3 Mean whole-blood levels of free chloramphenicol and its metabolites in newborn infants and older children after oral administration of chloramphenicol palmitate in single doses of 50 mg/kg body weight. A, age one to 11 years (mean of 13 subjects); B, age one to two days (mean of five subjects). (From Weiss *et al.*[25])

An interesting effect of chloramphenicol that has been examined in model animal systems is its ability to suppress the primary immune response at high doses.[27] The mechanism of the effect has not been well worked out, but it could involve an inhibition of the growth rate of the rapidly dividing, antigen-stimulated lymphocytes.[28] It has been shown that chloramphenicol inhibits the growth of leukemic lymphocytes at the same concentration at which it inhibits mitochondrial protein synthesis.[29] It is tempting to speculate that the immunosuppressive effect, like the bone-marrow toxicity, may be due to an inhibition of mitochondrial protein synthesis. Extensive depression of the ability of a patient's immune system to respond to an infection would be counterproductive. There is, however, no indication that chloramphenicol has a clinically significant immunosuppressive effect in the patient with infection.

Effects of Chloramphenicol on the Hematopoietic System

Chloramphenicol affects the hematopoietic system in two ways. One is a toxic phenomenon manifested by bone-marrow depression, and the other is an allergic or idiosyncratic response manifested by aplastic anemia.

Toxic Bone-marrow Depression

Chloramphenicol can cause a reversible, dose-related depression of bone-marrow function, which presents as an anemia, sometimes with leukopenia or thrombocytopenia.[30] This effect can occur in anyone receiving high doses of drug. For example, in one well-controlled study, bone-marrow depresssion developed in 2 of 20 patients given 2 gm and in 18 of 21 receiving 6 gm of the drug daily.[31] As a reference figure, approximately 4 gm of the drug per day is administered routinely to adults in the treatment of typhoid fever.

The mechanism of this toxic effect is not completely worked out, but there is considerable evidence supporting the argument that it is due to inhibition of mitochondrial protein synthesis.[32] Chloramphenicol readily penetrates mammalian mitochondria and binds to mitochondrial ribosomes. It inhibits protein synthesis in this organelle at concentrations of drug that exist in the serum during therapy.[33] Morphological changes have been demonstrated in the mitochondria of bone-marrow cells taken from patients receiving chloramphenicol.[34] These changes, like the toxicity, are reversible. Chloramphenicol inhibits protein synthesis in human marrow cell mitochondria *in vitro*, and antibiotics that are not myelotoxic have no effect.[32] Chloramphenicol reversibly inhibits the growth of bone-marrow colony-forming cells *in vitro*.[35]

Aplastic Anemia

Another type of response of the hematopoietic cells to chloramphenicol is the development of aplastic anemia. Only after three years of extensive use did it become evident that chloramphenicol was able to completely depress bone-marrow activity in some patients. It was in response to this three-year delay that the American Medical Association established the Registry on Blood Dyscrasias to collect data on such drug-associated reactions. Chloramphenicol has been implicated in more reports to the registry than any other single drug. This suppression of bone-marrow activity differs from the toxic phenomenon just discussed (Table 4-3). The response is characterized by pancytopenia with an aplastic marrow. It can appear during treatment, but it often appears long after treatment has ended. It is not related to the dose of the drug. The prognosis is very poor, with a high percentage of fatalities. Because it is not a frequent event, it is difficult to arrive at a good estimation of the risk of the aplastic response. A value in the range of 1 in 24,000 to 1 in 40,000 courses of treatment is probably reasonable, given the available data.[36]

The aplastic anemia is not a toxic reaction and it is very unlikely that it represents a drug hypersensitivity. Most workers in the field seem to feel that it is an idiosyncratic response; that is, it is a result of a genetically determined biochemical lesion.[37] This would account for the rarity of the event and the fact that aplastic anemia has been observed on at least one occasion in identical twins given chloramphenicol.[38] One could postulate a rare biochemical abnormality in the undifferentiated stem cell compartment of the marrow. One could also postulate rare individuals with altered routes of metabolism that produce a toxic metabolite of chloramphenicol. Neither of these hypotheses readily account for the long delay that sometimes exists between termination of therapy and the onset of the aplastic response.

The structural requirements for the production of the aplastic anemia are not known.[39] Thiamphenicol, an analog of chloramphenicol with similar antibacterial activity and the ability to produce the reversible dose-related anemia, has been in clinical

Table 4-3 **Features of two types of blood dyscrasia resulting from treatment with chloramphenicol**
There are two different responses of the hematopoietic system to chloramphenicol. Separation of the responses into the toxic effect (bone-marrow depression) and the aplastic response was first made by Yunis and Bloomberg.[30]

Feature	Toxic effect	Aplastic response
Appearance of bone-marrow smears	Normocellular	Hypoplastic or aplastic
Peripheral blood	Anemia (with or without leukopenia or thrombocytopenia)	Pancytopenia
Relation to dosage of drug given	Dose related	No dose relationship
Time of appearance	During therapy	Most often days to months after cessation of therapy
Most common presenting symptoms	Anemia	Purpura and/or hemorrhage
Prognosis	Recovery is usually complete on cessation of treatment	Fatal in many cases

use in Europe.[40] This compound has a methylsulfonyl group in place of the para-nitro group of chloramphenicol. Although it is too early to make any predictions regarding a rare event like bone-marrow aplasia, this complication has not been reported with thiamphenicol to date.[39,40]

Therapeutic Indications for Chloramphenicol

Chloramphenicol is a broad-spectrum drug. It inhibits the growth of both gram-positive and gram-negative bacteria as well as rickettsia and chlamydiae. The *Chlamydie* (formerly *Bedsonia*) include the agents responsible for psittacosis, lymphogranuloma venerum, trachoma, and inclusion conjunctivitis. When chloramphenicol came into clinical use, it was employed extensively in the treatment of a wide variety of infections. The clinical indications for its use became very restricted, however, when it became apparent that this drug could produce the fatal aplastic anemia and the reversible bone-marrow toxicity. Chloramphenicol is still the drug of choice for treatment of typhoid fever *(Salmonella typhosa)*. It should be noted, however, that in some regions of the world, for example Mexico, a significant percentage of the *Salmonella* isolates are now chloramphenicol-resistant.[41]

Chloramphenicol readily passes into the cerebrospinal fluid and it is effective against *Haemophilus influenzae*. It was used commonly for the treatment of meningitis caused by this organism until 1965 when it became clear that the less toxic drug ampicillin was also effective. Ampicillin then supplanted chloramphenicol as the drug of choice. It is difficult to determine which of these two antibiotics is the most efficacious drug for the treatment of *H. influenzae* meningitis.[42,43] In 1974, the picture changed somewhat in the United States because ampicillin-resistant strains of the bacterium began to appear.[44] The consequences of ineffective or delayed proper treatment of this condition are such that primary therapy for patients with confirmed or suspected infection due to *H. influenzae* should now include chloramphenicol. Thus, with patients over 2 months (with meningitis or epiglottitis due to *H. influenzae*) treatment can begin either with chloramphenicol alone or with chloramphenicol and ampicillin.[45] As soon as the ampicillin sensitivity of the organism is established, chloramphenicol therapy should be stopped and treatment continued with ampicillin.

The use of chloramphenicol in the treatment of *H. influenzae* meningitis is presented here for two reasons. First, it is one of the few clinical situations in which chloramphenicol is the drug of choice for initiation of therapy. Second, it provides a good example of how important it is for the physician to have accurate guidelines, immediately available, on drug usage. The status of a drug in the treatment of infectious disease varies continually with the introduction of new drugs, the development of large resistant populations, and the discovery of toxicities and hypersensitivity phenomena. One of the best ways for the physician to keep himself informed of the relative efficacy of drugs for the treatment of specific infections is to read *The Medical Letter*. This biweekly review of therapeutics publishes listings of the consensus recommendations of a number of experts in infectious disease therapy regarding the choice of antimicrobial drugs. The recommendations are updated continually as the therapeutic situation changes.

Chloramphenicol is effective against many anaerobic bacteria, the most common of which is *Bacteroides fragilis*. When a patient has a severe infection with *B. fragilis*, arising from a focus in the bowel or pelvis, either chloramphenicol or clindamycin is effective. Although the list of organisms susceptible to chloramphenicol is extensive, the drug has serious drawbacks and its usage should be restricted, as seen in the following guidelines:

1. *Chloramphenicol should be used as a drug of first choice only for the treatment of typhoid fever and meningitis or epiglottitis due to H. influenzae. Otherwise, it should be employed only in severe (life-threatening) infections in which the drugs of choice cannot be used and chloramphenicol is clearly the superior alternative. It should never be used for prophylaxis or for the treatment of mild or uncharacterized infections.*
2. *Prolonged usage and repeat exposure should be avoided.*
3. *Leukocyte counts with a differential should be taken two or three times per week, and therapy should be discontinued when leukopenia occurs.*

Resistance

The enteric bacteria generally become resistant to chloramphenicol by acquiring R-factors that determine the production of chloramphenicol acetyltransferase, an enzyme that inactivates the drug by acetylating an hydroxyl group.[46] These R-factors carry determinants for multiple drug resistances and they can be passed from *Salmonella* to drug-sensitive strains of *E. coli*.[47] This suggests that chloramphenicol resistance may be transmitted to enterobacteria in livestock in which the use of antibiotics in feed could enrich for the R-factor—carrying organisms. It has also been shown that chloramphenicol resistance can be transferred back from the induced-resistant *E. coli* to sensitive *Salmonella*.

The Use of Chloramphenicol

Chloramphenicol was introduced to the American drug market in 1949 under a patent issued to Parke, Davis and Co. It was found to be a useful broad-spectrum antibiotic noted for its relative lack of adverse side effects, By 1950, however, it has become apparent that chloramphenicol produced aplastic anemia, a fatal side effect, in a few patients. A continuing argument regarding the proper use of this drug then developed. On one side were the drug firm and a number of physicians who felt the risk of aplastic anemia to be trival when compared with the therapeutic usefulness of the antibiotic. On the other side were a steadily increasing number of authorities in the treatment of infectious disease, many hematologists, advisors in the Food and Drug Administration, and at least two congressional committees who held hearings on the drug (chaired by Senator Estes Kefauver in 1960 and by Senator Gaylord Nelson in 1968). The controversy did not concern the right of the company to market the drug or the right of the physician to use it. Rather it concerned the way in which the drug company advertised its product and the uninformed way many physicians employed the drug. Many critics felt that the company played down the problem of side effects in their advertisements to physicians. The story of the commericial side of the controversy has been reviewed in Consumer Reports.[48]

A great part of the problem with the use of this drug centers upon the way many physicians are exposed to information about drugs. The indications given for therapy with chloramphenicol in those cases of chloramphenicol-associated blood dyscrasia reported to the Registry on Blood Dyscrasias from 1953 through 1964 demonstrate how ignorant many physicians were of the proper use of this antibiotic.[49] As seen in Figure 4-4, the second most common indication for therapy was the treatment of the common cold, a virus infection against which the drug is totally useless. In other cases, the drug was prescribed for minor infections where therapy with chloramphenicol is definitely not indicated. One would think that after repeated warnings the unwarranted use of chloramphenicol would plummet—but this has not been the case. Periodically (usually immediately after Senate committee hearings) a new level of awareness is temporarily achieved, and use of the drug drops, but there has always been a gradual rebound in sales.[48] Since there is presumably no increase in the incidence of typhoid fever or severe infection for which other antibiotics cannot be used, one must assume that physicians are again using the drug indiscriminately. In a system in which the principal exposure of many physicians to drug information is through the drug industry itself (e.g., the Physician's Desk Refer-

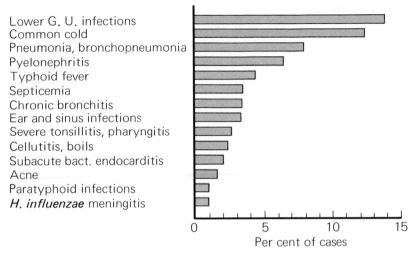

Figure 4-4   Some specific conditions for which chloramphenicol was given in instances of chloramphenicol-associated blood dyscrasia reported to the Registry on Blood Dyscrasias from 1953 through 1964. (From Best.[49])

ence with its product descriptions prepared by manufacturers, the drug company detailmen, and drug advertisements) there is simply not enough weight placed on unbiased reporting of the relative value of a drug in the best treatment of disease.

The use of chloramphenicol in some countries is much more lax than in the United States. In several countries, chloramphenicol is sold without a doctor's prescription.[50] A correspondent writes in the *New England Journal of Medicine* that chloramphenicol is used by many people in South America as " . . . a daily self-medication for all ills and aches. . . ."[51] In some places, appropriate warnings regarding the side effects and toxicities of chloramphenicol are not included in the drug package.[50] This is true even in cases when it was manufactured in countries like Great Britain and the United States where there are strict laws regarding the presentation of this information with chloramphenicol sold within the country.[52] We are warned that travelers to countries with lax laws or no laws protecting the consumer have died from aplastic anemia following ingestion of chloramphenicol contained in cough preparations and other formulations sold over the counter.[53]

ERYTHROMYCIN

Erythromycin is the only one of the macrolide antibiotics (a group that includes carbomycin, oleandomycin, and spiramycin) that is still used clinically. These antibiotics consist of a large lactone ring to which sugars are attached.

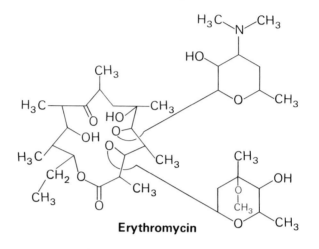

Erythromycin

Mechanism of Action

The Receptor

Erythromycin binds in a specific manner to the 50S subunit of the bacterial ribosome.[54] It does not bind to mammalian 80S ribosomes, and this accounts in part for its selective toxicity.[55] Like chloramphenicol, erythromycin can inhibit protein synthesis on ribosomes from mammalian mitochondria.[56] Competition experiments indicate that the erythromycin binding site on the 50S ribosome subunit overlaps with the binding sites for chloramphenicol and the lincomycins. The binding of [14C]chloramphenicol to bacterial ribosomes is prevented by erythromycin and lincomycin,[14] but the binding of [14C]erythromycin is not inhibited by chloramphenicol[57] or lincomycin.[58] The binding of [14C]lincomycin is inhibited by erythromycin.[59]

Experiments with drug-resistant mutants suggest that one 50S ribosomal protein in particular is important in the formation of the receptor site. A strain of *E. coli* resistant to erythromycin was isolated after exposure of a sensitive culture to a mutagenic nitro-soguanidine compound. The 50S ribosomal subunits from these cells did not bind erythromycin.[60] When the 50S protein components of the parent and resistant strains were compared using carboxymethyl-cellulose chromatography, one of the protein peaks in the resistant strain (component 50-8) had shifted position. This protein had undergone a mutation that altered its physical characteristics so that it eluted elsewhere. Genetic studies suggest that acquisition of erythromycin resistance and alteration in the 50-8 protein are due to one mutational event.[61] This altered protein may very well be a component of the receptor site for erythromycin. Chloramphenicol binds to the mutant ribosomes with decreased affinity, again suggesting that the receptor sites for chloramphenicol and erythromycin are closely related.[62] In another experiment, a strain of *E. coli* that is absolutely dependent on the presence of erythromycin for growth has been selected.[63] Lincomycin and chloramphenicol were also capable of permitting growth, although they were less effective than erythromycin. This also suggests a similarity in the interactions of the three structurally unrelated antibiotics with the 50S subunit.

Inhibition of Protein Synthesis

It is not completely clear which step in protein synthesis (cf. Figure 3-2) is the primary event inhibited by erythromycin. Studies on the drug effect both *in vivo* and *in vitro* strongly suggest that erythromycin inhibits the translocation step.[64,65] Other possibilities exist, however, and the reader is referred to the literature for a complete discussion of the data regarding the mechanism of inhibition.[1,66]

Cell-free protein synthesizing systems from both gram-positive and gram-negative bacteria are equally inhibited by erythromycin.[67] The drug, however, is clinically effective against gram-positive organisms but not most gram-negative bacilli. The concentration of erythromycin achieved in gram-positive organisms is 100 times greater than that in some gram-negative bacilli.[67] The drug is not actively transported into gram-positive organisms; rather, it enters by a passive process and is trapped by binding to the ribosomes. These observations are consistent with the interpretation that erythromycin cannot readily penetrate the cell envelope of gram-negative bacilli. The cell envelope of gram-negative cocci must be somewhat different, since erythromycin is effective against some *Neisseria*.

Erythromycin Resistance

An unusual type of inducible drug resistance has been observed in *Staphylococcus aureus*. Exposure of the organisms to erythromycin at low concentration (about $10^{-8}M$) results in resistance to high concentrations of erythromycin, the other macrolide antibiotics, and the lincosamides.[68] When the cells are initially exposed to high concentrations of erythromycin ($>10^{-7}M$), their growth is inhibited and induction of the resistance is blocked because of inhibition of protein synthesis. It has been shown that the RNA portion of the 50S ribosomal subunits of organisms exposed to a low concentration of erythromycin contains a unique methylated component (a dimethyl adenine).[69] Hybrid 50S ribosomal subunits have been assembled that utilize 23S RNA from drug-senstive or induced-resistant *S. aureus* and other protein and RNA constituants derived from *Bacillus stearothermophilus*. The complete hybrid ribosomes support phenylalanine incorporation, and lincomycin inhibits the synthesis when the ribosomes contain 23S RNA from the drug-sensitive parent but not when they contain the methylated 23S RNA from the induced-resistant cells.[70] This strongly suggests that the alteration in the RNA is responsible for the drug resistance. These staphylococci apparently have acquired a plasmid that contains the gene for an inducible RNA methylase. In the presence of small amounts of erythromycin (concentrations too low to inhibit protein synthesis), the enzyme is induced, causing a change in the RNA so that upon subsequent exposure to the usual growth-inhibitory concentrations of lincosamides or erythromycin, the drugs are no longer bacteriostatic.

Use and Pharmacology

Therapeutic Indications

Erythromycin is most often employed in the treatment of gram-positive infections, usually as an alternative drug in patients who are allergic to the penicillins. It is useful in the treatment of mild staphylococcal infection and respiratory tract infections due to pneumococci. The bacteriological cure rate obtained with oral erythromycin treatment of group A streptococcal pharyngitis is equivalent to that obtained with oral penicillin G.[71] The overall incidence of erythromycin resistance in group A β-hemolytic streptococci is less than 1 per cent of clinical isolates, but this may be slowly increasing.[72] Many of the bacterial infections that are likely to be sensitive to erythromycin are presented in Table 2-4. Erythromycin is useful in the treatment of infections due to *Mycoplasma pneumoniae* and the trachoma agent, a chlamydial organism (Table 4-8).

Pharmacology

Erythromycin base is labile in the acid gastric juice, and some activity may thus be lost in passage through the stomach. The absorption of the drug is better when the stomach is empty. The problem of acid lability has been solved in two ways. Many erythromycin preparations have an acid-resistant coating that allows them to pass safely through the low pH environment of the stomach to be absorbed in the small intestine. A propionyl derivative called erythromycin estolate is acid resistant and yields higher serum levels than the other forms.[73] Peak serum levels are achieved in about 2 hours.

Erythromycin diffuses well into most body spaces. Penetration into the cerebrospinal fluid is normally poor, but when the meninges are inflamed, the drug enters this space as well. Erythromycin also passes through the placenta.[74] The antibiotic is concentrated in the liver, and large amounts of the unaltered, biologically active form of the drug are excreted in the bile.

Clinically Undesirable Effects

Erythromycin has a good therapeutic index, although treatment is sometimes accompanied by mild gastrointestinal upset. Hypersensitivity reactions are uncommon, but one in particular is of special interest. Erythromycin estolate can cause a cholestatic hepatitis characterized by fever, abdominal pain, eosinophilia, and elevated serum bilirubin and transaminase.[75] Other forms of erythromycin do not have this effect. The first reaction usually occurs ten to 20 days after initiation of erythromycin estolate therapy, but in a patient who has had the reaction previously, it occurs within hours. The reaction is reversible upon withdrawal of the drug. Although this effect is often referred to as a hepato-toxicity, it has many of the characteristics of an allergic reaction. As yet, there has been no direct demonstration of an immunologi-cal mechanism in patients[76] and it has been suggested that the reaction may reflect an intrinsic toxicity to the liver coupled with a drug hypersensitivity.[77]

There are several observations that may contribute to a formula-tion of the mechanism of the hepatitis. The liver normally concen-trates erythromycin many-fold in the bile. Thus, the cells of this organ are exposed to very high concentrations of whichever erythromycin preparation is used. Erythromycin estolate is the lauryl sulfate salt of erythromycin propionate. Erythromycin pro-pionate has been shown to rapidly reduce bile flow in the isolated, perfused rat liver, whereas erythromycin base has a minimal effect.[77] Erythromycin propionate is clearly toxic to liver cells in suspension in concentrations at which other forms of the drug have no effect,[78,79] The demonstration that erythromycin propion-ate is toxic in these in vitro systems, whereas other forms of erythromycin are not, is completely consistent with the clinical observation that cholestatic hepatitis occurs only with this com-pound. The argument supporting the hepatotoxicity of erythro-mycin propionate is well substantiated. The rapid recurrence of symtoms when patients are rechallenged with the propionyl com-pound must be explained on an immunological basis. Thus, the interpretation that the cholestatic hepatitis is due to a summation of a hepatotoxic effect and a drug hypersensitivity seems a good one. There is one obvious clinical precaution that should be taken—erythromycin estolate should not be given to patients with impaired liver function.

Why isn't erythromycin more toxic? Like chloramphenicol, erythromycin and lincomycin inhibit protein synthesis on mam-mailian mitochondrial ribosomes. There is evidence that some toxic effects of chloramphenicol, such as reversible marrow suppression, may result from an inhibition of mitochondrial pro-tein synthesis in the cells of the patient. If that mechanism is valid, there must be a good reason why erythromycin and linco-mycin do not produce similar toxic effects. Chloramphenicol inhibits protein synthesis in isolated intact mitochondria, but erythromycin and lincomycin do not.[33] When the mitochondrial membrane is ruptured, however, both these antibiotics produce a marked inhibition. Thus, the mitochondrial membrane (and perhaps also the mammalian cell membrane) acts as an effective permeability barrier to erythromycin and lincomycin. This inability to penetrate into the mitochondria is probably an important factor in the selective toxicity of these agents.

LINCOMYCIN AND CLINDAMYCIN

Two lincosamide antibiotics are employed clinically, lincomycin and clindamycin. Lincomycin (see structure below) is produced by *Streptomyces lincolnensis*. Clindamycin is 7-chloro-lincomycin.

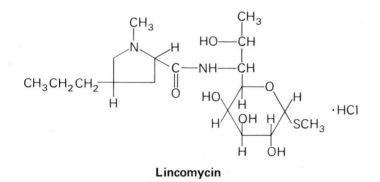

Lincomycin

Mechanism of Action

Lincomycin binds to the 50S ribosomal subunit.[59] As discussed in the preceding section on the mechanism of action of erythromycin, the lincomycin binding site appears to overlap the chloramphenicol and erythromycin receptor sites. The mechanism of protein synthesis inhibition, however, has not been worked out in detail. In *in vitro* systems, lincomycin interferes with peptide bond synthesis. But studies in intact bacteria suggest other mechanisms, including the possibility of inhibition of chain initiation.[80]

Therapeutic Use and Pharmacology

Therapeutic Indications

Lincomycin and clindamycin are active against many gram-positive cocci (including pneumococci, Group A streptococci, and staphylococci). They are useful in the treatment of severe infections due to several gram-positive organisms, particularly in patients who are allergic to the penicillins. The lincosamides can produce colitis, and less toxic alternatives should be chosen if the sensitivity of the organism permits. Clindamycin is more potent in vitro than lincomycin against most gram-positive organisms.[81] Clindamycin has been proven very effective in the treatment of infection due to anaerobic bacteria, particularly B. fragilis, and this constitutes an important indication for its clinical use (Table 2-4).[82,83]

Pharmacology

Clindamycin is much better absorbed from the gastrointestinal tract than lincomycin is, and higher blood levels are achieved with clindamycin.[81] Clindamycin phosphate is available for parenteral administration. This ester is inactive in vitro against microorganisms, but it is hydrolyzed in the body to clindamycin and high blood levels of the active drug are obtained.[84] The lincosamides distribute well into most body tissues and fluids except the cerebrospinal fluid. Clindamycin readily crosses the placenta.[74] Both lincomycin and clindamycin are extensively eliminated by hepatic mechanisms and dosage must be modified in patients with liver disease.[85] There is some excretion by the renal route (more with lincomycin than clindamycin), and in patients with chronic renal failure, the dosage of either of these antibiotics should be reduced.[86]

Clinically Undesirable Effects

Both these antibiotics can cause local irritation at intramuscular injection sites. Allergic reactions have been observed occasionally and blood dyscrasias occur rarely. A significant percentage of patients treated with parenteral clindamycin show reversible elevations in SGOT and SGPT.[84] The principal undesirable side effect associated with lincosamide therapy is colitis. The cardinal symptoms are diarrhea, diffuse abdominal cramping pain and distention, tenesmus, and fever.[87] The diarrhea can be very severe. Plaque-like lesions can be seen in air contrast X-ray studies of the colon. The histological findings upon biopsy of the colonic lesions are those of a pseudomembranous colitis.[88] The pseudomembrane is composed of polymorphonuclear leukocytes, fibrin, and necrotic cells. Pseudomembranous colitis has been reported to occur rarely with tetracyclines, chloramphenicol, and ampicillin therapy, but the incidence with the lincosamides is clearly higher than the others.

Antibiotics can cause a variety of untoward gastrointestinal effects.[89] Some symptoms, such as anorexia, nausea, vomiting, epigastric distress, abdominal distention, crampy abdominal pain, and diarrhea, occur on occasion with any oral antibiotic. These symptoms are apparently dose-related and probably are the result of direct irritation of the bowel mucosa. Diarrhea can also be due to superinfection with pathogenic organisms following suppression of the dominant bowel flora by the antibiotic. The pathophysiological basis for the pseudomembranous colitis is unknown. It is apparently not due to alterations in the bowel flora (although this is not yet ruled out) or to a direct irritant effect of the antibiotic.[87] Any adequate explanation will have to account for the fact that diarrhea sometimes begins after cessation of therapy. In at least one instance, lincosamide-associated pseudomembranous colitis has been reported in two members of the same family.[90] Another member of the same family also had pseudomembranous colitis without lincosamide therapy. These findings raise the possiblity that the syndrome in some patients may reflect a pharmacogenetic mechanism. Other possibilities include a virus, toxin, or possibly some type of immunological reaction.

The incidence of mild diarrhea occurring during lincosamide therapy is substantial (estimates range from 10 per cent to as high as 30 per cent). The incidence of intractable diarrhea due to pseudomembranous colitis has not been well defined. The physician should be aware of this adverse effect, and these drugs should not be employed for treating mild infections. The patient should be alerted to report significant diarrhea (more than five stools per day), and if it occurs, the drug should be discontinued. The processs is reversible.

ANTIBIOTICS THAT ACT ON THE 30S RIBOSOMAL SUBUNIT

SPECTINOMYCIN

Spectinomycin is an aminoglycoside, but its structure (see below) and mechanism of action are different fom other aminoglycosides (streptomycin, gentamicin, etc.).

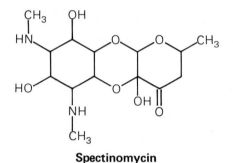

Spectinomycin

Spectinomycin inhibits protein synthesis in a reversible manner.[91] The drug interacts with the 30S ribosomal subunit.[92] Ribosome reconstitution experiments similar to those described for streptomycin have demonstrated that a single 30S ribosomal protein (P_4) is required for sensitivity to the drug to occur.[93] The *in vitro* inhibition of protein synthesis by spectinomycin requires the presence of guanylic or cytidylic acid in the synthetic RNA template.[92] The precise step in protein synthesis that is inhibited by spectinomycin has not been demonstrated directly. Some data are consistent with the interpretation that it inhibits the translocation process.

Spectinomycin is employed clinically in the treatment of only one infection—acute, uncomplicated gonococcal infection of the genitalia or rectum (Table 4-4).[94] Spectinomycin given in a single intramuscular administration is almost as effective in eradicating *Neisseria gonorrhoeae* as the preferred regimen for the parenteral treatment of uncomplicated gonococcal infection—procaine penicillin G with probenecid.[95] Spectinomycin is employed with patients who have a history of penicillin allergy. High-level resistance occurs in occasional clinical isolates of N. *gonorrhoeae*. It is due to alterations in the 30S ribosome subunit.[96] A single injection of spectinomycin can occasionally produce urticaria, dizziness, nausea, chills, and fever.

Table 4-4 **Recommended schedules for treatment of uncomplicated gonococ-cal infections in men and nonpregnant women**
(Center for Disease Control, U.S. Public Health Service[94])

Drug regimen of choice
    Aqueous procaine penicillin G, 4.8 million units intramuscularly, divided into two doses and injected into different sites at one visit, together with 1 gm of probenecid by mouth just before the injections.

Alternative regimens
    A. For patients in whom oral therapy is preferred: Ampicillin, 3.5 gm by mouth, together with 1 gm of probenecid administered at the same time.
    B. For patients who are allergic to the penicillins or probenecid:
        1. Tetracycline hydrochloride, 1.5 gm initially (orally) followed by 0.5 gm four times/day for 4 days (total dosage, 9.5 gm). Other tetracyclines are not more effective than tetracycline hydrochloride.
        2. Spectinomycin hydrochloride, 2.0 gm intramuscularly, in one injection.

TETRACYCLINES

The tetracycline antibiotics were isolated from various species of *Streptomyces* recovered by large-scale screening of soil samples.

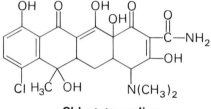

Chlortetracycline

The first of these compounds chlortetracycline (Aureomycin) was introduced in 1948. The tetracyclines are all very closely related, structurally. The structure of chlortetracycline is presented as an example of the basic polycyclic unit of all these compounds. The antimicrobial properties of these drugs are essentially the same. When resistance arises to one of the compounds there is (with rare exception) cross-resistance with the others.

Mechanism of Action

At the blood concentrations achieved in antibacterial therapy, the tetracyclines are bacteriostatic. At much higher concentrations, they are bactericidal. Various biochemical sites of action have been proposed for these drugs, based on reports of their inhibition of several bacterial enzyme systems, oxidative phosphorylation, glucose oxidation, and membrane transport.[97] One of the earliest studies demonstrated that protein synthesis is particularly sensitive to inhibition by the tetracyclines.[98] It is now clear that inhibition of protein synthesis is responsible for the inhibition of growth by these drugs.

The receptor for tetracyclines has not been defined as precisely as that for streptomycin or erythromycin. The tetracyclines bind to both ribosomes and mRNA. It is clearly the binding of the drug to the ribosome that inhibits protein synthesis.[99] This binding is largely reversible, and the bulk of the bound tetracycline is associated with the 30S ribosomal subunit.[100,101] A poly U-directed cell-free protein-synthesizing system from E. coli containing 30S ribosomal subunits from tetracycline-resistant cells is much less sensitive to inhibition by tetracycline than the same system containing 30S units from sensitive cells.[102] But it has not been demonstrated, as it has with streptomycin, that the 30S particles from resistant cells bind the drug less well.

In bacteria, tetracycline inhibits protein synthesis by blocking the binding of aminoacyl-tRNA to the mRNA-ribosome complex. As shown in Table 4-5, when tetracycline and phenylalanyl-tRNA are added simultaneously to a system containing 30S subunits and poly U, binding of the radioactive phenylalanyl-tRNA to the 30S subunits is markedly inhibited.[103] When the phenylalanyl-tRNA is added to the system 20 minutes before the tetracycline, inhibition of binding is much less. Thus, once the aminoacyl-tRNA is bound to the 30S particles, tetracycline cannot dissociate it.

There are two binding sites for aminoacyl-tRNA on the mRNA-70S-ribosome complex (see Chapter 2). An aminoacyl-tRNA can bind to the first site, the A site, when the 30S subunit is present. It is only when the 50S subunit is bound to the 30S ribosome subunit that a second binding site (the P site) is generated. This second binding site normally binds the tRNA to which the growing polypeptide is attached. It has been shown that tetracycline inhibits the binding of lysyl-tRNA to the ribosome but has no

Table 4-5 **The effect of tetracycline on the binding of phenylalanyl-tRNA to the 30S ribosomal subunit**

Phenylalanyl-tRNA binding to ribosomes was measured by incubating [3H]-labeled phenylalanyl-tRNA with poly U and 30S subunits at 24°C for 20 minutes. After incubation the samples were filtered and washed. The ribosome-bound ratioactivity remained on the filter, while the unbound radioactive aminoacyl-tRNA passed through. The values in the table represent the total phenylalanyl-tRNA bound per 7 μg of 30S subunit. (Data from Suzuka et al.[103])

| | Binding of [3H]phenylalanyl-tRNA: | |
Conditions of prebinding	Tetracycline added with 30S subunits	Tetracycline added 20 minutes after 30S subunits
Control	781	851
Tetracycline	226	674
$(4.5 \times 10^{-4}M)$		

effect on the binding of polylysyl-tRNA.[104] This indicates that the drug inhibits binding to the A site but not to the P site. A similar conclusion was reached by investigators who demonstrated that, although tetracycline inhibits virtually 100 per cent of the protein synthesis, it can only inhibit 50 per cent[105] of the binding of N-acetyl-phenylalanyl-tRNA. Protein synthesis then is halted at the same concentration of tetracycline that inhibits the binding of aminoacyl-tRNA to one-half of the tRNA binding sites on the ribosome.

The conclusion that tetracycline affects the binding to the acceptor site is supported by investigations using another antibiotic, puromycin, as an experimental tool. Puromycin is an analog of aminoacyl-tRNA.[106] It effects the separation of the growing peptide chain from the peptidyl-tRNA-messenger-ribosome complex, with the formation of peptidylpuromycin.[107] Puromycin does not prevent the binding of aminoacyl-tRNA to the A site nor does it effect the release of aminoacyl-tRNA from that site. It was reasoned that if tetracycline inhibits only the binding of amino-acyl-tRNA to the A site, then the one-half of the aminoacyl-tRNA that remains bound in the presence of tetracycline should be occupying the peptidyl-tRNA (P) site and should be released by puromycin. Correspondingly, only one-half of the aminoacyl-tRNA bound in the absence of the drug should be sensitive to puromycin. In the experiment presented in Table 4-6 and Figure 4-5, only one-half of the aminoacyl-tRNA was bound in the pres-

Table 4-6 **The release by puromycin of radioactive phenylalanyl-tRNA pre-bound to ribosomes: with and without tetracycline**

[14]C-labeled phenylalanyl-tRNA was bound to ribosomes with and without tetracycline. The phenylalanyl-tRNA was present in amounts sufficient to assure maximal binding. Puromycin was then added, the incubation was continued for 1 hour, and the amount of phenylalanyl-puromycin formed was extracted and assayed. Values represent the number of $\mu\mu$moles of phe-tRNA bound or phenylalanyl-puromycin released per incubation. (From Sarkar and Thach.[108])

Conditions of prebinding	Phenylalanyl-tRNA prebound ribosomes	Phenylalanyl-puromycin synthesized and released	Prebound phenylalanine released by puromycin
	($\mu\mu$ moles)		(%)
Control	14.1	6.74	˙47.7
Tetracycline ($6 \times 10^{-4}M$)	7.35	7.21	98.1

ence of tetracycline, and all of this was released as phenylalanyl-puromycin.[108] In the absence of tetracycline, twice as much aminoacyl-tRNA was bound, and only one-half of it (presumably that portion occupying the P site) was released as phenylalanyl-puromycin.

This use of one antibiotic to investigate the mechanism of action of another points up one important role that chemotherapeutic drugs have played outside the clinical field of infectious disease management. Many of these drugs are valuable investigative tools for the study of biological phenomena. Much of what we

Figure 4-5 The release by puromycin of phenylalanyl-tRNA bound to ribosomes with and without tetracycline. A. In the normal process of mRNA translation, the tRNA with the attached peptide occupies the P site (I). When puromycin is added, an aminoacyl-tRNA can still bind in the A site; puromycin, however, becomes linked by a peptide bridge to the carboxy terminal of the growing peptide (II), and this complex is released as peptidylpuromycin (III). (B) and (C). The experiment as carried out with tetracycline by Sarkar and Thach.[108] When phenyalanyl-tRNA is bound to ribosomes in the presence of tetracycline (B), tetracycline blocks binding to the A site, but binding to the P site is permitted. When the bound complex is exposed to puromycin, all the phenylalanine is released as phenylalanyl-puromycin. In the absence of tetracycline (C), phenylalanyl-tRNA can bind to both the A and P sites; therefore, twice as much is bound. Since puromycin can release only the phenylalanine occupying the P site, one-half of the bound puromycin is released as phenylalanyl-puromycin. P, puromycin; T, tetracycline; phe, phenylalanine; aa, amino acid.

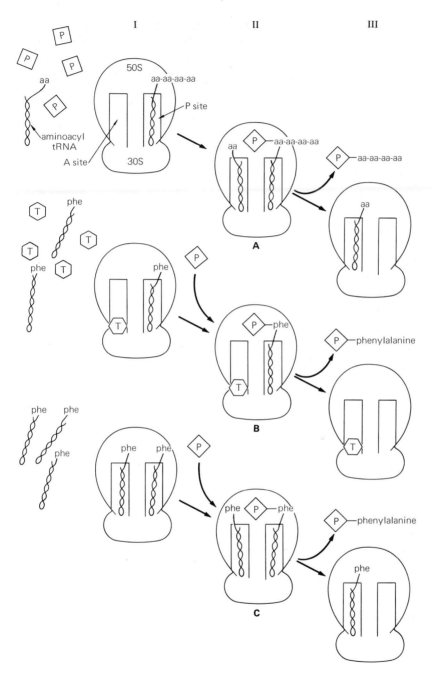

now know about intermediary metabolism, protein and nucleic acid synthesis, and the sequence of the cell cycle was determined by using drugs that specifically block particular biochemical events. The investigative use of these drugs is most productive when the mechanism of action of the drug is precisely defined. If they are employed when only scant data regarding their mechanism of action are available, interpretation of experimental results is impossible.

Basis for the Selective Toxicity of the Tetracyclines

Tetracyclines inhibit protein synthesis in cell-free systems from mammalian cells as well as from bacteria.[109] The selective toxicity of these antibiotics cannot be explained solely in terms of different drug sensitivities of the ribosomes from the two sources. An important component of their selective toxicity resides in their differential entry into bacterial cells. The tetracyclines are accumulated in both gram-negative and gram-positive bacteria by an energy-dependent process.[110,111] Mammalian cells (other than those involved in excretion of the drug) do not actively accumulate these antibiotics. Tetracyclines can extensively inhibit protein synthesis by mammalian cells in culture if their entry into the cell is facilitated by drugs, such as amphotericin B or polymyxin B, that alter membrane permeability.[112] Although an argument can be developed to explain some of the selective toxicity on the basis of differential entry, this explanation obviously does not apply to rickettsiae or the chlamydiae. These organisms grow intracellularly, and thus they must be more sensitive than the protein synthetic process of the host cells.

The predominant mechanism of tetracycline resistance in bacteria is by decreased uptake of the drug.[46] Usually, organisms become equally resistant to all of the tetracyclines, but in some resistant S. aureus strains, the organisms remain sensitive to minocycline. These tetracycline-resistant staphylococci take up less tetracycline than sensitive bacteria but both strains accumulate equivalent amounts of minocycline.[113]

Pharmacology of the Tetracyclines

Absorption and Distribution

The tetracyclines are absorbed from the stomach and the upper gastrointestinal tract. They form stable chelates with a number of metal ions, such as calcium, magnesium, iron and aluminum. The formation of an insoluble complex with any of these compounds decreases the absorption of the drug. Therefore, tetracyclines should never be administered with milk, which contains calcium, or with antacids, such as Maalox, which contains magnesium and aluminum hydroxide, or Amphojel, which is an aluminum hydroxide gel. Ferrous sulfate administered with a tetracycline markedly reduces the absorption of the antibiotic,[114] so even small doses of iron should be avoided during tetracycline therapy.

The tetracyclines are distributed in a space larger than the body water, and they readily penetrate most body cavities. Their concentration in the cerebrospinal fluid is much lower than in the blood, and penetration into the cerebrospinal fluid is not significantly affected by the presence of meningeal inflammation. The amount of drug bound to plasma protein varies from a low of 20 per cent with oxytetracyline to a high of 76 per cent with minocycline.[115,116]

There are some special aspects of the distribution of the tetracyclines that have suggested other uses for these antibiotics. The tetracyclines enter and are retained in certain neoplastic cells.[117] These compounds fluoresce when irradiated with ultraviolet light, and they can be readily visualized in histological preparations. The localization of tetracycline fluorescence in tumor cells recovered in gastric washings has been proposed as a cytological test for gastric carcinoma.[118] After administration of tetracyclines, the drug fluorescence can be observed in tumors of the oropharynx under ultraviolet illumination *in situ*.[119] Neither of these methods have proven to be clinically useful diagnostic aids because false negative results can occur. Tetracyclines are also retained in areas of the heart that have been damaged by ischemia.[120] The retention in the tissue may be related to the formation of a complex between the tetracycline and calcium released from the injured myocardial cells. The results of animal trials suggest that technetium-labeled tetracycline compounds may prove to be clinically useful in detecting and sizing myocardial infarctions by nuclear scanning techniques.[121] The tetracyclines are concentrated by the liver and secreted into the bile. They are also concentrated by the kidney during the process of excretion. Technetium-labeled tetracycline can be readily visualized by nuclear scanning as it is concentrated by these organs. This compound may prove to be clinically useful as a kidney and gallbladder imaging agent for diagnostic purposes.[122] These potential applications utilize several properties of the tetracyclines unrelated to their antibacterial effect, and they provide good examples of how new drugs can be developed by exploiting unique pharmacological properties of drugs in established use.

The concentration of the tetracyclines in the liver and kidneys is a transient phenomenon lasting only a few hours. The tetracyclines may be sequestered in bone for much longer periods of time. They are bound to newly forming bone but apparently not to bone that is already laid down.[123] Tetracycline is incorporated into calcifying tissue as a tetracycline-calcium orthophosphate complex. It is also incorporated into growing teeth and gives them a yellow or brownish color. If there is a deep yellow color it may be converted to brown, a process accelerated by exposure to light. The change in color is probably due to photooxidation products formed from tetracycline. The tetracyclines can cross the placenta, and their administration to pregnant women can discolor the deciduous teeth of the children they are carrying.[124] These drugs also appear in the milk of lactating patients. As would be expected, tetracycline taken by the mother during pregnancy does not affect the color of the child's permanent teeth.[125] Tetracycline deposited in the crown of the anterior teeth produces a cosmetically undesirable effect. Crown formation in these teeth is complete by 6 years in girls and 7 in boys.[126] Oxytetracycline binds calcium less readily than the other tetracyclines[127] and there is some suggestion that it is less likely to produce a noticeable discoloration.[126,128] In children under 12 years of age, the risk of discoloration of permanent teeth must be taken into account when the tetracyclines are being considered for therapy. Long-term therapy and repeat exposure should be avoided. The use of oxytetracycline (and possibly doxycycline) may further diminish the risk of dental staining.

Metabolism and Excretion

The tetracyclines are cleared from the plasma by the liver and excreted into the bile by an active transport mechanism.[129] The concentration of tetracyclines in the bile may be 20 to 30 times that in the serum. Much of the tetracycline released into the intestine in the bile is reabsorbed during passage through the rest of the gastrointestinal tract. Even if the drugs are given parenterally, they are found in high concentration in the bowel; this is an important observation, since enteritis can result from superinfection of the bowel after parenteral as well as oral therapy. The drug that is reabsorbed from the bowel in this enterohepatic cycle of events may again be cleared by the liver or excreted through the kidney by glomerular filtration. Some tetracyclines (minocycline, doxycycline) are excreted more slowly than others and have half-lives significantly longer than the 9 hours observed for tetracycline hydrochloride.

Untoward Effects of the Tetracyclines

The tetracyclines are irritative substances. Given intravenously, they can cause thrombophlebitis. Given orally, they cause epigastric burning, abdominal discomfort, nausea, and vomiting. If the irritation is severe, symptoms can sometimes be controlled, at the risk of some impairment of absorption, by having the patient take tetracyclines immediately after meals.

The tetracyclines can cause a hepatotoxicity, especially in patients with compromised renal function.[130] Pregnant women with renal disease are especially vulnerable.[131] The tetracyclines are eliminated to varying extents by the kidneys, and most of these drugs should not be administered to patients with compromised renal function. Doxycycline and minocycline depend less on the renal route of excretion than the others. If a tetracycline must be administered to a patient with decreased renal function, doxycycline is the preferred form.[132] Especial caution should be taken with patients with hepatic dysfunction.

The tetracyclines are potentially nephrotoxic. If possible, they should not be administered with other nephrotoxic drugs. A case in point is described, with the development of renal failure following the administration of methoxyfluorane anesthesia to patients receiving such nephrotoxic agents as tetracyclines or aminoglycosides.[133] Methoxyfluorane produces a dose-related nephrotoxicity that seems to be additive to that of these antibiotics. This example is presented to reenforce the general guideline that the physician should try to avoid, when possible, the use of more than one drug with a potential toxicity for a specific organ system. Another general point worth reenforcing here is that one should make it a habit to check the expiration date on any bottle of antibiotic before handing it to the patient. Both nephropathy[134] and the Fanconi syndrome[135] have been reported after ingestion of outdated tetracyclines.

As described in the previous section on drug distribution, the tetracyclines can stain the teeth if the fetus is exposed to the drug after the fourth month of gestation or if the drug is given to children under the age of twelve. This effect is clearly dose-related.

All the tetracyclines can cause a phototoxicity manifested by abnormal sunburn reactions or paresthesias (tingling sensations) in exposed parts.[136] These reactions are rapidly reversible. The mechanism is not defined. As mentioned above, the tetracyclines fluoresce when exposed to light in the ultraviolet range. The sunburn reaction is also precipitated by that component of light falling in the ultraviolet spectrum (260 to 320 nm). It is possible that ultraviolet irradiation promotes the formation of photodecomposition products that are responsible for the sunburn effect, but other explanations could also obtain. Demeclocycline and doxycycline cause these reactions more frequently than the other tetracyclines.[136,137]

When given in antibacterial doses over long periods of time, the tetracyclines can increase urinary nitrogen loss. In some cases, this loss may be substantial enough to result in an overall negative nitrogen balance.[138] It has been postulated that this is secondary to an antianabolic effect of inhibition of protein synthesis in the host, but there is no proof that this is the case. Tetracyclines sometimes cause the blood urea nitrogen (BUN) to become elevated. There may be several reasons for this including both prerenal and renal effects. Elevated BUN values are more frequently seen with patients who are also receiving diuretics.[139] This is probably not the result of a drug interaction but represents a nephrotoxic effect of the tetracyclines in patients with already compromised renal function.

Tetracyclines rarely elevate intracranial pressure in infants.[140] The mechanism of the effect is unknown, and withdrawal of the drug reverses it. Minocycline can produce vertigo, sometimes with weakness, nausea, and vomiting,[141] and some studies suggest that the incidence of these signs and symptoms may be very high.[142] The effect is reversible and the mechanism is unknown. Although the symptoms are exaggerated when the patient assumes the erect posture, this is not due to orthostatic hypotension.

The tetracyclines are bacteriostatic at therapeutic doses and thus require the bactericidal action of the host-defense mechanisms to eradicate the organism. It would be counterproductive if they affected the patient in such a manner as to decrease his ability to respond to the infection. Tetracyclines have been reported to inhibit chemotaxis and phagocytosis by human leukocytes[143,144] and to decrease the bactericidal effect of human serum.[145] This interference with the host response may not be significant in the patient with normal immunological defense mechanisms, but it might contribute to failure of therapy in the patient with borderline function.

Superinfection

The concept of superinfection has been presented in Chapter 1. Superinfection can occur with antibiotics that have a much narrower spectrum of action than the tetracyclines, but the frequency of this side effect is certainly higher with these broad-spectrum agents. Probably the most common superinfections outside of the gastrointestinal tract are caused by *Candida albicans*. When the normal flora are altered by antibiotic treatment, this organism can grow in the oropharynx, vagina, and perirectal area, causing itching and discomfort. Another common type of superinfection is due to overgrowth of the bowel with pathogenic bacteria. Diarrhea caused by the direct irritative effects of the tetracyclines on the bowel mucosa is relatively common and often difficult to distinguish from the less common diarrhea caused by superinfection with tetracycline-resistant bacteria or with *Candida*. In most cases, the symptomatology will reverse when tetracycline therapy is discontinued.

Certainly one of the least common but also one of the most dangerous types of superinfection is due to the growth of S. aureus in the gastrointestinal tract. Staphylococcal enterocolitis is a life-threatening condition, characterized by severe diarrhea, fever, and leukocytosis. It can be differentiated from the milder diarrhea that results from the irritative effect of the drug on the mucosa of the colon by the presence of large numbers of gram-positive cocci and leukocytes in the stool. When staphylococcal enteritis appears, tetracycline therapy must be stopped, vigorous fluid and electrolyte management begun, and oral treatment with vancomycin initiated immediately.

Superinfection with *Candida albicans* occurs in the oropharynx, vagina, and bowel; it can even occur as a systemic infection. Some tetracycline preparations contain both a tetracycline and nystatin, an antifungal agent included to suppress superinfection of the bowel with *Candida*. This does not constitute rational prophylactic use of an antibiotic. The use of these two drugs in a fixed-ratio combination has not been demonstrated to reduce the incidence of intestinal superinfection with *Candida*. As stated in a drug efficacy study conducted by the National Academy of Sciences, "It is preferable . . . to prescribe antifungal drugs when clinically indicated, rather than to use them indiscriminately as 'prophylaxis' against an uncommon clinical entity seen during therapy with tetracyclines and other antibiotics."[146] There are other negative features in these fixed-ratio combinations. The dose and route of administration of the second drug, nystatin, cannot be altered according to the severity and site of the fungal infection. Nystatin is not absorbed from the gastrointestinal tract and is useless against vaginal candidiasis, for example, when administered orally. Some physicians are simply not aware of this. Upon careful review of the patient, the physician often will find that the tetracycline therapy can be simply discontinued when superinfection intervenes. When this is not possible, then nystatin or another antifungal agent should be given in the appropriate form by the appropriate route. The use of this fixed-ratio drug combination represents a violation of several fundamental precepts of rational chemotherapy.

Tetracycline Preparations

The tetracycline preparations vary according to extent of plasma binding, rate of absorption, and rate of excretion. These differences dictate different dosages and schedules of administration. Variations in the extent of plasma binding, for example, determine differences in level of free drug obtained with a particular dose, but this has been taken into account in the therapeutic dosages recommended for each compound. Aside from these minor variations, the different tetracycline preparations do not vary significantly in clinical effectiveness. The antibacterial spectrum for all the tetracyclines is nearly the same. When resistance arises to one member of the group, it generally includes all the drugs. The drugs are usually given orally, but in severe infection they are given intravenously. They should never be given intrathecally.

One can legitimately ask what criteria, other than price, should affect one's choice of a tetracycline. The frequency of administration may be one consideration. The half-lives of tetracycline hydrochloride, chlortetracycline, and oxytetracycline are short enough to require oral administration every six hours, demeclocycline and methacycline can be given either twice or four times daily, and the half-lives of doxycycline and minocycline are long enough so that they are routinely given every 12 hours. In some cases, a special toxicity, such as minocycline-induced vertigo or the higher incidence of sunburn reaction with demeclocycline may, influence the choice. The site of infection may occasionally be important. For example, in the case in which a tetracycline is to be used in the treatment of a urinary tract infection, doxycycline would be inappropriate because it is not excreted in the urine in high concentration. Yet the lack of dependence on the renal route of excretion makes doxycycline the tetracycline of choice if one of these drugs must be given to a patient with compromised renal function. In general, the best recommendation to the physician is probably to pick one of the group, like tetracycline hydrochloride, and learn to use it well.

Although the clinical effectiveness of the various tetracyclines at recommended doses and at recommended frequencies of administration is roughly the same, there are nevertheless many generic and brand name preparations to choose from. A partial list of the preparations available is presented in Table 4-7. Tetracycline hydrochloride itself is available under a number of different trade names. This proliferation of different trade names for the same product injects a great deal of confusion into a physician's education. The tetracyclines are by no means a unique example, but they serve to point up the problems involved in the dual drug-naming system existing today. The immediate problem for the

Table 4-7 **Generic and brand names of some tetracycline preparations available in the United States**

Generic name	Brand name	Manufacturer
Tetracycline hydrochloride	Achromycin	Lederle
	Panmycin	Upjohn
	Tetracyn	Roerig
	Tetrachel	Rachelle
	Rexamycin	Rexall
	Kesso-Tetra	McKesson
Oxytetracycline	Terramycin	Pfizer
Chlortetracycline	Aureomycin	Lederle
Demeclocycline	Declomycin	Lederle
Methacycline	Rondomycin	Pfizer
Doxycycline	Vibramycin	Pfizer
Minocycline	Minocin	Lederle
	Vectrin	Parke Davis

medical student is that he first learns the generic name of the drug in the basic course in pharmacology. When he enters the clinical years, he is forced to completely overhaul his drug vocabulary in order to understand the clinician who, instead of referring to tetracycline hydrochloride, will talk about Achromycin, Panmycin, Tetrachel, or Tetracyn. All of these are brand names for the same compound, produced by different companies, and they indicate no clinically useful differences between the preparations.

The second problem resulting from this proliferation of names is that the practicing physician's awareness of new drug information can be considerably blunted. When a physician is informed of the advantages or disadvantages of a drug called by its brand name, he may not associate this information with other products that are identical. Chloramphenicol, for instance, is sold in the United States by several different companies under names like Chloromycetin, Amphicol, and Mychel, and it is sold abroad under numerous different brand names. This can of course make international communication between physicians difficult at times. It is clear that our redundant drug nomenclature system is not in the best interest of the physician or the patient. An example of one error mentioned in a German medical journal is that of a doctor who was treating a bronchitis patient with Paraxin, and when the patient remained febrile, he stopped Paraxin and initiated treatment with Leukomycin.[147] Paraxin and Leukomycin are both brand names for chloramphenicol.

Therapeutic Indications

The tetracyclines have a very broad spectrum of action. They inhibit the growth of many bacteria, actinomycetes, rickettsiae, mycoplasma, and agents of the psittacosis-lymphogranuloma venerum-trachoma group. The true viruses are not susceptible to the tetracyclines. Some protozoa are sensitive, and these drugs are occasionally used to treat infections due to *Entamoeba histolytica* and *Plasmodium falciparum* (see Chapters 10 and 11).

Tetracyclines used to be employed much more frequently in the treatment of infections due to gram-positive and gram-negative bacteria than they are today. Due to the development of drug resistance and the introduction of more specific bactericidal drugs, the tetracyclines are now largely employed as alternative agents in the treatment of the common bacterial infections. Bacteria in the community at large have remained more sensitive to the tetracyclines than those acquired in the hospital environment where there is more intensive antibiotic use.[148] The tetracyclines are very useful alternatives to the more toxic antibiotics and to the penicillins (in penicillin-allergic individuals) in the oral treatment of mild infections in outpatients [e.g., acute bronchitis, uncomplicated gonococcal infection (Table 4-4)]. A list of infections in which a tetracycline may be useful in therapy is presented in Table 2-4. There are very few specific bacterial infections for which a tetracycline may be considered a drug of first choice. These infections are rather uncommon and they include *Pseudomonas mallei* (glanders—a tetracycline with streptomycin), *Pseudomonas pseudomallei* (melioidosis—a tetracycline with or without chloramphenicol), *Brucella* (a tetracycline—with or without streptomycin), *Calymmatobacterium granulomatis* (granuloma inguinale), *Vibrio cholerae* (cholera), and *Borrelia recurrentis* (relapsing fever).

There are several diseases caused by rickettsia and chlamydiae in which tetracyclines are drugs of choice. These infections and the antibiotics employed in therapy are presented in Table 4-8. Either tetracycline or erythromycin is considered appropriate treatment of pneumonia due to *Mycoplasma pneumoniae*.

Table 4-8 **Some infections caused by filterable agents and rickettsiae in which tetracyclines are the appropriate drugs of first choice**

Organism	Disease	Alternatives to tetracycline therapy
Rickettsia	Rocky Mountain spotted fever, rickettsial pox, endemic typhus, scrub typhus, Q fever	Chloramphenicol
Mycoplasma	Primary atypical pneumonia— *Mycoplasma pneumoniae* (Eaton's agent)	Erythromycin
Chlamydia	Psittacosis—ornithosis	Chloramphenicol
	Trachoma (topical tetracycline)	Erythromycin (oral), chloramphenicol (topical), or a sulfonamide (oral)
	Lymphogranuloma venerum	Chloramphenicol or a sulfonamide
	Inclusion conjunctivitis (topical or oral tetracycline)	Chloramphenicol (topical)

Use of Tetracyclines in Acne

Tetracycline is given orally in low doses for the treatment of chronic severe acne vulgaris. The antibiotic is given on a long-term basis, and there are appropriate studies supporting the clinical effectiveness of this form of therapy.[149,150] The use of a broad-spectrum antibiotic in long-term therapy for a relatively minor clinical indication, like acne, requires special comment. With the usual therapeutic dosage, this form of therapy would be accompanied by an inappropriate risk of adverse drug effects. Although therapy of acne may be initiated with normal dosage, the low amount of antibiotic required to maintain the beneficial response (250 mg/day) has proven to be quite safe.[151] Occasionally, the development of Candida superinfection of the vagina and, rarely, the occurence of gram-negative folliculitis have required cessation of therapy.[152]

It is not completely clear why low dose tetracycline therapy works in the treatment of acne. Acne is an inflammatory lesion of the pilosebaceous follicle. The onset occurs when there is a marked increase in the activity of the sebaceous glands in response to androgenic hormones. The only bacteria regularly recoverable from acne lesions are Corynebacterium acnes and Staphylococcus epidermidis; both are normal resident skin bacteria.[153] These organisms may be important in producing the irritative stimulus. It has been shown that free fatty acids present in sebum are highly irritating to the skin.[154] Corynebacterium acnes synthesizes a lipase that splits triglycerides into the irritating free fatty acids.[155] Acne lesions contain bacteria, but it is not correct to consider the disease process an infection per se. It is easy to presume that tetracyclines affect the process by inhibiting the growth of C. acnes, thus reducing the production of the irritant free fatty acids. It is clear that this organism is often sensitive to tetracycline, and some investigators have found a decrease in the number of skin bacteria with antibiotic treatment.[156] The results of several studies suggest that other antibiotics, such as erythromycin, trimethoprim-sulfamethoxazole, and clindamycin (although the toxicity of this last drug makes it inappropriate for use in acne), are also effective and this strongly supports an antibacterial mechanism of action. Although some investigators have demonstrated changes in skin flora with tetracycline therapy, in one study tetracycline was found to significantly reduce the amount of free fatty acid in the skin without affecting the number of skin bacteria.[150] It has been shown that tetracycline is a rather potent inhibitor of the purified lipase enzyme from *C. acnes,* and such an inhibition could prove to be beneficial in addition to an antibacterial effect.[157] The response of acne to low dose therapy with tetracycline may represent a combination of a primary antibacterial effect and the fortuitous effect of the drug in inhibiting bacterial lipase.

In summary, the use of antibiotics in trivial acne is not justified, but most dermatologists would accept that long-term, low dose tetracycline therapy is appropriate in chronic severe acne.[149] The problem of unwanted side effects has been minimal because of the low doses employed. Demeclocycline should not be used because of photosensitivity. Erythromycin is apparently effective also. The primary mechanism of the beneficial effect is probably due to an antibacterial action on *C. acnes.*

REFERENCES

1. S. Pestka: Inhibitors of ribosome functions. *Ann. Rev. Microbiol.* 25:487 (1971).

2. C. L. Wisseman, J. E. Smadel, F. E. Hahn, and H. E. Hopps: Mode of action of chloramphenicol. I. Action of chloramphenicol on assimilation of ammonia and on synthesis of proteins and nucleic acids in *Escherichia coli. J. Bacteriol.* 67:662 (1954).

3. D. Vazquez: Uptake and binding of chloramphenicol by sensitive and resistant organisms. *Nature* 203:257 (1964).

4. H. K. Das, A. Goldstein, and L. C. Kanner: Inhibition by chloramphenicol of the growth of nascent protein chains in *Escherichia coli. Mol. Pharmacol.* 2:158 (1966).

5. A. G. So and E. W. Davie: The incorporation of amino acids into protein in a cell-free system from yeast. *Biochemistry* 2:132 (1963).

6. S. Perlman and S. Penman: Protein-synthesizing structures associated with mitochondria. *Nature* 227:133 (1970).

7. D. B. Roodyn and D. Wilkie, *The Biogenesis of Mitochondria,* London: Methuen and Co. Ltd., 1968. An extensive discussion of the possible evolutionary origin of mitochondria and a review of the effects of chloramphenicol on mitochondrial protein synthesis.

8. D. Vazquez: The binding of chloramphenicol by ribosmes from *Bacillus megaterium. Biochem. Biophys. Res. Commun.* 15:464 (1964).

9. K. H. Nierhaus and F. Dohme: Total reconstitution of functionally active 50S ribosomal subunits from *Escherichia coli. Proc. Natl. Acad. Sci. U.S.* 71:4713 (1974).

10. D. Nierhaus and K. H. Nierhaus: Identification of the chloramphenicol-binding protein in *Escherichia coli* ribosomes by partial reconstitution. *Proc. Natl. Acad. Sci. U.S.* 70:2224 (1973).

11. O. Pongs, R. Bald, and V. A. Erdman: Identification of chloram-

phenicol binding protein in *Escherichia coli* ribosomes by affinity labeling. *Proc. Natl. Acad. Sci. U.S.* 70:2229 (1973).

12. D. Vazquez: Binding of chloramphenicol to ribosomes; the effect of a number of antibiotics. *Biochim. Biophys. Acta* 114:277 (1966).

13. N. L. Oleinick, J. M. Wilhelm, and J. W. Corcoran: Nonidentity of the site of action of erythromycin A and chloramphenicol on *Bacillus subtilis* ribosomes. *Biochim. Biophys. Acta* 155:290 (1968).

14. M. Cannon, R. Krug, and W. Gilbert: The binding of sRNA by *Escherichia coli* ribosomes. *J. Mol. Biol.* 7:360 (1963).

15. C. Gurgo, D. Aprion, and D. Schlessinger: Polyribosome metabolism in *Escherichia coli* treated with chloramphenicol, neomycin, spectinomycin or tetracycline. *J. Mol. Biol.* 45:205 (1969).

16. S. Pestka: Studies on transfer ribonucleic acid-ribosome complexes: Effect of antibiotics on peptidyl puromycin synthesis on polysomes from *Escherichia coli*. *J. Biol. Chem.* 247:4669 (1972).

17. S. Pestka: Studies on the formation of transfer ribonucleic acid-ribosome complexes. XI. Antibiotic effects on phenylalanyloligonucleotide binding to ribosomes. *Proc. Natl. Acad. Sci. U.S.* 64:709 (1969).

18. J. L. Lessard and S. Pestka: Studies on the formation of transfer ribonucleic acid-ribosome complexes: Chloramphenicol, aminoacyl-oligonucleotides, and *Escherichia coli* ribosomes. *J. Biol. Chem.* 247:6909 (1972).

19. S. Pestka, T. Hishizawa, and J. L. Lessard: Studies on the formation of transfer ribonucleic acid-ribosome complexes: Aminoacyl oligonucleotide binding to ribosomes: Characteristics and requirements. *J. Biol. Chem.* 245:6208 (1970).

20. J. L. Lessard and S. Pestka: Studies on the formation of transfer ribonucleic acid-ribosome complexes: Binding of aminoacyl-oligonucleotides to ribosomes. *J. Biol. Chem.* 247:6901 (1972).

21. L. H. Taber, M. D. Yow, and F. G. Nieberg: The penetration of broad-spectrum antibiotics in to the cerebrospinal fluid. *Ann. N.Y. Acad. Sci.* 145:473 (1967).

22. G. Stramentinoli, A. Gazzaniga, and D. Della Bella: Increase of chloramphenicol glucuronidation in rats treated with phenobarbital. *Biochem. Pharmacol.* 23:1181 (1974).

23. A. A. Lindberg, L. H. Nilsson, H. Bucht, and L. O. Kallings: Concentration of chloramphenicol in the urine and blood in relation to renal function. *Br. Med. J.* 2:724 (1966).

24. L. G. Suhrland and A. S. Weisberger: Chloramphenicol toxicity in liver and renal disease. *Arch. Int. Med.* 112:747 (1963).

25. C. F. Weiss, A. J. Glazko, and J. K. Weston: Chloramphenicol in the newborn infant; a physiologic explanation of its toxicity when given in excessive doses. *New Eng. J. Med.* 262:787 (1960).

26. A. W. Craft, J. T. Brocklebank, E. N. Hey, and R. H. Jackson: The "grey toddler:" Chloramphenicol toxicity. *Arch. Dis. Child.* 49:235 (1974).

27. A. S. Weisberger and T. M. Daniel: Suppression of antibody synthesis by chloramphenicol analogs. *Proc. Soc. Exp. Biol. Med.* 131:570 (1969).

28. D. Della Bella, D. Petrescu, G. Marca, and M. Veronese: Humoral antibody, plaque, and rosette formation in mice treated with chloramphenicol. *Chemotherapy* 18:99 (1973).

29. D. F. Liberman and J. L. Roti Roti: Effect of chloramphenicol on the growth and viability of exponentially growing mouse leukemic cells (L5178Y). *Exp. Cell Res.* 77:346 (1973).

30. A. A. Yunis and G. R. Bloomberg: Chloramphenicol toxicity, clinical features and pathogenesis. *Progress in Hematology* 4:138 (1964).

31. J. L. Scott, S. M. Finegold, G. A. Belkin, and J. S. Lawrence: A controlled double-blind study of the hematologic toxicity of chloramphenicol. *New Eng. J. Med.* 272:1137 (1965).

32. O. J. Martelo, D. R. Manyan, U. S. Smith, and A. A. Yunis: Chloramphenicol and bone marrow mitochondria. *J. Lab. Clin. Med.* 74:927 (1969).

33. N. G. Ibrahim, J. P. Burke, and D. Beattie: The sensitivity of rat liver and yeast mitochondrial ribosomes to inhibitors of protein synthesis. *J. Biol. Chem.* 249:6806 (1974).

34. A. A. Yunis, U. S. Smith, and A. Restrepo: Reversible bone marrow supression from chloramphenicol: A consequence of mitochondrial injury. *Arch. Int. Med.* 126:272 (1970).

35. J. Ratzan, M. A. S. Moore, and A. A. Yunis: Effect of chloramphenicol and thiamphenicol on the *in vitro* colony-forming cell. *Blood* 43:363 (1974).

36. R. O. Wallerstein, P. K. Condit, C. K. Kasper, J. W. Brown, and F. R. Morrison: Statewide study of chloramphenicol therapy and fatal aplastic anemia. *J. Am. Med. Assoc.* 208:2045 (1969).

37. A. A. Yunis: Drug-induced bone marrow injury. *Adv. Int. Med.* 15:357 (1969).

38. T. Nagao and A. M. Mauer: Concordance for drug-induced aplastic anemia in identical twins. *New Eng. J. Med.* 281:7 (1969).

39. D. R. Manyan, G. K. Arimura, and A. A. Yunis: Comparative metabolic effects of chloramphenicol analogues. *Mol Pharmacol.* 11:520 (1975).

40. C. Keiser and U. Buchegger: Hematological side effects of chloramphenicol and thiamphenicol. *Helv. Med. Acta* 37:265 (1973).

41. G. Overturf, K. I. Marton, and A. W. Mathies: Chloramphenicol resistance among clinical isolates of *Salmonella typhosa* in Los Angeles, 1972—Epidemiologic and bacteriologic characteristics. *New Eng. J. Med.* 289:463 (1973).

42. P. G. Shackelford, J. E. Bobinski, R. D. Feigin, and J. D. Cherry: Therapy of Haemophilus influenzae meningitis reconsidered. *New Eng. J. Med.* 287:634 (1972).

43. F. F. Barrett, L. H. Taber, C. R. Morris, W. B. Stephenson, D. J. Clark, and M. D. Yow: A 12 year review of the antibiotic management of *Haemophilus influenzae* meningitis. *Pediatrics* 81:370 (1972).

44. Committee on Infectious Diseases: Ampicillin-resistant strains of *Haemophilus influenzae* type B. *Pediatrics* 55:145 (1975).

45. Editorial: Initial treatment of meningitis in children. *Med. Letter* 17:15 (1975).

46. R. Benveniste and J. Davies: Mechanisms of antibiotic resistance in bacteria. *Ann. Rev. Biochem.* 42:471 (1973).

47. R. M. Lawrence, E. Goldstein, and P. Hoeprich: Typhoid fever caused by chloramphenicol-resistant organisms. *J. Am. Med. Assoc.* 224:861 (1973).

48. *Consumer Reports,* October 1970, p. 616.

49. W. R. Best: Chloramphenicol-associated blood dyscrasias. *J. Am. Med. Assoc.* 201:99 (1967). Copyright 1967, American Medical Association.

50. M. Dunne, A. Herxheimer, M. Newman, and H. Ridley: Indications and warnings about chloramphenicol. *Lancet* 2:781 (1973).

51. S. Aladjem: Chloramphenicol in South America. *New Eng. J. Med.* 281:1369 (1969).

52. H. A. Schreier and L. Berger: On medical imperialism (Letter). *Lancet* 1:1161 (1974).

53. D. R. Ryrie, J. Fletcher, M. J. S. Langman, and H. E. Daniels: Chloramphenicol over the counter (Letter). *Lancet* 1:150 (1973).

54. J. C. H. Mao and M. Putterman: The intermolecular complex of erythromycin and ribosome. *J. Mol. Biol.* 44:347 (1969).

55. J. C. H. Mao, M. Putterman, and R. G. Wiegand: Biochemical basis for the selective toxicity of erythromycin. *Biochem. Pharmacol.* 19:391 (1970).

56. N. G. Ibrahim and D. S. Beattie: Protein synthesis on ribosomes isolated from rat liver mitochondria: Sensitivity to erythromycin. *FEBS Letters* 36:102 (1973).

57. K. Tanaka, H. Teraoka. T. Nagira, and M. Tamaki: [^{14}C] Eryhromycin-ribosome complex formation and non-enzymatic binding of aminoacyl-transfer RNA to ribosome-messenger RNA complex. *Biochim. Biophys. Acta* 123:435 (1966).

58. H. Teraoka, K. Tanaka, and M. Tamaki: The comparative study on the effects of chloramphenicol, erythromycin and lincomycin on polylysine synthesis in an *Escherichia coli* cell-free system. *Biochim. Biophys. Acta* 174:776 (1969).

59. F. N. Chang and B. Weisblum: The specificity of lincomycin binding to ribosomes. *Biochemistry* 6:836 (1967).

60. E. Otaka, H. Teraoka, M. Tamaki, K. Tanaka, and S. Osawa: Ribosomes from erythromycin-resistant mutants of *Escherichia coli* Q13 *J. Mol. Biol.* 48:499 (1970).

61. R. Takata, S. Osawa, K. Tanaka, H. Teraoka, and M. Tamaki: Genetic studies of the ribosomal proteins in *Escherichia coli* V. Mapping of erythromycin resistance mutations which lead to alteration of a 50S ribosomal protein component. *Mol. Gen. Genetics.* 109:123 (1970).

62. K. Tanaka and M. Tamaki: Low affinity for chloramphenicol of erythromycin resistant *Escherichia coli* ribosomes having an altered protein component. *Biochem. Biophys. Res. Commun.* 46:1979 (1972).

63. P. F. Sparling and E. Blackman: Mutation to erythromycin dependence in *Escherichia coli* K-12 *J. Bacteriol.* 116:74 (1973).

64. E. Cundliffe and K. McQuillen: Bacterial protein synthesis: The effects of antibiotics. *J. Mol. Biol.* 30:137 (1967).

65. S. Tanaka, T. Otaka, and A. Kaji: Further studies on the mechanism of erythromycin action. *Biochim. Biophys. Acta* 331:128 (1973).

66. J. C. H. Mao and E. E. Robishaw: Erythromycin, a peptidyltransferase effector. *Biochemistry* 11:4864 (1972).

67. J. C. H. Mao and M. Putterman: Accumulation in gram-positive and gram-negative bacteria as a mechanism of resistance to erythromycin. *J. Bacteriol.* 95:1111 (1968).

68. B. Weisblum, C. Siddhikol, C. J. Lai, and V. Demohn: Erythromycin-inducible resistance in *Staphylococcus aureus*: Requirements for induction. *J. Bacteriol.* 106:835 (1971).

69. C. J. Lai and B. Weisblum: Altered methylation of ribosomal RNA in an erythromycin-resistant strain of *Staphylococcus aureus*. *Proc. Natl. Acad. Sci. U.S.* 68:856 (1971).

70. C. J. Lai, B. Weisblum, S. R. Fahnstock, and M. Nomura: Alteration of 23S ribosomal RNA and erythromycin-induced resistance to lincomycin and spiramycin in *Staphylococcus aureus*. *J. Mol. Biol.* 74:67 (1973).

71. R. M. Shapera, K. A. Hable, and J. M. Matsen: Erythromycin therapy twice daily for streptococcal pharyngitis: Controlled comparison with erythromycin or penicillin phenoxymethyl four times daily or penicillin G benzathine. *J. Am. Med. Assoc.* 226:531 (1973).

72. J. M. S. Dixon and A. E. Lipinski: Infections with β-hemolytic *Streptococcus* resistant to lincomycin and erythromycin and observations on zonal-pattern resistance to lincomycin. *J. Infect. Dis.* 130:351 (1974).

73. R. S. Griffith and H. R. Black: Comparison of blood levels following pediatric suspensions of erythromycin estolate and erythromycin ethyl succinate. *Clin. Med.* 76 (June):16 (1969).

74. A Philipson, L. D. Sabath, and D. Charles: Transplacental passage of erythromycin and clindamycin. *New Eng. J. Med.* 288:1219 (1973).

75. P. Braun: Hepatotoxicity of erythromycin. *J. Infect. Dis.* 119:300 (1969).

76. K. G. Talman, J. J. Sannella, and J. W. Freston: Chemical structure of erythromycin and hepatotoxicity. *Ann. Int. Med.* 81:58 (1974).

77. J. Kendler, S. Anuras, O. Laborda, and H. J. Zimmerman: Perfusion of the isolated rat liver with erythromycin estolate and other derivatives. *Proc. Soc. Exp. Biol. Med.* 139:1272 (1972).

78. C. A. Dujovne, D. Shoeman, J. Biachine, and L. Lasagna: Experimental bases for the different hepatotoxicity of erythromycin preparations in man. *J. Lab. Clin. Med.* 79:832 (1972).

79. H. J. Zimmerman, J. Kendler, S. Libber, and L. Lukacs: Hepatocyte suspensions as a model for demonstration of drug hepatotoxicity. *Biochem. Pharmacol.* 23:2187 (1974).

80. E. Cundliffe: Antibiotics and polyribosomes. II. Some effects of lincomycin, spiramycin, and streptogramin A *in vivo*. *Biochemistry* 8:2063 (1969).

81. R. F. McGehee, C. B. Smith, C. Wilcox, and M. Finland: Comparative studies of antibacterial activity *in vitro* and absorption and excretion of lincomycin and clindamycin. *Am. J. Med. Sci.* 256:279 (1968).

82. J. G. Bartlett, V. L. Sutter, and S. Finegold: Treatment of anaerobic

infections with lincomycin and clindamycin. *New Eng. J. Med.* 287:1007 (1972).

83. R. J. Fass, J. F. Scholand, G. R. Hodges, and S. Saslaw: Clindamycin in the treatment of serious anaerobic infections. *Ann. Int. Med.* 78:853 (1973).

84. R. J. Fass and S. Saslaw: Clindamycin: Clinical and laboratory evaluation of parenteral therapy. *Am. J. Med. Sci.* 263:369 (1972).

85. R. Brandl, C. Arkenau, C. Simon, V. Malerczyk, and G. Eidelloth: The pharmacokinetics of clindamycin in the presence of abnormal liver function. *Dsch. Med. Wochenschr.* 97:1057 (1972).

86. A. M. Joshi and R. M. Stein: Altered serum clearance of intravenously administered clindamycin phosphate in patients with uremia. *J. Clin. Pharmacol.* 14:140 (1974).

87. J. L. LeFrock, A. S. Klainer, S. Chen, R. B. Gainer, M. Omar, and W. Anderson: The spectrum of colitis associated with lincomycin and clindamycin therapy. *J. Infect. Dis.* 131 Suppl.:S108 (1975).

88. F. J. Tedesco, R. J. Stanley, and D. H. Alpers: Diagnostic features of clindamycin-associated pseudomembranous colitis. *New Eng. J. Med.* 290:841 (1974).

89. F. R. Fekety: Gastrointestinal complications of antibiotic therapy. *J. Am. Med. Assoc.* 203:210 (1968).

90. M. J. Harrod, M. S. Brown, A. G. Weinberg, W. N. Harkness, and J. L. Goldstein: Familial pseudomembranous colitis and its relation to lincomycin therapy. *Digestive Dis.* 20:808 (1975).

91. J. Davies, P. Anderson, and B. D. Davis: Inhibition of protein synthesis by spectinomycin. *Science* 149:1096 (1965).

92. P. Anderson, J. Davies, and B. D. Davis: Effect of spectinomycin on polypeptide synthesis in extracts of *Escherichia coli. J. Mol. Biol.* 29:203 (1967).

93. A. Bollen, J. Davies, M. Ozaki, and S. Mizushima: Ribosomal protein conferring snesitivity to the antibiotic spectinomycin in *Escherichia coli. Science* 165:85 (1969).

94. Center for Disease Control: Gonorrhea: Recommended treatment schedules. *Ann. Int. Med.* 82:230 (1975).

95. R. E. Kaufman, R. E. Johnson, H. W. Jaffe, C. Thornsberry, G. H. Reynolds, P. J. Wiesner, and The Cooperative Study Group: National gonorrhea therapy monitoring study: Treatment results. *New Eng. J. Med.* 294:1 (1976).

96. M. J. Maness, G. C. Foster, and P. F. Sparling: Ribosomal resistance to streptomycin and spectinomycin in *Neisseria gonorrhoeae. J. Bacteriol.* 120:1293 (1974).

97. A. I. Laskin: Tetracyclines in D. Gotlieb and P. D. Shaw (ed.), *Antibiotics,* Vol. 1, New York: Springer-Verlag, 1967, pp. 331–359.

98. E. F. Gale and J. P. Folkes: The assimilation of amino acids by bacteria. Actions of antibiotics on nucleic acid and protein synthesis in *Staphylococcus aureus. Biochem. J.* 53:493 (1953).

99. L. E. Day: Tetracycline inhibition of cell-free protein synthesis. II Effect of the binding of tetracycline to the components of the system. *J. Bacteriol.* 92:197 (1966).

100. R. H. Connamacher and H. G. Mandel: Binding of tetracycline to the 30 S ribosomes and to polyuridylic acid. *Biochem. Biophys. Res. Commun.* 20:98 (1965).

101. I. H. Maxwell: Studies of the binding of tetracycline to ribosomes *in vitro. Mol. Pharmacol.* 4:25 (1968).

102. G. R. Craven, R. Gavin, and T. Fanning: The transfer RNA binding site of the 30S ribosome and the site of tetracycline inhibition. *Symp. Quant. Biol.* 34:129 (1969).

103. I. Suzuka, H. Kaji, and A. Kaji: Binding of specific sRNA to 30S ribosomal subunits: effect of 50S ribosomal subunits. *Proc. Natl. Acad. Sci. U.S.* 55:1483 (1966).

104. M. E. Gottseman: Reaction of ribosome-bound peptidyl transfer ribonucleic acid with aminoacyl transfer ribonucleic acid or puromycin. *J. Biol. Chem.* 242:5564 (1967).

105. G. Suarez and D. Nathans: Inhibition of aminoacyl-tRNA binding to ribosomes by tetracycline. *Biochem. Biophys. Res. Commun.* 18:743 (1965).

106. M. Yarmolinsky and G. de la Haba: Inhibition by puromycin of amino acid incorporation into protein. *Proc. Natl. Acad. Sci. U.S.* 45:1721 (1959).

107. J. D. Smith, R. R. Traut, G. M. Blackburn, and R. E. Monroe: Action of puromycin in polyadenylic acid-directed polylysine synthesis. *J. Mol. Biol.* 13:617 (1965).

108. S. Sarkar and R. E. Thach: Inhibition of formylmethionyl-transfer RNA binding to ribosomes by tetracycline. *Proc. Natl. Acad. Sci. U.S.* 60:1479 (1968).

109. T. J. Franklin: The inhibition of incorporation of leucine into protein of cell-free systems from rat liver and *Escherichia coli* by chlortetracycline. *Biochem. J.* 87:449 (1963).

110. T. J. Franklin and B. Higginson: Active accumulation of tetracycline by *Escherichia coli. Biochem. J.* 116:287 (1970).

111. M. E. Dockter and J. A. Magnuson: Characterization of the active transport of chlortetracycline in *Staphylococcus aureus* by a florescence technique. *J. Supramol. Structure* 2:32 (1974).

112. G. Medoff, C. N. Kwan, D. Schlessinger, and G. S. Kobayashi: Potentiation of rifampicin, rifampicin analogs, and tetracycline against animal cells by amphotericin B and polymyxin B. *Cancer Res.* 33:1146 (1973).

113. N. A. Kuck and M. Forbes: Uptake of minocycline and tetracycline by tetracycline-susceptible and -resistant bacteria. *Antimicrob. Agents Chemother.* 3:662 (1973).

114. P. J. Neuvonen, G. Gothoni, R. Hackman, and K. Bjorksten: Interference of iron with the absorption of tetracyclines in man. *Brit. Med. J.* 4:532 (1970).

115. C. M. Kunin and M. Finland: Clinical pharmacology of the tetracycline antibiotics. *Clin. Pharm. Ther.* 2:51 (1961).

116. H. Macdonald, R. G. Kelley, S. Allen, J. F. Noble, and L. A. Kanegis: Pharmacokinetic studies on minocycline in man. *Clin. Pharm. Ther.* 14:852 (1973).

117. D. P. Rall, T. L. Loo, M. Lane, and M. G. Kelley: Appearance and persistence of fluorescent material in tumor tissue after tetracycline administration. *J. Nat. Canc. Inst.* 19:79 (1957).

118. J. Klinger and R. Katz: Tetracycline fluorescence in diagnosis of gastric carcinoma. Preliminary report. *Gastroenterology* 41:29 (1961).

119. R. J. Dunn and K. D. Devine: Tetracycline-induced fluorescence of laryngeal, pharyngeal, and oral cancer. *Laryngoscope* 82:189 (1972).

120. P. Malek, J. Kolc, V. L. Zastava, F. V. Zak, and B. Peleska: Fluorescence of tetracycline analogues fixed in myocardial infarction. *Cardiologia* 42:303 (1963).

121. L. Holman, M. Lesch, F. G. Zweiman, J. Temte, B. Lown, and R. Gorlin: Detection and sizing of acute myocardial infarcts with ^{99m}Tc (Sn) tetracycline. *New. Eng. J. Med.* 291:159 (1974).

122. C. R. Fliegel, M. K. Dewanjee, L. B. Holman, M. A. Davis, and S. Treves: ^{99m}Tc-Tetracycline as a kidney and gallbladder imaging agent. *Radiology* 110:407 (1974).

123. R. A. Milch, D. P. Rall, and J. E. Tobie: Bone localization of the tetracyclines. *J. Nat. Canc. Int.* 19:87 (1957).

124. A. C. Douglas: The deposition of tetracycline in human nails and teeth. A complication of long-term treatment. *Brit. J. Dis. Chest* 57:44 (1963).

125. J. R. Anthony: Effect on deciduous and permanent teeth of tetracycline deposition *in utero*. *Postgrad. Med.* 48:165 (1970).

126. E. R. Grossman, A. Walchek, and H. Freedman: Tetracyclines and permanent teeth: The relation between dose and tooth color. *Pediatrics* 47:567 (1971).

127. M. Schach von Wittenau: Some pharmacokinetic aspects of doxycline metabolism in man. *Chemotherapy* 13:41 (1968).

128. I. S. Wallman an H. B. Hilton: Teeth pigmented by tetracycline. *Lancet* 1:827 (1962).

129. R. C. Lanman, S. Muranishi, and L. S. Schankar: Hepatic uptake and biliary excretion of tetracycline in the rat. *Am. J. Physiol.* 225:1240 (1973).

130. J. D. Loyd-Still, R. J. Grand, and G. F. Vawter: Tetracycline hepatotoxicity in the differential diagnosis of postoperative jaundice. *J. Pediat.* 84:366 (1974).

131. P. J. Whalley, R. H. Adams, and B. Combes: Tetracycline toxicity in pregnancy. *J. Am. Med. Assoc.* 189:103 (1964).

132. W. M. Bennett, I. Singer, and C. H. Coggins: Guide to drug usage in adult patients with impaired renal function. *J. Am. Med. Assoc.* 233:991 (1973).

133. M. J. Cousins and R. I. Mazze: Tetracycline, methoxyflurane anaesthesia, and renal dysfunction. *Lancet* 1:751 (1972).

134. F. Mavromatis: Tetracycline nephropathy. *J. Am. Med. Assoc.* 193:91 (1965).

135. J. M. Gross: Fanconi syndrome (adult type) developing secondary to the ingestion of outdated tetracycline. *Ann. Int. Med.* 58:523 (1963).

136. P. Frost, G. D. Weinstein, and E. C. Gomez: Phototoxic potential of minocycline and doxycycline. *Arch. Derm.* 105:681 (1972).

137. P. Frost, G. D. Weinstein, and E. C. Gomez: Methacycline and

demeclocycline in relation to sunlight. *J. Am. Med. Assoc.* 216:326 (1971).

138. M. E. Shils: Some metabolic aspects of the tetracyclines. *Clin. Pharm. Ther.* 3:321 (1962).

139. Boston Collaborative Drug Surveillance Program: Tetracycline and drug-attributed rises in blood urea nitrogen. *J. Am. Med. Assoc.* 17:377 (1972).

140. K. Opfer: The bulging fontanelle. *Lancet* 1:116 (1963).

141. R. N. Brogden, T. M. Speight, and G. S. Avery: Minocycline: A review of its antibacterial and pharmacokinetic properties and therapeutic use. *Drugs* 9:251 (1975).

142. D. N. Williams, L. W. Laughlin, and Y-H. Lee: Minocycline: Possible vestibular side-effects. *Lancet* 2:744 (1974).

143. R. R. Martin, G. A. Warr, R. B. Couch, H. Yeager, and V. Knight: Effects of tetracycline on leukotaxis. *J. Infect. Dis.* 129:110 (1974).

144. A. Forsgren, D. Schmeling, and P. G. Quie: Effect of tetracycline on the phagocytic function of human leukocytes. *J. Infect. Dis.* 130:412 (1974).

145. A. Forsgren and H. Gnarpe: Tetracyclines and host-defense mechanisms. *Antimicrob. Agents Chemother.* 3:711 (1973).

146. Editorial: *Candida* infections. *Med. Letter* 12:29 (1970).

147. W. Stille: Nil nocere! Arztliche Fehler bei der Antibiotika-Therapie. *Münchner Med. Wochenschr.* 110:144 (1968).

148. M. Finland: Twenty-fifth anniversary of the discovery of aureomycin: The place of the tetracyclines in antimicrobial therapy. *Clin. Pharm. Ther.* 15:3 (1974).

149. Ad Hoc Committee on the Use of Antibiotics in Dermatology: Systemic antibiotics for treatment of acne vulgaris. *Arch. Dermatol.* 111:1630 (1975).

150. W. J. Cunliffe, R. A. Forster, N. D. Greenwood, C. Hetherington, K. T. Holland, R. L. Holmes, S. Khan, C. D. Roberts, M. Williams, and B. Williamson: Tetracycline and acne vulgaris: A clinical and laboratory investigation. *Br. Med. J.* 4:332 (1973).

151. T. J. Delaney, B. J. Leppard, and D. M. MacDonald: Effects of long term treatment with tetracycline. *Acta Dermatovener* (Stockholm) 54:487 (1974).

152. J. J. Leyden, R. R. Marples, O. H. Mills, and A. M. Kligman: Gram-negative folliculitis—a complication of antibiotic therapy in acne vulgaris. *Br. J. Dermatol.* 88:533 (1973).

153. E. W. Rosenberg: Bacteriology of acne. *Ann. Rev. Med.* 20:201 (1969).

154. A. M. Kligman, V. R. Wheatley, and O. H. Mills: Comedogenicity of human sebum. *Arch. Dermatol.* 102:267 (1970).

155. R. M. Reisner, D. Z. Silver, M. Puhvel, and T. H. Sternberg: Lipolytic activity of *Corynebacterium acnes*. *J. Invest. Derm.* 51:190 (1968).

156. R. M. Marples and A. M. Kligman: Ecological effects of oral antibiotics on the microflora of human skin. *Arch. Dermatol.* 103:148 (1971).

157. G. S. Hassing: Inhibition of *Corynebacterium acnes* lipase by tetracycline. *J. Invest. Derm.* 56:189 (1971).

Chapter 5
The Antimetabolites
The Sulfonamides
The Sulfones
Para-aminosalicylic Acid
Trimethoprim
(Trimethoprim-sulfamethoxazole)

Discovery and Structure of the Sulfonamides

Sulfonamide-containing compounds were synthesized early in this century by German chemists for use as dyes. Their therapeutic potential was not exploited until 1935, when Domagk demonstrated that one of these dyes, prontosil, was effective in treating mice infected with streptococci. Later it was found that prontosil is metabolized in the tissues to para-aminobenzenesulfonamide, the chemotherapeutically active part of the molecule. Subsequently, thousands of compounds were synthesized, and many were introduced for the treatment of infection.

The sulfonamides are structural analogs of para-aminobenzoic acid (PABA). They differ from each other according to various substitutions on the sulfonamide group. The most active of the many sulfonamide compounds synthesized are those with a pK_a of about 6.5.[1]

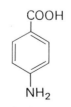

COOH

NH$_2$

para-Aminobenzoic acid

SO$_2$NHR

NH

Sulfonamides

MECHANISM OF ACTION

The Sulfonamides

The sulfonamides usually produce a bacteriostatic effect. When they are added to a culture of bacteria, there is a delay period of several cell replications before there is inhibition of growth (Figure 5-1). These drugs arrest cell growth by inhibiting the synthesis of folic acid by the bacterium. During the delay period, before cell growth is arrested, the bacterium is exhausting its stores of folic acid.

Folic acid is required for growth by both bacterial and mammalian cells. Because animal cells are unable to synthesize folate, this compound must be supplied in the diet. Folic acid is taken into mammalian cells by an active transport mechanism. Since it does not enter most bacterial cells, bacteria must therefore synthesize the compound intracellularly. This difference between the biochemistry of the bacterial and mammalian cell is the basis of the selective toxicity of the sulfonamides, para-aminosalicylic acid, and the sulfones.

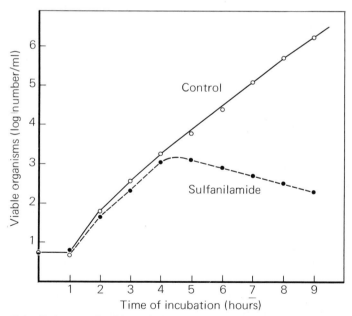

Figure 5-1 Early growth of hemolytic streptococci in blood broth without (o-o) and with (●--●) $10^{-5}M$ sulfanilamide. (From Woods.[2])

A reduced form of folic acid functions as a coenzyme, which transports one-carbon units from one molecule to another. Such one-carbon transfer reactions are essential for the synthesis of thymidine, all the purines, and several amino acids. Thymidine is necessary for DNA synthesis, and the purines are necessary for all nucleic acid synthesis in the cell. When folate synthesis is inhibited, cell growth is arrested due to the cell's inability to synthesize these essential macromolecular precursors.

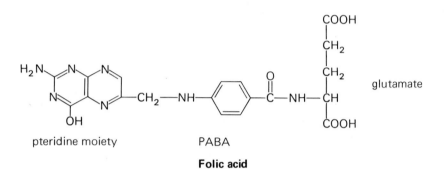

pteridine moiety   PABA

Folic acid

Folic acid consists of a pteridine unit, PABA, and glutamate. It was postulated some time ago that the sulfonamides, being structural analogs of PABA, might compete for the incorporation of this subunit into the folate molecule. Also, it was demonstrated that the effect of sulfonamides in bacteria capable of taking up folic acid could be reversed in a noncompetitive manner by adding to the culture such products of the inhibited reaction sequence as folic acid or leucovorin, a reduced and methylated form of folic acid. If the mechanism of growth inhibition by the sulfonamides is competition for PABA, then increasing the level of PABA in the culture medium should reverse the action of sulfonamide in a competitive manner. Figure 5-2 shows these effects in cultures of *Clostridium tetanomorphum*. Folic acid can enter these cells, and, in the presence of folic acid sufficient to maintain normal growth, the cell is not affected by any concentration of sulfonamide. In the presence of increasing concentrations of sulfanilamide, however, higher and higher concentrations of PABA are required to maintain growth.

The development of a cell-free system from bacteria that can form folate compounds from pteridines, PABA, and glutamic acid has permitted a more detailed analysis of the mechanism of

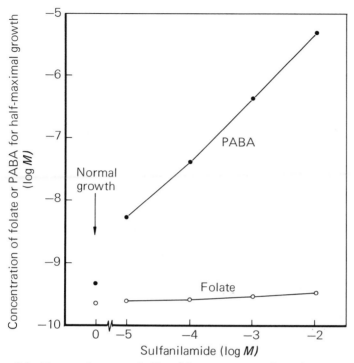

Figure 5-2 The requirement of *Clostridium tetanomorphum* for para-amino-benzoic acid or folic acid for growth in the presence of varying concentrations of sulfanilamide. Para-aminobenzoic acid (•-•); folic acid (o-o). (From Woods.[2])

sulfonamide action. Sulfonamides inhibit the incorporation of PABA into dihydropteroic acid in such a system, but inhibition is not solely competitive.[3] If sulfathiazole and PABA are added to the *in vitro* system simultaneously, then competition can be demonstrated. If the enzyme system is first preincubated with sulfathiazole, PABA cannot then completely reverse the inhibitory effect of the drug. The enzyme system in some bacteria incorporates a small amount of sulfonamide into a sulfonamide-containing analog of folic acid, and it is postulated that this product might itself be an inhibitor of the enzyme system. Therefore, the sulfonamides inhibit folic acid synthesis in two ways; the more important is competitive inhibition of PABA utilization. The enzyme that directs the incorporation of PABA and the pteridine moiety into dihydropteroic acid (dihydropteroate synthetase) has been purified 50-fold,[4] and definitive studies of the mechanism of sulfonamide action at the receptor level can now be carried out. Sulfadi-azine has been shown to inhibit the partially purified enzyme, and the kinetics of the inhibition are competitive.[5]

The inhibition of cell growth by sulfonamides may be reversed by adding the end products of one-carbon transfer reactions (thymidine, purines, methionine, and serine) to the growth medium. This reversal is of some clinical significance; in purulent infections the pus may contain a considerable amount of these substances as a result of cell breakdown. This may substantially decrease the efficacy of the sulfonamides in the treatment of these infections.[6] Also, the presence of PABA in the culture medium in which organisms are grown in the laboratory can lead to false conclusions regarding the drug sensitivity of clinical specimens. It is not uncommon to receive a report that a bacterium is resistant to sulfonamides when it is really quite sensitive and these drugs can be used in treatment.

Para-aminosalicylic Acid and the Sulfones

Para-aminosalicylic acid (PAS) and the sulfones are also struc-tural analogs of PABA, and their bacteriostatic action is antago-nized by PABA[7,8]; also PAS, like the sulfonamides, is joined to a pteroic acid moiety by the bacterial enzyme systems to produce PAS-containing folate analogs.[9] The sulfones, like the sulfon-amides, have been shown to be competitive inhibitors of partially purified dihydropteroate synthetase from *Escherichia coli*[5] and from the malarial parasite *Plasmodium berghei*[10].

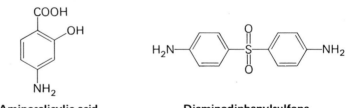

para-Aminosalicylic acid   Diaminodiphenylsulfone
                                                  (dapsone)

There is a great deal of difference between the spectrum of antibacterial action of PAS and that of the sulfonamides. Para-aminosalicylic acid is an effective drug in *Mycobacterium tuber-culosis*, but most organisms are not very sensitive to this compound. Sulfonamides are ineffective against M. tuberculosis, but they inhibit a number of organisms that are quite insensitive to PAS. There may be considerable variation in bacteria with regard to their relative permeability to these agents, but this cannot entirely explain the different sensitivities seen. Since both the sulfonamides and PAS inhibit growth by competing for PABA, it seems entirely possible that the enzyme responsible for incorporating PABA into the folate molecule may vary considerably from one type of bacterium to another. Thus, the PABA substrate site in M. tuberculosis may preferentially accept PAS over the sulfonamides. In other organisms, this same site may have another configuration, allowing good fit for PABA and the sulfonamides but not for PAS. This possibility is suggested by work carried out with mutant strains of pneumococci, which demonstrated varying degrees of resistance to the sulfonamides.[11] Cell-free extracts of the resistant cells, which incorporated PABA into folic acid, were found to require higher concentrations of sulfanilamide for inhibition of folate production than the wild type.[12] As shown in Table 5-1, the concentration of PAS required for inhibition of in vitro folate synthesis was higher in one resistant strain than the wild type; but in the other resistant strain, the enzyme was ten times more sensitive to PAS. Other experiments demonstrated that one of the altered enzymes (Fd) was heat sensitive and had an affinity for PABA that differed from that of the wild-type enzyme. A model system is available, therefore, which permits us to deduce that some of the great differences in sensitivity of different bacteria to growth inhibition by various members of three groups of drugs (the sulfonamides, PAS, and the sulfones) that act in a

Table 5-1 **Relative effect of sulfanilamide and PAS in inhibiting folic acid synthesis in cell-free extracts of pneumococci**
Cell-free extracts were prepared from two sulfanilamide-resistant strains of pneumococci and a wild type. The concentration of sulfanilamide or PAS required to reduce folic acid synthesis in each incubation to a fixed quantity was compared to that required for inhibition of the enzyme system from the wild type to the same level. (Data from Wolf and Hotchkiss.[12])

Strain	Sulfanilamide	PAS
Wild type	1	1
Fa	4	7.5
Fd	7	0.1

similar manner at the same receptor site may be explained by genetically determined variations in the structure of the receptor site.

The example of resistance we have just considered (altered dihydropteroate synthetase) is the result of a chromosomal mutation. Resistance to sulfonamides in clinical isolates, however, is usually mediated by R-factors. The biochemical mechanism of this extrachromosomal resistance is not known. There is some evidence that drug uptake may be reduced in the resistant organisms.[13] Apparently, drug metabolizing enzymes have not as yet been demonstrated.

Sulfonamides and "Thymineless Death"

The sulfonamides are generally regarded as bacteriostatic drugs, but under special growth conditions, they can be bactericidal. When bacteria are grown in medium containing amino acids and a source of purines, but no thymine, exposure to sulfonamide is bactericidal.[14] The killing effect is overcome by the addition of thymine. When the same organism is grown in the absence of amino acids, purines, and thymine, the sulfonamides are bacteriostatic. This poorly understood killing phenomenon is called "thymineless death," and it occurs when DNA synthesis is blocked (in this case because methylene tetrahydrofolate is required for the synthesis of thymidine monophosphate, which in turn is required for the synthesis of DNA) in the presence of continued protein synthesis. It is not merely of academic interest, since it has been shown that the sulfonamides can be bactericidal in human blood and urine as well as in synthetic media.[14,15] Thus, it is possible that these drugs are bactericidal in some body fluids containing little or no thymine. As mentioned earlier, sulfonamides are relatively ineffective in purulent wounds where liberation of thymine as a product of tissue breakdown may overcome any possible bactericidal effect. Obviously, if enough products of the blocked reactions are present, the drug will be ineffective.

PHARMACOLOGY AND UNDESIRABLE EFFECTS OF THE SULFONAMIDES

Absorption, Distribution, and Metabolism

The sulfonamides are absorbed well from the gastrointestinal tract, and they are routinely given orally. They readily pass into body fluids, including the pleural, synovial, and ocular fluids. They are one of the few groups of antibiotics that readily penetrate into the cerebrospinal fluid even in the absence of meningeal inflammation. This would seem, at first, to be of great benefit, but so many bacteria are resistant to the sulfonamides that they have rather limited usefulness in the treatment of central nervous system infections.

The sulfonamides bind to various extents to plasma protein,[16] occupying binding sites in common with those of bilirubin.[17] Thus, in the presence of sulfonamides, less bilirubin is bound and more of this compound circulates in the free form. In the newborn infant, free bilirubin can pass the blood-brain barrier and become deposited in the basal ganglia and subthalamic nuclei of the brain causing a toxic encephalopathy called kernicterus. Therefore, another drug should be used for treating the newborn infant. Since sulfonamides pass through the placenta and are excreted in the milk, they should not be administered during pregnancy approaching term or during nursing. The sulfonamides are metabolized to various degrees—primarily by acetylation and glucuronidation.

Excretion

Excretion of the sulfonamides is primarily renal. The sulfonamides are filtered and exhibit varying degrees of tubular reabsorption. In acid urine, some sulfonamides are quite insoluble and will precipitate out in crystalline aggregates. These crystal deposits in the kidney and ureters can produce symptoms of urinary tract obstruction. This used to be a fairly frequent complication, but it is unusual with modern therapy. The problem of sulfonamide insolubility has been approached in three ways:

1. Ensuring good urine output by a high daily fluid intake minimizes the problem. The sulfonamides are more soluble in an alkaline urine (see Table 5-2), so bicarbonate or lactate can be administered if the urine pH is very low.
2. Sulfonamide analogs with higher urine solubility have been synthesized to overcome this problem. Sulfisoxazole (gantrisin) is such a compound.
3. Moderate doses of three different sulfonamides are administered simultaneously. The presence of one sulfonamide does not decrease the solubility of another in the same aqueous solution. Thus, triple sulfonamides produce a higher total sulfonamide concentration than a single sulfonamide with-

Table 5-2 **Solubility of sulfonamides in acidic and alkaline urine**
(Data from Weinstein.[18])

Drug	Urine pH	Urine solubility at 37 °C (mg/100ml)
Sulfadiazine	5.5	18
	7.5	200
Sulfamerazine	5.5	35
	7.5	160
Sulfisoxazole	5.5	150
	7.5	14,500

out causing crystalluria. The triple sulfonamide combination, called trisulfapyrimidines, consists of sulfadiazine, sulfamerazine, and sulfamethazine (all short-acting drugs). Patients receiving trisulfapyrimidines for long periods of time should have their urine examined occasionally for the presence of sulfonamide crystals.

Undesirable Effects

Hypersensitivity reactions, particularly rashes, eosinophilia, and drug fever, occur in about 3 percent of patients receiving sulfisoxazole and sulfamethoxazole, two commonly used sulfonamides.[19] The incidence of untoward effects with these two drugs is compared with that of nitrofurantoin, a urinary tract antiseptic, in Table 7-1. Occasional photosensitivity reactions are seen. One hypersensitivity reaction that occurs rarely in therapy (with the penicillins, tetracyclines, or sulfonamides) is the Stevens-Johnson syndrome. This phenomenon can apparently also be initiated by a wide variety of antigenic substances other than drugs. It is characterized by fever, malaise, a severe erythema multiforme rash, and the formation of vesicles in the mucous membranes (mouth, conjunctivae, genitalia), which can erode and become hemorrhagic. The incidence of the Stevens-Johnson syndrome was thought to be especially high with the long-acting sulfonamides, which have been withdrawn from the market in the United States; but, it can occur with the short-acting drugs in current use.[20] Although the reaction occurs only rarely, it is important to identify it early, since it can be fatal.

Sulfonamides rarely cause hepatic necrosis. This also appears to be a hypersensitivity reaction.[21] Other rare allergic reactions include vasculitis, agranulocytosis, and thrombocytopenia. The crystalluria and kernicterus mentioned earlier in this section are toxic phenomena. There is a drug idiosyncrasy also associated with sulfonamide use. These drugs are among the large group of compounds that can cause hemolytic anemia in patients with a genetically determined deficiency of glucose-6-phosphate dehydrogenase activity in red blood cells. The mechanism of this effect is discussed in Chapter 10.

Three classes of drugs were developed by exploiting the side effects of the sulfonamides. It was observed that patients given sulfanilamide tended to develop metabolic acidosis with an alkaline urine. The finding that this was caused by the inhibition of carbonic anhydrase by sulfanilamide led to the development of acetazolamide and other diuretics of the carbonic anhydrase-inhibitor class. The observation that sulfonamide treatment caused hypoglycemia in some patients led to the development of the sulfonylurea group of oral antidiabetic agents. Finally, the observation that rats treated with sulfaguanidine developed goiters led to the development of the thiouracil group of antithyroid drugs. The interesting story of these developments is related in detail by Goldstein *et al.*[22]

SULFONAMIDE PREPARATIONS AND THERAPEUTIC INDICATIONS

The role of the sulfonamides as single drugs in the chemotherapy of bacterial infection has diminished continually as newer, more effective antibiotics have been introduced and the incidence of sulfonamide resistance has increased. The role of a sulfonamide in therapy in fixed-ratio combination with trimethoprim will be discussed later in this chapter. Sulfonamides are still very useful in the treatment of acute urinary tract infections, however. The sulfonamide most commonly employed for this purpose is sulfisoxazole. This short-acting drug has the best urine solubility of all the sulfonamides (Figure 5-3). Sulfisoxazole may be effective in prophylactic therapy when given continuously during the winter and spring to patients who have experienced recurrent otitis media.[23] The sulfonamides were often used to treat meningococcal infection, but resistance is now common.[24] They were also used to treat bacillary dysentery, but as discussed in Chapter 1, resistance spread rapidly among the enteric pathogens. The sulfonamides are still useful in the treatment of nocardiosis. Some *Chlamydia* (Table 4-8) are sensitive to the sulfonamides, although these are not the drugs of choice. Sulfonamides are useful in the

Figure 5-3 Structures and properties of the most commonly employed sulfonamides.

Name	Structure	Properties	Use and Comments
Trisulfapyrimidines Sulfadiazine	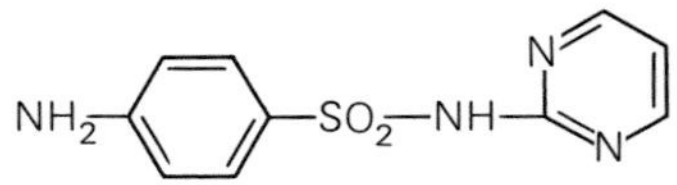	Rapidly absorbed, rapidly excreted, short acting	Administered in a single dosage containing equal amounts of each sulfonamide. Dosage interval, every 4 to 6 hours
Sulfamerazine	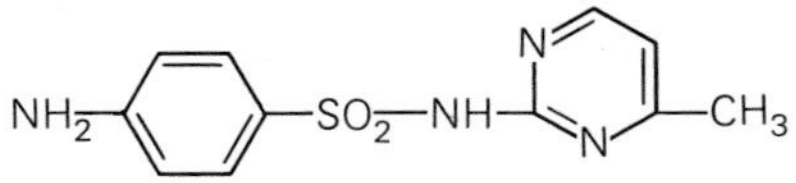		Most commonly used form (when a sulfonamide is not being employed in combination with trimethoprim). Dosage interval every 4 to 6 hours
Sulfamethazine	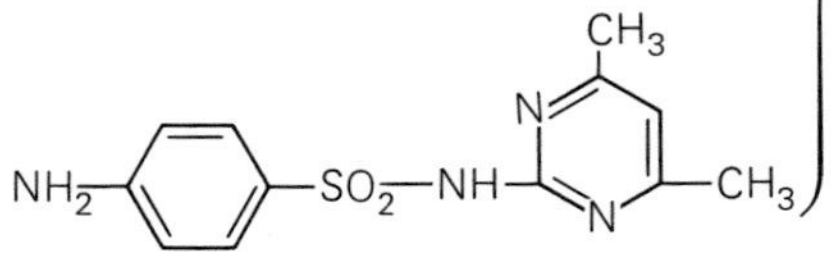		
Sulfisoxazole	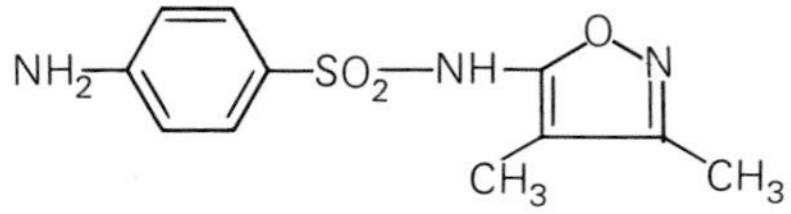	Best urine solubility, short acting	
Sulfamethoxazole	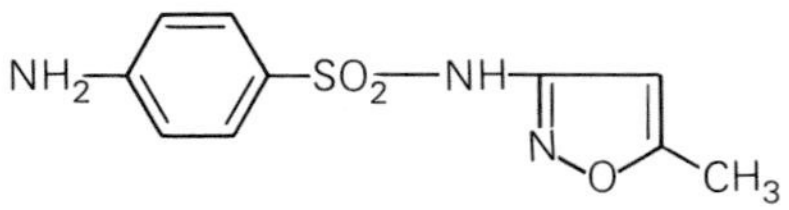	Urine solubility not as good as sulfisoxazole, intermediate acting	Usually administered as fixed-ratio combination with trimethoprim. Dosage interval every 12 hours
Mafenide (Sulfamylon)		Topical use only. Can be absorbed from burned skin	Used for the treatment of burn patients. Drawbacks include: (1) pain on application; (2) skin rashes; (3) metabolic acidosis when there is absorption from extensive burn area
Silver Sulfadiazine	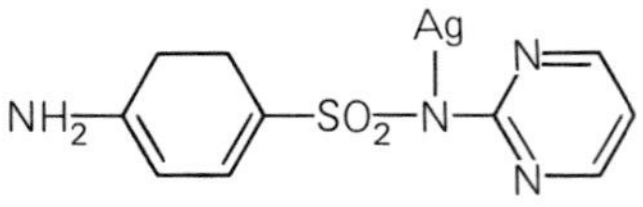	Topical use only. Mechanism of the antibacterial effect is different from the other sulfonamides	Used for treatment of burn patients. Application is generally painless. Causes skin rashes in 2 to 3 per cent of patients. Drug can be absorbed, but does not produce acidosis

treatment of several parasitic diseases including falciparum malaria and toxoplasmosis (see Chapters 10 and 11).

Some sulfonamides are used topically in burn patients (mafenide, silver sulfadiazine) or for treatment of infections of the eye (sulfacetamide). Sulfacetamide, a water-soluble sulfonamide, is marketed as an ophthalmic solution or ointment, whereas mafenide has been used for several years to prevent infection in burn patients. The latter drug is effective in reducing colonization of the burn wound by pathogenic bacteria.[25] It can produce pain upon application, and skin rashes occur in a few patients. Mafenide is absorbed through burned skin,[26] and when applied to an extensive burn area, enough of the drug can be absorbed to cause metabolic acidosis. The acidosis results from mafenide inhibition of carbonic anhydrase in the kidney, reducing the body's ability to excrete acid.

Silver sulfadiazine is another agent that has been used topically in burn patients. Application of this drug is generally painless, and it does not have to be applied as often as mafenide. Significant quantities of the drug are absorbed, and serum levels of sulfadiazine can approach those obtained with systemic administration.[27] The toxic reactions of the other sulfonamides are thus possible with silver sulfadiazine, although this has not been a clinical problem. In contrast to mafenide, the use of silver sulfadiazine is not complicated by metabolic acidosis.[28]

The mechanism of action of silver sulfadiazine is not entirely clear. The antibacterial effect of this drug is not prevented by para-aminobenzoic acid,[29] suggesting that the principal effect is due to the silver. This is not surprising in view of the fact that many silver compounds (e.g., silver nitrate) have antiseptic properties. It has been shown that the silver dissociates from the sulfadiazine and becomes associated with the bacteria.[30] Although it has been suggested that silver at low concentration may be bactericidal as a result of an interaction with DNA,[30] the mechanism of the cell-killing effect is really not known.[31,32] The spectrum of action of silver sulfadiazine is not restricted to bacteria. Several of the fungi that commonly infect the skin (dermatophytes) are sensitive to the drug.[33]

PARA-AMINOSALICYLIC ACID

Para-aminosalicylic acid (PAS) was formerly employed extensively in the treatment of tuberculosis. It is rarely utilized now, since newer drugs (ethambutol, rifampin) have taken its place in primary therapy. The chemotherapy of tuberculosis is discussed in Chapter 8. Para-aminosalicylic acid is well absorbed from the gastrointestinal tract. It distributes widely in the body and readily enters caseous tissue.[34] Levels of the drug in cerebrospinal fluid are low. Like the penicillins, PAS is actively transported out of the cerebrospinal fluid into the blood by a weak carboxylic acid transport system.[35] It is metabolized in the liver, primarily by acetylation. Isoniazid, one of the drugs used in combination with PAS in the treatment of tuberculosis, is extensively acetylated by a different enzyme. PAS is a weak competitive inhibitor of human isoniazid N-acetyltransferase in vitro.[36] This may account for the rather weak inhibition of isoniazid metabolism observed in tuberculosis patients also receiving large doses of PAS.[37]

The principal side effect of PAS is irritation of the gastrointestinal tract. This occurs very frequently, and many patients cannot be trusted to take the drug because of nausea and epigastric distress. Liver damage and decreased iodine uptake with enlargement of the thyroid gland are occasionally observed. A wide variety of allergic reactions can occur with PAS. Since there is a close structural similarity between PAS and salicylates, such as aspirin, one might predict that PAS would have some analgesic or antipyretic effect and that drug interaction would occur when both agents are used simultaneously. This is not the case, however, and PAS does not have an analgesic or antipyretic effect; although it has been reported that very high concentrations of salicylic acid will antagonize the bacteriostatic effect of PAS in vitro,[7] this is not clinically important.

THE SULFONES

The sulfones are the drugs of choice for the treatment of leprosy. The use and pharmacology of the sulfones has been described in detail by Weinstein.[38] Dapsone is the most commonly used member of the group, which also includes sulfoxone sodium, glucosulfone sodium, and acetosulfone. Sulfones are also occasionally used in the treatment of falciparum malaria.

The sulfones are toxic and can cause a variety of drug reactions.[39] They often produce a nonhemolytic anemia and, on occasion, an acute hemolytic anemia. During the treatment of leprosy, there may sometimes be an acute exacerbation of skin lesions with erythema, edema and flaking, acute neuritis, and fever.[40] These exacerbations can be serious, and permanent paralysis of the muscles supplied by the involved nerves may result. When this reaction occurs, sulfone therapy should be discontinued immediately and corticosteroid therapy instituted. The development of erythema nodosum is a common problem. If a patient has erythema nodosum associated with untreated leprosy, sulfone therapy should not be started until the reaction has regressed. At high dose levels, liver damage is sometimes seen. Patients with leprosy who are treated for years with these drugs, must be kept under constant clinical supervision because of the anemia and other side effects that can develop. Agranulocytosis has been reported with these compounds.

TRIMETHOPRIM–SULFAMETHOXAZOLE

MECHANISM OF ACTION OF TRIMETHOPRIM

Trimethoprim is a structural analog of the pteridine portion of dihydrofolic acid (Figure 5-4). It is a competitive inhibitor of dihydrofolate reductase,[41] the enzyme that reduces dihydrofolate (FAH_2) to tetrahydrofolate (FAH_4) in the presence of NADPH. This reduction must take place before the molecule can be converted to the various one-carbon cofactors required for the synthesis of thymidine, purines, methionine, glycine, and formylmethionine (Figure 5-5). Thus, when trimethoprim is added to a culture of bacteria growing in minimal medium, DNA, RNA, and protein synthesis are all affected.

In contrast to the sulfonamides, trimethoprim rapidly inhibits bacterial growth. Although the sulfonamides rapidly block synthesis of new folate, bacteria can continue to grow for several generations as their preexisting folate pools decline (Figure 5-1). In the presence of the trimethoprim block, FAH_4 is rapidly depleted and trapped in the unusable FAH_2 form.[42] Since the reutilization of dihydrofolate is prevented, growth inhibition occurs very early. In most of the one-carbon transfer reactions, the one-carbon unit is simply transferred to a precursor to make a product, and tetrahydrofolate is regenerated. But, when the one-carbon unit is transferred in the thymidylate synthetase reaction, dihydrofolic acid is formed. To keep the system running, the FAH_2 must be reduced to FAH_4 (Figure 5-6). Stoichiometric amounts of tetrahydrofolate cofactor are required for the critical synthetase reaction, and in the absence of dihydrofolate reductase

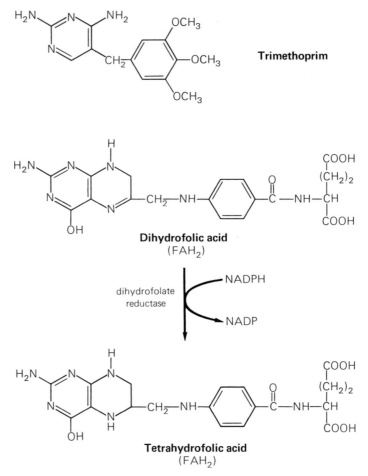

Figure 5-4 Trimethoprim and the reduction of dihydrofolate to tetrahydrofolate. Dihydrofolate must be reduced to tetrahydrofolate before the molecule can accept a one-carbon unit and act as a cofactor in subsequent reactions. This reaction is directed by dihydrofolate reductase and inhibited by trimethoprim. Trimethoprim is presented above to demonstrate its structural similarity to the pteridine portion of the normal substrate FAH_2.

activity, the supplies of active folate cofactors are rapidly depleted.[43]

The composition of the growth medium determines whether the response to trimethoprim will be cidal or static. When cells are grown in medium that does not contain any of the products of one-carbon metabolism, trimethoprim is bacteriostatic. When thymine is absent, but other products of one-carbon metabolism are supplied, trimethoprim is bactericidal. As is the case with sulfonamides, the addition of thymine reverses this effect.[44] Thus, the critical cellular lesion for the killing effect of the drug is inhibition of the thymidylate synthetase reaction.[45] In an appropriate low-thymine, amino acid-containing environment (e.g., human blood), bacteria exposed to trimethoprim will undergo "thymineless death."[46]

In the presence of trimethoprim and the low molecular weight

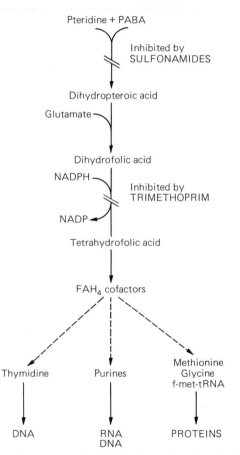

Figure 5-5 Schematic presentation of the sites of action of sulfonamides and trimethoprim in tetrahydrofolate synthesis. The FAH$_4$ cofactors denote (dashed lines) one-carbon fragments required for the synthesis of protein and nucleic acid precursors.

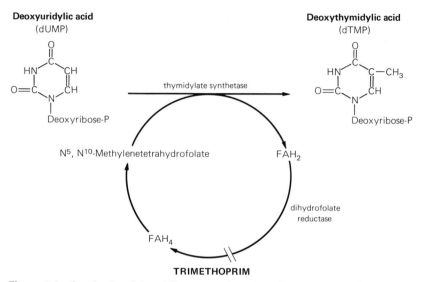

Figure 5-6 Synthesis of thymidine monophosphate from deoxyuridine mono-phosphate. In this critical reaction, a methyl group is transferred from the tetrahydrofolate cofactor to dUMP forming TMP and dihydrofolate (FAH_2). Tetrahydrofolate (FAH_4) is then regenerated by reduction of FAH_2. This reaction is blocked by trimethoprim, bringing the cycle to a halt with the folate in the inactive dihydro-form.

products of one-carbon metabolism, sustained exponential growth of *E. coli* can occur even when formylation of methionine-tRNA is undetectable.[47] In this case, one would expect cell growth to cease because formylmethionine-tRNA is utilized for the initiation of protein synthesis (Figure 3-1). The continuation of reduced cell growth in the absence of folate-dependent formation of f-met-tRNA is consistent with observations that suggest that the methionine-initiation-tRNA without the N-formyl group will permit some initiation of protein synthesis in intact bacteria.[48,49]

Selective Toxicity

The development of trimethoprim is an example of rational drug design based on the results of basic research. During the process of characterizing the properties (pH optima, Michaelis constants) of folate reductases from various sources, it became clear that large differences existed between the bacterial and mammalian enzymes.[41,50] Trimethoprim was one of several compounds that

Table 5-3 **Binding of trimethoprim to bacterial and mammalian dihydrofolate reductases**

Folate reductase, purified from bacteria or from mammalian livers, was incubated with 50 μM dihydrofolate, NADPH, and varying concentrations of trimethoprim. Enzyme activity was recorded by the change in absorbance at 340 nm. The values in the table represent the concentrations of trimethoprim required for 50 per cent inhibition of the enzyme activity. Thus, 60,000 times as much trimethoprim is required to inhibit the human enzyme as to inhibit that of *E. coli*. (Data from Burchall and Hitchings.[41])

Source of enzyme	Trimethoprim concentration required for 50 per cent inhibition (nM)
Bacterial	
Escherichia coli	5
Staphylococcus aureus	15
Proteus vulgaris	5
Mammalian	
Rat	260,000
Rabbit	370,000
Human	300,000

were synthesized to maximize selective toxicity by exploiting these differences. The inhibitory potency of trimethoprim against some bacterial and mammalian folate reductases is presented in Table 5-3. In this system, 20 to 60 thousand times as much drug is required to inhibit the human reductase as the bacterial enzymes. The difference in sensitivity probably reflects changes in the structure of the enzyme that occurred during the evolution of the higher organisms.

Synergism with Sulfonamides and Trimethoprim

The combination of trimethoprim (TMP) and a sulfonamide has been demonstrated to be synergistic in affecting cell growth. Although synergism has been shown with many sulfonamides,[51,52] the combined formulation used in therapy is that of trimethoprim–sulfamethoxazole (TMP–SMZ). In sensitive bacteria, TMP is usually 20 to 100 times more active on a molar basis than the sulfonamide.[53] The concentrations of TMP, SMZ, and TMP–SMZ required for inhibition of bacterial growth are presented in Table 5-4. The increase in activity obtained with the

Table 5-4 **Effect of trimethoprim and sulfamethoxazole alone and in combination on several common pathogenic bacteria growing *in vitro***
The minimum inhibitory concentration (MIC) of TMP alone, SMZ alone, or a mixture of one part TMP and 20 parts SMZ was determined for several bacteria in culture. (Data from Bushby.[53])

| | MIC (μg/ml) | | | |
| | Sulfamethoxazole | | Trimethoprim | |
Organism	alone	mixture	alone	mixture
Staphylococcus aureus	3	0.3	1	0.015
Streptococcus pneumoniae	30	2	2	0.1
Haemophilus influenzae	10	0.3	1	0.015
Shigella sonnei	10	1	0.3	0.05
Proteus vulgaris	30	3	3	0.15

combined formulation is substantial. There is a wide variation in sensitivity to TMP or SMZ, and the optimal ratio of the components in the mixture will also differ from one organism to another. Fortunately, potentiation occurs over a wide range of ratios, with the modal optimum being around one part trimethoprim to 20 parts sulfamethoxazole.[53] Synergy of the combined formulation of TMP–SMZ has been demonstrated after oral administration to animals with different bacterial infections.[53,54]

The synergism between sulfonamides and trimethoprim has been attributed to the fact that the drugs inhibit different enzymes in the same biosynthetic pathway.[55] It was proposed some time ago that such a sequential blockade might often produce a synergistic effect.[56,57] There are several well-documented examples of potentiation resulting from the combination of two drugs that produce sequential blockade. It has also been clearly demonstrated that sequential reactions can be inhibited by drugs without the occurrence of a synergistic response.[58] The concept of sequential blockade does not take into account the type of enzyme inhibition produced by the drug, the presence of rate-limiting steps in a series of reactions, or the complex series of events that control the synthesis and degradation of enzymes in intact cells. The basis for synergism between TMP and a sulfonamide is probably best considered as follows[42]: Trimethoprim is a competitor for the substrate dihydrofolate and its effect is reduced as FAH_2 accumulates, both as a result of the thymidylate synthetase reaction and new FAH_2 synthesis (Figure 5-5). When new synthesis is inhibited by a sulfonamide, there is less substrate to compete with TMP, and the effectiveness of the drug is enhanced. This is a reasonable explanation for this type of drug synergism.

As with the use of the individual drugs, the effect of TMP–SMZ depends upon the environment in which the bacteria are growing.[59] In minimal medium, the effect is bacteriostatic. In a low-thymine, amino acid-containing environment, the effect is bactericidal due to the production of "thymineless death." The TMP–SMZ formulation is bactericidal in human blood and urine, and its effect is overcome by the addition of thymine.[15] The addition of para-aminobenzoic acid to the medium will reduce the effect of the combination to that of trimethoprim alone.[59]

In addition to the production of synergism, TMP–SMZ may have a somewhat broader spectrum of clinically useful action than TMP or SMZ individually.[42] The use of two drugs concomitantly reduces the rate of emergence of resistance to therapy, and the combination is more consistently bactericidal than the drugs used alone.[59]

Resistance

Since there are two drugs in the TMP–SMZ formulation, there are several patterns of resistance to consider. An organism may remain sensitive to TMP and become resistant to sulfonamides. Such an organism generally retains a synergistic response to TMP–SMZ, and the combination can be used successfully in treatment.[60,61] With some TMP-sensitive, SMZ-resistant organisms, synergy is not observed.[62] Synergy with TMP–SMZ can also be seen with bacteria that are SMZ-sensitive and moderately TMP-resistant.[60] In most cases, it seems reasonable to expect a synergistic response if the minimum inhibitory concentration of trimethoprim can be attained. Bacteria can become resistant to both SMZ and TMP, and resistance to therapy can develop clinically.[63]

As in sulfonamide resistance, TMP resistance can be determined by an extrachromosomal mechanism. Trimethoprim resistance in the Enterobacteriaceae is carried on R-factors and can be transferred.[64] A unique mechanism of drug resistance has been demonstrated here. An R-factor determining TMP resistance was found to induce high levels of dihydrofolate reductase activity when it was transferred to sensitive cells.[65] The physical properties of the new enzyme differed from those of the original sensitive cell enzyme, and its affinity for trimethoprim was fourfold lower. These observations are consistent with the proposal that the plasmid carried a gene determining the formation of a variant target enzyme with a low affinity for the inhibitor. In contrast to the Enterobacteriaceae, resistance in S. aureus is apparently determined by chromosomal genes.[66] As discussed in Chapter 2, resistance to penicillins in staphylococci is generally carried on extrachromosomal loci.

USE, PHARMACOLOGY, AND UNDESIRABLE EFFECTS OF TRIMETHOPRIM–SULFAMETHOXAZOLE

Use

Trimethoprim has a broad spectrum of antimicrobial activity,[61] and TMP–SMZ is active against most of the common intestinal and urinary tract pathogens with the exception of Pseudomonas aeruginosa and Streptococcus faecalis. Urinary tract infections due to S. faecalis are better treated with ampicillin.[67] Failure to eradicate this organism with TMP–SMZ in many cases may be attributed to the fact that S. faecalis is one of the few bacteria capable of using exogenous folate cofactors. Thus, the blocks imposed by TMP and SMZ will be bypassed if folinic acid (formyl-FAH₄) is present in the urine. In the United States, TMP–SMZ is primarily used for the treatment of chronic and recurrent urinary tract infections due to such susceptible organisms as E. coli,[68] Proteus, Klebsiella, and Enterobacter. There has been a great deal more experience with this drug in Europe where it is often used for the treatment of gonorrhea and respiratory tract infections. Most Salmonella strains are sensitive to TMP–SMZ, and it is an effective agent for the treatment of patients with typhoid fever in which the Salmonella typhi has become resistant to both chloramphenicol and ampicillin. The reader is referred to a comprehensive review for a summary of the clinical experience with TMP–SMZ in therapy.[69]

Pharmacology

Trimethoprim–sulfamethoxazole tablets contain 400 mg SMZ and 80 mg TMP, a fixed ratio of 5:1. Both drugs are well absorbed from the gastrointestinal tract, and the usual adult dosage is two tablets taken every 12 hours. Sulfamethoxazole was chosen for the formulation because its pharmacokinetic properties are similar to those of trimethoprim. The mean half-life of SMZ is perhaps a little shorter (11 hours) than that of TMP (14 hours), but this difference does not greatly affect the ratio of SMZ to TMP in the blood.[70] The pharmacokinetics of TMP after oral administration are not significantly altered by simultaneous administration of SMZ.[70,71]

When the formulation is given orally every 12 hours, the plasma ratio of free SMZ to TMP is approximately 20:1. Thus, after the components of the original 5:1 preparation have been absorbed and are distributed throughout the body, the ratio of the active forms of the drugs in the plasma approximates the modal optimum ratio (20:1) for the production of synergy against bacteria.[70,72] Clearly, the ratio will vary considerably in the tissues and body fluids according to the distribution properties of each agent.[73] Appreciable synergy is observed over a wide range of ratios, however, and these differences should not have a large effect on the antibacterial efficacy. The TMP–SMZ combination cannot be criticized on the same basis that other fixed-ratio antibiotic combinations can be. Sulfamethoxazole readily distributes into the cerebrospinal fluid, and TMP enters when there is meningeal inflammation.

Both drugs are metabolized in the liver, and the primary route of excretion is by the kidney. The concentration of active (non-metabolized) TMP in the urine can be 100 times that of the plasma.[73] The concentration of SMZ in the urine is generally about three times that of the plasma. Therefore, bacteria in the urine are exposed to high levels of the active form of each drug at a low SMZ to TMP ratio of about 1:1. In the patient with renal failure, the rates of excretion of both drugs are decreased, and dosage reduction is advised.[74]

Undesirable Effects

Trimethoprim–sulfamethoxazole can cause all of the clinically undesirable effects associated with the sulfonamides. Cutaneous sensitivity and gastrointestinal reactions are the most common of the adverse effects.[75] Even though trimethoprim has a very large therapeutic index on the basis of its high affinity for bacterial reductases and its low affinity for the mammalian enzyme, there is the possibility that symptoms of folate deficiency may be produced in some patients. This has not been the experience with patients in a normal dietary state, but it has been cautioned that people with suboptimal folate nutrition (for example, pregnant patients, alcoholics, malnourished infants) who are exposed to long-term therapy may develop megaloblastic anemia, granulocytopenia, or thrombocytopenia.[76] It is reasonable to predict that folinic acid should reverse any bone-marrow effects based on inhibition of folate reductase activity. Folinic acid is transported into mammalian cells and, since it already contains a one-carbon group, it shunts around the block produced by trimethoprim. Reversal of megaloblastosis by folinic acid in patients receiving long-term trimethoprim therapy has been demonstrated clinically.[77] Folinic acid does not reduce the antibacterial effect, since it is not taken up by the bacteria. The only drawback to the approach is that folinic acid must be given parenterally.

It has been reported that TMP–SMZ can cause a deterioration in renal function, and caution should be employed when using the drug in patients with compromised function.[78] Sulfonamides rarely cause acute tubular necrosis, and the impaired renal function seen with the combined preparation may be due to the sulfamethoxazole component.

REFERENCES

1. P. H. Bell and R. O. Roblin: Studies in chemotherapy. VII. A theory of the relation of structure to activity of sulfanilamide type compounds. *J. Am. Chem. Soc.* 64:2905 (1942).

2. D. D. Woods: The biochemical mode of action of the sulfonamides. *J. Gen Microbiol.* 29:687 (1962).

3. G. M. Brown: The biosynthesis of folic acid: inhibition by sulfonamides. *J. Biol. Chem.* 237:536 (1962).

4. D. P. Richey and G. M. Brown: The biosynthesis of folic acid: Purification and properties of the enzymes required for the formation of dihydropteroic acid. *J. Biol. Chem.* 244:1582 (1969).

5. J. L. McCullough and T. H. Maren: Inhibition of dihydropteroate synthetase from *Escherichia coli* by sulfones and sulfonamides. *Antimicrob. Agents Chemother.* 3:665 (1973).

6. D. S. Feingold: Antimicrobial chemotherapeutic agents; the nature of their action and selective toxicity. *New Eng. J. Med.* 269:957 (1963).

7. H. Hurni: Über die quantitativen Verhältnisse bein Antagonisms zwischen p-Aminosalicylsaure (PAS) und p-Aminobenzoesaure (PABA). *Schweiz Z. Path. Bakt.* 12:282 (1949).

8. G. Brownlee, A. F. Green, and M. Woodbine: Sulfetrone; a chemotherapeutic agent for tuberculosis. *Brit. J. Pharmac. Chemother.* 3:15 (1948).

9. A Wacker, H. Kolm, and M. Ebert: Über den Stoffwecshel der p-Aminosalicylsaure and Salicylsaure bei *Enterococcus. Z. Naturforsch* 13b:147 (1958).

10. J. L. McCullough and T. H. Maren: Dihydropteroate synthetase from *Plasmodium berghei*: Isolation, properties, and inhibition by dapsone and sulfadiazine. *Mol. Pharmacol.* 10:140 (1974).

11. R. D. Hotchkiss and A. H. Evans: Fine structure of a genetically modified enzyme as revealed by relative affinities for modified substrate. *Fed. Proc.* 19:912 (1960).

12. B. Wolf and R. D. Hotchkiss: Genetically modified folic acid synthesizing enzymes of *Pneumococcus*. *Biochemistry* 2:145 (1963).

13. R. Benveniste and J. Davies: Mechanisms of antibiotic resistance in bacteria. *Ann. Rev. Biochem.* 42:471 (1973).

14. R. Then and P. Angehrn: Sulfonamide-induced "Thymineless Death" in *Escherichia coli*. *J. Gen. Microbiol.* 76:255 (1973).

15. R. Then and P. Angehrn: Nature of the bactericidal action of sulfonamides and trimethoprim, alone and in combination. *J. Infect. Dis.* 128 Suppl.:S498 (1973).

16. P. -L. Hsu, J. K. H. Ma, H. W. Jun, and L. A. Luzzi: Structure relationship for binding of sulfonamides and penicillins to bovine serum albumin by flurescence probe technique. *J. Pharmaceut. Sci.* 63:27 (1974).

17. A. H. Anton: Increasing activity of sulfonamides with displacing agents: A review. *Ann. N.Y. Acad. Sci.* 226:273 (1973).

18. L. Weinstein: "Sulfonamides" in *The Pharmacological Basis of Therapeutics* (ed. L. S. Goodman and A. Gilman). New York; Macmillan, 1970, p. 1197.

19. J. Koch-Weser, V. W. Sidel, M. Dexter, C. Parish, D. C. Finer, and P. Kanarek: Adverse reactions to sulfisoxazole, sulfamethoxazole, and nitrofurantoin: Manifestations and specific reaction rates during 2,118 courses of therapy. *Arch. Int. Med.* 128:399 (1971).

20. J. R. Bianchine, P. V. J. Macaraeg, L. Lasagna, D. L. Azarnoff, S. F. Brunk, E. F. Hvidberg, and J. A. Owen: Drugs as etiologic factors in the Stevens-Johnson syndrome. *Am. J. Med.* 44:390 (1968).

21. C. A. Dujovne, C. H. Chan, and H. J. Zimmerman: Sulfonamide hepatic injury: Review of the literature and report of a case due to sulfamethoxazole. *New Eng. J. Med.* 277:785 (1967).

22. A. Goldstein, L. Aronow, and S. M. Kalman: *Principles of Drug Action*, New York: John Wiley & Sons, 1974, pp. 766–773.

23. J. M. Perrin, E. Charney, J. B. MacWhinney, T. K. McInerny, R. L. Miller, and L. F. Nazarian: Sulfisoxazole as chemoprophylaxis for recurrent otitis media: A double blind crossover study in pediatric practice. *New Eng. J. Med.* 291:664 (1974).

24. Leading Article: Meningococcal infections. *Br. Med. J.* 3:295 (1974).

25. J. A. Boswick: "Topical therapy of the burn wound with mafenide acetate" in *Contemporary Burn Management* (ed. H. C. Polk and H. H. Stone). Boston: Little, Brown and Co., 1971, pp. 193–202.

26. H. N. Harrison, H. W. Bales, and F. Jacoby: The absorption into burned skin of sulfamylon acetate from 5 per cent aqueous solution. *J. Trauma* 12:994 (1972).

27. J. C. Ballin: Evaluation of a new topical agent for burn therapy: Silver sulfadiazine (Silvadene). *J. Am. Med. Assoc.* 230:1184 (1974).

28. C. R. Baxter: "Topical use of 1.0% silver sulfadiazine" in *Contem-*

porary *Burn Management,* ed. by H. C. Polk and H. H. Stone, Boston: Little, Brown and Co., 1971, pp. 217–225.

29. C. L. Fox, B. W. Rappole, and W. Stanford: Control of *Pseudomonas* infection in burns by silver sulfadiazine. *Surg. Gynecol. Obstet.* 128:1021 (1969).

30. S. M. Modak and C. L. Fox: Binding of silver sulfadiazine to the cellular components of *Pseudomonas aeruginosa. Biochem. Pharmacol.* 22:2391 (1973).

31. H. S. Rosenkranz and H. S. Carr: Silver sulfadiazine: Effect on the growth and metabolism of bacteria. *Antimicrob. Agents Chemother.* 2:367 (1972).

32. H. S. Rosenkranz and S. Rosenkranz: Silver sulfadiazine: Interaction with isolated deoxyribonucleic acid. *Antimicrob. Agents Chemother.* 2:373 (1972).

33. W. T. Speck and H. S. Rosenkranz: Activity of silver sulfadiazine against dermatophytes. *Lancet* 2:895 (1974).

34. A. Heller, R. H. Ebert, D. Koch-Weser, and L. J. Roth: Studies with C^{14} labelled para-aminosalicylic acid and isoniazid. *Am. Rev. Tuberc.* 75:71 (1957).

35. R. Spector and A. V. Lorenzo: The active transport of para-aminosalicylic acid from the cerebrospinal fluid. *J. Pharm. Expt. Ther.* 185:642 (1973).

36. J. W. Jenne: Partial purification and properties of the isoniazid transacetylase in human liver. Its relationship to the acetylation of para-aminosalicylic acid. *J. Clin. Invest.* 44:1992 (1965).

37. J. W. Jenne, F. M. MacDonald, and E. Mendoza: A study of the renal clearances, matabolic inactivation rates, and serum fall-off interaction of isoniazid and para-aminosalicylic acid in man. *Am. Rev. Resp. Dis.* 84:371 (1961).

38. L. Weinstein: "Drugs for leprosy" in *The Pharmacological Basis of Therapeutics* (ed. by L. S. Goodman and A. Gilman). New York: Macmillan, 1975, pp. 1216–1220.

39. L. E. Millikan and E. R. Harrell: Drug reactions to the sulfones. *Arch. Dermatol.* 102:220 (1970).

40. J. R. Trautman: The management of leprosy and its complications. *New Eng. J. Med.* 273:756 (1965).

41. J. J. Burchall and G. H. Hitchings: Inhibitor binding analysis of dihydrofolate-reductases from various species. *Mol. Pharmacol.* 1:126 (1965).

42. G. H. Hitchings: Mechanism of action of trimethoprim-sulfamethoxazole—I. *J. Infect. Dis.* 128 Suppl.:S433 (1973).

43. R. B. Dunlap, N. G. L. Harding, and F. M. Huennekens: Thymidylate synthetase and its relationship to dihydrofolate reductase. *Ann. N.Y. Acad. Sci.* 186:153 (1971).

44. A. E. Koch and J. J. Burchall: Reversal of the antimicrobial activity of trimethoprim by thymidine in commercially prepared media. *Appl. Microbiol.* 22:812 (1971).

45. B. A. Dale and G. R. Greenberg: Effect of the folic acid analogue, trimethoprim, on growth, macromolecular synthesis, and incorporation of exogenous thymine in *Escherichia coli. J. Bacteriol.* 110:905 (1972).

46. S. S. Cohen: On the nature of thymineless death. *Ann. N.Y. Acad. Sci.* 186:153 (1971).

47. R. J. Harvey: Growth and initiation of protein synthesis in *Escherichia coli* in the presence of trimethoprim. *J. Bacteriol.* 114:309 (1973).

48. C. E. Samuel, L. D'Ari, and J. C. Rabinowitz: Evidence against the folate-mediated formylation of formyl-accepting methionyl transfer ribonucleic acid in *Streptococcus faecalis* R. *J. Biol. Chem.* 245:5115 (1970).

49. M. J. Pine, B. Gordon, and S. S. Sarimo: Protein initiation without folate in *Streptococcus faecium*. *Biochim. Biophys. Acta* 179:439 (1969).

50. J. J. Burchall: Comparative biochemistry of dihydrofolate reductase. *Ann. N.Y. Acad. Sci.* 186:143 (1971).

51. S. R. M. Bushby and G. H. Hitchings: Trimethoprim, a sulfonamide potentiator. *Br. J. Pharmacol. Chemother.* 33:72 (1968).

52. J. H. Darrell, L. P. Garrod, and P. M. Waterworth: Trimethoprim: Laboratory and clinical studies. *J. Clin. Pathol.* 21:202 (1968).

53. S. R. M. Bushby: Trimethoprim-sulfamethoxazole: *In vitro* microbiological aspects. *J. Infect. Dis.* 128 Suppl.:S442 (1973).

54. E. Grunberg: The effect of trimethoprim on the activity of sulfonamides and antibiotics in experimental infections. *J. Infect. Dis.* 128 Suppl.:S478 (1973).

55. G. H. Hitchings and J. J. Burchall: "Inhibition of folate biosynthesis and function as a basis for chemotherapy" in *Advances in Enzymology*, Vol. 27 (ed. F. F. Nord). New York: John Wiley and Sons., 1965, pp. 417–468.

56. V. R. Potter: Sequential blocking of metabolic pathways *in vivo*. *Proc. Soc. Exp. Biol. Med.* 76:41 (1951).

57. M. L. Black: Sequential blockage as a theoretical basis for drug synergism. *J. Med. Chem.* 6:145 (1963).

58. R. J. Rubin, A. Reynard, and R. E. Handschumacher: An analysis of the lack of drug synergism during sequential blockade of *de novo* pyrimidine biosynthesis. *Cancer Res.* 24:1002 (1964).

59. S. R. M. Bushby: Combined antibacterial action *in vitro* of trimethoprim and sulfonamides: The *in vitro* nature of synergy. *Postgrad. Med. J.* 45:10 (1969).

60. J. F. Acar, F. Goldstein, and Y. A. Chabbert: Synergistic activity of trimethoprim-sulfamethoxazole on gram-negative bacilli: Observations *in vitro* and *in vivo*. *J. Infect. Dis.* 128 Suppl.:S470 (1973).

61. M. C. Bach, M. Finland, O. Gold, and C. Wilcox: Susceptibility of recently isolated pathogenic bacteria to trimethoprim and sulfamethoxazole separately and combined. *J. Infect. Dis.* 128 Suppl.:S508 (1973).

62. P. M. Waterworth: Practical aspects of testing sensitivity to trimethoprim and sulfamide. *Postgrad. Med. J.* 45:21 (1969).

63. R. W. Lacey, D. M. Bruten, W. A. Gillespie, and E. L. Lewis: Trimethoprim-resistant coliforms. *Lancet* 1:409 (1972).

64. N. Datta and R. W. Hedges: Trimethoprim resistance conferred by W plasmids in Enterobacteriaceae. *J. Gen. Microbiol.* 72:349 (1972).

65. O. Sköld and A. Widh: A new dihydrofolate reductase with low trimethoprim sensitivity induced by an R factor mediating high resistance to trimethoprim. *J. Biol. Chem.* 249:4324 (1974).

66. L. S. Nakhla: Genetic determinants of trimethoprim resistance in a strain of *Staphylococcus aureus. J. Clin. Path.* 26:712 (1973).

67. W. Brumfitt, J. M. T. Hamilton-Miller, and J. Kosmidis: Trimethoprim-sulfamethoxazole: The present position. *J. Infect. Dis.* 128 Suppl.:S778 (1973).

68. R. A. Gleckman: Trimethoprim-sulfamethoxazole vs. ampicillin in chronic urinary tract infections: A double-blind multicenter cooperative controlled study. *J. Am. Med. Assoc.* 233:427 (1975).

69. Various authors: Trimethoprim-sulfamethoxazole: Clinical experiences. *J. Infect. Dis.* 128Suppl.:613-777 (1973).

70. S. A. Kaplan, R. E. Weinfeld, C. W. Abruzzo, K. McFaden, M. L. Jack, and L. Weissman: Pharmacokinetic profile of trimethoprim-sulfamethoxazole in man. *J. Infect. Dis.* 128 Suppl.:S547 (1973).

71. H. Nolte and H. Büttner: Pharmacokinetics of trimethoprim and its combination with sulfamethoxazole in man after single and chronic oral administration. *Chemotherapy* 18:274 (1973).

72. P. Kremers, J. Duvivier, and C. Heusghem: Pharmacokinetic studies of co-trimoxazole in man after single and repeated doses. *J. Clin. Pharm.* 14:112 (1974).

73. D. E. Schwartz and J. Rieder: Pharmacokinetics of sulfamethoxazole and trimethoprim in man and their distribution in the rat. *Chemotherapy* 15:337 (1970).

74. P. G. Welling, W. A. Craig, G. L. Amidon, and C. M. Kunin: Pharmacokinetics of trimethoprim and sulfamethoxazole in normal subjects and in patients with renal failure. *J. Infect. Dis.* 128 Suppl.:S556 (1973).

75. J. M. Frisch: Clinical experience with adverse reactions to trimethoprim-sulfamethoxazole. *J. Infect. Dis.* 128 Suppl.:S607 (1973).

76. I. Chanarin and J. M. England: Toxicity of trimethoprim—sulfamethoxazole in patients with megaloblastic haemopoiesis. *Br. Med. J.* 1:651 (1972).

77. R. F. Jewkes, M. S. Edwards, and J. B. Grant: Haematological changes in a patient on long-term treatment with a trimethoprim-sulfonamide combination. *Postgrad. Med. J.* 46:723 (1970).

78. S. Kalowski, R. S. Nanra, T. H. Mathew, and P. Kinkaid-Smith: Deterioration in renal function in association with co-trimoxazole therapy. *Lancet* 1:394 (1973).

Chapter 6
Antibiotics that Affect
Membrane Permeability
Polymyxin B
Colistin
Gramicidin A and Tyrothricin

Introduction

This chapter will deal with the antibiotics that kill bacteria by virture of their effect on the permeability of the cell membrane. Some antibiotics, for example, bacitracin and vancomycin, have a locus of action at the membrane, but their principal effect is to specifically inhibit bacterial cell wall synthesis. The antibiotics to be considered here interact specifically with membranes, and this interaction alters the function of the cell membrane in a manner incompatible with the survival of the bacterium. There are two groups of membrane antibiotics employed in the therapy of bacterial infection: the polymixins, which are used for the treatment of certain infections by gram-negative bacteria, and the gramicidins, which are included in some topical antibiotic preparations. Some of the most interesting antibiotics acting on the cell membrane belong to the polyene group. These drugs do not affect bacteria; they are used only in the treatment of fungal infections, and they will be discussed in Chapter 9.

THE POLYMYXINS

Of the polymyxin group of antibacterial agents, polymyxin B and colistin (polymyxin E) are the least toxic and the only polymyxins used clinically. They contain both hydrophilic and hydrophobic portions and behave as cationic surface-active compounds at physiological pH. The antibacterial activity of the polymyxins decreases in the presence of anionic compounds, such as soap.[1]

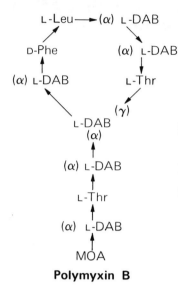

Polymyxin B

(α) and (γ) indicate the NH$_2$-groups involved in the peptide linkages

DAB = α, γ -Diaminobutyric acid residue

MOA = (+)-6-Methyloctanoic acid residue

Mechanism of Action

The Effect on Cell Permeability—An Explanation of the Cell Killing Effect

The polymyxins are bactericidal for a number of gram-negative bacilli. They cause leakage of small molecules, such as phosphate and nucleosides, from sensitive bacteria. The extent of the leakage; as measured by the amount of small molecular size material appearing in the growth medium, is proportional to the killing effect of the drug.[2] Changes in cellular permeability as a result of exposure to polymyxin have also been demonstrated with a dye compound. The dye N-tolyl-α-naphthylamine-8-sulfonic acid fluoresces under ultraviolet light when it is bound to protein. *Pseudomonas* cells exposed to the dye did not fluoresce; but when a polymyxin was added to the cell suspension, the permeability characteristics of the cell exterior were altered, the dye was permitted to penetrate the cell membrane, and flourescence resulted from the association of the dye with cellular protein.[3] This evidence of a change in the permeability of bacterial cells in the presence of polymyxins is supported by a number of other studies, which have been reviewed by Sebek.[4]

The Site of Action—The Cell Membrane

The polymyxins have been shown to associate with the cell membrane. Newton demonstrated that when *Pseudomonas aeruginosa* or *Bacillus megaterium* were exposed to a fluorescent DANSyl-derivative of polymyxin, the drug accumulated in the periphery of the cell.[5] Protoplasts obtained from such cells also fluoresced, and after disruption, the drug was recovered in the fraction containing the cell membrane. Preparations of cell membrane from organisms resistant to the polymyxins bind much less drug than those from sensitive cells.[6,7]

In the presence of polymyxin, the surface architecture of the cell is distorted, and these changes can be seen with the electron microscope.[8] The nature of the molecular association of the polymyxins with cell membranes has not been characterized in any detail. These drugs associate with phospholipids dispersed in water and they alter the physical properties of the small phospholipid spherules. From physical observations made on such phospholipid-drug complexes, it has been proposed that the fatty acid tail of the polymyxin penetrates into the hydrophobic regions of the phospholipid and the polypeptide ring binds electrostatically to the exposed phosphate groups of the lipid.[9] It is not yet known whether this model accurately reflects the orientation of the drug in the more complex structure of bacterial membranes.

The basis for the selective toxicity of the polymyxins has not been well defined. It is also not clear why gram-negative bacteria are more sensitive than gram-positive. Some studies suggest that polymyxin sensitivity is related to the phospholipid content of bacterial cell envelope preparations.[7,10] Liposomes prepared with lipids extracted from a gram-negative bacteria (e. g., *Escherichia coli*) are sensitive to polymyxin, whereas those prepared from lipids of gram-positive bacteria or sheep red blood cell membranes are less sensitive to the antibiotic.[11] Similar studies utilizing synthetic phospholipid suspensions indicate that one phospholipid in particular, phosphatidylethanolamine, may be especially important in determining the degree of sensitivity to polymyxins.[12]

In summary, it is clear that the bacterial cell membrane is the site of polymyxin action, that these drugs interact with the phospholipid components of the membrane, and preliminary observations suggest that the phospholipid composition may be important in determining sensitivity to the drugs. Resistance to these antibiotics can occur by mechanisms other than by changes in phospholipid content. For example, most strains of *Proteus* are resistant because the cell wall prevents access of the drug to the cytoplasmic membrane.[13,14] When *Proteus mirabilis* is converted to an L-form (without a cell wall), it becomes sensitive to polymyxin, and upon reconversion to the bacillary form, it becomes resistant again.[14] The polymyxins are toxic drugs. The toxicity is probably also due to their interaction with membranes. At low concentrations at which there is no gross effect on mammalian cells, polymyxin B nevertheless causes enough change in the permeability properties of the cell membrane to permit entry of such other antibiotics as the tetracyclines.[15] Similar effects have also been observed in fungi.[16]

Use and Pharmacology of the Polymyxins

Therapeutic Indications

Colistin and polymyxin B are used to treat infections caused by gram-negative bacteria. Since the introduction of less toxic antibiotics, their therapeutic indications have become very limited. The polymyxins are used to treat infections due to *Pseudomonas aeruginosa*[17] that is resistant to carbenicillin, gentamicin, and tobramycin. They are employed principally in the treatment of severe urinary tract infections. The polymyxins can be used to treat *Pseudomonas* bacteremia, but they are not of value in the treatment of tissue infections. Human serum decreases the activity of polymyxins against *Pseudomonas*.[18] Thus, these drugs may be less active in the patient than is suggested by *in vitro* sensitivity testing. The principal serum factor inhibiting drug action is calcium. It appears that calcium and other divalent cations antagonize the bactericidal effect of polymyxins by interacting with the cell wall and preventing these antibiotics from reaching their site of action in the cell membrane.[19] Polymyxin B is often used to treat superficial infections of the skin. The topical preparations usually contain another antibiotic, such as neomycin or bacitracin, and sometimes a corticosteroid is also included in the formulations. These topical antibiotic formulations are discussed briefly in the last section of Chapter 2.

Absorption, Distribution, and Excretion

Neiher polymyxin B nor colistin is absorbed from the gastrointestinal tract. They are sometimes given orally for the treatment of
diarrhea due to such gram-negative bacteria as enteropathogenic
E. coli. After oral administration, the drug remains in the intestinal lumen and is not present in the tissues of the bowel wall.
Thus, the clinical response in treatment of some intestinal infections, by *Shigella* for example, can vary considerably. Polymyxins
are also poorly absorbed by skin, even when it is partially denuded by burn. For systemic use, these drugs are administered
intramuscularly; this is often very painful.

The pharmacokinetics of polymyxn B and colistin are complex
and our understanding is incomplete. Both antibiotics have a high
volume of distribution because they are extensively bound in
certain tissues. The amounts of drug associated with liver and
kidney are particularly high.[20] It is known that polymyxins bind
to phospholipid components of mammalian tissues.[21] Polymyxins
do not enter the cerebrospinal fluid even when there is inflammation of the meninges (Table 3-5). Thus, when employed for the
treatment of meningitis due to gram-negative bacteria, they are
administered intrathecally.[22] Renal elimination of the polymyxins
is primarily by glomerular filtration. The slow rate of elimination
is due to the slow release of the drug from its depots in the body.
The persistence of the drug in the patient and the risk of toxicity
are markedly affected by the presence of renal failure, and a
substantial reduction in dosage is required in this case.[23,24] If
possible, another antibiotic should be used in patients with compromised renal function.

Sodium colistimethate (the methane sulfonate) is the form of
colistin used for parenteral injection. Colistimethate binds much
less to tissue components than the parent compound, colistin
sulfate,[25] and this probably explains why it is excreted faster and
is less toxic. Colistimethate appears to be partially converted to
colistin *in vivo.*[26]

Toxicity

The most common adverse effects of polymyxins are renal
damage and a variety of neurological reactions.[27] It has been
reported that, at intramuscular doses below 2.5 mg/kg daily, polymyxin B sulfate does not have a significant nephrotoxic effect.[28]
With higher doses, nephrotoxicity is seen. This rule of thumb

cannot be relied upon, and all patients receiving the drug parenterally should have their renal function monitored frequently. It has also been reported that there is no difference between the toxicity of colistin and polymyxin B when one takes into account the fact that the former has a less potent antibacterial effect and must be used in larger amounts.[29] Studies of renal function in dogs, however, indicate that colistin and colistimethate are less nephrotoxic than polymyxin B.[30,31] The mechanism of the nephrotoxicity is not known. High levels of polymyxin are bound by the kidneys, mostly in membranes.[20] Polymyxin can be extracted in an active bactericidal form from its association with the renal phospholipid.[32] It is entirely reasonable to postulate that the nephrotoxicity results from the interaction of the unaltered drug with renal cell membrane.

Parenteral administration of polymyxin is often accompanied by paresthesias of the distal extremities and lips, which diminish as the drug is excreted. Fever, dizziness, ataxia, weakness, dysphagia, and drowsiness also occur. A neuromuscular blockade with respiratory paralysis is a potentially fatal complication of parenterally administered polymyxins, particularly in patients with compromised renal function.[33] The respiratory paralysis is reversible. The mechanism is unknown, but it is clearly different from the neuromuscular blockade produced by the aminoglycosides (described in Chapter 3).[34] Neostigmine does not reverse it, but apparently calcium may have some effect.

GRAMICIDIN A AND TYROTHRICIN

There are several antibiotics that have been shown to cause rather specific changes in the cation permeability of membranes and lipid bilayers. Most of these agents are too toxic to be clinically useful; but two groups, the tyrocidines and the gramicidins, are present in some widely used topical antibiotic preparations. These compounds were originally isolated as a mixture from *Bacillus brevis*. The mixture was named tyrothricin, and it contains about 20 per cent gramicidin A and 60 per cent tyrocidines.[35] The tyrocidines are cyclic decapeptides. Gramicidin A is an open chain polypeptide, with 15 amino acid residues in which D- and L-forms alternate in the sequence (this can be seen in the structure presented below), since glycine is ambivalent.

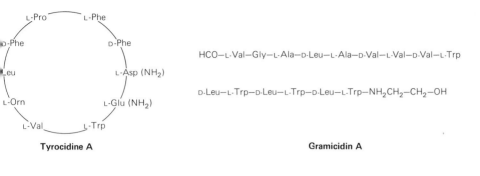

Tyrocidine A   Gramicidin A

Gramicidin A and the tyrocidines are only used topically. Gramicidin A is present in mixtures containing such other antibiotics as neomycin, bacitracin, or polymyxin B. The tyrocidines are only provided in combination with gramicidin A (tyrothricin). Gramicidin A is primarily active against gram-positive bacteria, whereas the tyrocidines are active against both gram-positive and gram-negative bacteria.

The tyrocidines act on bacterial cell membranes facilitating the transmembrane passage of monovalent cations.[36] In organisms sensitive to both compounds, gramicidin A is a more potent antibacterial agent than the tyrocidines. When tyrocidines are present in a mixture with gramicidin A (tyrothricin), they inhibit the action of the more potent antibiotic on the permeability of lipid bilayers.[37] The mechanism by which the tyrocidines alter membrane permeability is not well defined. It has been proposed that they act in a manner that is intermediate to that of the carrier and channel-forming types (Figure 6-1) of ionophore antibiotics.[38] The term ionophore refers to the ability of certain antibiotics to carry ions across such lipid barriers as cell membranes and artificial lipid bilayers. The study of these molecules has been very helpful in developing our understanding of membrane transport processes at the molecular level.

The lipid components of biological membranes are oriented in a more or less ordered way, such that their polar groups face the membrane surface whereas the nonpolar hydrocarbon chains form the membrane interior. The nonpolar components of the membrane form an extremely efficient barrier to the passage of such small ions as sodium or potassium. There are two principal mechanisms by which ionophores facilitate the passage of small ions across this barrier. Some ionophores, for example, valinomy-

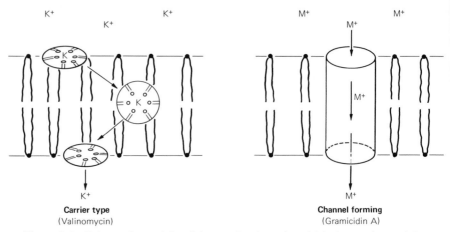

Figure 6-1 Schematic models of the mechanisms by which the carrier and the channel-forming type of ionophore antibiotics facilitate the passage of cations across biological and artificial membranes. The solid circles oriented at the membrane surface represent the polar head groups of the phospholipids, and the wavy lines denote the hydrophobic fatty acid chains. Valinomycin (an antibiotic not used clinically) is used as an example of the carrier type. In general, the carrier ionophores are much more specific with regard to the ions with which they interact, valinomycin being quite selective for potassium (K^+). The channel-formers are less selective, and in the case of gramicidin A, a variety of monovalent metal cations (M^+) are able to diffuse through the pore formed in the center of the antibiotic channel.

cin and nonactin, form a three-dimensional cage around the cation (Figure 6-1). The exterior of the antibiotic cage is quite hydrophobic and the ion-antibiotic complex is thus lipid soluble. The antibiotic binds a cation at one membrane interface by forming ion-dipole interactions that replace the water of hydration normally surrounding the ion. The antibiotic with the cation bound in its center is then able to diffuse to the opposite membrane surface where the cation is released (Figure 6-1). These antibiotics are called carrier type ionophores. They can be very efficient, one molecule facilitating the passage of thousands of ions per second.[39,40]

Another group of ionophores is called the channel-formers, and gramicidin A belongs to this group.[41] Here, the antibiotic forms a tube that passes from one surface of the membrane to the other (Figure 6-1). The ions enter the tube at one membrane interface and diffuse through the interior of the channel to the other side. Although the structure of gramicidin A has been presented above in linear form, it is clear that it can assume a three-dimensional conformation consistent with the formation of such an ion-conducting channel. From physical observations, it has been proposed that the antibiotic forms helical structures in nonpolar environments and that two of these helices can associate to form the channel.[42,43] One possible model of a double-helical gramicidin A dimer is presented in Figure 6-2. The channel formed by the

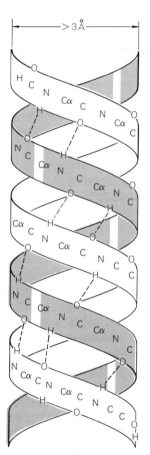

Figure 6-2 Scheme of a proposed double-helical conformation for the gramicidin dimer. One chain is shaded, whereas the other chain, oriented in antiparallel fashion, is not. The dotted lines denote hydrogen bonds. The covalent bonds between atoms have been omitted. The C_α represents all the amino acid except that portion participating in the peptide bond. A channel of greater than 3Å diameter is formed in the middle of the double helix. (Figure from Veatch *et al.*[43])

antibiotic permits the passage of univalent cations but completely excludes anions and polyvalent cations.[44] The gramicidin A channels are not static; they are constantly forming and disappearing. Gramicidin A is bactericidal. Cell death apparently results from changes in cellular cation content, principally the loss of potassium ion.[45]

REFERENCES

1. E. A. Bliss, C. A. Chandler, and E. B. Schoenbach: *In vitro* studies of polymyxin. *Ann. N.Y. Acad. Sci.* 51:944 (1949).

2. B. A. Newton: The release of soluble constituents from washed cells of *Pseudomonas aeruginosa* by the action of polymyxin. *J. Gen. Microbiol.* 9:54 (1953).

3. B. A. Newton: Site of action of polymyxin on *Pseudomonas aeruginosa;* antagonism by cations. *J. Gen. Microbiol.* 10:491 (1954).

4. O. K. Sebek: "Polymyxins and circulin" in *Antibiotics I* ed. by D. Gottlieb and P. D. Shaw. New York: Springer-Verlag, 1967, pp. 142–152.

5. B. A. Newton: A fluorescent derivative of polymyxin; its preparation and use in studying the site of action of the antibiotic. *J. Gen. Microbiol.* 12:226 (1955).

6. A. V. Few and J. H. Schulman: The absorption of polymyxin E by bacteria and bacterial cell walls and its bactericidal action. *J. Gen. Microbiol.* 9:454 (1953).

7. B. A. Newton: The properties and mode of action of the polymyxins. *Bact. Rev.* 20:14 (1956).

8. M. Koike, K. Iida, and T. Matsuo: Electron microscopic studies on mode of action of polymyxin. *J. Bacteriol.* 97:448 (1969).

9. W. Pache, D. Chapman, and R. Hillaby: Interaction of antibiotics with membranes: Polymyxin B and gramicidin S. *Biochim. Biophys. Acta* 255:358 (1972).

10. M. R. W. Brown and S. M. Wood: Relation between cation and lipid content of cell walls of *Pseudomonas aeruginosa, Proteus vulgaris* and *Klebsiella aerogenes* and their sensitivity to polymyxin B and other antibacterial agents. *J. Pharm. Pharmac.* 24:215 (1972).

11. M. Imai, K. Inoue, and S. Nojima: Effect of polymyxin B on liposomal membranes derived from *Escherichia coli* lipids. *Biochim. Biophys. Acta* 375:130 (1975).

12. C.-C. HsuChen and D. S. Feingold: The mechanism of polymyxin B action and selectivity toward biologic membranes. *Biochemistry* 12:2105 (1973).

13. I. J. Sud and D. S. Feingold: Mechanism of polymyxin B resistance in *Proteus mirabilis. J. Bacteriol.* 104:289 (1970).

14. M. Teuber: Susceptibility to polymyxin B of penicillin G-induced *Proteus mirabilis* L forms and spheroplasts. *J. Bacteriol.* 98:347 (1969).

15. G. Medoff, C. N. Kwan, D. Schlessinger, and G. S. Kobayashi: Potentiation of rifampicin, rifampin analogs, and tetracycline against

animal cells by amphotericin B and polymyxin B. *Cancer Res.* 33:1146 (1973).

16. S. N. Schwartz, G. Medoff, G. S.·Kobayashi, C. N. Kwan, and D. Schlessinger: Antifungal properties of polymyxin B and its potentiation of tetracycline as an antifungal agent. *Antimicrob. Agents Chemother.* 2:36 (1972).

17. I. B. R. Duncan: Susceptibility of 1,500 isolates of *Pseudomonas aeruginosa* to gentamicin, carbenicillin, colistin, and polymyxin B. *Antimicrob. Agents Chemother.* 5:9 (1974).

18. S. D. Davis, A. Iannetta, and R. J. Wedgewood: Activity of colistin against *Pseudomonas aeruginosa*: Inhibition by calcium. *J. Infect. Dis.* 124:610 (1971).

19. C.-C. HsuChen and D. S. Feingold: Locus of divalent cation inhibition of the bactericidal action of polymyxin B. *Antimicrob. Agents Chemother.* 2:331 (1972).

20. M. Jacobson, A. Koch, R. Kuntzman, and J. Burchall: The distribution and binding of tritiated polymyxin B in the mouse. *J. Pharm. Expt. Ther.* 183:433 (1972).

21. C. M. Kunin: Binding of antibiotics to tissue homogenates. *J. Infect. Dis.* 121:55 (1970).

22. B. L. Wise, J. L. Mathis, and E. Jawetz: Infections of the central nervous system due to *Pseudomonas aeruginosa*. *J. Neurosurg.* 31:432 (1969).

23. N. J. Goodwin and E. A. Friedman: The effects of renal impairment, peritoneal dialysis, and hemodialysis on serum sodium colistimethate levels. *Ann. Int. Med.* 68:984 (1968).

24. W. M. Bennett, I. Singer, and C. H. Coggins: Guide to drug usage in adult patients with impaired renal function: A supplement. *J. Am. Med. Assoc.* 223:991 (1973).

25. A. A. Al-Khayyat and A. L. Aronson: Pharmacologic and toxicologic studies with polymyxins II. Comparative pharmacologic studies of the sulfate and methanesulfonate salts of polymyxin B and colistin in dogs. *Chemotherapy* 19:82 (1973).

26. C. M. Kunin and A. Bugg: Binding of polymyxin antibiotics to tissues: The major determinant of distribution and persistence in the body. *J. Infect. Dis.* 124:394 (1971).

27. J. Koch-Weser, V. W. Sidel, E. B. Federman, P. Kanarek, D. C. Finer, and E. A. Eaton: Adverse effects of sodium colistimethate: Manifestations and specific reaction rates during 317 courses of therapy. *Ann. Int. Med.* 72:857 (1970).

28. E. M. Yow and J. H. Moyer: Toxicity of polymyxin B. *Arch. Int. Med.* 92:248 (1953).

29. N. M. Nord and P. D. Hoeprich: Polymyxin B and colistin, a critical comparison. *New Eng. J. Med.* 270:1030 (1964).

30. J. Vinnicombe and T. A. Stamey: The relative nephrotoxicities of polymyxin B sulfate, sodium sulfomethyl-polymyxin B, sodium sulfomethyl-colistin (colymycin), and neomycin sulfate. *Invest. Urol.* 6:505 (1969).

31. M. F. Pedersen, J. F. Pedersen, and P. O. Madsen: A clinical and

experimental comparative study of sodium colistimethate and poly-myxin B sulfate. *Invest. Urol.* 9:234 (1971).

32. C. M. Kunin and A. Bugg: Recovery of tissue bound polymyxin B and colistimethate. *Proc. Soc. Exp. Biol. Med.* 137:786 (1971).

33. L. A. Lindesmith, R. D. Baines, D. B. Bigelow, and T. L. Petty: Reversible respiratory paralysis associated with polymyxin therapy. *Ann. Int. Med.* 68:318 (1968).

34. M. P. McQuillen and L. Engbaek: Mechanism of colistin-induced neuromuscular depression. *Arch. Neurol.* 32:235 (1975).

35. *The Merck Index*, Eighth Edition. Rahway: Merck and Co., 1968, p. 1091.

36. S. N. Graven, H. A. Lardy, D. Johnson, and A. Rutter: Antibiotics as tools for metabolic studies. V. Effect of nonactin, monactin, dinactin, and trinactin on oxidative phosphorylation and adenosine triphosphatase induction. *Biochemistry* 5:1729 (1966).

37. M. C. Goodall: Structural effects in the action of antibiotics on the ion permeability of lipid bilayers. III. Gramicidins "A" and "S," and lipid specificity. *Biochim. Biophys. Acta* 219:471 (1970).

38. M. C. Goodall: Structural effects in the action of antibiotics on the ion permeability of lipid bilayers. II Kinetics of tyrocidine B. *Biochim. Biophys. Acta* 219:28 (1970).

39. P. Läuger: Carrier-mediated ion transport: Electrical relaxation experiments give insight into the kinetics of ion transport through artificial lipid membrane. *Science* 178:24 (1972).

40. B. C. Pressman: Properties of ionophores with a broad range of cation selectivity. *Fed. Proc.* 32:1698 (1973).

41. S. Krasne, G. Eisenman, and G. Szabo: Freezing and melting of lipid bilayers and the mode of action of nonactin, valinomycin, and gramicidin. *Science* 174:412 (1971).

42. D. W. Urry, M. C. Goodall, J. D. Glickson, and D. F. Mayers: The gramicidin A transmembrane channel: Characteristics of head-to-head dimerized helices. *Proc. Natl. Acad. Sci. U.S.* 68:1907 (1971).

43. W. R. Veatch, E. T. Fosel, and E. R. Blout: The conformation of gramicidin A. *Biochemistry* 13:5249 (1974).

44. S. B. Hladky and D. A. Haydon: Ion transfer across lipid mem-branes in the presence of gramicidin A. I. Studies of the unit conductance channel. *Biochim. Biophys. Acta* 274:204 (1972).

45. F. M. Harold and J. R. Baarda: Gramicidin, valinomycin and cation permeability of *Streptococcus faecalis. J. Bacteriol.* 94:53 (1967).

Chapter 7

The Urinary Tract Antiseptics
Nalidixic Acid and Oxolinic Acid
Nitrofurantoin
Methenamine

Introduction

Several of the drugs that have already been discussed are used in the treatment of urinary tract infections. The soluble sulfonamides, ampicillin, and the tetracyclines are the principal drugs employed in treating acute, uncomplicated infections of the urinary tract. Trimethoprim—sulfamethoxazole (TMP—SMZ) is often used to treat chronic or recurrent infection. Others, such as the aminoglycosides, cephalosporins, and carbenicillin, are used much less often for restricted indications. There are several drugs that are concentrated in the urine and that are employed only in treating patients with infection of the urinary tract. These drugs are called urinary tract antiseptics, and the group includes nalidixic acid, oxolinic acid, nitrofurantoin, and methenamine. The treatment of persistent infection in the urinary tract is often difficult and frustrating both for the physician and the patient. The reader is referred to two short textbooks for a clinical review of the natural history, diagnosis, and management of urinary tract infections.[1,2]

NALIDIXIC ACID AND OXOLINIC ACID

Naladixic acid is active *in vitro* against many of the gram-negative bacteria commonly involved in urinary tract infections.[3] For example, 90 per cent of *Escherichia coli*, 70 per cent of *Klebsiella*, 80 per cent of *Proteus mirabilis*, and 100 per cent of indole-positive *Proteus* strains are killed by the concentration of active drug achieved in the urine of adults receiving normal therapeutic doses (*Pseudomonas* is not sensitive).[4] Oxolinic acid is structurally similar to nalidixic acid, and it has a similar, if not identical, mechanism of action.

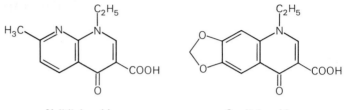

| Nalidixic acid | Oxolinic acid |

Mechanism of Action

Nalidixic acid is more effective against gram-negative than gram-positive bacteria. It rapidly inhibits DNA synthesis in susceptible bacterial cells, while protein and RNA synthesis continue unabated for some time after exposure to the drug[5]; DNA synthesis in mammalian cells is not affected. Replication of DNA in chloroplasts of the protozoan *Euglena gracilis* is inhibited at concentrations of drug that have no effect on nuclear DNA replication.[6] The mechanism by which nalidixic acid inhibits DNA synthesis is not at all clear, but there is good evidence that this is the primary metabolic effect responsible for bacterial cell killing.[7] When cells exposed to nalidixic acid are placed in a drug-free medium, growth resumes.[8] Thus, the inhibition of DNA synthesis is reversible.

Attempts to localize the component of the DNA replication process affected by nalidixic acid have not been successful, but the results of experiments in both intact bacteria and in cell-free systems show that numerous potential mechanisms of action are quite unlikely. Nalidixic acid has no effect when it is added to an *in vitro* DNA-synthesizing system containing purified DNA, DNA polymerase I, and the appropriate nucleoside triphosphate precursors.[9] The drug does not bind to purified DNA,[10] and DNA obtained from *E. coli* after nalidixic acid treatment is not cross-linked.[9] It has also been shown in cell-free systems that the drug does not inhibit numerous enzymes involved in the synthesis of DNA precursors or the modification of DNA.[9,11] There is no evidence that nalidixic acid is changed to an active compound by the bacterium.[10] When *E. coli* is treated with toluene, the premeability of the cell membrane is altered such that deoxynucleoside triphosphates added to the growth medium can pass directly into the cell and become incorporated into DNA.[12] Nalidixic acid inhibits the direct incorporation of radioactive nucleotides into DNA in toluene-treated cells, again suggesting that precursor formation is not inhibited.[11,13]

It is clear that semiconservative DNA synthesis is inhibited by nalidixic acid. It has been reported that the drug has some effect on post-irradiation synthesis, which suggests that DNA repair may be affected as well.[14] But there is other evidence indicating that DNA synthesis taking place on a single-stranded DNA template (as in the resynthesis step of excision repair) may not be inhibited by nalidixic acid. For example, in toluene-treated cells deficient in DNA polymerase I, nalidixic acid inhibits semiconservative DNA synthesis but it does not affect ultraviolet light-simulated repair synthesis.[15] Also, in another study, it was shown that the conversion of single-stranded M-13 phage DNA into the double-stranded form is not affected by nalidixic acid, whereas DNA synthesis by the double-stranded replicative form is completely inhibited.[16]

The conclusion to be drawn from all these observations is that nalidixic acid affects replication at a stage beyond the production of deoxynucleoside triphosphates; synthesis taking place on double-stranded DNA template is inhibited but the drug does not inhibit synthesis by affecting any known purified enzyme involved in DNA metabolism. It is possible that nalidixic acid inhibits the function of an as yet uncharacterized component required for semiconservative replication. The drug has been shown to inhibit semiconservative replication carried out by cell-free systems from E. coli that depend on the presence of soluble macromolecules other than DNA polymerase I or II.[10,17] The precise role of these components in the complex process of double-stranded DNA replication is not known, but it is reasonable to speculate that one or more of them might represent the receptor for nalidixic acid (Figure 7-1). Any model of the mechanism of action of nalidixic acid must account for the dominance of sensitivity over resistance to the drug in partial diploids for the nal A marker.[18] In this respect, it is interesting to note that a soluble, heat-sensitive, macromolecular component from nalidixic-acid sensitive cells confers partial sensitivity on a lysate from drug-resistant cells.[10] One can speculate that this protein represents the site of action of nalidixic acid.

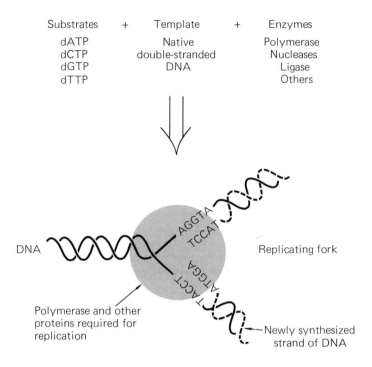

Substrates	+	Template	+	Enzymes
dATP		Native		Polymerase
dCTP		double-stranded		Nucleases
dGTP		DNA		Ligase
dTTP				Others

DNA

Replicating fork

Polymerase and other
proteins required for
replication

Newly synthesized
strand of DNA

Replication Complex

Figure 7-1 Scheme of the replication of double-stranded DNA. The process of semiconservative replication requires deoxyribonucleoside triphosphates, double-stranded DNA template, and multiple enzymes. New strands are synthesized in short sections, called Okazaki fragments, which are joined together by ligases to form a high molecular weight DNA. This complex process requires multiple components, some of which have not been characterized. From the experimental observations reviewed in the text, one may speculate that an as yet unidentified component of the DNA replication apparatus is the site of action for nalidixic acid.

Pharmacology and Undesirable Effects of Nalidixic Acid and Oxolinic Acid

Nalidixic acid is used principally for treating patients with recurrent urinary tract infections. Development of resistance during therapy has been reported to be a common problem,[19,20] and the physician must be guided by the results of *in vitro* sensitivity tests. Oxolinic acid is similar in its spectrum of action to nalidixic acid, and resistance is a clinical problem with this drug as well.[21] Oxolinic acid is more potent than nalidixic acid on a weight basis, but the principal difference is that it has a longer half-life, which permits administration on a twice daily regimen rather than four times daily.[21]

Absorption, Distribution, Metabolism, and Excretion

Nalidixic acid is almost completely (96 per cent) absorbed from the gastrointestinal tract.[22] It is rapidly metabolized in the liver to the biologically active compound hydroxynalidixic acid and to glucuronide conjugated products, which are inactive.[22] One-third of the biologically active drug in the plasma is present as the hydroxylated metabolite, which is 63 per cent bound to plasma protein, and the rest is the parent compound, which is 93 per cent bound.[23] The distribution of nalidixic acid has been studied in monkeys. In this study, the drug did not associate with tissues, and the kidney was the only organ found to have a higher level of drug than plasma.[22] Nalidixic acid does not distribute into prostatic fluid.[24] This is important, since chronic bacterial prostatitis is a very common cause of recurrent urinary tract infections in male patients. Thus, even in the presence of effective clearance of bacteria from the urinary tract in response to the drug, the organism can become reinstated due to seeding of the urine from foci of infection in the prostate, which is not exposed to the antibacterial action. Although the drug has been tried in the treatment of infections outside the urinary tract it was not proven useful. At least part of the reason for the poor response is due to the very poor drug distribution into tissues.

Excretion is almost completely via the kidney, and the concentration of antibacterially active compounds achieved in the urine is several-fold that of the plasma. Over 80 per cent of the drug in the urine is present as the inactive glucuronide conjugate. Of the remainder, most is present as the biologically active hydroxylated metabolite (which is 16 times more potent than nalidixic acid itself).[23] The therapeutic effect of this drug in the treatment of the urinary tract infection is thus primarily due to the action of its metabolite, hydroxynalidixic acid.

In patients with advanced renal failure, bactericidal levels of drug are still achieved in the urine.[25] In spite of the presence of severely compromised renal function, antibacterially active drug does not accumulate in the serum during continuous therapy.[25] This observation leads us to compare nalidixic acid metabolism and excretion with the way chloramphenicol is processed by the liver and kidney (Chapter 4). Chloramphenicol is also extensively conjugated to the glucuronide. In patients with renal failure, the nontoxic, biologically inactive conjugates of chloramphenicol accumulate in the body, but there is no increase in the serum level of unchanged drug. It is not clear whether conjugation of nalidixic acid and hydroxynalidixic acid to the glucuronide renders these compounds completely nontoxic. Thus, the potential toxicity of high serum levels of the glucuronides in renal failure is unknown. Even though increased toxicity has not been observed with nalidixic acid given in usual doses to people with severely compromised renal function, the physician should exert special caution with this patient group in monitoring for untoward drug effects.

Untoward Effects

Nausea is the most frequent side effect experienced by patients taking nalidixic acid.[20] Other gastrointestinal complaints include vomiting, diarrhea, and abdominal pain. Occasional allergic reactions, including rashes, urticaria, itching, and eosinophilia are observed. In addition to nonspecific rashes, nalidixic acid can produce a photosensitivity response most commonly manifested as a sunburn-like reaction and rarely as a bullous eruption.[26] Patients taking the drug should be cautioned against excessive exposure to direct sunlight. A variety of visual disturbances have been reported to occur occasionally; these include blurring of vision, diplopia, difficulty of accommodation, photophobia, and changes in color perception. The visual abnormalities all reverse upon cessation of therapy.

Nalidixic acid occasionally produces central nervous system side effects. Patients may complain of mild problems such as drowsiness, weakness, headache, and dizziness, but in some people severe reactions such as convulsions and toxic psychosis have been reported. The drug should not be given to patients with convulsive disorders or symptoms of cerebral vascular insufficiency. When used in young children and infants, nalidixic acid has occasionally produced intracranial hypertension with papilledema and bulging fontanelles.[27][28] It has been the experience that this reverses upon cessation of therapy. The mechanism of production of pseudotumor cerebri is not known. Because of it some pediatricians have been reluctant to use the drug for younger patients. Nalidixic acid is not recommended for infants less than 1 month of age or for pregnant women during the first trimester.

Nalidixic acid has rarely been associated with the production of cholestatic jaundice, blood dyscrasias, and hemolytic anemia (sometimes associated with glucose-6-phosphate dehydrogenase deficiency—see Chapter 10). The glucuronic acid liberated from the glucuronide conjugates of nalidixic acid and hydroxynalidixic acid in the urine can cause a false-positive reaction for glucose with certain test procedures. In general, the type and incidence of side effects with oxolinic acid are comparable to those with nalidixic acid.[20] The severe central nervous system side effects of intracranial hypertension and convulsions have not been reported with oxolinic acid, but excitative responses, such as restlessness, insomnia, and nervousness, are more common than with nalidixic acid.[29]

NITROFURANTOIN

Several nitrofuran derivatives are being used clinically. Nitrofurazone, for example, has a broad antibacterial effect against common skin pathogens. It is available in topical formulations. Furazolidone is a nitrofuran compound, which is marketed in oral preparations for treating enteritis caused by such organisms as Salmonella, Shigella, and Vibrio cholerae. The efficacy of many of these preparations in clinical use is not well founded. Nitrofurantoin is available for use as a urinary tract antiseptic. It is concentrated in the urine and is active in vitro against a wide spectrum of gram-positive and gram-negative bacteria. At the concentrations achieved in the urine, the drug is effective against most clinical isolates of E. coli, Klebsiella, Enterobacter, staphylococci, and enterococci. The majority of Proteus strains and Pseudomonas aeruginosa are resistant.[30]

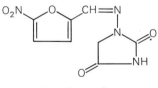

Nitrofurantoin

With standard oral therapy, nitrofurantoin does not yield sufficient serum or tissue levels of antimicrobial activity to permit its use in treating infection outside the urinary tract. It is employed for treatment of acute urinary tract infections with organisms not sensitive to other drugs. Its use for the initial treatment of acute infections has declined over the years because of the rather high frequency of gastrointestinal side effects associated with administration at the recommended doses (50 to 100 mg every 6 hours for adults). But it has been shown that nitrofurantoin given in smaller amounts (50 mg as a single night-time dose) on a daily basis over a period of many months will markedly reduce the frequency of recurrent urinary tract infections in women.[31] Continuous prophylaxis has also been reported to be beneficial in selected male patients with chronic or recurrent urinary tract infections.[32] Organisms isolated from the urine of women with recurrent infections often remain sensitive to nitrofurantoin even after many courses of therapy.[1] This is probably due to the fact that nitrofurantoin does not appear in measurable amounts in the stool and consequently the sensitivity of intestinal flora is not altered, since reinfection from the bowel flora is the most common cause of recurrence of uncomplicated urinary tract infections in females[1]; the fact that these organisms remain sensitive to nitrofurantoin is an advantage in both continuous prophylaxis and repeated courses of therapy.

Mechanism of Action and Pharmacology

Nitrofurnatoin inhibits a wide variety of enzyme systems in bacteria. Despite many studies, which have been reviewed in other texts,[33,34] its primary mechanism of action is not known. Nitrofurans can enter mammalian cells and they have been shown to affect several enzymes in these cells as well.[33] The basis for the selective toxicity of nitrofurantoin probably rests largely on its pharmacological properties. The drug is concentrated in urine, and plasma levels are very low. Also, it is rapidly destroyed by enzymes in the tissues.[35] The antibacterial action of nalidixic acid and oxolinic acid is antagonized *in vitro* by nitrofurantoin.[36] The mechanism of this antagonism is unknown. The two drugs should not be used together.

Two effects of nitrofurantoin on mammalian cells are of particular interest. Several of the nitrofuran derivatives have been shown to arrest spermatogenesis in animals.[33] At high local concentrations, nitrofurantoin immobilizes human sperm, and it has been suggested that irrigation of the vas deferans with the drug during male sterilization may eliminate the postoperative interval before the viable sperm count drops to zero.[37] Nitrofurantoin and nitrofurazone have also been shown to have radiosensitizing properties in hypoxic cells.[38] This suggests the potential application of this class of compounds in the radiotherapy of tumors with hypoxic regions.

Absorption, Distribution, Metabolism, and Excretion

Nitrofurantoin is completely absorbed from the gut and only very low levels of antibacterial activity are achieved in the plasma. The serum half-life is short (20 minutes in humans with normal renal function)[39] because the drug is both rapidly excreted by the kidney and rapidly degraded in the tissues. The drug is excreted by both glomerular filtration and tubular secretion, and there is significant reabsorption (30 per cent) when the urine is acid.[40] Although the urine concentration of nitrofurantoin can be increased by alkalization, the antibacterial efficacy is decreased. Thus, efforts to increase urine pH are non-productive. The drug has been shown by autoradiographic techniques to be present in the interstitial fluid of the renal medulla[41] and by bacteriological methods to achieve a several-fold higher concentration in the lymphatics draining the medulla than in the plasma.[42] With normal renal function, high concentrations of nitrofurantoin are obtained in the urine. But the recovery of drug from the urine is linearly related to the rate of creatinine clearance, and the concentration in the urine of uremic patients is not high enough to inhibit common urinary tract pathogens.[43] Nitrofurantoin is contraindicated in patients with impaired renal function (creatinine clearance less than 60 ml/minute)[43] both because inadequate urine concentrations are achieved and the danger of developing neuropathy may be increased.[44]

Untoward Effects

The most common undesirable effects associated with nitrofurantoin therapy are nausea and vomiting.[45] There are several reports that the incidence of gastrointestinal reactions may be lower with the macrocrystalline preparation.[46] The crystalline and macrocrystalline forms are therapeutically equivalent. The incidence of untoward effects with nitrofurantoin therapy was compared with those of sulfisoxazole and sulfamethoxazole (cf. Chapter 5, Figure 5-3) in a large prospective study involving over 2,000 courses of therapy.[45] The incidence of reactions to these two classes of drugs commonly employed in the treatment of urinary tract infection is presented in Table 7-1. Reactions to sulfonamides were primarily allergic in nature, whereas nitrofurantoin therapy was accompa-

Table 7-1 Incidence of adverse reactions to nitrofurantoin and two soluble sulfonamides commonly used to treat urinary tract infections

Adverse reactions were monitored during 2,118 courses of therapy with sulfisoxazole, sulfamothoxazole, or nitrofurantoin in a prospective study. (Data from Koch-Weser et al.[45])

Drug	Courses of therapy: No.	Total reactions: No.	Reaction rate (%)	Toxic reactions: No.	Reaction rate (%)	Allergic reactions: No.	Reaction rate (%)
Sulfisoxazole	1,002	30	3.1	3	0.3	28	2.8
Sulfamethoxazole	359	12	3.3	1	0.3	11	3.0
Nitrofurantoin	757	70	9.2	39	5.1	31	4.1

nied by both toxic and allergic effects in a substantial percentage of cases. In this study, the overall frequency of adverse reactions severe enough to require discontinuation of nitrofurantoin therapy was 9.2 per cent. The allergic reactions to nitrofurantoin include a variety of rashes, urticaria, angioneurotic edema, eosinophilia, and drug fever.

Nitrofurantoin causes two types of pulmonary reactions. The acute reaction is characterized by fever, cough, and dyspnea.[47] The chest X-ray generally shows infiltration, especially in the base of the lungs, and pleural effusion often occurs. Eosinophilia is present in over 30 per cent of cases, but it clears rapidly when the drug is stopped. Several features of this acute reaction suggest that it is immunologically mediated, in particular, the fact that the entire syndrome rapidly recurs after rechallenge with the drug.[48] There is some evidence implicating cell-mediated immunity as a possible mechanism for this type of nitrofurantoin sensitivity.[49] The second type of pulmonary reaction is rare, and it occurs after treatment for more than 6 months. In this chronic reaction, the symptoms are insidious in onset, and they consist primarily of exertional dyspnea and cough.[50] The pathological features are those of interstitial fibrosis with or without interstitial pneumonitis. It is most likely that this reaction also has an immunological basis. In some cases, there may be improvement with termination of nitrofurantoin and institution of steroid therapy.

Occasionally, nitrofurantoin has been associated with the development of polyneuropathy. This is typically an ascending sensorimotor peripheral neuropathy and the mechanism is unknown.[51] Impaired renal function probably increases the risk of developing neuropathy.[44] Megaloblastic anemia and cholestatic jaundice occur rarely with nitrofurantoin therapy. The drug can cause hemolysis in patients with glucose-6-phosphate dehydrogenase deficiency (Chapter 10). Since several of the nitrofurans inhibit spermatogenesis and have radiomimetic and mutagenic properties, the carcinogenic activity of several compounds was examined in the rat.[52] Although some of the 5-nitrofuran derivatives were found to be active, nitrofurantoin and nitrofurazone were not carcinogenic.

METHENAMINE

Methenamine has been used as a urinary tract antiseptic for many years and most of the details of its pharmacology and action were worked out in 1913.[53] Methenamine itself is not bactericidal, but

Methenamine

it becomes hydrolyzed at acid pH to ammonia and formaldehyde, which is the active bactericidal agent. Formaldehyde is probably bactericidal by virture of its ability to denature protein. If bacteria are exposed to formaldehyde and then washed and suspended in formaldehyde-free medium, there is a delay before the remaining viable organisms begin growing again.[54] This bacteriostatic effect may be useful in therapy, since the organisms that remain in the

$$N_4(CH_2)_6 + 6H_2O + 4H^+ \rightarrow 4NH_4^+ + 6HCHO$$

bladder after voiding may function as a less effective inoculum in the fresh urine that is subsequently produced.

Methenamine is well absorbed from the gastrointestinal tract. Some drug is lost due to hydrolysis in the stomach, and enteric-coated preparations have been made available with the intention of reducing this loss. Methenamine distributes widely in the body spaces. But since almost no formaldehyde is generated at physiological pH, there is no antibacterial activity in blood, tissues, or body fluids. Since formaldehyde is formed only in an acid environment, it is essential that the pH of the patient's urine be kept at or below 5.5. Thus, it is necessary to administer an acidifying agent, like ascorbic acid, and to have the patient monitor the acidity of the urine with pH paper several times a day. Methenamine may be obtained as the mandelic or hippuric acid salt. It is unclear whether the presence of the mandelate or hippurate moiety significantly affects the pH of the urine, but these organic acids have some antibacterial effect of their own. Their antibacterial action is due to the undissociated form of the acid, which is only present in significant amounts at acid pH. It is not known if therapeutically important differences exist among the various methenamine preparations, although the mandelate and hippurate are prescribed more often.

Methenamine is used only for prophylactic or suppressive therapy. Methenamine mandelate, together with an acidifying agent, has been shown to be useful in the management of recurrent urinary tract infection in females,[55] although it does not appear to be as effective as trimethoprim–sulfamethoxazole administered once daily.[56] Methenamine has also been reported to be useful in prophylactic therapy of males with chronic bacteriuria.[32] The drug cannot be used to treat infections of the upper urinary tract because there is inadequate time for the generation of sufficient amounts of formaldehyde during the passage of urine through the kidney. Thus, methenamine is employed to sterilize the lower urinary tract between acute episodes of infection that are better treated with other drugs. Methenamine is generally not useful against such urea-splitting organisms as *Proteus*. These bacteria produce urease, an enzyme that breaks down urea into ammonia, thus raising the pH of the urine. In the presence of these organisms, it may be difficult or impossible to acidify the urine to the point at which sufficient formaldehyde is generated from methenamine. It has been shown that acetohydroxamic acid, a urease inhibitor, is synergistic with methenamine against *Proteus* in some culture systems *in vitro*.[57] Such a combined approach could prove useful in therapy if a nontoxic urease inhibitor were available.

Methenamine is usually well tolerated, with gastric distress and allergic reactions occurring occasionally. Some patients complain of symptoms of bladder irritation (dysuria, frequency, hematuria, urgency). The mandelic acid salt should not be given to patients in renal failure, since it can cause crystalluria if urine flow is inadequate.

REFERENCES

1. C. M. Kunin: *Detection, Prevention and Management of Urinary Tract Infections*. Philadelphia: Lea and Febiger, 1972, pp. 1–230.

2. Multiple Authors: *Urinary Tract Infection and Its Management*. ed by D. Kaye. Saint Louis: The C. V. Mosby Co., 1972, pp. 1–290.

3. W. Brumfitt and R. Pursell: Observations on bacterial sensitivies to nalidixic acid and critical comments on the 6-centre survey. *Postgrad. Med. J.* 47 Suppl.:16 (1971).

4. T. A. Stamey: Observations on the clinical use of nalidixic acid. *Postgrad. Med. J.* 47 Suppl.:21 (1971).

5. W. A. Goss, W. H. Deitz, and T. M. Cook: Mechanism of action of nalidixic acid on *Escherichia coli* II. Inhibition of deoxyribonucleic acid synthesis. *J. Bacteriol.* 89:1068 (1965).

6. P. Pienkos, A. Walfield, and C. L. Hershberger: Effect of nalidixic acid on *Euglena gracilis*: Induced loss of chloroplast deoxyribonucleic acid. *Arch. Biochem. Biophys.* 165:548 (1974).

7. A. Bauernfeind: Mode of action of nalidixic acid. *Antibiotics and Chemotherapy* 17:122 (1971).

8. W. H. Deitz, T. M. Cook, and W. A. Goss: Mechanism of action of nalidixic acid on *Eshericia coli*. III. Conditions required for lethality. *J. Bacteriol.* 91:768 (1966).

9. J. V. Boyle, T. M. Cook, and W. A. Goss: Mechanism of action of nalidixic acid on *Escherichia coli*. VI. Cell-free studies. *J. Bacteriol.* 97:230 (1969).

10. G. J. Bourguignon, M. Levitt, and R. Sternglanz: Studies on the mechanism of action of nalidixic acid. *Antimicrob. Agents Chemother.* 4:479 (1973).

11. A. M. Pedrini, D. Geroldi, A. Siccardi, and A. Falaschi: Studies on the mode of action of nalidixic acid. *Eur. J. Biochem.* 25:359 (1972).

12. R. E. Moses and C. C. Richardson: Replication and repair of DNA in cells of *Escherichia coli* treated with toluene. *Proc. Natl. Acad. Sci. U.S.* 67:674 (1970).

13. R. M. Burger and D. A. Glaser: Effect of nalidixic acid on DNA replication by toluene-treated *Escherichia coli*. *Proc. Natl. Acad. Sci. U.S.* 70:1955 (1973).

14. H. Eberle and W. E. Masker: Effect of nalidixic acid on semiconservative replication and repair synthesis after ultraviolet irradiation in *Escherichia coli*. *J. Bacteriol.* 105:908 (1971).

15. T. J. Simon, W. E. Masker, and P. C. Hanawalt: Selective inhibition of semiconservative DNA synthesis by nalidixic acid in permeabilized bacteria. *Biochim. Biophys. Acta* 349:271 (1974).

16. P. K. Schneck, W. L. Staudenbauer, and P. H. Hofschneider: Replication of bacteriophage M-13. Template specific inhibition of DNA synthesis by nalidixic acid. *Eur. J. Biochem.* 38:130 (1973).

17. H. Schaller, B. Otto, V. Nüsslein, J. Huf, R. Herrman, and F. Bonhoeffer: Deoxyribonucleic acid replication *in vitro*. *J. Mol. Biol.* 63:183 (1972).

18. M. Hane and T. Wood: *Escherichia coli* K-12 mutants resistant to nalidixic acid: Genetic mapping and dominance studies. *J. Bacteriol.* 99:238 (1969).

19. A. R. Ronald, M. Turck, and R. G. Petersdorf: A critical evaluation of nalidixic acid in urinary-tract infections. *New Eng. J. Med.* 275:1081 (1966).

20. E. Atlas, H. Clark, F. Silverblatt, and M. Turck: Nalidixic acid and oxolinic acid in the treatment of chronic bacteriuria. *Ann. Int. Med.* 70:713 (1969).

21. K. Mohring and P. O. Madsen: Treatment of urinary tract infections with oxolinic acid in patients with normal and impaired renal function. *Del. Med. J.* 43:376 (1971).

22. E. W. McChesney, E. J. Froelich, G. Y. Lesher, A. V. R. Crain, and D. Rosi: Absorption, excretion and metabolism of a new antibacterial agent, nalidixic acid. *Toxicol. & Appl. Pharmacol.* 6:292 (1964).

23. G. A. Portmann, E. W. McChesney, H. Stander, and W. E. Moore: Pharmacokinetic model for nalidixic acid in man. II. Parameters for absorption, metabolism and elimination. *J. Pharmaceut. Sci.* 55:72 (1966).

24. T. A. Stamey, E. M. Meares, and D. G. Winningham: Chronic bacterial prostatitis and the diffusion of drugs into prostatic fluid. *J. Urol.* 103:187 (1970).

25. T. A. Stamey, N. J. Nemoy, and M. Higgins: The clinical use of nalidixic acid: A review and some observations. *Invest. Urol.* 6:582 (1969).

26. D. A. Birkett, M. Garretts, and C. J. Stevenson: Phototoxic bullous eruptions due to nalidixic acid. *Br. J. Derm.* 81:342 (1969).

27. D. N. Cohen: Intracranial hypertension and papilledema associated with nalidixic acid therapy. *Am. J. Ophthalmol.* 76:680 (1973).

28. K. G. Rao: Pseudotumor cerebri associated with nalidixic acid. *Urology* 4:204 (1974).

29. C. E. Cox: Oxolinic acid therapy of recurrent urinary tract infections. *Del. Med. J.* 42:327 (1970).

30. W. J. Holloway: Nitrofurantoin in urinary tract infections. *Del. Med. J.* 44:99 (1972).

31. R. R. Bailey, A. P. Roberts, P. E. Gower, and H. E. deWardener: Prevention of urinary-tract infection with low-dose nitrofurantoin. *Lancet* 2:1112 (1971).

32. R. B. Freeman, W. M. Smith, J. A. Richardson, P. J. Hennelly, R. J. Thurm, C. Urner, J. A. Vaillancourt, R. J. Griep, and L. Bromer: Long-term therapy for chronic bacteriuria in men: U.S. Public Health Service cooperative study. *Ann. Int. Med.* 83:133 (1975).

33. H. E. Paul and M. F. Paul: "The Nitrofurans—Chemotherapeutic Properties" (first of two parts) in *Experimental Chemotherapy, vol. 2* (ed. R. J. Schnitzer and F. Hawking). New York: Academic Press, 1964, pp. 307–370.

34. H. E. Paul and M. F. Paul: "The Nitrofurans—Chemotherapeutic Properties" (second of two parts) in *Experimental Chemotherapy, vol. 4* (ed. R. J. Schnitzer and F. Hawking). New York: Academic Press, 1966. pp. 521–536.

35. M. F. Paul, H. E. Paul, R. C. Bender, F. Kopko, C. M. Harrington, V. R. Ells, and J. A. Buzard: Studies on the distribution and excretion of certain nitrofurans. *Antibiotics and Chemotherapy* 10:287 (1960).

36. G. P. C. Westwood and W. L. Hooper: Antagonism of oxolinic acid by nitrofurantoin. *Lancet* 1:460 (1975).

37. P. S. Albert, D. J. Mininberg, J. E. Davis: Nitrofurans: Sperm-immobilizing agents. Their tissue toxicity and clinical application. *Urology* 4:307 (1974).

38. J. D. Chapman, A. P. Reuvers, J. Borsa, A. Petkau, and D. R. McCalla: Nitrofurans as radiosensitizers of hypoxic mammalian cells. *Cancer Res.* 32:2616 (1972).

39. H. K. Reckendorf, R. G. Castringius, and H. K. Spingler: Comparative pharmacodynamics, urinary excretion, and half-life determinations of nitrofurantoin sodium. *Antimicrobial Agents and Chemotherapy— 1962* pp. 531–537 (1963).

40. J. Schirmeister, F. Stephani, H. Willmann, and W. Hallauer: Renal handling of nitrofurantoin in man. *Antimicrobial Agents and Chemotherapy—1965* pp. 223–226 (1966).

41. G. A. Currie, P. J. Little, and S. J. McDonald: The localization of cephaloridine and nitrofurantoin in the kidney. *Nephron* 3:282 (1966).

42. Y. J. Katz, A. T. K. Cockett, and R. S. Moore: Renal lymph and antibacterial levels in the treatment of pyelonephritis. *Life Sci.* 3:1249 (1964).

43. J. Sachs, T. Geer, P. Noell, and C. M. Kunin: Effect of renal function on urinary recovery of orally administered nitrofurantoin. *New Eng. J. Med.* 278:1032 (1968).

44. J. H. Felts, D. M. Hayes, J. A. Gergen, and J. F. Toole: Neural, hematologic and bacteriologic effects of nitrofurantoin in renal insufficiency. *Am. J. Med.* 51:331 (1971).

45. J. Koch-Weser, V. W. Sidel, M. Dexter, C. Parish, D. C. Finer, and P. Kanarek: Adverse reactions to sulfisoxazole, sulfamethoxazole, and nitrofurantoin. *Arch. Int. Med.* 128:399 (1971).

46. S. Kalowski, N. Radford, and P. Kincaid-Smith: Crystalline and macrocrystalline nitrofurantoin in the treatment of urinary-tract infection. *New Eng. J. Med.* 290:385 (1974).

47. F. J. Hailey, H. W. Glascock, and W. F. Hewitt: Pleuropneumonic reactions to nitrofurantoin. *New Eng. J. Med.* 281:1087 (1969).

48. T. M. Nicklaus and A. B. Snyder: Nitrofurantoin pulmonary reaction: A unique syndrome. *Arch Int. Med.* 121:151 (1968).

49. H. R. Pearsall, J. Ewalt, M. S. Tsoi, S. Sumida, D. Bachus, R. H. Winterbauer, D. R. Webb, and H. Jones: Nitrofurantoin lung sensitivity: Report of a case with prolonged nitrofurantoin lymphocyte sensitivity and interaction of nitrofurantoin-stimulated lymphocytes with alveolar cells. *J. Lab. Clin. Med.* 83:728 (1974).

50. E. C. Rosenow, R. A. DeRemee, and D. E. Dines: Chronic nitrofurantoin pulmonary reaction: Report of five cases. *New Eng. J. Med.* 279:1258 (1968).

51. J. F. Toole and M. L. Parrish: Nitrofurantoin polyneuropathy. *Neurology* 23:554 (1973).

52. J. E. Morris, J. M. Price, J. J. Lalich, and R. J. Stein: The carcinogenic activity of some 5-nitrofuran derivatives in the rat. *Cancer Res.* 29:2145 (1969).

53. P. J. Hanzlik and R. J. Collins: Hexamethyleneamin: The liberation of formaldehyd and the antiseptic efficiency under different chemical and biological conditions. *Arch. Int. Med.* 12:578 (1913).

54. D. M. Musher and D. P. Griffith: Generation of formaldehyde from methenamine: Effect of pH and concentration, and antibacterial effect. *Antimicrob. Agents Chemother.* 6:708 (1974).

55. N. H. Holland and C. D. West: Prevention of recurrent urinary tract infections in girls. *Am. J. Dis. Child.* 105:560 (1963).

56. G. K. M. Harding and A. R. Ronald: A controlled study of antimicrobial prophylaxis of recurrent urinary infection in women. *New Eng. J. Med.* 291:597 (1974).

57. D. M. Musher, D. P. Griffith, M. Tyler, and A. Woelfel: Potentiation of the antibacterial effect of methenamine by acetohydroxamic acid. *Antimicrob. Agents Chemother.* 5:101 (1974).

Chapter 8
Chemotherapy of Tuberculosis
Isoniazid
Ethambutol
Rifampin
Streptomycin, Para-aminosalicylic Acid, Pyrazinamide, Ethionamide, Cycloserine, Viomycin, Kanamycin, Capreomycin

Introduction

The treatment of tuberculosis is a special problem within the field of chemotherapy. Some of the drugs used in treating this disease [streptomycin, para-aminosalicylic acid (PAS), cycloserine, kanamycin] have been presented in earlier chapters, since it was more convenient to consider them along with other agents having a similar mechanism of action. Many of the drugs employed in antituberculosis therapy are used only in treating infections caused by mycobacteria. The drugs used to treat tuberculosis may be divided into two groups according to their clinical usefulness. The major agents include isoniazid, ethambutol, streptomycin, and rifampin. If organisms prove resistant and cannot be treated with an appropriate combination of drugs from this group, then the less common and generally more toxic agents must be employed. These minor drugs include PAS, cycloserine, viomycin, pyrazinamide, kanamycin, capreomycin, and ethionamide .

Treatment of the active case of tuberculosis virtually always includes simultaneous therapy with two or more of the major drugs. It was observed some time ago that organisms resistant to a single drug are rather readily selected from populations of tubercle bacilli. Combinations of drugs are used to decrease the rate of emergence of resistance as well as increase the antibacterial effect. Combination chemotherapy has become a cornerstone of the treatment of tuberculosis.

The choice of drugs to be used in treating tuberculosis depends on many factors including the organ system involved, the severity of the disease, the state of the patient's renal and hepatic function, the in vitro sensitivity of the organism, and any history of relapse or failure to respond to previous therapy. The reader is referred to the therapeutic literature for specific recommendations regarding therapy. This introduction will be concerned only with brief mention of the therapeutic rationale behind some approaches used in treating pulmonary tuberculosis and the concept of preventive therapy.

Standard Daily Therapy

In general, therapy of pulmonary tuberculosis involves a prolonged period of treatment lasting for 18 to 20 months. In severe disease, a two-phase chemotherapeutic approach is almost always employed. This includes an initial period of intensive drug therapy when the bacterial population is large, followed by a long period of less intensive treatment.[1,2] Virtually all therapeutic regimens include isoniazid. In far advanced cavitary disease of the chest, for example, therapy is often initiated with isoniazid, ethambutol, and streptomycin. Streptomycin is very effective, but it has its drawbacks: it must be given by intramuscular injection and it is rather toxic. When the sputum no longer contains acid-fast bacilli, streptomycin administration is usually stopped. Since both isoniazid and ethambutol are given orally, therapy then becomes more convenient. In cases of minimal to moderate pulmonary tuberculosis, streptomycin therapy is usually not necessary and a regimen of isoniazid and ethambutol may be given for the complete course of treatment.

Some physicians prefer to keep the newer drug rifampin in reserve for retreatment of patients who have relapsed or failed to respond to the initial drug regimen. But rifampin can be used very effectively in the initial treatment of severe tuberculosis. It has been shown that far-advanced cavitary disease can be treated as well with an oral regimen consisting of isoniazid and rifampin as with the two-phase approach starting with isoniazid, ethambutol, and streptomycin.[3] This form of therapy may become more common, since there is some evidence that conversion to a negative sputum occurs sooner and earlier outpatient treatment may be facilitated.

Intermittent Therapy

In standard daily therapy, the drugs must be taken for a long enough period of time to ensure that the disease will not become reactivated—ordinarily for 2 years.[4] In many patient populations, the long period of continued therapy after the disease appears to be cured is compromised by erratic compliance and premature termination of therapy. Several investigators have suggested that with these patients programs of intermittent chemotherapy may be preferable to irregular self-administration. The intermittent programs usually consist of an initial phase of 1 to 3 months of daily therapy followed by the completely supervised, twice weekly administration of isoniazid and streptomycin.[5,6] The effectiveness of combinations of oral drugs in biweekly adminis- tration is also being evaluated.

Short-course Therapy

It would be of great advantage if the duration of chemotherapy for tuberculosis could be significantly shortened. In order to test this possibility, an extensive therapeutic trial was conducted with several drug regimens.[7,8] The results suggest that daily therapy with streptomycin, isoniazid, and rifampin for 6 months may be as effective in treating pulmonary tuberculosis as the standard 18- month program. This regimen has the drawback of requiring a daily injection (streptomycin), but it may prove possible to achieve success with a shorter term of streptomycin administra- tion or with a combination of oral agents alone. The possibility that pulmonary tuberculosis could be cured with only 6 months of treatment is indeed attractive.

Preventive Therapy

The term chemoprophylaxis is not appropriately applied with respect to tuberculosis.[1] In tuberculosis, instead of trying to pre- vent infection, a drug is being given in order to prevent the development of clinically apparent disease in people who are already infected. Preventive daily therapy is carried out with isoniazid for 1 year. At the dosage used for preventive therapy, isoniazid can produce hepatitis. The likelihood that a person will develop hepatitis increases with age, and because of this all persons who are positive tuberculin reactors are not automatic candidates for preventive therapy. The following recommenda- tions serve as guidelines for determining which patients with positive tuberculin tests should be considered for preventive ther- apy with isoniazid.[9]

Preventive therapy is mandatory for patients up to 7 years of age and highly recommended to age 35. Among positive reactors over 35, the risk of hepatitis precludes the routine use of preventive

Table 8-1   **Risk factors to be considered in determining candidates for preventive therapy with isoniazid**
(According to guidelines presented by the American Thoracic Society.[9])

A. Household members and other close associates of persons with recently diagnosed tuberculous disease
B. Positive tuberculin reactors with findings on chest X-ray consistent with nonprogressive tuberculous disease, without positive bacteriological findings, and without a history of adequate chemotherapy
C. Newly infected persons
D. Positive tuberculin reactors in the following special clinical situations:
  1. Prolonged therapy with glucocorticoids
  2. Immunosuppressive therapy
  3. Some hematological and reticuloendothelial diseases, such as leukemia or Hodgkin's disease
  4. Diabetes mellitus
  5. Silicosis
  6. After gastrectomy

therapy unless one of the additional risk factors presented in Table 8-1 is present. When these risk factors are not present, positive reactors in this age group should be considered for preventive therapy on an individual basis. This consideration is based on the likelihood of serous consequences to contacts who may become infected. Appropriate examples include those who live in a closed environment, people who work with infants, children, or patients with impaired immune systems. Contraindications to preventive therapy include pregnancy, acute liver disease, and a history of previous isoniazid-associated hepatic injury or other severe reaction to the drug.

ISONIAZID

Isoniazid has been used to treat tuberculosis for many years. A great deal of information has become available regarding its mechanism of action, the genetic control of its metabolism, and the biochemical basis of its hepatotoxic effect.

Isoniazid

Mechanism of Action

Isoniazid is bactericidal against actively growing tubercle bacilli; is is less effective against resting tubercle cells.[10] Isoniazid has been reported to affect a number of cellular functions,[11] but the results of several studies suggest that the primary drug effect is to inhibit synthesis of mycolic acids.[12,13] Mycolic acids are β-hydroxy acids substituted at the α-position with a long aliphatic side chain, and they are important components of the cell walls of mycobacteria. When actively growing cultures of *Mycobacterium tuberculosis* are exposed to bactericidal concentrations of isoniazid, the cells rapidly lose their ability to incorporate precursors into mycolic acid.[14] The inhibition of mycolic acid synthesis is the earliest effect observed upon uptake of isoniazid into the bacterium, preceding the loss in cell viability by several hours. The mycolic acid-synthesizing system is inhibited at very low concentrations of the drug[15] and there is evidence that isoniazid prevents the elongation of a 26-carbon fatty acid, thus inhibiting the synthesis of very long chain fatty acids that are precursors of the mycolic acids.[16] It is not clear, however why the formation of a mycolate-deficient cell wall results in the loss of cell viability. Gross morphological changes are observed in isoniazid treated cells by 24 hours.[17] It is possible that mycolate-depleted cell walls are structurally weak, and distortion of cell architecture and finally cell rupture occur.

A primary effect of isoniazid on mycolic acid synthesis would explain both the limited spectrum of action and the basis for the selective toxicity of the drug. The clinical usefulness of isoniazid is limited to *M. tuberculosis* and some atypical mycobacterial infections. Organisms of other genera and fungi are not affected unless extremely high concentrations are present *in vitro*. The mycolic acids are the major lipid components of the lipid-rich cell wall and other parts of the cell envelope of mycobacteria, and they appear to be unique to this class of organism. Since mycolic acids are not present in animal cells, there is selective toxicity with respect to the host.

Concentration and Duration of Exposure

The effect of isoniazid *in vitro* and *in vivo* is related to both the concentration of and the duration of exposure to the drug.[18] This observation is of some clinical importance, since insoniazid levels rise and fall with each drug administration. At low concentration, the drug effect is bacteriostatic, and at higher levels, it is bactericidal. With multiple pulses of isoniazid there is a cumulative effect in vitro that is not observed if the pulses are too far apart.[18] When isoniazid is given to patients on an intermittent schedule, there are limits on how far apart the doses can be spaced and still retain the drug effect.[19] For example, with people who rapidly inactivate isoniazid (fast acetylators), therapeutic efficacy decreases sharply if the drug is given less often than twice a week.[20] This is, of course, what would be expected if the drug killed a certain percentage of the organisms and in the interval remaining before the next dose viable organisms multiplied sufficiently rapidly to restore the bacterial population. But there may be an additional explanation at the subcellular level. If M. tuberculosis, H37RA strain, is exposed to isoniazid for 60 minutes in vitro (by this time there is virtually complete inhibition of mycolate synthesis)[14] and then permitted to grow in the absence of the drug, the mycolic acid-synthesizing capacity slowly returns to normal.[21] There is no recovery of activity if the exposure time is 10 hours (by this time there is 90 per cent loss of cell viability) or longer. Thus, the biochemical effect of isoniazid is reversible if too much time has not elapsed. Effective drug treatment may depend upon preventing the occurrence of this reversal.

Resistance

Several studies suggest that mycobacteria resistant to isoniazid may take up less drug than sensitive cells.[11] The mechanism of drug accumulation is not well understood. The drug becomes concentrated in the tubercle bacillus[23] and uptake is blocked by anoxia and metabolic poisons.[11] Isoniazid is metabolized by the tubercle bacillus to the biologically inactive isonicotinic acid.[11] Resistance is not due to an increased rate of drug inactivation.[24] It seems likely that the affinity of the resistant cells for isoniazid has decreased, or less drug passes into the organism.

It is clear that resistant mutants occur at random and spontaneously in growing populations of tubercle bacilli.[25] In the presence of the drug, there is a selection for resistant organisms. The larger the initial population of bacilli, the greater the likelihood that significant numbers of resistant cells exist before initiation of therapy. Selection of single-drug resistant mutants is discouraged by combination chemotherapy, but tubercle bacilli can acquire resistance to several drugs during therapy. This multiple-drug resistance in mycobacteria is a consequence of multiple mutations and not multiple-drug resistance transfer as occurs with R-factors in enterobacteria. It should be noted, however, that there is evidence for the occurrence of a plasmid for streptomycin resistance in M. smegmatis and that the resistance can be transferred by mycobacteriophage.[26] Both sensitivity and resistance to isoniazid have been transduced in another strain of the same organism.[27] Sensitivity is transduced at a higher frequency than resistance.

Pharmacology of Isoniazid

Absorption and Administration

Isoniazid is rapidly absorbed, primarily from the intestine.[28] Lower peak serum levels are obtained if antacids are given concomitantly.[29] Peak plasma levels are achieved in 1 to 2 hours, there is no protein binding, and the drug is distributed throughout the body water.[30] Substantial levels of drug are found in pleural effusions and in the cerebrospinal fluid (20 per cent of plasma levels) of both normal subjects and patients with tuberculous meningitis.[30] Isoniazid passes through the placenta, and concentrations in breast milk are similar to those in plasma. Studies of the distribution of radioactive isoniazid in man have shown that the drug readily passes into, and is retained in, caseous tuberculous lesions.[30]

Metabolism

The primary route of isoniazid metabolism in man is by acetylation to acetyl isoniazid.[31] The enzyme responsible for the metabolism is an N-acetyltransferase that is located in the soluble fraction of liver cells.[32] In this reaction, an acetyl moiety from acetyl-Coenzyme A (acetyl-CoA) is first transferred to the enzyme, forming an acetylated enzyme intermediate (1). The acetyl group

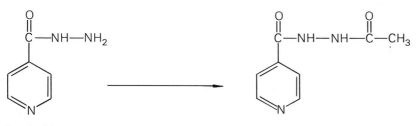

Isoniazid   Acetylated isoniazid

is then transferred to the drug, and the nonacetylated enzyme is regenerated (2). In humans, sulfamethazine and dapsone are acetylated by the same enzyme.[33]

(1) N-Acetyltransferase + acetyl-CoA $\rightleftharpoons$
Acetyl N-acetyltransferase + CoA
(2) Acetyl-N-acetyltransferase + isoniazid $\rightleftharpoons$
Acetyl isoniazid + N-acetyltransferase

The metabolism of isoniazid is noninducible, and the rate of metabolism is constant in any one patient. But there are large differences from one person to another in the rate of isoniazid acetylation. The great majority of individuals can be characterized as either slow or rapid metabolizers of the drug.[33,34] Slow acetylation is inherited as an autosomal recessive trait.[34] Thus, a slow acetylator is homozygous for two allelic genes, whereas rapid acetylators are either heterozygotes or homozygous for the rapid gene (see the table, below). The phenotype appears with varying frequency in populations of different racial origin. Estimates of the frequency of slow acetylators range from as low as 5 per cent among Canadian Eskimos to as high as 83 per cent among Egyp-

Genotype	Phenotype
slow-slow	Slow
slow-rapid	Rapid
rapid-rapid	Rapid

tians.[34] In the United States, 58 per cent of Caucasians are slow acetylators. Since acetylation is the primary route determining the rate at which isoniazid is eliminated from the body,[35] slow acetylators will tend to have elevated levels of the drug in the plasma. This relationship is presented in Figure 8-1. In this study, isoniazid was given intravenously to over 300 Finnish patients, and serum drug levels and half-lives were determined.[36] The mean half-life for isoniazid in fast acetylators is about 80 minutes (range 40 to 110 minutes), and it is 180 minutes (range 110 to more than 270 minutes) in slow acetylators. The average serum concentration of active drug in rapid acetylators is 30 to 50 per cent of that in the slow metabolizing individuals.

N-Acetyltransferase has been partially purified from the livers of both rapid and slow acetylators. The enzymes from the two acetylator phenotypes behave similarly upon purification and they have the same kinetic properties and the same specificity for a variety of substrates.[32,34] There is, as yet, no evidence for any qualitative difference between the human enzymes from the two

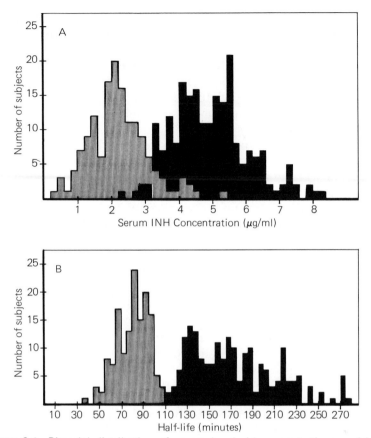

Figure 8-1 Bimodal distribution of serum isoniazid concentrations and half-lives in a large group of Finnish patients. More than 300 patients were given intravenous injections of 5 mg/kg of isoniazid (INH). Serum drug concentrations were assayed at multiple times after injection. (A) The distribution of the serum half-lives of isoniazid; the stippled histograms represent rapid inactivators, and the solid histograms, slow inactivators. (B) The distribution of serum concentrations of isoniazid for patients of each group 180 minutes after injection. (From Tiitinen.[36])

groups. Thus, it has been suggested that the difference in acetylating capacity reflects different levels of the same enzyme protein.[32] As is often the case, more detailed studies in animal models indicate that the situation is more complex. Using a rabbit model, Weber and his colleagues have found that N-acetyltransferase exists in more than one form.[37] The liver of rapid acetylating rabbits contains two isoenzymes with physical characteristics and substrate specificities that differ from those of the single enzyme obtained from the liver of slow acetylators. If these more definitive observations can be extrapolated to humans, there is the distinct possibility that the difference between rapid and slow acetylators may be due to subtle qualitative differences in N-acetyltransferases. Like humans, rabbits also have enzymes in extrahepatic tissues capable of N-acetylating a variety of substrates. These transferases are not under the same genetic control as the liver isoenzymes, but studies conducted both in vitro and in vivo demonstrate that, for certain substrates, extrahepatic N-acetyltransferase activity contributes significantly to the total acetylating capacity of the animal.[38,39]

The genetic variations in the rate of isoniazid metabolism are of fundamental clinical importance, both in explaining limitations on the types of treatment schedules that can be employed in intermittent therapy and in the manifestation of drug toxicity. When isoniazid is being given on a daily basis, as in standard therapy, the acetylator status of an individual does not affect the therapeutic result.[35] But the acetylator phenotype is very important in weekly intermittent therapy in which rapid acetylators have fared considerably worse than slow acetylators.[35] Some untoward reactions are more likely to occur in slow acetylating individuals. Peripheral neuropathy, a common adverse effect of isoniazid, is clearly dose-related[40] and occurs more often in slow acetylators. In contrast, isoniazid hepatitis appears to occur with a higher frequency in rapid acetylators. There is an interesting drug interaction between isoniazid and diphenylhydantoin that is related to the acetylation polymorphism. Isoniazid is a noncompetitive inhibitor of diphenylhydantoin metabolism,[41] and when both drugs are given, patients who are slow acetylators are more likely to develop symptoms of diphenylhydantoin toxicity.[42]

Excretion

Isoniazid and its metabolites are excreted in the urine. In man, the major metabolites are acetylisoniazid and isonicotinic acid.[43] A small amount of unaltered drug is also excreted. The ratio of acetylisoniazid to free isoniazid in the urine of rapid acetylators is much greater than that of the slow acetylators.[30,43] The metabolites of isoniazid are less toxic and are more rapidly excreted by the kidney.[35] Although the principal limitation on the rate of excretion of isoniazid is the rate of its metabolism, the drug will accumulate in patients with markedly impaired renal function (serum creatinine greater than 12), and isoniazid serum concentrations should be monitored in this group.[44] It is reasonable to predict (although it has not been proven) that the effect of renal failure would be of more concern in slow acetylators. The effect of liver disease on isoniazid levels is not well documented. There is some evidence that serum concentrations of total isoniazid are higher in patients with chronic·liver disease.[45]

Untoward Effects of Isoniazid

Neurotoxicity

Isoniazid can produce a variety of effects in the central and peripheral nervous systems. The most common effect is peripheral neuritis. This dose-related effect[40] is more likely to occur in malnourished individuals, chronic alcoholics, and slow acetylators. The symptoms usually consist of numbness and tingling in the lower extremities.[46] Sometimes paresthesias occur in the hands and fingers as well. Frequently, there is also muscle aching, which is made worse by activity. Although sensory complaints dominate, weakness and rarely ataxia can occur. The syndrome reverses rapidly if the drug is withdrawn soon after the onset of symptoms, but if therapy is continued for more than a few weeks, residual difficulties may persist for as long as a year. The incidence is probably about 1 per cent in patients taking 3 to 5 mg/kg of isoniazid daily but is considerably higher with larger doses. The syndrome can be prevented by daily administration of pyridoxine (100 mg). The pyridoxine does not affect the antibacterial action of isoniazid.[30]

Central nervous system side effects include symptoms of excitability, which extend from irritability and restlessness to seizures. Isoniazid overdosage (sometimes as intentional ingestion) can result in hyperglycemia, metabolic acidosis, and seizures. Death or prolonged coma from persistent seizure activity has occurred upon administration of conventional doses, and caution should be used in patients with a known history of seizures. Although the basis for the seizure activity is not clear, it is interesting to note that isoniazid markedly alters the levels of brain gamma-aminobutyric acid (GABA) in experimental animals. Moreover, the simultaneous administration of pyridoxine with a convulsant dose of isoniazid both prevents the onset of seizures and attenuates the fall in GABA levels in chicks.[47] Large doses of intravenous pyridoxine have also been reported to terminate seizures in patients with isoniazid overdosage.[48] Caution must be exercised when giving isoniazid to patients who are also receiving diphenylhydantoin. For reasons noted above, diphenylhydantoin toxicity (lethergy, incoordination) is more likely to occur in slow isoniazid inactivators receiving both drugs. A variety of psychological effects may be seen with isoniazid. These range from complaints of depression and impairment of memory to the manifestation of acute toxic psychosis (more common in patients with a history of mental instability).[49] Other rare but serious neurological complications include toxic encephalopathy and optic neuritis.

Allergic Reactions and Drug Side Effects

Isoniazid occasionally causes allergic reactions including fever and a variety of rashes.[50] It is one of several drugs that can produce a syndrome very similar to lupus erythematosis.[51] The syndrome includes vasculitis and other clinical features of lupus as well as the serological abnormalities. Antinuclear antibodies have been found in a substantial percentage of tuberculosis patients treated with isoniazid.[52] The clinically manifest lupus syndrome occurs only rarely, however, and it usually disappears when therapy is stopped. Other antimicrobial agents that have been implicated in the etiology of lupus include penicillins, sulfonamides, tetracycline, streptomycin, PAS, and griseofulvin.[51] Isoniazid has rarely been associated with the production of blood dyscrasias, including anemia and agranulocytosis.[46]

Symptoms and signs of pellagra (including skin lesions) can be precipitated in malnourished individuals treated with isoniazid. They respond to administration of niacinamide. Anemia due to a pyridoxine deficiency can occur. Occasionally, patients receiving isoniazid will complain of dry mouth, gastrointestinal distress, or difficulty in micturation.

Hepatotoxicity

Although there were a few reports of hepatotoxicity in patients receiving isoniazid during the first two decades of its use, the extent of the problem was not clearly recognized until 1970 when it was reported that 19 of 2,321 persons developed hepatitis while receiving the drug in a program of preventive therapy.[53] In response to this disclosure, the U.S. Public Health Service set up a nationwide program of surveillance of new recipients of isoniazid to identify the nature and extent of the risk associated with the drug. Several studies were also initiated to determine the pathophysiological and biochemical basis of the problem. The work carried out between 1971 and 1975 is reviewed in the proceedings of a conference held at the National Institutes of Health.[54] These investigations are an excellent example of well-coordinated and well-designed research in clinical pharmacology.

From 10 to 20 per cent of patients receiving isoniazid in preventive therapy develop evidence of subclinical hepatic injury as indicated by abnormal serum transaminase (SGOT) and bilirubin values.[55] Most patients who develop biochemical evidence of hepatic injury recover completely while continuing to take isoniazid. A few progress to the stage of clinically overt hepatitis. It is not clear why some patients are able to adapt to the liver injury while others progress. There is a definite relationship between the development of overt hepatitis and the age of the patient. Progressive liver damage is rarely seen in patients under 20 years of age, but the incidence is 1.2 per cent in the 35- to 49-year group and up to 2.3 per cent in those 50 years and over.[9] Histological examination of liver biopsies from patients with clinical hepatitis reveals mainly hepatocellular damage—in some cases there is submassive or massive necrosis.[56] Prior to the onset of jaundice, patients may complain of gastrointestinal symptoms (anorexia, nausea, vomiting, abdominal distress), weakness, and fatigue.[56] Hepatic injury may occur at any time during therapy. For example, in one study, 54 per cent of the patients had received isoniazid for periods of 2 to 11 months before hepatic injury was noted.[56]

There is no correlation between plasma drug concentration and susceptibilitity to isoniazid-induced liver injury. In the Public Health Service survey, which involved almost 14,000 patients, it was noted that people of Oriental ancestry were more susceptible to isoniazid liver injury than other populations.[56] A very high percentage (85 to 90 per cent) of Orientals are rapid acetylators.[34] In a group of 21 non-Oriental patients, who had recovered from probable isoniazid hepatitis, 86 per cent were found to be rapid inactivators, whereas the expected frequency should have been about 45 per cent.[43] An examination of the isoniazid metabolites in the two phenotypes revealed that rapid acetylators hydrolyze much more isoniazid to isonicotinic acid and the free hydrazine moiety (Figure 8-2) than slow acetylators. The hydrazine formed is primarily acetylhydrazine, and it is probable that this is the product that injures the liver.

Acetylhydrazine has been shown to produce liver cell necrosis in rats. Toxicity may result from metabolic activation of acetylhydrazine to compounds that subsequently link covalently to

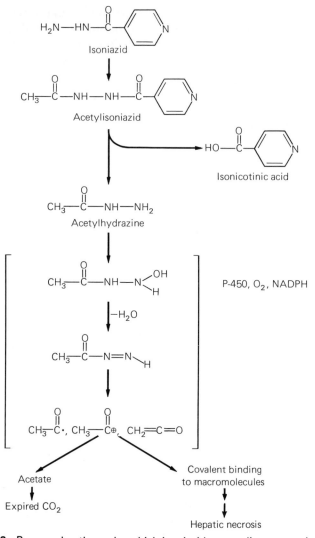

Figure 8-2 Proposed pathway by which isoniazid causes liver necrosis. Isoniazid is first converted to acetylisoniazid by N-acetyltransferase. Most of the acetylisoniazid is hydrolyzed to acetylhydrazine and isonicotinic acid (which is not hepatotoxic). There is evidence that acetylhydrazine is converted by the hepatic P-450 drug metabolizing system to one or more reactive intermediates that can covalently bind to components of liver cells. The compounds presented within brackets represent a suggested scheme for the production of the intermediates. (From Mitchell *et al.*[54])

macromolecules in the liver. Studies in rats suggest that the metabolic activation requires the participation of the hepatic P-450 enzyme system.[54] Pretreatment of rats with phenobarbital (a compound that induces P-450—dependent drug metabolizing activity) increases the extent of liver necrosis and the amount of covalent binding of hydrazine after administration of either acetylisoniazid or acetylhydrazine.[54] It is clear that isonicotinic acid does not produce liver necrosis. If acetylisoniazid or isoniazid is radiolabeled in the pyridine ring and given to rats, no radioactivity becomes covalently associated with liver components. But if the animals are given acetylisoniazid labeled in the acetyl side chain, or labeled acetylhydrazine, there is significant covalent binding (as much as 0.5 nmoles/mg of hepatic protein).[54] These observations on metabolic activation and covalent binding have also been carried out with liver preparations in vitro.[54]

Rarely, individuals with isoniazid hepatitis have presented with features suggestive of an allergic phenomenon.[57] In some patients, isoniazid hepatitis may have an allergic basis, but this is not generally the case, and there are many facets of the syndrome that are not consistent with a hypersensitivity mechanism.[54] The schema of events leading to isoniazid-mediated liver injury presented in Figure 8-2 is a reasonable proposal on the basis of the observations in humans and in animal models. The difference in the incidence of hepatitis for rapid versus slow acetylators is probably due to the fact that rapid acetylators are exposed to about 50 per cent more free acetylhydrazine than the slow acetylators.[43] Almost all of the isonicotinic acid excreted in the urine comes from acetylisoniazid rather than isoniazid.[43] Thus, the predominant hydrazine produced is acetylhydrazine, and the rate of production of this compound depends upon the rate of drug acetylation (Figure 8-2). The fact that older people are more likely to develop clinical hepatitis may simply reflect a decreased ability to rapidly repair hepatitic damage with advancing age. At present, the model assumes that acylation of macromolecules in the liver leads to hepatic necrosis. This may be true, but the mechanism is not known.

ETHAMBUTOL

The efficacy of ethambutol in the initial treatment of pulmonary tuberculosis is well established.[58,59] It has the advantages of oral administration and low toxicity. Tubercle bacilli can become resistant, however, so the drug is always given in combination with one or two other agents.

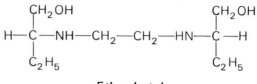

Ethambutol

Mechanism of Action

Ethambutol is effective only against mycobacteria. It is active against dividing organisms but there is no effect on the survival of nonproliferating cells.[60] Ethambutol rapidly enters mycobacteria by passive diffusion, but growth inhibition is not apparent until many hours after addition of the drug to a culture. Both the association of radiolabeled ethambutol with mycobacteria and growth inhibition are prevented in a nonspecific manner by cations and polyamines.[61] The amount of growth inhibition obtained depends upon length of exposure to the drug.[62] It is not known what biochemical process is primarily affected by ethambutol. The early effects of the drug are reversible, and when cells from inhibited cultures are resuspended in drug-free medium, growth resumes after a prolonged lag period. There is no lag, however, if the cells had been exposed to the drug at low temperature. The lag period is thought to represent the time required for repair of the biochemical damage incurred during growth in the presence of the drug.[63]

Pharmacology

Ethambutol (80 to 90 per cent of a dose) is rapidly absorbed from the gastrointestinal tract, and the peak serum concentration is achieved in about 2 hours.[64,65] The drug enters the cerebrospinal fluid in therapeutic concentrations (the levels here range from 10 to 50 per cent of the serum concentration), whether or not there is inflammation of the meninges.[66,67] Ethambutol is metabolized to a small extent (about 20 per cent) in the liver, being converted first to an aldehyde and then an acid.[65] The drug has been shown to be a substrate for purified alcohol dehydrogenase.[68] The rate of metabolism remains constant even when the drug is given daily over a prolonged period of time.[65] The unchanged drug and its metabolites are eliminated by the kidney with a normal half-life in the range of 8 hours. Since the kidney is the principal route of excretion, serum levels should be measured and dosage adjusted accordingly in patients with poor renal function.[69] Ethambutol produces a substantial increase in serum uric acid concentration in about 60 per cent of patients.[70] This is due to the fact that it decreases the renal clearance of urate, but the details of the mechanism are not known.[70]

Untoward Effects

Ethambutol is generally well tolerated. It occasionally produces mild gastrointestinal upset, allergic reactions (including dermatitis, pruritis, and rarely, anaphylaxis), dizziness, mental confusion, fever, malaise, and headache. Precipitation of acute gout (due to interference with urate excretion) has been reported. Rarely, peripheral neuritis (mainly sensory) occurs.[71] The principal untoward effect of ethambutol is retrobulbar neuritis. This is a dose-related effect.[72] In one study, the incidence of optic neuritis was about 1 per cent in patients on a regimen of 25 mg/kg daily for 60 days, followed by a maintenance dose of 15 mg/kg daily.[73] There are two types of retrobulbar neuritis.[72] In the most common type, the central fibers of the optic nerve are involved, and the signs are loss of central vision and disturbance in color discrimination. In the less common type, the peripheral fibers of the optic nerve are affected; here there may be no loss of visual acuity, but there is constriction of peripheral fields of vision. Vision may be unilaterally or bilaterally affected. The neuritis usually occurs after 2 months of therapy and is reversible on withdrawal of the drug in the majority of cases. No changes are evident on fundascopic examination.[73] All patients should have a comprehensive ophthalmologic examination before initiation of therapy to establish an accurate base line for reference. The value of routine testing of vision during therapy, however, is unclear. In the experience of some observers, visual tests fail to detect ocular toxicity before symptoms (blurring of vision, loss of color discrimination) occur,[74] but others recommend periodic assessment of visual acuity.[75] Clearly, patients should be advised to report any visual disturbances to the physician, and they should be questioned about their vision during each office visit.

RIFAMPIN

Rifampin is one of a large number of semisynthetic derivatives of the antibiotic rifamycin B. Rifampin is very active against myco-bacteria, gram-positive organisms and *Neisseria* species. There is considerably less activity against gram-negative bacilli because the drug does not readily penetrate the cell envelope. The actions of the rifamycins have been reviewed by Wehrli and Staehelin.[76]

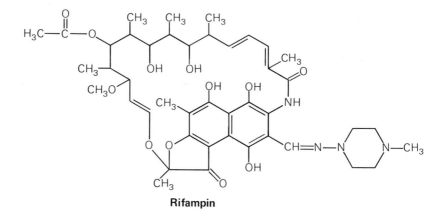

Rifampin

Mechanism of Action

The bactericidal effect of rifampin is due to inhibition of RNA synthesis.[77] The drug inhibits RNA synthesis by interacting directly with DNA-dependent RNA polymerase. Rifampin binds in a very tight,[78] but non-covalent[79] manner to the enzyme from sensitive bacteria but not to RNA polymerases from resistant strains.[78,80] Quantitative measurements have shown that one mole of rifampin is bound per mole of enzyme.[76]

Bacterial RNA polymerases are composed of several polypep-tide chains. The core enzyme from *Escherichia coli*, for example, contains at least four subunits (2α, 1β, and $1\beta'$). In addition, the enzyme core binds another unit, the σ factor. The σ factor effects recognition of the promoter regions of the DNA where transcrip-tion is initiated. The subunits of the core enzyme can be disso-ciated, separated from one another by electrophoresis, and then reassociated, to form a complex with enzyme activity.[81] This technique has permitted reconstitution experiments utilizing components purified from rifampin-sensitive and rifampin-resistant RNA polymerases. The effect of rifampin on the function of such reconstituted enzymes is shown in Table 8-2. The reconstituted enzymes are only about 20 per cent as active as the original drug-sensitive and drug-resistant polymerases from which the subunits were derived, but it is clear that the β subunit must be derived from the drug-sensitive polymerase for substantial rifampin inhibition to take place.[81]

The β subunits of RNA polymerases from resistant bacterial strains have in some cases been found to have different physical properties from the analogous drug-sensitive subunits.[82,83] Rifampin associates weakly with the isolated β subunit of drug-sensitive polymerase,[84] but binding to the reconstituted enzyme is much tighter.[79] Thus, the receptor for rifampin is the β subunit of bacterial, DNA-dependent RNA polymerase. Rifampin is bound most tightly when the β subunit is in the conformation it assumes in the holo enzyme ($\alpha_2\beta\beta'\sigma$). The DNA polymerases are unaffected by the drug.

Rifampin inhibits the initiation of RNA synthesis, but synthesis in progress at the time of drug exposure is not affected.[85] If rifampin is added to RNA polyerase that has been preincubated with DNA template, the subsequent initiation of RNA chain syn-

Table 8-2 Demonstration that the β subunit is required for rifampin inhibition of bacterial RNA polymerase

Purified polymerases from rifampin-sensitive and rifampin-resistant bacteria were dissociated, and the α, β, and β' subunits were separated by electrophoresis. The subunits were then mixed in stoichiometric ratio, σ factor was added, and the units were permitted to reassociate. The activity of the reconstituted enzymes was then assayed in the presence or absence of rifampin. The subscript r refers to subunits derived from the rifampin-resistant polymerase. Enzyme activity is expressed as milliunits per milligram enzyme protein. (From Heil and Zillig.[81])

	Specific activity of enzyme (mU/mg)		Inhibition by rifampin (%)
	Minus rifampin	Plus rifampin	
Original sensitive enzyme	242	1.5	99
Original resistant enzyme	124	120	3
Reconstituted enzyme			
$\alpha + \beta + \beta' + \sigma$	52	1.4	97
$\alpha_r + \beta_r + \beta_r' + \sigma$	27	25.6	5
$\alpha_r + \beta + \beta' + \sigma$	40	0.6	98
$\alpha + \beta_r + \beta' + \sigma$	88	69	22
$\alpha + \beta + \beta_r' + \sigma$	17.5	1.4	92

thesis is not inhibited.[86] The drug, however, does not block the formation of the complex between RNA polymerase and DNA.[87] It has been proposed that rifampin prevents the conversion of the enzyme-template complex to the appropriate tight binding state required for the addition of the first ribonucleoside triphosphate.[88] In merodiploids, which contain roughly equal amounts of both drug-sensitive and drug-resistant β subunits, rifampin sensitivity is dominant.[89] It has been suggested that the drug-bound sensitive molecules may block the template so that the resistant polymerase cannot initiate RNA synthesis.[89]

Rifampin is selectively toxic because mammalian RNA polymerases are not affected by the drug. The RNA polymerases of sensitive bacteria are generally inhibited by concentrations in the range of 0.005 to 0.1 μg/ml. The RNA polymerase isolated from human placenta is not inhibited at 5 μg/ml.[90] Polymerase from rat liver nuclei is not affected until a concentration of 200 μg/ml is reached.[91] The same insensitivity has been found for nuclear polymerases from a variety of eukaryotic cells.[76]

There are several reports that RNA synthesis in mitochondria and chloroplasts is inhibited by rifampin.[92,93] The concentration of drug required for the effect, however, is more than 100 times that required to inhibit the bacterial enzymes. The fact that this RNA synthesis can be inhibited by rifampin has been used as an argument in favor of the proposal that these organelles resemble bacteria in their mechanism of RNA transcription. In view of the high concentrations required for inhibition, the rifampin effect may not provide good evidence for this proposal.[76]

Many rifamycin derivatives have been synthesized in the hope that greater activity against viral polymerases may be obtained. Some of these derivatives inhibit normal (and perhaps viral) RNA synthesis in mammalian cells, but only at high concentrations. In addition, synthesis of DNA and other biosynthetic processes are inhibited, so the specificity of the drug effect can be seriously questioned.[94]

Use and Pharmacology of Rifampin

Use

In the United States, rifampin is used to treat mycobacterial infections and meningococcal carriers. Its efficacy in the treatment of tuberculosis is well established. It is more active than ethambutol and virtually as effective as isoniazid in the treatment of experimental tuberculosis in animal models.[95] Rifampin in combination with isoniazid or isoniazid *and* ethambutol is effective in the initial treatment of moderate and far advanced pulmonary tuberculosis.[3] Rifampin should be included in retreatment regimens in patients who did not receive the drug during initial therapy.[96] Rifampin is also useful in treating extrapulmonary disease, including miliary tuberculosis and tuberculous meningitis. When the drug is used alone, resistance develops readily, and the emergence of resistance is directly related to the inoculum size.[97] Thus, rifampin is always used in combination with other drugs in the treatment of tuberculosis. As with other organisms, mycobacteria become resistant by developing altered DNA-dependent RNA polymerases.[98] There is no cross-resistance with other antimicrobial drugs.

Some atypical mycobacteria are sensitive to rifampin and these infections are often treated with a three-drug regimen of isoniazid, ethambutol, and rifampin. *Mycobacterium leprae*, the causative agent of leprosy, also responds to rifampin. In patients with lepromatous leprosy, death of *M. leprae* occurs more rapidly with rifampin treatment than with oral dapsone (Chapter 5).[99]

Rifampin is effective in the treatment of meningococcal carriers.[100] Drug-resistant meningococcal strains emerge readily,[101] even with treatment periods as short as 2 days.[102] Rifampin is recommended for the short-term treatment (adults, 600 mg daily for 4 days) of asymptomatic carriers of *Neisseria meningitidis*, but because of resistance, it is generally not used to treat clinical infection.

Pharmacology

Rifampin is well absorbed from the gastrointestinal tract, and maximum serum levels are achieved in 2 to 3 hours.[103] Absorption is impaired if the drug is taken right after a meal[103] or concomitantly with PAS.[104] Rifampin distributes widely in the tissues and body fluids,[103] and therapeutic levels are achieved in the cerbrospinal[105] and pleural fluids.[106] Levels of drug exceeding the minimum inhibitory concentrations for sensitive strains of *N. meningitidis* have been measured in saliva.[107] About 85 per cent of the drug in serum is bound to plasma protein.[108]

Rifampin is metabolized in the liver by deacetylation and excreted in the bile.[109,110] The dacetylated metabolite is also biologically active. Unaltered drug is reabsorbed from the gastrointestinal tract in an enterohepatic cycle, but the deacetyl metabolite is very poorly reabsorbed. A small amount (10 to 20 per cent) of the drug and the metabolite are excreted in the urine, but the dosage of rifampin does not have to be modified in the presence of renal insufficiency. When hepatic function is impaired, however, serum levels of the drug increase.[45]

Rifampin can delay the clearance of bromosulfophthalein and unconjugated bilirubin from the plasma.[111] This effect is apparently due to its ability to compete for the uptake of these substances at the plasma membrane of liver cells.[112] The uptake of rifampin by the liver is significantly depressed by probenecid.[113] This results in a near doubling of the peak serum level.

The half-life and peak serum values of rifampin change during the course of therapy. After the first dose of 600 mg to an adult (the usual therapeutic dosage), the half-life is about 3.5 hours. But after daily administration for a week or two, it is approximately 2 hours[114] and remains constant there after.[115] The levels of rifampin in plasma assayed at 6 and 12 hours after drug adminstration also fall during the first few days of therapy. This change in kinetics is apparently due to the fact that rifampin induces its own metabolizing enzymes in the liver.[110] The variation in the kinetics of rifampin during the initial period of daily administration is pharmacologically interesting, but it apparently does not affect the therapeutic outcome, since the plasma levels achieved after prolonged daily administration are in the therapeutic range.

Untoward Effects of Rifampin

Several interactions between rifampin and other drugs have already been mentioned: interference with rifampin absorption by PAS, interference with hepatic uptake of BSP by rifampin, and increased rifampin serum levels in the presence of probenecid. Rifampin has also been reported to compete for the uptake of contrast substances used in cholecystography, to reduce the effect of the coumarin anticoagulants (perhaps by increasing the rate of their metabolism),[116,117] and to decrease the effectiveness of oral contraceptives.[118] The incidence of menstrual disorders is apparently increased in women taking both rifampin and anti-fertility drugs.[118] Rifampin itself can cause liver damage, and it should be used with caution with other hepatotoxic drugs. Disturbance in liver function may be more frequent when rifampin is given with isoniazid, which is hepatotoxic, than with ethambutol.[119]

Rifampin and its metabolites sometimes appear red-orange in urine, feces, saliva, sweat, and tears. Patients should be warned of this to prevent unnecessary anxiety.

The effect of rifampin on the liver is usually manifested by a reversible elevation of serum bilirubin and transaminase. This is observed in a significant percentage of patients,[119,120] and it is more likely to occur in those with preexisting liver disease, such as alcoholics. It is difficult to determine the exact incidence of the hepatotoxicity because patients usually receive several drugs together. Jaundice and severe hepatotoxic reactions have been reported and deaths have resulted.

A higher incidence of adverse reactions has been reported with biweekly and once-weekly intermittent therapy with rifampin in high dosage.[121,122] Clinical symptoms of a systemic reaction, including fever, chills, aches, nausea, and vomiting, start within an hour or two after drug ingestion. In addition, immune thrombocytopenia, immune hemolytic anemia, and acute renal failure have been reported in intermittent therapy. There is some evidence that anti-rifampin antibodies may be present, but it is not at all clear why the systemic reaction characteristically occurs in patients on intermittent rather than daily therapy.

The most common side effects seen with daily rifampin administration are gastrointestinal disturbances (epigastric pain, abdominal cramps, nausea, vomiting, and diarrhea). Headache, drowsiness, ataxia, dizziness, fatigue, and other nervous system complaints occur occasionally. Rashes, pruritis, urticaria, eosinophilia, and leukopenia are also seen.

Rifampin has been reported to have immunosuppressive properties in various animal test systems.[123] The mechanism is not defined. Rifampin in high concentrations can inhibit phytohemagglutinin-stimulated thymidine incorporation and RNA synthesis in human lymphocytes.[124] The significance of any immunosuppressive action in man is not known, although rifampin has been reported to attenuate cutaneous hypersensitivity to purified protein derivative in patients.[125] Rifampin therapy has also been associated with the production of light-chain proteinuria.[126] Again, the mechanism is not known.

STREPTOMYCIN

Streptomycin was the first drug shown to be effective against tuberculosis in humans. It is an aminoglycoside antibiotic and the mechanism of action, pharmacology, and adverse effects of these bactericidal drugs have been described in detail in Chapter 3. The toxic effects of streptomycin on the kidney and ear (balance, hearing) and the necessity for parenteral administration make it less attractive than such potent oral drugs as isoniazid and rifampin. Accordingly, the use of streptomycin in the initial therapy of tuberculosis is declining as the effectiveness of combination regimens without the drug is established.

THE MINOR ANTITUBERCULOSIS DRUGS

The minor antituberculosis drugs are used primarily in the retreatment of patients in whom initial therapy failed because of the presence of resistant organisms. As with the other drugs, they are used in combination regimens.

Para-aminosalicylic Acid

An inhibitor of folic acid synthesis, the mechanism of action and pharmacology of PAS are described in Chapter 5. It produces a rather high incidence of gastrointestinal disturbances and allergic reactions are common.

Pyrazinamide

Pyrazinamide is an oral tuberculostatic drug that can produce severe liver damage, urate retention, and photosensitivity.

Ethionamide

This is an oral drug that frequently produces gastrointestinal disturbances. It is very toxic. Adverse effects include liver damage, hypersensitivity reactions, peripheral neuropathy, optic neuritis, hypothyroidism, and gynecomastia. The control of diabetes may become very difficult when this drug is used.

Cycloserine

Cycloserine is given orally. It is tuberculocidal by virtue of its ability to inhibit cell wall synthesis, and the mechanism of its action is described in detail in Chapter 2. Cycloserine can be quite toxic to the central nervous system, and it can cause headache, tremors, twitching, seizures, confusion, and psychosis. Peripheral neuropathy, hepatic damage, and malabsorption occur occasionally.

Viomycin

Viomycin is similar to the aminoglycoside antibiotics. It must be given by intramuscular injection. It causes eighth-nerve damage, renal damage, rashes, and electrolyte disturbances.

Kanamycin

Kanamycin is an aminoglycoside (Chapter 3). As with other aminoglycosides, caution must be used in patients with impaired renal function.

Capreomycin

Capreomycin is also given by intramuscular injection. It causes renal damage, hearing loss, and disturbance of balance; allergic reactions are also seen. Like the aminoglycosides, the drug can cause neuromuscular blockade, which is reversed by calcium gluconate and neostigmine.

REFERENCES

1. R. F. Johnson and K. H. Wildrick: "State of the Art" Review. The impact of chemotherapy on the care of patients with tuberculosis. *Am. Rev. Resp. Dis.* 109:636 (1974).

2. W. Fox: The John Barnwell Lecture: Changing concepts in the chemotherapy of pulmonary tuberculosis. *Am. Rev. Resp. Dis.* 97:767 (1968).

3. R. Newman, B. Doster, F. J. Murray, and S. F. Woolpert: Rifampin in initial treatment of pulmonary tuberculosis: A U.S. Public Health Service tuberculosis therapy trial. *Am. Rev. Resp. Dis.* 109:216 (1974).

4. Medical Research Council: Long term chemotherapy in the treatment of chronic pulmonary tuberculosis with cavitation. *Tubercle* 43:201 (1962).

5. L. D. Hudson and J. A. Sbarbaro: Twice weekly tuberculosis chemotherapy. *J. Am. Med. Assoc.* 223:139 (1973).

6. C. V. Ramakrishnan, S. Devadatta, C. Evans, W. Fox, N. K. Menon, O. Nazareth, S. Radhakrishna, S. Sambamoorthy, H. Stott, S. P. Tripathy, and S. Velu: A four year follow-up of patients with quiescent pulmonary tuberculosis at the end of a year of chemotherapy with twice-weekly isoniazid plus streptomycin or daily isoniazid plus PAS. *Tubercle* 50:115 (1969).

7. East African/British Medical Research Councils: Controlled clinical trial of four short-course (6-month) regimens of chemotherapy for treatment of pulmonary tuberculosis. *Lancet* 1:1331 (1973).

8. W. Fox and D. A. Mitchison: State of the art: Short-course chemotherapy for pulmonary tuberculosis. *Am. Rev. Resp. Dis.* 111:325 (1975).

9. A joint statement of the American Thoracic Society, American Lung Association, and the Center for Disease Control: Preventive therapy of tuberculous infection. *Am. Rev. Resp. Dis.* 110:371 (1974).

10. W. B. Schaefer: The effect of isoniazid on growing and resting tubercle bacilli. *Am. Rev. Tuberc.* 69:125 (1954).

11. J. Youatt: A review of the action of isoniazid. *Am. Rev. Resp. Dis.* 99:729 (1969).

12. F. G. Winder and S. A. Rooney: The effects of isoniazid on the carbohydrates of *Mycobacterium tuberculosis* BCG. *Biochem. J.* 117:355 (1970).

13. F. G. Winder and P. B. Collins: Inhibition by isoniazid of synthesis of mycolic acids in *Mycobacterium tuberculosis. J. Gen. Microbiol.* 63:41 (1970).

14. K. Takayama, L. Wang, and H. L. David: Effect of isoniazid on the *in vivo* mycolic acid synthesis, cell growth, and viability of *Mycobacterium tuberculosis. Antimicrob. Agents Chemother.* 2:29 (1972).

15. L. Wang and K. Takayama: Relationship between the uptake of isoniazid and its action on *in vivo* mycolic acid synthesis in *Mycobacterium tuberculosis. Antimicrob. Agents Chemother.* 2:438 (1972).

16. K. Takayama, H. K. Schnoes, E. L. Armstrong, and R. W. Boyle: Site of inhibitory action of isoniazid in the synthesis of mycolic acids in *Mycobacterium tuberculosis. J. Lipid Res.* 16:308 (1975).

17. K. Takayama, L. Wang, and R. S. Merkal: Scanning electron microscopy of the H37RA strain of *Mycobacterium tuberculosis* exposed to isoniazid. *Antimicrob. Agents Chemother.* 4:62 (1973).

18. A. R. Armstrong: Further studies on the time concentration relationships of isoniazid on tubercle bacilli *in vitro. Am. Rev. Resp. Dis.* 91:440 (1965).

19. J. H. Vivien, R. Thibier, and A. Lepeuple: Recent studies on isoniazid. *Adv. Tuberc. Res.* 18:148 (1972).

20. Tuberculosis Chemotherapy Centre, Madras: A controlled comparison of a twice-weekly and three once-weekly regimens in the initial treatment of pulmonary tuberculosis. *Bull. Wld. Hlth. Org.* 43:143 (1970).

21. K. Takayama, E. L. Armstrong, and H. L. David: Restoration of mycolate synthetase activity in *Mycobacterium tuberculosis* exposed to isoniazid. *Am. Rev. Resp. Dis.* 110:43 (1974).

22. K. S. Sriprakash and T. Ramakrisnan: Isoniazid-resistant mutants of *Mycobacterium tuberculosis* H37RV: Uptake of isoniazid and properties of NADase inhibitor. *J. Gen. Microbiol.* 60:125 (1970).

23. W. H. Beggs and J. W. Jenne: Capacity of tubercle bacilli for isoniazid accumulation. *Am. Rev. Resp. Dis.* 102:94 (1970).

24. D. Fishbain, G. Ling, and D. J. Kushner: Isoniazid metabolism and binding by sensitive and resistant strains of *Mycobacterium smegmatis. Can. J. Microbiol.* 18:783 (1972).

25. H. L. David and C. M. Newman: Some observations on the genetics of isoniazid resistance in the tubercle bacilli. *Am. Rev. Resp. Dis.* 104:508 (1971).

26. W. D. Jones and H. L. David: Preliminary observations on the occurrence of a streptomycin R-factor in *Mycobacterium smegmatis. Tubercle* 53:35 (1972).

27. D. Saroja and K. P. Gopinathan: Transduction of isoniazid susceptibility-resistance and streptomycin resistance in mycobacteria. *Antimicrob. Agents Chemother.* 4:643 (1973).

28. J. F. Barley, D. F. Evered, and S. M. Tromon: Transport of isoniazid in rat small intestine *in vitro. Biochem. Parmacol.* 21:2660 (1972).

29. A. Hurwitz and D. L. Schlozman: Effects of antacids on gastrointestinal absorption of isoniazid in rat and man. *Am. Rev. Resp. Dis.* 109:41 (1974).

30. J. M. Robson and F. M. Sullivan: Antituberculosis drugs. *Pharmac. Rev.* 15:169 (1963).

31. J. H. Peters, K. S. Miller, and P. Brown: Studies on the metabolic basis for the genetically determined capacities for isoniazid inactivation in man. *J. Pharm. Exp. Ther.* 150:298 (1965).

32. J. W. Jenne: Partial purification and properties of the isoniazid transacetylase in human liver. Its relationship to the acetylation of p-aminosalicylic acid. *J. Clin. Invest.* 44:1992 (1965).

33. W. W. Weber: "The relationship of genetic factors to drug reactions" in *Drug Induced Diseases, Vol. 4* (ed. L. Meyler and H. M. Peck). Amsterdam: Excerpta Medica, 1972, pp. 33–59.

34. W. W. Weber: "Acetylation of drugs" in *Metabolic Conjugation and Metabolic Hydrolysis* (ed. W. H. Fishman). New York: Academic Press, 1973, pp. 249–296.

35. G. A. Ellard: Variations between individuals and populations in the acetylation of isoniazid and its significance for the treatment of pulmonary tuberculosis. *Clin. Pharm. Ther.* 19:610 (1976).

36. H. Tiitinen: Isoniazid and ethionamide serum levels and inactivation in Finnish subjects. *Scand. J. Resp. Dis.* 50:110 (1969).

37. W. W. Weber, G. Drummond, J. N. Miceli, and R. Szabadi: "Genetic control and isozymic composition of drug acetylating enzymes" in *Isoenzymes, Vol. 4* (ed. C. Markert). New York: Academic Press, 1975, pp. 813–828.

38. D. J. Hearse and W. W. Weber: Multiple N-acetyltransferases and drug metabolism: Tissue distribution, characterization and significance of mammalian N-acetyltransferase. *Biochem. J.* 132:519 (1973).

39. W. W. Weber, J. N. Miceli, D. J. Hearse, and G. S. Drummond: N-acetylation of drugs: Pharmacogenetic studies in rabbits selected for their acetylator characteristics. *Drug Metab. Disp.* 4:94 (1976).

40. S. Devadatta, P. R. J. Gangadharam, R. H. Andrews, W. Fox, C. V. Ramakrishnan, J. B. Selkon, and S. Velu: Peripheral neuritis due to isoniazid. *Bull. Wld. Hlth. Org.* 23:587 (1960).

41. H. Kutt, K. Verebely, and F. McDowell: Inhibition of diphenylhydantoin metabolism in rats and rat liver microsomes by antitubercular drugs. *Neurology* 18:706 (1968).

42. H. Kutt, W. Winters, and F. H. McDowell: Depression of parahydroxylation of diphenylhydantoin by antituberculous chemotherapy. *Neurology* 16:594 (1966).

43. J. R. Mitchell, U. P. Thorgeirsson, M. Black, J. A. Timbrell, W. R. Snodgrass, W. Z. Potter, D. J. Jollow, and H. R. Keiser: Increased incidence of isoniazid hepatitis in rapid acetylators: Possible relation to hydrazine metabolites. *Clin. Pharm. Ther.* 18:70 (1975).

44. D. W. Bowersox, R. H. Winterbauer, G. L. Stewart, B. Orme, and E. Barron: Isoniazid dosage in patients with renal failure. *New Eng. J. Med.* 289:84 (1973).

45. G. Acocella, L. Bonollo, M. Garimoldi, M. Mainardi, L. T. Tenconi, and F. B. Nicolis: Kinetics of rifampicin and isoniazid administered alone and in combination to normal subjects and patients with liver disease. *Gut* 13:47 (1972).

46. A. L. Goldman and S. S. Braman: Isoniazid: A review with emphasis on adverse effects. *Chest* 1:62 (1972).

47. J. D. Wood and S. J. Peesker: The effect on GABA metabolism in brain of isonicotinic acid hydrazide and pyridoxine as a function of time after administration. *J. Neurochem.* 19:1527 (1972).

48. G. A. Katz and G. C. Jobin: Large doses of pyridoxine in the treatment of massive ingestion of isoniazid. *Am. Rev. Resp. Dis.* 101:991 (1970).

49. W. S. Weidorn and F. Ervin: Schizophrenic-like psychotic reaction with administration of isoniazid. *Arch. Neurol. Psychiat.* 72:321 (1954).

50. S. J. Berté, J. D. DiMase, and C. S. Christianson: Isoniazid, PAS, and streptomycin intolerance in 1744 patients. An analysis of reactions to single drugs and drug groups plus data on multiple reactions, type and time of reactions, and desensitization. *Am. Rev. Resp. Dis.* 90:598 (1964).

51. D. Alarcon-Segovia: Drug-induced lupus syndromes. *Mayo Clin. Proc.* 44:664 (1969).

52. D. Alarcon-Segovia, E. Fishbein, and H. Alcala: Isoniazid acetylation rate and development of antinuclear antibodies upon isoniazid treatment. *Arth. Rheum.* 14:748 (1971).

53. R. A. Garibaldi, R. E. Drusin, S. H. Ferebee, and M. B. Gregg: Isoniazid-associated hepatitis: Report of an outbreak. *Am. Rev. Resp. Dis.* 106:357 (1972).

54. J. R. Mitchell, H. J. Zimmerman, K. G. Ishak, U. P. Thorgeirsson, J. A. Timbrell, W. R. Snodgrass, and S. D. Nelson: Isoniazid liver injury: Clinical spectrum, pathology, and probable pathogenesis. *Ann. Int. Med.* 84:181 (1976).

55. J. R. Mitchell, M. W. Long, U. P. Thorgeirsson, and D. J. Jollow: Acetylation rates and monthly liver function tests during one year of isoniazid preventive therapy. *Chest* 68:181 (1975).

56. M. Black, J. R. Mitchell, H. J. Zimmerman, K. G. Ishak, and G. R. Epler: Isoniazid-associated hepatitis in 114 patients. *Gastroenterology* 69:289 (1975).

57. W. C. Maddrey and J. K. Boitnott: Isoniazid hepatitis. *Ann. Int. Med.* 79:1 (1973).

58. B. Doster, F. J. Murray, R. Newman, and S. F. Woolpert: Ethambu-

tol in the initial treatment of pulmonary tuberculosis: U.S. Public Health Service tuberculosis therapy trials. *Am. Rev. Resp. Dis.* 107:177 (1973).

59. I. D. Bobrowitz: Ethambutol-isoniazid versus streptomycin-ethambutol-isoniazid in original treatment of cavitary tuberculosis. *Am. Rev. Resp. Dis.* 109:548 (1974).

60. M. Forbes, N. A. Kuck, and E. A. Peets: Mode of action of ethambutol. *J. Bacteriol.* 84:1099 (1962).

61. W. H. Beggs and F. A. Andrews: Nonspecific ionic inhibition of ethambutol binding by *Mycobacterium smegmatis. Antimicrob. Agents Chemother.* 4:115 (1973).

62. W. H. Beggs and J. W. Jenne: Growth inhibition of *Mycobacterium tuberculosis* after single-pulsed exposures to streptomycin, ethambutol, and rifampin. *Infect. Immunol.* 2:479 (1970).

63. M. Forbes, N. A. Kuck, and E. A. Peets: Effect of ethambutol on nucleic acid metabolism in *Mycobacterium smegmatis* and its reversal by polyamines and divalent cations. *J. Bacteriol.* 89:1299 (1965).

64. V. A. Place and J. P. Thomas: Clinical pharmacology of ethambutol. *Am. Rev. Resp. Dis.* 87:901 (1963).

65. E. A. Peets, W. M. Sweeney, V. A. Place, and D. A. Buyske: The absorption, excretion, and metabolic fate of ethambutol in man. *Am. Rev. Resp. Dis.* 91:51 (1965).

66. U. Gundert-Remy, M. Klett, and E. Weber: Concentration of ethambutol in cerebrospinal fluid in man as a function of non-protein-bound drug fraction in serum. *Europ. J. Clin. Pharmacol.* 6:133 (1973).

67. I. D. Bobrowitz: Ethambutol in tuberculous meningitis. *Chest* 61:629 (1972).

68. E. A. Peets and D. A. Buyske: Comparative metabolism of ethambutol and its L-isomer. *Biochem. Parmacol.* 13:1403 (1964).

69. I. Strauss and F. Erhardt: Ethambutol absorption, excretion and dosage in patients with renal tuberculosis. *Chemother.* 15:148 (1970).

70. A. E. Poslethwaite and W. N. Kelley: Studies on the mechanism of ethambutol-induced hyperuricemia. *Arthritis Rheum.* 15:403 (1972).

71. P. Tugwell and S. L. James: Peripheral neuropathy with ethambutol. *Postgrad. Med. J.* 48:667 (1972).

72. J. E. Leibold: The ocular toxicity of ethambutol and its relation to dose. *Ann. N.Y. Acad. Sci.* 135:904 (1966).

73. G. J. Barron, L. Tepper, and G. Iovine: Ocular toxicity from ethambutol *Am. J. Ophthalmol.* 77:256 (1974).

74. K. M. Citron: Ethambutol: A review with special reference to ocular toxicity. *Tubercle* 50 Suppl.:32 (1969).

75. W. M. Grant: *Toxicology of the Eye*, Second Edition, Springfield: Charles C. Thomas, 1974, pp. 459–462.

76. W. Wehrli and M. Staehelin: Actions of the rifamycins. *Bact. Rev.* 35:290 (1971).

77. G. Lancini, R. Pallanza, and L. G. Silvestri: Relationships between bactericidal effect and inhibition of ribonucleic acid nucleotidyltransferase by rifampicin in *Escherichia coli* K-12. *J. Bacteriol.* 97:761 (1969).

78. W. Wehrli, F. Knüsel, K. Schmid, and M. Staehelin: Interaction of rifamycin with bacterial RNA polymerase. *Proc. Natl. Acad. Sci.* 61:667 (1968).

79. U. I. Lill and G. R. Hartmann: On the binding of rifampicin to the DNA-directed RNA polymerase from *Escherichia coli*. *Eur. J. Biochem.* 38:336 (1973).

80. E. di Mauro, L. Snyder, P. Marino, A. Lamberti, A. Coppo, and G. P. Tocchini-Valentini: Rifampicin sensitivity of the components of DNA-dependent RNA polymerase. *Nature* 222:533 (1969).

81. A. Heil and W. Zillig: Reconstitution of bacterial DNA-dependent RNA-polymerase from isolated subunits as a tool for the elucidation of the role of the subunits in transcription. *FEBS Letters* 11:165 (1970).

82. D. Rabussay and W. Zillig: A rifampicin resistant RNA-polymerase from *E. coli* altered in the β-subunit. *FEBS Letters* 5:104 (1969).

83. T. Linn, R. Losick, and A. L. Sonenschein: Rifampin resistance mutation of *Bacillus subtilis* altering the electrophoretic mobility of the beta subunit of ribonucleic acid polymerase. *J. Bacteriol.* 122:1387 (1975).

84. W. Zillig, K. Zechel, D. Rabussay, M. Schachner, V. S. Sethi, R. Palm, A. Heil, and W. Seifert: On the role of different subunits of DNA-dependent RNA polymerase from *E. coli* in the transcription process. *Cold Spring Harbor Symp. Quant. Biol.* 35:47 (1970).

85. A. Sippel and G. Hartman: Mode of action of rifamycin on the RNA polymerase reaction. *Biochim Biophys. Acta* 157:218 (1968).

86. A. E. Sippel and G. R. Hartmann: Rifampicin resistance of RNA polymerase in the binary complex with DNA. *Eur. J. Biochem.* 16:152 (1970).

87. D. C. Hinkle, W. F. Mangel, and M. J. Chamberlin: Studies of the binding of *Escherichia coli* RNA polymerase to DNA. IV. The effect of rifampicin on binding and on RNA chain initiation. *J. Mol. Biol.* 70:209 (1972).

88. R. E. Kerrich-Santo and G. R. Hartmann: Influence of temperature on the action of rifampicin on RNA polymerase in presence of DNA. *Eur. J. Biochem.* 43:521 (1974).

89. S. J. Austin, I. P. B. Tittawella, R. S. Hayward, and J. G. Scaife: Amber mutations of *Escherichia coli* RNA polymerase. *Nature New Biol.* 232:133 (1971).

90. H. P. Voigt, R. Kaufmann, and H. Matthei: Solubilized DNA-dependent RNA polymerase from human placenta; A magnesium-dependent enzyme. *FEBS Letters* 10:257 (1970).

91. W. Wehrli, J. Nüesch, F. Knüsel, and M. Staehelin: Action of rifamycins on RNA polymerase. *Biochim. Biophys. Acta* 157:215 (1968).

92. B. D. Reid and P. Parsons: Partial purification of mitochondrial RNA polymerase from rat liver. *Proc. Natl. Acad. Sci. U.S.* 68:2830 (1971).

93. J. J. Armstrong, S. J. Surzycki, B. Moll, and R. P. Levine: Genetic transcription and translation specifying chloroplast components in *Chlamydomonas reinhardi. Biochemistry* 10:692 (1971).

94. E. Busiello, A. D. Girolamo, L. Fisher-Fantuzzi, and C. Vesco: Multiple effects of rifamycin derivatives on animal-cell metabolism of macromolecules. *Eur. J. Biochem.* 35:251 (1973).

95. F. Grumbach: Experimental *in vivo* studies of new antituberculosis drugs; capreomycin, ethambutol, rifampicin. *Tubercle* 50 Suppl: 12 (1969).

96. A. Vall-Spinosa, W. Lester, T. Moulding, P. T. Davidson, and J. K. McClatchy: Rifampin in the treatment of drug-resistant *Mycobacteria tuberculosis* infections. *New Eng. J. Med.* 283:616 (1970).

97. F. Kradolfer and R. Schnell: Incidence of resistant pulmonary tuberculosis in relation to initial bacterial load. *Chemotherapy* 15:242 (1970).

98. R. J. White, G. C. Lancini, and L. G. Silvestri: Mechanism of action of rifampin on *Mycobacterium smegmatis. J. Bacteriol.* 108:737 (1971).

99. Leprosy Chemotherapy Committee of the U.S. Leprosy Panel and the Leonard Wood Memorial: Rifampin therapy of lepromatous leprosy. *Am. J. Trop. Med. Hyg.* 24:475 (1975).

100. W. B. Deal and E. Sanders: Efficacy of rifampin in treatment of meningococcal carriers. *New Eng. J. Med.* 281:641 (1969).

101. W. E. Beam, N. R. Newberg, L. F. Devine, W. E. Pierce, and J. A. Davies: The effect of rifampin on the nasopharyngeal carriage of *Neisseria meningitidis* in a military population. *J. Infect. Dis.* 124:39 (1971).

102. L. F. Devine, D. P. Johnson, S. L. Rhode, C. R. Hagerman, W. E. Pierce, and R. D. Peckinpaugh: Rifampin: Effect of two-day treatment on the meningococcal carrier state and the relationship to the levels of drug in sera and saliva. *Am. J. Med. Sci.* 261:79 (1971).

103. S. Furesz, R. Scotti, R. Pallanza, and E. Mapelli: Rifampicin: A new rifamycin III: Absorption, distribution, and elimination in man. *Arzneim.-Forsch.* 17:536 (1967).

104. G. Boman: Serum concentration and half-life of rifampicin after simultaneous oral administration of aminosalicylic acid or isoniazid. *Eur. J. Clin. Pharmacol.* 7:217 (1974).

105. J. J. G. Oliveira: Cerebrospinal fluid concentrations of rifampin in meningeal tuberculosis. *Am. Rev. Resp. Dis.* 106:432 (1972).

106. G. Boman and A.-S. Malmborg: Rifampicin in plasma and pleural fluid after single oral doses. *Eur. J. Clin. Pharmacol.* 7:51 (1974).

107. L. F. Devine, D. P. Johnson, C. R. Hagerman, W. E. Pierce, S. L. Rhode, and R. O. Peckinpaugh. Rifampin: Levels in serum and saliva and effect on the meningococcal carrier state. *J. Am. Med. Assoc.* 214:1055 (1970).

108. G. Boman and V.-A. Ringberger: Binding of rifampicin by human plasma proteins. *Eur. J. Clin. Pharmacol.* 7:369 (1974).

109. G. Acocella, F. B. Nicolts, and A. Lamarina: A study on the kinetics of rifampicin in man. *Chemother.* 5:87 (1967).

110. S. Furesz: Chemical and biological properties of rifampicin. *Antibiot. Chemother.* 16:316 (1970).

111. H. D. Cohn: Clinical studies with a new rifamycin derivative. *J. Clin. Pharmacol.* 9:118 (1969).

112. S. Kenwright and A. J. Levi: Sites of competition in the selective hepatic uptake of rifamycin-SV, flavaspidic acid, bilirubin, and bromsulphthalein. *Gut* 15:220 (1974).

113. S. Kenwright and A. J. Levi: Impairment of hepatic uptake of rifamycin antibiotics by probenecid, and its therapeutic implications. *Lancet* 2:1401 (1973).

114. G. Acocella, V. Pagani, M. Marchetti, G. C. Baroni, and F. B. Nicholis: Kinetic studies on rifampicin. I. Serum concentration analysis

in subjects treated with different oral doses over a period of two weeks. *Chemotherapy* 16:356 (1971).

115. V. Nitti, F. Delli Veneri, A. Ninni, and G. Meola: Rifampicin blood serum levels and half-life during prolonged administration in tuberculosis patients. *Chemotherapy* 17:121 (1972).

116. G. Beran: Der Einfluss der Rifampizintherapie auf die orale Antikoagulation mit Acenocoumarol. *Prax. Pneumol.* 26:350 (1972).

117. J. A. Romankiewicz and M. Ehrman: Rifampin and warfarin: A drug interaction. *Ann. Int. Med.* 82:224 (1975).

118. Medical News: Rifampicin, 'pill' do not go well together. *J. Am. Med. Assoc.* 227:608 (1974).

119. A. W. Lees, G. W. Allen, J. Smith, W. F. Tyrrell, and R. J. Fallon: Toxicity from rifampin plus isoniazid and rifampin plus ethambutol therapy. *Tubercle* 52:182 (1971).

120. K. Mattson: Side effects of rifampicin: A clinical study. *Scand. J. Resp. Dis.* Suppl. 82: 1–52 (1973).

121. G. Poole, P. Stradling, and S. Worlledge: Potentially serious side effects of high-dose twice-weekly rifampicin. *Br. Med. J.* 3:343 (1971).

122. M. Aquinas, W. G. L. Allan, P. A. L. Horsfall, P. K. Jenkins, W. Hung-Yan, D. Girling, R. Tall, and W. Fox: Adverse reactions to daily and intermittent rifampicin regimens for pulmonary tuberculosis in Hong Kong. *Br. Med. J.* 1:765 (1972).

123. L. Bassi, L. DiBerardino, V. Arioli, L. G. Silvestri, and E. L. Chérié Lignière: Conditions for immunosuppression by rifampicin. *J. Infect. Dis.* 128:736 (1973).

124. B. G. T. Pogo: Specific inhibition by rifampicin of transcription in human lymphocytes stimulated by phytohemagglutinin. *J. Cell. Biol.* 55:515 (1972).

125. P. Mukerjee, S. Schuldt, and J. E. Kasik: Effect of rifampin on cutaneous hypersensitivity to purified protein derivative in humans. *Antimicrob. Agents Chemother.* 4:607 (1973).

126. C. D. Graber, J. Jebaily, R. L. Galphin, and E. Doering: Light chain proteinuria and humoral immunoincompetence in tuberculosis patients treated with rifampin. *Am. Rev. Resp. Dis.* 107:713 (1973).

Part II
Drugs Employed in the Treatment of Fungal Infection

Introduction

The treatment of fungal disease can be divided into two quite different problems according to the location of the infection. The most common fungal infections are superficial and are either treated with the oral drug griseofulvin or with one of several topical drugs. The systemic mycoses constitute quite a different therapeutic problem and have an impressive fatality rate. The systemic mycoses are sometimes considered in two groups according to the infecting organism. The "opportunistic infections" refer to those mycoses—candidosis, aspergillosis, cryptococcosis, and phycomycosis—that commonly occur in debilitated and immunosuppressed patients. These infections are a particular problem in patients with leukemias and lymphomas, in people who are receiving immunosuppressive therapy, and in patients with such predisposing factors as diabetes mellitus. Other systemic mycoses—for example, blastomycosis, histoplasmosis, coccidioidomycosis, and sporotrichosis—tend to have a relatively low incidence that may vary considerably according to geographical area. The chemotherapy of the systemic mycoses has been reviewed by Bennett.[1] There are two principal drugs employed in therapy, amphotericin B (a polyene antibiotic) and flucytosine.

THE POLYENE ANTIBIOTICS

Structures and Physical Properties

The polyene antibiotics are a large group of compounds, but many of them are too toxic to be used in therapy. Amphotericin B, nystatin, and candicidin, the only compounds used clinically in the United States, are produced by soil actinomycetes.

The polyenes are large molecules with a hydroxylated portion, which is hydrophilic, and a portion containing four to seven conjugated double bonds, which is lipophilic.[2] The unsaturated chromophore region is subject to photooxidation, and this contributes to the instability of these compounds in solution. This

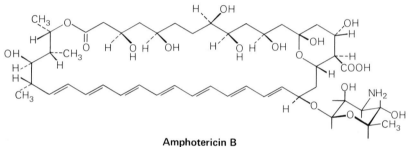

Amphotericin B
(Structure according to Ganis *et al.*[3])

lipophilic portion also dictates a poor solubility in aqueous media.

Mechanism of Action

The Effect on Cell Permeability—
An Explanation of the Cell Killing Effect

Research on the mechanism of action of the polyene antibiotics has been reviewed by Kinsky.[4] Early experiments demonstrated that exposure of intact sensitive yeast cells to nystatin or amphotericin B affected a number of biochemical functions including respiration and glycolysis. Investigators found that adding K^+ or NH_4^+ to the buffer solution in which the yeast cells were suspended prevented inhibition of glycolysis occurring at neutral pH.[5] The amount of nystatin taken up by the yeast cell was not altered by NH_4^+ or K^+, and nystatin treatment rapidly depleted intracellular K^+. These observations suggested that glycolysis inhibition was secondary to the loss of K^+ resulting from a nystatin-induced change in membrane permeability. The demonstration that polyenes did not inhibit glycolysis by yeast extracts or respiration by yeast mitochondrial suspensions support this conclusion.[6] Indeed, the polyenes have not been shown to inhibit the function of any enzyme system in vitro.[6]

Although the effect of the polyenes on glycolysis in intact cells can be reversed by K^+ or NH_4^+, their fungicidal action is not reversed.[5] This could be explained by the leakage of other cellular components needed for cell survival but not for glycolysis. When polyene antibiotics are added to yeast cell cultures, there is a marked decrease in dry weight of the cells and a rapid leakage of a number of small molecules from the cell (including nucleotides, amino acids, inorganic phosphate, and phosphorylated and free sugars).[7,8] These changes are accompanied by a decreased density of the cell cytoplasm as viewed by electron microscopy[9] and a rapid loss of integrity of fungal protoplasts.[10] At low concentrations, amphotericin B primarily affects the permeability of membranes to small ions. At higher concentrations, there is leakage of larger molecules from the cell. The sequelae of the polyene-induced change in cellular permeability would seem to account for the fungicidal action of this group of antibiotics.

The cell killing effect of the polyenes and other antibiotics that act by affecting membrane permeability (e.g., polymyxins, gramicidin A) does not require growth of the organism. This is in contrast to the penicillins, for example, which only have a killing effect on growing organisms.

The Site of Action—The Cell Membrane

The polyene antibiotics are bound only to cells sensitive to their killing effect.[11] These drugs are bound by isolated cell walls and protoplast membranes derived from yeasts, but they are not taken up by bacteria. They can be extracted from the cell with organic solvents, which suggests that the binding is not covalent. That the binding is of high affinity is implicit in the finding that bound, radioactive-labeled nystatin cannot be readily displaced by adding unlabeled drug to the medium. Virtually all the polyene antibiotic bound by protoplasts is found in the cell membrane.[12]

As will become clear, the specificity of polyene action is defined by the association of the drug with the membranes of sensitive cells. These drugs inhibit the growth of fungi, protozoa, and algae, but bacteria neither bind the drugs nor are they sensitive to them. This difference in the sensitivity of different organisms is determined by the presence of sterols in their cell membranes. In sensitive yeast cells, for example, nystatin is distributed in various subcellular fractions in direct proportion to sterol content.[12] The higher algae contain sterols in their membranes and are sensitive to the polyenes. The blue-green algae do not contain sterols and are insensitive. There are no sterols in bacterial cell membranes, and even bacterial protoplasts will not bind polyenes.[13]

The sterol requirement for polyene sensitivity, has been demonstrated even more directly. If membranes from sensitive cells that bind nystatin are extracted with ethanol-acetone, the membranes' ability to bind nystatin is abolished (see Table 9-1). The binding capacity can be partially restored by incubating the extracted particles with ergosterol. One of the clearest demonstrations of the correlation between sterol in the cell membrane and sensitivity to the polyene antibiotics was carried out with *Mycoplasma laidlawii*. In contrast to most mycoplasma, this saprophytic organism does not require sterols for growth.[14] In a sterol-free medium, these organisms are resistant to polyene antibiotics, but when they are grown in a cholesterol-containing medium, they incorporate sterol into the membrane and are sensitive to amphotericin B[15] and filipin,[16] a potent polyene antibiotic that is not used clinically (see Table 9-2).

Table 9-1 **The effect of sterol on the ability of a particulate fraction from *Neurospora crassa* to bind nystatin**
A particulate fraction was prepared from pulverized, lyophylized, mycelial mats of *Neurospora crassa* by high speed centrifugation. A portion was extracted with ethanol-acetone, and reconstituted particles were prepared by adding the ethanol-acetone extract or ergosterol back to the extracted particulate fraction. The reconstituted particles were then dried, suspended in buffer, and assayed for their capacity to bind nystatin at a concentration of 10 μg/ml. Values represent micrograms of nystatin bound by equivalent 0.4 ml aliquots of particulate fraction per hour. (Data from Kinsky.[13])

Particle treatment		Nystatin bound
None	None	13.3
Extracted	None	0
Extracted	Extract	10.1
Extracted	Ergosterol	6.8

Table 9-2 **Interconversion of *Mycoplasma laidlawii* between sensitivity and resistance to amphotericin B by growth in the presence and absence of cholesterol**

Mycoplasma laidlawii were grown in medium with (sensitive, S cells) and without (resistant, R cells) 20 μg/ml cholesterol. Both types of cells were harvested, washed, suspended in cholesterol-free medium, and assayed for viability with and without 25 μg/ml of amphotericin B. Cholesterol was then added to the R cells, and each parent culture was divided in half for further incubation at either 4 or 37°C. At the end of this second incubation, viability tests were performed as before. *Mycoplasma laidlawii* has a generation time of about 2 hours; therefore, if the drug had no effect on cell growth during the 2-hour incubation in the presence of amphotericin B, the number of cells would be expected to double and approach 200 per cent of the initial viability assay. If the drug had a killing effect, then the per cent survivors would be less than 100 per cent (that is, less than the initial viability assay carried out before exposure to the drug). Growing the R cells at 37°C in cholesterol medium sure to the drug). Growing the R cells at 37°C in cholesterol medium makes them drug sensitive, whereas the S cells are made drug insensitive by growth at 37°C without cholesterol. (From Feingold[15])

Cell type	Survivors after a 2-hour exposure to amphotericin B (%)
S cells	2
R cells	200
S cells incubated in cholesterol-free medium for 2 hours at	
37 °C	150
4 °C	5
R cells incubated in cholesterol-containing medium for 2 hours at	
37 °C	3
4 °C	180

Further understanding of the mechanism of action of the polyenes and other antibiotics that affect membrane function is limited by our knowledge of the fundamental structure and action of biological membranes. One of the areas of research that adds to this knowledge is the study of synthetic membrane systems. The effects of the polyenes on a number of model membranes, such as lipid monolayers, bilayers, and liposomes, have been investigated.[4] Some of the most intriguing work in this area concerns the effect of the polyenes on the rate of release of small ions and glucose from liposomes. Liposomes are artificial spherules of phospholipid formed, in this instance, by mixing lecithin and dicetyl phosphate in the presence or absence of cholesterol. The lipids are permitted to swell in the presence of a small molecule (e.g., glucose). The resulting spherules, which contain the sequestered markers, are then dialyzed to eliminate soluble (extra-spherular) glucose from the suspending buffer. Test substances, such as the polyene antibiotics, can then be added to the liposome suspension, and the rate of release of sequestered glucose from the trapped to the free form can be measured as a function of both sterol content and antibiotic concentration. It has been demonstrated that the polyenes increase the rate of release of glucose[17] and also of such small ions as $CrO_4^=$ and $H_2PO_4^-$ from phospholipid spherules[18] that contain a sterol (see Figure 9-1). In the absence of a sterol, there is little effect. Thus, an *in vitro* system has been prepared that mimics some of the characteristics of the response of the far more complex biological membranes to the polyenes.

The polyenes do not all associate with membranes in the same way. Sterols must satisfy quite specific structural requirements in

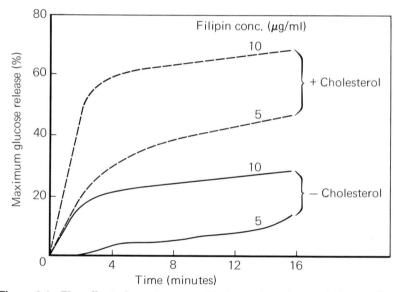

Figure 9-1 The effect of a polyene antibiotic on the release of glucose from liposomes made with and without cholesterol. Liposomes were prepared from egg lecithin, dicetyl phosphate, and glucose in the presence or absence of cholesterol. After dialysis to remove free glucose, filipin was added to equivalent suspensions of liposomes, and the release of sequestered glucose to the free form was measured by a spectrophotometric assay. The rate of release and the extent of release are much larger in the liposomes containing cholesterol (dotted line). (Figure adapted from Kinsky *et al.,*[17] Fig. 8.) Similar results have been obtained for the effect of nystatin and amphotericin B on the release of $CrO_4^=$ and $H_2PO_4^-$ from liposomes prepared with and without a sterol.[18]

order to be bound maximally to filipin,[19,20] for example, whereas amphotericin B does not display the same degree of selectivity.[20,21] The formation of the sterol polyene complex involves primarily hydrophobic forces. The exact geometry of the binding complex has not been defined, and it is not at all clear how this complex disrupts the fungal membrane.

The effects of amphotericin B and nystatin on the ion permeability of artificial lipid bilayers differ somewhat from their effects on fungi. The antibiotic-treated synthetic membranes are quite selective in permitting the passage of anions.[22] This stands in contrast to the effect of some other polyenes (e.g., candicidin) that are cation selective in the lipid bilayer system[23] and to the effect of amphotericin B and nystatin on K^+ passage through fungal membranes. The effect on the artificial membrane is reversible, and the passage of anion (and consequently the electrical conductance) is markedly augmented when the antibiotic is present on both sides of the membrane.[22] The effect here, as in natural membranes and in the liposome vesicles described in Figure 9-1, is sterol dependent. In the thin lipid membrane model, the binding of amphotericin B and nystatin to sterols apparently results in the formation of nonstatic aqueous channels permeable to small ions. Thus, the mechanism of the permeability effect in this system may be similar to that of the channel-forming ionophore antibiotics described in Chapter 6 (e.g., gramicidin A). One of several models poposed for the mechanism of pore formation by amphotericin B is shown in Figure 9-2.[24] The model is presented to give the reader a framework upon which to fit a concept of amphotericin B-membrane interactions. The model does not account for the anion selectivity of the amphotericin B effect in this system, and it is not supposed to represent the mechanism of the drug effect as it occurs in complex membranes of fungi and higher organisms.

Effects of Polyenes on Mammalian Cell Membranes

If the presence of sterols in a membrane is a determinant for sensitivity to the polyene antibiotics, then, since mammalian cell membranes contain sterols, one might expect that these drugs would affect the permeability of host cells. This is indeed the case. Polyenes have been shown to affect a variety of cells from higher organisms. One cell system in which polyene effects have been studied in some detail is the human red blood cell. Erythrocytes suspended in isotonic saline rupture on exposure to high

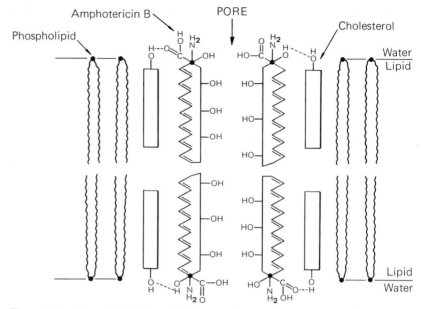

Figure 9-2   A hypothetical model of a pore formed by amphotericin B in a lipid bilayer membrane. Considerable evidence supports the hypothesis that amphotericin B and nystatin can form pores in artificial lipid bilayer membranes. These pores are quite anion selective. Since sucrose (radius = 5.2 Å) is not permitted to pass through, the radius of the pore is thought to be less than 4 to 5 Å.[25] The pore is formed by several polyene molecules packed side by side in a cylinder formation. The principal interactions between the antibiotic and the membrane involve hydrophobic bonds between the lipophilic heptaene segment of the antibiotic and the sterols. The dashed lines represent possible hydrogen bonds. The solid circles oriented at the membrane surfaces represent the polar head groups of the phospholipids, and the wavy lines denote the hydrophobic fatty acid chains. In this configuration, amphotericin B is 20 to 24 Å long and would extend approximately one-half the distance of a bilayer. The ion conductance of artificial bilayer membranes is markedly potentiated when the antibiotic is added to both sides, presumably because continuous pores passing from one membrane surface to the other can be readily formed.[23] (Adapted from Andreoli,[24] Figure 11.)

concentrations of amphotericin B.[26] The effect can be inhibited by serum—probably because polyenes bind to serum cholesterol so that the concentration of free drug available for association with membrane sterols is effectively lowered. Upon exposure to amphotericin B, human erythrocytes lose potassium at a rate that is related to the drug concentration.[27] The interaction of the polyenes with the red cell membrane also seems to be sterol dependent. This is suggested by the observation that erythrocytes from patients with spur-cell anemia are especially sensitive to amphotericin B.[28] These cells have abnormally high amounts of membrane cholesterol.

The precise mechanism of amphotericin B-induced hemolysis is not well defined. It is clear that, since the permeability to small ions is altered, there is a substantial shift of water into the erythrocyte and cell rupture occurs.[29] Thus it would seem that rupture results from osmolysis and is not a function of massive disruption of the erythrocyte membrane by the amphotericin B molecule itself. Some polyenes can cause gross changes in the architecture of red cell membranes. Filipin, for example, causes pits to form in red cell membranes as well as in lecithin-cholesterol dispersions.[30] These pits can be demonstrated by electron microscopy. The formation of pits is dependent on the presence of cholesterol. It is clear from the results of freeze-etching experiments that the pits caused by filipin do not represent large membrane pores, as has been suggested, and it is also clear that amphotericin B does not cause pit formation.[31]

Another effect of amphotericin B on mammalian cells deserves special mention. When cells in culture are exposed to combinations of amphotericin B and other cytotoxic drugs, a synergistic response is sometimes seen.[32] This suggests that amphotericin B may be able to alter the permeability of mammalian cells enough to permit the increased entry of other drugs (e.g., the tetracyclines) that act on intracellular processes.[33] Some of the cytotoxic drugs employed in the chemotherapy of cancer do not readily enter cells, and it is conceivable that a combined drug approach, such as the above, could increase the therapeutic effect. When mice bearing a transplantable leukemia were treated with a single injection of amphotericin B followed 24 hours later by a single injection of BCNU [1,3-bis(2-chloroethyl)-1-nitrosurea], an anti-cancer drug, a significant number of long-term survivors was obtained.[34] Control mice treated with either drug alone survived only a few days. The mechanism of the amphotericin B effect in the leukemic mice appears to be more complex than that seen in cell culture systems. Another polyene compound, vitimin A, has been shown to have adjuvent properties (like bacillus Calmette-Guerin, BCG),[35] and it has been suggested that amphotericin B itself can modify host immune responses.[36] Even though the effects of amphotericin B in the intact animal may reflect more than one action, the possibility of a new therapeutic approach using membrane-active antibiotics is certainly attractive.

It is possible that membrane-active drugs may someday be used to counteract drug resistance based on altered cellular permeability. For example, resistance to the anticancer drug actinomycin D can result from decreased drug entry into tumor cells.[37,38] But when amphotericin B was added to cultured human cells (HeLa), which had been selected for this type of resistance, the cells were again sensitive to the actinomycin D.[39] In this study it was also demonstrated that amphotericin B treatment resulted in the increased entry of radioactive actinomycin D into the cells.

Given that the polyenes clearly affect the cell membranes of higher organisms, it is important to ask—What then is the basis for the selective toxicity of the polyenes for fungi? The answer to this question is by no means clear. First, it should be noted that these are very toxic drugs. They have a very low therapeutic index. Second, cell membrane constituents vary from one organism or cell type to another. It is possible that sensitivity to the polyenes may vary somewhat with the phospholipid to sterol ratio in the membrane[40] and that it may differ in host cells and fungi. It has also been suggested that amphotericin B has a greater affinity for ergosterol than for cholesterol. Selective toxicity could be explained on this basis, since ergosterol is the principal sterol in fungal membranes and cholesterol is the principal sterol in animal cell membranes.[41]

Potentiation of the Antifungal Effects of Other Drugs by Amphotericin B

It now seems clear that the combination of amphotericin B and flucytosine can be synergistic in several types of fungi growing in vitro including *Cryptococcus neoformans* and several species of *Candida*.[42,43,44] *Candida* organisms growing in culture take up much more radioactive flucytosine into the acid-precipatable fraction when amphotericin B is present.[43] Thus, it is reasonable to suggest that the synergism is due to the ability of amphotericin B to alter the permeability of the fungal membrane to flucytosine. This potentiation may occur after administration of the drugs to animals. In experimental cryptococcal and candidal infections in mice, amphotericin B and flucytosine used together have produced additive and possibly synergistic effects.[45,46,47] Clinical experience with the combined therapy has been very limited. The combination was used successfully in a pilot study in which several patients with disseminated cryptococcosis were treated.[48] It was suggested here that the combined approach might permit a smaller dosage of amphotericin B to be used for a shorter period of time.

The action of rifampicin is also potentiated by amphotericin B. Rifampicin, an inhibitor of RNA synthesis, is employed in the treatment of tuberculosis and some other bacterial infections (Chapter 8). It is not particularly effective against fungi, apparently because it cannot readily enter these organisms. In the presence of low concentrations of amphotericin B, however, rifampicin has antifungal activity in vitro. This potentiation has been shown in several species of fungi including Candida albicans, Histoplasma capsulatum, and Coccidoides imitis.[49,50,51] Determinations of the rate of incorporation of radioactive uridine into fungal RNA support the hypothesis that the effectiveness of the combination is due to increased rifampicin entry and consequent inhibition of RNA synthesis.[43,50]

Rifampicin, and perhaps other antibiotics, may prove to be more useful in combination with amphotericin B than flucytosine. Flucytosine is not active against many fungi, whereas rifampicin and other agents may prove to have a broad spectrum of antifungal activity. Given the early status of the work on the combined drug approach, it is not possible to accurately predict its future role in antifungal therapy. The possibility that one drug may be used to allow another drug to achieve effective intracellular concentrations is in itself an intriguing concept. The use of agents that alter cell permeability in combination therapy may eventually find clinical application not only in the treatment of infectious disease and cancer but elsewhere in therapeutics.

Resistance to the Polyenes

The development of resistance to the polyenes during therapy of fungal infection is uncommon. Under clinical conditions of relapse of disease after a course of amphotericin B therapy, the more recent isolate is usually of the same order of susceptibility as the initial specimens. There is a report of resistance occurring in Candida tropicalis during therapy of a patient with funguria.[52] Both the amphotericin B-resistant isolates from this patient were shown to have an altered sterol content. Polyene-resistant strains of fungi have been selected in vitro, and these organisms have also been found to have changes in their sterol content. The resistant fungi seem generally to fall into one of two classes: (1) fungi with a reduced ability to synthesize ergosterol; (2) mutant fungi that synthesize increased quantities of other sterols, which have a lower affinity for the polyene (these resistant fungi also produce less ergosterol).[53] The principal sterols of the highly nystatin-resistant strains of *Saccharomyces cerevisiae* are ergosterol precursors.[54] It appears quite likely that the emergence of polyene-resistant fungi represents a selection for organisms with impaired enzymatic functions required for sterol synthesis.

Studies on *Candida albicans* sensitivity to amphotericin during different growth phases show that organisms in exponential growth are more sensitive to the drug than those in the stationary phase.[55] The difference was not observed in spheroplasts (forms of the organism lacking a cell wall) derived from exponential and stationary phase fungi. This suggests that the change in sensitivity may reflect differences in the fungal cell wall. If extramembranal structures affect the ability of the antibiotic to reach its site of action in the cell membrane, it is possible that a future chemotherapeutic approach could include combinations of polyenes and (as yet unidentified) inhibitors of fungal cell wall synthesis. If the cell wall impedes drug entry, this could contribute to the intrinsic differences in amphotericin B sensitivity observed among the various fungi.

Therapeutic Use

Nystatin, amphotericin B, and candicidin are all used in the treatment of superficial *Candida* infection. They are provided in a variety of forms for topical administration. These include creams, lotions, and ointments for application to the skin; suspensions for treatment of oropharyngeal candidiasis; and tablets for vaginal administration. Nystatin and amphotericin B are also provided in oral tablet form for the treatment of intestinal *Candida* infections. Since there is very little absorption of these drugs from the intestinal tract, oral administration for intestinal candidiasis constitutes a local use of the drug analogous to local topical therapy. *Candida albicans* is the fungus most commonly involved in superinfection in patients receiving anti-bacterial therapy. There are tetracycline preparations that also contain nystatin for the purpose of preventing fungal overgrowth in the bowel. The use of these fixed-ratio combinations has not been proven effective and does not reflect rational therapy (see Chapter 4 for discussion of the nystatin–tetracycline preparations). Systemic candidiasis is treated with intravenous amphotericin B, either alone or in combination therapy with flucytosine. The incidence of systemic candidiasis is much higher in patients who have Hodgkin's disease or lymphoproliferative and myeloproliferative disorders and in patients who are receiving antibiotics and immunosuppressive drugs.[56]

Amphotericin B is the only polyene available for parenteral use. It is given intravenously in the treatment of systemic mycoses (Table 9-3). The minimum inhibitory concentration for susceptible fungi ranges from 0.02 to 1.0 $\mu g/ml$, and at about twice the minimum inhibitory concentration, the drug is fungicidal. The tolerance to amphotericin B varies substantially from patient to patient, and because of the extensive toxicity and side effects therapy is instituted at a lower dosage than the maintenance dose. The manufacturer recommends an initial dose of 0.25 mg/kg. The daily dosage is then increased gradually as nephrotoxicity permits. There is no fixed maintenance dosage, but the dose arrived

Table 9-3 **Drugs employed in the treatment of selected fungal infections**

Infecting fungus	Drugs of choice	Alternatives
SUPERFICIAL INFECTIONS		
Dermatophytes	Topical agents	Topical agents
Epidermophyton	Miconazole	Tolnaftate
Microsporon	Clotrimazole	Undecylenic acid
Trichophyton		Oral therapy
		Griseofulvin
Candida albicans		
Superficial	Miconazole or	Nystatin (topical)
	clotrimazole	
	(topical)	
Intestinal	Nystatin (oral)	
SYSTEMIC INFECTIONS		
Candida albicans	Amphotericin B (with	
Cryptococcus neoformans	or without	Flucytosine
Aspergillus	Flucytosine)	
Histoplasma capsulatum		
Coccidioides immitis	Amphotericin B	None
Mucor		
Blastomyces dermatitidis	Amphotericin B	Hydroxystilbamidine
(N. American)		
Sporothrix schenkii	Iodides	Amphotericin B
		Griseofulvin

at is usually between 0.3 and 1.0 mg/kg daily. Under no circumstances should a total dose of 1.0 mg/kg in daily therapy or 1.5 mg/kg in alternate day treatment be exceeded.

Another method of administration[1] is to deliver an initial test dose of 1 mg over a 30-minute time interval; the patient's pulse and temperature are then monitored every 30 minutes for 4 hours; and if little fever occurs, the dosage is raised by 5-mg increments on subsequent days until a maintenance dosage of about 0.3 mg/kg is achieved. This method of administration may permit the patient to develop some tolerance to the drug fever, but therapeutic doses are not achieved quickly. In patients with serious, progressive systemic fungal infections, the first day's dose should be in the therapeutic range, 0.3 mg/kg. This may be increased to about 0.6 mg/kg daily as nephrotoxicity permits.

When the daily maintenance dosage has been achieved, the patient can be gradually changed to a schedule in which a double dose is given every other day. It has been shown that such alternate day therapy maintains appropriate serum concentrations, and it is more convenient and usually well tolerated by the patient.[57] This is an important consideration, since systemic fungal infections require many weeks of intravenous amphotericin B therapy.

It would seem that the most accurate way to determine when a patient is receiving an adequate dosage of amphotericin B would be to test the ability of the patient's serum to kill the isolated fungus in vitro. This would allow the dose to be individually adjusted according to the sensitivity of the organism. Drutz et al.[58] have published a study in which they treated patients daily with enough amphotericin B to provide peak serum levels at least twice those required to inhibit the fungal isolate. This method has not been widely applied because the concentration of amphotericin B required to inhibit a fungus depends greatly on assay technique,[1] and this varies considerably among different laboratories. Also, it is not clear that the blood level of amphotericin B reflects appropriate fungicidal levels in infected tissues. The distribution and pharmacokinetic properties of the drug are not well understood.

Amphotericin B has permitted the treatment of a number of systemic mycoses. The chemical, pharmacological, and toxic properties of the drug make its administration difficult. Several different dosage regimens have been presented here to enforce this point and to emphasize the largely empirical basis of therapy.

In the sections on the pharmacology and toxicity of amphotericin B, additional problems of drug administration will be discussed.

Pharmacology of the Polyenes

Absorption and Method of Administration

Amphotericin B is poorly absorbed from the gastrointestinal tract. Several attempts have been made to use amphotericin B orally, but the drug blood levels achieved are low and inconsistent.[59] Amphotericin B is essentially insoluble in water; therefore, in preparing the drug for intravenous administration it is brought into a colloidal dispersion with sodium deoxycholate. The drug-deoxycholate mix is supplied as a dry powder, which is first suspended in sterile water and then added to a 5 per cent solution of dextrose in water. The final concentration of the drug in the infusion fluid should be 0.1 mg/ml. Since the drug will precipitate from saline solutions and solutions containing preservatives, they should never be employed. The personnel administering this drug must be cautioned to watch for precipitate formation. If a precipitate forms, the solution should be immediately discarded.

Amphotericin B should be administered slowly over a period of about 6 hours. Rapid infusion of therapeutic doses is dangerous because untoward reactions may result. With patients who tolerate the drug poorly, 25 to 50 mg of hydrocortisone sodium succinate may be helpful in controlling fever and other side effects. Perhaps by virtue of its effect on cell membranes, amphotericin B is very irritating, and it is associated with a high incidence of thrombophlebitis. The risk of this complication is lowered by using a small needle and a very slow drip. Since the course of therapy is often long, the physician can preserve the maximum amount of vein for future infusion by alternating therapy between extremities and by starting the infusion site distally and moving it proximally if necrosis or occlusion of the veins occurs.

Amphotericin B is slowly degraded by light. When stored in the powder form, it should be kept in the dark. The intravenous solution should be administered promptly after preparation. It has been recommended that amphotericin B be kept from light during the infusion, but when the infusion bottle is covered with a paper bag or tinfoil, it is awkward to monitor the rate of drug administration. It has been shown that there is no significant loss in biological activity over the course of 8 hours at room temperature under normal lighting conditions.[60,61] Thus, it is not necessary to cover the infusion bottle during drug administration.

The levels of drug in the spinal fluid after intravenous administration are very low compared to the blood levels,[57] and intrathecal administration of amphotericin B is required for treatment of some fungal infections of the central nervous system like coccidioidal meningitis and refractory cases of cryptococcal meningitis. For intrathecal administration, 0.5 mg of the drug is dissolved in 5 ml of cerebrospinal fluid and injected into either the lumbar area or directly into the cisterna magna. It is usually given two to three times a week. Intrathecal administration is accompanied by such side effects as radiculitis, paresthesias, paresis, headache, and visual impairment.[62]

Other methods of introducing the drug into the cerbrospinal fluid have been tried; one method permits the direct injection of amphotericin B into the lateral cerebral ventricle.[63] A burr hole is made in the skull and a subcutaneous dome of siliconized rubber is fitted into the hole. A catheter extends from the dome into the ventricle. The drug is injected into the reservoir, and intermittent gentle pressure on the skin over the reservoir promotes mixing of the drug via the catheter with the cerebrospinal fluid. This method of administration is useful in some patients, but it is accompanied by a high incidence of complications related to technical problems of insertion and maintenance of the reservoir and the production of arachnoiditis and bacterial infection.[64]

Another intriguing approach to intrathecal amphotericin B administration is suggested by some animal experiments in which hyperbaric solutions of drugs were used.[65] Monkeys were injected in the lumbar area with amphotericin B dissolved in 10 per cent dextrose in water and placed in the Trendelenburg position (the body is at a 30 degree tilt with the head downward). The specific gravity of the dextrose solution is greater than that of the cerebrospinal fluid and it migrates downhill to the cisterna magna, carrying the amphotericin B with it. It is possible that this technique, or a modification of it, may prove useful in treating patients with fungal meningitis.

Distribution and Excretion

The data available on distribution of amphotericin B in both man and animals are very limited. Much of the work carried out in humans has involved measuring blood and cerebrospinal fluid levels by bioassay techniques after intravenous administration. It is very difficult to interpret data gathered by withdrawing a sample of blood and determining the antifungal activity of the serum. When properly controlled, such measurements will give a fairly good indication of the amount of free drug present in the serum but not of the total drug. Drug bound to β-lipoprotein in the serum,[57] for example, would not be included. Sterols in the serum inhibit polyene action on fungi,[66] and it is possible that such assays may vary considerably according to the patient's serum cholesterol content. These studies are therefore inadequate if one is trying to answer the pharmacological question—What is the distribution of the drug? On the other hand, they are the best method available for determining the answer to the therapeutically important question—What is the level of antifungal activity achieved in the serum? Even bioassay methods can give results that are in error. Values will be too high, for instance, if the assay conditions allow dissociation of a drug from the serum-bound to the biologically active, free form.[67]

Bindschadler and Bennett have carried out serum bioassays for amphotericin B after infusion of the drug at various doses every day or every other day.[57] They demonstrated that at the end of an infusion no more than 10 per cent of the biologically active drug could be found in the serum and no more than 40 per cent, by calculation, in the extracellular fluid. Only a small percentage of the drug was removed by excretion during the period of the drug infusion. The investigators noted that as the dose of the drug was increased, inactivation and/or storage mechanisms increased also. After cessation of therapy, the drug could be detected in the serum for 3 weeks, a finding confirmed by other studies. The results of Bindshadler and Bennett's study are consistent with the hypothesis that amphotericin B is rapidly sequestered in the body and then slowly released from its depot into the blood. It is possible that this depot consists of the cell membranes that contain sterols and bind the polyenes.

No data are available to demonstrate that the concentration of free antibiotic in infected tissues parallels the concentration in the patient's serum. With intravenous administration it is clear that the concentrations achieved in the cerebrospinal fluid and some other body spaces, such as the aqueous humor,[68] are much lower than concentrations in the blood. The distribution of amphotericin B across the placenta is apparently not known, but several patients treated with the drug during the last two trimesters of pregnancy have given birth to normal infants.[69]

The primary route of drug excretion is via the kidney, but the rate of elimination is very slow. In the presence of compromised renal function, the serum concentration of amphotericin B does not rise, and no dosage adjustment need be made.[57,70] Amphotericin B is poorly dialyzable, but again there is no need to adjust the dosage in patients with renal insufficiency when they undergo hemodialysis.[71]

Toxicity of the Polyenes

When given orally for the treatment of intestinal candidiasis, nystatin and amphotericin B may cause nausea, vomiting, and diarrhea. When given topically, there are essentially no side effects, other than occasional irritation.

The intravenous use of amphotericin B is associated with a wide variety of side effects.[1,72] Virtually every patient is affected by one or more toxic phenomenon. The initial infusions of the drug often cause chills and fever. In one study, for example, 27 of 29 patients experienced fever.[73] Occasionally, hypotension and delirium occur along with the fever. Because the initial response to the drug can be severe, a small test dose (1 mg) should be given to assess the patient's tolerance and the daily drug dosage is increased slowly in small increments. If therapy is resumed after the patient has been off the drug for more than a week, the initial dosage procedure should be followed. Nausea, vomiting, and abdominal pain occur even though the drug is not being given orally. Headache, anorexia, and phlebitis also occur frequently, whereas cardiac arrhythmias occur rarely.

Amphotericin B causes a normochromic, normocytic anemia. It seems clear that this is due to a reversible suppression of erythrocyte production.[74] The hemolysis discussed earlier in this chapter occurs only at concentrations higher than those achieved in the serum during therapy.[27] Rarely, leukopenia and thrombocytopenia occur.

Virtually all patients who receive a therapeutic course of intravenous amphotericin B demonstrate some degree of nephrotoxicity. For example, in one study of 56 patients, elevated blood urea nitrogen values were observed in 93 per cent of the patients, and 83 per cent had high serum creatinine values.[75] Permanent impairment of renal function is generally not clinically significant in patients receiving a cumulative dosage of less than 4 gm during a normal therapeutic interval of several weeks. With a total dosage greater than 4 gm, significant persistent renal damage occurs.[75]

Specimens of renal tissue obtained at biopsy or postmortem examination show tubular degenerative changes with intratubular and interstitial calcium deposits.[76] Amphotericin B nephropathy is manifested by abnormal urine sediment, azotemia (elevated blood urea nitrogen), and renal tubular acidosis.[77] Hypokalemia develops in a significant number of patients, who will require potassium replacement. Renal potassium wasting and nephrocalcinosis may both result from a tubular defect in acid excretion.[77] Studies of the nephrotoxicity in animal models also support the concept that amphotericin B affects the renal tubule, modifying its ability to acidify the urine.[78,79] It is clear that amphotericin B can interact with mammalian cell membranes and alter their permeability to small cations like hydrogen and potassium.[27] A significant part of the nephrotoxicity of amphotericin B may be due to a similar effect in the membranes of the cells of the distal tubule.

The data from some animal studies suggest that it may be possible to reduce the nephrotoxicity of amphotericin B. It has been shown that administration of sodium bicarbonate can reduce nephrotoxicity in rats.[79] The simultaneous administration of mannitol reduced the rise in blood urea nitrogen caused by amphotericin B in dogs.[80] This second approach has received a preliminary trial in a few renal transplant patients undergoing amphotericin B therapy.[81] The four patients in this study were successfully cleared of fungal infection without experiencing a significant change in blood urea nitrogen or serum creatinine. A larger clinical trial is warrented.

Some degree of renal damage is almost inevitable when amphotericin B is given intravenously. Indeed, it is frequently the extent of the nephrotoxicity and not the therapeutic response that determines the duration of treatment. In view of the problems of administration and toxicity, a number of precautions should be observed when amphotericin B is given intravenously. The drug should be used only for severe deep fungal infection. It should not be used when positive skin or serological tests alone are present without symptomatology indicating a potentially fatal fungal infection. It should be used only with hospitalized patients. Before therapy is begun the physician should obtain a complete hemogram, urinalysis, liver function tests, serum electrolytes, and BUN. During therapy, these tests should be performed at least weekly, and BUN should be determined two to three times weekly. The total daily dose should never exceed 1.5 mg/kg.

FLUCYTOSINE

Flucytosine, the 5-fluoro-substituted analog of cytosine, was originally synthesized as a potential anticancer drug. And although it was found not to be cytotoxic for mammalian cells, it was active against some fungi.

Mechanism of Action and Resistance

Flucytosine is transported into fungal cells where it is deaminated by cytosine deaminase to 5-fluorouracil (Figure 9-3). The uptake of

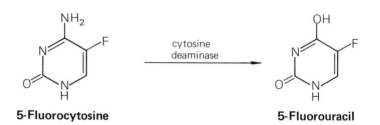

5-Fluorocytosine   **5-Fluorouracil**

5-fluorocytosine, and thus the inhibition of growth, can be blocked by cytosine.[82] The anticancer drug cytosine arabinoside will also block the flucytosine effect by competing for uptake of the drug.[83] The conversion of flucytosine to 5-fluorouracil is an absolute requirement for drug activity; mutant fungi with no cytosine deaminase activity are resistant to flucytosine.[84,85]

As can be seen from Figure 9-3, 5-fluorouracil is converted to 5-fluorouracil-ribose monophosphate. This reaction in fungi seems to depend primarily on uridine-monophosphate (UMP) pyrophosphorylase.[86] Mutant fungi that are resistant to very high concentrations of both 5-fluorocytosine and 5-fluorouracil have been isolated.[87] Their resistance is often the result of a mutation that affects the production of UMP pyrophosphorylase. The exact action of the drug on fungi is not well defined. It is clear that a significant amount of the 5-fluorouracil is converted to the triphosphate and incorporated into RNA.[88,89] It is not clear, however, that the fungistatic effect of flucytosine is entirely due to "faulty" RNA production by the fungus.

In mammalian cells, 5-fluorouracil is a very toxic compound, which is used as an anticancer drug. For 5-fluorouracil to be cytotoxic, it must first be converted to 5-fluorouracil-ribose mono-

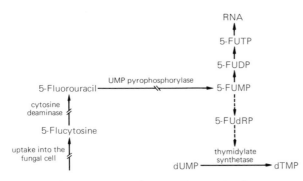

Figure 9-3 Action of flucytosine in fungi. 5-Flucytosine is transported into the fungal cell where it is deaminated to 5-fluorouracil (5-FU). The 5-FU is then converted to 5-fluorouracil-ribose monophosphate (5-FUMP). Additional phosphates are added and the triphosphorylated form of the pyrimidine (5-FUTP) is incorporated into fungal RNA. The arrows with break marks represent those reactions that have been shown to be absent in various flucytosine-resistant fungi. Mammalian cells have the capacity to convert the ribose in 5-FUMP to deoxyribose, to form 5-FUdRP (dashed arrows), which is a potent inhibitor of thymidylate synthetase. As yet, there is no evidence that this enzyme is inhibited in fungi.

phosphate (5-FUMP); the sugar is then reduced to 5-fluoro-2′-deoxyuridine-5′-monophosphate (5-FUdRP). This compound inhibits thymidylate synthetase. It thus blocks the production of thymidine monophosphate (dashed arrows, Figure 9-3) to inhibit DNA synthesis.[90] As yet, there is no evidence that this mechanism exists in fungi.[89] One would expect flucytosine to be toxic to the patient, since 5-fluorouracil is such a toxic compound. This, however, is not the case. In man, flucytosine is not metabolized further;[91] and none of the toxicity of the drug can be attributed to 5-fluorouracil production. The selective toxicity of flucytosine is explained by the difference in the abilities of the host and the fungus to convert it to 5-fluorouracil.

Many fungi are not sensitive to clinically achievable concentrations of flucytosine. About 60 per cent of *Candida* spp. and most *Cryptococcus* are initially sensitive, but resistance can develop during treatment. This is a major therapeutic problem when the drug is used alone in therapy.[87,92] There are many possible mechanisms of resistance to flucytosine, several of which have been demonstrated in resistant strains isolated from patients. These include (Figure 9-3) a decrease in the activity of the cytosine-specific permease responsible for drug entry into the fungus,[87] a loss of cytosine deaminase activity,[93] or a decrease in UMP pyrophosphorylase activity.[87,94] Mutant organisms created in the laboratory have been shown to be resistant by all these mechanisms and also by the absence of a feedback inhibition of pyrimidine synthesis.[84] This last mechanism is especially interesting. Normally, aspartic transcarbamylase, the first enzyme in the pyrimidine biosynthetic pathway, is under feedback inhibitory control by UTP. A mutation resulting in a loss of this regulation leads to increased endogenous synthesis of uridine nucleotides, which compete with the fluorine-containing uridine analogs created from the drug to overcome the antifungal effect.

Use, Pharmacology, and Untoward Effects of Flucytosine

Use

Flucytosine is effective against many strains of *Cryptococcus neoformans*, *Candida albicans*, and *Torulopsis glabrata*.[1] It has been used successfully in single drug therapy of urinary tract infections and fungemia due to *Candida* and in the treatment of cryptococcal meningitis. As discussed earlier in this chapter, the combination of amphotericin B and flucytosine is sometimes additive or synergistic both *in vitro* and in laboratory animals infected with sensitive fungi. In serious mycoses due to sensitive strains, flucytosine should probably be combined with amphotericin B for therapy.[1] The use of the combination may have several advantages: (1) There may be a more potent antifungal effect than with either drug alone; (2) it may permit a lower dose of amphotericin B to be used, thus avoiding some of the toxicity inherent to this drug;[48] and (3) the rate of emergence of resistance to therapy should be much lower than with flucytosine alone.

Absorption, Distribution, and Excretion

Unlike amphotericin B, flucytosine is well absorbed from the gastrointestinal tract and is routinely given orally. It readily passes into the cerebrospinal fluid, yielding levels that are about 75 per cent of the serum level.[83,95] It also enters the aqueous humor and the bronchial secretions in concentrations in the range of efficacy for sensitive fungi.[96,97] Flucytosine is poorly bound by serum protein.[71] It is excreted primarily by glomerular filtration, there is no detactible metabolism in man,[91] and high concentrations of the unaltered drug are found in the urine.[83]

When renal function is impaired, the dosage schedule must be modified.[95,98] One recommended method is to increase the dosage interval, using the creatinine clearance as a guide to renal function—one dose every 6 hours for a creatinine clearance over 40 ml/minute, every 12 hours for a clearance of 20 to 40 ml; and every 24 hours for a clearance between 10 and 20.[98] The drug is not recommended for patients with a creatinine clearance below 10 ml/minute. The elimination kinetics of flucytosine differ greatly from those of amphotericin B, which is eliminated very slowly and does not require dosage modification in patients with renal failure. It must be remembered when the two drugs are used together in therapy that amphotericin B is a nephrotoxic drug. In the patient with compromised renal function, the serum level of flucytosine can be measured by bioassay even in the presence of amphotericin B.[99]

Untoward Effects

Flucytosine often causes nausea, skin rashes, and eosinophilia. Reversible hepatic dysfunction is manifested by mild elevations in serum transaminases and alkaline phosphatase. There have also been occasional instances of confusion, hallucinations, headache, and vertigo. The principal toxicity associated with the drug is a reversible neutropenia, with an occasional thrombocytopenia.[48,100] A few cases of irreversible bone-marrow failure have been reported,[101,102] and patients with a limited marrow reserve (for example, patients with lymphoreticular disorders or patients on cytotoxic drug regimens) may be more prone to develop hematological complications. The mechanism of the bone-marrow suppression is not known. If the entry of flucytosine into the cells of the marrow is facilitated by the amphotericin B at the doses used in combined therapy, then bone-marrow depression may prove to be more of a problem with this form of treatment.

In summary, flucytosine offers many pharmacological advantages over amphotericin B; these include oral administration, good penetration into the central nervous system, and less toxicity. Many fungi, however, are insensitive to the drug, and in other fungi, resistance can readily develop during treatment with flucytosine alone. It has been difficult to define the role of flucytosine in the therapy of systemic mycoses,[103] but it is becoming clear that the clinical indications for its use are quite restricted (primarily to cryptococcal and candidal infections). In serious infection, it should probably be used in combination with amphotericin B.[1] Frequent blood counts should be performed and hepatic enzymes and renal function should be monitored routinely during therapy. Bone-marrow toxicity is more common in patients with impaired renal function and their dosage interval should be carefully adjusted.

HYDROXYSTILBAMIDINE

2-Hydroxystilbamidine is a close analog of other diamidine compounds (e.g., pentamidine) that are used in the treatment of some protozoal infections. Hydroxystilbamidine is active against a few protozoa (Chapter 11), but it is employed therapeutically only in the treatment of North American blastomycosis[104]—amphotericin B, however, is the drug of choice (Table 9-3). The drug is given daily by slow intravenous infusion and must be kept from light to prevent inactivation. The untoward effects of hydroxystilbamidine are similar to those described for pentamidine (Chapter 11) and include nausea, malaise, hepatotoxicity, paresthesias, and rashes. If infusion is too rapid, hypotension and tachycardia can occur.

DRUGS USED IN THE TREATMENT OF SUPERFICIAL FUNGAL INFECTION

GRISEOFULVIN

Mechanism of Action

The dermatophytes and yeasts, such as *Candida albicans,* are responsible for most superficial fungal infections. The dermophytic infections are treated either with topical drugs or with the systemic agent griseofulvin (Table 9-3). Griseofulvin has been isolated from a number of molds of the genus *Penicillium.* The drug is inactive against bacteria, yeasts, and fungi that cause systemic disease, and its use in the chemotherapy of infection is limited to the treatment of dermatophytic infections.

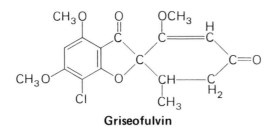

Griseofulvin

Although it is not clear whether griseofulvin as it is used in therapy has a predominantly fungistatic or fungicidal action, experiments with cultured fungi demonstrate that it can act as a fungicide. For griseofulvin to exert a killing effect, the organism must be growing.[105] The drug is concentrated as much as 100-fold by *Microsporum gypseum*.[106] The uptake of griseofulvin by fungi is energy dependent, and correlated with the sensitivity of the organism to the drug.[107] When growing fungi are exposed to griseofulvin, the total DNA and phosphorus content increases, but there is no change in protein, carbohydrate, lipid, and RNA content.[108] The drug causes gross morphological changes in the fungus including the production of binucleate and multinucleate cells.[109] Thus, one of the major cellular effects of griseofulvin is inhibition of fungal mitosis.

At high concentrations, griseofulvin causes metaphase arrest in mammalian cells growing *in vitro*. Much of the information on the mechanism of action of griseofulvin has come from studies of the effect of the drug on mammalian cells. The gross effect of griseofulvin is similar to that of colchicine; the mitotic spindle is disrupted.[110] Upon entering the cell, griseofulvin binds to soluble protein.[111] The principal cellular receptors for griseofulvin are the microtubules, the proteins that form the mitotic spindle. These spindle fibers are long strands consisting of bundles of microtubules that connect the two centrioles of the dividing cell; some spindle fibers connect the kinetochores of the chromosomes to the centrioles. The spindle fibers determine the appropriate segregation of the sister chromatids to opposite poles during anaphase. In telophase, the microtubules disappear when the nuclear envelope forms. Several drugs, including colchicine, vinblastine, and vincristine, bind to the microtubules to inhibit mitosis. Unlike these drugs that inhibit microtubule assembly in the cell, griseofulvin appears to affect the function of the polymerized microtubule.[112]

It has been postulated that the migration of chromosomes may depend upon the ability of adjacent microtubules to slide over one another, thus causing a contraction of spindle fibers and the segregation of the chromosomes in opposite poles of the cell.[113] It is possible that this contractile process is inhibited by griseofulvin.[112] The exact way in which the drug interacts with the microtubule is not known, but it is clear that the binding sites are not the same as those for colchicine or the *Vinca* alkaloids.[114]

Although we have focused on the effect of griseofulvin on mitosis in this discussion, microtubules also have important roles in other cellular events. The griseofulvin-microtubule interaction may be responsible for such additional effects as the gross morphological changes (e.g., curling of hyphae) that have been observed after exposure to the drug.

Pharmacology and Untoward Effects of Griseofulvin

Griseofulvin is given orally for the treatment of infection of the skin, hair, and nails by dermatophytes. These fungi include members of the genera *Microsporum, Trichophyton,* and *Epidermophyton.* Other fungi are not sensitive to the drug.

Absorption, Distribution, and Metabolism

Griseofulvin is essentially insoluble in water. Absorption of the drug from the gastrointestinal tract is enhanced by employing the ultra-fine particle form. Absorption is increased when the drug is taken with a fatty meal.[115] In animals, it has been shown that much higher plasma levels are obtained when the drug is given in an oil-water emulsion.[116] It is not known whether the drug itself passes through the mucosa of small intestine by diffusion or whether it is taken up in the form of a mixed micelle with fat. At least 50 per cent of the ultra-fine particle form of the drug is absorbed from the intestine.[117] Griseofulvin, applied topically, penetrates into all levels of the stratum corneum, but (for unknown reasons) it is only effective in treating fungal infection of the skin when given orally.[118]

The dermatophytic fungi reside in superficial keratinized tissue, and it is the distribution of the drug into this compartment that is particularly important with regard to its therapeutic effect. Griseofulvin binds to keratin and high concentrations of the drug occur in the stratum corneum, the outermost layer of the epidermis that contains the keratinized cells. There are apparently two routes by which the drug reaches the skin surface: (1) by passive diffusion in the epidermal fluid and (2) by secretion in the sweat.[119] Griseofulvin binding by keratin is of high enough affinity to account for selective localization in the skin, but it is clearly reversible. As the blood concentration of the drug decreases, the concentration of the drug in the stratum corneum declines at roughly the same rate.[120] The average course of therapy for tinea of the body is 3 to 6 weeks. Infections of intertriginous areas and the thick skin of the palms and the soles require 4 to 8 weeks of therapy.

Two other sites of dermatophyte infection of special interest are the hair and the nails. It was shown some time ago that when guinea pigs with ringworm infection were treated for a few days with oral griseofulvin, the fungus was eradicated from the hair follicle and the base of the hair shaft but the tips of the hair remained infected.[121] Subsequently, it was shown that orally administered griseofulvin became associated with hair.[122] It thus seems that the griseofulvin becomes associated with keratin in the hair follicle, and as the hair grows, fungi are not able to grow in the griseofulvin-containing region. This unique aspect of the drug distribution is an important component of its clinical effectiveness in treating infection by dermatophytic fungi.

There is another biological effect of griseofulvin, in addition to the action on microtubules, that may contribute to its clinical effectiveness. It has been shown that some dermatophytes produce enzymes that digest keratin.[123] These keratinases may be important in helping the fungus penetrate and parasitize keratinous structures, and some data suggest that griseofulvin-containing hair may not be as good a substrate for these enzymes as normal hair.[124]

Dermatophyte infection of the nails requires long-term griseofulvin therapy. The duration of drug administration is in part determined by the time required for complete growth of the nail. The drug probably becomes associated with keratin as the nail is being formed. Apparently, griseofulvin cannot diffuse through the nail structure in the same way that it can pass through the layers of the skin, and fungi continue to infect the portion of the nail that was formed before initiation of therapy. Infection of the finger nails requires therapy for 3 to 6 months and infection of the toe nails 6 to 12 months and sometimes longer.

The distribution properties of griseofulvin are uniquely appropriate to its clinical use in dermatophyte infections. Chemotherapy requires a minimum of several weeks (this varies with the location of the infection), but the patient's symptoms are relieved within a few days.

Metabolism of griseofulvin is principally by demethylation and glucuronide formation in the liver.[117] About 50 per cent of a dose of griseofulvin is excreted in the urine within 5 days, mostly in the form of the metabolites.[117] In the rat, the rate of metabolism of griseofulvin is somewhat increased by phenobarbital,[125] a drug that induces activity of the hepatic microsomal drug metabolizing system. Concomitant administration of clinically usual doses of phenobarbital significantly reduces the blood levels of griseofulvin in man. It should not be presumed that the reduced blood level in man is due to an increased rate of metabolism. Studies in subjects receiving griseofulvin intravenously or orally indicate that the major effect of phenobarbital is to decrease the gastrointestinal absorption of griseofulvin.[126] Griseofulvin itself apparently increases the rate of metabolism of the coumarin anticoagulants and diminishes the effect of these drugs.

Untoward Effects

A common side effect of griseofulvin is headache. This may occur in as many as 10 to 15 per cent of patients. The headache usually disappears within a few days despite continuation of therapy. Rarely, lapses of memory, impairment of judgment, and other effects on the nervous system have been reported, and this contraindicates the use of the drugs in pilots and bus drivers. Griseofulvin occasionally causes gastrointestinal distress, skin rashes, and photosensitivity reactions. Superinfection with *Candida* can occur during therapy. Leukopenia has been reported, and occasional blood counts are advisable during the first few weeks of therapy. Griseofulvin apparently increases porphyrin excretion in mice, and it has been reported to increase fecal porphyrin execretion in man.[127] The increased porphyrin metabolism results from the induction of increased levels of δ-aminolevulinic acid synthetase, a rate-limiting enzyme in porphyrin metabolism.[128] The effect of griseofulvin on porphyrin metabolism in humans is probably not of great clinical consequence,[129] but the drug should not be used in people with porphyria.

As mentioned earlier, griseofulvin in high doses causes metaphase arrest in mammalian cells growing *in vitro*. Like colchicine, griseofulvin has an anti-inflammatory effect, and it has been shown to produce some relief in patients with acute gouty arthritis and the shoulder-hand syndrome of rheumatoid arthritis. As with any drug inhibiting mammalian cell division, there was initially some concern over the possibility that griseofulvin might have an adverse effect on rapidly dividing systems like the cells of the bone marrow and spermatogonia. The available evidence, however, supports the conclusion that griseofulvin at the doses used clinically does not affect spermatogenesis.[130] At very high doses, the drug is teratogenic in mice.[131] Although there is no evidence of teratogenicity in humans, it is prudent to withhold the drug from pregnant women.

UNDECYLENIC ACID

Several compounds are employed for the topical treatment of superficial fungal infections in addition to those already discussed (nystatin, amphotericin B, and candicidin). Undecylenic acid is one of a number of fatty acids possessing anti-fungal activity. The reason for this activity is not known. Undecenylic acid is sold in various proprietary preparations for the treatment of tinea pedis (athlete's foot).

TOLNAFTATE

Tolnaftate is used in the treatment of a wider spectrum of dermatophytic infections than is undecylenic acid. It is quite effective in the treatment of infection with *Trichophyton rubrum*, a fungus that is often resistant to other topical agents and to griseofulvin. *Candida* spp. are not sensitive. The mechanism of action of tolnaftate is unknown. There are no known untoward effects.

MICONAZOLE AND CLOTRIMAZOLE

Several imidazole derivatives (e.g., thiabendazole, mebendazole, and metronidazole) have been introduced for the treatment of parasitic infections (Chapter 11), whereas two imidazole compounds, miconazole and clotrimazole, have significant antifungal activity and are employed in the topical treatment of superficial mycoses.

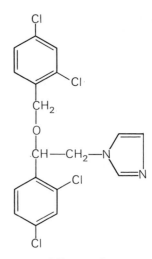

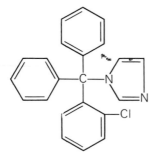

Clotrimazole   **Miconazole**

Both miconazole and clotrimazole have a broad spectrum of antifungal action, with good *in vitro* activity against most fungi of clinical interest.[132,133] For example, the minimum molar concentration of clotrimazole required to inhibit the *in vitro* growth of *Cryptococcus neoformans, Candida albicans,* and *Coccidioides immitis* is lower than that of amphotericin B.[134] In addition to their antifungal activity, miconazole and clotrimazole are active against gram-positive bacteria, although gram-negative bacteria are not sensitive. At high concentrations, clotrimazole is trichomonacidal.[133]

The biochemical mechanism of action of these imidazole derivatives is not well understood. At low concentrations they are fungistatic and at higher concentrations fungicidal. Electron microscopic studies of the effects of both drugs at fungicidal concentrations show marked changes in plasma membrane and intracellular membrane morphology.[135,136] Also at these high concentrations, there is leakage of ions, amino acids, and other molecules from the cell.[137,138] Gross morphological alterations may result from drug-induced changes in cell permeability. At low concentrations, miconazole apparently affects the uptake of purines into the cell.[139] Again this may suggest that an important site of drug action is the plasma membrane. When *Candida* growing in log phase are exposed to radiolabeled miconazole, most of the radioactivity is recovered in the fraction containing cell walls and plasma membrane.[139] With stationary phase cells, most of the drug is found in the microsomal fraction.

These studies do not permit us to define either the site of action or the primary events affected by the imidazole derivatives. It is hypothesized, however, that miconazole and clotrimazole affect the permeability of fungi by acting directly on the cell wall or plasma membrane. No substantial differences in the actions of the two drugs have been observed at the biochemical level, but it is possible that they do not affect cells the same way.

Miconazole and clotrimazole are available in the United States for the topical treatment of common fungal infections of the skin and vagina. They are effective in the treatment of dermatophyte infections,[140,141] but neither drug has been demonstrated to be effective in treating fungal infection of the nails. Both drugs are as effective as nystatin in vaginal candidiasis.[133,142,143] In mixed skin infections with both dermatophytes and *Candida,* these drugs are especially useful (Table 9-3).

Clotrimazole has been used to treat systemic mycoses orally, but it has not been proven effective,[1] and oral administration is accompanied by a serious gastrointestinal intolerance.[134] Serum levels of the drug after topical application to the skin or vagina are very low to undetectable.[144] Both drugs are well tolerated upon topical application, but occasional burning and irritation have been reported.

REFERENCES

1. J. E. Bennett: Chemotherapy of systemic mycoses. *New Eng. J. Med.* 290:30–32, 320–323 (1974).

2. J. M. T. Hamilton-Miller: Chemistry and biology of the polyene macrolide antibiotics. *Bact. Rev.* 37:166 (1973).

3. P. Ganis, G. Auitabile, W. Mechlinski, and C. P. Schaffner: Polyene macrolide antibiotic amphotericin B. Crystal structure of the N-iodoacetyl derivative. *J. Amer. Chem. Soc.* 93:4560 (1971).

4. S. C. Kinsky: Antibiotic interactions with model membranes. *Ann. Rev. Pharmacol.* 10:119 (1970).

5. F. Marini, P. Arnow, and J. O. Lampen: The effect of monovalent cations on the inhibition of yeast metabolism by nystatin. *J. Gen. Microbiol.* 24:51 (1961).

6. J. O. Lampen: "Interference by polyenic antifungal antibiotics (especially nystatin and filipin) with specific membrane functions" in *Biochemical Studies of Antimicrobial Drugs,* ed. by B. A. Newton and P. E. Reynolds. London: Cambridge University Press. 1966, pp. 111–130.

7. S. C. Kinsky: Alterations in the permeability of Neurospora crassa due to polyene antibiotics. J. Bacteriol. 82:889 (1961).

8. D. Gottlieb, H. E. Carter, J. H. Sloneker, L. C. Wu, and E. Gaudy: Mechanisms of inhibition of fungi by filipin. Phytopathology 51:321 (1961).

9. G. R. Gale: Cytology of Candida albicans as influenced by drugs acting on the cytoplasmic membrane. J. Bacteriol. 86:151 (1963).

10. S. C. Kinsky: Effect of polyene antibiotics on protoplasts of Neurospora crassa. J. Bacteriol. 83:351 (1962).

11. J. O. Lampen and P. M. Arnow: Significance of nystatin uptake for its antifungal action. Proc. Soc. Exptl. Biol. Med. 101:792 (1959).

12. J. O. Lampen, P. M. Arnow, Z. Borowska, and A. I. Laskin: Location and role of sterol at nystatin-binding sites. J. Bacteriol. 84:1152 (1962).

13. S. C. Kinsky: Nystatin binding by protoplasts and a particulate fraction of Neurospora crassa, and a basis for the selective toxicity of polyene antifungal antibiotics. Proc. Natl. Acad. Sci. U.S. 48:1049 (1962).

14. S. Razin, M. Argaman, and J. Avigan: Chemical composition of Mycoplasma cells and membranes. J. Gen. Microbiol. 33:477 (1963).

15. D. S. Feingold: The action of amphotericin B on Mycoplasma laidlawii. Biochem. Biophys. Res. Commun. 19:261 (1965).

16. M. W. Weber and S. C. Kinsky: Effect of cholesterol on the sensitivity of Mycoplasma laidlawii to the polyene antibiotic filipin. J. Bacteriol. 89:306 (1965).

17. S. C. Kinsky, J. Haxby, C. B. Kinsky, R. A. Demel, and L. L. M. Van Deenen. Effect of cholesterol incorporation on the sensitivity of liposomes to the polyene antibiotic, filipin. Biochim. Biophys. Acta 152:174 (1968).

18. G. Weissmann and G. Sessa: The action of polyene antibiotics on phospholipid-cholesterol structures. J. Biol. Chem. 242:616 (1967).

19. A. W. Norman, R. A. Demel, B. de Kruyff, and L. L. M. van Deenen: Studies on the biological properties of polyene antibiotics. Evidence for the direct interaction of filipin with cholesterol. J. Biol. Chem. 247:1918 (1972).

20. R. Bittman and S. A. Fischkoff: Fluorescence studies of the binding of the polyene antibiotics filipin III, amphotericin B, nystatin, and lagosin to cholesterol. Proc. Natl. Acad. Sci. U.S. 69:3795 (1972).

21. R. Bittman, W. C. Chen, and O. R. Anderson: Interaction of filipin III and amphotericin B with lecithin-sterol vesicles and cellular membranes. Spectral and electron microscope studies. Biochemistry 13:1364 (1974).

22. R. W. Holz: The effects of the polyene antibiotics nystatin and amphotericin B on thin lipid membranes. Ann. New York Acad. Sci. 235:469 (1974).

23. A. Cass, A. Finkelstein, and V. Krespi: The ion permeability induced in thin lipid membranes by the polyene antibiotics nystatin and amphotericin B. J. Gen. Physiol. 56:100 (1970).

24. T. E. Andreoli: The structure and function of amphotericin B-cholesterol pores in lipid bilayer membranes. Ann. New York Acad. Sci. 235:448 (1974).

25. R. Holz and A. Finkelstein: The water and nonelectrolyte permeability induced in thin lipid membranes by the polyene antibiotics nystatin and amphotericin B. *J. Gen. Physiol.* 56:125 (1970).

26. S. C. Kinsky: Comparative responses of mammalian erythrocytes and microbial protoplasts to polyene antibiotics and vitamin A. *Arch. Biochem. Biophys.* 102:180 (1963).

27. W. T. Butler and E. Cotlove: Increased permeability of human erythrocytes induced by amphotericin B. *J. Infect. Dis.* 123:341 (1971).

28. J. A. McBride and H. S. Jacob: Abnormal kinetics of red cell membrane cholesterol in acanthocytes: Studies in genetic and experimental abetalipoproteinemia and in spur cell anemia. *Br. J. Hematol.* 18:383 (1970).

29. W. T. Butler, D. W. Alling, and E. Cotlove: Potassium loss from human erythrocytes exposed to amphotericin B. *Proc. Soc. Exptl. Biol. Med.* 118:297 (1965).

30. S. C. Kinsky, S. A. Luse, D. Zopf, L. L. M. Van Deenen, and J. Haxby: Interaction of filipin and derivatives with erythrocyte membranes and lipid dispersions; electron microscopic observations. *Biochim. Biophys. Acta* 135:844 (1967).

31. A. J. Verkleij, B. deKruijff, W. F. Gerritsen, R. A. Demel, L. L. M. van Deenen, and P. H. J. Ververgaert: Freeze-etch electron microscopy of erythrocytes, *Acholeplasma laidlawii* cells and liposomal membranes after the action of filipin and amphotericin B. *Biochim. Biophys. Acta* 291:577 (1973).

32. G. Medoff, C. N. Kwan, D. Schlessinger, and G. S. Kobayashi: Potentiation of rifampicin, rifampicin analogs, and tetracycline against animal cells by amphotericin B and polymyxin B. *Cancer Res.* 33:1146 (1973).

33. G. Medoff, C. N. Kwan, D. Schlessinger, and G. S. Kobayashi: Permeability control in animal cells by polyenes: A possibility. *Antimicrob. Agents Chemother.* 3:441 (1973).

34. G. Medoff, F. Valeriote, R. G. Lynch, D. Schlessinger, and G. S. Kobayashi: Synergistic effect of amphotericin B and 1,3-bis(2-chloroethyl)-1-nitrosurea against a transplantable AKR leukemia. *Cancer Res.* 34:974 (1974).

35. M. Jurin and I. F. Tannock: Influence of vitamin A on immunological response. *Immunology* 23:283 (1972).

36. M. Z. Thomas, G. Medoff, and G. S. Kobayashi: Changes in murine resistance to *Listeria monocytogenes* infection induced by amphotericin B. *J. Infect. Dis.* 127:373 (1973).

37. D. Kessel and I. Wodinski: Uptake *in vivo* and *in vitro* of actinomycin D by mouse leukemia as factors in survival. *Biochem. Pharmacol.* 17:161 (1968).

38. D. Kessel and H. B. Bosmann: On the characteristics of actinomycin D resistance in L5178Y cells. *Cancer Res.* 30:2695 (1970).

39. J. Medoff, G. Medoff, M. N. Goldstein, D. Schlessinger, and G. S. Kobayashi: Amphotericin B-induced sensitivity to actinomycin D in drug-resistant HeLa cells. *Cancer Res.* 35:2548 (1975).

40. R. A. Demel, F. J. L. Crombag, L. L. M. Van Deenen, and S. C.

Kinsky: Interaction of polyene antibiotics with single and mixed lipid monolayers. *Biochim. Biophys. Acta* 150:1 (1968).

41. J. Kotler-Brajtburg, H. D. Price, G. Medoff, D. Schlessinger, and G. S. Kobayashi: Molecular basis for the selective toxicity of amphotericin B for yeast and filipin for animal cells. *Antimicrob. Agents Chemother.* 5:377 (1974).

42. G. Medoff, M. Comfort, and G. S. Kobayashi: Synergistic action of amphotericin B and 5-fluorocytosine against yeast-like organisms. *Proc. Soc. Exptl. Biol. Med.* 138:571 (1971).

43. G. Medoff, G. S. Kobayashi, C. N. Kwan, D. Schlessinger, and P. Venkov: Potentiation of rifampicin and 5-fluorocytosine as antifungal antibiotics by amphotericin B. *Proc. Natl. Acad Sci. U.S.* 69:196 (1972).

44. J. Z. Montgomerie, J. E. Edwards, and L. B. Guze: Synergism of amphotericin B and 5-fluorocytosine for *Candida* species. *J. Infect. Dis.* 132:82 (1975).

45. E. R. Block and J. E. Bennett: The combined effect of 5-fluorocytosine and amphotericin B in the therapy of murine cryptococcosis. *Proc. Soc. Exptl. Biol. Med.* 142:476 (1973).

46. E. Titsworth and E. Grunberg: Chemotherapeutic activity of 5-fluorocytosine and amphotericin B against *Candida albicans* in mice. *Antimicrob. Agents Chemother.* 4:306 (1973).

47. S. Rabinovich, B. D. Shaw, T. Bryant, and S. T. Donta: Effect of 5-fluorocytosine and amphotericin B on *Candida albicans* infection in mice. *J. Infect. Dis.* 130:28 (1974).

48. J. P. Utz, I. L. Garriques, M. A. Sande, J. F. Warner, G. L. Mandel, R. F. McGehee, R. J. Duma, and S. Shadomy: Therapy of cryptococcosis with a combination of flucytosine and amphotericin B. *J. Infect. Dis.* 132:368 (1975).

49. W. H. Beggs, G. A. Sarosi, and F. A. Andrews: Synergistic action of amphotericin B and rifampin on *Candida albicans*. *Am. Rev. Resp. Dis.* 110:671 (1974).

50. G. S. Kobayashi, S. C. Cheung, D. Schlessinger, and G. Medoff: Effects of rifamycin derivatives, alone and in combination with amphotericin B, against *Histoplasma capsulatum*. *Antimicrob. Agents Chemother.* 5:16 (1974).

51. D. Rifkind, E. D. Crowder, and R. N. Hyland: *In vitro* inhibition of *Coccidoides immitis* strains with amphotericin B plus rifampin. *Antimicrob. Agents Chemother.* 6:783 (1974).

52. R. A. Woods, M. Bard, I. E. Jackson, and D. J. Drutz: Resistance to polyene antibiotics and correlated sterol changes in two isolates of *Candida tropicalis* from a patient with an amphotericin B-resistant funguria. *J. Infect. Dis.* 129:53 (1974).

53. M. Bard: Biochemical and genetic aspects of nystatin resistance in *Saccharomyces cerevisiae*. *J. Bacteriol.* 111:649 (1972).

54. M. Fryberg, A. C. Oehlschlager, and A. M. Unrau: Sterol biosynthesis in antibiotic-resistant yeast: Nystatin. *Arch. Biochem. Biophys.* 160:83 (1974).

55. E. F. Gale, A. M. Johnson, D. Kerridge, and T. Y. Koh: Factors affecting the changes in amphotericin sensitivity of *Candida albicans* during growth. *J. Gen. Microbiol.* 87:20 (1975).

56. P. D. Hart, E. Russell, and J. S. Remington: The compromised host and infection. II. Deep fungal infection. *J. Infect. Dis.* 120:169 (1969).

57. D. D. Bindschadler and J. E. Bennett: A pharmacologic guide to the clinical use of amphotericin B. *J. Infect. Dis.* 120:427 (1969).

58. D. J. Drutz, A. Spickard, D. E. Rogers, and M. G. Koenig: Treatment of disseminated mycotic infections. *Am. J. Med.* 45:405 (1968).

59. H. M. Kravetz, V. T. Andriole, M. A. Huber, and J. P. Utz: Oral administration of solubilized amphotericin B. *New Eng. J. Med.* 265:183 (1961).

60. S. Shadomy, D. L. Brummer, and A. V. Ingroff: Light sensitivity of prepared solutions of amphotericin B. *Am Rev. Resp. Dis.* 107:303 (1973).

61. E. R. Block and J. E. Bennett: Stability of amphotericin B in infusion bottles. *Antimicrob. Agents Chemother.* 4:648 (1973).

62. J. P. Utz: Current and future chemotherapy of central nervous system fungal infections. *Adv. Neurol.* 6:127 (1974).

63. R. A. Ratcheson and A. K. Oyama: Experience with the subcutaneous cerebrospinal-fluid reservoir: Preliminary report of 60 cases. *New Eng. J. Med.* 279:1025 (1968).

64. R. D. Diamond and J. E. Bennett: A subcutaneous reservoir for intrathecal therapy of fungal meningitis. *New Eng. J. Med.* 288:186 (1973).

65. N. P. Alazraki, J. Fierer, S. E. Halpern, and R. W. Becker: Use of a hyperbaric solution for administration of intrathecal amphotericin B. *New Eng. J. Med.* 290:641 (1974).

66. D. Gottlieb, H. Carter, J. H. Sloneker, and A. Amman: Protection of fungi against polyene antibiotics by sterols. *Science* 128:361 (1958).

67. B. T. Fields, J. H. Bates, and R. S. Abernathy: Amphotericin B serum concentrations during therapy. *Appl. Microbiol.* 19:955 (1970).

68. W. R. Green, J. E. Bennett; and R. D. Goos: Ocular penetration of amphotericin B: A report of laboratory studies and a case report of postsurgical cephalosporium endophthalmitis. *Arch. Ophthalmol.* 73:769 (1965).

69. P. M. Silberfarb, G. A. Sarosi, and F. E. Tosh: Cryptococcosis and pregnancy. *Am. J. Obstet. Gynecol.* 112:714 (1972).

70. H. A. Feldman, J. D. Hamilton, and R. A. Gutman: Amphotericin B in an anephric patient. *Antimicrob. Agents Chemother.* 4:302 (1973).

71. E. R. Block, J. E. Bennett, L. G. Livotti, W. J. Klein, R. R. MacGregor, and L. Henderson: Flucytosine and amphotericin B: Hemodialysis effects on the plasma concentration and clearance. *Ann. Int. Med.* 80:613 (1974).

72. R. P. Miller and J. H. Bates: Amphotericin B. toxicity: A follow-up report of 53 patients. *Ann. Int. Med.* 71:1089 (1969).

73. J. H. Seabury and H. E. Dascomb: Experience with amphotericin B. *Ann. New York Acad. Sci.* 89:202 (1960).

74. M. W. Brandriss, S. M. Wolff, R. Moores and F. Stohlman: Anemia induced by amphotericin B. *J. Am. Med. Assoc.* 189:663 (1964).

75. W. T. Butler, J. E. Bennett, D. W. Alling, P. T. Wertlake, J. P. Utz, and G. J. Hill: Nephrotoxicity of amphotericin B; early and late effects in 81 patients. *Ann. Int. Med.* 61:175 (1964).

76. P. T. Wertlake, W. T. Butler, G. J. Hill, and J. P. Utz: Nephrotoxic

tubular damage and calcium deposition following amphotericin B therapy. *Am. J. Path.* 43:449 (1963).

77. D. K. McCurdy, M. Frederic and J. R. Elkinton: Renal tubular acidosis due to amphotericin B. *New Eng. J. Med.* 278:124 (1968).

78. P. R. Steinmetz and L. R. Lawson: Defect in urinary acidification induced *in vitro* by amphotericin B. *J. Clin. Invest.* 49:596 (1970).

79. T. H. Gouge and V. T. Andriole: An experimental model of amphotericin B nephrotoxicity with renal tubular acidosis. *J. Lab. Clin. Med.* 78:713 (1971).

80. A. A. Hellebusch, F. Salama, and E. Eadie: The use of mannitol to reduce the nephrotoxicity of amphotericin B. *Surg. Gynecol. Obstet.* 134:241 (1972).

81. J. J. Olivero, J. Lozano-Mendez, E. M. Ghafary, G. Eknoyan, and W. N. Suki: Mitigation of amphotericin B nephrotoxicity by mannitol. *Br. Med. J.* 1:550 (1975).

82. A. Polak and H. J. Scholer: Fungistatic activity, uptake and incorporation of 5-fluorocytosine in *Candida albicans* as influenced by pyrimidines and purines. I. Reversal experiments. *Pathol. Microbiol.* 39:148 (1973).

83. R. J. Holt and R. L. Newman: The antimycotic activity of 5-fluorocytosine. *J. Clin. Pathol.* 26:167 (1973).

84. R. Jund and F. Lacrute: Genetic and physiological aspects of resistance to 5-fluoropyrimidines in *Saccharomyces cerevisiae. J. Bacteriol.* 102:607 (1970).

85. R. Giege and J. H. Weil: Étude des tRNA de levure ayant incorporé du fluorouracile provenant de la désamination *in vivo* de la 5-fluorocytosine. *Bull. Soc. Chim. Biol.* 52:135 (1970).

86. M. Grenson: The utilization of exogenous pyrimidines and the recycling of uridine-5′-phosphate derivatives in *Saccharomyces cerevisiae,* as studied by means of mutants affected in pyrimidine uptake and metabolism. *Eur. J. Biochem.* 11:249 (1969).

87. E. R. Block, A. E. Jennings, and J. E. Bennett: 5-fluorocytosine resistance in *Cryptococcus neoformans. Antimicrob. Agents Chemother.* 3:649 (1973).

88. A. Polak and H. J. Scholer: Fungistatic activity, uptake and incorporation of 5-fluorocytosine in *Candida albicans* as influenced by pyrimidines and purines. II. Studies on distribution and incorporation. *Pathol. Microbiol.* 39:334 (1973).

89. A. Polak and H. J. Scholer: Mode of action of 5-fluorocytosine and mechanisms of resistance. *Chemotherapy* 21:113 (1975).

90. C. Heidelberger: Cancer chemotherapy with purine and pyrimidine analogues. *Ann. Rev. Pharmacol.* 7:101 (1967).

91. B. A. Koechlin, F. Rubio, S. Palmer, T. Gabriel, and R. Duschinsky: The metabolism of 5-fluorocytosine-2^{14}C and of cytosine-^{14}C in the rat and the disposition of 5-fluorocytosine-2^{14}C in man. *Biochem. Pharmacol.* 15:435 (1966).

92. S. Shadomy: Further *in vitro* studies with 5-fluorocytosine. *Infection and Immunity* 2:484 (1970).

93. P. D. Hoeprich, J. L. Ingraham, E. Kleker, and M. J. Winship: Development of resistance to 5-fluorocytosine in *Candida parapsilosis* during therapy. *J. Infect. Dis.* 130:112 (1974).

94. S. Normark and J. Schönebeck: In vitro studies of 5-fluorocytosine resistance in Candida albicans and Torulopsis glabrata. Antimicrob. Agents Chemother. 2:114 (1972).

95. E. R. Block and J. E. Bennett: Pharmacological studies with 5-fluorocytosine. Antimicrob. Agents Chemother. 1:476 (1972).

96. A. B. Richards, B. R. Jones, J. Whitwell, and Y. M. Clayton: Corneal and intra-ocular infection by Candida albicans treated with 5-fluorocytosine. Trans. Ophthalmol. Soc. U.K. 89:867 (1970).

97. J. E. Pennington, E. R. Block, and H. Y. Reynolds: 5-Fluorocytosine and amphotericin B in bronchial secretions. Antimicrob. Agents Chemother. 6:324 (1974).

98. J. Schönebeck, A. Polak, M. Fernex, and H. J. Scholer: Pharmacokinetic studies on the oral antimycotic agent 5-fluorocytosine in individuals with normal and impaired kidney function. Chemotherapy 18:321 (1973).

99. R. L. Kasper and D. J. Drutz: Rapid, simple bioassay for 5-fluorocytosine in the presence of amphotericin B. Antimicrob. Agents Chemother. 7:462 (1975).

100. A. G. Vandevelde, A. A. Mauceri, and J. E. Johnson: 5-Fluorocytosine in the treatment of mycotic infections. Ann. Int. Med. 77:43 (1972).

101. C. O. Record, J. M. Skinner, P. Sleight, and D. C. E. Speller: Candida endocarditis treated with 5-fluorocytosine. Br. Med. J. 1:262 (1971).

102. R. Meyer and J. L. Axelrod: Fatal aplastic anemia resulting from flucytosine. J. Am. Med. Assoc. 228:1573 (1974).

103. J. A. Krick and J. S. Remington: Treatment of fungal infections. Ann. Int. Med. 135:344 (1975).

104. J. F. Busey: Blastomycosis III. A comparison study of 2-hydroxystilbamidine and amphotericin B therapy. Am. Rev. Resp. Dis. 105:812 (1972).

105. E. J. Foley and G. A. Greco: Studies on the mode of action of griseofulvin. Antibiotics Annual, p. 670 (1959–60).

106. M. A. El-Nakeeb and J. O. Lampen: Uptake of griseofulvin by the sensitive dermatophyte, Microsporum gypseum. J. Bacteriol. 89:564 (1965).

107. M. A. El-Nakeeb and J. O. Lampen: Uptake of griseofulvin by microorganisms and its correlation with sensitivity to griseofulvin. J. Gen. Microbiol. 39:285 (1965).

108. F. M. Huber and D. Gottlieb: The mechanism of action of griseofulvin. Can. J. Microbiol. 14:111 (1968).

109. K. Gull and A. P. J. Trinci: Griseofulvin inhibits fungal mitosis. Nature 244:292 (1973).

110. S. E. Malawista, H. Sato, and K. G. Bensch: Vinblastine and griseofulvin reversibly disrupt the living mitotic spindle. Science 160:770 (1968).

111. W. A. Creasey, K. G. Bensch, and S. E. Malawista: Colchicine, vinblastine and griseofulvin: Pharmacological studies with human leukocytes. Biochem. Pharmacol. 20:1579 (1971).

112. L. M. Grisham, L. Wilson, and K. Bensch: Antimitotic action of griseofulvin does not involve disruption of microtubules. Nature 244:294 (1973).

113. J. R. McIntosh, P. K. Helper, and D. G. Van Wie: Model for mitosis. *Nature* 224:659 (1969).

114. L. Wilson: Properties of colchicine binding protein from chick embryo brain. Interactions with vinca alkaloids and podophyllotoxin. *Biochemistry* 9:4999 (1970).

115. R. G. Crounse: Effective use of griseofulvin. *Arch. Dermatol.* 87:86 (1963).

116. P. J. Carrigan and T. R. Bates: Biopharmaceutics of drugs administered in lipid-containing dosage forms. I: GI absorption of griseofulvin from an oil-in-water emulsion in the rat. *J. Pharmaceutical Sci.* 62:1476 (1973).

117. C. C. Lin, J. Magat, R. Chang, J. McGlotten, and S. Symchowicz: Absorption, metabolism and excretion of ^{14}C-griseofulvin in man. *J. Pharm. Exptl. Ther.* 187:415 (1973).

118. W. L. Epstein, V. P. Shah, H. E. Jones, and S. Riegelman: Topically applied griseofulvin in prevention and treatment of *Trichophyton mentagrophytes*. *Arch. Dermatol.* 111:1293 (1975).

119. V. P. Shah, W. L. Epstein, and S. Riegelman: Role of sweat in accumulation of orally administered griseofulvin in skin. *J. Clin. Invest.* 53:1673 (1974).

120. W. L. Epstein, V. P. Shah, and S. Riegelman: Griseofulvin levels in stratum corneum. Study after oral administration in man. *Arch. Dermatol.* 106:344 (1972).

121. J. C. Gentles: Experimental ring worm in guinea pigs: Oral treatment with griseofulvin. *Nature* 182:476 (1958).

122. J. C. Gentles, M. J. Barnes, and K. H. Fantes: Presence of griseofulvin in hair of guinea pigs after oral administration. *Nature* 183:256 (1959).

123. J. P. Collins, S. F. Grappel, and F. Blank: Role of keratinases in dermatophytosis. II. Fluorescent antibody studies with keratinase II of *Trichophyton mentagrophytes*. *Dermatologica* 146:95 (1973).

124. R. J. Yu and F. Blank: On the mechanism of action of griseofulvin in dermatophytosis. *Sabouraudia* 11:274 (1973).

125. D. Busfield, K. J. Child, and E. G. Tomich: An effect of phenobarbitone on griseofulvin metabolism in the rat. *Brit. J. Pharmacol.* 22:137 (1964).

126. S. Riegelman, M. Rowland, and W. L. Epstein: Griseofulvin-phenobarbital interaction in man. *J. Am. Med. Assoc.* 213:426 (1970).

127. C. Rimington, P. N. Morgan, K. Nicholls, J. D. Everall, and R. R. Davies: Griseofulvin administration and porphyrin metabolism. *Lancet* 2:318 (1963).

128. S. Granick: Induction of the synthesis of δ-aminolevulinic acid synthetase in liver parenchyma cells in culture by chemicals that induce acute porphyria. *J. Biol. Chem.* 238:2247 (1963).

129. C. J. Watson, F. Lynch, I. Bossenmaier, and R. Cardinal: Griseofulvin and porphyrin metabolism. Special reference to normal fecal porphyrin excretion. *Arch. Dermatol.* 98:451 (1968).

130. L. Goldman: Griseofulvin. *Med. Clin. N. Am.* 54:1339 (1970).

131. M. F. Klein and J. R. Beall: Griseofulvin: A teratogenic study. *Science* 175:1483 (1972).

132. P. R. Sawyer, R. N. Brogden, R. M. Pinder, T. M. Speight, and G. S. Avery: Micronazole: A review of its antifungal activity and therapeutic efficacy. *Drugs* 9:406 (1973).

133. P. R. Sawyer, R. N. Brogden, R. M. Pinder, T. M. Speight, and G. S. Avery: Clotrimazole: A review of its antifungal activity and therapeutic efficacy. *Drugs* 9:424 (1975).

134. P. D. Hoeprich and A. C. Huston: Susceptibility of *Coccidioides immitis, Candida albicans* and *Cryptococcus neoformans* to amphotericin B, flucytosine, and clotrimazole. *J. Infect. Dis.* 132:133 (1975).

135. K. Iwata, Y. Kanda, H. Yamaguchi, and M. Osumi: Electron microscopic studies on the mechanism of action of clotrimazole on *Candida albicans. Sabouraudia* 11:205 (1973).

136. S. De Nollin and M. Borgers: The ultrastructre of *Candida albicans* after *in vitro* treatment with miconazole. *Sabouraudia* 12:341 (1974).

137. K. Iwata, H. Yamagouchi, and T. Hiratani: Mode of action of clotrimazole. *Sabouraudia* 11:158 (1973).

138. K. H. S. Swamy, M. Sirsi, and G. R. Rao: Studies on the mechanism of action of miconazole: Effect of miconazole on respiration and cell permeability of *Candida albicans. Antimicrob. Agents Chemother.* 5:420 (1974).

139. H. van den Bossche: Biochemical effects of miconazole on fungi. I. Effects on the uptake and/or utilization of purines, pyrimidines, nucleosides, amino acids and glucose by *Candida albicans. Biochem. Pharmacol.* 23:887 (1974).

140. G. Poleman: Clinical experience in the local treatment of dermatomycoses with clotrimazole. *Post. Grad. Med. J.* Suppl. 1, vol. 50:54 (1974).

141. S. J. Mandy and T. C. Garrott: Miconazole treatment for severe dermatophytoses. *J. Am. Med. Assoc.* 230:72 (1974).

142. J. M. Proost, F. M. Maes-Dockx, M. O. Nelis, and J. M. van Cutsem: Miconazole in the treatment of mycotic vulvovaginitis. *Am. J. Obstet. Gynecol.* 112:688 (1972).

143. Various authors: Clotrimazole. *Post. Grad. Med. J.* Suppl. 1, vol. 50: pp. 78–88 (1974).

144. B. Duhm, H. Medenwald, J. Peutter, W. Maul, K. Patzschke, and L. A. Wegner: The pharmacokinetics of clotrimazole ^{14}C. *Post. Grad. Med. J.* (Suppl. 1) 50:13 (1974).

Part III
Drugs Employed in the Treatment of Parasitic Disease

The parasitic diseases, which are prevalent under conditions of crowding, poverty, and poor sanitation, constitute one of the major health problems of man. Parasitic infections generally are not responsible for producing a fulminant, life-threatening situation; rather, they are often chronic in nature, and in hyperendemic areas where there is substantial undernutrition as well, the chronic disability may have far-reaching effects on the society. In many areas of the world, chronic parasitic infection is accepted as a part of life by the rural population. Large numbers of people living under conditions of poor sanitation in tropical areas may be infected simultaneously with a number of different parasites. Children are, as a rule, more frequently affected than adults. Because they lack acquired humoral and tissue immunity, the morbidity and mortality is also greater in children. Particularly in the developing countries in the tropics, the constant infection and accompanying malnutrition may result in a decreased intellectual function in the people who grow up under these conditions. This, in turn, may seriously affect the rate at which the people in these areas can acquire the technical skills to provide better living standards that would contribute greatly to the solution of the problem of parasitic disease. A circular process is thus set up by the presence of parasitic infection in which the debilitating physical and mental effects contribute to a decreased capacity for food production, mass sanitary improvement, and other corrective measures. The successful control of parasitic disease is one of the major goals of the health professions in the last quarter of this century.

Chapter 10
The Chemotherapy of Malaria

INTRODUCTION

Malaria is still one of the major health concerns of the world, affecting millions of people annually. But the great progress made in eradication of the disease from most of Europe and North America and in reduction of the incidence of the disease in Africa, Asia, and South America establishes the fight against malaria as a major achievement in the public health field. Improvement has taken place at many levels. The greatest contribution made in controlling the disease has been the effort to control the mosquito vector. Thus, in a very real sense, the chemical that has been most effective in controlling the incidence of malaria is DDT. Another level of attack has been, of course, the development of drugs that specifically act on the parasite in the patient.

For centuries the mainstay of antimalarial therapy was quinine. The fascinating history of this drug is well worth reading.[1] The access to and control of quinine production has had considerable influence on world history over the past 400 years; malaria has literally determined the fates of nations. The possession of antimalarial drugs and the development of new, more effective antimalarials has been and still is intimately bound up with the establishment of national spheres of influence, which have risen and declined over the past 200 years. A great portion of the current research on antimalarial drugs is funded or carried out by the military.

The field of malariology is highly specialized, and many aspects of antimalarial chemotherapy will not be discussed in this chapter. The emphasis will be on the mechanisms of drug action and on pharmacology. Treatment of malaria differs greatly from one region to another depending upon the type of plasmodium and the degree of drug resistance. For more extensive information, the reader is referred to specialized texts and reviews.[2-5]

The Disease

Malaria is characterized clinically by paroxysms of severe chills, fever, and profuse sweating. These episodes sometimes occur at reasonably well-defined intervals determined by the life cycle of the invading plasmodium (Fig. 10-1). When untreated, after recovery from the acute attack, the disease can become chronic with repeated relapses. Malarial organisms confer a low grade but specific immunity on the host.[7] The disease is the result of infection with protozoa of the genus *Plasmodium*. There are more than

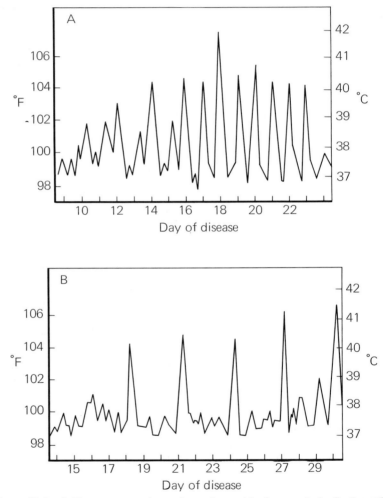

Figure 10-1 A. Temperature chart of a patient with vivax malaria. Both tertian (every other day) and quotidian (every day) fever patterns can be seen. B. Temperature chart of a patient with quartan malaria demonstrating fever spikes with 2 days between each episode. (From Coggeshall[6] in Beeson and McDermott: *Textbook of Medicine*. 1963.)

40 species of this genus of which only four affect man—*P. vivax*, *P. falciparum*, *P. malariae*, and *P. ovale*. Malaria caused by the last organism is rare, and only the first three will be discussed in this chapter. The organisms are transmitted to man in the saliva of the female *Anopheles* mosquito. The lapse between the invasion time and the onset of clinical symptoms varies according to the species of the plasmodium, as does the frequency of the febrile paroxysms. As summarized in Table 10-1, the most common type of malaria is the tertian variety, caused by *P. vivax*, which is distinguished by febrile paroxysms occurring every other day. The second most common, and the type producing the severest symptomatology, is caused by *P. falciparum*. This form is called malignant tertian malaria, and it is characterized by paroxysms of somewhat longer duration occurring at irregular intervals. Quartan malaria is caused by *P. malariae*. This is the least common of the three and is generally characterized by fever spikes occurring every 72 hours.

The Life Cycle of the Parasite

In order to understand the rationale behind the therapy of malaria, it is necessary to understand the life cycle of the plasmodium. The various stages are presented in schematic form in Figure 10-2. The vector for this disease, the female *Anopheles* mosquito, becomes a carrier of the plasmodium by ingesting the blood of a host that contains the male and female sexual forms of the parasite. In the stomach of the mosquito, the male gametocyte produces hairlike bodies that detach and fertilize the female gametocyte—to form the zygote. The parasite then penetrates the stomach wall and forms a cyst on its outer surface. Numerous cell divisions take place to produce an oocyst containing thousands of sporozoites. The cyst bursts, releasing the sporozoites into the body cavity. The sporozoites migrate to the salivary glands, and, when the mosquito bites a suitable host, some of the sporozoites are injected into the bloodstream of the host. The sporozoites rapidly disappear from the blood and appear within the parenchymal cells of the liver. They divide inside the liver cells to form an hepatic (exoerythrocytic) schizont containing numerous merozoites. The different latency times for the disease are defined by variations in the length of this hepatic phase. The patient is asymptomatic during this time. After this latent period, the affected hepatic cells burst, releasing merozoites into the bloodstream. Some of these may reinvade the liver cells, producing secondary hepatic schi-

Table 10-1 **Some characteristics of the three common malarias**

Common name	Agent	Frequency of occurrence	Latency after infection	Frequency of febrile paroxysms	Severity
Tertian malaria	*Plasmodium vivax*	Most common	26 days	Every 2 days	Mild
Malignant tertian (estivoautumnal)	*Plasmodium falciparum*	Less common	~12 days	Irregular	Severe
Quartan malaria	*Plasmodium malariae*	Least common	18–40 days	Every 3 days	Intermediate

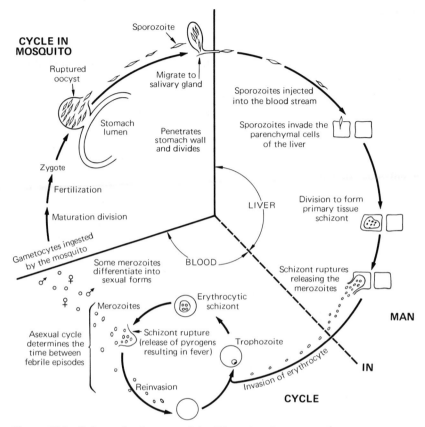

CYCLE IN MOSQUITO

Sporozoite

Ruptured oocyst

Migrate to salivary gland

Sporozoites injected into the blood stream

Stomach lumen

Penetrates stomach wall and divides

Sporozoites invade the parenchymal cells of the liver

Zygote

Fertilization

LIVER

Division to form primary tissue schizont

Maturation division

Gametocytes ingested by the mosquito

Some merozoites differentiate into sexual forms

BLOOD

Schizont ruptures releasing the merozoites

MAN

Merozoites

Erythrocytic schizont

Asexual cycle determines the time between febrile episodes

Schizont rupture (release of pyrogens resulting in fever)

Trophozoite

Reinvasion

Invasion of erythrocyte

IN

CYCLE

Figure 10-2 Schematic diagram of the life cycle of the malarial parasite.

zonts, but the vast majority invade the erythrocytes where they again multiply asexually. A mature erythrocytic schizont is formed, which then ruptures, and again merozoites are released. The rupture of the parasitized erythrocyte is accompanied by the release of pyrogenic substances, which cause the rapid rise in body temperature. The released merozoites have two fates. The asexual forms can reinvade erythrocytes to give rise to continued cycles of division and rupture. In those cases in which the fever becomes periodic, the length of the interval between fever paroxysms is determined by the rate of which this synchronized intra-erythrocytic growth takes place. A few of the merozoites produced with each erythrocyte cycle undergo a sexual division to form the male and female gametocytes, which are then ingested by the mosquito, and the life cycle in the vector is continued.

THE THERAPEUTIC RATIONALE

The erythrocytic stages of the plasmodium cycle are the most sensitive to antimalarial drugs. The exo-erythrocytic (liver) stage is more difficult to treat, while the sporozoites injected by the mosquito into the bloodstream are not sensitive to any of the antimalarial drugs. Since the sporozoite is not affected, it is not possible to prevent viable plasmodia from reaching the liver. Therefore, therapy must be directed toward the hepatic or the erythrocytic stages of the parasite cycle. Unfortunately, effective treatment of the erythrocytic stage of the cycle, although it will make the person asymptomatic, often does not get rid of the parasite completely. When therapy is stopped symptoms can resume because merozoites are released into the bloodstream from the liver. To completely rid the body of *P. vivax* or *P. malariae* it is necessary to administer drugs that are effective against the hepatic forms of the parasite. Often, however, when a person will remain in an area where malaria is endemic and continual reinvasion is a virtual certainty, it is not reasonable to attempt complete eradication of the parasite from the body. In such a case, therapy is aimed at suppressing the symptomatology by inhibiting the erythrocytic stages of the cycle.

There are two characteristics of *P. falciparum* that modify treatment. On rupture of the hepatic schizont, the merozoites of this organism are not likely to reinvade the liver and cause secondary tissue schizonts, thus, successful treatment of the initial acute attack usually results in complete eradication of the organism from the patient. A second characteristic of *P. falciparum* is that it becomes resistant to drug therapy much more readily than the other strains. As stated by Hunsicker, "Falciparum malaria has proved to be the *Staphylococcus aureus* of the malarias, and has demonstrated its ability to develop resistance to all the agents currently in use."[8]

Several drug regimens employed in the treatment of malaria are presented in Table 10-2. The therapeutic goals include suppressive therapy, treatment of the acute attack (clinical cure), and radical cure.

(1) *Suppressive treatment:* In most cases, chloroquine, which is effective against the erythrocytic forms of the parasite, is administered once a week as long as the patient remains in the endemic malarial area. When exposure to infection ends, daily primaquine therapy is added to eradicate any parasites that may be present in the liver. The U.S. military has carried out suppressive treatment

by administering tablets containing both chloroquine and primaquine. These are given once a week during exposure and for an
additional period after the patient leaves the malaria area. These
combination tablets are effective, but they extend exposure to
primaquine, which is potentially toxic.[9] Many drug combinations
have been tried for suppressive treatment for people visiting
regions where chloroquine-resistant falciparum malaria is common. Usually these regimens include either a sulfonamide or a
sulfone combined with an appropriate form of a folate reductase
inhibitor (cycloguanil or pyrimethamine).[10]

The physician practicing medicine in Europe or North America
is concerned with suppressive therapy only when he must provide protection for a person who is traveling abroad. In this case,
he should contact the public health authorities for information
regarding the type of malaria and the frequency of chloroquine
resistance found in the travel area. Physicians in the military and
those who practice medicine in Africa, Asia, and South America
follow this form of treatment routinely and are familiar with the
drug regimen that is required for their locality. Occasionally,
suppressive therapy is employed on a mass scale, and every
member of a population is treated. The purpose of such mass drug
administration is to eliminate the disease in a local area. In this
case, mass suppressive therapy is carried out in conjunction with
a comprehensive program to eliminate the mosquito vector. There
are numerous practical problems associated with this form of
drug administration, and there is also the clear risk of promoting
the selection of drug-resistant strains of plasmodia.[5]

(2) *Treatment of the acute attack:* The clinical attack of malaria
is treated with drugs effective against the erythrocytic stage of the
plasmodium. With *P. vivax* and *P. malariae* the drug of choice is
chloroquine. Chloroquine-resistant strains of falciparum malaria
require treatment with other drugs in a combined therapeutic
approach (Table 10-2). The biochemical basis for some of these
drug combinations will be examined later in the chapter. The
severe attack of falciparum malaria is a life-threatening situation
that requires intravenous quinine therapy. The problem of malarial treatment is sometimes complicated by the presence of simultaneous infection with two types of plasmodia. Such mixed infections require different drug combinations for successful therapy.[11]
Some stains of *P. falciparum* have developed resistance to multiple antimalarial drugs, and these infections can present an especially complex therapeutic problem.[12,13]

(3) *Radical cure:* In order to prevent relapse after a clinical

Table 10-2 Drug regimens for the treatment of malaria (Dosages are for adults.)

Therapeutic goal	Drug regimen of choice	Alternative
SUPPRESSIVE PROPHYLAXIS		
Suppression of disease in an endemic area (all except regions with choroquine-resistant *P. falciparum*)	Chloroquine phosphate (300 mg base weekly; continue for 8 weeks after last exposure)	Amodiaquine dihydrochloride (400 mg base weekly; continue for 8 weeks after last exposure)
	plus	plus
	Primaquine phosphate (15 mg base daily for 14 days after last exposure)	Primaquine phosphate (15 mg base daily for 14 days after last exposure)
Regions with chloroquine-resistant falciparum malaria[10]	Sulfadoxine (500 mg weekly) plus pyrimethamine (25 mg weekly)	Sulfalene (500 mg weekly) plus pyrimethamine (25 mg weekly)
TREATMENT OF THE ACUTE ATTACK		
All except chloroquine-resistant *P. falciparum* Uncomplicated attack	Chloroquine phosphate (1 gm, 600 mg base, then 0.5 gm in 6 hours, then 0.5 gm daily for 2 days)	Amodiaquine dihydrochloride (600 mg base first day, then 400 mg base daily for 2 days)
Severe attack	Chloroquine hydrochloride (250 mg, 200 mg base, i.m. every 6 hours until oral therapy possible)	Quinine dihydrochloride as for treatment of severe illness with *P. falciparum*

Chloroquine-resistant *P. falciparum*

Uncomplicated attack

Quinine sulfate (650 mg every eight hours for 14 days)

plus

Pyrimethamine (25 mg every 12 hours for 3 days)

plus either

Sulfadiazine (500 mg every 6 hours for 5 days) or dapsone (25 mg daily for 28 days)

Quinine sulfate (650 mg every 8 hours for 3 days)

plus

A tetracycline (500 mg every 6 hours for 7 days)

Severe attack

Quinine dihydrochloride (600 mg in 300 ml normal saline, i.v., over no less than 30 minutes, repeat every 6 to 8 hours until oral therapy is possible)

RADICAL CURE

Eradication of persistent exo-erythrocytic parasites after clinical cure (all except *P. falciparum*)

Primaquine phosphate (15 mg base daily for 14 days)

attack of *P. vivax* or *P. malariae* has been treated, it is necessary to administer a drug that is effective against the hepatic forms of the parasite. Primaquine is usually employed for this purpose. As mentioned above, radical cure of *P. falciparum* is usually achieved with successful treatment of the acute attack. In people who might have become infected with *P. falciparum* while receiving suppressive therapy, radical cure is ensured by continuing the medication for 8 weeks after the last exposure.

ANTIMALARIALS EFFECTIVE AGAINST ERYTHROCYTIC FORMS OF THE PLASMODIUM

4-Aminoquinolines (Chloroquine and Amodiaquine)

Structures

The two most widely used 4-aminoquinolines are chloroquine and amodiaquine. They are very effective against the asexual erythrocytic forms of both *P. vivax* and *P. falciparum*. They are also active against the sexual forms of *P. vivax* but not those of *P. falciparum*. These drugs are virtually inactive against the hepatic forms of the plasmodia.

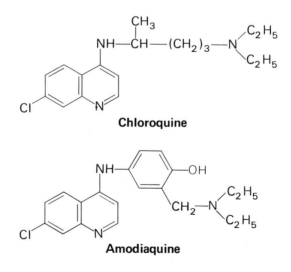

Chloroquine

Amodiaquine

Mechanism of Action

Chloroquine has been demonstrated to have a number of biochemical effects in parasitized erythrocytes.[2,3] It is not yet possible to state with confidence that a particular biochemical event is the primary event responsible for the killing action. One of the effects of chloroquine that has been examined in detail is its ability to inhibit the synthesis of nucleic acid. The following discussion will focus on this effect. This work points out some of the difficulties involved in relating biochemical observations made in subcellular systems to the mechanism of the effect of a drug in intact parasites.

There is a great deal of difference between studying the mechanism of action of a growth-inhibiting agent in bacteria and in an intracellular parasite like the plasmodium. Compared to bacteria, much less is known about the biochemistry of parasites, and it is difficult to set up good experimental systems with which to study mechanisms of drug action in these organisms *in vitro*. Inability to maintain parasites under controlled conditions *in vitro* has been a major impediment to obtaining data on the biochemical mechanism of action of antiparasitic drugs. Experimental models have been developed, however, that permit the investigator to study drug effects in plasmodia growing in synchrony within red blood cells *in vitro*.[14] One of these model systems utilizes the erythrocytic stage of *Plasmodium knowlesi*, a parasite that normally infects monkeys. This organism has a complete erythrocytic cycle of 24 hours. Erythrocytes harvested from heavily infected monkeys during the first 3 or 4 hours of the erythrocytic cycle are suspended in a culture medium with radioactive precursor molecules. The development of the plasmodium is followed morphologically and can be correlated with the rate of nucleic acid and protein synthesis during the different stages of growth. Since nonnucleated erythrocytes do not synthesize nucleic acids or protein, the incorporation of labeled substrates reflects plasmodial metabolism. The relationships of macromolecular synthesis to the erythrocytic growth stages of the parasite are presented in Figure 10-3.

If chloroquine is added to this culture system, the synthesis of both plasmodial nucleic acids and protein is inhibited.[15] Nucleic acid synthesis is inhibited more than protein synthesis. The inhibition of nucleic acid synthesis confirms observations made in red blood cells infected with avian plasmodia.[16] The maximal effect

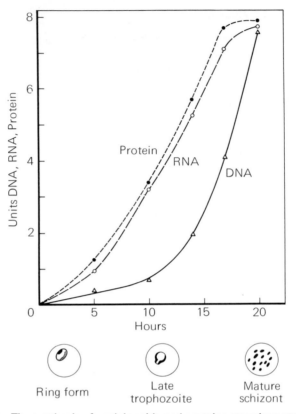

Figure 10-3 The synthesis of nucleic acids and proteins at various stages of the erythrocytic cycle of *Plasmodium knowlesi.* Red blood cells obtained from an infected monkey are suspended in a culture medium. Radioactive orotic acid or leucine is added to replicate cultures, and the cumulative incorporation of radioactivity into the isolated macromolecules is assayed at various times. One unit of the ordinate is equivalent to 75 cpm per culture for DNA, 300 cpm per culture for RNA, and 450 cpm per culture for protein. Incorporation into DNA, RNA, and protein of uninfected control cultures has been subtracted. The drawings below the graph are made from photomicrographs of Giemsa-stained cells taken at the corresponding times of the culture period noted on the abcissa. (Adapted from Polet and Barr.[14])

of chloroquine on DNA synthesis occurs at a concentration in the culture medium of approximately 10^{-6} M. The concentration of chloroquine achieved in the blood during therapy is also in this range.[17] Thus, the inhibition of DNA synthesis is an early event and it occurs at an appropriate drug concentration.

Since it is difficult to work with parasite systems, it is not surprising that investigators chose to examine the mechanism of chloroquine inhibition of DNA synthesis in bacteria. When a culture of *Bacillus megaterium* is exposed to chloroquine at high concentrations, there is a rapid killing effect preceded by inhibition of nucleic acid and protein synthesis.[18] This effect is observed at about one hundred times the concentration of drug required for inhibition of nucleic acid synthesis in the parasitized erythrocyte.

The ability of chloroquine to inhibit nucleic acid synthesis can be demonstrated in purified systems in which DNA or RNA synthesis is carried out under the direction of DNA template and a purified polymerase enzyme from *Escherichia coli*.[19] Again, high concentrations of drug are required for inhibition. There are three major components to this reaction system: the enzyme, the DNA template, and the nucleoside triphosphate precursors. Chloroquine could inhibit the system by interacting with any of these components. If chloroquine inhibits DNA synthesis by decreasing the effectiveness of the enzyme or the DNA template, then the addition of that component in large amounts to the system might reverse the chloroquine effect. It was shown that the effect of chloroquine is reversed as larger amounts of DNA template are added to the enzyme reaction. Changing the amount of enzyme had no effect on the extent of inhibition. The added DNA primer overcame the chloroquine inhibition competitively. The same observations made in the DNA polymerase reaction were also made with an RNA polymerase reaction system, although RNA synthesis was somewhat less sensitive to the drug (which was consistent with the effects observed in plasmodia). These experimental results show that chloroquine inhibits nucleic acid synthesis by affecting the ability of DNA to act as a template.

The interaction of chloroquine with DNA has been demonstrated by a number of physical methods. Chloroquine, for example, can alter the temperature at which native, double-standed DNA uncoils to form denatured, single-stranded DNA.[20] This indicates a binding between the drug and the nucleic acid. The strong interaction between chloroquine and DNA can be recorded as a change in the absorption spectrum of the drug.[20] This effect can be seen in Figure 10-4.

The results of a number of observations, including physical studies on the effect of chloroquine on the coiling of closed

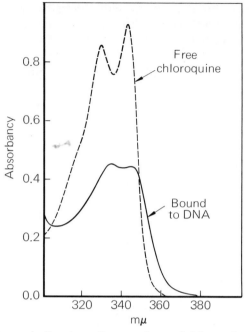

Figure 10-4   Change in the absorption spectrum of chloroquine resulting from the interaction of the drug with DNA. The dotted line represents the absorption spectrum of 4.8×10^{-5} M chloroquine is 15 mM potassium phosphate buffer, pH 5.9, at 22 °C. In the presence of calf thymus DNA (solid line), there is binding of the drug and the bound form of the drug is less able to absorb light energy. (From Cohen and Yielding.[20])

circular DNA,[21] demonstrate that the drug intercalates between the base pairs of the double-stranded DNA helix. This relationship is presented schematically in Figure 10-5. Studies of chloroquine interaction with synthetic polynucleotides indicate that no strict base specificity for drug binding exists in contrast to the binding of some other intercalating agents, such as actinomycin D.[23,24] Observations on the interaction of chloroquine with nucleotides in solution suggest that association of the drug with purines (adenine and guanine) is much stronger than that with pyrimidines (cytidine and thymine).[25]

In summary, chloroquine intercalates between the base pairs in DNA to prevent it from functioning as a template for nucleic acid synthesis. At lower concentrations, the drug inhibits nucleic acid synthesis in parasitized red blood cells. It is unclear whether the two effects are related. It has been shown that the parasitized erythrocyte concentrates chloroquine at least 100-fold more than the unparasitized erythrocyte.[26] The fact that the drug is concentrated in the target cell has been used to link the observations of the drug effects made in the parasite with those in bacterial systems. But even though the total amount of drug in the parasitized red cell is sufficient to account for a primary effect on DNA according to the intercalation model, it is unclear whether this chloroquine is free to associate with nucleic acid.

A number of researchers have studied chloroquine uptake by plasmodia, and there are several hypotheses as to how the drug is concentrated. At least part of the concentrating mechanism is energy dependent.[27,28] According to one hypothesis, chloroquine may pass to the inside of the cell by diffusion and be selectively retained in lysosomes.[29] In the low pH environment of the lyso-

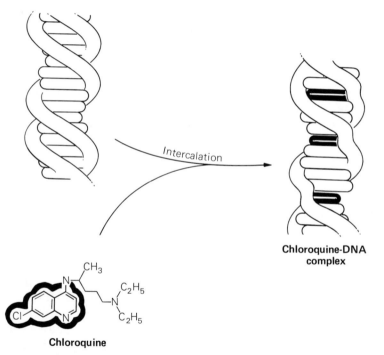

Intercalation

Chloroquine-DNA
complex

Chloroquine

Figure 10-5 Schematic model of the intercalation of chloroquine into DNA. The open, wafer-shaped units represent the base pairs and the coils signify the deoxyribose phosphate backbone of the DNA double helix. The solid, wafer-shaped units on the right represent chloroquine (viewed in the plane of the double ring portion of the molecule), which is intercalated between base pairs. (Adapted from Lerman.[22])

some, the drug would be more ionized and thus be unable to pass out through the membrane. According to another hypothesis, chloroquine is trapped in the cell by association with high affinity binding sites.[28,30] The role of energy in the process is unclear (Is it required for synthesis of lysosomal vacuoles, synthesis of binding sites, for active transport?). Most importantly with regard to the DNA intercalation model, it appears that most of the chloroquine concentrated in the cell may be trapped in lysosomes or bound to molecules other than DNA.

The fact that malarial organisms resistant to chloroquine are deficient in their ability to concentrate the drug clearly indicates that more knowledge of the concentration process is germane to understanding the mechanism of chloroquine action.[26,31] It would be wrong to conclude from current data that the malarial parasite is resistant because it takes up less drug. The difference in drug uptake by red cells parasitized by sensitive and resistant organisms is not enough to account for the high degree of resistance. Indeed, it seems likely that the explanation may be quite the reverse—parasite resistance may depend on some other mechanism, and this biochemical alteration determining drug resistance also leads to less drug accumulation. One attractive hypothesis is that the resistant cell contains less drug receptor. This would explain both the absence of the drug effect and the decrease in high affinity binding of chloroquine.[31]

Binding of Chloroquine in Mammalian Tissues

Since the basic structure of DNA is quite similar in different types of cells, it is not surprising that at the high concentrations of drug that affect nucleic acid synthesis in bacteria chloroquine inhibits cell replication and nucleic acid synthesis in cultured mammalian cells.[32] It has been shown that the binding affinity of chloroquine for DNA isolated from mammalian tissues is the same as that for purified plasmodial DNA.[33] Since significant DNA binding occurs at approximately 100 times the serum concentration required for the schizontocidal effect, chloroquine does not produce side effects due to cytotoxic action on rapidly dividing cell systems (bone-marrow depression, hair loss, gastrointestinal ulceration, etc.).

Chloroquine is taken up by human cells in culture and, as with plasmodia, it has been suggested that some of the drug may be trapped in the low pH environment of the lysosomes.[34] A lot of the chloroquine is also bound to tissue constituents. Drug distribution studies in animals have demonstrated extensive tissue binding, particularly in the kidney, liver, and lung.[35] The drug binds to protein and to RNA[36] as well as to DNA. The amount of chloroquine bound by some tissues is nearly as high as that found in parasitized red blood cells. This argues strongly against any hypothesis of selective toxicity based purely on preferential concentration of the drug in the infected red cell.

The sequestration of chloroquine in the patient's cells is responsible for two clinically important phenomena that must be considered in administering the drug. When initiating therapy with chloroquine, it is necessary to administer a loading dose that is twice the maintenance dose. This is done to saturate tissue binding and to reach effective free drug levels. For suppressive therapy, a maintenance dose of 500 mg (300 mg base) is given only once a week. The long interval between doses is possible because the drug has a half-life of several days. The long half-life is due to a slow release from tissue-binding sites. When the drug is withdrawn, several weeks pass before it disappears from the tissues. The avidity of quinine binding in the tissues is much less than that of chloroquine. Quinine has a short half-life, and no priming dose is required. Quinacrine, a polycyclic drug that is no longer used to treat malaria, binds to DNA and inhibits nucleic acid synthesis. This yellow compound is bound in tissues to a greater extent than chloroquine.[35] During therapy, the tissue-bound drug produced a yellowish discoloration of the skin.

Pharmacology and Untoward Effects of Chloroquine

Absorption, Distribution, and Excretion

Chloroquine and amodiaquine are both absorbed rapidly from the gastrointestinal tract. Chloroquine is distributed widely in the body with extensive tissue binding. The principal metabolite of chloroquine in man is desethylchloroquine.[37] The drug is excreted very slowly in the urine ($t_{1/2}$ = 6 to 7 days), 70 per cent as chloroquine and 23 per cent as the desethyl metabolite.[38] Chloroquine can be recovered from the urine many weeks after termination of therapy. Chloroquine is metabolized by the liver microsomal drug metabolizing system. In the presence of an inhibitor of this metabolizing system, SKF-525A, the plasma half-life of the drug is prolonged.[39] This is an important observation because it allows one to predict that the plasma level of free chloroquine may be depressed if the patient is being treated concomitantly with any of the growing number of drugs known to induce the hepatic drug metabolizing system. This consideration is not crucial in short-term treatment of the acute malarial attack, but it should be kept in mind during suppressive therapy, when low blood levels of the free drug are maintained for long periods of time. Experiments in animals have shown that the plasma levels of chloroquine are prolonged by primaquine, another antimalarial drug that is sometimes administered concomitantly.[39]

Toxicity and Side Effects

Chloroquine is a safer drug than the studies of its mechanism of action would predict. In doses used for treatment of acute attacks, it can cause dizziness, headache, difficulty in visual accommodation, itching, vomiting, and skin rashes. At the low blood levels of drug employed for suppressive therapy the drug does not have significant toxicity. With the use of high doses of chloroquine for prolonged periods in the treatment of intestinal amebiasis, lupus erythematosis, and discoid lupus, toxic effects in the skin, blood, and eyes occur. Skin eruptions, photosensitivity, alopecia, and bleaching of the hair have been seen. Occasionally there is leukopenia.

Ocular damage can take the form of a temporary, reversible blurring of vision, and with large doses, there may be severe eye damage and even permanent blindness. The cause of the retinopathy resulting from chloroquine treatment is not known.[40] Chloroquine is localized in the melanin-containing areas of the eye,[41] and it binds extensively to preparations of choroidal melanin both *in vivo* and *in vitro*.[42] The drug binds to melanin in the skin as well,[43] and studies of the binding of iodoquine (the iodine-containing analog of chloroquine) to purified melanin and DNA suggest that it binds more strongly to melanin than to nucleic acid.[44] It is not known whether the avid association of the drug with the retinal pigment is in some way responsible for the retinopathy. At high drug concentrations, chloroquine inhibits the incorporation of amino acids into protein in samples of retinal pigment epithelium.[45] Although this particular observation does not expand our knowledge of the mechanism of the chloroquine effect, it raises the possibility that the basis for the retinopathy may be studied *in vitro*. The retinal lesion appears as a hyperpigmentation of the macula surrounded by a zone of depigmentation that in turn is encircled by another ring of pigment.[46] This bull's-eye lesion is most commonly seen in patients who have received chloroquine, but similar lesions have been observed rarely in patients who have never received the drug.[47] It has been reported that the lesion can occur months after cessation of chloroquine therapy.[48]

Prolonged high-dose therapy with chloroquine is rarely accompanied by ototoxicity.[49] Again, a careful study of the distribution of chloroquine in the inner ear of rats demonstrates that the drug is located in the melanin-containing tissues of the stria vascularis and the planum semilunatum.[50] The importance of melanin in localization of the drug was confirmed by the absence of radioactive chloroquine in the inner ear tissue of albino rats. In contrast to the aminoglycosides, which are also ototoxic drugs (Chapter 3), chloroquine is not concentrated in the fluids of the inner ear.[50]

There is a form of toxicity that should be considered when any drug that interacts with DNA is given to large populations on a chronic basis—the drug may be mutagenic. Chloroquine, amodiaquine, quinacrine, and quinine all interact with DNA and are employed chronically in large populations. Many agents of similar structure, such as the acridine dyes that intercalate between the base pairs in DNA, are potent mutagens and carcinogens.

Cinchona Alkaloids (Quinine)

The cinchona alkaloids are all compounds isolated from the bark of the cinchona tree. The most important member of the group is quinine. Until the 1920s, when more potent synthetic antimalarials were first introduced, the cinchona alkaloids were the only specific antimalarial drugs. The use of quinine in antimalarial therapy would probably be merely of historical interest if it were not for the recent development of resistance to the more potent drugs in *P. falciparum*. For reasons that are still unknown, resistance has not readily developed to quinine,[51] and, in spite of its lesser potency, the drug again has a role in the treatment of malaria.

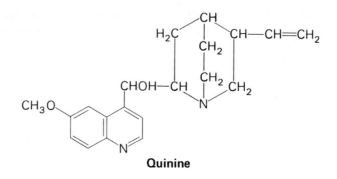

Quinine

Mechanism of Action

Quinine has a structure similar to the 4-aminoquinolines. As with chloroquine, several studies have focused on the ability of quinine to bind to DNA and inhibit nucleic acid synthesis.[52,53,54] The drug has been shown to produce a variety of other biochemical effects,[2] but the observations cannot yet be put together into a coherent model for a mechanism of action.

Absorption, Distribution, and Excretion

Quinine sulfate is well absorbed from the gastrointestinal tract, and it should not be given by intramuscular or subcutaneous injection. Quinine hydrochloride is the form of the drug employed for intravenous administration. Quinine is widely distributed in the body; but it does not accumulate in the tissues like chloroquine. Most of the quinine is metabolized in the liver, primarily by hydroxylation, and the hydroxylated products are rapidly excreted by the kidney.[55] The rapid metabolism and excretion define a short half-life for the drug, and to obtain a maximum therapeutic effect in treating the acute malarial attack it must be given every 6 to 8 hours.[56]

Toxicity

Quinine has a large number of pharmacological effects. The effects of quinine on the central and peripheral nervous system and the cardiovascular system will not be considered here except as they relate to the toxicity observed when the drug is used in the treatment of malaria. The administration of quinine in high doses for treatment of the acute malaria attack is often accompanied by tinnitus, blurred vision, nausea, headache, and a decrease in hearing acuity. This symptom complex is similar to salicylism and is called cinchonism. Permanent damage to vision, balance, and hearing can result. In high concentrations, quinine, like its dextro-isomer quinidine, can directly depress the myocardium. Quinine also causes vasodilation by a direct effect on vascular smooth muscle. During intravenous therapy, high blood levels of quinine are achieved; as a result of the myocardial depression and vasodilation, the patient can go into shock. The drug therefore must be given very slowly when the intravenous route is employed.

Quinine can cause contraction of uterine muscle, and it has been used in medicine to stimulate contraction during labor. It does not have significant effect until labor has begun. At toxic doses, quinine can cause abortion. It is unclear whether the abortifacient effect is due to its action on the uterus or to fetal poisoning. If other antimalarial drugs can be used, quinine should not be given to pregnant women. Quinine rarely causes hemolysis and bone-marrow depression. Occasional rashes and photosensitivity reactions occur during quinine therapy. Patients who have a history of cardiac arrythmia, episodes of hemolysis, tinnitus, or optic neuritis should be treated with other drugs whenever possible. Quinine has the poorest ratio between therapeutic potency and toxicity of all the antimalarial drugs.

ANTIMALARIALS EFFECTIVE AGAINST EXO-ERYTHROCYTIC FORMS OF THE PLASMODIUM

8-Aminoquinolines (Primaquine)

The only commonly employed member of the 8-aminoquinoline group is primaquine. Other drugs in this group include pamaquine and quinocide. The ring structure of these drugs is the same as that of chloroquine, and as one might expect, they also bind to DNA.[57] But the similarity between the two groups of compounds seems to end here. The 8-aminoquinolines are effective against the exo-erythrocytic stages of the parasite. They have no clinically useful activity against the erythrocytic forms of the parasite, but they do kill the sexual forms in the blood. The mechanism of

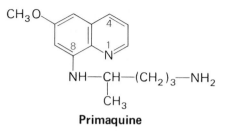

Primaquine

action is unknown. There is evidence that primaquine may become associated with the mitochondria of the exo-erythrocytic forms of plasmodia growing in culture[58] and that exposure to primaquine causes the mitochondria to swell and become vacuolated.[59] Primaquine at high concentration inhibits the growth of B. megaterium, and protein synthesis is inhibited early in the time-course of the drug effect.[60] The interpretation of this observation is subject to the same reservations as the inhibition of bacterial nucleic acid synthesis by chloroquine. Inhibition of protein synthesis at high primaquine concentrations has been demonstrated in a subcellular system from rat liver that incorporates amino acids into polypeptide under the direction of synthetic mRNA.[61,62] Chloroquine in high concentration also inhibits protein synthesis in this system. These experiments are not definitive, and there is no suggestion that the primary effect of the drug is either in the mitochondrion or at the level of protein synthesis. There is reason to believe that some of the effect of primaquine may be due to products of metabolism and not to the drug itself. This possibility injects an element of doubt into the meaning of *in vitro* studies of the biochemical effects of primaquine.

Pharmacology of Primaquine

Primaquine is rapidly absorbed from the gastrointestinal tract. All the 8-aminoquinolines are metabolized rapidly. It is clear that, at least for pamaquine and pentaquine, some of the metabolites are more potent antimalarials than the parent compounds.[63,64] This would also seem to be the case with primaquine. Peak plasma concentrations of primaquine are achieved 4 to 6 hours after drug administration, but the prophylactic effect of a single dose of the drug is maximal when it is administered 12 hours before infection.[64] The difference between the time of peak plasma levels of the unaltered drug and peak therapeutic effect may be due to the fact that more active forms of the drug are being produced by metabolism in the patient. The 8-aminoquinolines do not bind in the tissues like 4-aminoquinolines. As a result of their rapid metabolism, the rapid renal excretion of the metabolites, and the absence of tissue binding, these drugs have a relatively short half-life in the body and are administered daily.

Toxicity. Primaquine has a good therapeutic index. The ratio of the maximum tolerated dose to the smallest dose capable of preventing nearly all relapses is about ten. The same ratio for pamaquine is one.[65] For this reason, pamaquine is no longer used. With primaquine, there is occasional gastrointestinal distress, nausea, headache, pruritis, and leukopenia.[66] Very rarely agranulocytosis may occur.[66] The most important side effect is hemolytic anemia, which occurs in people with a glucose-6-phosphate dehydrogenase (G6PD) deficiency.

Primaquine Sensitivity (Glucose-6-phosphate Dehydrogenase Deficiency)

Although most patients tolerate primaquine quite well, in about 5 to 10 per cent of Negro males therapeutic doses can precipitate an acute hemolytic anemia. This response is also seen in darker-hued Caucasians (such as Indians), in Asians, and in people from or living in the countries bordering the Mediterranean.[67] People who are primaquine sensitive have a genetically determined deficiency of G6PD in their red blood cells (for a review, see reference 68). This enzyme (Figure 10-6) is responsible for the oxidation of glucose-6-phosphate to 6-phosphogluconic acid. This reaction is necessary to produce NADPH, which functions as a proton doner in the glutathione reductase reaction. In this second reaction, reduced glutathione is produced from oxidized glutathione. Reduced glutathione is necessary for the maintenance of red cell integrity. The hemolysis seen in the reduced glutathione-deficient state is apparently the result of an increased susceptibility of the erythrocyte to mechanical breakage. A metabolite of primaquine acts in the erythrocyte as an oxidizing agent and converts reduced glutathione to oxidized glutathione.[69] With a deficiency of G6PD, the cell is unable to produce enough NADPH to regenerate the reduced form of glutathione, and hemolysis takes place.

It is possible that red cell membranes become fragile because they have undergone oxidative damage. There is evidence that in the red cell glutathione peroxidase may be the major mechanism

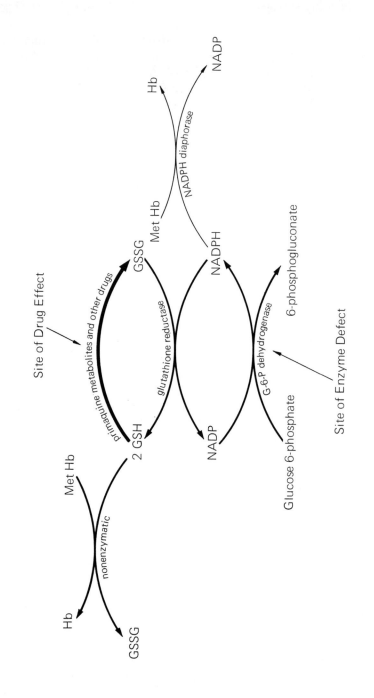

of defense against oxidative damage.[70] This enzyme catalyzes the reduction of hydrogen peroxide with the generation of water and oxidized glutathione. In addition, it can catalyze the reduction of lipid peroxides. It has been suggested that the action of glutathione peroxidase may break the autocatalytic chain reaction of lipid peroxidation and thus protect the red cell membrane from oxidative damage.[71] In the presence of primaquine, the G6PD-deficient patient may not produce enough reduced glutathione to provide adequate reducing equivalents for this reaction, and the resulting oxidative damage to the membrane may predispose the red cell to lysis.

In addition to hemolysis, patients who are deficient in G6PD may develop methemoglobinemia upon treatment with primaquine. There is evidence that the action of glutathione peroxidase in red cells is the major method of protecting hemoglobin from oxidation to methemoglobin by hydrogen peroxide.[70] Thus, in the G6PD-deficient patient, the red cell is less efficient at eliminating hydrogen peroxide and more methemoglobin could be produced. The reconversion of methemoglobin to hemoglobin may also be impaired. Methemoglobin can be converted to hemoglobin by several systems. One of these systems derives its reduced equivalents from NADPH, and another is a nonenzymatic process in which the proton donor is reduced glutathione.[72] These reactions are illustrated schematically in Figure 10-6.

Glucose-6-phosphate dehydrogenase deficiency is inherited as a sex-linked trait. Primaquine is not the only drug that causes hemolysis in people with this enzyme deficiency. A number of drugs, including the sulfonamides, the cinchona alkaloids, the

Figure 10-6 Scheme of the principal reactions related to the hemolysis and methemoglobinemia that occur in primaquine-sensitive patients. In the presence of primaquine metabolites and a number of other drugs, reduced glutathione (GSH) is converted to oxidized glutathione (GSSG). In erythrocytes from normal individuals the GSH level is maintained at a constant amount by the glutathione reductase reaction, which requires NADPH. The principal source of NADPH in the cell is the glucose-6-phosphate dehydrogenase (G6PD) reaction. In primaquine-sensitive individuals, G6PD activity is low, and the cell consequently cannot provide enough NADPH to keep up the levels of GSH in the presence of hemolyzing drugs. The depressed levels of GSH apparently render the erythrocyte susceptible to mechanical breakage. Low amounts of both NADPH and GSH in the cell may contribute to the methemoglobinemia occasionally observed in these patients.

sulfones, the 4-aminoquinolines, and chloramphenicol, can produce hemolytic anemia in these people.[73] The effect of an oxidizing agent on the glutathione content of normal and G6PD-defi-
cient red cells is presented in Figure 10-7.[74] The glutathione
content in erythrocytes was measured after incubation with acetylphenylhydrazine, one of the most effective hemolytic compounds. Before exposure to acetylphenylhydrazine, the erythrocytes from normal controls and G6PD-deficient individuals
contain the same amount of reduced glutathione. After 2 hours of
incubation in the presence of the oxidant, the erythrocytes from
the G6PD-deficient individuals have a much lower level of

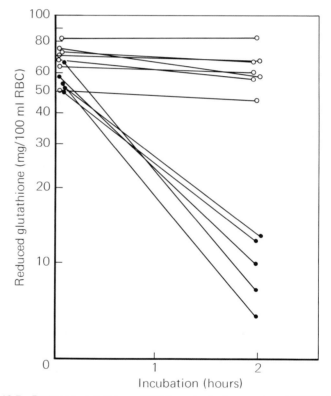

Figure 10-7 Reduced glutathione (GSH) content of normal and G6PD-deficient
red blood cells. Assays for GSH were performed on blood samples from seven
non-sensitive (o-o) and five primaquine-sensitive subjects (•-•). The erythrocytes were then incubated in the presence of acetylphenylhydrazine for 2 hours,
and the GSH assay was repeated. (From Beutler.[74])

reduced glutathione. Rapid clinical tests are now routinely available for identifying the G6PD-deficient patient.

ANTIMALARIALS THAT INHIBIT BOTH ERYTHROCYTIC AND EXO-ERYTHROCYTIC FORMS OF THE PLASMODIUM

The Inhibitors of Folic Acid Synthesis

Introduction

Several compounds that inhibit the synthesis of folic acid have been developed for antimalarial use; these include pyrimethamine, trimethoprim, chloroguanide, and cycloguanil embonate. Of this group, pyrimethamine is most widely used clinically. These

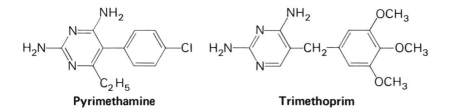

Pyrimethamine   Trimethoprim

drugs are schizontocidal for both the erythrocytic and exo-erythrocytic forms of P. *falciparum*. They have some effect on the exo-erythrocytic forms of P. *vivax* but not enough to make them useful in the radical cure of malaria caused by this organism.

Chloroguanide is less potent than pyrimethamine, and there is good evidence that chloroguanide itself is not the active form of the drug. It was demonstrated some time ago that chloroguanide has no effect on the exo-erythrocytic forms of P. *gallinaceum in vitro*. When the drug was incubated with minced liver tissue, however, it proved very effective.[75] The active dihydrotriazine metabolite produced by the liver is a closed ring form that has a structure similar to that of pyrimethamine (Figure 10-8).

Mechanism of Action

Early investigations carried out in bacteria demonstrated that pyrimethamine, like trimethoprim, inhibits the synthesis of

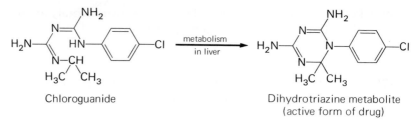

Chloroguanide

Dihydrotriazine metabolite
(active form of drug)

Figure 10-8 Chloroguanide is inactive as an antimalarial compound until it is altered by ring closure in the body to form the active dihydrotriazine metabolite.

reduced forms of folic acid.[76] Since the mechanism of action of this type of dihydrofolate reductase inhibitor has been discussed in detail in Chapter 5, the effect of pyrimethamine will be reviewed here only briefly. It is suggested that both sections be read for a comprehensive understanding of the drug effect.

It has been shown that plasmodia synthesize dihydrofolate *de novo* in much the same way bacteria do (Figure 10-9).[77] Dihydrofolate is then reduced in the presence of dihydrofolate reductase to tetrahydrofolate. This is the form of the compound that can function as the one-carbon carrier molecule required for the synthesis of methionine, glycine, thymidine, and the purines. Pyrimethamine inhibits the dihydrofolate reductase enzyme isolated

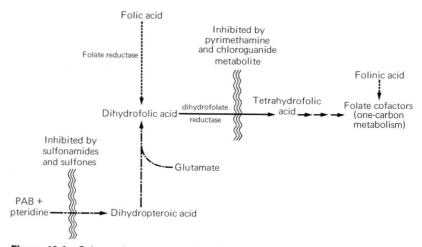

Figure 10-9 Schematic representation of sites of action for inhibitors of dihydrofolate synthesis and reduction. Reactions occurring in parasite only (—·—·—), man only (-------), and parasite and man (——).

from *P. berghei* is only about $5 \times 10^{-10} M$, whereas a concentration of $1.8 \times 10^{-6} M$ is required to inhibit human dihydrofolate reduc- with the natural substrate dihydrofolate. In Figure 10-10, the structure of pyrimethamine is redrawn to show the similarity between the drug and the pteridine moiety of dihydrofolate.

The reduction of folic acid compounds is a necessary step in the normal biochemistry of the host as well as the plasmodium (Figure 10-9). Inhibition of this enzyme by the drug would be expected to have a severe adverse effect in the patient (easily demonstrated with other antifolates, such as methotrexate). This is not the case, however. The selective toxicity of pyrimethamine is based on the fact that it binds very strongly to the dihydrofolate reductase from plasmodia and very weakly to the human enzyme.[79,80,81] This relationship is presented in Table 10-3. The concentration of pyrimethamine required to inhibit the enzyme

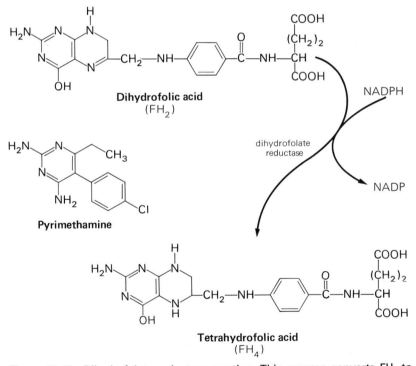

Figure 10-10 Dihydrofolate reductase reaction. This enzyme converts FH₂ to FH₄. It is inhibited by pyrimethamine, which is presented here to demonstrate the structural similarity to the pteridine portion of the normal substrate FH₂.

Table 10-3 **Inhibition of dihydrofolate reductases by pyrimethamine and trimethoprim**

Dihydrofolate reductase was purified from several sources. The concentration of drug (nanomolar) required to inhibit the activity of each enzyme preparation by 50 per cent is shown. (Data compiled from Ferone et al.[80] and Burchall and Hitchings.[81])

| | 50 Per cent inhibitory concentration (nM) | |
Source of enzyme	Pyrimethamine	Trimethoprim
Protozoal		
Plasmodium berghei	0.5	70
Bacterial		
Escherichia coli	2,500	5
Mammalian		
Human liver	1,800	300,000

from *P. berghei* is only about 5×10^{-10} M, whereas a concentration of 1.8×10^{-6} M is required to inhibit human dihydrofolate reductase. This amounts to a 3,600-fold difference in the sensitivity of the two enzymes to the drug. The different sensitivities probably reflect differences in the amino acid composition at or near the active site of the enzyme. The difference between the spectrum of enzyme inhibition by pyrimethamine and that of trimethoprim can also be appreciated from the data in Table 10-3. Pyrimethamine acts quite selectively on the plasmodial enzyme. Trimethoprim is most active against the bacterial enzyme, but it also has considerable selective toxicity for the plasmodial reductase.

Combination Therapy with Sulfones and Sulfonamides

Since the plasmodium must synthesize dihydrofolic acid, such drugs as the sulfonamides and sulfones, which compete for the utilization of para-aminobenzoic acid in that synthetic pathway, should be active as antimalarial agents. This is the case. These drugs act mainly on the asexual erythrocytic forms of the parasite. When used alone they have a relatively poor efficacy against *P. vivax* and a good but slow action against *P. falciparum*.[4] When sulfonamides or sulfones are administered with a dihydrofolate reductase inhibitor like pyrimethamine, a synergistic effect may be obtained in antimalarial therapy.[82] This can be seen in the experiment presented in Figure 10-11, which demonstrates that the presence of very low concentrations of sulfadiazine markedly

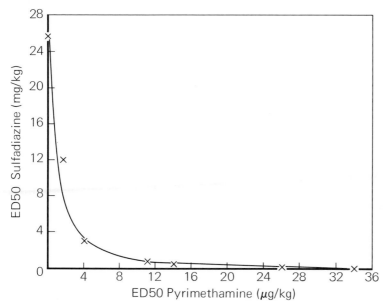

Figure 10-11 Synergism observed with sulfadiazine and pyrimethamine in chicks infected with *P. gallinaceum.* The figure presents the doses of pyrimethamine and sulfadiazine, administered both singly and together in various proportions, which were required to reduce parasitemia to 50 per cent of controls. (From Rollo.[82])

reduces the amount of pyrimethamine required for the therapeutic effect. The combination of a sulfonamide and trimethoprim is used in the treatment of a variety of bacterial infections. The biochemical basis for the synergism often observed with combinations of a dihydrofolate reductase inhibitor and a sulfonamide or sulfone is discussed in detail in Chapter 5.

Resistance to Pyrimethamine

Malarial organisms can develop resistance to pyrimethamine[83]; and cross-resistance to trimethoprim usually occurs. Plasmodia may be resistant because they contain increased amounts of dihydrofolate reductase or an altered enzyme with decreased affinity for the drug or both.[78] For some reason, resistance has been much more of a problem with *P. falciparum* than with other plasmodia.[84] The use of pyrimethamine in combination with a sulfonamide or sulfone should decrease the rate of selection for resistant organisms. The drug combination, however, should be used for suppressive treatment only in areas where there is a significant incidence of chloroquine-resistant falciparum malaria to minimize the selection of resistant strains (Table 10-2). The sulfonamide—pyrimethamine combination is often clinically effective even against strains with a moderate level of resistance to pyrimethamine itself.[85] The potentiating effect of the drug combination has been shown in mice infected with either sulfonamide-resistant or moderately pyrimethamine-resistant plasmodia (see the discussion of resistance under trimethoprim—sulfamethoxazole in Chapter 5).[86]

The possibility that drug resistance may be transferable from one species of plasmodium to another is suggested by an intriguing experiment performed with malarial organisms that parasitize rodents.[87] In this study, mice were simultaneously inoculated with pyrimethamine-resistant *Plasmodium vinckei* and pyrimethamine-sensitive *P. berghei*, and both organisms were allowed to multiply. Both plasmodia were then transferred from the mice to a hamster that was subsequently treated with high doses of pyrimethamine. Since *P. vinckei* is not able to grow in hamsters, the hamster can serve as a biological filter to select for *P. berghei* that have become drug resistant. Drug-resistant *P. berghei* was recovered from the hamster. The dihydrofolate reductase enzyme prepared from these newly resistant plasmodia behaved similarly to the altered enzyme of the original drug-resistant *P. vinckei*. Thus, it is postulated that there was transfer of genetic material from the drug-resistant to the drug-sensitive plasmodium. The mechanism by which transfer took place is not known; but the observation brings to mind the infectious type of drug resistance described in Chapter 1, in which resistance information contained in episomes is transferred from one type of bacterium to another.

Pharmacology

Pyrimethamine and chloroguanide are well absorbed from the gastrointestinal tract. Pyrimethamine is bound in the tissues to a greater extent than chloroguanide and is extensively metabolized. As mentioned earlier in this chapter, chloroguanide is metabolized to at least one active metabolite. Excretion is predominantly renal. About 60 per cent of the chloroguanide is excreted as the parent compound and about 40 per cent as its metabolites.[88] Because tissue binding is less and excretion by the kidneys is more rapid, chloroguanide is shorter acting than pyrimethamine. For this reason, and because of its higher potency, pyrimethamine is the more popular drug. Pyrimethamine has a half-life of about 4 days,[89] and after a single dose, suppressive levels are maintained in the blood for at least 2 weeks.[90] Pyrimethamine is secreted in human milk, and breast feeding yields suppressive levels of the drug in the infant.[91] Cycloguanil pamoate (embonate), a repository preparation of the dihydrotriazine metabolite of chloroguanide, has been developed. A single intramuscular dose of this compound will protect experimental animals and man for weeks against clinical attack.[92]

For treatment of the acute malarial attack, pyrimethamine is used with quinine and a short-acting sulfonamide or sulfone. For suppressive prophylaxis against chloroquine-resistant falciparum malaria, the dihydrofolate reductase inhibitor and the antimetabolite are chosen according to the interval desired for drug administration.[10] Thus, cycloguanil pamoate can be administered by injection at 3-month intervals with acedapsone, a repository form of dapsone. For weekly oral therapy, pyrimethamine is given with a long-acting sulfonamide, such as sulfadoxine or sulfalene (Table 10-2). Sulfadoxine has a half-life in the range of 7 to 9 days.[93] The long plasma half-lives of the components suggest that the pyrimethamine–sulfadoxine combination may be effective in suppression if given at biweekly or perhaps even monthly intervals.[94] If daily drug administration is desired, a short-acting reductase inhibitor, chlorguanide, is used, usually in combination with dapsone.[10]

Weekly administration of pyrimethamine at the dosage recommended for suppressive prophylaxis is well tolerated.[2] Higher doses or particularly long-term therapy may produce a megaloblastic anemia. The anemia will clear quickly when the drug is stopped, or it can be reversed by folinic acid. As can be seen in Figure 10-9, folinic acid cannot be utilized by the plasmodium.[77] It is taken into the mammalian cell and shunts around the drug-blocked reaction. The marrow-depressant effect of pyrimethamine has been exploited with the use of higher doses in the treatment of polycythemia rubra vera. If possible, the drug should not be given during pregnancy.

Antibiotics

It has been known for many years that some antibiotics (e.g., the tetracyclines, chloramphenicol) have antimalarial activity. Studies with infected animals suggest an effect on both the erythrocytic and tissue forms of the organisms. When tetracyclines are given alone, the rate of clearance of *P. falciparum* is slow.[95] Although the tetracyclines are not optimal antimalarial agents, the emergence of multidrug-resistant strains of *P. falciparum* have given them a role in therapy. Because the infection usually does not respond for 3 or 4 days it is essential to administer a rapid-acting blood schizontocide, like quinine, at the beginning of the course of therapy.[95,96,97] Since there is a risk of changing the drug sensitivity of pathogenic bacteria, the tetracyclines should not be used on a long-term basis. Clindamycin is another antibiotic that can effect a radical cure of *P. falciparum*.[98] It also acts slowly, and a rapid-acting drug such as quinine must be given initially. The possibility of developing colitis should be remembered if clindamycin is being considered for therapy (see Chapter 4).

REFERENCES

1. M. B. Kreig: "The incredible history of quinine." in *Green Medicine*. New York; Rand McNally, 1964, pp. 165–206.

2. P. E. Thompson and L. M. Werbel: *Antimalarial Agents. Chemistry and Pharmacology*, New York: Academic Press, 1972.

3. W. Peters: Recent advances in antimalarial chemotherapy and drug resistance. *Adv. Parasitol.* 12:69 (1974).

4. R. S. Rozman: Chemotherapy of malaria. *Ann. Rev. Pharmacol.* 13:127 (1973).

5. *Chemotherapy of Malaria and Resistance to Antimalarials. World Health Organization Techn. Rep. Ser.*, No. 529 (1973).

6. L. T. Coggeshall: "Malaria" in *Textbook of Medicine*, ed. by P. B. Beeson and W. McDermott. Philadelphia: W. B. Saunders, 1963, pp. 383–389.

7. I. N. Brown: Immunological aspects of malaria infection. *Adv. Immunol.* 11:267 (1969).

8. L. G. Hunsicker: The pharmacology of the antimalarials. *Arch. Int. Med.* 123:645 (1969).

9. E. Barrett-Connor: Chemoprophylaxis of malaria for travelers. *Ann. Int. Med.* 81:219 (1974).

10. D. F. Clyde: Treatment of drug-resistant malaria in man. *Bull. Wld. Hlth. Org.* 50:243 (1974).

11. M. B. Miller, J. L. Bratton, J. P. Hanson, M. Cohen, R. D. Reynolds, D. C. Lohr, J. Hunt, and D. Jilek: Experience with mixed infections of *Plasmodium falciparum* and *vivax*. *Military Med.* 138:567 (1973).

12. R. H. Glew, L. H. Miller, W. E. Collins, W. A. Howard, D. J. Wyler, E. Chaves-Carballo, and F. A. Neva: Response to treatment in man of multi-drug resistant *Plasmodium falciparum* from Panama. *Am. J. Trop. Med. Hyg.* 23:1 (1974).

13. D. Willerson, L. Kass, H. Frischer, K. H. Rieckmann, P. E. Carson, and L. Richard: Chemotherapeutic results in a multi-drug resistant strain of *Plasmodium falciparum* malaria from Vietnam. *Military Med.* 139:175 (1974).

14. H. Polet and C. F. Barr: DNA, RNA, and protein synthesis in erythrocytic forms of *Plasmodium knowlesi. Am. J. Trop. Med. Hyg.* 17:672 (1968).

15. H. Polet and C. F. Barr: Chloroquine and dihydroquinine; *In vitro* studies of their antimalarial effect upon *Plasmodium knowlesi. J. Pharm. Exp. Ther.* 164:380 (1968).

16. K. A. Schellenberg and G. R. Coatney: The influence of antimalarial drugs on nucleic acid synthesis in *Plasmodium gallinaceum* and *Plasmodium berghei. Biochem. Pharmacol.* 6:143 (1961).

17. A. S. Alving, L. Eichelberger, B. Craige, R. Jones, C. M. Whorton, and T. N. Pullman: Studies on the chronic toxicity of chloroquine (SN-7618). *J. Clin. Invest.* 27 Suppl. :60(1948).

18. J. Ciak and F. E. Hahn: Chloroquine: Mode of action. *Science* 151:347 (1966).

19. S. N. Cohen and K. L. Yielding: Inhibition of DNA and RNA polymerase reactions by chloroquine. *Proc. Natl. Acad. Sci. U.S.* 54:521 (1965).

20. S. N. Cohen and K. L. Yielding: Spectrophotometric studies of the interaction of chloroquine with deoxyribonucleic acid. *J. Biol. Chem.* 240:3123 (1965).

21. M. Waring: Variation of the supercoils in closed circular DNA by binding of antibiotics and drugs: Evidence for molecular models involving intercalation. *J. Mol. Biol.* 54:247 (1970).

22. L. S. Lerman: Acridine mutagens and DNA structure. *J. Cell. Comp. Physiol.* 64 Suppl. 1:1 (1964).

23. L. W. Blodgett and K. L. Yielding: Comparison of chloroquine binding to DNA, and polyadenylic and polyguanylic acids. *Biochim. Biophys. Acta* 169:451 (1968).

24. C. R. Morris, L. V. Andrew, L. P. Wichard, and D. J. Holbrook: The binding of antimalarial aminoquinolines to nucleic acids and polynucleotides. *Mol. Pharmacol.* 6:240 (1970).

25. H. Sternglanz, K. L. Yielding, and K. M. Pruitt: Nuclear magnetic resonance studies of the interaction of chloroquine diphosphate with adenosine 5'-phosphate and other nucleotides. *Mol. Pharmacol.* 5:376 (1969).

26. P. B. Macomber, R. L. O'Brien, and F. E. Hahn: Chloroquine: Physiological basis of drug resistance in *Plasmodium berghei. Science* 152:1374 (1966).

27. H. Polet and C. F. Barr: Uptake of chloroquine-3-H³ by *Plasmodium knowlesi* in vitro. *J. Pharm. Exptl. Ther.* 168:187 (1969).

28. C. D. Fitch, N. G. Yunis, R. Chevli, and Y. Gonzalez: High-affinity accumulation of chloroquine by mouse erythrocytes infected by *Plasmodium berghei, J. Clin. Invest.* 54:24 (1974).

29. C. A. Homewood, D. C. Warhurst, W. Peters, and V. C. Baggaley: Lysosomes, pH and the anti-malarial action of chloroquine. *Nature* 235:50 (1972).

30. P. A. Kramer and J. E. Matusik: Location of chloroquine binding sites in *Plasmodium berghei*. *Biochem. Pharmacol.* 20:1619 (1971).

31. C. D. Fitch: Chloroquine resistance in malaria: A deficiency of chloroquine binding. *Proc. Nat. Acad. Sci. U.S.* 64:1181 (1969).

32. J. D. Gabourel: Effects of hydroxychloroquine on the growth of mammalian cells *in vitro. J. Pharm. Exptl. Ther.* 141:122 (1963).

33. W. E. Gutteridge, P. I. Trigg, and P. M. Bayley: Effects of chloroquine on *Plasmodium knowlesi in vitro. Parasitol.* 64:37 (1972).

34. H. Polet: Influence of sucrose on chloroquine-3-H³ content of mammalian cells *in vitro:* The possible role of lysosomes in chloroquine resistance. *J. Pharm. Exptl. Ther.* 173:71 (1970).

35. R. W. Berliner, D. P. Earle, J. V. Taggart, C. G. Zubrod, W. J. Welch, N. J. Conan, E. Bauman, S. T. Scudder, and J. A. Shannon: Studies on the chemotherapy of human malarias: VI. The physiological disposition, anti-malarial activity, and toxicity of several derivatives of 4-aminoquinoline. *J. Clin. Invest.* 27 Suppl.: 98 (1948).

36. J. L. Irvin, E. M. Irvin, and F. S. Parker: The interaction of antimalarials with nucleic acids. *Science* 110:426 (1949).

37. E. W. McChesney, W. D. Conway, W. F. Banks, J. E. Rogers, and J. M. Shekosky: Studies of the metabolism of some compounds of the 4-amino-7-chloroquinoline series. *J. Pharm. Exptl. Ther.* 151:482 (1966).

38. E. W. McChesney, M. J. Fasco, and W. F. Banks: The metabolism of chloroquine in man during and after repeated oral dosage. *J. Pharm. Exptl. Ther.* 158:323 (1967).

39. L. E. Gaudette and G. R. Coatney: A possible mechanism of prolonged antimalarial activity. *Am. J. Trop. Med. Hyg.* 10:321 (1961).

40. H. E. Hobbs, A. Sorsby, and A. Freedman: Retinopathy following chloroquine therapy. *Lancet* 2:478 (1959).

41. H. Bernstein. N. Zvaifler, M. Rubin, and A. M. Mansour: The ocular deposition of chloroquine. *Invest. Ophth.* 2:384 (1963).

42. A. M. Potts: The reaction of uveal pigment *in vitro* with polycyclic compounds. *Invest. Ophth.* 3:405 (1964).

43. W. M. Sams and J. E. Epstein: The affinity of melanin for chloroquine. *J. Invest. Derm.* 45:482 (1965).

44. M. Blois: Melanin binding properties of iodoquine. *J. Invest. Derm.* 50:250 (1968).

45. L. M. Gonasun and A. M. Potts: *In vitro* inhibition of protein synthesis in the retinal pigment epithelium by chloroquine. *Invest. Ophthal.* 13:107 (1974).

46. A. L. Scherbel, A. H. Mackenzie, J. E. Nousek, and M. Atdjian: Ocular lesions in rheumatoid arthritis and related disorders with particular reference to retinopathy. *New Eng. J. Med.* 273:360 (1965).

47. E. E. Weise and L. A. Yanuzzi: Ring maculopathies mimicking chloroquine retinopathy. *Am. J. Ophthal.* 78:204 (1974).

48. R. P. Burns: Delayed onset of chloroquine retinopathy. *New Eng. J. Med.* 275:693 (1966).

49. E. C. Toone, G. D. Hayden, and H. M. Ellman: Ototoxicity of chloroquine. *Arthritis Rheum.* 8:475 (1965).

50. L. Dencker and N. G. Lindquist: Distribution of labeled chloroquine in the inner ear. *Arch. Otolaryngol.* 101:185 (1975).

51. L. H. Schmidt: Chemotherapy of the drug-resistant malarias. *Ann. Rev. Microbiol.* 23:427 (1969).

52. F. E. Hahn, R. L. O'Brien, J. Ciak, J. L. Allison, and J. G. Olenick: Studies on modes of action of chloroquine, quinacrine, and quinine and on chloroquine resistance. *Military Med.* 131:1071 (1966).

53. R. L. O'Brien, J. G. Olenick, and F. E. Hahn: Reactions of quinine, chloroquine, and quinacrine with DNA and their effects on the DNA and RNA polymerase reactions. *Proc. Nattl. Acad. Sci. U.S.* 55:1511 (1966).

54. R. D. Estensen, A. K. Krey, and F. E. Hahn: Studies on a deoxyribonucleic acid-quinine complex. *Mol. Pharmacol.* 5:532 (1969).

55. B. B. Brodie, J. E. Baer, and L. C. Craig: Metabolic products of the cinchona alkaloids in human urine. *J. Biol. Chem.* 188–567 (1951).

56. R. D. Powell: The chemotherapy of malaria. *Clin. Pharm. Ther.* 7:48 (1966).

57. L. P. Whichard, C. R. Morris, J. M. Smith, and D. J. Holbrook: The binding of primaquine, pentaquine, pamaquine, and plasmocid to deoxyribonucleic acid. *Mol. Pharmacol.* 4:630 (1968).

58. M. Aikawa and R. L. Beaudoin: *Phasmodium fallax:* High-resolution autoradiography of exoerythrocytic stages treated with primaquine *in vitro. Exp. Parasit.* 27:454 (1970).

59. M. Aikawa and R. L. Beaudoin: Morphological effects of 8-aminoquinolines on the exoerythrocytic stages of *Plasmodium fallax. Military Med.* 134:986 (1969).

60. J. G. Olenick and F. E. Hahn: Mode of action of primaquine: Preferential inhibition of protein biosynthesis in *Bacillus megaterium. Antimicrob. Agents Chemother.* 1:259 (1972).

61. R. Roskoski and S. R. Jaskunas: Chloroquine and primaquine inhibition of rat liver cell-free polynucleotide-dependent polypeptide synthesis. *Biochem. Pharmacol.* 21:391 (1972).

62. C. F. Lefler, H. S. Lilja, and D. J. Holbrook: Inhibition of aminoacylation and polypeptide synthesis by chloroquine and primaquine in rat liver *in vitro. Biochem. Pharmacol.* 22:715 (1973).

63. D. J. Taylor, E. S. Josephson, J. Breenberg, and G. R. Coatney: The *in vitro* activity of certain antimalarials against erythrocytic forms of *Plasmodium gallinaceum. Am. J. Trop. Med. Hyg.* 1:132 (1952).

64. A. S. Alving, R. D. Powell, G. J. Brewer, and J. D. Arnold: "Malaria, 8-aminoquinolines and haemolysis" in *Drugs, Parasites and Hosts,* ed. by L. G. Goodwin and R. H. Nimmo-Smith. Boston: Little, Brown, 1962, pp. 83–111.

65. J. H. Edgcomb, J. Arnold, E. H. Yount, A. S. Alving, and L. Eichelberger: Primaquine, SN13272, a new curative agent in vivax malaria: A preliminary report. *J. Nat. Malaria Soc.* 9:285 (1950).

66. H. Most: Treatment of common parasitic infections of man encountered in the United States (Second of two parts). *New Eng. J. Med.* 287:698 (1972).

67. E. Beutler: The hemolytic effect of primaquine and related compounds; a review. *Blood* 14:103 (1959).

68. E. Beutler: Drug-induced hemolytic anemia. *Pharmacol. Rev.* 21:73 (1969).

69. I. M. Fraser and E. S. Vesell: Effects of metabolites of primaquine

and acetanilid on normal and glucose-6-phosphate dehydrogenase deficient erythrocytes. *J. Pharm. Exp. Ther.* 162:155 (1968).

70. G. Cohen and P. Hochstein: Glutathione peroxidase: The primary agent for the elimination of hydrogen peroxide in erythrocytes. *Biochemistry* 2:1420 (1963).

71. Y. C. Awasthi, E. Beutler, and S. K. Srivastava: Purification and properties of human erythrocyte glutathione peroxidase. *J. Biol. Chem.* 250:5144 (1975).

72. P. S. Gerald and E. M. Scott: "The hereditary methemoglobinemias" in *The Metabolic Basis of Inherited Disease,* ed. by J. B. Stanbury, J. B. Wyngaarden and D. S. Fredrickson, New York: McGraw-Hill, 1966 p. 1095.

73. P. A. Marks and J. Banks: Drug-induced hemolytic anemias associated with glucose-6-phosphate dehydrogenase deficiency; a genetically heterogeneous trait. *Ann. N.Y. Acad. Sci.* 123:198 (1965).

74. E. Beutler: The glutathione instability of drug sensitive red cells; A new method for the *in vitro* detection of drug sensitivity. *J. Lab. Clin. Med.* 49:84 (1957).

75. F. Hawking and W. L. M. Perry: Activation of paludrine. *Brit. J. Pharmacol.* 3:320 (1948).

76. R. C. Wood and G. H. Hitchings: Effect of pyrimethamine on folic acid metabolism in *Streptococcus faecalis* and *Escherichia coli. J. Biol. Chem.* 234:2377 (1959).

77. R. Ferone and G. H. Hitchings: Folate cofactor biosynthesis by *Plasmodium berghei.* Comparison of folate and dihydrofolate as substrates. *J. Protozool* 13:504 (1966).

78. R. Ferone: Dihydrofolate reductase from pyrimethamine-resistant *Plasmodium berghei. J. Biol. Chem.* 245:850 (1970).

79. J. J. Burchall: Comparative biochemistry of dihydrofolate reductase. *Ann. N.Y. Acad. Sci.* 186:143 (1971).

80. R. Ferone, J. J. Burchall, and G. H. Hitchings: *Plasmodium berghei* dihydrofolate reductase; isolation, properties, and inhibition by antifolates. *Mol. Pharmacol.* 5:49 (1969).

81. J. J. Burchall and G. H. Hitchings: Inhibitor binding analysis of dihydrofolate reductases from various species. *Mol. Pharmacol.* 1:126 (1965).

82. I. M. Rollo: The mode of action of sulfonamides, proguanil and pyrimethamine on *Plasmodium gallinaceum. Brit. J. Pharmacol.* 10:208 (1955).

83. G. H. Hitchings: Pyrimethamine: The use of an antimetabolite in the chemotherapy of malaria and other infections. *Clin. Pharm. Ther.* 1:570 (1960).

84. L. H. Schmidt: Chemotherapy of the drug-resistant malarias. *Ann. Rev. Microbiol.* 23:427 (1969).

85. W. Chin, P. G. Contacos, G. R. Coatney, and H. K. King: The evaluation of sulfonamides, alone or in combination with pyrimethamine, in the treatment of multi-resistant falciparum malaria. *Am. J. Trop. Med. Hyg.* 15:823 (1966).

86. W. Peters: Potentiating action of sulfalene-pyrimethamine mixtures against drug-resistant strains of *Plasmodium berghei. Chemotherapy* 16:389 (1971).

87. R. Ferone, M. O'Shea, and M. Yoeli: Altered dihydrofolate reductase associated with drug-resistance transfer between rodent plasmodia. *Science* 167:1263 (1970).

88. C. G. Smith, J. Ihrig, and R. Menne: Antimalarial activity and metabolism of biguanides. *Am. J. Trop. Med. Hyg.* 10:694 (1960).

89. D. R. Stickney, W. S. Simmons, R. L. DeAngelis, R. W. Rundles, and C. A. Nichol: Pharmacokinetics of pyrimethamine (PRM) and 2,4-diamino-5-(3',4'-dichlorophenyl)-6-methyl pyrimidine (DMP) relevent to meningeal leukemia. *Proc. Am. Assoc. Canc. Res.* 14:52 (1973).

90. M. H. Brooks, J. P. Malloy, P. J. Bartelloni, T. W. Sheehy, and K. G. Barry: Quinine, pyrimethamine, and sulphorthodimethoxine: Clinical response, plasma levels, and urinary excretion during the initial attack of naturally acquired falciparum malaria. *Clin. Pharm. Ther.* 10:85 (1969).

91. D. F. Clyde: Prolonged malaria prophylaxis through pyrimethamine in mother's milk. *East African Med. J.* 37:659 (1960).

92. G. R. Coatney, P. G. Contacos, J. S. Lunn, J. W. Kilpatrick, and H. A. Elder: The effect of a repository preparation of the dihydrotriazine metabolite of chlorguanide, CI-501, against the Chesson strain of *Plasmodium vivax* in man. *Am. J. Trop. Med.* 12:504 (1963).

93. C. C. Peck, A. N. Lewis, and B. E. Joyce: Pharmacokinetic rationale for a malarial suppressant administered once monthly. *Ann. Trop. Med. Parasitol.* 69:141 (1975).

94. A. N. Lewis and J. T. Ponnampalam: Suppression of malaria with monthly administration of combined sulphadoxine and pyrimethamine. *Ann. Trop. Med. Parasitol.* 69:1 (1975).

95. E. J. Colwell, R. L. Hickman, and S. Kosakal: Quinine-tetracycline and quinine-bacterim treatment of acute falciparum malaria in Thailand. *Ann. Trop. Med. Parasitol.* 67:125 (1973).

96. E. J. Colwell, R. L. Hickman, and S. Kosakal: Tetracycline treatment of chloroquine-resistant falciparum malaria in Thailand. *J. Am. Med. Assoc.* 220:684 (1972).

97. E. J. Colwell, R. L. Hickman, R. Intraprasert, and C. Tirabutana: Minocycline and tetracycline treatment of acute falciparum malaria in Thailand. *Am. J. Trop. Med. Hyg.* 21:144 (1972).

98. L. H. Miller, R. H. Glew, D. J. Wyler, W. A. Howard, W. E. Collins, P. G. Contacos, and F. A. Neva: Evaluation of clindamycin in combination with quinine against mutidrug-resistant strains of *Plasmodium falciparm. Am. J. Trop. Med. Hyg.* 23:565 (1974).

Chapter 11
Chemotherapy of Protozoal Diseases

Introduction

The incidence of parasitic disease will surely decline as improvements in the economy and nutrition and sanitary standards continue, particularly in the nations of Africa, Asia, and South America. During the next few generations, however, other parasitic diseases will have to be attacked world wide in much the same way that malaria has been. Large-scale programs of chemotherapy are important in controlling some of these parasitic diseases, but they have less impact than efforts devoted to the control of vectors, elimination of reservoirs of infection, and amelioration of the poor sanitary conditions and living conditions responsible for transmission of parasites.

The problem of the chemotherapy of parasitic diseases is complicated by a number of factors. First, the size of the population infected with parasites or living in areas where parasitic diseases are endemic is huge. Second, therapy is complicated by the fact that quite often individuals are infected with several organisms simultaneously. To provide such people with appropriate medical care it is necessary to carry out numerous diagnostic and follow-up laboratory tests and institute multiple-drug therapy. After this is done in a careful way, the person often returns to an environment in which multiple parasites are endemic, and optimum conditions for recurrent infection exist. Third, many people are used to being infected and are not well enough educated to understand and be conscientious in following the treatment recommended by the physician. This is linked to the fact that health workers (often from an alien culture) are sometimes considered outsiders whose efforts are felt as threatening to well-established life patterns.

At present, there are no immunization procedures for protection against protozoal and helminthic disease.[1] The physician must rely on drugs which are discussed in this chapter and in the following one, for treatment of these conditions. Not a great deal is known about the mechanisms of action or mechanisms behind the toxic effects and side effects of many of these drugs.

DRUGS EMPLOYED IN THE TREATMENT OF AMEBIASIS AND OTHER PROTOZOAL INFECTIONS THAT OCCUR IN NORTH AMERICA AND EUROPE

Amebiasis

Amebiasis results from infection by the protozoan *Entamoeba histolytica*. The disease occurs in all parts of North America and throughout the world. As with malaria and many other parasitic diseases, it is important to know the life cycle of the protozoan and the normal progression of the disease process in order to understand the therapy. Man is the principal host and main source of infection by *E. histolytica*. The patient becomes infected by ingesting mature cysts, which are resistant to the acidic environment of the stomach and pass to the small intestine (Figure 11-1). The cyst disintegrates in the small intestine, releasing four amebas, which divide to form eight trophozoites. The trophozoites pass into the large intestine where they may live and multiply for a time in the crypts of the bowel. Some of the trophozoites are able to invade the intestinal epithelium, and encystation and ulceration of the intestinal wall takes place. The presence of bacteria is required for survival of the protozoan in the intestine of the host. Although diarrhea is often seen, ulceration does not usually result in prolonged diarrhea or abdominal pain. Indeed many affected patients have no complaints. The cysts formed from the trophozoites on the surface of the colon are passed in formed stools. Thus, people readily become asymptomatic carriers of the disease by passing cysts in the stool for long periods of time. Patients with active diarrhea do not spread the disease because the trophozoites are not able to mature into the active cyst forms in the hyperactive bowel. The lesions produced by *E. histolytica* are primarily located in the large bowel, although secondary systemic invasion can occur. The organisms may pass up the portal vein to the liver producing hepatitis and abscesses. Encystation rarely occurs in organs other than the liver.

Metronidazole is effective against all forms of the parasite—the intestinal cysts, the trophozoites in the intestinal lumen, and the extraintestinal cysts. At low doses, it is effective in the treatment of liver abscess,[2,3] and at higher doses, it is effective in treating amebic dysentery.[4,5] It is now considered the drug of choice for both these forms of the disease (Table 11-1).[6] Metronidazole is also used to treat patients who are asymptomatic cyst passers, but in about 10 per cent of such patients, the usual course of therapy

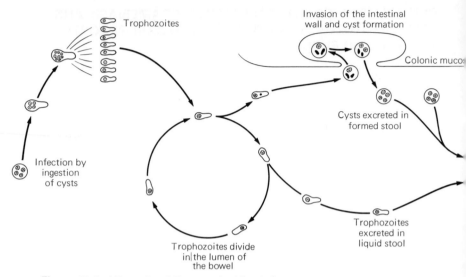

Trophozoites

Invasion of the intestinal
wall and cyst formation

Colonic mucos

Cysts excreted in
formed stool

Infection by
ingestion
of cysts

Trophozoites
excreted in
liquid stool

Trophozoites divide
in the lumen of
the bowel

Figure 11-1   Life cycle of *Entamoeba histolytica.*

fails to eradicate intestinal infection.[7] Diiodohydroxyquin is useful in the treatment of both asymptomatic cyst passers and
patients with mild amebic dysentery, but it cannot be used in the
treatment of hepatic abscess.

Severe intestinal disease can be treated with emetine or dehydroemetine, usually in combination with an antibiotic. Although
the emetines have a direct amebicidal effect on the trophozoites,
the role of the antibiotics in this case is interesting since, with the
exception of paromomycin (Chapter 3), which has been demonstrated to have a direct amebicidal effect *in vitro,*[8] the antibiotics
do not affect the amebae directly but inhibit the growth of amebas
by reducing the bacterial population of the bowel. The amebas are
dependent upon bacteria in the bowel for growth.[9] The drugs that
are effective in treating only the intestinal forms of the parasite
include the antibiotics tetracyclines and paromomycin, diiodohydroxyquin, and diloxanide furoate (available as an investigational
drug in the United States).[10,11] In contrast, chloroquine is effective
in the treatment of hepatic abscess but is ineffective against the
intestinal forms (Table 11-2). In the treatment of amebic hepatic
abscess, chloroquine and either dehydroemetine or emetine are
combined in therapy.[12] Although this older drug regimen is more
toxic to the patient than metronidazole alone, it is useful in
treating those few patients with hepatic abscess in which the
latter drug does not effect a cure.

Table 11-1 Drugs used to treat intestinal protozoa and other protozoal infections that occur in North America and Europe
The tetracyclines are presented in Chapter 4; choroquine and pyrimethamine, Chapter 10; quinacrine, Chapter 12. (Adapted from *The Medical Letter*.[6])

Infecting organism	Drug of choice	Alternative
Entamoeba histolytica		
Asymptomatic cyst passer	Diiodohydroxyquin	Metronidazole
Mild intestinal disease	Metronidazole	Paromomycin plus diiodohydroxyquin
Severe intestinal disease	Metronidazole	Dehydroemetine or emetine plus paromomycin followed by diiodohydroxyquin
Hepatic abscess	Metronidazole	Dehydroemetine or emetine plus chloroquine phosphate
Giardia lamblia	Quinacrine hydrochloride	Metronidazole Diiodohydroxyquin
Balantidium coli	Oxytetracycline	A tetracycline
Dientamoeba fragilis	Diiodohydroxyquin	Topical agents
Trichomonas vaginalis	Metronidazole	Pentamidine
Pneumocystis carinii	Trimethoprim– sulfamethoxazole	
Toxoplasma gondii	Pyrimethamine plus trisulfapyrimidines	None

Metronidazole

Metronidazole has proven to be therapeutically useful in the treatment of several parasitic diseases. Subsequent to the first demonstration of its efficacy against E. *histolytica*,[13] it has become the drug of choice for the treatment of amebiasis. It also is very active against *Trichomonas vaginalis*. Until this compound was introduced, trichomoniasis was treated with a variety of topical agents. Complete cure of the disease was difficult to achieve, and infection often recurred as a result of reintroduction of the parasite by the sexual partner. Metronidazole given orally (often to both partners) has proven to be a very effective therapy for this common genital infection.[14] Metronidazole can be useful

Table 11-2 **The site of action of the antiamebic drugs**

Drug	Effective against:	
	Intestinal disease	Hepatic abscess
Metronidazole	+	+
Dehydroemetine and emetine	+	+
Diiodohydroxyquin	+	−
Antibiotics	+	−
Diloxanide furoate	+	−
Chloroquine	−	+

in the treatment of giardiasis (infection with the intestinal flagellate *Giardia lamblia*), one of the most common intestinal parasitic infections of travelers. The cure rate with metronidazole alone is not as good as with quinacrine hydrochloride, the drug of choice, but it can be used as a second course of treatment in the unusual case of quinacrine failure.[15]

The spectrum of drug action is not limited to protozoa. There are some reports that metronidazole may be effective in the treatment of dracontiasis[16,17] (infection with the guinea-worm *Dracunculus medinensis*), but its usefulness in this condition has been questioned.[18] Metronidazole is active against several anaerobic bacteria including *Clostridium perfringens* and *Bacteroides fragilis*. It is bactericidal at concentrations that are achieved in the serum during therapy with a dosage of 250 mg every 8 hours.[19,20] Metronidazole has been used successfully in the treatment of Vincent's angina, an acute ulcerative gingivitis caused by anaerobic bacteria.[21]

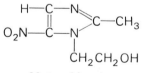

Metronidazole

Mechanism of Action of Metronidazole

All the organisms susceptible to metronidazole are anaerobic or micro-aerophilic. These organisms have developed unique mechanisms of energy production and electron transfer that permit their survival in the absence of oxygen. It has been shown that metronidazole inhibits hydrogen production in cultures of the anaerobic bacterium *C. perfringens* and the protozoan *Trichomonas vaginalis*.[22,23] The principal mechanism of hydrogen evolution in these organisms is by the pyruvate phosphoroclastic reaction. In this complex reaction, pyruvate is converted to acetyl phosphate with the evolution of carbon dioxide and hydrogen. There are two enzyme systems involved:

(1) Pyruvate + phosphate $\rightarrow$ acetyl phosphate + CO_2 + $2H^+$
(2) $2H^+ + 2e \rightarrow H_2$

Metronidazole inhibits the generation of H_2 without affecting the rate of acetyl phosphate synthesis.[24] Thus, it is the second reaction that is inhibited by the drug. This reaction requires the participation of an electron transfer protein (ferredoxin in clostridia), which has a redox potential of about -450 mV. The redox potential of metronidazole is -560 mV, and it acts as an electron sink, drawing off electrons from the reduced electron transfer protein.

There are several ways in which this could be toxic to the cell. First, the reducing equivalents may be needed to synthesize compounds (e.g., NADH, NADPH) vital to cell survival. Second, in drawing off electrons via the nitro group, the drug appears to become irreversibly reduced and the ring is cleaved.[23] This reduced drug product could be the primary toxic form. This is an intriguing possibility, since the organism would, in effect, be carrying out a "lethal synthesis" by converting a relatively innocuous substance into a toxic compound. Regardless of the mechanism of cell death, the selective toxicity of metronidazole is explained, in this model, by the assumption that only anaerobic organisms have redox systems of the appropriate negative potential with which the nitroimidazoles can interact. Although the model for the mechanism of action has not been completely worked out, it offers a reasonable explanation for the available biochemical data and an attractive hypothesis.

Radioactive metronidazole enters and is retained by *E. histolytica*, but at the same concentration and with the same experimental methods, no drug became associated with cultured human cells.[24] If this observation reflects a difference in the permeability of the host cell and the target cell to the drug, this difference could also contribute to the selective toxicity. Although mammalian cells under normal conditions can tolerate quite high concentrations of metronidazole, the drug has been shown to radiosensitize hypoxic cells.[25] Some other antimicrobial agents, such as nitro-furantoin and nitrofurazone (Chapter 7), have been shown to have a similar radiosensitizing effect.[26] The mechanism is not known, but the effect may prove useful as an adjunct to radiation therapy of certain tumors containing significant numbers of hypoxic cells.

Pharmacology and Untoward Effects of Metronidazole

Metronidazole is given orally. In most cases, absorption from the gastrointestinal tract is good, but therapeutic failure due to low blood levels possibly resulting from poor intestinal absorption has been reported.[27] Metronidazole distributes into a volume of about 80 per cent of the body weight and the half-life of elimination is about 8.5 hours.[28,29] High levels are achieved in the cerebrospinal fluid, and there is almost no binding to serum protein. Metronidazole is extensively metabolized by oxidation and glucuronide formation. The principal route of excretion is via the kidney, with about 10 per cent of the drug being excreted unchanged[28] and the rest in the form of metabolites that have little or no antimicrobial activity.[30]

The most frequently encountered undesirable effects of metronidazole are nausea, vomiting, epigastric distress, diarrhea, and headache. The drug can produce a metallic taste, and when given in the higher doses usually employed for the treatment of amebiasis, the metabolites can discolor the urine. Reversible leukopenia sometimes occurs. Rarely, nervous system toxicity, including weakness, paresthesias, vertigo, and ataxia, has been observed. Metronidazole can also produce unpleasant sensations in some patients when they drink alcoholic beverages. Because of this disulfiram-like effect metronidazole was at one time tried for the treatment of alcoholism but it was not found to be useful. Metronidazole inhibits liver alcohol dehydrogenase, but since this inhibition occurs at concentrations approximately 100 times those found in the serum during therapy, it is unlikely that this is related to the effect.[31,32] In the course of evaluating its usefulness in the therapy of alcoholism, it was found that the simultaneous administration of metronidazole and disulfiram can produce psychosis.[33] The basis of this drug interaction is not known.

Metronidazole has been found to be both carcinogenic and mutagenic. Rats fed large amounts of the drug have an increased incidence of lung cancer,[34] and the mutation rate of bacteria exposed to the drug is increased.[35] Most disturbing is the observation that bacteria (excision-repair-deficient test strains) show a marked increase in mutation rate when exposed to urine from patients receiving doses of the drug that are normal for the treatment of trichomoniasis.[36] Thus, metronidazole usage, especially on a widespread basis, as in treating trichomoniasis, carries a certain risk. The drug has been used in pregnant patients without gross evidence that it produces fetal malformation,[37] but it is prudent to avoid use during pregnancy whenevery possible.

Trichomonas vaginalis can be made resistant to metronidazole, but this has not been a problem during therapy.[38] Failure of therapy has been reported to occur because of metabolism of the drug by vaginal bacteria.[39]

Emetine and Dehydroemetine

Emetine was the mainstay of treatment of severe intestinal and extraintestinal amebiasis for many years. The emetines kill the trophozoite forms of the amebas directly, but they are not very active against the cyst form of E. hystolytica in the intestinal wall. In the treatment of hepatic abscess, the combination of an ementine and chloroquine is more effective and relapses occur less frequently than with either drug alone.[40] Emetine and dehydroemetine have similar potencies in vitro, and when an identical dose of either drug is given in combination with chloroquine in the treatment of hepatic abscess, the therapeutic result is the same.[41]

Mechanism of Action of the Emetines

Emetine is one of several compounds that inhibit protein synthesis in eukaryotic but not in prokaryotic (e.g., bacteria) cells. Thus, the emetines block the synthesis of protein in both parasites and mammalian cells. Much of the information regarding the mechanism of action has been obtained by studying the drug effects in mammalian systems. When emetine is added to human cells in culture, there is a rapid and irreversible inhibition of protein synthesis and a lesser and delayed effect on RNA synthesis (Figure 11-2).[42] There is also rapid inhibition of DNA synthesis, but this is most probably secondary to a primary effect on protein synthesis, since in animal cells, protein synthesis is required for concurrent synthesis of DNA.

Emetine has been shown to immobilize the polyribosome structure in both cultured human cells[42] and in amebae.[43] This observation and other evidence obtained in cell-free protein synthesiz-

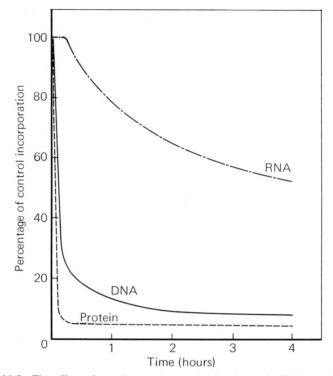

Figure 11-2   The effect of emetine on the synthesis of protein, RNA, and DNA in HeLa cells. HeLa cell suspensions were incubated with emetine ($10^{-6}M$) and radioactive precursors of DNA, RNA, and protein. The amount of incorporation was determined for 10-minute periods and is expressed as a percentage of the incorporation seen in control suspensions without the drug. (Redrawn from Grollman.[42])

ing systems[44] suggest that emetine inhibits polypeptide chain elongation, not initiation (cf. Figure 3-2). Emetine is structurally similar to cycloheximide (Figure 11-3).[45] Cycloheximide also inhibits protein synthesis in eukaryotic cells but not in prokaryotic systems; and like emetine, it blocks polypeptide chain elongation and immobilizes the polysomes. In the presence of emetine, puromycin releases nascent peptide chains bound to ribosomes.[46,47] This suggests that emetine does not inhibit peptide bond formation. Since cycloheximide blocks puromycin release of nascent peptide chains, its action may differ somewhat from that of emetine.[47] Thus, the available data are consistent with the interpretation that emetine inhibits that portion of the translocation process involving movement of the ribosome along the

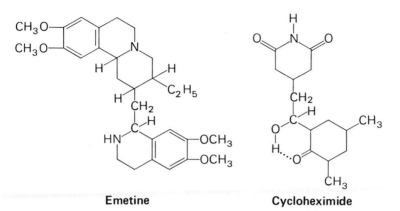

Emetine   **Cycloheximide**

Figure 11-3 Structures of emetine and cycloheximide. The dotted line between the ketone and hydroxyl groups of cycloheximide represents hydrogen bonding. The similarity of structure between such glutarimide antibiotics as cyclohex-imide and the ipecac alkaloids (emetine) was demonstrated by Grollman.[45]

mRNA. It is not clear what part of the protein synthesizing system contains the emetine receptor site.

Since the protein synthesizing machinery is inhibited in the cells of both the parasite and the host, there must be some other basis for the selective toxicity of emetine at the doses used to treat amebiasis. For example, entry of the drug into the mammalian cell may be restricted, or the consequences of partial inhibition of protein synthesis may be more severe in the parasite than in the host. As might be predicted, emetine has been shown to have some anti-tumor activity in model animal systems. The life-span of mice bearing Ehrlich ascites carcinoma[48] or leukemia L1210[49] is increased by treatment with emetine.

Pharmacology and Untoward Effects of the Emetines

Emetine and dehydroemetine are administered subcutaneously or intramuscularly. Oral administration is not used, since the drug often produces nausea and vomiting by this route. Because the drug is cardiotoxic, the intravenous route is contraindicated. Animal studies indicate that more emetine is concentrated in the liver, kidney, spleen, and lung than in heart muscle[50] The relative sensitivity of the heart to the toxic effects of the emetines therefore cannot be explained by selective concentration of the drug in that organ, but concentration of the drug in the liver may very well contribute to its efficacy in treating hepatic amebiasis. The nature and extent of the metabolism of emetine in man are not known. The principal route of excretion in humans has been assumed to be the kidney, but this is not well documented. After intraperitoneal administration of radioactive emetine to guinea pigs, 95 per cent of the radioactivity was recovered in the feces, whereas only 5 per cent appeared in the urine.[51] The rate of excretion is slow and high drug levels can readily build up in the body. The total dosage administered must, therefore, be carefully monitored. The drug is given at a dose of 1 mg/kg daily (up to a maximum of 60 mg) for no more than 10 days. This total dosage limit (600 mg) should not be exceeded.

The emetines are irritating compounds and their administration is often accompanied by pain, tenderness, and muscle weakness at the site of injection. Nausea and vomiting are occasionally observed even though the drug is given parenterally. This is probably due to a central action. Emetine can also induce diarrhea. This effect, as well as the hypotensive effect of emetine, may occur as a result of a blockade of the sympathetic nervous system.[52,53] The fact that the drug itself causes diarrhea can complicate assessment of the response to therapy in the patient who has amebic dysentery. The cardiotoxic effects of emetine include tachycardia, abnormalities in the electrocardiogram, dyspnea, and sometimes precordial pain.[54] Electrocardiographic abnormalities, such as lengthening of the P-R and Q-T intervals and flattening or inversion of the T waves, occurred in approximately 50 per cent of the patients in one large study.[54] Changes in cardiac rhythm are unusual. The electrocardiographic abnormalities rarely regress unless the drug is discontinued. Both electrocardiographic changes and signs of myositis may appear after cessation of therapy. The neuromuscular effect, characterized by general muscle weakness and aching, may be due to a blocking action of emetine at or near the neuromuscular junction.[53] True neuritis probably does not occur. The side effects of dehydroemetine are similar to those of emetine, although it appears to be less cardiotoxic.[51,55] In the United States, dehydroemetine may be obtained from the Center for Disease Control, Atlanta, Georgia.

The mechanism of the cardiotoxic effect of emetine is not known. A number of studies indicate that the drug has a direct and primary depressant action on the myocardium.[56] At extraordinarily high concentrations, emetine inhibits oxidative phosphorylation in suspensions of dog heart mitochondria[57]; it is unlikely, however, that this inhibition is responsible for the cardiotoxicity. In one study, it was shown that emetine at low concentration (10^{-7} M) inhibits the incorporation of radioactive leucine into protein in rat heart muscle preparations.[58] It is not clear whether this represents a direct or an indirect inhibition of protein synthesis. It is significant that inhibition of amino acid incorporation was observed in heart muscle specimens prepared from animals injected with emetine at a dosage (1.3 mg/kg daily for 3 days) near the therapeutic range. It is possible (although there are certainly many other potentially valid explanations) that the therapeutic and cardiotoxic effects of emetine result from inhibition of the same biochemical process (protein synthesis) in the parasite and the host.

It is clear that certain precautions in patient management are warranted in view of the toxicity of the emetines. An electrocardiogram should be taken before therapy is initiated and repeatedly thereafter. The patient should remain sedentary during therapy and for a while thereafter. Emetine should not be used in patients with heart disease, in children, or in pregnant women unless absolutely necessary—that is, if metronidazole and chloroquine are ineffective. If a 10-day course of emetine therapy is not successful, one should wait 2 months before initiating a second course.

Diiodohydroxyquin

Several iodinated 8-hydroxyquinolines are effective in the treatment of intestinal amebiasis; these include diiodohydroxyquin, iodochlorhydroxyquin, and chiniofon. Diiodohydroxyquin is most commonly used in the United States. These drugs are amebicidal, and their mechanism of action is not known.

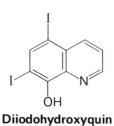

Diiodohydroxyquin

Diiodohydroxyquin is used alone (650 mg three times a day for 20 days) to treat asymptomatic cyst passers and in combination with a tetracycline to treat the patient with mild intestinal disease (Table 11-1). In the case of severe intestinal disease, diiodohydroxyquin may be given after completion of a short course of emetine therapy. The drug is a luminal amebicide and has no effect on hepatic abscesses. This lack of effectiveness against *E. histolytica* in the liver probably reflects the low concentration of the drug in this organ. Amebae in the gut would be exposed to much higher concentrations.

Diiodohydroxyquin is considered by many specialists to be the drug of choice for the treatment of *Dientamoeba fragilis* infection and an alternative to the tetracyclines in *Balantidium coli* infection (balantidiasis). The dosage here is the same as for treating amebiasis, but the duration of therapy is half as long (10 days). In the United States, these two applications are still considered to be under investigational status. Diiodohydroxyquin, at high dosage and upon chronic administration, is reputed to be useful in the treatment of acrodermatitis enteropathica, a hereditary disease characterized by vesiculobullous and eczematoid skin lesions and diarrhea.[59] The pathophysiology of this condition is not known, and reports of the effectiveness of treatment with diiodohydroxyquin are, as yet, largely anecdotal in nature.

Diiodohydroxyquin is not readily absorbed from the gastrointestinal tract. About 5 per cent of a single oral dose can be recovered in the urine as the glucuronide conjugate and a small amount is excreted as the sulfate.[60] Considerably more iodochlorhydroxyquin than diiodohydroxyquin is absorbed—about 25 per cent of an oral dose.[61] The small amount of diiodohydroxyquin that is absorbed has a plasma half-life of about 12 hours.[61]

Diiodohydroxyquin occasionally causes headache, diarrhea, nausea, vomiting, skin rashes, and anal pruritis. Although the systemic absorption of this iodinated drug is limited, slight enlargement of the thyroid gland is occasionally observed. The drug can interfere with some thyroid function tests. It should not be given to people who have a known iodine sensitivity. The most important untoward effect associated with the 8-hydroxyquinolines is subacute myelo-optic neuropathy. This syndrome includes dysesthesia, weakness, and other manifestations of peripheral neuropathy; it is sometimes accompanied by loss of visual acuity and even optic atrophy with permanent blindness. The mechanism of the toxicity is unknown. It was first noticed in Japan where iodochlorhydroxyquin was being sold without prescription.[62] Although the bulk of the cases have involved iodochlorhydroxyquin, blindness can result from diiodohydroxyquin administration as well.[63] Before this effect was recognized, the halogenated hydroxyquinolines were used to treat chronic non-specific diarrhea in children and to prevent, as well as treat, "traveler's" diarrhea.[64] Such nonspecific use of these drugs is clearly unwarranted.

DRUGS EMPLOYED IN THE TREATMENT OF LEISHMANIASIS AND TRYPANOSOMIASIS

The Diseases

There are three principal diseases caused by *Leishmania:* visceral leishmaniasis (kala-azar), the result of infection with L. *donovani;* cutaneous leishmaniasis (oriental sore), L. *tropica;* and American mucocutaneous leishmaniasis, L. *braziliensis.* The *Leishmania* organisms, which assume the flagellated form in the insect vector and in culture, are ovoid unflagellated organisms in man; they are transmitted from a reservoir of numerous species of small animals and rodents to the human host by the bite of sandflies of the genus *Phlebotomus.* Visceral leishmaniasis is a disease of gradual onset characterized by fever, weight loss, hepatosplenomegaly, lymphadenopathy, hemorrhage, and hepatic malfunction. When untreated, this disease is fatal in a high percentage of cases. Cutaneous leishmaniasis is characterized by a superficial ulceration of the skin at the site of the bite. The organism can be identified in scrapings from the edge of the ulcerations, which are prone to superinfection. American mucocutaneous leishmaniasis occurs in several different forms. There may be extensive ulceration of the mucous membrane of the mouth, palate, pharynx, and nose. Progressive and grossly disfiguring erosion takes place.

Trypanosomiasis also occurs in three forms. The first two forms produce a similar clinical picture, and both are called African trypanosomiasis (sleeping sickness). One form is caused by *Trypanosoma gambiense,* the other by *Trypanosoma rhodesiense.* Both are transmitted to humans by the bite of an infected *Glossina* (tsetse fly). The first stage of the disease is characterized by invasion of the lymphatic system, with lymphadenopathy, hepatosplenomegaly, intermittent febrile attacks, dyspnea, and tachycardia. The chronic, sleeping-sickness stage is initiated by invasion of the central nervous system. This stage is marked by headache, increasing mental dullness and apathy, and disturbances in coordinated neurological functions. In the final stages, the patient sleeps continually, emaciation becomes profound, and coma and death result. Although the symptomatology of the two diseases is similar, the symptoms develop sooner, and the disease progresses more rapidly with T. rhodesiense. The third form of the disease, called South American trypanosomiasis (Chagas' disease), is caused by Trypanosoma cruzi and is transmitted to man by reduviid bugs. These organisms evoke a symptom complex quite unlike the African trypanosomes. Myocarditis is a prominent feature of Chagas' disease. The various diseases caused by the blood and tissue flagellates have been reviewed in a Ciba Foundation Symposium.[65]

The drugs most commonly employed in the treatment of leishmaniasis are the pentavalent antimonial preparations (e.g., sodium stibogluconate). Antimonials are also used extensively for the treatment of schistosomiasis and they are discussed in the section on the treatment of fluke infections in Chapter 12. Pentamidine, amphotericin B, and cycloguanil pamoate are also effective against some forms of leishmaniasis (Table 11-3). African trypa-

Table 11-3 **Drugs used to treat leishmaniasis and trypanosomiasis**
Amphotericin B and primaquine are presented in Chapters 9 and 10, respectively. Sodium stibogluconate, a pentavalent antimony compound, is presented with other antimonial drugs in Chapter 12.

Infecting organism	Drug of choice	Alternative
Leishmaniasis	Sodium	
Leishmania donovani (kala-azar, visceral leishmaniasis)	stibogluconate	Pentamidine
Leishmania tropica (oriental sore, cutaneous leishmaniasis)	Sodium stibogluconate	
Leishmania braziliensis (American mucocutaneous leishmaniasis)	Sodium stibogluconate	Amphotericin B or cycloguanil pamoate
African Trypanosomiasis		
Trypanosoma gambiense	Pentamidine	Suramin
Trypanosoma rhodesiense	Suramin	Pentamidine
Either T. gambiense or T. rhodesiense in late disease with central nervous system involvement	Melarsoprol	Tryparsamide plus suramin
South American Trypanosomiasis (Chagas' disease)		
Trypanosoma cruzi	Nifurtimox	Primaquine

nosomiasis in the hemolymphatic stage is effectively treated with pentamidine or suramin. After the parasite has invaded the central nervous system, melarsoprol is the drug of choice. Until recently, no drugs were known to be effective in the treatment of Chagas' disease. Primaquine is useful in destroying the extracellular trypanosomes in the blood, but it is not effective against the intracellular form of the parasite. The investigational drug nifurtimox is reported to be effective against the intracellular stage as well. Physicians in the United States must obtain many of these drugs (pentamidine, suramin, melarsoprol, nifurtimox) from the Center for Disease Control, Atlanta, Georgia.

Pentamidine

Pentamidine is one of a number of diamidine compounds, including propamidine and stilbamidine, which have trypanocidal activity. Another diamidine, hydroxystilbamidine, is occasionally used in the treatment of North American blastomycosis (Chapter 9). Pentamidine isethionate is useful in the treatment of early trypanosomiasis before central nervous system involvement and in chemoprophylaxis. Pentamidine is also effective against some forms of leishmaniasis. The physician practicing in Europe or North America does not come into contact with these diseases, although very rarely they are diagnosed in travelers who become symptomatic after returning home.[66] The experience of the American physician with this drug has been primarily in the treatment of infection by Pneumocystis carinii. This organism is often classed as a protozoan, but its taxonomic position is not completely clear. Pneumocystis carinii is an opportunistic organism, since it produces pneumonitis almost exclusively in the compromised host, most commonly in patients with malignant disease or organ transplants who are receiving immunosuppressive therapy.[67,68] Pentamidine has been the drug of choice for treatment of Pneumocystis carinii pneumonitis (Table 11-1),[68,69] but this infection also responds well to trimethoprim–sulfamethoxazole (Chapter 5)[70] or pyrimethamine plus sulfadiazine (Chapter 10).[71]

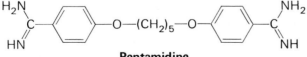

Pentamidine

The mechanism of action of pentamidine is not yet defined. Other trypanocidal diamidines with structures analogous to pentamidine (hydroxystilbamidine, berenil) have been shown to bind to DNA and polynucleotides, but they do not intercalate between the base pairs as does chloroquine (Figure 10-5).[72] In the case of the diamidines, it is possible that the DNA binding may be related to the trypanocidal action. When diamidines are added to trypanosomes growing in culture, they interact selectively with kinetoplast DNA[73,74] The kinetoplast is a specialized structure that contains its own DNA (as opposed to the nuclear DNA), and in trypanosomes, this prominent body is a part of the mitochondrial system. The diamidines cause a disorganization of the kinetoplast DNA and the organelle eventually loses its nucleic acid. It has been proposed that the bound drug may interfere with kinetoplast DNA replication.[75]

Pentamidine is not well absorbed from the gastrointestinal tract and it is routinely administered by intramuscular injection (it can also be given intravenously). The regimen for treatment of pneumocystosis or trypanosomiasis is 4 mg/kg daily for 12 to 14 days. For prophylaxis against African trypanosomiasis, the same dosage is given once every 3 to 6 months. In mice, pentamidine is stored in the tissues and slowly excreted in the urine, predominantly or totally as the unchanged drug.[76] The available data also suggest that the drug in man is retained by tissue binding and excreted over an extended period of time.[76] The highest levels of pentamidine are found in the kidney, a localization that may contribute to its renal toxicity.[76] In experimental animals, the drug can be found in such tissues as the liver and kidney months after treatment has stopped. This retention is probably important in permitting the drug to be effective for several months when used for chemoprophylaxis of African trypanosomiasis. Pentamidine does not enter the central nervous system to any extent. Therefore, it cannot be used to treat trypanosomiasis during the later phases of the disease, which are marked by central nervous system involvement.

The administration of pentamidine sometimes causes pain at the injection site, and this can be followed by abscess formation and tissue necrosis. The drug is quite toxic. In one survey, for example, 69 out of 164 patients experienced side effects.[69] Immediate reactions, including hypotension, tachycardia, and vomiting, are seen, especially when the drug is given intravenously. Pentamidine can cause hypoglycemia and particular care must be taken in the treatment of the diabetic. Reversible renal and hepatic damage occur in a substantial percentage of patients. Blood dyscrasias have also been reported.

Suramin

Suramin is a compound developed from a group of nonmetallic dyes, such as trypan blue, that are known to have trypanocidal activity. It is used in the treatment of both types of African trypanosomiasis in the early stages of the disease. Suramin is also effective in the treatment of infection by one of the filaria, *Onchocerca volvulus*. In this case, it is employed in combination with or following a course of therapy with diethylcarbamazine.

Suramin

Exposure of trypanosomes to suramin *in vitro* at concentrations as low as 10^{-5} M reduces their infectivity, but even at 10^{-2} M the drug does not affect the motility or respiration of the cells.[77] At concentrations of 10^{-5} to 10^{-4} M, suramin inhibits a wide variety of enzymes. It is interesting that the kinetics of the enzyme inhibition are sometimes competitive. For example, the drug reversibly inhibits several components of the complement system in an apparently competitive manner.[78] It has been suggested that the large, negatively charged drug just binds nonspecifically to cationic sites on proteins, and in the case of some enzymes, the binding is sufficient to produce a reversible inactivation. Its selective toxicity in trypanosomes has not been explained. Suramin does not diffuse across mammalian or yeast cell membranes and it is probably selectively taken into trypanosomes, perhaps by pinocytosis. If it could enter host cells, the drug would be too toxic to be useful in therapy. That the poor permeability property of the drug is critical to limiting its toxicity is pointed up by the effect of suramin on the sodium pump in red blood cells. Exposure of intact red cells to low concentrations of suramin does not affect the activity of (Na^+-K^+)-activated ATPase. But when the red cell membrane is ruptured and suramin is allowed to enter the cell, it is a potent inhibitor of the ATPase at the inside surface of the membrane.[79]

Suramin is administered by slow intravenous injection. Because the drug can occasionally cause serious immediate reactions (nausea, vomiting, shock, and loss of consciousness), a 100- to 200-mg test dose is given initially to assess the patient's tolerance. If this is not attended by severe reaction, a dose of 1 gm is given on days 1, 3, 7, 14, and 21 in the therapy of sleeping sickness and at weekly intervals for *O. volvulus* infection. If there is intolerance to the test dose, therapy should not be initiated. The cause of the intolerance is not known. Suramin does not penetrate into the central nervous system, and in the treatment of trypanosomiasis with central nervous system involvement, an arsenical must also be employed. The drug binds tightly to proteins, a predictable effect for a dye derivative. This avid protein binding causes the drug to persist in the circulation for a long time. The slow release from plasma protein and the slow excretion by the kidney permit the drug to be administered on a bimonthly basis for chemoprophylaxis of sleeping sickness.

Suramin causes a variety of nervous system side effects including paresthesias, hyperesthesia of the palms and soles, peripheral neuropathy, and photophobia. It can precipitate immediate urticaria and pruritus as well as delayed skin rashes. The drug is nephrotoxic, and frequent urinalyses should be performed to monitor for the proteinuria that often occurs during therapy. Hematuria and cylinduria occur when renal damage is extensive, and special caution must be exercised in patients with preexisting renal disease. Rarely, blood dyscrasias and hemolytic anemia have been reported with therapy.

The Arsenicals

There are several organic arsenical drugs that have been employed in treating trypanosomiasis. Because of toxicity their use in all but the meningoencephalitic stages of sleeping sickness has been discontinued, and pentamidine and suramin are used instead. The arsenicals are produced in trivalent (melarsoprol) and pentavalent (tryparsamide) forms with the toxic and antiparasitic actions produced by the trivalent form. Tryparsamide, some of which is converted to the trivalent form *in vivo,* is no longer widely used; it is not available in the United States.

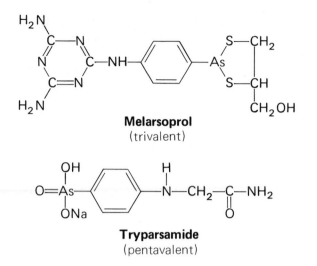

Melarsoprol
(trivalent)

Tryparsamide
(pentavalent)

The arsenicals interact with sulfhydryl (SH) groups in proteins, and they have been shown to inactivate a wide variety of enzymes. The integrity of SH groups is essential in maintaining the appropriate structure and consequently the function of a number of enzymes. Many of the toxic effects, as well as the trypanocidal action of organic arsenicals, are probably due to inactivation of SH groups.

Given a nonspecific mechanism of action such as this, one could predict that the arsenicals are very toxic drugs. The prediction is true; side effects are common. The basis of the selective toxicity of these agents is not completely clear, but a differential permeability between the host cells and trypanosomes may be important. Resistance to the arsenical drugs occurs, and there is evidence that the parasites become resistant because they take up less drug.[80] The nonmetallic moiety of the drug probably contributes to some specificity of action. Of the many enzymes that can be affected, the terminal glycolytic enzyme pyruvate kinase may be the primary site of the trypanocidal action.[81] There are differences between pyruvate kinases of mammalian and trypanosomal origin.[82] Some of the selective toxicity of the organic arsenical drugs may be attributable to the special sensitivity of this critical enzyme in the trypanosome.

Melarsoprol and tryparsamide would not be used in therapy but for the fact that they penetrate into the cerebrospinal fluid. Melarsoprol is the drug of choice for the treatment of trypanosomal meningoencephalitis (Table 11-3).[83] Melarsoprol is also active against the earlier stages of the disease, but it is not used before central nervous system involvement occurs because of its potential for causing encephalopathy. It is administered by slow intravenous injection. The drug is very irritating to tissues and special care must be taken to ensure that extravasation does not take place during injection. As with many of the drugs used in the treatment of parasitic infections, the dosage schedule is complex. For example, in one regimen it is given once a day on three consecutive days in doses of 1.5, 2, and 2.2 mg/kg, followed, after a 7-day interval, by doses of 2.5, 3, and 3.6 mg/kg, and finally, after another 7-day interval, by a third 3-day course of 3.6 mg/kg.[66] In children and underweight patients even more cautious dosage regimens are employed.[84] Doses of more than 3.6 mg/kg are not used. Patients who are severely debilitated are treated with suramin before initiation of melarsoprol therapy.[83] The concentration of drug achieved in cerebrospinal fluid is only 2 to 20 per cent that of plasma, but this is sufficient for the trypanocidal effect.[85] The rate of drug elimination is fairly rapid—after a 3-day course of therapy, the plasma level of active drug in man drops by 50 per cent in about 24 hours.[85]

Melarsoprol therapy is often accompanied by side effects, which include hypertension, abdominal pain, vomiting, albuminuria, peripheral neuropathy, arthralgia, angioneurotic edema, and rashes.[84] The first administration of drug is sometimes followed by an exacerbation of fever. This is thought to represent a Herxheimer-type reaction. A serious and potentially fatal side effect is the development of reactive encephalopathy. This central nervous system reaction is the most common side effect, occurring in 12.5 per cent of patients in one large study.[84] Melarsoprol should only be given in the hospital since the patient's condition must be closely monitored.

Nifurtimox

In contrast to the trypanosomes that cause African sleeping sickness, T. cruzi, the etiological agent of Chagas' disease, multiplies intracellularly as the amastigote form. Its intracellular location has contributed to the difficulty in finding therapeutically useful drugs against the disease. The development of a method of growing T. cruzi within cells in tissue culture facilitated the conduction of large-scale drug screening programs. With the help of cell cultures and animal screening models, a nitrofuran derivative, nifurtimox, was found to be active against both the intracellular amastigote and the extracellular mastigote stages of the parasite.[86] Nifurtimox irreversibly inhibits development of the intracellular parasite at concentrations that do not damage human cells in culture.[87] The mechanism of the drug action is unknown.

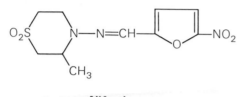

Nifurtimox

(Bayer 2502)

Nifurtimox is effective in eradicating the parasite both from patients with acute infection[88] and those with the chronic stage of the disease[89] (characterized by myocardiopathy and colonic and esophageal dilation). The drug is given orally according to a complicated dosage schedule. The duration of therapy is 120 days. Nifurtimox is well absorbed from the gastrointestinal tract and rapidly and extensively metabolized. The metabolites are excreted predominantly by the kidney—there is virtually no unaltered drug in the urine.[90,91] The incidence of undesirable side effects attributable to the drug is unclear because many placebo-treated Chagas' disease patients have the same complaints.[88] Side effects appear to be more common in adults than children; they are generally mild, however, and therapy must be discontinued in only about 5 per cent of patients. The most commonly reported untoward reactions (complaint by more than 10 per cent of adults under treatment) are anorexia, nausea, and vomiting; stomach pain; nervous excitation; vertigo; headache; myalgia; insomnia; and skin rashes.[88]

REFERENCES

1. R. S. Desowtiz: Antiparasite chemotherapy. *Ann. Rev. Pharmacol.* 11:351 (1971).

2. S. J. Powell, A. J. Wilmot, and R. Elsdon-Dew: Further trials of metronidazole in amoebic dysentery and amoebic liver abscess. *Ann. Trop. Med. Parasit.* 61:511 (1969).

3. S. J. Powell, A. J. Wilmot, and R. Elsdon-Dew: Single and low dosage regimens of metronidazole in amoebic dysentery and amoebic liver abscess. *Ann. Trop. Med. Parasit.* 63:139 (1969).

4. F. Scott and M. J. Miller: Trials with metranidazole in amebic dysentery. *J. Am. Med. Assoc.* 211:118 (1970).

5. S. J. Powell: New developments in the therapy of amoebiasis. *Gut* 11:967 (1970).

6. Drugs for parasitic infections. *Med. Letter* 16:5 (1974).

7. S. J. Powell and R. Elsdon-Dew: Some new nitroimidazole derivatives: Clinical trials in amebic liver abscess. *Am. J. Trop. Med. Hyg.* 21:518 (1972).

8. M. W. Fisher and P. E. Thompson: "Antibiotics with specific affinities. Part 3: Paromomycin" in *Experimental Chemotherapy* (ed. R. J. Schnitzer and F. Hawking). New York: Academic Press, 1964, pp. 329–345.

9. B. P. Phillips and P. A. Wolfe: The use of germfree guinea pigs in studies on the microbial interrelationships in amoebiasis. *Ann. N.Y. Acad. Sci.* 78:308 (1959).

10. M. S. Wolfe: Nondysenteric intestinal amebiasis: Treatment with diloxanide furoate. *J. Am. Med. Assoc.* 224:1601 (1973).

11. S. J. Powell and E. J. Stewart-Wynne: Metronidazole combined with diloxanide furoate in amoebic liver abscess. *Ann. Trop. Med. Parasitol.* 67:367 (1973).

12. P. D. Marsden and M. G. Schultz: Intestinal parasites. *Gastroenterology* 57:724 (1969).

13. S. J. Powell, I. MacLeod, A. J. Wilmot, and R. Elsdon-Dew: Metronidazole in amoebic dysentery and amoebic liver abscess. *Lancet* 2:1329 (1966).

14. H. C. Hesseltine and G. Lefebvre: Treating vaginal trichomoniasis with metronidazole. *J. Am. Med. Assoc.* 184:1011 (1963).

15. M. S. Wolfe: Giardiasis. *J. Am. Med. Assoc.* 233:1362 (1975).

16. K. O. Padonu: A controlled trial of metronidazole in the treatment of dracontiasis in Nigeria. *Am. J. Trop. Med. Hyg.* 22:42 (1973).

17. J. A. Antani, H. V. Srinivas, K. R. Krishnamurthy, and A. N. Bargaonkar: Metronidazole in dracunculiasis: Report of further trials. *Am. J. Trop. Med. Hyg.* 21:178 (1972).

18. D. W. Belcher, F. K. Wurapa, and W. B. Wardi: Failure of thiabendazole and metronidazole in the treatment and suppression of guineaworm disease. *Am. J. Trop. Med. Hyg.* 24:444 (1975).

19. L. J. Nastro and S. M. Finegold: Bactericidal activity of five antimicrobial agents against *Bacteroides fragilis*. *J. Infect. Dis.* 126:104 (1972).

20. A. W. Chow, V. Patten, and L. B. Guze: Susceptibility of anaerobic bacteria to metronidazole: Relative resistance of non-spore-forming gram-positive bacilli. *J. Infect. Dis.* 131:182 (1975).

21. K. W. Stephen, M. F. McLatchie, D K. Mason, H. W. Noble, and D. M. Stevenson: Treatment of acute ulcerative gingivitis (Vincent's type). *Br. Dent. J.* 121:313 (1966).

22. D. I. Edwards and G. E. Mathison: The mode of action of metronidazole against *Trichomonas vaginalis*. *J. Gen. Microbiol.* 63:297 (1970).

23. D. I. Edwards, M. Dye, and H. Carne: The selective toxicity of antimicrobial nitroheterocyclic drugs. *J. Gen. Microbiol.* 76:135 (1973).

24. H. B. Tanowitz, M. Wittner, R. M. Rosenbaum, and Y. Kress: In vitro studies on the differential toxicity of metronidazole in protozoa and mammalian cells. *Ann. Trop. Med. Parasitol.* 69:19 (1975).

25. H. B. Stone and H. R. Withers: Tumor and normal tissue response to metronidazole and irradiation in mice. *Radiology* 113:441 (1974).

26. J. D. Chapman, A. P. Reuvers, J. Borsa, A. Petkau, and D. R. McCalla: Nitrofurans as radiosensitizers of hypoxic mammalian cells. *Cancer Res.* 32:2616 (1972).

27. P. O. Kane, J. A. McFadzean, and S. Squires: Absorption and excretion of metronidazole. *Br. J. Vener. Dis.* 37:276 (1961).

28. D. E. Schwartz and F. Jeunet: Comparative pharmacokinetic studies of ornidazole and metronidazole in man. *Chemotherapy* 22:19 (1976).

29. E. D. Ralph, J. T. Clarke, R. D. Libke, R. P. Luthy, and W. M. M. Kirby: Pharmacokinetics of metronidazole as determined by bioassay. *Antimicrob. Agents Chemother.* 6:691 (1974).

30. E. D. Ralph and W. M. M. Kirby: Bioassay of metronidazole with either anaerobic or aerobic incubation. *J. Infect. Dis.* 132:587 (1975).

31. J. A. Edwards and J. Price: Metronidazole and human alcohol dehydrogenase. *Nature* 214:190 (1967).

32. N. K. Gupta, C. L. Woodley, and R. Fried: Effect of metronidazole on liver alcohol dehydrogenase. *Biochem. Pharmacol.* 19:2805 (1970).

33. E. Rothstein and D. D. Clancy: Toxicity of disulfiram combined with metronidazole. *New Eng. J. Med.* 180:1006 (1969).

34. M. Rustia and P. Shubik: Induction of lung tumors and malignant lymphomas in mice by metronidazole. *J. Natl. Canc. Inst.* 48:721 (1972).

35. C. E. Voogd, J. J. Van der Stel, and J. J. Jacobs: The mutagenic action of nitroimidazoles. I Metronidazole, nimorazole, dimetridazole and ronidazole. *Mutat. Res.* 26:483 (1974).

36. M. S. Legator, T. H. Connor, and M. Stoeckel: Detection of mutagenic activity of metronidazole and niridazole in body fluids of humans and mice. *Science* 188:1118 (1975).

37. W. F. Peterson, J. E. Stauch, and C. D. Ryder: Metronidazole in pregnancy. *Am. J. Obstet. Gynecol.* 94:343 (1966).

38. I. de Carneri, G. Achilli, G. Monti, and F. Trane: Induction of in-vivo resistance of *Trichomonas vaginalis* to metronidazole. *Lancet* 2:1308 (1969).

39. C. S. Nicol, A. J. Evans, J. A. McFadzean, and S. L. Squires: Inactivation of metronidazole. *Lancet* 2:441 (1966).

40. J. N. Scragg and S. J. Powell: Emetine hydrochloride and dehydroemetine combined with chloroquine in the treatment of children with amoebic liver abscess. *Arch. Dis. Child.* 43:121 (1968).

41. S. J. Powell, A. J. Wilmot, I. N. MacLeod, and R. Elsdon-Dew: A comparative trial of dehydroemetine and emetine hydrochloride in identical dosage in amoebic liver abscess. *Ann. Trop. Med. Parasitol.* 61:26 (1967).

42. A. P. Grollman: Inhibitors of protein synthesis: Effects of emetine on protein and nucleic acid biosynthesis in HeLa cells. *J. Biol. Chem.* 243:4089 (1968).

43. C. J. Flickinger: Ribosomal aggregates in amebae exposed to the protein synthesis inhibitor emetine. *Exptl. Cell. Res.* 74:541 (1972).

44. H. F. Lodish, D. Housman and M. Jacobsen: Initiation of hemoglobin synthesis: Specific inhibition by antibiotics and bacteriophage ribonucleic acid. *Biochemistry* 10:2348 (1971).

45. A. P. Grollman: Structural basis for inhibition of protein synthesis

by emetine and cycloheximide based on an analogy between ipecac alkaloids and glutarimide antibiotics. *Proc. Natl. Acad. Sci. U.S.* 56:1867 (1966).

46. A. P. Grollman and M. T. Huang: Inhibitors of protein synthesis in eukaryotes: Tools in cell research. *Fed. Proc.* 32:1673 (1973).

47. B. S. Baliga, S. A. Cohen, and H. N. Munro: Effect of cycloheximide on the reaction of puromycin with polysome-bound peptidyl-tRNA. *FEBS Letters* 8:249 (1970).

48. R. K. Johnson and W. R. Jondorf: Some inhibitory effects of (−)-emetine on growth of Ehrlich ascites carcinoma. *Biochem. J.* 140:87 (1974).

49. W. R. Jondorf, B. J. Abbott, N. H. Greenberg, and J. A. R. Mead: Increased lifespan of leukemic mice treated with drugs related to (−)-emetine. *Chemotherapy* 16:109 (1971).

50. A. I. Gimble, C. Davison, and P. K. Smith: Studies on the toxicity, distribution and excretion of emetine. *J. Pharmacol. Exptl. Ther.* 94:431 (1948).

51. D. E. Schwartz and J. Herrero: Comparative pharmacokinetic studies of dehydroemetine and emetine in guinea pigs using spectrofluorometric and radiometric methods. *Am. J. Trop. Med. Hyg.* 14:78 (1965).

52. K. K. F. Ng: A new pharmacological action of emetine. *Brit. Med. J.* 1:1278 (1966).

53. K. K. F. Ng: Blockade of adrenergic and cholinergic transmissions by emetine. *Br. J. Pharmac. Chemother.* 28:228 (1966).

54. G. Klatskin and H. Friedman: Emetine toxicity in man; studies on the nature of early toxic manifestations, their relation to dose level, and their significance in determining safe dosage. *Ann. Int. Med.* 28:892 (1948)

55. S. J. Powell, I. N. MacLeod, A. J. Wilmot, and R. Elsdon-Dew: The treatment of acute amebic dysentery. *Ann. Trop. Med. Parasit.* 59:205 (1965).

56. A. Bianchi, V. deMarino, G. R. deVleeschhouwer, and A. Marino: Effects of emetine on heart, coronary circulation and blood pressure (Research *in vitro* on the guinea pig heart and coronary flow; Research *in vivo* on the dog heart, coronary flow and blood pressure). *Arch. Int. Pharmacodyn.* 156:238 (1965).

57. M. L. Murphy, R. T. Bulloch, and M. B. Pearce: The correlation of metabolic and ultrastructural changes in emetine myocardial toxicity. *Am. Heart. J.* 87:105 (1974).

58. B. M. Beller: Observations on the mechanism of emetine poisoning of myocardial tissue. *Circulation Res.* 22:501 (1968).

59. K. H. Neldner, L. Hagler, W. R. Wise, F. B. Stifel, E. G. Lufkin, and R. H. Herman: Acrodermatitis enteropathica: A clinical and biochemical survey. *Arch. Dermatol.* 110:711 (1974).

60. L. Berggren and O. Hansson: Absorption of intestinal antiseptics derived from 8-hydroxyquinolines. *Clin. Pharm. Ther.* 9:67 (1968).

61. D. B. Jack and W. Riess: Pharmacokinetics of iodochlorhydroxyquin in man. *J. Pharmaceut. Sci.* 62:1929 (1973).

62. G. P. Oakley: The neurotoxicity of the halogenated hydroxyquinolines: A commentary. *J. Am. Med. Assoc.* 225:395 (1973).

63. D. I. Fleisher, R. S. Hepler, and J. W. Landau: Blindness during diiodohydroxyquin (Diodoquin) therapy: A case report. *Pediatrics* 54:106 (1974).

64. American Academy of Pediatrics Committee on Drugs: Blindness and neuropathy from diiodohydroxyquin-like drugs. *Pediatrics* 54:378 (1974).

65. Ciba Foundation Symposium: *Trypanosomiasis and Leishmaniasis with special reference to Chagas' disease,* Amsterdam: Associated Scientific Publishers, 1974.

66. H. C. Spencer, J. J. Gibson, R. E. Brodsky, and M. G. Schultz: Imported African trypanosomiasis in the United States. *Ann. Int. Med.* 82:633 (1975).

67. W. T. Hugues, R. A. Price, H.-K. Kim, T. P. Coburn, D. Grigsby, and S. Feldman: *Pneumocystis carinii* pneumonitis in children with malignancies. *J. Pediat.* 82:404 (1973).

68. P. D. Walzer, D. P. Perl, D. J. Krogstad, P. G. Rawson, and M. G. Schultz: *Pneumocystis carinii* pneumonia in the United States. *Ann. Int. Med.* 80:83 (1974).

69. K. A. Western, D. R. Perera, and M. G. Schultz: Pentamidine isethionate in the treatment of *Pneumocystic carinii* pneumonia. *Ann. Int. Med.* 73:695 (1970).

70. W. T. Hughes, S. Feldman, and S. K. Sanyal: Treatment of *Pneumocystis carinii* pneumonitiis with Trimethoprim-sulfamethoxazole. *Can. Med. Assoc. J.* 112 (Spec. No. 13):47S (1975).

71. H. B. Kirby, B. Kenamore, and J. C. Guckian: *Pneumocystis carinii* pneumonia treated with pyrimethamine and sulfadiazine. *Ann. Int. Med.* 75:505 (1971).

72. B. Festy and M. Daune: Hydroxystilbamidine. A nonintercalating drug as a probe of nucleic acid conformation. *Biochemistry* 12:4827 (1973).

73. E. Delain, Ch. Brack, G. Riou, and B. Festy: Ultrastructural alterations of *Trypanosoma cruzi* kinetoplast induced by the interaction of a trypanocidal drug (hydroxystilbamidine) with kinetoplast DNA. *J. Ultrastruct. Res.* 37:200 (1971).

74. Ch. Brack, E. Delain, G. Riou, and B. Festy: Molecular organization of the kinetoplast DNA of *Trypanosoma cruzi* with berenil, a DNA interacting drug. *J. Ultrastruct. Res.* 39:568 (1972).

75. Ch. Brack, E. Delain, and G. Riou: Replicating, covalently closed, circular DNA from kinetoplasts of *Trypanosoma cruzi. Proc. Natl. Acad. Sci. U.S.* 69:1642 (1972).

76. T. P. Waalkes, C. Denham, and V. T. DeVita: Pentamidine: Clinical pharmacologic correlations in man and mice. *Clin. Pharm. Ther.* 11:505 (1970).

77. B. A. Newton: "The chemotherapy of trypanosomiasis and leishmaniasis: towards a more rational approach" in *Trypanosomiasis and Leishmaniasis with Special Reference to Chagas' Disease,* Amsterdam: Associated Scientific Publishers, 1974, pp. 285–301.

78. J. S. C. Fong and R. A. Good: Suramin—a potent reversible and competitive inhibitor of complement systems. *Clin. Exp. Immunol.* 10:127 (1972).

79. P. A. G. Fortes, J. C. Ellory, and V. L. Lew: Suramin: A potent ATPase inhibitor which acts on the inside surface of the sodium pump. *Biochim. Biophys. Acta* 318:262 (1973).

80. F. Hawking: "Chemotherapy of trypanosomiasis" in *Experimental Chemotherapy Vol. I* (ed. R. J. Schnitzer and F. Hawking). New York: Academic Press, 1963, pp. 129–256.

81. I. B. R. Bowman, I. W. Flynn, and A. H. Fairlamb: Carbohydrate metabolism of pleomorphic strains of *Trypanosoma rhodesiense* and sites of action of arsenical drugs. *J. Parasitol.* 56:402 (1970).

82. I. W. Flynn and I. B. R. Bowman: Further studies on the mode of action of arsenicals on trypanosome pyruvate kinase. *Trans. Roy. Soc. Trop. Med. Hyg.* 63:121 (1969).

83. F.I.C. Apted: Four year's experience of melarsen oxide/BAL in the treatment of late stage Rhodesian sleeping sickness. *Trans. Roy. Soc. Trop. Med. Hyg.* 51:75 (1957).

84. D. H. H. Robertson: The treatment of sleeping sickness (mainly due to *Trypanosoma rhodesiense*) with melarsoprol. I. Reactions observed during treatment. *Trans. Roy. Soc. Trop. Med. Hyg.* 57:122 (1963).

85. F. Hawking: The concentration of melarsoprol (Mel B) and Mel W in plasma and cerebrospinal fluid estimated by bioassay with trypanosomes *in vitro. Trans. Roy. Soc. Trop. Med. Hyg.* 56:354 (1963).

86. A. Haberkorn and R. Gönnert: Animal experimental investigation into the activity of nifurtimox against *Trypanosoma cruzi. Anzneim.-Forsch.* 22:1570 (1972).

87. R. Gönnert and M. Bock: The effect of nifurtimox on *Trypanosoma cruzi* in tissue cultures. *Arzneim.-Forsch.* 22:1582 (1972).

88. D. H. G. Wegner and R. W. Rohwedder: The effect of nifurtimox in acute Chagas' infection. *Arzneim.-Forsch.* 22:1624 (1972).

89. D. H. G. Wegner and R. W. Rohwedder: Experience with nifurtimox in chronic Chagas' infection: Preliminary report. *Arzneim.-Forsch.* 22:1635 (1972).

90. H. Medenwald, K. Brandau, and K. Schlossman: Quantitative determination of nifurtimox in body fluids of rat, dog and man. *Arzneim.-Forsch.* 22:1613 (1972).

91. B. Duhm, W. Maul, H. Medenwald, K. Patzschke, and L. A. Wegner: Investigations on the pharmacokinetics of nifurtimox-^{35}S in the rat and dog. *Arzneim.-Forsch.* 22:1617 (1972).

Chapter 12
Chemotherapy of Helminthic Diseases

Introduction

The helminthic, or worm, diseases are caused by members of two phyla. The nematodes (roundworms) belong to the phylum Nemathelminthes. Diseases caused by this group of organisms include, for example, ascaris, whipworm, pinworm, and hookworm infections, trichinosis, and elephantiasis. The cestodes, or tapeworms, and the trematodes, a group including the various flukes (e.g., the schistosomes), are both members of the phylum Platyhelminthes (flatworms). These worms are multicellular organisms that possess crude organ systems. Their complex life cycles usually include a stage of development in the human intestinal tract.

The interaction between the drugs used to treat helminthic disease and the biochemistry of the worms has been reviewed by Saz and Bueding[1] and by Cavier and Hawking.[2] Bueding has made some observations about the basis of anthelminthic chemotherapy that are well worth presenting here.[3] The pathogenic forms of most of the worm infections amenable to chemotherapy are the adult, nongrowing stages of the parasite's life cycle. Therefore, drugs that are inhibitors of growth in many cases may not be particularly useful as anthelminthic agents. There are two processes in the worm that stand out as appropriate targets for chemotherapeutic attack: the mechanisms essential for the motor activity of the organisms and the reactions that generate metabolic energy. The selective effect of the anthelminthic drugs is sometimes based on differences between the biochemistry of the host and the parasite. In other cases in which there is no selective toxicity, the parasite is exposed to high concentrations of the drug in its intestinal habitat by the use of orally administered, nonabsorbable drugs. The discussion of the drugs used to treat the worm infections will expand upon these observations.

DRUGS EMPLOYED IN THE TREATMENT OF FLUKE INFECTIONS

Schistosomiasis

Schistosomiasis (also called bilharziasis) is one of the most prevalent diseases of man and therefore one of the most serious health problems in the world today. An accurate census of the number of people in the world with the disease is impossible—a reasonable estimate may be in the range of 150 million. In Egypt, approximately one-half the population is infected with schistosomes.[4] The economic cost to the country, to say nothing of the human misery, is very high.

Schistosomes are multicellular flukes with primitive excretory, nervous, and circulatory systems and specialized organs of reproduction. These organisms penetrate the skin of the human host and migrate to the liver via the bloodstream, residing for a time in the hepatic vessels. After a few weeks, a retrograde migration to various areas of the abdominal vascular plexuses occurs; *Schistosoma hematobium* lives in the venules of the vesicle plexus and *Schistosoma mansoni* and *Schistosoma japonicum* in the mesenteric veins. Here the organisms mate, depositing eggs that are excreted in the urine and feces. The reservoir for these parasites is the freshwater snail. The disease symptomatology is protean in nature and cannot be described in a few words. In the early stages of infection, chemotherapy is very successful. If the disease has been present for some time, however, the intestine and particularly the liver become fibrosed, and chemotherapy cannot reverse the pathology.

The Organic Antimonials

A number of antimonial compounds have been used to treat leishmaniasis (Table 11-3) and schistosomiasis (Table 12-1). Sodium stibogluconate and meglumine antimoniate (not available in the United States) are pentavalent compounds used to treat leishmaniasis. The trivalent antimonials, like stibophen, antimony dimercaptosuccinate, and antimony potassium tartrate, are used in the chemotherapy of schistosomiasis. The flagellate form of leishmanial organisms in culture can grow in the presence of high concentrations of pentavalent antimonials, and it is probably necessary for the metal to be reduced to the trivalent form before these drugs are active against the parasite.[5] The trivalent antimonials are active against leishmania[6] and schistosomes[7] both *in vivo* and *in vitro*.

Table 12-1 Drugs used to treat flatworm infections

In the United States, niridazole, antimony dimercaptosuccinate, bithionol, dehydro-emetine, and niclosamide may be obtained from the Parasitic Diseases Drug Service, Center for Disease Control, Atlanta, Georgia.

Infecting organism	Drug of choice	Alternatives
Flukes (Trematodes)		
Schistosoma haematobium	Niridazole	Antimony sodium dimercaptosuccinate Stibophen
Schistosoma mansoni	Stibophen	Antimony sodium dimercaptosuccinate Niridazole
Schistoma japonicum	Antimony potassium tartrate	Antimony sodium dimercaptosuccinate Stibophen
Clonorchis sinensis (liver fluke)	Chloroquine phosphate	Bithionol
Paragonimus westermani (lung fluke)	Bithionol	Chloroquine phosphate
Fasciola hepatica (sheep liver fluke)	Bithionol or emetine	Chloroquine phosphate
Tapeworms (Cestodes)		
Diphyllobothrium latum (fish tapeworm)	Niclosamide	Paromomycin
Taenia saginata (beef tapeworm)	Niclosamide	Paromomycin
Taenia solium (pork tapeworm)	Niclosamide	Paromomycin
Hymenolepis nana (dwarf tapeworm)	Niclosamide	Paromomycin

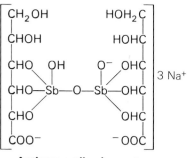

Antimony stibogluconate
(a pentavalent antimonial)

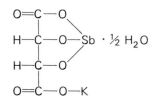

Antimony potassium tartrate
(a trivalent antimonial)

Mechanism of Action

The biochemical locus of action of the trivalent antimonials is well defined. These drugs inhibit glycolysis in the parasite by inhibiting phosphofructokinase, a rate-limiting enzyme in the pathway for the anaerobic metabolism of glucose. The survival of certain organisms like *Schistosoma mansoni,* depends almost entirely on the anaerobic metabolism of carbohydrate. The rate of utilization of glucose in schistosomes is very high. The mature S. *mansoni,* for example, can metabolize in 1 hour an amount of glucose equal to one-fifth its dry weight.[8] Inhibition of this metabolism results in the death of the parasite. Concentrations of trivalent antimonials in the range of the therapeutic dose inhibit glycolysis in the intact schistosome[8] and in subcellular extracts prepared from the worm.[9]

The activity of the glycolytic pathway (Figure 12-1) can be easily assayed in schistosome homogenates by measuring the rate of production of lactic acid from glucose. When glucose or fructose-6-phosphate is added to a broken cell homogenate of schistosomes, the rate of production of lactic acid is inhibited by the trivalent antimonials. But when fructose-1,6-diphosphate is provided as the substrate, lactic acid production is unaffected by the drugs (Figure 12-2).[9] This indicates that it is the conversion of fructose-6-phosphate to fructose-1,6-diphosphate, the reaction catalyzed by phosphofructokinase, that is inhibited by the drug. If purified mammalian phosphofructokinase is added to a schistosome homogenate, inhibition of lactate production from glucose by trivalent antimonials is reversed (Table 12-2).[10] Schistosome phosphofructokinases are 65 to 80 times more sensitive than the mammalian enzymes to the inhibitory effects of trivalent antimonials.[11] This difference in enzyme sensitivity is the basis for the selective toxicity of these drugs. Although phosphofructokinase has been purified from mammalian sources, the enzyme has not been purified from schistosomes, and the mechanism of the drug inhibition has not been elaborated in detail. At high enough concentrations, trivalent antimonials inhibit a variety of enzymes, probably as a result of interactions with sulfhydryl groups. This type of interaction may account for the inhibition of phosphofructokinase and for the toxic effects of these drugs. The inhibition of phosphofructokinase by trivalent antimonials is readily reversible both *in vitro* and *in vivo.*

An interesting change in the location of schistosome organisms in the body occurs when doses of antimonials that are sublethal to

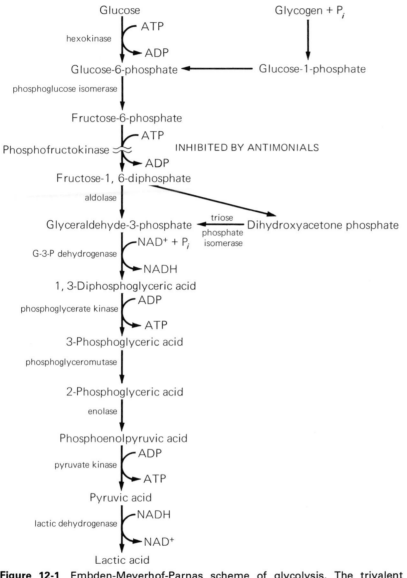

Figure 12-1 Embden-Meyerhof-Parnas scheme of glycolysis. The trivalent arsenicals inhibit the anaerobic production of energy and lactate from glucose by inhibiting the glycolytic enzyme phosphofructokinase in the parasite.

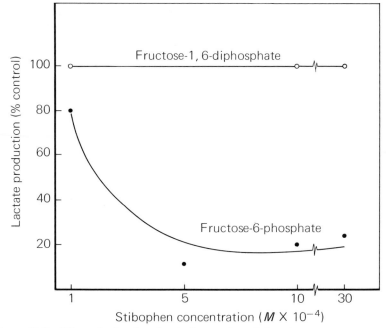

Figure 12-2 Effect of stibophen (a trivalent antimonial) on lactic acid production from fructose-6-P and fructose-1,6-diphosphate by schistosome extracts. (From Mansour and Bueding.[9])

the worms are administered. About 1 hour after a single dose of an antimonial drug is administered to mice infected with S. mansoni, the worms have shifted from the mesenteric veins to the liver.[12] Later, the organisms migrate back to the mesenteric veins. This reverse migration is correlated with a return of their phosphofructokinase activity to normal levels.[11] The reason for this shift of the organism in response to anti-schistosomal drugs is not completely clear. It seems probable that the organisms require energy to attach to the mesenteric vessels and to move against the direction of blood flow, and that when the anaerobic energy production mechanism is inhibited, they are passively carried to the liver with the normal portal blood flow.

Pharmacology and Untoward Effects of the Organic Antimonials

The organic antimonials are administered by intramuscular or slow intravenous injection. The trivalent antimonials bind in the tissues to a greater extent than the pentavalent compounds. Prob-

Table 12-2 **Effect of an antimonial drug and mammalian phosphofructo-kinase on lactic acid production by homogenates of *Schistosoma mansoni***

Replicate samples of a homogenate of *S. mansoni* were incubated for 30 minutes at 37 °C with glucose and ATP. Stibophen ($1 \times 10^{-4}M$), potassium antimony tartrate ($5 \times 10^{-5}M$), or phosphofructokinase (PFK) from rabbit muscle (0.5 units/ml) were added. At the end of the incubation period, lactic acid was assayed and the results are expressed as μmoles lactic acid produced per milligram of protein in 30 minutes. (Data from Beuding and Mansour,[10] Table 1.)

Additions	Production of lactate from glucose
None	1.2
Stibophen	0.4
PFK (rabbit muscle)	2.0
Stibophen + PFK	1.9
Potassium antimonial tartrate	0.4
Potassium antimonial tartrate + PFK	1.7

ably for this reason the pentavalent compound sodium stibogluconate is excreted much more rapidly than the trivalent drugs.[13] Some of the pentavalent antimony is reduced in the liver to the trivalent state,[13] and trivalent antimonials are taken up and retained by the liver.[14] When patients with S. *hematobium* infection were injected with radioactively labeled antimony sodium dimercaptosuccinate (a trivalent compound), antimony from the drug was found to have been concentrated (about 400-fold with respect to the plasma concentration) in parasite eggs recovered from the urine.[15] The trivalent antimonials are excreted primarily via the kidney.[16] After a single dose, the rate of elimination is rapid for the first few hours and much slower thereafter.[15,16]

Pentavalent antimonials are less toxic than the trivalent drugs. Antimony potassium tartrate is the most toxic of the antimonials. The adverse effects of the other trivalent drugs are similar to those of antimony potassium tartrate, but they occur less frequently and are usually less severe. During intravenous infusion of antimony potassium tartrate, paroxysms of coughing and vomiting may occur. The trivalent antimonials frequently cause vomiting, myalgia, and arthralgia. Electrocardiographic changes are often seen during therapy; these changes are reversible, and interruption of treatment is not usually required. Bradycardia occurs frequently with antimony potassium tartrate. The drug is contraindicated in the presence of cardiac disease. The trivalent antimonials can also cause rashes, pruritus, abdominal pain, diarrhea, weakness, dizziness, renal damage, and occasionally shock. Hepatocellular damage with jaundice and abnormal liver function is a rare side effect, and the drug is contraindicated in the presence of liver disease of non-schistosomal origin.

As with so many of the antiprotozoal and antiparasitic drugs, the antimonials are toxic compounds and are difficult to administer. People with schistosomiasis will frequently discontinue therapy because of side effects and the fact that numerous parenteral injections are required.

The Organic Antimonial Preparations

Sodium Stibogluconate

This drug is a pentavalent compound that has become a drug of choice for the treatment of many forms of leishmaniasis (Table 11-3). See reference 17 for a review. It is especially important in the treatment of visceral infections (kala-azar) where it elicits a prompt clinical and parasitological response. It is also useful in treating cutaneous and mucocutaneous leishmaniases. Sodium stibogluconate is given intramuscularly or intravenously and it is well tolerated.

Antimony Potassium Tartrate

This is both the most therapeutically potent and the most toxic and irritating of the trivalent antimonials. It is used primarily in the treatment of S. *japonicum* infection (Table 12-1) and is given only by the intravenous route. It is irritating to tissues and special care must be taken during its administration so that extravasation into perivascular tissue does not take place because this may lead to necrosis. The drug should be injected slowly, since coughing, vomiting, and even circulatory collapse can occur when it is given too fast.

Stibophen

Stibophen is most often used in the treatment of S. *mansoni* and S. *hematobium* infections, S. *mansoni* being the schistosome most commonly encountered in the United States, primarily among the inhabitants of Puerto Rico.[18] Stibophen comes in 5-ml ampules containing 8.5 mg of trivalent antimony. It is given intramuscularly. Usually the patient's tolerance is assessed by administering a smaller initial dosage (1.5 ml followed 2 days later by 3.5 ml), and therapy is continued by injecting 4 to 5 ml every other day until a total course of 80 to 100 ml has been given. The principal toxic effect is vomiting; but muscle and joint pains are common.

Antimony Sodium Dimercaptosuccinate

This drug is also administered intramuscularly, with only one or two injections per week required. The total dosage for a course of therapy is 40 mg/kg and it is given in five divided doses. Skin eruptions are more common with this trivalent compound than with stibophen.

Niridazole

Niridazole is used to treat infection due to S. *hematobium* and S. *mansoni* (Table 12-1). It has also been reported to be useful in the treatment of dracontiasis (infection with the guinea worm *Dracunculus medinensis*, Table 12-3).[19,20] Niridazole is active against E. *histolytica*, but it is not used in treating amebiasis because it is more toxic than other effective drugs. The biochemistry, pharmacology, adverse effects, and the therapeutic trials conducted with this drug, have been reviewed in a symposium.[20] The drug's biochemical mechanism of action is not known. Although it clearly does not inhibit glycolysis as the antimonials do, niridazole affects carbohydrate metabolism in schistosomes by increasing the rate of breakdown of glycogen stores in the parasite.[21] The decrease in glycogen is brought about by a drug-induced reduction in the rate of conversion of active schistosome glycogen phosphorylase to the inactive form. The rate of glycogen phosphorylase inactivation in the host's skeletal muscle is also decreased but to a much lesser degree.[21] Thus, the effect is somewhat selective. The consequences of increased glycogen breakdown in the parasite are not clear.

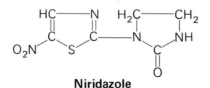

Niridazole

Niridazole is absorbed from the gastrointestinal tract over a period of several hours. A course of therapy for schistosomiasis usually consists of 12.5 mg/kg twice a day for 7 days. The onset of drug action is slow: the worms do not shift to the liver until 4 days after administration.[2] The drug is extensively metabolized in the liver, but the period of time required for metabolism does not account for the delay in schistosomicidal action. This was demonstrated by incubating schistomes in vitro with plasma from untreated animals containing added niridazole and with plasma from treated animals containing the as yet unidentified metabolites but no niridazole. Only the niridazole-containing plasma damaged the schistosomes.[22] The concentrations of both the drug and its metabolites have been measured in blood obtained from the portal system and from the inferior vena cava of experimental animals given radiolabeled niridazole.[23] Although the total radioactivity from each source was the same, the portal blood contained three to four times the concentration of unchanged niridazole. The drug is excreted almost entirely in the form of metabolites in both urine and feces.[24]

Children in general tolerate niridazole better than adults. Adults taking niridazole frequently experience gastrointestinal disturbances (vomiting, cramping, and diarrhea), headaches, and dizziness. Occasionally, electrocardiographic changes and rashes occur. The stage of the disease process being treated is very important in niridazole therapy. The side effects seen in the treatment of patients with the intestinal form of the disease are generally not severe. But in patients who have hepatosplenic damage the levels of both niridazole and its metabolites in the blood are markedly elevated.[22] Treatment of patients with impaired liver function is accompanied by central nervous system disturbances (including EEG changes, psychosis, and convulsions) in a significant percentage of cases.[25] Extreme care should be taken if the drug is administered to patients who have a history of psychosis or convulsions. Niridazole has been shown to produce hemolysis in glucose-6-phosphate dehydrogenase-deficient erythrocytes.

Niridazole reversibly inhibits spermatogenesis in experimental animals.[26] This has not been observed in humans receiving doses in the therapeutic range.[27] Niridazole has been reported to be a potent inhibitor of cell-mediated hypersensitivity in experimental animals,[28] and some delayed hypersensitivity responses are suppressed in humans receiving the drug in therapeutic dosage.[29]

This drug has been given to a large number of people and its use has not been associated with increased susceptibility to infection or neoplastic disease in spite of possible depression of T cell function. Niridazole does not produce the bone-marrow depression associated with some other classes of immunosuppressive drugs. Niridazole has been shown to be mutagenic to bacteria (excision-repair-deficient test strains).[30] The mutagenic effect does not require large amounts of drug. Indeed, it was found that the urine of a patient being treated with niridazole was strongly mutagenic in the test.[30]

Bithionol

Fluke infections are common in domesticated animals. Because of the large economic impact of these diseases in livestock extensive drug screening has been carried out to find agents useful in therapy.[31] For the most part, the drugs developed for animal use have proven to be too toxic for administration to man. Bithionol is one of the few drugs that have come into human use by this route. It is the drug of choice for treating infection by the lung fluke *Paragonimus westermani*.[32,33] Although the emetines (Chapter 11) are most frequently used to treat fascioliasis (Table 12-1), bithionol has been used with beneficial effect in a few cases.[34] There is no drug that can cure infection with *Clonorchis sinensis*, an Asian liver fluke.[18] Prolonged therapy with chloroquine[35] or bithinol[34] will temporarily suppress egg production. Bithionol is given orally. Vomiting, diarrhea, abdominal pain, rashes, and skin photosensitivity reactions are common side effects.

DRUGS EMPLOYED IN THE TREATMENT OF TAPEWORM INFECTIONS

Tapeworm Infection

Tapeworm infection (cestodiasis) occurs when uncooked meat or fish containing the encysted larval forms of the organism are ingested. In the intestine of the host, the head of the tapeworm, or scolex, attaches to the intestinal wall. The worm then grows by producing large numbers of egg-containing segments. Growth can continue until, in the fish tapeworm *(Diphyllobothrium latum)*, for example, there are three to four thousand segments and the worm is 30 feet long. Tapeworms are hermaphroditic, and the fertilized eggs are excreted as the segments are passed with the feces. The eggs can then be ingested by the intermediate host in which the larval form develops, thus completing the cycle. In some cases, the normal course of events is altered when man accidently ingests the eggs instead of the larvae. This happens with the pork tapeworm (Taenia solium) where man is the usual definitive host and the intermediate host is the pig. If tapeworm eggs are accidentiy ingested by man, the larvae can develop in human tissues.

The clinical symptoms of tapeworm infection by adult forms growing in the intestine are surprisingly mild in the well-nourished, otherwise healthy patient. There may be vague abdominal discomfort and pain, which is relieved by food, as well as weakness, weight loss, epigastric fullness, and anemia. Intestinal obstruction due to the mass of the worms is rare. Ingestion of eggs that produce migratory larvae can be very serious, since the larvae may develop in the orbit, brain, or other organs to form growing, space-occupying masses. There is no chemotherapeutic treatment for infection by these intermediate stages of the life cycle of the tapeworm, but surgical removal of the mass is sometimes possible.

Niclosamide

Niclosamide is very effective in the treatment of tapeworm infections in man.[36] Cures are obtained in more than 90 per cent of patients with Taenia saginata, D. latum, and Hymenolepsis nana infections.[37] The cure rate with T. solium is about 85%.[38] Niclosamide appears to act by inhibiting the anaerobic production of ATP. It has also been reported to uncouple oxidative phosphorylation in mammalian mitochondria.[39] At low concentrations, niclosamide inhibits the anaerobic incorporation of inorganic phosphate into ATP by the tapeworm Hymenolepsis diminuta.[40]

Niclosamide

Tapeworms, like the adult forms of many other helminths, derive their major source of energy from anaerobic rather than aerobic metabolism of carbohydrate.[2] This is consonant with their location in the lumen of the intestine, where oxygen tension is very low. Their heavy dependence on anaerobic metabolism of carbohydrate renders them especially sensitive to the action of the drug.

Niclosamide is given orally. It is not absorbed from the gastrointestinal tract. Thus, the parasite is exposed to very high drug concentrations and a selective toxicity is obtained. A course of therapy for an adult consists of four 500 mg tablets taken in a single dose and chewed thoroughly before swallowing. Treatment of *H. nana* requires the same dosage on each of 5 consecutive days.[41] No serious side effects of niclosamide have been reported. Patients may experience some abdominal discomfort and soft or loose stools on the day of treatment.[42] After niclosamide administration, the segments of the tapeworm are destroyed, and large numbers of viable eggs are released into the intestine. In the case of the pork tapeworm (*T. solium*), for which man can be an intermediate host, this could possibly result in the dissemination of the larval forms to the tissues (cysticercosis). To reduce the risk of cysticercosis, magnesium sulfate purges are given to patients with *T. solium* infection shortly after niclosamide administration.[37]

Paromomycin

Paromomycin is an aminoglycoside antibiotic that has been shown to be effective in treating cestodiasis. Cure rates of better than 90 per cent have been reported.[43,44] Therapy for an adult with *Taenia* or *Diphyllobothrium* infection consists of 1 gm every 15 minutes for a total of four doses. In the case of *H. nana* infection, the dose is 45 mg/kg daily for 5 days.[44] Like the other aminoglycosides, paromomycin is very poorly absorbed from the gastrointestinal tract. The pharmacology and adverse effects of the aminoglycosides have been presented in Chapter 3. In oral paromomycin therapy, diarrhea and abdominal pain are the main side effects, but the occasional patient complains of nausea or dizziness.[44] The ototoxicity and renal toxicity that occur with systemic aminoglycoside administration have not been reported with this form of therapy, but the bacterial population of the bowel can be altered and superinfection of the gastrointestinal tract is possible.

Patients with *T. solium* infection should be given an oral purgative 2 hours after paromomycin administration for the reasons outlined under niclosamide.

Quinacrine

Quinacrine is an acridine derivative formerly used as an antimalarial agent. Before the introduction of niclosamide, quinacrine was the drug most commonly employed in treating tapeworm infections.[45] In many areas it is still used for this purpose. Quinacrine is the drug of choice for treating giardiasis, an intestinal infection caused by the flagellated protozoan *Giardia lamblia* (Table 11-1).[46] Quinacrine, like chloroquine, binds to DNA and inhibits nucleic acid synthesis.[47] It is not known whether this effect is related to the antiparasitic action. The drug is employed in an acute manner at high local concentrations for the eradication of tapeworms from the bowel.

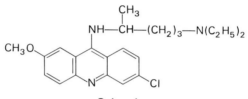

Quinacrine

Quinacrine is taken orally. It commonly causes nausea and vomiting. For the treatment of tapeworm infection, quinacrine can be administered by duodenal tube directly into the upper small intestine. This results in less vomiting and a higher drug concentration in the intestinal lumen.[34] The patient should be fasting and should have been on a fluid diet the preceding day. When it is taken orally, the tendency to vomit can be reduced by the concomitant administration of sodium bicarbonate. A saline purge is required about 2 hours after quinacrine is given. This is done regardless of which tapeworm is involved. Quinacrine frequently causes headache and dizziness and occasionally toxic psychosis, anemia, and exfoliative dermatitis (patients with psoriasis are especially prone to develop this last complication). The drug should not be given to patients with a history of psychosis. Aplastic anemia and acute hepatic necrosis have been reported on rare occasion. One of the more annoying side effects to the patient is a yellowish discoloration of the skin due to binding of the drug in the tissues (see Chapter 10). When quinacrine was used for prolonged therapy of malaria, occasional blue discoloration of the nailbeds occurred. This resembles cyanosis but is due to a deposition of blood pigment. Quinacrine is strongly bound in the liver and slowly eliminated from the body. The metabolism of primaquine can be inhibited as long as 10 to 12 weeks after the last dose of quinacrine. The free blood levels of primaquine are elevated in the presence of quinacrine, and therefore, treatment with primaquine is a contraindication for quinacrine use.

Quinacrine has another use in medicine. The binding of quinacrine to DNA in chromosomal structure creates fluorescent bands in regions with a high $(A + T)/(G + C)$ ratio.[48] Thus quinacrine fluorescence in human genetics has been of great help in identifying portions of human chromosomes and in defining the lesions involved in many inherited diseases.

DRUGS EMPLOYED IN THE TREATMENT OF ROUNDWORM INFECTIONS

Ascariasis

Ascariasis is the most common of all human parasitoses. The disease affects approximately one-third of the world population, or at least one billion people (Figure 12-3).[49] Infection with

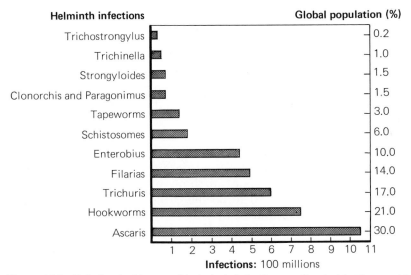

Figure 12-3 Relative incidence of helminth infections estimated in the world population. (Adapted from Standen.[49])

Ascaris is more prevalent in tropical countries, but it occurs all over the world. The adult worm, which looks rather like an earthworm, lives in the lumen of the small intestine. Humans become infected by ingesting embryonated eggs. When the eggs reach the duodenum, the larvae hatch and begin a remarkable odyssey that eventually returns them to the intestinal lumen. The larvae penetrate the wall of the small intestine and are carried through the right heart to the lungs. They then penetrate the walls of the pulmonary capillaries, emerge into the air sacs, and migrate up the pulmonary tree to the epiglottis. This period of larval migration is occasionally accompanied by cough, fever, and pulmonary infiltration. Signs of hypersensitivity, such as eosinophilia and urticaria, may be observed. Occasionally, the larvae reach the general circulation and become lodged in tissues where they can provoke local reactions.

The larvae are swallowed after they reach the epiglottis, and upon their second arrival in the small intestine they develop into adult male and female worms. The patient at this stage of infection may be asymptomatic or have vague symptoms of abdominal distress (epigastric pain, nausea, vomiting, and anorexia). More serious problems can arise as a result of migration of the adult worms into the pancreatic and bile ducts, gallbladder, and liver or from complete obstruction of the appendix or intestinal lumen. The by-products of living or dead worms can produce severe reactions in sensitized patients. It is interesting that migration of the adult worms, and the resulting complications, can be stimulated by drug therapy. A number of people who are infected with *Ascaris* are also infected with other parasites, such as hookworm.[49] Treatment of hookworm infection with tetrachlorethylene, for example, can provoke the migration of *Ascaris*. In this case, the symptoms that arise as a side effect of tetrachlorethylene therefore are due to an effect of the drug on an entirely different parasite from that being treated. When there is infection by more than one type of intestinal helminth, *Ascaris* is usually treated first in order to avoid promoting migration of the worm. Piperazine and pyrantel pamoate are both effective in therapy; the latter is often considered to be the drug of choice for the treatment of ascariasis (Table 12-3).

Piperazine

Piperazine citrate is very effective in treating both roundworm (*Ascaris*) and pinworm (*Enterobius vermicularis*) infection. A

Table 12-3   Drugs used to treat nematode (roundworm) infections

Infecting organism	Drug of choice	Alternative
Intestinal roundworms		
Ascaris lumbricoides	Pyrantel pamoate	Piperazine
Enterobius (Oxyuris)	Pyrantel pamoate	Piperazine
vermicularis (pinworm)	Mebendazole	Pyrvinium pamoate
Trichuris trichiura	Mebendazole	Thiabendazole
(whipworm)		
Strongyloides stercoralis	Thiabendazole	Pyrvinium pamoate
Necator americanus		
(hookworm)	Pyrantel pamoate	Bephenium
Ancylostoma duodenale	Mebendazole	Thiabendazole
(hookworm)		
Filaria		
Wuchereria bancrofti		
Wuchereria (Brugia)	Diethylcarbamazine	None
malayi		
Loa loa		
Onchocerca volvulus	Diethylcarbamazine plus suramin	None
Dracunculus medinensis	Niridazole	Metronidazole
(guinea worm)		

single course of therapy for ascariasis (75 mg/kg to a maximum of 3.5 gm/day for 2 days) results in a cure in 95 per cent of the cases.[50] Piperazine acts by paralyzing the worm. The paralyzed worm, unable to maintain its position in the intestinal tract, is then passively expelled by the normal peristaltic action of the bowel; no purgative is required.

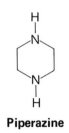

Piperazine

If piperazine citrate is added to a bath containing an *Ascaris* attached to a strain gauge, the irregular contraction of the worm ceases after a few minutes and the worm remains in flaccid paralysis (Figure 12-4, A).[51] The delay may reflect the time

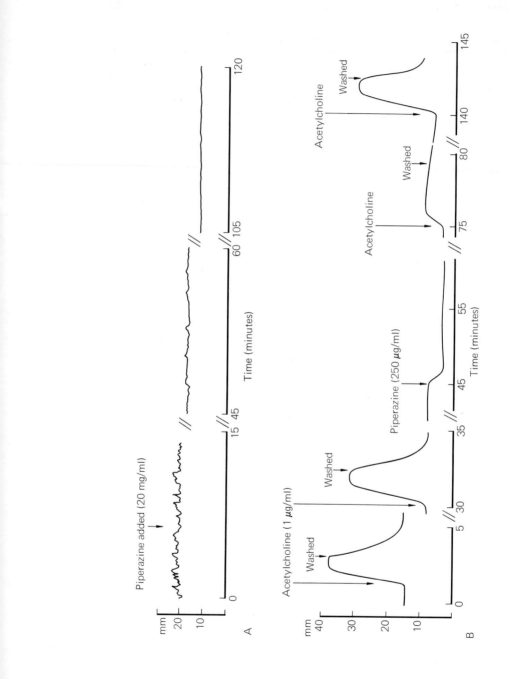

required for the drug to reach its site of action. The time of onset of the paralysis in the intact worm preparation decreases with increasing doses of the drug. If a crudely dissected section from *Ascaris* is suspended in a similar bath, there is no spontaneous movement of the muscle. The muscle contracts readily upon addition of acetylcholine, and the response to acetylcholine is reversibly antagonized by piperazine (Figure 12-4, B).[51] Electrical stimulation of the muscle of the body wall causes a contraction that is not blocked by piperazine. These observations were felt to be consistent with the conclusion that piperazine paralyzes *Ascaris* by a blocking action at the myoneural junction. If this is true, one would then have to explain why piperazine does not have this effect on mammalian muscle preparations.[52]

Piperazine is readily absorbed from the intestinal tract, and the basis for its selective toxicity is not explained by the fact that the parasite is exposed to very high concentrations of drug in comparison with the host. The basis for the selective action of this drug is not entirely clear. The following model is one of several that have been proposed. Although the data are somewhat sketchy, it appears that contraction of *Ascaris* muscle is initiated by rhythmic spike potentials generated by pacemakers in the muscle membrane itself.[53] Acetylcholine depolarizes the muscle cells, thereby increasing the frequency of the spike potentials and the degree of muscle contraction. The results of electrophysiological studies suggest that piperazine increases the resting potential of the muscle so that pacemaker activity is suppressed, and flaccid paralysis ensues.[54] Piperazine may therefore act as an inhibitory neurotransmitter. Indeed, it could be an analog of a natural inhibitory transmitter in *Ascaris*. The difference in the response of the host and the parasite to the drug would rest on the development of different control mechanisms at the muscle membrane in the

Figure 12-4   A. The effect of piperazine on the spontaneous contraction of a whole *Ascaris* attached to a strain gauge. When a whole *Ascaris* is exposed to piperazine, there is a delay period followed by the development of flaccid paralysis. A 10-mm deflection on the record is equivalent to a 2-gm increase in tension. (The tracing is adapted from Norton and deBeer.[51]) B. The effect of piperazine on the response of a crude nerve-muscle preparation of *Ascaris* to acetylcholine. The anterior portion of a worm (containing the main ganglia) was cut off, the worm was split, and the intestinal tract removed. The remainder was attached to a strain gauge and suspended in Ringer's solution. Piperazine decreases the response of the preparation in a reversible manner. (The tracing is adapted from Norton and DeBeer.[51])

more advanced species man. That is, through differentiation, the receptor may have been lost or altered in higher life forms.

Piperazine is administered orally as a tablet, or as a liquid preparation for children. It is also prepared in a number of salt combinations. There is no important pharmacological difference between the citrate, the phosphate, and the adipate.[55] The drug is readily absorbed from the gastrointestinal tract and much of an oral dose is excreted in the urine within 24 hours.[56] The drug generally is quite safe. Occasional rashes and dizziness are observed. Rarely, patients experience difficulty in focusing as a side effect of the drug. Piperazine can produce a neurotoxicity characterized by incoordination and hypotonia.[57] This cerebellar type of ataxia ("worm wobble") is rare, but it is more likely to occur in patients with compromised renal function and possibly in those receiving concomitant phenothiazine therapy.[58] Patients who are epileptic may have an exacerbation of seizures and another drug should be used.

Pyrantel Pamoate

Several pyrantel derivatives were found to have excellent activity against a variety of worms that parasitize livestock.[59] In human trials, it was found that pyrantel is well tolerated and highly effective in treating enterobiasis,[60] ascariasis,[61] and hookworm infection.[62] The daily dosage is 11 mg/kg taken as a single dose to a maximum of 1 gm. A single administration is all that is required for a cure rate of better than 90 per cent in ascariasis or *Ancylostoma duodenale* infection. With pinworm, it is advisable to repeat the single dose 2 weeks later because reinfection is so common. For *Necator americanus*, it is necessary to continue treatment for 3 consecutive days.

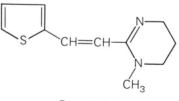

Pyrantel

Pyrantel acts by paralyzing the worms, which are then passed out of the intestine with the normal fecal flow. In *Ascaris* preparations, pyrantel has been shown to have a depolarizing action, causing contracture of the worm.[63] This spastic paralysis is the opposite of the effect described for piperazine, which produces hyperpolarization and paralysis in relaxation. Indeed, in micro-electrode studies, piperazine has been shown to antagonize the effects of pyrantel on the membrane potential of single muscle cells in *Ascaris*.[63] Pyrantel also behaves as a depolarizing neuro-muscular blocking agent in several mammalian systems.[63,64] Two factors apparently determine the selective effect: (1) Pyrantel is incompletely absorbed and the worms are exposed to high con-centrations in the intestine; (2) the neuromuscular junction of the worm is more sensitive to the drug than that of the host. Pyrantel is more than 100 times as active as acetylcholine in causing contraction of strip muscle preparations from *Ascaris*.

Most of a dose of pyrantel pamoate is excreted unchanged in the feces. Although systemic absorption is limited, enough occurs to cause occasional systemic side effects like headache, dizziness, and drowsiness.[42] The principal adverse effects involve the gas-trointestinal tract—nausea, vomiting, diarrhea, and cramps.

Pyrvinium Pamoate

Pyrvinium is one of the cyanine dyes. These are basic dyes char-acterized by a quaternary nitrogen linked to a tertiary nitrogen by a conjugated chain of an odd number of carbon atoms. The mech-anism of action of pyrvinium is not well defined. It has been

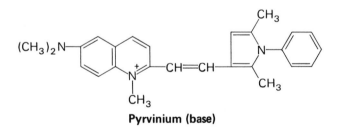

Pyrvinium (base)

demonstrated that cyanine dye compounds inhibit oxygen con-sumption by the adult filarial worm *Litomosoides carinii*,[1] whereas oxygen consumption by mammalian cells is not inhib-ited even at drug concentrations several orders of magnitude higher than those affecting the parasite. Pyrvinium pamoate is used clinically in the treatment of infections by roundworms, which live in the anaerobic environment of the intestine. The action of dithiazanine (another cyanine dye formerly used in therapy) has been studied in the canine whipworm *Trichuris vulpis,* an intestinal parasite that is primarily anaerobic. On the basis of several observations made in this system, it was concluded that the drug interferes with the transport of glucose into the worm.[65] The effects of cyanine dyes on oxygen consumption and glucose utilization are apparently unrelated.[1] The second effect is probably pertinent to the usual application of pyrvinium in treating intestinal worm infections in humans.

Pyrvinium pamoate is effective in the treatment of pinworm infection. A single oral dose (5 mg/kg to a maximum of 250 mg) results in a high rate of cure (96 per cent).[66] Because reinfection is common, the dose is usually repeated after 2 weeks and patients should be examined for the presence of eggs at the anus several weeks after treatment. Pyrvinium pamoate given for 5 to 7 days is useful in the treatment of strongyloidiasis.[67] The drug is not absorbed from the intestinal tract and it is generally well tolerated. Nausea, vomiting, cramping, and diarrhea occur occasionally, and patients should be warned that the stool is frequently red in color. Pyrvinium is a red dye and it is this color that is seen as the drug is eliminated in the feces.

Thiabendazole

Thiabendazole is a benzimidazole derivative with a broad spectrum of action against gastrointestinal helminths infecting both humans and animals.[68] The literature on this drug has been summarized in a symposium[69] and a review.[70] The mechanism of

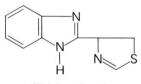

Thiabendazole

the anthelminthic effect is not completely defined. The broad spectrum of drug action suggests that a critical reaction common to many different worms is affected. Thiabendazole ($10^{-4}M$) has been shown to inhibit the fumarate reductase enzyme system in mitochondrial preparations from *Haemonchus contortus,* an intestinal roundworm that infects sheep.[71] In a number of helminths, fumarate is the terminal electron acceptor in anaerobic metabolism and this enzyme system is important for the production of both ATP and NAD (Figure 12-5).[72] The reaction is an essential component of the mechanism of energy production in the parasite but not in the host. The observation that the drug does not inhibit fumarate reductase activity in a particulate preparation from a thiabendazole-resistant strain supports the proposal that this enzyme represents the primary site of the drug effect in helminths.[73] Thiabendazole also has broad-spectrum antifungal activity, and studies in plant fungi suggest that the primary site of inhibition in this case is the terminal electron transport system.[74] In the concentration range at which it affects fumarate reductase in helminths and electron transport in fungi, thiabendazole inhibits several enzyme functions in mitochondria prepared from beef heart.[74] Thus, the basis for the selective effect of thiabendazole may depend in part upon differential entry into the parasite or pharmacological properties of distribution, metabolism, etc., in the host.

Thiabendazole (25 mg/kg orally twice a day for 2 days) is highly effective in the treatment of infection by *Strongyloides stercor-*

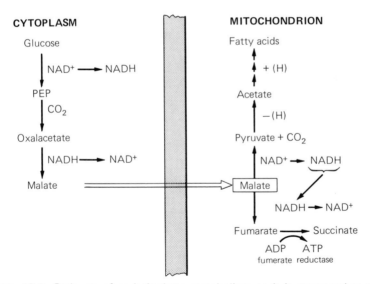

Figure 12-5 Pathway of carbohydrate metabolism as it is proposed to take place in *Ascaris* muscle. The fumarate reductase enzyme may be the primary site of thiabendazole action. (From Saz.[72])

alis, for which cure rates of almost 100 per cent have been reported.[75,76] The drug is also used to treat guinea worm infection (dracontiasis) and, occasionally, hookworm (Table 12-3).[69] It is active against pinworms and Ascaris, although other more effective, less toxic drugs are used for therapy.

In addition to affecting adult worms, thiabendazole also prevents the development of nematode eggs and larvae.[68,69] This observation has led to the use of thiabendazole in the treatment of human disease by larval forms, as in trichinosis and cutaneous larva migrans. Cutaneous larva migrans, also called creeping eruption, is caused by larvae of canine and feline hookworms that penetrate and migrate under the skin. Their presence causes intense irritation and itching. Administered orally, thiabendazole produces a rapid and effective clinical response in this condition,[77] and it can also be effectively administered topically.[69] Young children sometimes ingest the eggs of Toxocara worms of dogs and cats. The larvae that emerge in the intestine penetrate the gut wall and are carried about the body. In the human host, the larvae are unable to complete their usual development, but they can cause fever, eosinophilia, hepatomegaly, and pneumonitis. This infection is called visceral larva migrans and there are reports that thiabendazole treatment for several days produces rapid clinical improvement.[78] The limited experience with thiabendazole in the treatment of trichinosis indicates that it has a prompt effect,[79] with decreased temperature and muscle pain; but not all the larvae in man are killed by the drug.[80] It is possible that the beneficial action reported in trichinosis is due in part to an anti-inflammatory effect of thiabendazole.[81]

Thiabendazole is rapidly absorbed after oral administration, and plasma levels reach their peak in 1 hour. The drug is excreted principally as its glucuronide and sulfate ester metabolites by the kidney within 24 to 48 hours.[69,70] Transient side effects, including anorexia, nausea, vomiting, and dizziness, are frequently encountered with thiabendazole. Less commonly, there may be leukopenia and crystalluria (both reversible), rashes, hallucinations, and xanthopsia, a disturbance of color vision in which objects appear yellow. Patients may notice a malodorous urine and sweat. This is caused by a metabolite that is excreted by these routes. Occasionally, vomiting of live Ascaris occurs. Rare side effects include tinnitus, collapse, hyperglycemia, enuresis, decrease in pulse rate and systolic blood pressure, and a transitory rise in cephalin flocculation and SGOT.

Hookworm

The two types of hookworm causing infection in man are *Necator americanus* and *Ancylostoma duodenale*. Upon coming in contact with the skin, hookworm larvae actively burrow through the skin to the lymphatics or venules where they are carried via the blood through the right heart to the lungs. The larvae are unable to pass through the capillaries and they break through capillary walls to the alveoli. Then, like *Ascaris*, they migrate up the bronchi and the trachea and are swallowed, finally reaching the lumen of the intestine. By the time they reach the intestine the larvae have developed a buccal capsule by which they become attached to the intestinal mucosa. Ulcerations are created at the point of contact. The worms ingest blood from the mucosal vessels of the patient and lay eggs, which are passed with the feces. Definitive diagnosis depends upon finding eggs in the feces.

The penetration of the larvae into the skin produces localized erythema and severe itching, and the passage of large numbers of worms through the lungs may produce signs of pneumonitis. The adult worms in the intestine can produce gastrointestinal symptoms, such as abdominal fullness and epigastric pain; often, there are no acute symptoms. The symptoms of hookworm infection are characteristic of a progressive, hypochromic, microcytic anemia of the nutritional deficiency type. Anemia is secondary to chronic blood loss, which is superimposed on such contributing factors as malnutrition and an iron-deficient diet in many infected individuals. Several drugs are effective in treating hookworm infections; these include mebendazole, pyrantel pamoate, bephenium hydroxynaphthoate, and thiabendazole (Table 12-3).

Mebendazole

Mebendazole, like thiabendazole, is a benzimidazole derivative with a broad-spectrum anthelminthic activity. Mebendazole is the drug of choice for treating trichuriasis. Cure rates ranging from 65

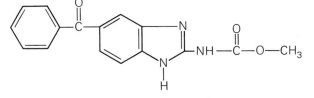

Mebendazole

to 95 per cent have been reported with a single course of treatment consisting of 100 mg twice daily for 3 days.[82,83,84] Until the introduction of mebendazole, whipworm infections had proven to be quite refractory to drug therapy. Mebendazole is clearly superior to thiabendazole. The same drug regimen also yields high cure rates in hookworm (95 per cent)[82] and *Ascaris* (91 to 99 per cent)[82,85] infections. A single dose is over 90 per cent effective against pinworms (enterobiasis).[86,87] The three most common nematodes infecting man are *Ascaris lumbricoides*, *Trichuris trichuria*, and *Enterobius vermicularis*, and many people are simultaneously infected with all three.[49] The broad spectrum of action and virtual atoxicity of mebendazole make it particularly attractive in the treatment of patients with multiple worm infections and for mass treatment of highly infected populations.

Although mebendazole is derived from the same class of compound as thiabendazole, its mechanism of action and pharmacology are both quite different. Many benzimidazole derivatives are potent uncouplers of oxidative phosphorylation in mammalian mitochondria.[88] At high concentration, mebendazole has been shown to inhibit phosphorylation in mitochondria of *Ascaris* muscle[89]; the anthelminthic effect, however, is achieved at much lower concentrations of drug. At these low drug levels, mebendazole inhibits the uptake of exogenous glucose into *Ascaris*.[89] This is followed by a depletion of glycogen in the parasite and ultimately by a decreased ability to generate ATP. The drug apparently acts primarily on the passage of hexose into the cell and not on utilization of carbohydrate. In addition to its effect on adult worms, mebendazole is toxic to nematode eggs.[90] Even at high concentration there is no effect on fully formed hookworm larvae; but when rats were fed large amounts of the drug, a slow but lethal effect was observed against the encysted phase of *Trichenella* larvae.[91]

In contrast to thiabendazole, very little mebendazole is absorbed from the gastrointestinal tract. Only 5 to 10 per cent of an oral dose is recovered in the urine, principally as the decarboxylated derivative.[86] There are surprisingly few side effects with mebendazole therapy. This is probably because of very limited drug absorption. Abdominal pain and diarrhea have occurred with expulsion of worms in patients with massive infection, but no direct side effects of the drug have been reported in humans. Large doses are very well tolerated by various animal species.[92] But the manufacturer warns that (in spite of the limited absorption of the drug) embryotoxic and teratogenic activity have been demonstrated in rats at single oral doses as low as 10 mg/kg. Accordingly, mebendazole is contraindicated in pregnant women.

Bephenium Hydroxynaphthoate

Bephenium is a quaternary ammonium compound that is effective against both N. *americanus* and A. *duòdenale*. It is also active against *Ascaris* as well as a number of nematodes that infect livestock.[93] The structure of bephenium is similar to that of acetylcholine, and when it is added to a preparation of *Ascaris*

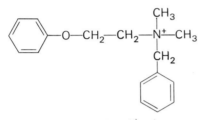

Bephenium (base)

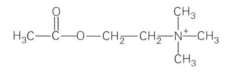

Acetylcholine

muscle, it causes contraction.[94] It is five times more potent than acetylcholine in causing contraction of isolated *Ascaris* muscle strips. The stimuatory effect of bephenium on *Ascaris* muscle, like that of acetylcholine, is blocked by piperazine and d-tubocurarine. When bephenium is added to a bath containing whole *Ascaris*, the worms first contract and then relax.[95] In the patient, hookworms are unable to maintain their attachment in the intestinal tract and are expelled with the normal fecal flow.

Essentially no bephenium is absorbed from the intestinal tract. Less than 0.5 per cent of an oral dose is excreted in the urine.[96] Since bephenium is bitter, it is generally given in a liquid that will mask its taste. The drug occasionally causes nausea, vomiting, or diarrhea. There are no other side effects. Although bephenium possesses some activity against other worms, it is used in medicine specifically for the treatment of hookworm infections (Table 12-3). *Ancylostoma duodenale* is more sensitive to bephenium than. *Necator americanus*. The usual adult regimen for *A. duodenale* infection is one 5-gm packet (2.5-gm bephenium base) given twice in one day. This yields a cure rate of about 85 per cent.[97] For *N. americanus*, the above regimen is administered on 3 consecutive days. There has been a great deal of variation in the cure rates reported with this infection.[45]

Tetrachloroethylene

Tetrachloroethylene (C_2Cl_4) is a colorless volatile liquid that is very effective in the treatment of *Necator americanus* infection. The drug must be stored in a cool, dark place; if exposed to air at warm temperatures, it will oxidize to phosgene. How this drug eliminates hookworms from the intestine is not known. A single dose will cure 80 per cent of *N. americanus* infections.[98] The cure rate in *A. duodenale* infection is very low—approximately 25 per cent. The reason for the different sensitivities of these two organisms to the drug is unknown.

The absorption of tetrachloroethylene from the gastrointestinal tract is minimal in the absence of fat or alcohol. To reduce the absorption of the drug, fatty foods and alcohol should not be ingested before and for 24 hours after the drug is administered. The drug may cause nausea, vomiting, dizziness, and a burning sensation in the stomach. Rarely, tetrachloroethylene causes a loss of consciousness, so the patient should be kept at rest for 4 hours after it is administered. This drug is contraindicated if the patient is infected with *Ascaris* as well as hookworm. As mentioned earlier, tetrachloroethylene stimulates the migration of *Ascaris*, thereby increasing the risk of serious complications due to organ invasion and obstruction by these worms. When *Ascaris* organisms are present, they must first be eliminated with piperazine. When *Ascaris* eggs are no longer found in the feces, the hookworm infection can then be treated with tetrachloroethylene. Tetrachloroethylene is only available as a veterinary preparation in the United States, but it can be used effectively and safely in humans. Although physicians in North America rarely use this drug now, it costs very little and in some countries it is used frequently.

Diethylcarbamazine in the Treatment of Filariasis

Filaria worms, a subgroup of nematodes, are transmitted to man by insects. The adult forms of filaria inhabit the tissues or body cavities of a vertebrate host. Some of the more important members of this family are *Wuchereria bancrofti, W. malayi, Loa loa,* and *Onchocerca volvulus.*

Diethylcarbamazine is the drug of choice (Table 12-3) for the treatment of *W. bancrofti, W. malayi,* and *Loa loa.*[99] The drug removes almost all of the microfilaria (the prelarval forms of the organism) from the blood. Diethylcarbamazine has also been reported to kill the adult forms of *W. malayi* and *Loa loa.*[100] In patients with *Onchocerca,* treatment results in a temporary removal of microfilariae from the skin, but, since the adult worms are not killed, the microfilariae return after a few weeks.[100] Although diethylcarbamazine is a derivative of piperazine, unsubstituted piperazine has no filaricidal action. The mechanism of the filaricidal action of diethylcarbamazine is unknown. The effect on the microfilariae is rapid. The drug does not become selectively associated with either microfilariae or adult worms.[101]

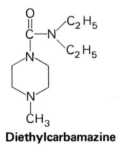

Diethylcarbamazine

Diethylcarbamazine is absorbed well from the gastrointestinal tract, peak blood levels are achieved in 4 hours, and all of the drug is excreted (both as the parent drug and metabolites) by the kidney within 48 hours.[102] Reactions to the drug are of two types. Patients may experience headache, malaise, weakness, nausea, and vomiting as a direct effect of the drug. A second complex of side effects represents allergic reactions to substances released from the killed microfilariae. These reactions are usually mild in the case of *W. bancrofti* or *B. malayi,* but they are often severe when the drug is used to treat *O. volvulus.* Symptoms include swelling and edema of the skin, intense itching, enlargement and tenderness of the inguinal lymph nodes, rash, fever, tachycardia, and headache. Nodular swellings may develop along the course of the lymphatics. These symptoms persist for 3 to 7 days and then subside; then, quite high doses can be tolerated without further reaction. For this reason the following schedule may be used in treating *O. volvulus* infection (adult dosages): 25 mg daily for 3 days; 50 mg daily for 3 days, 100 mg daily for 3 days, and 150 mg daily for 12 days. Caution must also be exercised in the use of diethylcarbamazine in *Loa loa* because it can provoke an encephalopathy in addition to the Herxheimer-like reactions.

REFERENCES

1. H. J. Saz and E. Bueding: Relationships between anthelmintic effects and biochemical and physiological mechanisms. *Pharm. Rev.* 18:871 (1966).

2. R. Cavier and F. Hawking: *Chemotherapy of Helminthiasis.* New York: Pergamon Press, 1973, pp. 1–537.

3. E. Bueding: Some biochemical effects of anthelmintic drugs. *Biochem. Pharmacol.* 18:1541 (1969).

4. M. Farooq: Progress in Bilharziasis control: The situation in Egypt. *Wld. Hlth. Org. Chron.* 21:175 (1967).

5. E. Beveridge: "Chemotherapy of Leishmaniasis" in *Experimental Chemotherapy Vol. I,* ed. R. J. Schnitzer and F. Hawking. New York: Academic Press, 1963, pp. 257–287.

6. J. D. Fulton and L. P. Joyner: Studies on protozoa. Part I. The metabolism of Leishman-Donovan bodies and flagellates of *Leishmania donovani. Trans. Roy. Soc. Trop. Med. Hyg.* 43:273 (1949).

7. E. Bueding and E. Schiller: "Mechanism of action of antischistosomal drugs" in *Mode of Action of Antiparasitic Drugs,* ed. J. Rodrigues da Silva and M. J. Ferreira. New York: Pergamon Press, 1968, pp. 81–86.

8. E. Bueding: Carbohydrate metabolism of *Schistosoma mansoni. J. Gen. Physiol.* 33:475 (1950).

9. T. E. Mansour and E. Bueding: The actions of antimonials on glycolytic enzymes of *Schistosoma mansoni. Brit. J. Pharmacol.* 9:459 (1954).

10. E. Bueding and J. M. Mansour: The relationship between inhibition of phosphofructokinase activity and the mode of action of trivalent organic antimonials on *Schistosoma mansoni. Brit. J. Pharmacol.* 12:159 (1957).

11. E. Bueding and J. Fisher: Factors affecting the inhibition of phosphofructokinase activity of *Schistosoma mansoni* by trivalent organic antimonials. *Biochem. Pharmacol.* 15:1197 (1966).

12. G. A. H. Buttle and M. T. Khayyal: Rapid hepatic shift of worms in mice infected with *Schistosoma mansoni* after a single injection of tartar emetic. *Nature* 194:780 (1962).

13. L. G. Goodwin and J. E. Page: A study of the excretion of organic antimonials using a polarographic procedure. *Biochem. J.* 37:198 (1943).

14. S. E. Smith: Uptake of antimony potassium tartrate by mouse liver slices. *Br. J. Pharmacol.* 37:476 (1969).

15. A. R. Schulert, H. G. Browne, and H. H. Salem: Human disposition of antimony sodium dimercaptosuccinate: With an analysis of antimony concentration in excreted *Schistosoma haematobium* ova. *Trans. Roy. Soc. Trop. Med. Hyg.* 58:48 (1964).

16. F. C. Bartter, D. B. Cowie, H. Most, A. T. Ness, and S. Forbush: The fate of radioactive tartar emetic administered to human subjects. I. Blood concentration and excretion following single and multiple intravenous injections. *Am. J. Trop. Med.* 27:403 (1947).

17. E. A. Steck: "The leishmaniases" in *Progress in Drug Research: Tropical Diseases I,* ed. E. Jucker. Basel: Birkhäuser Verlag, 1974, pp. 289–351.

18. H. Most: Treatment of common parasitic infections of man encountered in the United States [second of two parts]. *New Eng. J. Med.* 287:698 (1972).

19. C. R. Reddy, M. M. Reddy, and M. D. Sivaprasad: Niridazole (Ambilhar) in the treatment of dracunculiasis. *Am. J. Trop. Med. Hyg.* 18:516 (1969).

20. Symposuim: The pharmacological and chemotherapeutic properties of niridazole and other antischistosomal compounds. *Ann. N.Y. Acad. Sci.* 160:423–946 (1969).

21. E. Bueding and J. Fisher: Biochemical effects of niridazole on *Schistosoma mansoni. Mol. Pharmacol.* 6:532 (1970).

22. J. W. Faigle and H. Keberle: Metabolism of niridazole in various species, including man. *Ann. N.Y. Acad. Sci.* 160:544 (1969).

23. C. R. Lambert: Transaminases et rôle du filtre hépatique lors du traitement au CIBA 32644-Ba. *Acta Tropica* Suppl. 9:28 (1966).

24. Symposium: Thérapeutique nouvelle de la Bilharziose et de l'amibiase. *Acta Tropica* Suppl. 9 (1966). The entire issue is about niridazole; several papers present aspects of the drug's distribution and excretion.

25. A. Coutinho and F. T. Barreto: Treatment of hepatosplenic schistosomiasis mansoni with niridazole: Relationships among liver function, effective dose and side effects. *Ann. N.Y. Acad. Sci.* 160:612 (1969).

26. C. R. Lambert, V. S. Sinari, and J. Tripod: Effect of CIBA 32644-Ba on spermatogenesis in laboratory animals. *Acta Tropica* 22:155 (1965).

27. M. D. Prates and A. L. T. Franco: Action du CIBA 32644-Ba sur la spermatogénèse: Etude preliminaire. *Acta Tropica* Suppl. 9:287 (1966).

28. A. A. F. Mahmoud, M. A. Mandel, K. S. Warren, and L. T. Webster: Niridazole: II. A potent long-acting suppressant of cellular hypersensitivity. *J. Immunol.* 114:279 (1975).

29. L. T. Webster, A. E. Butterworth, A. A. F. Mahmoud, E. N. Mngola, and K. S. Warren: Suppression of delayed hypersensitivity in schistosome-infected patients by niridazole. *New. Eng. J. Med.* 292:1144 (1975).

30. M. S. Legator, T. H. Connor, and M. Stoeckel: Detection of mutagenic activity of metronidazole and niridazole in body fluids of humans and mice. *Science* 188:1118 (1975).

31. G. Lämmler: Chemotherapy of trematode infections. *Adv. Chemother.* 3:153 (1968).

32. S. Yang and C. Lin: Treatment of paragonimiasis with bithionol and bithionol sulfoxide. *Dis. Chest* 52:220 (1967).

33. S. J. Oh: Bithionol treatment in cerebral paragonimiasis. *Am. J. Trop. Med. Hyg.* 16:585 (1967).

34. P. D. Marsden and M. G. Schultz: Intestinal parasites. *Gastroenterology* 57:724 (1969).

35. J. A. Rider, R. G. Devereaux, and H. C. Moeller: Clonorchiasis. Treatment with chloroquine phosphate. *Gastroenterology* 52:267 (1967).

36. J. E. D. Keeling: "The chemotherapy of Cestode infections" in *Advances in Chemotherapy*, ed. by A. Goldin, F. Hawking, and R. J. Schnitzer. New York: Academic Press, 1968, pp. 109–152.

37. D. R. Perera, K. A. Western, and M. G. Schultz: Niclosamide treatment of cestodiasis: Clinical trials in the United States. *Am. J. Trop. Med. Hyg.* 19:610 (1970).

38. I. Gherman: Observations on the treatment of taeniases with niclosamide. *Bull. Soc. Pathol. Exot.* 61:432 (1968).

39. L. Runeberg: Uncoupling of oxidative phosphorylation in rat liver mitochondria with desaspidin and related phlorobutyrophenone derivatives. *Biochem. Pharmacol.* 11:237 (1962).

40. L. W. Scheibel, H. J. Saz, and E. Bueding: The anaerobic incorporation of ^{32}P into adenosine triphosphate by *Hymenolepsis diminuta*. *J. Biol. Chem.* 243:2229 (1968).

41. H. Most, M. Yoeli, J. Hammond, and G. P. Scheinesson: Yomesan (niclosamide) therapy of *Hymenolepis nana* infections. *Am. J. Trop. Med. Hyg.* 20:206 (1971).

42. H. Most: Treatment of common parasitic infections of man encountered in the United States [first of two parts]. *New Eng. J. Med.* 287:495 (1972).

43. D. Botero: Paromomycin as effective treatment of *taenia* infections. *Am. J. Trop. Med. Hyg.* 19:234 (1970).

44. M. Wittner and H. Tanowitz: Paromomycin therapy of human cestodiasis with special reference to hymenolepiasis. *Am. J. Trop. Med. Hyg.* 20:433 (1971).

45. O. D. Standen: "Chemotherapy of helminthic infections" in *Experimental Chemotherapy*, ed. R. J. Schnitzer and F. Hawking. New York: Academic Press, 1963, pp. 701–892.

46. M. S. Wolfe: Giardiasis. *J. Am. Med. Assoc.* 233:1362 (1975).

47. R. L. O'Brien, J. G. Olenick, and F. E. Hahn: Reactions of quinine, chloroquine, and quinacrine with DNA and their effects on the DNA and RNA polymerase reactions. *Proc. Natl. Acad. Sci. U.S.* 55:1511 (1966).

48. B. Weisblum and P. L. deHaseth: Quinacrine, a chromosome stain specific for deoxyadenylate-deoxythymidylate-rich regions in DNA. *Proc. Natl. Acad. Sci. U.S.* 69:629 (1972).

49. P. A. J. Janssen: Recent advances in the treatment of parasitic infections in man. *Drug Research* 18:191 (1974) and O. D. Standen: Chemotherapy of intestinal helminthiasis. *Drug Research* 19:158 (1975).

50. H. W. Brown, K.-F. Chan, and K. L. Hussey: Treatment of enterobiasis and ascariasis with piperazine. *J. Am. Med. Assoc.* 161:515 (1956).

51. S. Norton and E. J. deBeer: Investigations on the action of piperazine on *Ascaris lumbricoides. Am. J. Trop. Med. Hyg.* 6:898 (1957).

52. P. A. Mason and G. Sturman: Some pharmacological properties of piperazine. *Br. J. Pharmacol.* 44:169 (1972).

53. J. T. DeBell, J. Del Castillo, and V. Sanchez: Electrophysiology of the somatic muscle cells of *Ascaris lumbricoides. J. Cell Comp. Physiol.* 62:159 (1963).

54. J. Del Castillo, W. C. De Mello, and T. Morales: Mechanism of the paralyzing action of piperazine on *Ascaris* muscle. *Brit. J. Pharmacol.* 22:463 (1964).

55. O. D. Standen, L. G. Goodwin, E. W. Rogers, and D. Stephenson: Activity of piperazine. *Br. Med. J.* 2:437 (1955).

56. S. Hana and A. Tang: Human urinary excretion of piperazine citrate from syrup formulations. *J. Pharmaceut. Sci.* 62:2024 (1973).

57. A. C. Parsons: Piperazine neurotoxicity: "Worm wobble." *Br. Med. J.* 4:792 (1971).

58. B. M. Boulos and L. E. Davis: Hazard of simultaneous administration of phenothiazine and piperazine. *New Eng. J. Med.* 280:1245 (1969).

59. W. C. Austin, W. Courtney, J. C. Danilewicz, D. H. Morgan, L. H. Conover, H. L. Howes, J. E. Lynch, J. W. McFarland, R. L. Cornwell, and V. J. Theodorides: Pyrantel tartrate, a new anthelmintic effective against infections of domestic animals. *Nature* 212:1273 (1966).

60. T. S. Bumbalo, D. J. Fugazzotto, and J. W. Wyczalek: Treatment of enterobiasis with pyrantel pamoate. *Am. J. Trop. Med. Hyg.* 18:50 (1969).

61. W. J. Bell and S. Nassif: Comparison of pyrantel pamoate and piperazine phosphate in the treatment of ascariasis. *Am. J. Trop. Med. Hyg.* 20:584 (1971).

62. R. S. Desowitz, T. Bell, J. Williams, R. Cardines, and M. Tamarua: Anthelmintic activity of pyrantel pamoate. *Am. J. Trop. Med. Hyg.* 19:775 (1970).

63. M. L. Aubry, P. Cowell, M. J. Davey, and S. Shevde: Aspects of the pharmacology of a new anthelmintic: Pyrantel. *Br. J. Pharmacol.* 38:332 (1970).

64. P. Eyre: Some pharmacodynamic effects of the nematocides: Methyridine, tetramisole and pyrantel. *J. Pharm. Pharmacol.* 22:26 (1970).

65. E. Bueding, E. Kmetec, C. Swartzwelder, S. Abadie, and H. J. Saz: Biochemical effects of dithiazanine on the canine whipworm, *Trichuris vulpis. Biochem. Pharmacol.* 5:311 (1961).

66. J. W. Beck, D. Saavedra, G. J. Antell, and B. Tejeiro: Treatment of pinworm infections in humans (enterobiasis) with pyrvinium pamoate. *Am. J. Trop. Med. Hyg.* 8:349 (1959).

67. E. D. Wagner: Pyrvinium pamoate in the treatment of strongyloidiasis. *Am. J. Trop. Med. Hyg.* 12:60 (1963).

68. H. D. Brown, A. R. Matzuk, I. R. Ilves, L. H. Peterson, S. A. Harris, L. H. Sarett, J. R. Egerton, J. J. Yakstis, W. C. Campbell, and A. C. Cuckler: Antiparasitic drugs. IV. 2-(4'-thiazolyl)-benzimidazole, a new anthelmintic. *J. Am. Chem. Soc.* 83:1764 (1961).

69. Multiple authors: Thiabendazole symposium. *Texas Rep. Biol. Med.* 27(Suppl. 2):533–708 (1969).

70. A. C. Cuckler and K. C. Mezey: The therapeutic efficacy of thiabendazole for helminthic infections in man. *Arzneim.-Forsch.* 16:411 (1966).

71. R. K. Prichard: Mode of action of the anthelminthic thiabendazole in *Haemonchus contortus*. *Nature* 228:684 (1970).

72. H. J. Saz: "Comparative biochemistry of carbohydrates in Nematodes and Cestodes" in *Comparative Biochemistry of Parasites,* ed. by H. Van den Bossche. New York: Academic Press, 1972, pp. 33–47.

73. M. F. Malkin and M. Remedios: The effect of thiabendazole on fumarate reductase from thiabendazole-sensitive and resistant *Haemonchus contortus*. *J. Parasitol.* 58:845 (1972).

74. P. M. Allen and D. Gottlieb: Mechanism of action of the fungicide thiabendazole, 2-(4'-thiazolyl) benzimidazole. *Appl. Microbiol.* 20:919 (1970).

75. K. H. Franz, W. J. Schneider, and M. H. Pohlman: Clinical trials with thiabendazole against intestinal nematodes infecting humans. *Am. J. Trop. Med. Hyg.* 14:383 (1965).

76. H. M. Most, W. C. Yoeli, W. C. Campbell, and A. C. Cuckler: The treatment of *Strongyloides* and *Enterobius* infections with thiabendazole. *Am. J. Trop. Med. Hyg.* 14:379 (1965).

77. O. J. Stone and J. F. Mullins: Thiabendazole effectiveness in creeping eruption. *Arch. Dermatol.* 91:427 (1965).

78. R. J. A. Aur, C. B. Pratt, and W. W. Johnson: Thiabendazole in visceral larva migrans. *Am. J. Dis. Child.* 121:227 (1971).

79. O. J. Stone, C. T. Stone, and J. F. Mullins: Thiabendazole: Probable cure for trichinosis. *J. Am. Med. Assoc.* 187:536 (1964).

80. B. H. Kean and D. W. Hoskins: Treatment of trichinosis. *J. Am. Med. Assoc.* 190:852 (1964).

81. W. C. Campbell: Anti-inflammatory and analgesic properties of thiabendazole. *J. Am. Med. Assoc.* 216:2143 (1971).

82. A. P. Chavarria, J. C. Swartzwelder, V. M. Villarejos, and R. Zeledon: Mebendazole, an effective broad-spectrum anthelmintic. *Am. J. Trop. Med. Hyg.* 22:592 (1973).

83. R. G. Sargent, A. M. Savory, A. Mina, and P. R. Lee: A clinical evaluation of mebendazole in the treatment of trichuriasis. *Am. J. Trop. Med. Hyg.* 23:375 (1974).

84. S. Maqbool, D. Lawrence, and M. Katz: Treatment of trichuriasis with a new drug, mebendazole. *J. Pediat.* 86:463 (1975).

85. M. S. Wolfe and J. M. Wershing: Mebendazole: Treatment of trichinosis and ascariasis in Bahamian children. *J. Am. Med. Assoc.* 230:1408 (1974).

86. J. P. Brugmans, D. C. Thienpont, I. van Wijngaarden, O. F. Vanparijs, V. L. Schuermans, and H. L. Lauwers: Mebendazole in enterobiasis: Radiochemical and pilot clinical study in 1,278 subjects. *J. Am. Med. Assoc.* 217:313 (1971).

87. M. J. Miller, I. M. Krupp, M. D. Little, and C. Santos: Mebendazole: An effective anthelmintic for trichuriasis and enterobiasis. *J. Am. Med. Assoc.* 230:1412 (1974).

88. O. T. G. Jones and W. A. Watson: Properties of substituted 2-trifluoromethylbenzimidazoles as uncouplers of oxidative phosphorylation. *Biochem. J.* 102:564 (1967).

89. H. Van den Bossche: "Biochemical effects of the anthelmintic drug mebendazole" in *Comparative Biochemistry of Parasites*, ed. by H. Van den Bossche. New York: Academic Press, 1972, pp. 139–157.

90. E. D. Wagner and A. P. Chavarria: In *vivo* effects of a new anthelmintic, mebendazole (R-17,635) on the eggs of *Trichuris trichuria* and hookworm. *Am. J. Trop. Med. Hyg.* 23:151 (1974).

91. S. De Nollin, M. Borgers, O. Vanparijs, and H. Van den Bossche: Effects of mebendazole on the encysted phase of *Trichinella spiralis* in the rat: An electron-microscope study. *Parasitol.* 69:55 (1974).

92. R. Marsboom: Toxicologic studies on mebendazole. *Toxicol. Appl. Pharmacol.* 24:371 (1973).

93. L. G. Goodwin, L. G. Jayewardene, and O. D. Standen: Clinical trials with bephenium hydroxynaphthoate against hookworm in Ceylon. *Br. Med. J.* 2:1572 (1958).

94. A. W. J. Broome: "Mechanisms of anthelminthic action with particular reference to drugs affecting neuromuscular activity" in *Drugs, Parasites and Hosts*, ed by L. G. Goodwin and R. H. Nimmo-Smith. Boston: Little, Brown, 1962, pp. 43–61.

95. A. I. Krotov and S. N. Federova: Effect of bephenium hydroxynaphthoate on ascarids. *Fed. Proc.* (Translation supplement) 23:T55 (1964).

96. E. W. Rogers: Excretion of bephenium salts in urine of human volunteers. *Br. Med. J.* 2:1576 (1958).

97. H. H. Salem, W. M. Morcos, and H. M. El-Ninny: Clinical trials with bephenium hydroxynaphthoate against *A. duodenale* and other intestinal helminths. *J. Trop. Med.* 68:21 (1965).

98. R. C. Jung and J. E. McCroan: Efficacy of bephenium and tetrachloroethylene in mass treatment of hookworm infection. *Am. J. Trop. Med. Hyg.* 9:492 (1960).

99. E. F. Elslager: New perspectives on the chemotherapy of malaria, filariasis, and leprosy. *Drug Research* 18:99 (1974).

100. F. Hawking: "Chemotherapy of filariasis" in *Experimental Chemotherapy*, Vol. I, ed. by R. J. Schnitzer and F. Hawking. New York: Academic Press, 1963, pp. 893–912.

101. D. R. Bangham: The mode of action of diethylcarbamazine investigated with ^{14}C-labelled drug. *Br. J. Pharmacol.* 10:406 (1955).

102. M. Lubran: Determination of hetrazan in biological fluids. *Br. J. Pharmacol.* 5:210 (1950).

Part IV
Drugs Employed in the Treatment of Viral Infection

Medical efforts to combat viral infection include a variety of approaches.[1] As with the parasitic diseases, vector control is helpful in limiting those viral infections transmitted by insects (e.g., yellow fever transmitted by mosquitos) and animals (e.g., rabies transmitted by dogs). In some cases, isolation of infected patients will limit the spread of a virus in the community. Other efforts to control viral infection have been directed at active stimulation of the immune response by eliciting specific antibody production (immunization) or at passive assistance to the patient's defense mechanism by the use of human gamma globulin, equine antiserums, and, more recently, antiserum from successfully vaccinated humans. In addition to these approaches, there are a few drugs available for the treatment and prevention of selected viral infections.

Prophylaxis by immunization has been the most effective form of control for many viral infections. Mass immunization with live (attenuated) virus vaccines is currently effectively employed to prevent diseases like polio, mumps, measles, and yellow fever. The use of vaccinia virus immunization to prevent smallpox has been so successful that the disease has been virtually eradicated. The use of killed virus vaccines against influenza provides partial protection against serious infection. Influenza vaccines are currently used during epidemics to protect the elderly, the young, and people debilitated because of chronic disease (these are the groups that suffer the greatest morbidity and mortality during influenza epidemics).

In addition to a variety of host defenses, such as antibody production, macrophage action, and cell-mediated immunity, viruses stimulate the production of interferon by certain host cells.[2,3] This protein, in turn, elicits antiviral activity in other host cells. Two methods have been employed experimentally to increase the amount of interferon in the body. The first is the administration of exogenous interferon and the second is the use of compounds that induce interferon production by the host. This second method holds some promise of providing a new class of effective antiviral drugs, and it will be discussed in the following chapter.

Three groups of drugs are currently marketed in the United States for antiviral chemotherapy: the pyrimidine analogs, amantadine, and the isatin-β-thiosemicarbazones. There is no broad-spectrum antiviral drug available for clinical use, and the application of each of these drug groups is severely restricted to the

410

Table IV-1 Approaches to specific control of viral infections
(From Hilleman,[1] Table 1.)

Approach	Level of effectiveness	Characteristics: Antiviral spectrum	Duration of effect
Immunological	Usually high	Very narrow	Relatively long to lifetime
Host resistance (interferon)	Moderate to high	Very broad	Relatively short term
Chemical	Low to moderate	Narrow	Short term

treatment of only a few viral infections. The drugs used to treat viral diseases have been the subject of several reviews and texts.[4-8] A comparison of the three approaches to antiviral therapy (immunization, interferon production, and chemotherapy) is presented in Table IV-1.

REFERENCES

1. M. R. Hilleman: Toward control of viral infections of man. *Science* 164:506 (1969).

2. T. C. Merigan: Host defenses against viral disease. *New Eng. J. Med.* 290:323 (1974).

3. G. W. Jordan and T. C. Merigan: Enhancement of host defense mechanisms by pharmacological agents. *Ann. Rev. Pharmacol.* 15:157 (1975).

4. W. H. Prusoff and B. Goz: Potential mechanisms of action of antiviral agents. *Fed. Proc.* 32:1679 (1973).

5. J. G. Tilles: Antiviral agents. *Ann. Rev. Pharmacol.* 14:469 (1974).

6. [Multiple Authors]: *Chemotherapy of Viral Diseases*, Section 61, vol. I of *International Encyclopedia of Pharmacology and Therapeutics*, New York: Pergamon Press, 1972, 431 pp.

7. W. A. Carter (ed.): *Selective Inhibitors of Viral Functions*, Cleveland: CRC Press, 1973, 377 pp.

8. Y. Becker: *Antiviral Drugs: Mode of Action and Chemotherapy of Viral Infections of Man*, Basel: S. Karger, 1976, 130 pp.

Chapter 13
Chemotherapy of Viral Infections

INTRODUCTION

Definition and Classification of Viruses

Viruses are organisms composed of a nucleic acid core (the genome may be either DNA or RNA) surrounded by a protein-containing shell; they reproduce only inside living cells. They derive their energy supply and their substrates from the infected cell; they also use its synthetic machinery to produce the virus-specific protein required for production of the mature viral particle. Mature virus particles possess only one type of nucleic acid, and they lose their organized form during replication of the genome in the host cell. These characteristics distinguish the viruses from intracellular parasites like the chlamydiae (psittacosis-lymphogranuloma venerum-trachoma group of organisms), which possess both DNA and RNA in their infectious particles and retain their organized form in the intracellular phase, dividing by binary fission.[1] Still more complex intracellular parasites like the plasmodia, the leprosy bacillus, and the rickettsiae have even higher levels of cellular organization, possessing protein-synthesizing and energy-generating systems of their own.

The animal viruses are classified according to various characteristics, such as nucleic acid content (RNA viruses, DNA viruses), gross morphology, location of viral multiplication (in the cytoplasm or nucleus of the infected cell), composition of the virus shell (enveloped or non-enveloped), and serological typing. A selected list of the viruses that infect man is presented in Table 13-1.

The Biology of Viral Reproduction

It is impossible in this text to provide a background review of the molecular biology of animal viruses. But by presenting examples of some of the biochemical events that take place during a viral infection, we can provide a basis for understanding some of the possible sites where the process of viral infection can be selectively inhibited by drugs. The process of viral infection can be

Table 13-1 Classification of some viruses infecting man
(Adapted from Luria and Darnell,[2] Table 1-1.)

Group	Agent	Characteristics
RNA VIRUSES		
Small RNA viruses		Cubic symmetry, no envelope, multiply in cytoplasm, RNA about 2×10^6 daltons
Enteroviruses	Polio	
	Coxsackie A	
	Coxsackie B	
	ECHO	
Rhinoviruses		
Reoviruses		Cubic symmetry, no envelope, multiply in cytoplasm, double-stranded RNA
Myxoviruses		Enveloped virions
Subgroup I		Nuclear phase in replication cycle
	Influenza	Three serotypes (A,B,C,); type A most frequent, causes large epidemics
Subgroup II		Multiplies in cytoplasm; very large RNA (6 to 8×10^6 daltons)
	Parainfluenza	
	Mumps	
	Measles	
Arboviruses		Small, enveloped virions with central RNA-containing core; transmitted by arthropods, cause encephalitis
Subgroup A		Includes Western and Eastern equine encephalomyelitis
Subgroup B		Includes yellow fever and denge
DNA VIRUSES		
Poxviruses		Large, brick-shaped enveloped virions containing at least ten proteins and a large DNA molecule, multiply in cytoplasm
	Variola	Causes smallpox
	Vaccinia	Used for vaccination against smallpox
Herpesvirus		Large, enveloped virions with well-defined icosahedral capsid
	Herpes simplex	Causes fever blisters
	Varicella	Causes chickenpox
	Cytomegalovirus	Infection leads to giant cell formation
Adenovirus		Icosahedral, non-enveloped virions
	Human subgroup	Causes upper respiratory disease and conjunctivitis
Small DNA viruses		Icosahedral, non-enveloped virions containing circular DNA molecules
	Human papilloma	Causes warts
	SV-40	Can transform cultured human cells

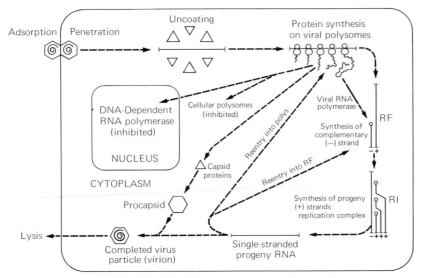

Figure 13-1   The replication cycle of poliovirus. RF, replicative form; RI, replicative intermediate. (From Pearson.[4])

conveniently considered in three stages: (I) entry of the virus into the host cell and release of nucleic acid; (II) replication of the genome and synthesis of viral proteins; and (III) assembly of the virion and release from the cell. A schematic summary of the replication cycle of poliovirus,[3] a non-enveloped RNA virus, is presented in Figure 13-1 for reference during the following discussion.

Stage I—Adsorption, Penetration, and Uncoating

The initial attachment of viruses to mammalian cells appears to be mediated by an electrostatic interaction between the virus capsid or outer envelope and the cell membrane. In some cases, specific receptors for a virus have been demonstrated on the surface of mammalian cells. Polio, for example, a virus that possesses a protein capsid composed of 60 repeating units (four separate proteins per unit), becomes attached to receptors found only in membranes of susceptible cells.

After attachment, a variety of mechanisms operate to introduce the virus into the cell. Certain bacterial viruses (the T-even bacteriophages, for example) have developed elaborate mechanisms for injecting their nucleic acid through the cell wall and membrane into the cytoplasm, but these mechanisms do not pertain to animal viruses. Viruses penetrate animal cells by a process of pinocytosis, but in general, their entry mechanisms are not well understood. Certain viruses (e.g., influenza viruses and other myxoviruses) are surrounded by an envelope containing carbohydrate, lipid, and protein. It is possible that proteins in viral envelopes perform an active role in initiating and facilitating cell penetration.

Some poxviruses have developed elaborate mechanisms of becoming uncoated and releasing their nucleic acid after they have entered the cell. For example, the vaccinia virus, a large DNA virus with an envelope, undergoes a two-stage uncoating process in the cell.[5] In the first stage, the virion is attacked by host cell enzymes that partially degrade the virus particle, which loses some of its protein and all of its phospholipid. The resulting particle, called a core, is composed of DNA surrounded by protein. Poxvirus cores contain a DNA-dependent RNA polymerase,[6] and they can synthesize mRNA.[7] The second stage of the uncoating process proceeds only after a delay, releasing the viral DNA into the cell cytoplasm. This second uncoating process is prevented by inhibitors of protein synthesis.[5] The most plausible model of this sequence of events is that a portion of the DNA in the virus core is available to act as a template for the synthesis of an mRNA that in turn directs the synthesis of a virus-specific uncoating enzyme that then degrades the core, releasing naked vaccinia DNA. The delay between the first and second stage of the uncoating process represents the time required for synthesis of the virus-specific mRNA and uncoating protein.

These examples of viral penetration and uncoating point up the complicated interaction between the virus and the host cell that is required for the initiation of a viral infection. The infective process can be interrupted here at the first stage of the virus-cell interaction. Antiviral antibodies, for example, can prevent attachment of the virus to the cell by reacting with the coat protein of the virion; when added shortly after adsorption of the virus to the cell surface, they can, in some cases, prevent initiation of infection. Amantadine, one of the clinically useful antiviral drugs, acts at this first stage of the infection process. In the presence of amantadine the virus can adsorb to the cell surface, but penetration and uncoating are apparently inhibited. As has just been demonstrated, drugs that inhibit animal cell protein synthesis may in some cases inhibit the uncoating process; such drugs, however, are not useful in therapy because their effect is not selective.

Stage II—Synthesis of Viral Components

In the second stage of viral infection, the genome of the virus is duplicated, and the viral proteins are synthesized in the appropriate sequence. The events that take place in the second stage involve a variety of control mechanisms that direct the energy-producing and synthetic functions of the cell to serve in the synthesis of viral nucleic acid and protein. When some DNA viruses infect a population of growing cells, for example, they inhibit the synthesis of host DNA, thus reserving the pools of nucleic acid precursors for their own use. This inhibition of host cell DNA synthesis is apparently mediated by a virus-specific protein.

Although viruses use cellular enzymes in the synthesis of viral components, they also produce their own enzymes for specialized functions. For example, polymerases produced after infection with some of the small RNA viruses are necessary for replicating the RNA genome. As far as is known at present, RNA does not serve a template function in virus-free mammalian cells, and specific enzymes, coded in the viral genome, must be produced so that the genetic information of these RNA viruses can be replicated. One of these enzymes, produced after infection by poliovirus is RNA replicase; it requires a single-stranded RNA for a template and directs the synthesis of a second strand of RNA. This second strand (−) is complementary to the first strand (+), which contains the genetic information of the virus, and it can, in turn, serve as a template from which multiple viral RNA genomes, (+) strands, are synthesized. This enzyme is completely different from the RNA polymerase of the host cell, which uses double-stranded DNA as a template. It is also different from other viral polymerases, such as the RNA-dependent DNA polymerase (or reverse transcriptase) that synthesizes DNA from single-stranded viral RNA template.[8]

The production and function of key virus-specific enzymes like nucleic acid polymerases and enzymes involved in synthesizing nucleic acid precursors stand out as logical points for selective attack by chemotherapeutic agents. Several compounds inhibit viral nucleic acid synthesis. Guanidine[9] and 2-(α-hydroxybenzyl)-benzimidazole[10] are both active against certain small RNA viruses (e.g., poliovirus, Coxsackie B virus, and many ECHO viruses) as a result of a primary inhibition of viral RNA production. The mechanisms by which these compounds inhibit RNA synthesis have not been precisely defined, but it appears that initiation of RNA chains is inhibited by guanidine (and possibly also by the benzimidazoles). Several antibiotics (e.g., streptovaricins, rifamycins, distamycin A) inhibit some of the virus-specific nucleic acid polymerases and have antiviral activity in selected systems in vitro. None of these agents has yet been shown to be useful in the chemotherapy of viral diseases.

The detailed study of the viral enzymes responsible for nucleic acid synthesis may yield new viral-inhibitory drugs. The substrate site of the viral enzyme, for example, may "accept" nucleotide analogs not accommodated by the mammalian polymerases. Such nucleotide analogs could then have an antiviral effect either by blocking the function of the viral enzyme or by being incorporated into viral nucleic acid, to produce a faulty inactive RNA or DNA. In either case, a selective toxicity would obtain. Iododeoxyuridine (IUdR) is a clinically useful antiviral drug that is incorporated into DNA in place of thymidine. The IUdR-containing DNA behaves abnormally in several ways and there is a consequent marked decrease in viral infectivity. The incorporation of IUdR into DNA is not a very selective event, since the drug is incorporated into the DNA of the patient's cells as well as into that of the virus. Another thymidine analog, 5-iodo-5'-amino-2',5'-dideoxyuridine, selectively inhibits herpes simplex virus (type 1) replication in vitro.[11] This compound is not incorporated into DNA in uninfected cells, but in virus-infected cultures it is phosphorylated and incorporated into the nucleic acid. The unique biological activity of this drug suggests that much greater selectivity of action may be obtainable with the nucleoside analog approach.

The production of viral proteins in all DNA viruses requires the synthesis of mRNAs, which are then translated by the protein synthesizing machinery (ribosomes, tRNAs, amino acids, activating enzymes, etc.) of the host cell. Many single-stranded RNA viruses contain (−)RNA (that is, RNA as the antimessenger) and this must serve as a template for the production of (+)RNA under the direction of a viral transcriptase before protein synthesis can take place. In the case of some single-stranded RNA viruses (e.g., polio, Coxsackie, ECHO), the virus itself contains the (+)RNA that serves both as a messenger for protein synthesis and as a template for (−)RNA synthesis. Poliovirus RNA is translated in a single continuous process. Thus, a very large protein is formed, and this is systemically cleaved by protease to yield the viral enzymes and structural proteins. With many of the more complex viruses, the mRNAs for proteins involved in the replication of the viral genome and in the direction of host cell synthesis of viral-specific components are produced earlier in the infection process than the mRNA for proteins like the capsid proteins, which are not required until the end when assembly of the virion takes place. This statement is somewhat of an oversimplification, but it points out the fact that production of the various components of the virus is subject to some control.

The synthesis of viral-specific proteins is another potential biochemical site for selective inhibition by chemotherapeutic drugs. Indeed, one of the clinically useful antiviral compounds, N-methylisatin-β-thiosemicarbazone, appears to inhibit the multiplication of poxviruses by selectively affecting the late RNA to inhibit the synthesis of late viral structural proteins.

Stage III—Assembly and Release of the Virus

In the final stage of the infection process, the viral components are assembled into a mature virion. During replication, the viral nucleic acid is not associated with viral structural protein. The capsid proteins accumulate in the cell late in the infection. The viral genome then is encased by capsid proteins and, once associated with them, can no longer replicate. In the case of nonenveloped viruses (e.g., poliovirus, adenovirus), the virion is complete and is released from the cell. With other viruses, however, the capsid is enveloped by a membrane, the carbohydrate and lipid portions of which are derived from host cell membranes. The poxviruses are even more complex. They contain a large DNA molecule surrounded by many viral proteins and more than one membrane. These complex viruses are synthesized in cytoplasmic factories, and they possess a higher degree of organization than the other viruses.

The release of mature virions from the cell may be rapid and may be accompanied by cell death and lysis; this is often the case with the simpler nonenveloped viruses like polio. In contrast to this method of release, some enveloped viruses are released (often over a long period of time) by a process of budding at the cell membrane. In this case the cytoplasmic membrane remains intact during the release of the viruses, and the cell may survive.

The antibiotic rifampin may exert its antiviral action by affecting events in the late stage of the infection cycle. Rifampin is used to treat tuberculosis and some other bacterial infections, and its mechanism of action has been reviewed in detail in Chapter 8. The antibacterial effect of rifampin clearly results from its specific inhibition of bacterial RNA polymerases. Some rifamycin derivatives are inhibitors of tumor virus DNA polymerases,[12] but they also inhibit mammalian polymerases and the degree of specificity of action is small. At high concentrations, rifampin itself is active in vitro against some poxviruses, such as vaccinia.[13,14] The mechanism of the drug effect is not at all clear, but it is probably not related to its antibacterial action. Concentrations of rifampin that inhibit viral growth do not inhibit RNA polymerase activity associated with the mature vaccinia virus particle or the virus core.[15] Further, it has been demonstrated that viral DNA, RNA, and protein synthesis continues in the presence of rifampin, but that assembly into mature virus particles is prevented.[16] This drug effect is reversible. If rifampin is removed, the virus particles are assembled into mature virions even in the absence of new protein synthesis. It is possible that the receptor for rifampin in both bacteria and viruses is RNA polymerase. In bacteria the association of the drug with the receptor inhibits enzyme activity, and in the virus the rifampin-RNA polymerase complex, although enzymatically active, may be structurally altered so that it is unable to interact with other parts of the virus as a necessary component of the virus core. Thus, the result of the as yet undefined rifampin effect appears to be an inhibition of maturation or assembly of viral components into an infective virion.

The replication of influenza virus in tissue culture can be inhibited by a specific inhibitor of neuraminidase, 2-deoxy-2,3-dehydro-N-trifluoroacetylneuraminic acid.[17] Neuraminidase is an enzyme that cleaves sialic acid off glycoprotein, and it's activity is important for either the assembly or release of some myxoviruses.

Because viruses parasitize many of the functions of their host cells, there are many biochemical mechanisms common to both the infecting agent and the animal cell. This, of course, limits the number of functions that may be selectively interrupted by chemical agents.

It is hoped that this introduction has served to underscore the fact that fundamental research into the molecular biology of viral replication is providing a basis for the rational development of antiviral drugs. One of the problems in chemotherapy of viral infection is that the clinical symptoms of infection are often not evident until there has already been extensive viral replication, and the immune responses of the host are already building an effective deterrent to the virus. Thus, for many common viral infections chemotherapy may not be an appropriate modality of treatment. This is especially true in those cases in which the usual presentation is one of mild disease. There are already firm indications that antiviral drugs are useful in prophylaxis against and treatment of a few severe viral infections. A clear need exists for drugs with a greater antiviral potency and selectivity of action for use in patients with severe viral infections requiring systemic drug administration.

INTERFERON

Interferons are carbohydrate-containing proteins produced by animal cells infected with viruses. They are released from the cells in which they are produced, and they cause inhibition of virus multiplication in other cells. The lymphoreticular system produces much of the circulating interferon in the body, with both DNA and RNA viruses being interferon inducers. In addition, a wide variety of other intracellular parasites, microbial extracts, synthetic polymers, and some small molecular weight compounds can elicit the production of interferon (see Table 13-2). Interferon is also produced by sensitized lymphocytes on exposure to specific antigen and by normal lymphocytes on exposure to mitogens.[18] The interferons produced by different animals are quite species specific.[19] That is, they inhibit viral multiplication only in cells of the same animal species (or closely related ones) in which they were produced. In contrast, the antiviral action of the interferons is very broad. There is a large literature dealing with interferon production and action, and the reader is referred to specific reviews for detailed discussion[18,19,20]

Studies on the Mechanism of Induction of Interferon

Much indirect evidence suggests that interferon is produced as a result of the induction of new host cell protein synthesis by viral components. Pure double-stranded RNAs of both synthetic and viral origin are good interferon inducers, and it is likely that nucleic acid is the viral component that is the active inducing moiety. The production of virus-induced and synthetic RNA-induced interferon is blocked by inhibitors of both RNA and protein synthesis. These observations are consistent with (but do not prove) the hypothesis that interferon-inducing substances

Table 13-2   List of interferon inducers
(Modified from DeClercq and Merigan,[19] Table 1, and Ho and Armstrong,[18] Table 1.)

Microorganisms

*Viruses (both DNA and RNA)
  Chlamydia (trachoma, inclusion conjunctivitis)
  Rickettsiae
  Mycoplasma
  Bacteria (e.g., *Escherichia coli, Bacillus abortus, Haemophilus influenzae*)
  Protozoa (e.g., *Toxoplasma gondii,*
    Plasmodium berghei, Trypanosoma cruzi)

Microbial extracts

*Viral extracts (double-stranded RNAs from several viruses)
  Bacterial extracts (endotoxin)
  Fungal polysaccharide (mannan)

Synthetic polymers

  Polycarboxylates (maleic anhydride copolymers, polyacrylic and polymethyla-
    crylic acids)
  Polysulfates (polyvinylsulfate)
  Polyphosphates
  *Polyribonucleotide homopolymer pairs (e.g., poly rI:rC and poly rA:rU)
  Alternating polyribonucleotides
  Phosphorylated polysaccharides (e.g., dextran phosphate)
  Polythiophosphate (thiophosphate analogs of polyribonucleotides)

Low molecular weight compounds

  Tilorone
  Basic dyes (e.g., Methylene blue, Acridine orange)

The best inducers are marked by an asterisk

cause the mammalian cell to transcribe a specific cellular gene into mRNA to produce interferon. (It is not known whether one gene or multiple structural genes are expressed in cells induced to synthesize interferon.)

The sequence of events occurring prior to mRNA synthesis has not been defined. It is not yet clear whether entry of the high molecular weight inducers into the cell is required for induction or whether they bind to surface receptors and initiate a chain of intracellular events leading to interferon induction. Since double-stranded RNAs are the most potent of the synthetic interferon inducers, they have been used as a probe to find possible cellular receptors. There are at least four requirements for these polynucleotides to be effective inducers: (1) a double-stranded form; (2) a sufficiently high T_m; (3) a high molecular weight; and (4) intact ribose 2'-OH groups.[21] Poly rI:rC and other synthetic double-stranded RNAs bind to the cell surface, but this interaction alone does not appear to be sufficient to initiate interferon production.[22] Uptake of poly rI:rC into the cell also takes place. When the polynucleotide is attached to a solid carrier that is too large to enter the cell, induction still occurs, but this could be caused by small amounts of polynucleotide that are released from the carrier and taken into the cell.[23] Thus, it is not yet known for certain where interferon inducers initially interact with the critical cell components responsible for producing the induction effect.

Studies on the Mechanism of Action of Interferon

It is well established that interferon does not interact directly with viruses or affect their adsorption or penetration into the cell and that virus replication is blocked at a stage prior to assembly. Interferon binds tightly to cell surfaces,[24] but the mechanism by which it produces an antiviral effect has not been established. Perhaps in response to the surface binding, a series of events are triggered that require cellular RNA and protein synthesis. These conclusions were made on the basis of experiments using RNA and protein synthesis inhibitors to block the antiviral action.[25,26] This has been interpreted as an indication that interferon itself is an inducer molecule that derepresses the host cell genome, producing a protein that inhibits virus multiplication. Since viral protein synthesis appears to be primarily affected in several interferon-treated experimental systems,[27,28,29] the putative induced product has been called translation inhibitory protein.

The data concerning the viral process that is primarily affected are at this point somewhat confusing, and the reader must consult recent reviews to accurately appreciate the situation as it evolves. Several studies made in intact virus-infected cells,[28,29] however, have supported the model proposed by Marcus and Salb[30] that viral mRNA cannot combine with ribosomes after interferon treatment. Also, studies in cell-free systems have shown that protein-synthesizing extracts of interferon-treated cells are impaired in their ability to translate viral mRNA but that translation of poly U and cellular mRNA proceeds normally.[32,33] It is not known how the inhibitory factor (the results of one study suggest that it is a ribosome-associated protein with a molecular weight of 48,000)[31] produced in response to interferon distinguishes between cellular and viral mRNAs. Although many studies have supported a mechanism based on a primary inhibition of viral mRNA translation, there are also a few reports of interferon-induced inhibition of transcription,[33,34] and we are clearly still at an early stage of understanding the interferon effect. One problem is that interferon preparations often contain more than one biologically active component,[35] and thus more than one mechanism of action may be possible.

Interferon Inducers as Antiviral Drugs

Of the three approaches to the specific control of viral infections, immunization provides the longest lasting protection, but its usefulness is restricted to those infections in which there are only a few serotypes. In the case of viruses causing many common illnesses, there are so many different serotypes, and immunity is so short lived, that control by immunization is not practical. The chemotherapeutic agents developed to date have a very narrow spectrum of action, and their effects are transient, whereas interferon has a broad spectrum of activity, and it does not have the delay period inherent to the development of the antibody response in immunization. Exploitation of the antiviral effect of interferon would thus seem to be a potential therapeutic approach. This could be done in two ways: the administration of purified interferon or the administration of compounds that stimulate the production of interferon by the cells of the host.

Because of species specificity, interferon prepared for human use must be purified from human (or perhaps primate) cells. This is a costly procedure, and it yields only limited amounts of the compound. At present, interferon is prepared from human leukocytes and only enough is available for small pilot studies. In a randomized, placebo-controlled trial, local administration of interferon (given by nasal spray in divided doses one day before and for three days after infection) produced a statistically significant amelioration of symptoms and reduction in seroconversion and virus shedding in volunteers challenged with rhinovirus type 4.[36] A similar antiviral effect has not yet been demonstrated with systemically administered interferon in humans, although antiviral protection has been shown in animal models.[37] It is clear, however, that levels of circulating interferon exceeding those observed in naturally occurring viral diseases can be achieved with intravenous or intramuscular administration in man.[38] Studies of interferon pharmacokinetics in animals (reviewed by Ho[39]) show half-lives of only a few minutes after rapid intravenous injection. After continuous intravenous infusion in man, however, the half-life is 2.8 hours.[38] This makes it likely that it may be possible to maintain sufficient serum levels for prolonged periods. The following example also suggests that systemically administered interferon may produce an antiviral action. Interferon was administered subcutaneously or intramuscularly to a few patients with chronic hepatitis B infection and chronic active hepatitis. It produced a rapid fall in Dane-particle–associated DNA, DNA polymerase activity, and hepatitis B core antigen.[40] The Dane particles are the presumed causative virus of Type B hepatitis. It is not clear whether this effect is due to a direct antiviral action or to some effect of interferon on the immune system. But these observations indicate that interferon could some day prove useful in limiting carrier infectivity or in eradicating chronic hepatitis B infection. It is very encouraging that systemic administration of large doses of interferon has been accompanied by quite low toxicity,[38] although it should be noted that mild reversible hematopoietic suppression has been observed.[40] As might be predicted from its high molecular weight, very low levels of interferon are achieved in the cerebrospinal fluid.[38]

The second potential therapeutic approach utilizes interferon inducers to stimulate endogenous interferon production. Some microbial extracts and synthetic polymers that induce the production of interferon are listed in Table 13-2. The most potent of the synthetic interferon inducers is poly rI:rC, a double-stranded homopolymer of inosine and cytosine. This compound has been shown to protect cells in culture from a variety of viruses, including the production of resistance to some common respiratory viruses in cultured human cells.[41,42] It also elicits antiviral activity in animals.[37] Poly rI:rC has a number of side effects,[43] including endotoxin-like effects,[44] pyrogenicity,[45] and embryotoxicity[46] (at high concentrations). Poly rI:rC is also immunogenic in some strains of mice that spontaneously develop an autoimmune disorder resembling human systemic lupus erythematosus,[47] a condition in which anti-nucleic acid antibodies are commonly found. The possibly severe side effects of such inducers as poly rI:rC and tilorone have prevented systemic application in man. Prophylactic intranasal administration of poly rI:rC has been reported to slightly reduce symptoms in volunteers challenged with rhinovirus 13.[48] A more impressive effect was obtained in a study in which a substituted propanediamine interferon inducer was administered as nosedrops on the day before and the day of challenge with rhinovirus Type 21.[49] In this study interferon appeared in nasal washings in a high titer, symptoms were somewhat alleviated, and there was decreased virus shedding. But one major problem with this approach to therapy is that people become hyporeactive on repeated exposure to the inducers. This drawback and the fact that effectiveness has only been shown in humans when the inducer is applied locally and prophylactically will make it difficult to extend the approach to a successful field trial.

AMANTADINE

Structure and Mechanism of Action

Amantadine hydrochloride is a water-soluble amine with a unique cage-like structure. It inhibits the replication of some

$NH_2 \cdot HCl$

Amantadine

myxoviruses *in vitro*[50]; these include the influenza A group,[51] parainfluenza strains,[51] and rubella,[52] among others. Influenza B viruses are resistant to amantadine.[51]

The biochemical mechanism of amantadine action is unknown, but the locus of its effect in the sequence of events that take place during virus replication is fairly well defined. Amantadine does not inactivate the virus or prevent its adsorption to the cell membrane and there is no effect on either the synthesis of viral components or on virion assembly and release.[53,54] In experiments in which one cycle of virus replication is permitted, amantadine must be present at the time of infection to be effective.[53,54] In a study of the drug action on influenza A_2 replication in cultured cells, it was observed that the virus that is adsorbed to cells in the presence of amantadine is susceptible to inactivation by antiviral antibody several hours after infection (Figure 13-2).[53] On the basis of this type of data, it was suggested that the primary effect of amantadine is to inhibit viral penetration into the cell, leaving the

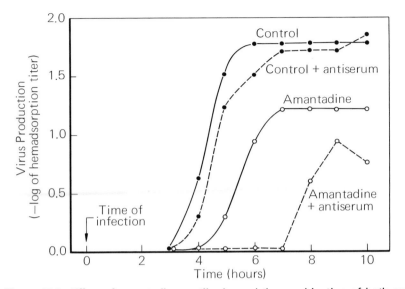

Figure 13-2 Effect of amantadine, antibody, and the combination of both on virus production in chick embryo fibroblasts infected with influenza A2/AA/2/60. Control (●-●); control, plus antiserum (●--●); amantadine (○-○); amantadine plus antiserum (○--○). Monolayer cultures of chick embryo fibroblasts were infected with influenza A$_2$, and, after 15 minutes of incubation, the unadsorbed virus was removed by washing the cells. Amantadine (20 μg/ml) was present from 15 minutes before to 2 hours after infection. Antibody-treated cultures were exposed to specific virus rabbit antiserum for a 15-minute period between 1.75 and 2 hours postinfection. The amount of virus produced was determined by a hemadsorption test. It is clear that the antiserum had little effect on the production of virus when added to the control cultures during the indicated period. Amantadine alone produced a delay in the initial appearance of virus as well as a reduction in the total amount of virus. Amantadine plus antiserum resulted in a long delay in the appearance of virus as well as a reduction in the total amount of virus produced. These results have been interpreted as evidence for the concept that in the presence of amantadine virus remains adsorbed at the cell surface. (Redrawn from Hoffmann et al.[53])

virus attached to the surface in a form that can react with antibodies. Subsequent observations of the effect of amantadine on fowl plague virus (an avian influenza A virus) replication support a mechanism in which the primary effect is on viral uncoating.[54,55] Although there is a slight inhibition of penetration in this system, virus was observed to pass into intracellular vacuoles in the presence of amantadine. Fowl plague virus labeled with Neutral red remained sensitive to photoinactivation when the drug was present (Figure 13-3).[54] Loss of photosensitivity of Neutral red-

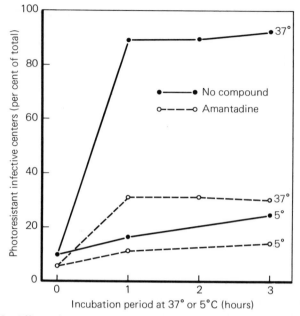

Figure 13-3 Effect of amantadine on uncoating of fowl plague virus in chick embryo cells. Cells were infected with 0.01 plaque-forming units/cell of Neutral red-labeled virus. After 30 minutes at 5 °C the cells were washed and then incubated at 5 or 37 °C. Assays were made for total and for photoresistant infective centers. The number of photoresistant infective centers is expressed as a percentage of the total amount in respective cultures. After uncoating, the virus is no longer inactivated by light. Amantadine was present at a concentration of 25 μg/ml from the time of virus inoculation until the end of light irradiation. (From Kato and Eggers.[54])

labeled virus occurs with uncoating. From this and other observations, it has been concluded that the predominant effect of amantadine is to prevent viral uncoating.[54,55]

The Clinical Use of Amantadine

Despite the *in vitro* sensitivity of influenza A and A_1, some parainfluenza viruses, and rubella, amantadine is clinically useful only in the treatment of influenza A_2 infection. It is currently recommended that the use of amantadine be restricted to prophylaxis against influenza A_2 (Asian) and that it should not be used in the treatment of patients who have been symptomatic with A_2 influenza for more than a few hours.[56] This recommendation is based on the results of clinical trials comparing the incidence and severity of infection in subjects treated with the drug or a placebo. The interpretation of the results of several of the early clinical trials has been questioned because of a number of deficiencies in their design, including an inadequate number of patients, an occasional failure to confirm the infection serologically, inappropriate matching of control and drug-treated groups, and lack of double-blind procedures in administration and patient evaluation.[57]

It is easy to understand the difficulty in determining the effectiveness of an antiviral drug in reducing the incidence of naturally acquired infection during an influenza epidemic. The experimental protocol has to be prepared and the participating investigators organized before the epidemic has developed. Otherwise, it is difficult to assure uniformity of methods and adequate sample sizes. Consistent and accurate methods of identifying index cases, defining the presence of infection, and quantitating its severity and duration must be employed. Appropriate serological identification of the infection must be carried out, and antibody titers should be followed in all control and treated patients to determine possible effects of the drug on subclinical infection and to control for those patients suffering from virus infection other than influenza A_2. The population studied must be assigned to drug-treated or control groups by an appropriate random process, and the groups must be compared, at the end, to assure that they are matched according to age and sex. Finally, the drug or placebo should be administered and the patient response assessed according to double-blind procedure.

Several studies have been carried out that follow this protocol; they demonstrate that amantadine, given before the onset of clinical symptoms, decreases the occurrence of Asian influenza in humans when the infection is experimentally induced[58,59] and when it is naturally acquired.[60] The results of one of these studies are presented in Table 13-3. They demonstrate that amantadine treatment of contacts (people living in the same household) of active cases of influenza A_2 results in both a decreased incidence of clinical influenza and a significant reduction in subclinical infection (i.e., where there is only serological evidence). The sample size in this study is not large, but the results are representative. Amantadine certainly does not provide complete protection, but the results have been encouraging enough to warrant its use with high risk patients.

Table 13-3 **The effect of amantadine on the incidence of infection in contacts of serologically confirmed, active cases of influenza A$_2$**

Index cases were identified during an influenza A$_2$ epidemic, and their families were divided at random into drug-treated and placebo groups. All members of one family except the index case received the same treatment (drug or placebo). Index cases received only the placebo, so as not to reduce the possible spread of influenza virus among contacts. Treatment consisted of 100 mg of amantadine (adult dose) every 12 hours for 10 days from the time the index case was first seen. The drug, or placebo, was given on a double-blind basis. Blood samples were taken from everybody on the first visit and again 2 to 3 weeks later. During the 10 days, the family members were visited regularly with daily recording of temperature and the presence of a cough. A cough accompanied by a temperature of 100 °F or higher was accepted as the criterion for a diagnosis of clinical influenza. Subclinical infection was identified by a fourfold or greater rise in antibody titer to A$_2$/England/10/67 virus without cough and temperature elevation. The data presented in the table refer only to family members of index cases in which there was serological confirmation of influenza A$_2$ infection. (Data taken from Galbraith *et al.*[60] Tables II and III.)

Contacts who developed clinical influenza within 10 days of entering the study:						
Treatment	All cases			Confirmed serologically		
	Number	Percent	Probability	Number	Percent	Probability
Amantadine	2/55	3.6		0/48	0	
			0.07			0.05–0.01
Placebo	12/85	14.1		10/69	14.5	

Contacts with serological evidence of influenza infection:					
Treatment	Clinical and subclinical infections			Subclinical infections only	
Amantadine	7/48	14.6		7/48	14.6
			<0.01		0.2
Placebo	27/69	39.1		17/69	24.6

There is also some indication, that the clinical course of influenza A$_2$ infection may be altered by the administration of amantadine after the appearance of symptoms. Several double-blind, placebo-controlled studies with serologically confirmed cases of naturally occurring A$_2$ influenza suggest that amantadine treatment results in more rapid defervesence and a milder clinical course.[61,62,63] The clinical improvement is probably due to a reduction in the number of additional cells infected by the virus. Thus, this drug may be of some use in the treatment, as well as the prophylaxis, of influenza A$_2$ infection if given within 24 hours of the onset of symptoms. At present, the prophylactic effect of amantadine justifies its administration on a continuous basis for up to 90 days to reduce the likelihood of infection in high risk patients during A_2 influenza epidemics. The drug may be used with or without vaccine.

Pharmacology and Untoward Effects of Amantadine

Amantadine is rapidly and completely absorbed from the gastrointestinal tract.[64] There is no evidence of metabolism of the drug in man, and the primary route of excretion is renal (56 per cent of a dose is excreted in the urine in 24 hours and 86 per cent in 4 days).[64]

Amantadine given for many months at many times the comparable human dosage did not produce organ pathology in animals.[65] At the usual adult dosage of 200 mg/day, amantadine is generally well tolerated. Since the drug is excreted in the unchanged form by the kidney, it is prudent to use caution in administering the drug to patients with compromised renal function. Acute neurotoxicity, consisting of tremors, hallucinations, and bizarre behavior, has been reported in a patient with chronic renal failure receiving amantadine.[66] Although amantadine is well tolerated, patients sometimes complain of subjective central nervous system side effects, including feelings of depression, confusion, detachment, lethargy, nervousness, and dizziness. Nausea, vomiting, dryness of the mouth, ataxia, slurred speech, edema, and livedo reticularis occur occasionally.

Although some patients experience tremors as a side effect, exactly the opposite response was noted in one parkinsonian patient who experienced a remission of her symptoms of rigidity, tremor, and akinesia while being treated with amantadine for prophylaxis during an influenza epidemic.[67] This serendipitous observation has been followed up by clinical trials that demonstrate that amantadine is of significant benefit for the patient with mild Parkinson's disease,[68,69] and it now has an accepted role in the treatment of that condition.[70] The mechanism of the beneficial effect is not well understood, but amantadine may have both an indirect dopamine-releasing action and the ability to directly stimulate dopamine receptors.[71] There is little support for the model in which amantadine is said to increase local dopamine concentrations by inhibiting its reuptake. The pharmacological actions and adverse effects of amantadine have been reviewed in detail by Parkes.[72]

METHISAZONE

Structure and Mechanism of Action

Methisazone (N-methylisatin-β-thiosemicarbazone) is one of a group of derivatives of isatin-β-thiosemicarbazone that possess antiviral activity. Other thiosemicarbazones have been shown to have antibacterial or antitumor activity.[73]

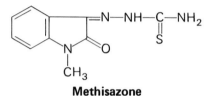

Methisazone

The mechanism by which methisazone inhibits poxvirus replication is not well defined. Studies of the effect of the parent compound isatin-β-thiosemicarbazone on vaccinia virus replication in HeLa cells suggest that the drug affects the ability of late virus mRNA to express itself normally.[74,75] The viral mRNA, which is synthesized in cells during the first 3 hours of infection, is normal in size and fully functional in the presence of the drug. The late viral mRNA (produced after 3 hours) is apparently of normal size when synthesized, and it can enter polysomes; but within a very short period, the RNA decreases in size, and protein synthesis is drastically reduced. It is not clear whether the decline in protein synthesis represents a primary or secondary effect of the drug, however, and it appears that the synthesis of all "late" proteins may not be inhibited.[76]

Viruses, like bacteria, can become drug resistant. Resistance to all the antiviral drugs in clinical use (amantadine,[77] the pyrimidine analogs,[78] and the isatin-β-thiosemicarbazones[79]) has been demonstrated. A strain of rabbitpox virus made resistant to isatin-β-thiosemicarbazone was also resistant to methisazone, and this suggests that the mechanism of action of the two drugs may be similar. Both isatin-β-thiosemicarbazone–dependent (IBT^D) and –resistant (IBT^R) mutants of vaccinia virus have been selected.[80] When mixed infections were produced in HeLa cells, it was found that the drug-sensitive wild type vaccinia was able to grow in the presence of the drug when either mutant strain (IBT^D or IBT^R) was the coinfecting agent. Also, the presence of either wild type or

IBT[R] assisted the growth of IBT[D] in the absence of the drug. These observations suggest that a protein coded by the genome of one of the strains enables particles of all strain types to be made even under unfavorable conditions (with drug for the wild type and without drug for the dependent strain).

The basis for the antiviral activity of some analogs of IBT is clearly different from the inhibition of "late" viral protein synthesis described for the effect of IBT or methisazone on poxviruses. A study of the effects of busatin (a dibutyl-derivative of IBT) on poliovirus replication demonstrates that this analog inhibits viral RNA synthesis and, to some extent, cellular DNA synthesis, but not cellular RNA synthesis.[81] Inhibition was also demonstrated in a cell-free poliovirus RNA polymerase reaction.

Methisazone inactivates the transforming activity of Rous sarcoma virus on contact and it also inhibits the RNA-dependent DNA polymerase of that virus.[82] This effect is a consequence of the ability of the thiosemicarbazones to bind certain metallic ions. Some thiosemicarbazones have been found to possess antitumor activity in animals, which is also a consequence of their metal ion complexing effect.[73]

Clinical Use and Pharmacology of Methisazone

Although methisazone inhibits the reproduction of several RNA and DNA viruses in vitro, it has a very limited application in the treatment of human infections. The drug is clinically useful for the prophylaxis of smallpox in people exposed to active cases.[83,84] It has the advantage of being active during the incubation period of the virus at a time when vaccination would be too late to prevent the development of infection.

A trial of the prophylactic effect of methisazone against smallpox was carried out in Madras, India in 1963.[83] Drug treatment of close contacts was begun 1 to 2 days after hospital admission of the patient with active smallpox. Of 2,610 contacts treated, there were 18 cases of smallpox (0.69%), and 4 cases died. In the control sample of 2,710 contacts, there were 113 cases of active smallpox (4.17%), and 21 cases died. Methisazone also appears to reduce the incidence of variola minor (alastrim) in contacts of active cases.[85] Although it exhibits a clinically milder course, this disease is caused by a virus that is closely related to variola major, the causative agent of smallpox. Methisazone is not effective in the active case of smallpox, but there are several case reports and uncontrolled studies (summarized by Bauer[86]) suggesting that it may be useful in treating eczema vaccinatum and vaccinia gangrenosa.

Methisazone is taken orally and its pharmacology is largely unknown. Patients frequently experience vomiting, but the incidence of this side effect varies widely from one report to another.[86] With the projected elimination of smallpox from the earth during the next few years methisazone may lose its role in medicine.

PYRIMIDINE AND PURINE ANALOGS

IDOXURIDINE

Structures and Mechanism of Action

Idoxuridine (5-iodo-2'-deoxyuridine, IUdR) was synthesized by Prusoff in 1959,[87] and it is one of many purine and pyrimidine analogs that have been tested for antiviral, antitumor, and immunosuppressive activity. Idoxuridine, a halogenated derivative of deoxyuridine, is an analog of thymidine. The presence of a halogen in lieu of methyl group alters the electron configuration of the pyrimidine, resulting in a more acidic dissociation constant. The iodine atom has a van der Waals' radius of 2.15 Å. This is approximately the size of a methyl group 2.00 Å; therefore, IUdR is able to replace thymidine in many reactions.

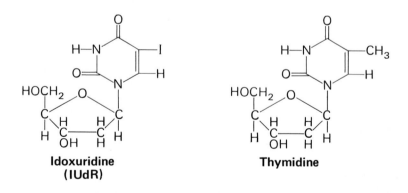

Idoxuridine
(IUdR)

Thymidine

In tissue culture, idoxuridine inhibits the replication of such DNA viruses as herpes simplex, vaccinia, pseudorabies, varicella zoster, SV-40 and polyoma virus.[88] The RNA viruses are not inhibited. Studies on the mechanism of the antiviral action of

IUdR have been reviewed by Prusoff and Goz.[89,90] There are two levels at which IUdR could affect the biochemistry of the DNA-containing viruses. First, the drug or its phosphorylated derivatives could inhibit the formation of DNA by blocking production of the required precursor molecules or their polymerization into DNA. Second, the incorporation of IUdR into the DNA could prevent it from functioning normally.

In cells, IUdR is converted to the triphosphorylated derivative by the same enzymes that convert thymidine to thymidine triphosphate. The drug itself competitively inhibits the thymidine kinase reaction, and IUdR monophosphate competitively inhibits thymidylate kinase.[91] In addition, 5-iodo-2'-deoxyuridine triphosphate functions, like the natural compound deoxythymidine triphosphate, as a feedback inhibitor of several enzymes involved in the synthesis of pyrimidine nucleotides.[89] The inhibitory effects of IUdR or its mono- or triphosphate derivative are competitive, they are readily reversible, and there is no difference in the susceptibility of enzymes to inhibition in uninfected versus virus infected cells.[89] The triphosphate of IUdR competes with thymidine triphosphate as a substrate for DNA polymerases, and it becomes incorporated into both viral and mammalian DNAs.

At present, it is reasonable to conclude that the primary antiviral action of IUdR is the result of its incorporation into viral DNA. The DNA containing the halogenated compound is altered in a number of ways. The drug-containing viral DNA is more susceptible to strand breakage[92]; the mutation rate is increased; there are errors in subsequent RNA and protein synthesis; and when complete viral particles are formed in the presence of the drug, their infectivity is decreased. The observations regarding the consequences of idoxuridine incorporation into DNA have varied somewhat according to the system being examined. Studies of the effect of IUdR on pseudorabies virus multiplication, for example, suggest that non-functional viral proteins are produced.[93] Both viral DNA and proteins are synthesized and accumulate in the IUdR-treated cells; but there is little or no assembly of these viral components into viral particles. In experiments with herpes simplex and vaccinia viruses, it was found that viral particles were formed in drug-treated cells, but they were abnormal in appearance.[90,94] When phage T4 in which 60 per cent or more of the DNA thymidine was replaced with IUdR was used to infect E. coli growing in the absence of drug, very poor induction of viral enzymes was observed.[95,96] These diverse observations could be explained by a common mechanism if the presence of IUdR in DNA results in sufficient abnormal base-pairing during transcription such that altered (and in some cases non-functional) viral proteins are subsequently produced.

Use and Pharmacology of Idoxuridine

The principal use of IUdR in clinical medicine is in the treatment of herpes simplex keratitis. Several well controlled double-blind studies have demonstrated its efficacy against this corneal infection.[97,98] The drug is applied to the eye locally in drops or as an ointment. Although it hastens recovery from the infection, idoxuridine itself causes both local allergic reactions and irritation.[99] The inherent selectivity of action of IUdR for the DNA virus compared to the host cell is low. When IUdR is employed topically to treat viral infections in the eye, additional selective effect is probably achieved. The replication of viruses in the cell requires the rapid, sustained synthesis of DNA, whereas normal mammalian cells in the conjunctiva of the eye are not synthesizing DNA at a high rate. The cells involved in the healing process, however, may be dividing rapidly and animal studies of the effects of IUdR in the absence of herpetic infection suggest that it inhibits stromal repair and decreases the strength of healing stromal wounds.[100]

The topical application of IUdR results in high local concentrations of the drug, but systemic levels remain low and toxic effects beyond the local area are avoided. Adverse reactions including inflammation, itching and edema of the eyelids, photophobia, and lacrimal duct occlusion are observed with local application to the conjunctiva.

Idoxuridine-resistant herpes simplex can be selected in vitro.[78] This acquired resistance is stable to multiple passages in the absence of drug,[101] but the mechanism is apparently unknown. In most clinical situations, however, failure of therapy may not be due to the development of drug resistance. When herpes isolates from 12 "clinically idoxuridine-resistant" patients were examined for drug susceptibility in vitro, ten were immediately sensitive and the other two were fully sensitive by the fourth passage.[102] The mechanism of clinical failure with these viruses is not well understood. It has been suggested that some strains of herpes may be more pathogenic than others and may show less response to the drug because of their greater invasiveness.[103] Patients with corneal ulcers that are resistant to or deteriorating in spite of IUdR therapy often will respond to adenine arabinoside.[104] This purine analog has also been shown to be effective *in vitro* against a strain of herpes simplex that was biochemically resistant to IUdR.[105]

The usefulness of topical IUdR in treating herpes simplex infection of the skin and mucous membranes has not been clearly established. Although there are several reports of favorable clinical results, the responses obtained are certainly not dramatic, and in some studies, a therapeutic effect has not been demonstrated.[88,106] Several studies in the form of case reports and uncontrolled trials suggested that IUdR might be useful in the intravenous treatment of herpes simplex encephalitis.[88,107] But a subsequent, controlled double-blind study of the effect of the drug (100 mg/kg as two rapid intravenous administrations daily) in patients with biopsy-proven herpetic encephalitis was terminated because of unacceptable marrow toxicity and failure of the drug to prevent death.[108] Topical application of IUdR dissolved in DMSO has been shown to significantly decrease the duration of pain and to accelerate healing in patients infected with varicella zoster, a DNA virus closely related to herpes simplex.[109,110]

Systemic administration of IUdR can produce stomatitis, leukopenia, and thrombocytopenia,[108,111] a complex of symptoms seen with many drugs that are cytotoxic to mammalian cells . Idoxuridine is also hepatotoxic. In addition to its being toxic, the systemic use of the drug is compromised by its rapid metabolism in tissues.[112] Because of this fast inactivation, intravenous infusion must be rapid in order to obtain significant blood levels.[113]

Since halogenated pyrimidines are mutagenic in bacteria, and since they produce chromosomal damage in eukaryotic cells, there is a clear basis for concern regarding the possibility, with systemic administration of IUdR of producing genetic damage in man.[114] It has been shown that exposure of certain non-virus-producing cells in culture to IUdR can initiate virus production. This has been observed, for example, in cell lines prepared from mouse embryos that produce high titers of infectious murine leukemia virus in the presence of the drug.[115] The production of Epstein-Barr virus-related antigens is initiated in non-producing human lymphoblastoid cells exposed to IUdR.[116] These and similar observations in several systems reenforce the possibility that a potential risk of IUdR administration may be oncogene activation—that is, the expression of normally repressed cancer virus genomes.

Idoxuridine-containing DNA is especially sensitive to the effects of radiation (strand breakage occurs, as well as cross-linking of thymidine residues, which results in covalent linkage between the two strands in the DNA helix). For this reason, the halogenated pyrimidines have been studied as possible adjuncts to X-irradiation of cancer. The IUdR-containing DNA is sensitive to ultraviolet irradiation, an effect that may contribute to the therapeutic action of the drug in the treatment of superficial infection of the cornea, which is exposed to some solar ultraviolet radiation.[117]

CYTARABINE

Cytarabine (cytosine arabinoside) is a pyrimidine in which the orientation of the hydroxyl group on the two carbon of the sugar is reversed from that of cytidine; thus, it becomes an analog of 2'-deoxycytidine. In cell culture, cytarabine inhibits DNA virus replication as well as the growth of a variety of mammalian cells. It inhibits DNA synthesis in mammalian cells while permitting RNA and protein synthesis to continue for long periods. This effect is competed for, and at an early point, reversed by, deoxycytidine.

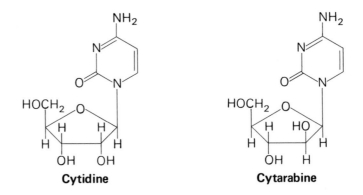

The precise mechanism of action of cytarabine is not yet completely clear. It was first hypothesized that the phosphorylated form of the drug inhibited the reduction of ribonucleosides to deoxyribonucleosides.[118] Nucleotides of arabinosylcytosine, however, were found to be only weak inhibitors of the reduction reaction, and this effect probably does not contribute greatly to the observed inhibition of DNA synthesis.[119] The triphosphory-lated drug, ara-CTP, is incorporated to a slight extent into DNA.[120] Some investigators have suggested that the cytarabine acts as a DNA chain terminator,[121] but in some systems there is no correlation between its extent of incorporation into mammalian DNA and the degree of lethality.[122] Ara-CTP competitively inhibits the polymerization of the natural nucleotide (deoxycytidine triphosphate) into DNA by mammalian DNA polymerase preparations.[122,123] In cells infected with pseudorabies virus, the degree of inhibition of virus production parallels inhibition of DNA synthesis.[124] Cytarabine prevents DNA synthesis and the formation of intact virions when added to cells 3 to 6 hours after infection with herpes simplex virus.[125] When added at a later stage of the viral growth cycle, the drug does not inhibit the coating of the already formed viral DNA or the yield of the infectious virus. These studies suggest that cytarabine exerts its primary antiviral effect by inhibiting DNA synthesis after its phosphorylation to the triphosphate. Cells that lack the ability to phosphorylate cytarabine are resistant to inhibition.

The primary application of cytarabine in clinical medicine is in the treatment of leukemia. Since it inhibits the multiplication of several DNA viruses in vitro, however, it has been used systemically to treat infections caused by the herpes group viruses in man. Because most of the available information consists of case reports and uncontrolled studies, the possible usefulness of the drug has not been defined. A good example of the value of a randomized, placebo-controlled, double-blind therapeutic trial in evaluating an antiviral agent is provided by the study of Stevens and co-workers.[126] In this study, cytosine arabinoside was delivered by continuous intravenous infusion to patients with disseminated varicella zoster infection. It was found that, contrary to the impression gained from some uncontrolled studies, cytosine arabinoside (at the dosage employed) had no beneficial effect on the disease, and in some immunologically compromised patients the disease was even prolonged, probably as a result of the drug's action in further depressing the host responses.[126]

Cytarabine is given intravenously, by injection or by continuous infusion. It is not active when taken orally. The drug is rapidly deaminated by cytidine deaminase in the liver and kidney.[127] The deaminated product uracil arabinoside is inactive and accounts for approximately 90 per cent of the drug eliminated in the urine. Cytarabine exerts its primary toxic effects on the bone marrow (marrow depression, leukopenia, thrombocytopenia, and anemia), the gastrointestinal tract (vomiting, diarrhea, and stomatitis), and the liver.

ADENINE ARABINOSIDE

Adenine arabinoside (9-β-D-arabinofuranosyladenine, ara-A) is a purine derivative that inhibits a variety of DNA viruses in vitro at concentrations that are not toxic to host cells. The extensive work carried out with this drug prior to 1975 has been reviewed in a symposium.[128]

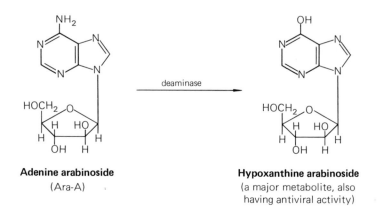

Adenine arabinoside
(Ara-A)

Hypoxanthine arabinoside
(a major metabolite, also
having antiviral activity)

Like cytarabine, ara-A inhibits both ribonucleotide reductases[119] and DNA polymerases,[129] and from the available data it appears that the primary cytotoxic effect is an inhibition of DNA polymerase by ara-A triphosphate.[130] Some studies in herpes simplex virus-infected cells suggest that ara-A acts selectively to inhibit virus-specific DNA synthesis.[131,132] Since crude DNA polymerase preparations from virus-infected and uninfected cells were found to have the same sensitivity to inhibition by ara-ATP,[132] the basis for the selective action is not yet understood.

The value of adenine arabinoside in treating infections outside the eye has not been established. The pharmacology of the drug after systemic administration in humans has been reviewed.[128] An ophthalmic ointment (which has not yet been finally approved for commercial distribution in the United States) is used to treat herpes simplex infection of the eye. In double-blind clinical studies comparing the effects of ara-A and IUdR on herpetic ulcers, no significant difference in healing time was observed but there were fewer reactions to ara-A.[104,128] Patients who were intolerant of IUdR because of toxicity or hypersensitivity were able to use ara-A without adverse reaction.[104,128] Adenine arabinoside has also been found effective in cases of herpetic keratitis that had not responded to IUdR therapy.[104,128]

Adenine arabinoside is also being evaluated for its effectiveness in deeper infections, such as herpetic uveitis. Topical application of the drug apparently has some effect in patients who have unhealthy, disrupted epithelium, which suggests that effective intraocular drug concentrations are at least partially dependent on a breakdown of the tear-epithelium barrier.[133] In studies on the intraocular penetration of topically applied idoxuridine and ara-A in animal models and in humans, both drugs were recovered from the aqueous humor as metabolites.[133] Idoxuridine is broken down to uracil, which has no antiviral activity, whereas ara-A is deaminated to hypxanthine arabinoside, an active antiviral compound.[134]

At present, ara-A appears to be as effective as idoxuridine in the therapy of routine epithelial herpes, but it has an advantage because of its relative lack of toxicity and allergenicity.

REFERENCES

1. J. T. Grayston and S. Wang: New knowledge of Chlamydiae and the diseases they cause. *J. Infect. Dis.* 132:87 (1975).

2. S. E. Luria and J. E. Darnell: *General Virology* (second ed.), New York: John Wiley, 1967.

3. D. H. Spector and D. Baltimore: The molecular biology of poliovirus. *Scientific American* 232:25 (1975).

4. G. D. Pearson: *The Inhibition of Poliovirus Replication by N-Methylisatin-β-4':4'-dibutylthiosemicarbazone.* Ph.D. Thesis, Stanford University, 1968.

5. W. K. Joklik: The intracellular uncoating of poxvirus DNA, II. The molecular basis of the uncoating process. *J. Mol. Biol.* 8:277 (1964).

6. J. R. Kates and B. R. McAuslan: Poxvirus DNA-dependent RNA polymerase. *Proc. Natl. Acad. Sci. U.S.* 58:134 (1967).

7. J. R. Kates and B. R. McAuslan: Messenger RNA synthesis by a "coated" viral genome. *Proc. Natl. Acad. Sci. U.S.* 57:314 (1967).

8. H. M. Temin and S. Mizutani: RNA-dependent DNA polymerase in virions of Rous sarcoma virus. 226:1211 (1970).

9. A. Caliguiri and I. Tamm: "Guanidine" in *International Encyclopedia of Pharmacology and Therapeutics* (Section 61, vol. 1), New York: Pergamon Press, 1972, pp. 181–230.

10. I. Tamm and L. A. Caliguiri: "2-(α-Hydroxybenzyl)benzimidazole and related compounds" in *International Encyclopedia of Pharmacology and Therapeutics* (Section 61, vol. 1), New York: Pergamon Press, 1972, pp. 115–179.

11. M. S. Chen, D. C. Ward and W. H. Prusoff: Specific herpes simplex virus-induced incorporation of 5-iodo-5′-amino-2′,5′-deoxyuridine into deoxyribonucleic acid. *J. Biol. Chem.* 251:4833 (1976).

12. M. Green, J. Bragdon, and A. Rankin: 3-Cyclic amine derivatives of rifamycin: Strong inhibitors of the DNA polymerase activity of RNA tumor viruses. *Proc. Natl. Acad. Sci. U.S.* 69:1294 (1972).

13. J. H. Subak-Sharpe, M. C. Timbury, and J. F. Williams: Rifampicin inhibits the growth of some mammalian viruses. *Nature* 222:341 (1969).

14. E. Heller, M. Argaman, H. Levy, and N. Goldblum: Selective inhibition of vaccinia virus by the antibiotic rifampicin. *Nature* 222:273 (1969).

15. B. Moss, E. Katz, and E. N. Rosenblum: Vaccinia virus directed RNA and protein synthesis in the presence of rifampicin. *Biochem. Biophys. Res. Commun.* 36:858 (1969).

16. B. Moss, E. N. Rosenblum, E. Katz, and P. M. Grimley: Rifampicin: a specific inhibitor of vaccinia virus assembly. *Nature* 229:1280 (1969).

17. P. Palese, J. L. Schulman, G. Bodo, and P. Meindl: Inhibition of influenza and parainfluenza virus replication in tissue culture by 2-deoxy-2,3-dehydro-N-trifluoroacetylneuraminic acid (FANA). *Virology* 59:490 (1974).

18. M. Ho and J. A. Armstrong: Interferon. *Ann. Rev. Microbiol.* 29:131 (1975).

19. E. DeClercq and T. Merigan: Current concepts of interferon and interferon induction. *Ann. Rev. Med.* 21:17 (1970).

20. N. B. Finter (ed.): *Interferons and Interferon Inducers*, Amsterdam: North Holland Publishing Co., 1973, 598 pp.

21. E. DeClercq, P. F. Torrence, and B. Witkop: Interferon induction by synthetic polynucleotides: Importance of purine N-7 and strandwise rearrangement. *Proc. Natl. Acad. Sci. U.S.* 71:182 (1974).

22. P. M. Pitha, H. D. Harper, and J. Pitha: Dependence of interferon induction on cell membrane integrity. *Virology* 59:40 (1974).

23. P. Pitha and J. Pitha: Interferon induction site: Poly IC on solid substrate carriers. *J. Gen. Virol.* 21:31 (1973).

24. R. M. Friedman: Interferon binding: The first step in establishment of antiviral activity. *Science* 156:1760 (1967).

25. J. Taylor: Studies on the mechanism of action of interferon. I. Interferon action and RNA synthesis in chick embryo fibroblasts infected with Semliki Forest virus. *Virology* 25:340 (1965).

26. S. Levine: Effect of actinomycin D and puromycin dehydrochloride on action of interferon. *Virology* 24:586 (1964).

27. R. M. Friedman: Inhibition of arbovirus protein synthesis by interferon. *J. Virol.* 2:1081 (1968).

28. H. B. Levy and W. A. Carter: Molecular basis of the action of interferon. *J. Mol. Biol.* 31:561 (1968).

29. W. K. Joklik and T. C. Merigan: Concerning the mechanism of action of interferon. *Proc. Natl. Acad. Sci. U.S.* 56:558 (1966).

30. P. I. Marcus and J. M. Salb: Molecular basis of interferon action: Inhibition of viral RNA translation. *Virology* 30:502 (1966).

31. R. M. Friedman, D. H. Metz, R. M. Esteban, D. R. Tovell, L. A. Ball, and I. M. Kerr: Mechanism of interferon action: Inhibition of viral messenger ribonucleic acid translation in L-cell extracts. *J. Virol.* 10:1184 (1972).

32. C. F. Samuel and W. K. Joklik: A protein synthesizing system from interferon treated cells that discriminates between cellular and viral messenger RNAs. *Virology* 58:476 (1974).

33. M. N. Oxman and M. J. Levin: Interferon and transcription of early virus-specific RNA in cells infected with simian virus 40. *Proc. Natl. Acad. Sci. U.S.* 68:299 (1971).

34. P. I. Marcus, D. L. Engelhardt, J. M. Hunt, and M. J. Sekellick: Interferon action: Inhibition of vesicular stomatitis virus RNA synthesis induced by virion-bound polymerase. *Science* 174:593 (1971).

35. E. T. Torma and K. Paucker: Purification and characterization of human leukocyte interferon components. *J. Biol. Chem.* 251:4810 (1976).

36. T. C. Merigan, S. E. Reed, T. S. Hall, and D. A. J. Tyrrell: Inhibition of respiratory virus infection by locally applied interferon. *Lancet* 1:563 (1973).

37. N. B. Finter: "Interferons and inducers *in vivo*: I. Antiviral effects in experimental animals" in *Interferons and Interferon Inducers*, ed. by N. B. Finter. Amsterdam: North Holland Publishing Co., 1973, pp. 295–361.

38. G. W. Jordan, R. P. Fried, and T. C. Merigan: Administration of human leukocyte interferon in herpes zoster. I. Safety, circulating antiviral activity and host responses to infection. *J. Infect. Dis.* 130:56 (1974).

39. M. Ho: "Pharmacokinetics of interferons" in *Interferons and Interferon Inducers*, ed. by N. B. Finter. Amsterdam: North Holland Publishing Co., 1973, pp. 241–249.

40. H. B. Greenberg, R. B. Pollard, L. I. Lutwick, P. B. Gregory, W. S. Robinson, and T. C. Merigan: Effect of human leukocyte interferon on hepatitis B virus infection in patients with chronic active hepatitis. *New Eng. J. Med.* 295:517 (1976).

41. M. R. Hilleman: Double-stranded RNA's (poly I:C) in the prevention of viral infections. *Arch. Int. Med.* 126:109 (1970).

42. D. A. Hill, S. Baron, and R. M. Chanock: Sensitivity of common respiratory viruses to an interferon inducer in human cells. *Lancet* 2:187 (1969).

43. E. DeClercq and T. Merigan: Induction of interferon by nonviral agents. *Arch. Int. Med.* 126:94 (1970).

44. M. Absher and W. R. Stinebring: Toxic properties of a synthetic double-stranded RNA. *Nature* 223:715 (1969).

45. H. L. Lindsay, P. W. Trown, J. Brandt, and M. Forbes: Pyrogenicity of poly I: poly C in rabbits. *Nature* 223:717 (1969).

46. R. H. Adamson and S. Fabro: Embryotoxic effect of poly I. poly C. *Nature* 223:718 (1969).

47. A. D. Steinberg, S. Baron, and N. Talal: The pathogenesis of autoimmunity in New Zealand mice, I. Induction of antinucleic acid antibodies by polyinosinic polycytidylic acid. *Proc. Natl. Acad. Sci. U.S.* 63:1103 (1969).

48. D. A. Hill, S. Baron, J. C. Perkins, M. Worthington, J. E. Van Kirk, J. Mills, A. Z. Kapikian, and R. M. Chanock: Evaluation of an interferon inducer in viral respiratory disease. *J. Am. Med. Assoc.* 219:1179 (1972).

49. C. Panusarn, E. D. Stanley, V. Dirda, M. Ribenis, and G. G. Jackson: Prevention of illness from rhinovirus infection by a topical interferon inducer. *New Eng. J. Med.* 291:57 (1974).

50. C. E. Hoffman: "Amantadine HC1 and related compounds" in *Selective Inhibitors of Viral Functions*, ed. by W. A. Carter. Cleveland: CRC Press, 1973, pp. 199–211.

51. E. M. Neumayer, R. F. Haff, and C. E. Hoffman: Antiviral activity of amantadine hydrochloride in tissue culture and *in ovo*. *Proc. Soc. Exptl. Biol. Med.* 119:393 (1965).

52. H. F. Maassab and K. W. Cochran: Rubella virus: Inhibition *in vitro* by amantadine hydrochloride. *Science* 145:3639 (1964).

53. C. E. Hoffmann, E. M. Neumayer, R. F. Haff, and R. A. Goldsby: Mode of action of the antiviral activity of amantadine in tissue culture. *J. Bacteriol.* 90:623 (1965).

54. N. Kato and H. J. Eggers: Inhibition of fowl plague virus by 1-adamantanamine hydrochloride. *Virology* 37:632 (1969).

55. W. F. Long and J. Olusanya: Adamantamine and early events following influenza virus infection. *Archiv. für Ges. Virusforsch.* 36:18 (1972).

56. L. Weinstein and T. W. Chang: The chemotherapy of viral infections. *New Eng. J. Med.* 289:725 (1973).

57. A. B. Sabin: Amantadine hydrochloride. *J. Am. Med. Assoc.* 200:135 (1967).

58. Y. Togo, R. B. Hornick, and A. T. Dawkins: Studies on induced influenza in man. I. Double-blind studies designed to assess prophylactic efficacy of amantadine hydrochloride against A2/Rockville/1/65 strain. *J. Am. Med. Assoc.* 203:1089 (1968).

59. A. T. Dawkins, L. R. Gallager, Y. Togo, R. B. Hornick, and B. A. Harris: Studies on induced influenza in man. II. Double-blind study designed to assess the prophylactic efficacy of an analogue of amantadine hydrochloride. *J. Am. Med. Assoc.* 203:1095 (1968).

60. A. W. Galbraith, J. S. Oxford, G. C. Schild, and G. I. Watson: Protective effect of 1-adamantanamine hydrochloride on influenza A2 infections in the family environment. *Lancet* 2:1026 (1969).

61. W. L. Wingfield, D. Pollack, and R. R. Grunert: Therapeutic efficacy of amantadine HCl and rimantidine HCl in naturally occurring influenza A2 respiratory illness in man. *New Eng. J. Med.* 281:579: (1969).

62. Y. Togo, R. B. Hornick, V. J. Felitti; M. L. Kaufman, A. T. Dawkins, V. E. Kilpe, and J. L. Claghorn: Evaluation of therapeutic efficacy of amantadine in patients with naturally occurring A_2 influenza. *J. Am. Med. Assoc.* 211:1149 (1970).

63. A. W. Galbraith, J. S. Oxford, G. C. Schild, C. W. Potter, and G. I. Watson: Therapeutic effect of 1-adamantanamine hydrochloride in naturally occurring influenza A_2/Hong Kong infection. A controlled double-blind study. *Lancet* 2:113 (1971).

64. W. E. Bleidner, J. B. Harmon, W. E. Hewes, T. E. Lynes, and E. C. Hermann: Absorption, distribution and excretion of amantadine hydrochloride. *J. Pharm. Exptl. Ther.* 150:484 (1965).

65. V. G. Vernier, J. B. Harmon, J. M. Stump, T. E. Lynes, J. P. Marvel, and D. H. Smith: The toxicologic and pharmacologic properties of amantadine hydrochloride. *Toxic. Appl. Pharmacol.* 15:642 (1969).

66. K. F. W. Armbruster, A. C. Rahn, T. S. Ing, I. S. Halper, J. H. Oyama, and H. L. Klowans: Amantadine toxicity in a patient with renal insufficiency. *Nephron* 13:183 (1974).

67. R. S. Schwab, A. C. England, D. C. Poskanzer, and R. R. Young: Amantadine in the treatment of Parkinson's disease. *J. Am. Med. Assoc.* 208:1168 (1969).

68. R. S. Schwab, D. C. Poskanzer, A. C. England, and R. R. Young: Amantadine in Parkinson's disease: Review of more than two years' experience. *J. Am. Med. Assoc.* 222:792 (1972).

69. R. B. Bauer and J. T. McHenry: Comparison of amantadine, placebo, and levodopa in Parkinson's disease. *Neurology* 24:715 (1974).

70. M. D. Yahr and R. C. Duvoisin: Drug therapy of parkinsonism. *New. Eng. J. Med.* 287:20 (1972).

71. E. V. Bailey and W. T. Stone: The mechanism of action of amantadine in Parkinsonism: A review. *Arch. Int. Pharmacodyn.* 216:246 (1975).

72. D. Parkes: Amantadine. *Adv. in Drug Res.* 8:11 (1974).

73. W. Levinson: "Inhibition of viruses, tumors, and pathogenic microorganisms by isatin β-thiosemicarbazone and other thiosemicarbazones" in *Selective Inhibitors of Viral Functions*, ed. by W. A. Carter. Cleveland: CRC Press, 1973, pp. 213–226.

74. W. K. Joklik: "Studies on the mode of action of two antiviral agents: Isatin-β-thiosemicarbazone and interferon" in *Medical and Applied Virology*. ed. by M. Sanders and E. H. Lennette, St. Louis: Warren H. Green, 1968, pp. 299–326.

75. B. Woodson and W. K. Joklik: The inhibition of vaccinia virus multiplication by isatin-β-thiosemicarbazone. *Proc. Natl. Acad. Sci. U.S.* 54:946 (1965).

76. E. Katz, E. Margalith, B. Winer, and N. Goldblum: Synthesis of vaccinia virus polypeptides in the presence of isatin-β-thiosemicarbazone. *Antimicrob. Agents Chemother.* 4:44 (1973).

77. J. S. Oxford, I. S. Logan, and C. W. Potter: In vivo selection of an influenza A_2 strain resistant to amantadine. *Nature* 226:82 (1970).

78. H. E. Renis and D. A. Buthala: Development of resistance to antiviral drugs. *Ann. N.Y. Acad. Sci.* 130:343 (1965).

79. G. Appleyand and H. J. Way: Thiosemicarbazone-resistant rabbitpox virus. *Brit. J. Exptl. Path.* 47:144 (1966).

80. E. Katz, E. Margalith, B. Winer, and A. Lazar: Characterization and mixed infections of three strains of vaccinia virus: Wild type, IBT-resistant and IBT-dependent mutants. *J. Gen. Virol.* 21:469 (1973).

81. G. D. Pearson and E. F. Zimmerman: Inhibition of poliovirus replication by N-methylisatin-β-4':4'-dibutylthiosemicarbazone. *Virology* 38:641 (1969).

82. W. Levinson, A. Faras, B. Woodson, J. Jackson, and J. M. Bishop: Inhibition of RNA-dependent DNA polymerase of rous sarcoma virus by thiosemicarbazones and several cations. *Proc. Natl. Acad. Sci. U.S.* 70:164 (1973).

83. D. J. Bauer, L. St. Vincent, C. H. Kempe, P. A. Young, and A. W.

Downie: Prophylaxis of smallpox with methisazone. *Am. J. Epidemiol.* 90:130 (1969).

84. A. R. Rao, E. S. Jackobs, K. Kamalakshi, S. Bradbury, and A. Swamy: Chemoprophylaxis and chemotherapy in variola major. Part I. An assessment of CG 662 and Marboran in prophylaxis of contacts of variola major. *Indian J. Med. Res.* 57:477 (1969).

85. L. A. R. de Valle, P. R. de Melo, L. F. De Salles Gomez, and L. M. Proenca: Methisazone in prevention of variola minor among contacts. *Lancet* 2:976 (1965).

86. D. J. Bauer: "Thiosemicarbazones" in *International Encyclopedia of Pharmacology and Therapeutics* (Section 61, vol. 1), New York: Pergamon Press, 1972, pp. 35–113.

87. W. H. Prusoff: Synthesis and biological activities of iododeoxyuridine, an analog of thymidine. *Biochim. Biophys. Acta* 32:295 (1959).

88. F. M. Schabel and J. A. Montgomery: "Purines and pyrimidines" in *International Encyclopedia of Pharmacology and Therapeutics* (Section 61, vol. 1), New York: Pergamon Press, 1972, pp. 35–113.

89. B. Goz and W. H. Prusoff: Pharmacology of viruses. *Ann. Rev. Pharmacol.* 10:143 (1970).

90. W. H. Prusoff and B. Goz: Potential mechanisms of action of antiviral agents. *Fed. Proc.* 32:1679 (1973).

91. Y. S. Bakhle and W. H. Prusoff: The effect of 5-iodo-2'-deoxyuridine and its mono- and triphosphates on some enzymes concerned with the biosynthesis of DNA in cell-free extracts of murine neoplastic cells. *Biochim. Biophys. Acta* 174:302 (1969).

92. J. F. McCrea and M. B. Lipman: Strand-length measurements of normal and 5-iodo-2'-deoxyuridine-treated vaccinia virus deoxyribonucleic acid released by the Kleinschmidt method. *J. Virol.* 1:1037 (1967).

93. A. S. Kaplan and T. Ben-Porat: Mode of antiviral action of 5-iodouracil deoxyriboside. *J. Mol. Biol.* 19:320 (1966).

94. K. O. Smith and C. D. Dukes: Effects of 5-iodo-2'-deoxyuridine (IDU) on herpesvirus synthesis and survival in infected cells. *J. Immunol.* 92:550 (1964).

95. B. Goz and W. H. Prusoff: The ability of phage containing 5-iodo-2'-deoxyuridine-substitiuted deoxyribonucleic acid to induce enzymes. *J. Biol. Chem.* 243:4750 (1968).

96. B. Goz and W. H. Prusoff: The regulation of antiviral activity of IUdR to gene function in phage. *Ann. N.Y. Acad. Sci.* 173:379 (1970).

97. R. P. Burns: A double-blind study of IDU in human herpes simplex keratitis. *Arch. Ophthalmol.* 70:381 (1963).

98. P. R. Laibson and I. H. Leopold: An evaluation of double blind IDU therapy in 100 cases of herpetic keratitis. *Trans. Am. Acad. Ophthalmol. Oto-laryngol.* 68:22 (1964).

99. J. McGill, H. Williams, J. McKinnon, A. D. Holt-Wilson, and B. R. Jones: Reassessment of idoxuridine therapy of herpetic keratitis. *Trans Ophthal. Soc. U.K.* 94:542 (1974).

100. R. H. S. Langston, D. Pavan-Langston, and C. H. Dohlman: Antiviral medication and corenal wound healing. *Arch. Ophthalmol.* 92:509 (1974).

101. T. W. Sery and R. M. Nagy: A stable mutation of herpes virus resistance to IUdR. *Invest. Ophthalmol.* 4:947 (1965).

102. E. Jawetz, V. R. Coleman, C. R. Dawson, and P. Thygeson: The dynamics of IUdR action in herpetic keratitis and the emergence of IUdR resistance in vitro. *Ann. N.Y. Acad. Sci.* 173:282 (1970).

103. E. Jawetz, R. Schultz, V. Coleman and M. Okumoto: Studies on herpes simplex. XI. The antiviral dynamics of 5-iodo-2-deoxyuridine in vivo. *J. Immunol.* 95:635 (1965).

104. D. Pavan-Langston: Clinical evaluation of adenine arabinoside and idoxuridine in the treatment of ocular herpes simplex. *Am. J. Ophthalmol.* 80:496 (1975).

105. A. B. Nesburn, C. Robinson, and R. Dickinson: Adenine arabinoside effect on experimental idoxuridine-resistant herpes simplex infection. *Invest. Ophthalmol.* 13:302 (1974).

106. B. E. Juel-Jensen and F. O. Maccallum: *Herpes Simplex Varicella and Zoster,* London: W. Heinemann. 1972, 194 pp.

107. D. C. Nolan, C. B. Lauter, and A. M. Lerner: Idoxuridine in herpes simplex virus (type 1) encephalitis. *Ann. Int. Med.* 78:243 (1973).

108. Boston Interhospital Virus Study Group and the NAID-Sponsored Cooperative Antiviral Clinical Study: Failure on high dose 5-iodo-2'-deoxyuridine in the therapy of herpes simplex virus encephalitis. *New. Eng. J. Med.* 292:599 (1975).

109. B. E. Juel-Jensen, F. O. MacCallum, A. M. R. Mackenzie, and M. C. Pike: Treatment of zoster with idoxuridine in dimethyl sulfoxide. Results of two double-blind controlled trials. *Br. Med. J.* 4:776 (1970).

110. R. Dawber: Idoxuridine in herpes zoster: Further evaluation of intermittent topical therapy. *Brit. Med. J.* 2:526 (1974).

111. P. Calabresi: Current status of clinical investigations with 6-azauridine, 5-iodo-2'-deoxyuridine, and related derivatives. *Cancer Res.* 23:1260 (1963).

112. A. D. Welch and W. H. Prusoff: A synopsis of recent investigations of 5-iodo-2'-deoxyuridine. *Cancer Chem. Rep.* 6:29 (1960).

113. A. M. Lerner and E. J. Bailey: Concentrations of idoxuridine in serum urine and cerebrospinal fluid of patients with suspected diagnoses of Herpesvirus hominis encephalitis. *J. Clin. Invest.* 51:45 (1972).

114. A. D. Welch: Some mechanisms involved in selective chemotherapy. *Ann. N.Y. Acad. Sci.* 123:19 (1965).

115. W. P. Rowe, D. R. Lowy, N. Teich, and J. W. Hartley. Some implications of the activation of murine leukemia virus by halogenated pyrimidines. *Proc. Nat. Acad. Sci. U.S.* 69:1033 (1972).

116. K. Sugauara and T. Osato: Two distinct antigenic components in an Epstein-Barr virus-related early product induced by halogenated pyrimidines in non-producing human lymphoblastoid cells. *Nature New Biol.* 243:209 (1973).

117. R. Thiel and A. Wacker: Behandlung der Keratitis herpetica mit Thymin-alalogen Verbindungen. *Klin. Monatsbl. Augenheilk.* 141:94 (1962).

118. M. Y. Chu and G. A. Fisher: A proposed mechanism of action of 1-β-D-arabinofuranosylcytosine as an inhibitor of the growth of leukemic cells. *Biochem. Pharmacol.* 11:423 (1962).

119. E. C. Moore and S. S. Cohen: Effects of arabinonucleotides on ribonucleotide reduction by an enzyme system from rat tumor. *J. Biol. Chem.* 242:2116 (1967).

120. M. Y. Chu and G. A. Fisher: The incorporation of ^{3}H-cytosine arabinoside and its effect on murine leukemic cells (L5178 Y). *Biochem. Pharmacol.* 17:753 (1968).

121. M. A. Waqar, L. A. Burgoyne, and M. R. Atkinson: Deoxyribonucleic acid synthesis in mammalian nuclei. Incorporation of deoxyribonucleotides and chain-terminating nucleotide analogues. *Biochem. J.* 121:803 (1971).

122. F. L. Graham and G. F. Whitamore: Studies in mouse L-cells on the incorporation of 1-β-D-arabinofuranosylcytosine into DNA and on inhibition of DNA polymerase by 1-β-D-arabinofuranosylcytosine-5'-triphosphate. *Cancer Res.* 30:2636 (1970).

123. J. J. Furth and S. S. Cohen: Inhibition of mammalian DNA polymerase by the 5'-triphosphate of 1-β-D-arabinofuranosylcytosine and the 5'-triphosphate of 9-β-D-arabinofuranosyladenine. *Cancer Res.* 28:2061 (1968).

124. T. Ben-Porat, M. Brown, and A. S. Kaplan: Effect of 1-β-D-arabinofuranosylcytosine on DNA synthesis. II. In rabbit kidney cells infected with herpes viruses. *Mol. Pharmacol.* 4:139 (1968).

125. J. Levitt and Y. Becker: The effect of cytosine arabinoside on the replication of herpes simplex virus. *Virology* 31:129 (1967).

126. D. A. Stevens, G. W. Jordan, T. F. Waddell, and T. C. Merigan: Adverse effect of cytosine arabinoside on disseminated zoster in a controlled trial. *New Eng. J. Med.* 289:873 (1973).

127. W. A. Creasy, R. J. Papac, M. E. Markiw, P. Calabresi, and A. D. Welch: Biochemical and pharmacological studies with 1-β-D-arabinofuranosylcytosine in man. *Biochem. Pharmacol.* 15:1417 (1966).

128. D. Pavan-Langston, R. A. Buchanan, and C. A. Alford (Eds.): *Adenine Arabinoside: An Antiviral Agent,* New York: Raven Press, 1975, 425 pp.

129. J. J. Furth and S. S. Cohen: Inhibition of mammalian DNA polymerase by the 5'-triphosphate of 9-β-D-arabinofuranosyladenine. *Cancer Res.* 28:2061 (1968).

130. L. T. Ch'ien, F. M. Schabel, and C. A. Alford: "Arabinosyl nucleosides and nucleotides" in *Selective Inhibitors of Viral Functions,* ed. by W. A. Carter. Cleveland: CRC Press, 1973, pp. 227–256.

131. W. M. Shannon: "Adenine arabinoside: Antiviral activity *in vitro*" in *Adenine Arabinoside: An Antiviral Agent,* ed. by D. Pavan-Langston, R. A. Buchanan, and C. A. Alford. New York: Raven Press, 1975, pp. 1–43.

132. L. L. Bennett, W. M. Shannon, P. W. Allan, and G. Arnett: Studies on the biochemical basis for the antiviral activities of some nucleoside analogs. *Ann. N.Y. Acad. Sci.* 225:342 (1975).

133. D. Pavan-Langston, C. H. Dohlman, P. Geary, and D. Szulczewski: "Intraocular penetration of adenine arabinoside and idoxuridine—Therapeutic implications in clinical herpetic uveitis" in *Adenine Arabinoside: An Antiviral Agent,* ed. by D. Pavan-Langston, R. A. Buchanan, and C. A. Alford. New York: Raven Press, 1975, pp. 293–306.

134: D. Pavan-Langston, R. H. S. Langston, and P. A. Geary: Prophylaxis and therapy of experimental ocular herpes simplex: Comparison of idoxuridine, adenine arabinoside, and hypoxanthine arabinoside. *Arch. Ophthalmol.* 92:417 (1974).

Index

Abscesses, 8
Acedapsone, 339
Acetohydroxamic acid, 227
Acetosulfone, 188. See also Sulfones
Acetylcholine, 115, 390
Acetyltransferase, 188, 237–40
Acidifying urine, 226
Acidosis, metabolic, 185
Acridines, 386
Acrodermatitis enteropathica, 358
Adenine arabinoside, 437, 440, 441
Agranulocytosis
    from chloramphenicol, 136, 137
    from isoniazid, 242
    from primaquine, 329
    from sulfonamides, 184
    from sulfones, 189
Alastrim, 433
Alcohol, 252
Allergic reactions. See also names of
specific drugs
    desensitization, 64
    interstitial nephritis, 65
    to isoniazid, 242
    major determinants and, 58–65
    mechanism of penicillin, 56–59
    minor determinants and, 58–65
    to nalidixic acid, 220
    to PAS, 188
    to penicillins, 55–66
    penicilloyl-polylysine, 59–65
    precautions, 64–65
    skin testing, 59–63
    to sulfonamides, 184
    treatment of allergic patient, 63–65
Allopurinol, 66
Amantadine
    adverse effects of, 431
    clinical trials, 428–31
    mechanism of action, 416, 426–28
    in Parkinson's disease, 431

pharmacology of, 431
    resistance to, 432
    therapeutic use, 428, 431
Amebiasis, 347–49
Amikacin, 111. See also Amino-
glycosides
Aminoglycosides
    absorption, 103, 104
    administration, 104
    anesthetics and, 115, 119
    distribution, 104, 105
    ethacrynic acid and, 116
    inhibition of protein synthesis by,
    89–94
    mechanism of action of, 89–94
    methoxyfluorane and, 119
    misreading of genetic code by, 97–
    100
    myasthenia gravis and, 115
    nephrotoxicity, 119
    neuromuscular blockade, 104, 115
    ototoxicity, 104, 115–19
    phenotypic suppression by, 97–99
    receptor for, 94–97
    renal failure and, 106–9, 116
    resistance to, 94–97, 100
Amodiaquine, 314, 316
Amphotericin B
    administration, 276–80
    adverse effects of, 282–83
    distribution and excretion, 280–82
    dosage, 276–79
    effects on mammalian cells, 271–
    74
    flucytosine and, 274, 275, 277
    in leishmaniasis, 360
    mechanism of action of, 266–74
    resistance to, 275, 276
    structure of, 266
    and synergism, 274, 275
    therapeutic use, 276–79